MW00353239

DISCARD

North
American
Plantfile

North American Plantfile

A Visual Guide to
Plant Selection
— for Use in
Landscape
Design

by
Gary L. Hightshoe
and
harlen d. Groe

McGraw-Hill
New York   San Francisco   Washington, D.C.   Auckland   Bogotá
Caracas   Lisbon   London   Madrid   Mexico City   Milan
Montreal   New Delhi   San Juan   Singapore
Sydney   Tokyo   Toronto

1 2 3 4 5 6 7 8 9 0   11MP/11MP   9 0 2 1 0 9 8 7

ISBN 0-07-028816-X

The sponsoring editor for this book was Wendy Lochner.

Printed and bound by Printvision.

McGraw-Hill books are available at special quantity discounts to use as
premiums and sales promotions, or for use in corporate training programs. For
more information, please write to the Director of Special Sales, McGraw-Hill,
11 West 19th Street, New York, NY 10011. Or contact your local bookstore.

This book is printed on recycled, acid-free paper.

Dedication

I dedicate this book to my parents, Clarence and Alda Hightshoe. Their appreciation of the beauty and wonder of nature has always impressed me. Our frequent family outings to parks, gardens and especially the wild places—to discover the little dramas between the plants and animals that make their home there, to feel the spirit of each place, to be inspired and invigorated by it all—are the memories and gentle teachings that are often on my mind and always in my heart. Their reverence for and celebration of the beauty and mystery of those special places is perhaps their greatest gift to me.

— G.H.

This book is dedicated to the many friends, faculty, staff, and students —past and present— for their endurance in waiting. I would also like to thank the many arboreta and botanical garden's for their assistance with our requests and needs for this book. To Clarence —Gary's father— for his humor on the special trips —thanks, and to all who allow the woodland landscape as their garden. A special thanks to my wife, Mary for her persistence with my studies.

— h. G.

Acknowledgments

The authors wish to thank the many students, colleagues, family, and friends whose encouragement and suggestions were vital to the successful completion of this work. The authors also wish to thank the many persons involved in the design and preparation of the **North American Plant*f*ile**. To the many students whose faith in and work on the book were unwavering, we salute you. Indeed, without your generous contribution of time and talent, this work would not have been finished. Those students who made a major contribution and what they did are:

- **Information collection**: Lisa Nunamaker Orgler, Terry Powell, Beth Stevens, Todd Wiebenga.

- **Plantfile template design**: Linda Kleinschmidt.

- **Pictorial symbol design**: Curtis Stemsrud, Kyle Swanson.

- **Plant photography**: Brett Black, Rob Maurizi.

- **Plant distribution maps**: Kathy Berger, Jodi Gee, Robin Hein, Ann Reinhardt, Tom Simmons.

- **Information entry**: Kathy Berger, Bridget Bode, Paige Bulkeley, Jin Chen, Chris Chockley, Joy Clemsen, Kelly Donahue, Gregg Hadish, Robin Hein, Jenny Rae, Ann Reinhardt, Tom Simmons, Brad Snider, Beth Stevens, Nancy Suprenant.

- **Special recognition goes to:** Joan, Jessica, Katie, and Tobin Hightshoe for their assistance with the plant photography and information entry.

- **Special thank you goes to:** Nancy Spiess and Cheryl Sansgaard for their secretarial skills and dedication in typing the many drafts of the text and plant lists.

The authors are especially indebted to the many botanical gardens, arboreta, and university campuses that granted permission to use their facilities and photograph plant materials. Throughout much of the summer of 1988 we traveled in a recreational vehicle and were able to visit many of those locations. At several of the places visited, we were the first to be granted the privilege of "camping" overnight on the arboretum grounds. It was a wonderful experience and we thank them for their generosity.

Arizona-Sonora Desert Museum,
Tucson, AZ

Arnold Arboretum,
Jamaica Plain (Boston), MA

Brooklyn Botanic Gardens,
New York, NY

Desert Botanical Garden,
Phoenix, AZ

Fairchild Tropical Gardens,
Coral Gables, FL

Foster Botanical Gardens,
Honolulu, HI

Fruit and Spice Park,
Homestead, Florida

Holden Arboretum,
Mentor, OH

Iowa State University Campus,
Ames, IA

Leu Gardens,
Orlando, FL

Longwood Gardens,
Kennet Square, PA

Los Angeles State
and County Arboretum,
Arcadia, CA

Missouri Botanical Gardens,
St. Louis, MO

Morton Arboretum,
Lisle, IL

New York Botanical Gardens,
New York, NY

Old Westbury Gardens,
New York, NY

Planting Fields Arboretum,
New York, NY

Shelby Botanical Gardens,
Sarasota, FL

Strybing Arboretum,
San Francisco, CA

Tilden County Arboretum,
Oakland, CA

Thomas Edison House and Gardens,
Fort Meyers, FL

U.C.—Berkeley Arboretum,
University of California,
Berkeley, CA

Contents

Preface

The **North American Plantfile** is the result of the talents and dedication of many persons over a five year period. Toward the end of that time it was unclear as to whether we would even be able to complete the work. The mountain of plant information, photographs, and maps to be collected and transferred to the plant files seemed an impossible task.

Finally, the authors realized that another five years could easily be invested to bring the project closer to the original vision proposed in 1988. Even then there would be information and photography missing. What remains to be finished, however, is small in comparison to the wealth of information that has been assembled. Colleagues, students, and local practitioners, eager to use the plant files on current projects, argued that the plant files in their present form were complete enough to greatly enhance their work. They lobbied that the manual should be made available as soon as possible. We conceded to their wisdom and sincerely believe you will also find the **North American Plantfile** to be useful for many planting design situations.

It is our intent to continue to assemble the remaining plant information and to incorporate those into a second edition. We invite you to send any suggestions you have that would improve the content or utility of the **North American Plantfile**. If you find any of the plant information to be inaccurate or incomplete based on your experience, please let us know.

A second, though less important, need is to improve and complete the photographic portion of the book. The utility of the **North American Plantfile** for plant selections depends solely on reviewing the design data (icon symbols). Photographs of a plants physiological aspects —form, leaves, fruit or flower— are not necessary, but do help to confirm the appropriateness of the chosen plant. In this supplemental way, photographs serve a useful purpose. That one or two photographs of a particular plant are missing has no influence on whether that plant is suitable for a given design situation.

Completing the plant photography would be a nice thing to do. However, it is a practical impossibility to travel the breadth of the United States to photograph a plant in bloom and to return or go elsewhere to photograph it's fruit and so on. We need your help! Anyone having 35mm color slides or black-and-white negatives of missing or poorly represented plant characteristics are encouraged to call or write, that we might copy and incorporate them into the plantfile. All contributions will be fully acknowledged in the second edition. The **North American Plantfile** is indeed an ambitious project. With your help, we can make it even better; a tool unlike all others in its utility as a plant selection reference with quick find capability.

The greatest wealth of information was extracted from horticultural, botany, and forestry references. They appear in the bibliography. We are indebted to the writers of those respected and popular works.

Introduction

The **North American Plant∫ile** presents a summary of the important information for the common and not so common woody plants used in American landscape design. Over 3,600 native and exotic trees, shrubs, and vines are featured. The book provides the amateur, student, and professional plantsman with a unique plant selection and planting design reference that categorizes the environmental suitabilities, aesthetic qualities, cultural requirements, and functional uses for each plant. Over 350 design criteria are organized in a creative new photographic and pictorial format we call the "plantfile". Use of the plantfile enables quick analysis and plant selection for most landscaping situations.

The **North American Plant∫ile** is the most complete summary treatment of woody plant information for landscape use available. Previously the landscaping industry and landscape designers needed to consult many different, often lengthy, references to make plant use decisions. This process was painfully time-consuming and often costly. What was clearly needed was a reference book that incorporated comprehensive, rapid plant search capabilities across all climatic regions of the United States, southern Canada, and northern Mexico. We believe the innovative design of the **North American Plant∫ile** to be the answer.

The **North American Plant∫ile** meets the need of many persons for a rapid, comprehensive, user-friendly plant selection and planting design tool. This reference book should enhance the planning, introduction, and maintenance of native and exotic plants on home grounds, in parks, along highways, and in many other public and private places throughout urban and rural America.

What is the North American Plant∫ile and who might use it?

The **North American Plant∫ile** is an easy-to-use system to keep plant information organized and up-to-date. The opportunity to introduce a diversity of species and a variety of plant expression to urban and rural American landscapes requires a disciplined and systematic approach in the selection and use of those materials.

The North American Plant∫ile was created in order to:

- Bring the popular plant information used in landscape design into one comprehensive source and tool.

- Offer a quick pictorial plant-find alternative to the large volume of planting design references that must be read.

- Develop a standardized pictorial language that enhances communication between amateur, student, and professional persons with an interest in plant selection.

- Classify critical plant information into four areas of primary design consideration; aesthetic merit, cultural requirements, environmental suitability, and functional uses.

The **North American Plant*f*ile** contains over 3,600 plants, 10,500 photographs, and more than 140,000 plant characteristics organized in an easily accessible system. Persons wanting to select woody plant materials for parks, gardens, plazas, or city streets that satisfy explicit design criteria will find the **North American Plant*f*ile** to be a most useful tool. The plantfile can also assist botanists, foresters, landscape architects, homeowners and others in the proper identification of plants growing in forest, field, or yard.

Your North American Plant*f*ile can process many different types of plant search.

Selection of plant materials for a landscape project using the plantfile is accomplished by making a list of specific design criteria that the chosen plants are required to meet. A quick scan of the plantfile should enable you to:

- discover what plants match selected aesthetic criteria of size, shape, color, and texture.

- discover what plants match selected cultural conditions of soil, sun or shade, rate of growth, longevity, and resistance to insects and disease.

- discover what plants are suitable/adaptable to selected conditions of the natural environment including habitat and region.

- discover what plants will best satisfy selected utilitarian criteria, such as plants that function well on arbors, as bonsai, as border edging, in windbreaks, or in a rock garden.

- discover what plants match a combination of criteria from the areas above.

Additional search operations include:

- finding a particular plant in the file and reviewing all of the pictorial design infmation and photographs (referred to as a plant signature) at a glance.

- changing your criteria to a more general or specific purpose and expanding or reducing the number of plants that meet those criteria.

- manipulating your criteria to reflect **and**, **or** and **not** considerations, such as searching the plantfile for a shrub with mounded form **and** showy flowers with yellow **or** orange coloration but **not** attracting bees.

Plant Information:

Plant information is displayed in the plantfile in a way that is similar to the subject catalogue cards found in a library's card catalogue system. Books about trees, shrubs, and vines are separate subject files found in the catalogue. The **North American Plant*file*** also features separate files covering those subjects.

This distinction accounts, in part, for the name given this book. There are two master files (deciduous and evergreen). Each of the master files are divided into three separate life-form files (trees, shrubs, and vines). The three life-form files are subdivided into 11 size files (large, medium and small trees; very large, large, medium, small and very small shrubs; and tall, medium and low vines).

Each size file has up to 165 plant signatures. Each plant signature consists of the BOTANIC and COMMON names and the names of selected popular horticultural varieties, along with information about the plant's FORM, BARK, LEAF, FLOWER, FRUIT, CULTURE, USES, and REGION. This information appears in various forms that include black-and-white photographs; numeric, alphabetic, and pictorial symbols (icons); bargraphs, key word text, and maps (Figure 1).

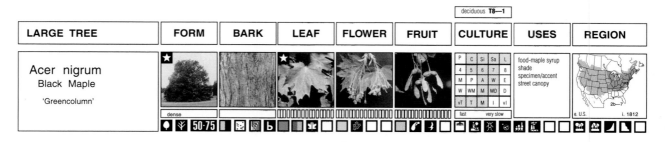

*Figure 1: Typical plant signature in the **North American Plant*file.***

The various plantfiles are interactive with the design criteria or conditions set by the designer. Figure 2, illustrated on the following page, shows that the desired plant characteristics must be an exact duplication or **true** reflection of the design criteria. In this illustration all 15 criteria must have true conditions for a plant to be acceptable. If a condition is false, it aborts the sequence and the search moves to the next plant signature in the file. A false condition for the second criterion in Figure 2 is acceptable because it is linked to the first criterion (ovoid **or** globular shape) for which the condition is true.

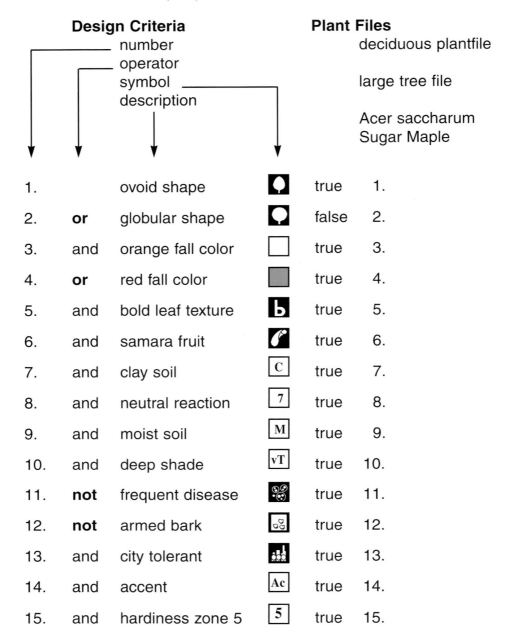

Design Criteria   **Plant Files**

number   deciduous plantfile

operator

symbol   large tree file

description

Acer saccharum
Sugar Maple

1.		ovoid shape		true	1.
2.	**or**	globular shape		false	2.
3.	and	orange fall color		true	3.
4.	**or**	red fall color		true	4.
5.	and	bold leaf texture	**b**	true	5.
6.	and	samara fruit		true	6.
7.	and	clay soil	C	true	7.
8.	and	neutral reaction	7	true	8.
9.	and	moist soil	M	true	9.
10.	and	deep shade	vT	true	10.
11.	**not**	frequent disease		true	11.
12.	**not**	armed bark		true	12.
13.	and	city tolerant		true	13.
14.	and	accent	Ac	true	14.
15.	and	hardiness zone 5	5	true	15.

Figure 2: Interactive relationship between the design criteria and the plantfile.

Selecting plants that meet specified planting design objectives for any landscape project is easily accomplished with the **North American Plant*f*ile** by observing the following steps:

1. Select your criteria for a specified planting situation,
2. Prioritize your criteria from most to least important,
3. Search the file, and
4. Prepare a list of the selected plants that meet your combined criteria.

Criteria selection:

There are over 350 individual plant characteristics called *design criteria* used in describing each plant species in detail. The organization of this criteria has been divided into eight design categories in order to simplify and hasten the plant search process. The design categories are presented in Figure 3.

Figure 3: Eight design categories help simplify the plant search process.

Appendices **A** through **H** give detailed descriptions of each category and criterion. You may select any number of criteria from as many categories as you want. There is no advantage in creating long lists of criteria, however. Lengthy criteria will result in no plants found that meet all the requested design conditions. Conversely, too many plants will be found that meet short lists with few criteria.

Placing criteria in order of importance:

The order of your selected criteria is helpful, since any of the selected criteria may not be met by any plant in the file. List the most important criteria first, least important last. Figure 4 shows how the criteria might be arranged in order of importance.

Random Listing	Prioritized Listing
1. blue-green foliage	6. zone 3
2. alkaline soil reaction	5. windbreak
3. dense form	2. alkaline soil reaction
4. conical form	4. conical form
5. windbreak	1. blue-green foliage
6. zone 3	3. dense form

Figure 4: Comparison of random and prioritized criteria.

The rationale for the order of importance expressed in Figure 4 is based on the following:

- zone 3 —highest importance, because if a plant is not adaptable to the climate of the project locale, all other criteria is of no consequence.
- windbreak —the functional use to which the plant must be suited. Such plants

must be wind firm and tolerant of drought and heat; few plants in the plantfile are suitable for windbreaks.

- alkaline soil reaction —relatively few plants are tolerant of alkaline soils, therefore this becomes the third most limiting factor influencing plant selection.

- conical form —most of the coniferous evergreens have a conical form.

- blue-green foliage —many evergreen conifers have blue-green colored leaves.

- dense form —is of the least importance because most evergreens are densely clothed with branches and foliage.

Notice that the three most important criteria (zone 3, windbreak, and soil reaction) are also the most restrictive, in the sense that relatively few plants in the plantfile have these characteristics. There is a very large group of plants that share the last three criteria. Time is saved by narrowing the field of suitable plants as quickly as possible. This is the primary advantage in listing your criteria in order of importance; that is to say, finding an appropriate number of plants for a particular planting situation in the fewest steps.

How to use the North American Plant*f*ile:

Selecting plants from the plantfile for any landscape project is accomplished easily by observing these six steps.

1. Determine whether evergreen or deciduous plants are desired. The plantfile groups all evergreens together, the same for deciduous.

2. Determine the plant life-form you want for a particular planting situation. Select from trees, shrubs, or vines.

3. Specify the size category of the plants you are looking for. Figure 5 reveals the eleven size files with their corresponding range of height (in feet) and their chapter file names.

plant Size	range of Height in feet	chapter File name
large tree	> 50	T8
medium tree	35 — 50	T7
small tree	20 — 35	T6

plant Size	range of Height in feet	chapter File name
very large shrub	12 — 20	S5
large shrub	6 — 12	S4
medium shrub	3 — 6	S3
small shrub	1 — 3	S2
very small shrub	< 1	S1
tall vine	> 50	V3
medium vine	20 — 50	V2
low vine	0 — 20	V1

*Figure 5: List of size files in the **North American Plantfile** with the corresponding heights and chapter files.*

After you have selected the size file you want, turn to that chapter.

4. Review at a glance those plants that match the combination of design qualities (criteria) you are searching for.

5. Determine the landscape region you are working in and check the USDA hardiness map to learn if the chosen plant(s) will grow in your region.

6. Consult a landscape architect, nurserymen, or your horticulture extension specialist to confirm the local adaptability and availability of the chosen plant(s).

How the North American Plantfile is organized:

The plantfile's information is organized into eight categories (columns) of design consideration. The first five are aesthetic and include FORM, BARK, LEAF, FLOWER, and FRUIT information. The sixth and seventh categories include CULTURAL information and appropriate plant USES, respectively. The eighth category, REGION, includes plant nativity or adaptability and its most suitable habitat. Use of the plantfile for selecting plants for any one of the eight categories or any combination of considerations is accomplished by making a list of the specific design criteria which the chosen plant(s) is/are required to meet.

Consider for the moment that you are selecting plant material to cover an arbor that spans an entry courtyard to a residential house. In this example, your design criteria requires plants to be a (1) *deciduous*, (2) *climbing vine* of (3) *medium* size. Other criteria include (4) *bold* or *extra bold* leaf texture, (5) vivid *yellow* autumn coloration, and (6) *showy* fruits of any type. You believe a (7) *twining vine* or vine with *tendrils* would best cover the arbor. The seven criteria listed above are all aesthetic considerations. The choice(s) must also be adaptable to (8) USDA climate *zone 6*. Your first search has a total of eight criteria that must be satisfied. A quick scan of the plantfile in this example, reveals all those plants that satisfy that combination of criteria (FIGURE 6).

Ampelopsis brevipedunculata	Porcelainberry
Ampelopsis cordata	Heartleaf Ampelopsis
Cocculus carolinus	Carolina Moonseed
Smilax hispida	Bristly Greenbrier
Smilax rotundifolia	Common Greenbrier
Vitus labrusca	Fox Grape

Figure 6: *List of plants in the **North American Plantfile** that match the combination of design criteria including (1) deciduous, (2) climbing vine, (3) medium size, (4) bold or extra bold leaf texture, (5) yellow autumn coloration, (6) showy fruit, (7) tendrils or twining habit, and (8) hardy in USDA zone 6.*

Basic procedure for information retrieval:

The standard approach is to scan the plantfile (size file) as one would read the page of a book—from top to bottom and left to right. This is appropriate if your criteria have no particular order of importance. For the arbor illustration above, arrange your written criteria in a sequence that correlates with each of the 8 categories/columns in the plantfile.

First scan down the FORM column looking for those pictorial symbols that signify a *climbing* vine with *tendrils* or *twining* habit. The presence of both symbols means that plant meets those criteria. Next, scan across (to the right) to the LEAF column. Look for the symbols that signify *yellow* fall color and *bold* or *extra bold* texture. If neither or only one symbol are present, then that plant is no longer a consideration. If both symbols are present, four of the eight criteria have now been met. Again, scan right to the FRUIT column and look for the **star** symbol in the upper left corner of the fruit photograph. The star means the fruit has a showy ornamental quality. If the star is present, the fifth criterion is met. Again, scan right to the REGION column. Look to see if the approximate location of your project falls within the green zone on the USDA hardiness map. If you aren't sure if the project area is covered by green on the map, then read the number and letter description that accompanies the map to confirm your suspicion.

Failure to see any corresponding numeric, alphabetic, or pictorial symbol for any criterion drops a plant out for consideration and you move down to the next plant signature. Return to the FORM column and repeat the search sequence. If the plant matches all eight criteria, then you have found the first suitable plant. Move down the file to the next plant and repeat the process. After you have scanned the selected file, you should end up with a list of plants that meet all the criteria. Which plant(s) from the list you decide to choose is based on designer/client preference, plant availability, and/or cost. If you have prioritized your criteria you may, of course, scan the file in a column sequence that corresponds to their order of importance to you.

It's that simple! What if you go through a file and find no suitable plants? If this happens you must modify one or several criteria to make them less specific. In the previous illustration you would add more plants to the suitable list if you were willing to also accept vines with medium leaf texture. If your list includes twenty or more suitable plants, then your criteria are too general; additional criteria will narrow the possibilities.

Illustrations of Information Retrieval:

Plant selection based on aesthetic criteria

Consider for the moment that you are selecting plant material for a specific location drawn on a planting plan for a private residential client. A typical request might be to identify (1) *deciduous,* (2) *shrubs,* with (3) *small* size, (4) *mounded* form and with (5) *fine* or *extra fine* leaf texture. Additional criteria to be met include the identification of all shrubs displaying (6) *yellow* flowers which are (7) seasonally effective in *summer.* The last criterion is that the plants selected be (8) adaptable to hardiness *zone 8.* There are a total of eight criteria to be met. Figure 7 reveals all of the plants in the file that fulfill the combination of criteria.

Cytisus supinus	Bigflower Broom
Diervilla sessilifolia	Southern Bush-honeysuckle
Genista germanica	German Woodwaxen
Genista lydia	Lydia Woodwaxen
Genista radiata	
Genista tinctoria	Dyer's Greenwood
Hypericum androsaemum	Tutsan St. Johnswort
Hypericum frondosum	Golden St. Johnswort
Hypericum kalmianum	Kalm St. Johnswort
Hypericum uralum	Ural St. Johnswort

Figure 7: *List of plants in the **North American Plantfile** that match the combination of design criteria including (1) deciduous, (2) shrub, (3) small size, (4) mounded form, (5) fine or extra fine leaf, (6) yellow flowers, (7) in summer, and (8) hardy in USDA zone 8.*

Plant selection based on ecological considerations.

Plant selection must be more closely related to the site as a habitat or mosaic of habitats where climate, slope aspect, and characteristics of soil will be more sensitively considered. All planting design must proceed with an awareness that failure to respect the landscape heritage of each place and the environmental forces that shape it has deep implications that greatly influence plant health and function. The use of native plants that are adapted to the physical and climatological influences of the project site and region is encouraged. Energy intensive landscape design that depends on irrigation, high chemical inputs of fertilizer, herbicides, and insecticides, and other regular maintenance to sustain poorly adapted exotic species are generally to be avoided.

In this illustration, the Iowa Department of Natural Resources (DNR) is considering plant materials for a revegetation site. The program calls for the planting of several hundred acres of mudflat along the water margin of a large reservoir located in the southeastern part of that state. The criteria specifies that (1) *native* plants be used that are (2) tolerant of *heavy clay* soils that have (3) a *strong acid* reaction. Species tolerant of (4) frequently *wet* sites with (5) *minimal to poor* drainage are desired. Plants that are (6) *large*, (7) *deciduous*, (8) *trees* with (9) *high food value* for wildlife are favored by wildlife biologists managing this area. Figure 8 lists all the plants that meet the nine criteria set by the DNR staff.

Acer saccharinum	Silver Maple
Betula nigra	River Birch
Quercus bicolor	Swamp White Oak
Quercus palustris	Pin Oak

Figure 8: List of plants in the **North American Plantfile** that match the combination of design criteria including (1) native to Southeast Iowa, (2) tolerant of heavy clay soils, (3) strong acid reaction, (4) wet sites, (5) minimal to poor drainage that are (6) large, (7) deciduous, (8) trees with (9) high food value for wildlife.

Plant Selection for urban environments.

Vegetation modifies and enhances urban and rural environments making them enjoyable and livable. Nowhere is there a greater need for plant material than in the city. In parks and plazas, along streets and rivers, or in scattered forest reserves, vegetation must grow and survive the hostile conditions of environment common to many metropolitan landscapes. The more hostile the environment, the more limited the selection of tolerant plant material.

Cultural characteristics of this environment including air pollution, high heat albedos, deficient or excess soil moisture, improper drainage, compacted soils, infertile soils, salt spray from winter road maintenance, and night lighting are limiting factors. For a description of the environmental factors characteristic of large cities and their impact on plant material, see Appendix G. Extensive tree mortality and maintenance must be avoided in favor of plant species and varieties that are culturally and functionally adapted.

The last illustration of information retrieval shows how the cultural and plant use criteria in the plantfile can assist in identifying species best adapted to the urban environment of a large northern city such as Milwaukee or Pittsburgh. A tree planting program prescribes that selected plants be (1) *large*, (2) *deciduous*, (3) *trees* to be used as a (4) *street canopy* tree. Additional criteria to be fulfilled include (5) tolerance of the *city* environment and (6) hardy in USDA *zone 4*. All trees fulfilling the six criteria are listed in Figure 9.

Betula nigra	River Birch
Catalpa speciosa	Northern Catalpa
Ginkgo biloba	Ginkgo
Gleditsia tricanthos	Common Honeylocust
Liriodendron tulipifera	Tuliptree
Nyssa sylvatica	Black Tupelo
Platanus **x** acerifolia	London Planetree
Tilia **x** euchlora	European Linden
Tilia petiolaris	Silverpendent Linden
Tilia platyphyllos	Bigleaf Linden
Tilia tomentosa	Silver Linden
Ulmus **x** hollandica	Dutch Elm
Ulmus procera	English Elm
Ulmus pumila	Siberian Elm

Figure 9: List of plants in the **North American Plantfile** *that match the combination of design criteria including (1) large, (2) deciduous, (3) trees to be used as a (4) street canopy tree (5) tolerant of the city environment and (6) hardy in USDA zone 4.*

Summary

The **North American Plantfile** is a unique tool that can greatly assist professional and amateur designers. Analysis and selection of plant materials that satisfy complex criteria requirements are easily and quickly accomplished and with confidence. Planting plans that feature a wonderful diversity of species and varieties that are better adapted to the project site and region are now probable. The result is the creation of beautiful and healthy landscapes that serve a useful purpose, give human enjoyment, and are more sustainable.

Whether used as an aid to plant identification in the field or as a quick find plant selection tool, the **North American Plantfile's** creative pictorial and photographic presentation promises to be invaluable to many persons.

Deciduous master file

LARGE TREE	FORM	BARK	LEAF	FLOWER	FRUIT	CULTURE	USES	REGION

Acer nigrum
Black Maple

'Greencolumn'

CULTURE: P C Si Sa L / 4 5 6 7 8 / M P A W E / W WM M MD D / vT T M I vl / dense / moderate

USES: food - maple syrup / shade / specimen / accent / street canopy

REGION: 2b—7 / i. 1812 / e. U.S

FORM: 50-75

Acer pseudoplatanus
Sycamore Maple
Planetree Maple

'Brilliantissimum' 'Spaethii'
'Purpureum'

CULTURE: P C Si Sa L / 4 5 6 7 8 / M P A W E / W WM M MD D / vT T M I vl / dense / moderate

USES: screen / shade / specimen / accent / street canopy

REGION: 5b—7 / i. e. col. x. / Europe

FORM: 50-75

Acer rubrum
Red Maple

'Autumn Flame' 'Schlesinger'
'Columnare' 'Scanlon'

CULTURE: P C Si Sa L / 4 5 6 7 8 / M P A W E / W WM M MD D / vT T M I vl / dense / moderate / fast

USES: bee tree / seacoast / shade / specimen / accent / street canopy

REGION: 3b—10 / c. 1656 / e. N. America

FORM: 50-75

Acer saccharinum
Silver Maple

'Blair' 'Pyramidale'
'Silver Queen' 'Wieri'

CULTURE: P C Si Sa L / 4 5 6 7 8 / M P A W E / W WM M MD D / vT T M I vl / open / fast / short

USES: bee tree / shade / street canopy / windbreak

REGION: 3—9a / i.1725 / e.U.S.

FORM: >75

Acer saccharum
Sugar Maple

'Bonfire' 'Temple's Upright'
'Globosum' 'Green Mountain'

CULTURE: P C Si Sa L / 4 5 6 7 8 / M P A W E / W WM M MD D / vT T M I vl / slow / moderate / moderate

USES: food- maple syrup / shade / specimen / street canopy

REGION: 3b—7b / i.1735 / e. N. America

FORM: 50-75

Aesculus indica
Indies Horsechestnut

'Sidney Pierce'

bee tree
shade
specimen / accent

Himalayas

4b—8

i.1851

P	C	Si	Sa	L
4	5	6	7	8
M	P	A	W	E
W	WM	M	MD	D
vT	T	M	I	vI

moderate

50·75

Aesculus octandra
Yellow Buckeye
Sweet Buckeye

preservation
shade
specimen / accent

Central U. S

(4b)—8

i.1764

P	C	Si	Sa	L
4	5	6	7	8
M	P	A	W	E
W	WM	M	MD	D
vT	T	M	I	vI

slow

moderate

50·75

Alnus rubra
Red Alder
Oregon Alder

naturalizing
shade
specimen / accent

w. N. America

(5a)—8

i.b.1880

P	C	Si	Sa	L
4	5	6	7	8
M	P	A	W	E
W	WM	M	MD	D
vT	T	M	I	vI

fast   short

moderate

open

20·35

Avicennia marina
Black Mangrove

bee tree
culinary
jams, jellies
naturalizing
preservation
seacoast
specimen / accent

s.e. U.S.

9—10

P	C	Si	Sa	L
4	5	6	7	8
M	P	A	W	E
W	WM	M	MD	D
vT	T	M	I	vI

fast   short

moderate

50·75

Betula alleghaniensis
syn. B. lutea
Yellow Birch

mass planting
patio garden
shade
specimen / accent

e. N. America

3—8b

i.1767

P	C	Si	Sa	L
4	5	6	7	8
M	P	A	W	E
W	WM	M	MD	D
vT	T	M	I	vI

moderate   moderate

moderate

50·75

...deciduous

T8—2

..deciduous **T8—3**

LARGE TREE	FORM	BARK	LEAF	FLOWER	FRUIT	CULTURE	USES	REGION

Betula costata
Japanese Birch

open · 50-75

CULTURE: P C Si Sa L / 4 5 6 7 8 / M P A W E / W WM M MD D / vT T M I vl / moderate / short

USES: mass planting, patio garden, shade, specimen / accent

REGION: Japan · 6—8 · i.1880

Betula lenta
Sweet Birch
Cherry Birch

moderate · 50-75

CULTURE: P C Si Sa L / 4 5 6 7 8 / M P A W E / W WM M MD D / vT T M I vl / slow / moderate

USES: mass planting, naturalizing, patio garden, shade

REGION: e. U.S. · (3b)—7 · i.1759

Betula maximowicziana
Monarch Birch

open · 50-75

CULTURE: P C Si Sa L / 4 5 6 7 8 / M P A W E / W WM M MD D / vT T M I vl / fast / moderate

USES: mass planting, patio garden, shade, specimen / accent

REGION: Japan · (5b)—7 · c.1890

Betula nigra
River Birch
Red Birch
'Heritage'

moderate · 50-75

CULTURE: P C Si Sa L / 4 5 6 7 8 / M P A W E / W WM M MD D / vT T M I vl / fast / short

USES: mass planting, naturalizing, patio garden, shade, specimen / accent, street canopy

REGION: e. U.S. · 4—9 · i.1736

Betula papyrifera
Paper Birch
Canoe Birch

open · 35-50

CULTURE: P C Si Sa L / 4 5 6 7 8 / M P A W E / W WM M MD D / vT T M I vl / moderate / short

USES: mass planting, patio garden, shade, specimen / accent

REGION: n. N.America · 2—6 · i.1750

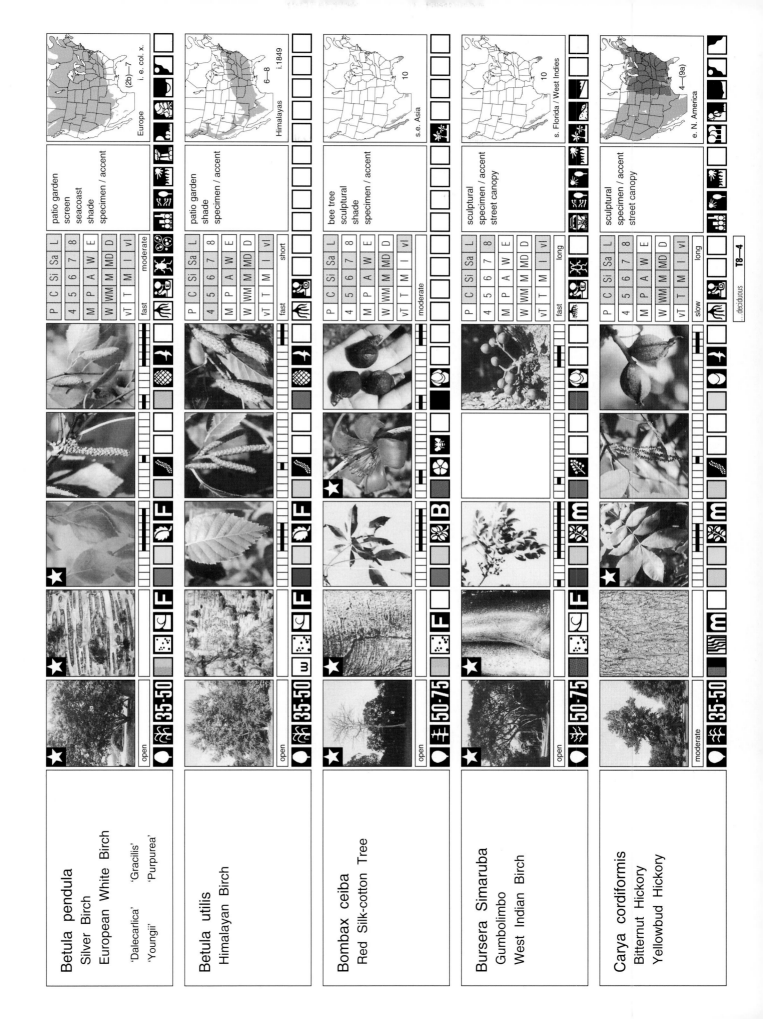

Betula pendula
Silver Birch
European White Birch

'Dalecarlica'   'Gracilis'
'Youngii'   'Purpurea'

P	C	Si	Sa	L
4	5	6	7	8
M	P	A	W	E
W	WM	M	MD	D
vT	T	M	I	vI

patio garden
screen
seacoast
shade
specimen / accent

Europe   (2b)—7   i. e. col. x.

open   35-50   fast   moderate

Betula utilis
Himalayan Birch

P	C	Si	Sa	L
4	5	6	7	8
M	P	A	W	E
W	WM	M	MD	D
vT	T	M	I	vI

patio garden
shade
specimen / accent

Himalayas   6—8   i.1849

open   35-50   fast   short

Bombax ceiba
Red Silk-cotton Tree

P	C	Si	Sa	L
4	5	6	7	8
M	P	A	W	E
W	WM	M	MD	D
vT	T	M	I	vI

bee tree
sculptural
shade
specimen / accent

s.e. Asia   10

open   50-75   moderate

Bursera Simaruba
Gumbolimbo
West Indian Birch

P	C	Si	Sa	L
4	5	6	7	8
M	P	A	W	E
W	WM	M	MD	D
vT	T	M	I	vI

sculptural
specimen / accent
street canopy

s. Florida / West Indies   10

open   50-75   fast   long

Carya cordiformis
Bitternut Hickory
Yellowbud Hickory

P	C	Si	Sa	L
4	5	6	7	8
M	P	A	W	E
W	WM	M	MD	D
vT	T	M	I	vI

sculptural
specimen / accent
street canopy

e. N. America   4—(9a)

moderate   35-50   slow   long

…deciduous   T8—4

LARGE TREE	FORM	BARK	LEAF	FLOWER	FRUIT	CULTURE	USES	REGION

Carya glabra
Pignut Hickory
Broom Hickory

moderate · 35-50

CULTURE: P C Si Sa L · 4 5 6 7 8 · M P A W E · W WM M MD D · vT T M I vI · slow — long

USES: preservation, shade, specimen / accent

REGION: 5b—9 · e. N.America

Carya illinoensis
Pecan

'Cheyene' 'Chickasaw'
'Elliot' 'Stuart'

moderate · 6-12

CULTURE: P C Si Sa L · 4 5 6 7 8 · M P A W E · W WM M MD D · vT T M I vI · moderate — long

USES: naturalizing, orchard, preservation, seacoast, shade, specimen / accent

REGION: (5b)—9 · i.1760 · N.America

Carya laciniosa
Big Shellbark Hickory
King Nut

'Bradley' 'Fayette'
'Chetopa' 'Nieman'

moderate · 35-50

CULTURE: P C Si Sa L · 4 5 6 7 8 · M P A W E · W WM M MD D · vT T M I vI · slow — long

USES: orchard, preservation, shade, specimen / accent

REGION: 5—8 · i.1804 · n.e. U.S.

Carya ovata
Shagbark Hickory
Shellbark Hickory

'Abundance' 'Porter'
'Fox' 'Wilcox'

moderate · 35-50

CULTURE: P C Si Sa L · 4 5 6 7 8 · M P A W E · W WM M MD D · vT T M I vI · slow — long

USES: naturalizing, orchard, shade, specimen / accent

REGION: (4a)—8 · c.1629 · e. N.America

Carya texana
Black Hickory

moderate · 50-75

CULTURE: P C Si Sa L · 4 5 6 7 8 · M P A W E · W WM M MD D · vT T M I vI · slow — long

USES: orchard, shade, specimen / accent

REGION: (5b)—9a · s.c. U.S.

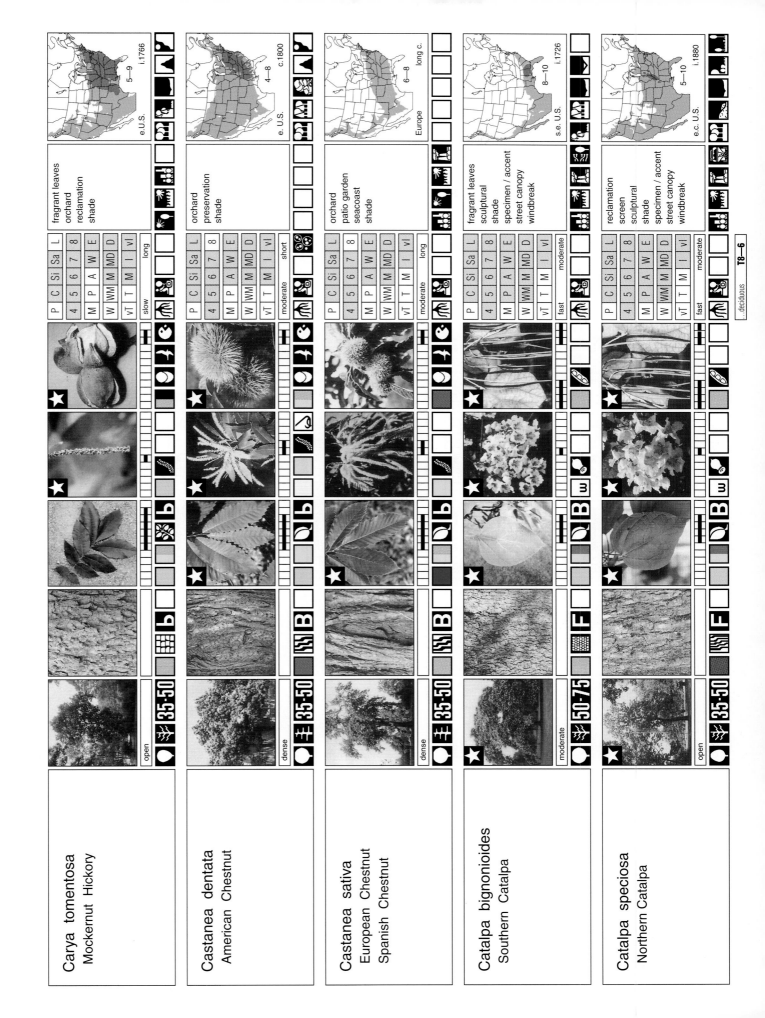

Carya tomentosa — Mockernut Hickory
e.U.S. — i.1766 — 5–9
open — 35–50
Uses: fragrant leaves, orchard, reclamation, shade
P C Si Sa L / 4 5 6 7 8 / M P A W E / W WM M MD D / vT T M I vl — slow — long

Castanea dentata — American Chestnut
e. U.S. — c.1800 — 4–8
dense — 35–50
Uses: orchard, preservation, shade
P C Si Sa L / 4 5 6 7 8 / M P A W E / W WM M MD D / vT T M I vl — moderate — short

Castanea sativa — European Chestnut, Spanish Chestnut
Europe — long c. — 6–8
dense — 35–50
Uses: orchard, patio garden, seacoast, shade
P C Si Sa L / 4 5 6 7 8 / M P A W E / W WM M MD D / vT T M I vl — moderate — long

Catalpa bignonioides — Southern Catalpa
s.e. U.S. — i.1726 — 8–10
moderate — 50–75
Uses: fragrant leaves, sculptural, shade, specimen / accent, street canopy, windbreak
P C Si Sa L / 4 5 6 7 8 / M P A W E / W WM M MD D / vT T M I vl — fast — moderate

Catalpa speciosa — Northern Catalpa
e.c. U.S. — i.1880 — 5–10
open — 35–50
Uses: reclamation, screen, sculptural, shade, specimen / accent, street canopy, windbreak
P C Si Sa L / 4 5 6 7 8 / M P A W E / W WM M MD D / vT T M I vl — fast — moderate

…deciduous   **T8—6**

LARGE TREE	FORM	BARK	LEAF	FLOWER	FRUIT	CULTURE	USES	REGION

Celtis australis
European Hackberry

moderate / 50-75

CULTURE: P C Si Sa L / 4 5 6 7 8 / M P A W E / W WM M MD D / vT T M I vI / slow — moderate

USES: screen / shade / specimen / accent / street canopy

REGION: s. Europe / 7—9 / i.1736

Celtis jessoensis
Korean Hackberry

moderate / 50-75

CULTURE: P C Si Sa L / 4 5 6 7 8 / M P A W E / W WM M MD D / vT T M I vI / moderate — moderate

USES: shade / specimen / accent / street canopy

REGION: Korea / 6—9 / i.1892

Celtis laevigata
Sugarberry
Sugar Hackberry

'All Seasons'

moderate / 50-75

CULTURE: P C Si Sa L / 4 5 6 7 8 / M P A W E / W WM M MD D / vT T M I vI / moderate — moderate

USES: shade / specimen / accent / street canopy / windbreak

REGION: s.e. U.S. / 6—10 / c.1811

Celtis occidentalis
Common Hackberry

'Prairie Pride'

moderate / 50-75

CULTURE: P C Si Sa L / 4 5 6 7 8 / M P A W E / W WM M MD D / vT T M I vI / moderate — long

USES: shade / specimen / accent / street canopy

REGION: e.c. N.America / 3—8 / i.1656

Celtis sinensis
Chinese Hackberry
Yunnan Hackberry

moderate / 50-75

CULTURE: P C Si Sa L / 4 5 6 7 8 / M P A W E / W WM M MD D / vT T M I vI / slow — moderate

USES: bonsai / hedge / patio garden / seacoast / specimen / accent / street canopy / windbreak

REGION: China / 6—9 / i.1793

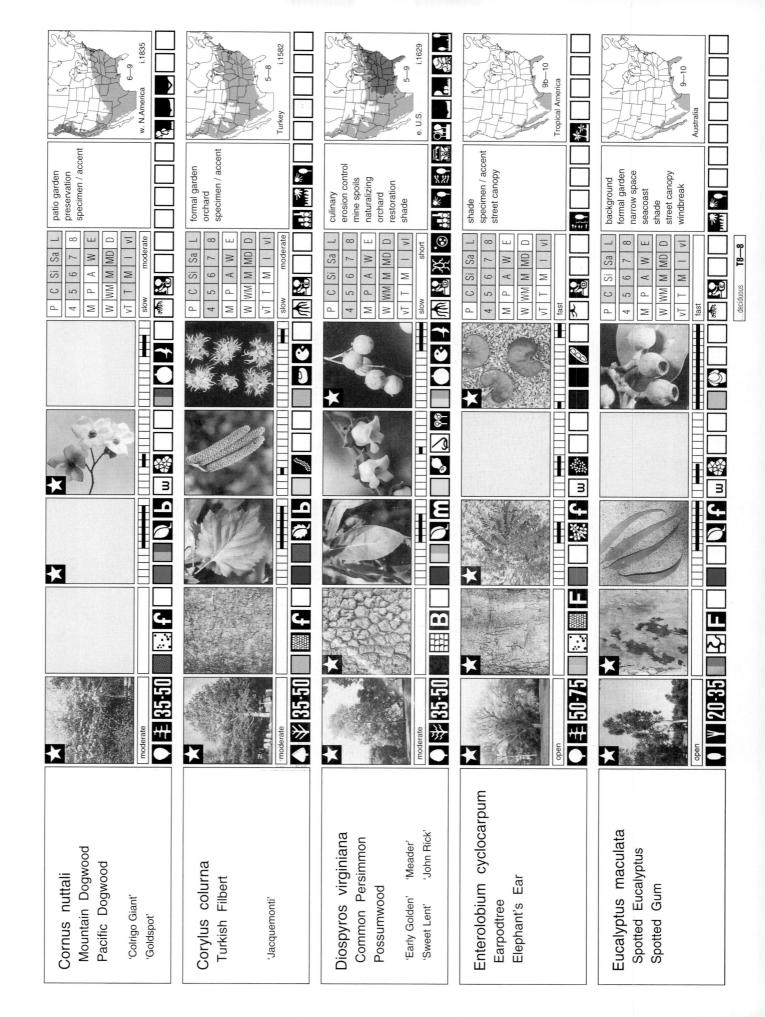

Cornus nuttali
Mountain Dogwood
Pacific Dogwood

'Colrigo Giant'
'Goldspot'

P	C	Si	Sa	L
4	5	6	7	8
M	P	A	W	E
W	WM	M	MD	D
vT	T	M	I	vI

patio garden
preservation
specimen / accent

slow   moderate

w. N.America   6—9   i.1835

35-50   moderate

Corylus colurna
Turkish Filbert

'Jacquemonti'

P	C	Si	Sa	L
4	5	6	7	8
M	P	A	W	E
W	WM	M	MD	D
vT	T	M	I	vI

formal garden
orchard
specimen / accent

slow   moderate

Turkey   5—8   i.1582

35-50   moderate

Diospyros virginiana
Common Persimmon
Possumwood

'Early Golden'   'Meader'
'Sweet Lent'   'John Rick'

P	C	Si	Sa	L
4	5	6	7	8
M	P	A	W	E
W	WM	M	MD	D
vT	T	M	I	vI

culinary
erosion control
mine spoils
naturalizing
orchard
restoration
shade

slow   short

e. U.S.   5—9   i.1629

35-50   moderate

Enterolobium cyclocarpum
Earpodtree
Elephant's Ear

P	C	Si	Sa	L
4	5	6	7	8
M	P	A	W	E
W	WM	M	MD	D
vT	T	M	I	vI

shade
specimen / accent
street canopy

fast

Tropical America   9b—10

50-75   open

Eucalyptus maculata
Spotted Eucalyptus
Spotted Gum

P	C	Si	Sa	L
4	5	6	7	8
M	P	A	W	E
W	WM	M	MD	D
vT	T	M	I	vI

background
formal garden
narrow space
seacoast
shade
street canopy
windbreak

fast

Australia   9—10

20-35   open

...deciduous   **T8—8**

LARGE TREE	FORM	BARK	LEAF	FLOWER	FRUIT	CULTURE	USES	REGION

Fagus grandifolia — American Beech

- FORM: 50-75, dense
- CULTURE: P C Si Sa L / 4 5 6 7 8 / M P A W E / W WM M MD D / vT T M I vl / slow / long
- USES: hedge / barrier, preservation, sculptural, shade, specimen / accent
- REGION: e. N. America, i.1766, 4—9a

Fagus orientalis — Oriental Beech

- FORM: 35-50, dense
- CULTURE: P C Si Sa L / 4 5 6 7 8 / M P A W E / W WM M MD D / vT T M I vl / slow / long
- USES: hedge / barrier, shade, specimen / accent, topiary
- REGION: Asia, i.1904, 5b—7

Fagus sylvatica — European Beech

'Asplenifolia' 'Atropunicia'
'Fastigiata' 'Pendula'

- FORM: 50-75, dense
- CULTURE: P C Si Sa L / 4 5 6 7 8 / M P A W E / W WM M MD D / vT T M I vl / slow / long
- USES: hedge / barrier, sculptural, seacoast, shade, shelter belt, specimen / accent, topiary
- REGION: Europe, long c., 4—9

Ficus aurea — Florida Strangler Fig / Golden Fig

- FORM: >75, moderate
- CULTURE: P C Si Sa L / 4 5 6 7 8 / M P A W E / W WM M MD D / vT T M I vl / fast / long
- USES: sculptural, shade, specimen / accent
- REGION: s. Florida, 10

Ficus religiosa — Botree Fig / Peepul

- FORM: 50-75, moderate
- CULTURE: P C Si Sa L / 4 5 6 7 8 / M P A W E / W WM M MD D / vT T M I vl / fast / long
- USES: religious, sacred tree, shade, specimen / accent
- REGION: India, 7—10

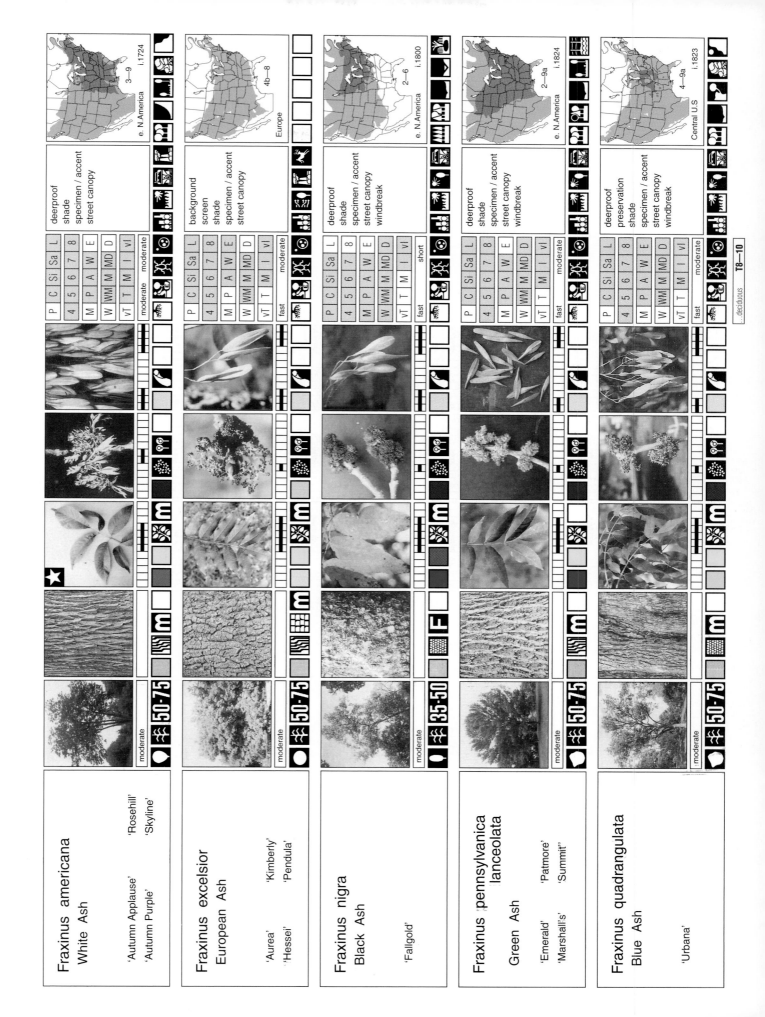

Fraxinus americana
White Ash

'Autumn Applause'   'Rosehill'
'Autumn Purple'   'Skyline'

deerproof
shade
specimen / accent
street canopy

e. N.America   i.1724   3—9

P	C	Si	Sa	L
4	5	6	7	8
M	P	A	W	E
W	WM	M	MD	D
vT	T	M	I	vI

moderate   moderate

moderate   50-75

Fraxinus excelsior
European Ash

'Aurea'   'Kimberly'
'Hessei'   'Pendula'

background
screen
shade
specimen / accent
street canopy

Europe   4b—8

P	C	Si	Sa	L
4	5	6	7	8
M	P	A	W	E
W	WM	M	MD	D
vT	T	M	I	vI

fast   moderate

moderate   50-75

Fraxinus nigra
Black Ash

'Fallgold'

deerproof
shade
specimen / accent
street canopy
windbreak

e. N.America   i.1800   2—6

P	C	Si	Sa	L
4	5	6	7	8
M	P	A	W	E
W	WM	M	MD	D
vT	T	M	I	vI

fast   short

moderate   35-50

Fraxinus pennsylvanica lanceolata
Green Ash

'Emerald'   'Patmore'
'Marshall's'   'Summit''

deerproof
shade
specimen / accent
street canopy
windbreak

e. N.America   i.1824   2—9a

P	C	Si	Sa	L
4	5	6	7	8
M	P	A	W	E
W	WM	M	MD	D
vT	T	M	I	vI

fast   moderate

moderate   50-75

Fraxinus quadrangulata
Blue Ash

'Urbana'

deerproof
preservation
shade
specimen / accent
street canopy
windbreak

Central U.S   i.1823   4—9a

P	C	Si	Sa	L
4	5	6	7	8
M	P	A	W	E
W	WM	M	MD	D
vT	T	M	I	vI

fast   moderate

moderate   50-75

...deciduous   **T8—10**

LARGE TREE	FORM	BARK	LEAF	FLOWER	FRUIT	CULTURE	USES	REGION

Ginkgo biloba
Ginkgo
Maidenhairtree

'Autumn Gold' 'Lakeview'
'Fastigiata'

FORM: open 50-75
CULTURE:
P	C	Si	Sa	L
4	5	6	7	8
M	P	A	W	E
W	WM	M	MD	D
vT	T	M	I	vl
slow — long

USES: bonsai / low maintenance / patio garden / shade / specimen / accent / street canopy

REGION: e. China 4—9 i.1727

Gleditsia aquatica
Waterlocust

FORM: open 50-75
CULTURE:
P	C	Si	Sa	L
4	5	6	7	8
M	P	A	W	E
W	WM	M	MD	D
vT	T	M	I	vl
fast — short

USES: naturalizing / seacoast / specimen / accent / windbreak

REGION: s.e. U.S. 5b—9 i.1723

Gleditsia triacanthos
Common Honeylocust

'Imperial' 'Moraine'
'Shademaster' 'Skyline'

FORM: open 50-75
CULTURE:
P	C	Si	Sa	L
4	5	6	7	8
M	P	A	W	E
W	WM	M	MD	D
vT	T	M	I	vl
fast — moderate

USES: screen / shade / street canopy / windbreak

REGION: e.c. U.S. 4—9 i.1700

Gymnocladus dioica
Kentucky Coffeetree

FORM: moderate 35-50
CULTURE:
P	C	Si	Sa	L
4	5	6	7	8
M	P	A	W	E
W	WM	M	MD	D
vT	T	M	I	vl
moderate — moderate

USES: naturalizing / sculptural / shade / specimen / accent / windbreak

REGION: c. U.S. 4—8

Juglans cinerea
Butternut
White Walnut

'Ayers' 'Chamberlin'
'Booth' 'My Joy'

FORM: moderate 35-50
CULTURE:
P	C	Si	Sa	L
4	5	6	7	8
M	P	A	W	E
W	WM	M	MD	D
vT	T	M	I	vl
fast — short

USES: orchard / preservation / shade

REGION: e. N. America 3b—7 c.1633

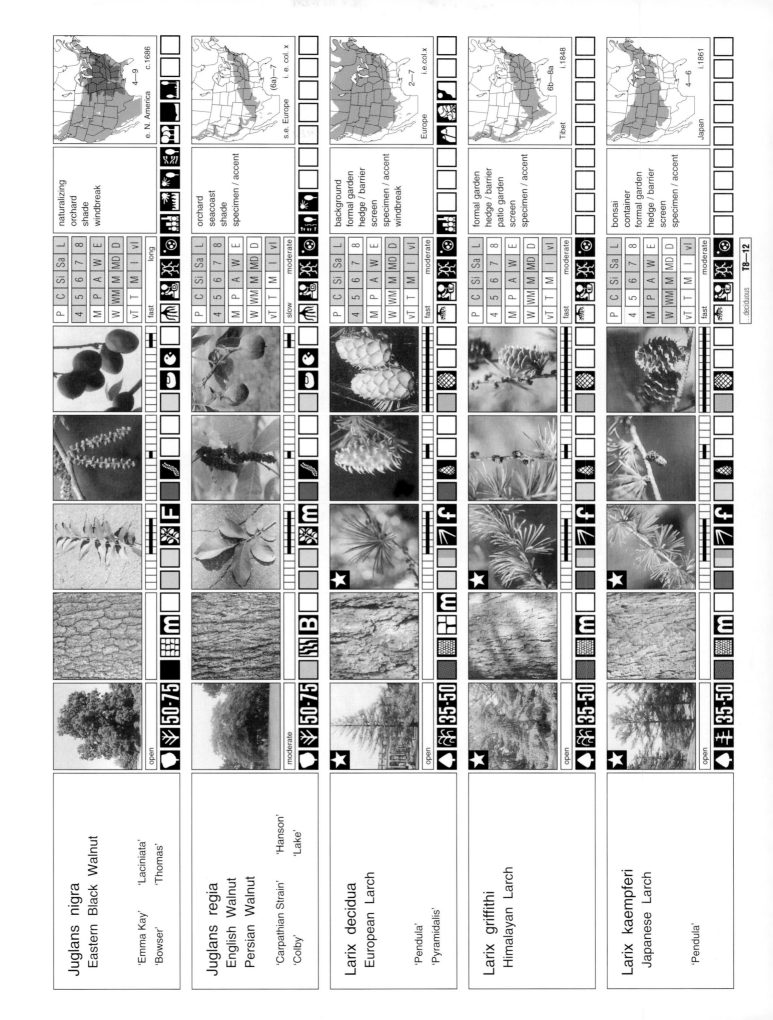

Juglans nigra
Eastern Black Walnut

'Emma Kay'   'Laciniata'
'Bowser'   'Thomas'

e. N. America   c.1686   4—9

naturalizing
orchard
shade
windbreak

P	C	Si	Sa	L
4	5	6	7	8
M	P	A	W	E
W	WM	M	MD	D
vT	T	M	I	VI

fast   long
open   50-75

Juglans regia
English Walnut
Persian Walnut

'Carpathian Strain'   'Hanson'
'Colby'   'Lake'

s.e. Europe   i. e. col. x   (6a)—7

orchard
seacoast
shade
specimen / accent

P	C	Si	Sa	L
4	5	6	7	8
M	P	A	W	E
W	WM	M	MD	D
vT	T	M	I	VI

moderate
moderate   50-75

Larix decidua
European Larch

'Pendula'
'Pyramidalis'

Europe   i.e.col. x   2—7

background
formal garden
hedge / barrier
screen
specimen / accent
windbreak

P	C	Si	Sa	L
4	5	6	7	8
M	P	A	W	E
W	WM	M	MD	D
vT	T	M	I	VI

slow   moderate
fast   moderate
open   35-50

Larix griffithi
Himalayan Larch

Tibet   i.1848   6b—8a

formal garden
hedge / barrier
patio garden
screen
specimen / accent

P	C	Si	Sa	L
4	5	6	7	8
M	P	A	W	E
W	WM	M	MD	D
vT	T	M	I	VI

fast   moderate
open   35-50

Larix kaempferi
Japanese Larch

'Pendula'

Japan   i.1861   4—6

bonsai
container
formal garden
hedge / barrier
screen
specimen / accent

P	C	Si	Sa	L
4	5	6	7	8
M	P	A	W	E
W	WM	M	MD	D
vT	T	M	I	VI

fast   moderate
open   35-50

...deciduous   **T8—12**

LARGE TREE	FORM	BARK	LEAF	FLOWER	FRUIT	CULTURE	USES	REGION

Larix laricina
Eastern Larch
Tamarack
'Newport Beauty'

- FORM: open — 35-50
- CULTURE: P C Si Sa L / 5 6 7 8 / M P A W E / W WM M MD D / vT T M I vl — fast — moderate
- USES: background, bog garden, formal garden, screen, specimen / accent
- REGION: n. N. America — 2–6 — i.1760

Larix occidentalis
Western Larch
'Repens'

- FORM: open — 35-50
- CULTURE: P C Si Sa L / 4 5 6 7 8 / M P A W E / W WM M MD D / vT T M I vl — slow — long
- USES: background, formal garden, screen, specimen / accent, windbreak
- REGION: w. N. America — 2–6 — i.1880

Liquidambar styraciflua
American Sweetgum
'Burgendy'   'Palo Alto'
'Festival'   'Autumn Gold'

- FORM: moderate — 50-75
- CULTURE: P C Si Sa L / 4 5 6 7 8 / M P A W E / W WM M MD D / vT T M I vl — very fast — very short
- USES: background, screen, shade, specimen / accent, street canopy
- REGION: e. U.S. — 5–10 — i.17th cent.

Liriodendron tulipifera
Tuliptree
Tulip Poplar
'Arnold'   'Majestic Beauty'
'Fastigiatum'

- FORM: moderate — 50-75
- CULTURE: P C Si Sa L / 4 5 6 7 8 / M P A W E / W WM M MD D / vT T M I vl — fast — moderate
- USES: bee tree, bonsai, formal garden, screen, shade, specimen / accent, street canopy
- REGION: e. U.S. — 4b–9 — c.1688

Magnolia acuminata
Cucumbertree Magnolia
'Golden Glow'
'Miss Honeybee'

- FORM: moderate — 50-75
- CULTURE: P C Si Sa L / 4 5 6 7 8 / M P A W E / W WM M MD D / vT T M I vl — moderate — moderate
- USES: formal garden, shade, specimen / accent, street canopy
- REGION: e. N. America — 4b–9a — i.1736

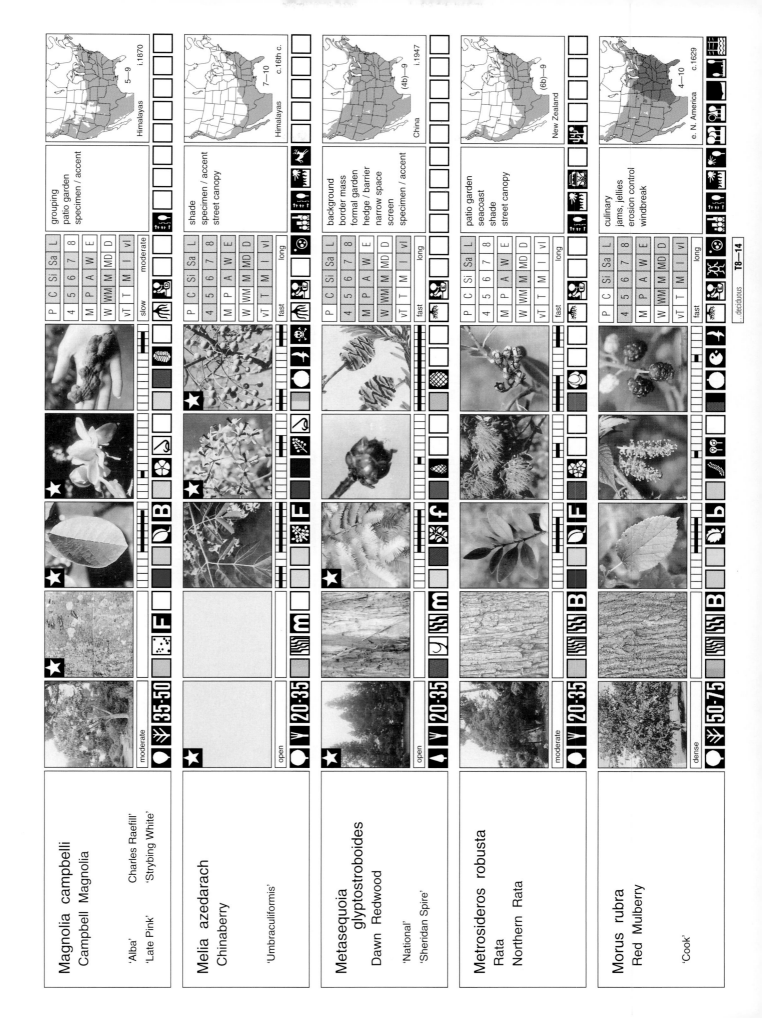

Magnolia campbelli
Campbell Magnolia

'Alba' Charles Raefill'
'Late Pink' 'Strybing White'

grouping
patio garden
specimen / accent

Himalayas 5—9 i:1870

P	C	Si	Sa	L
4	5	6	7	8
M	P	A	W	E
W	WM	M	MD	D
vT	T	M	I	vl

slow / moderate

moderate 35-50

Melia azedarach
Chinaberry

'Umbraculiformis'

shade
specimen / accent
street canopy

Himalayas 7—10 c.16th c.

P	C	Si	Sa	L
4	5	6	7	8
M	P	A	W	E
W	WM	M	MD	D
vT	T	M	I	vl

fast / long

open 20-35

Metasequoia glyptostroboides
Dawn Redwood

'National'
'Sheridan Spire'

background
border mass
formal garden
hedge / barrier
narrow space
screen
specimen / accent

China (4b)—9 i.1947

P	C	Si	Sa	L
4	5	6	7	8
M	P	A	W	E
W	WM	M	MD	D
vT	T	M	I	vl

fast / long

open 20-35

Metrosideros robusta
Rata
Northern Rata

patio garden
seacoast
shade
street canopy

New Zealand (6b)—9

P	C	Si	Sa	L
4	5	6	7	8
M	P	A	W	E
W	WM	M	MD	D
vT	T	M	I	vl

fast / long

moderate 20-35

Morus rubra
Red Mulberry

'Cook'

culinary
jams, jellies
erosion control
windbreak

e. N. America 4—10 c.1629

P	C	Si	Sa	L
4	5	6	7	8
M	P	A	W	E
W	WM	M	MD	D
vT	T	M	I	vl

fast / long

dense 50-75

...deciduous **T8—14**

LARGE TREE	FORM	BARK	LEAF	FLOWER	FRUIT	CULTURE	USES	REGION

Nyssa sylvatica
Black Tupelo
Black Gum
Pepperidge

dense · 50-75

P	C	Si	Sa	L
4	5	6	7	8
M	P	A	W	E
W	WM	M	MD	D
vT	T	M	I	vl

slow / moderate

border mass
naturalizing
seacoast
shade
specimen / accent
street canopy

e. U.S.   i:1750   4—9

Platanus x acerifolia
London Planetree

'Bloodgood'   'Yarwood'
'Pyramidalis'

open · 50-75

P	C	Si	Sa	L
4	5	6	7	8
M	P	A	W	E
W	WM	M	MD	D
vT	T	M	I	vl

fast / long

background
screen
seacoast
shade
specimen / accent
street canopy

hybrid   6—9a   o.1663

Platanus occidentalis
American Planetree
American Sycamore

open · >75

P	C	Si	Sa	L
4	5	6	7	8
M	P	A	W	E
W	WM	M	MD	D
vT	T	M	I	vl

fast / long

mass planting
seacoast
shade
specimen / accent
street canopy
windbreak

e.c.U.S.   4—9a   i.1636

Platanus orientalis
Oriental Planetree

open · 50-75

P	C	Si	Sa	L
4	5	6	7	8
M	P	A	W	E
W	WM	M	MD	D
vT	T	M	I	vl

fast / long

mass planting
seacoast
shade
specimen / accent
street canopy

s.e. Europe   6b—9a

Platanus racemosa
California Planetree
Buttonwood

open · 50-75

P	C	Si	Sa	L
4	5	6	7	8
M	P	A	W	E
W	WM	M	MD	D
vT	T	M	I	vl

fast / long

erosion control
shade
specimen / accent
street canopy
windbreak

s. California   7b—10   i:1870

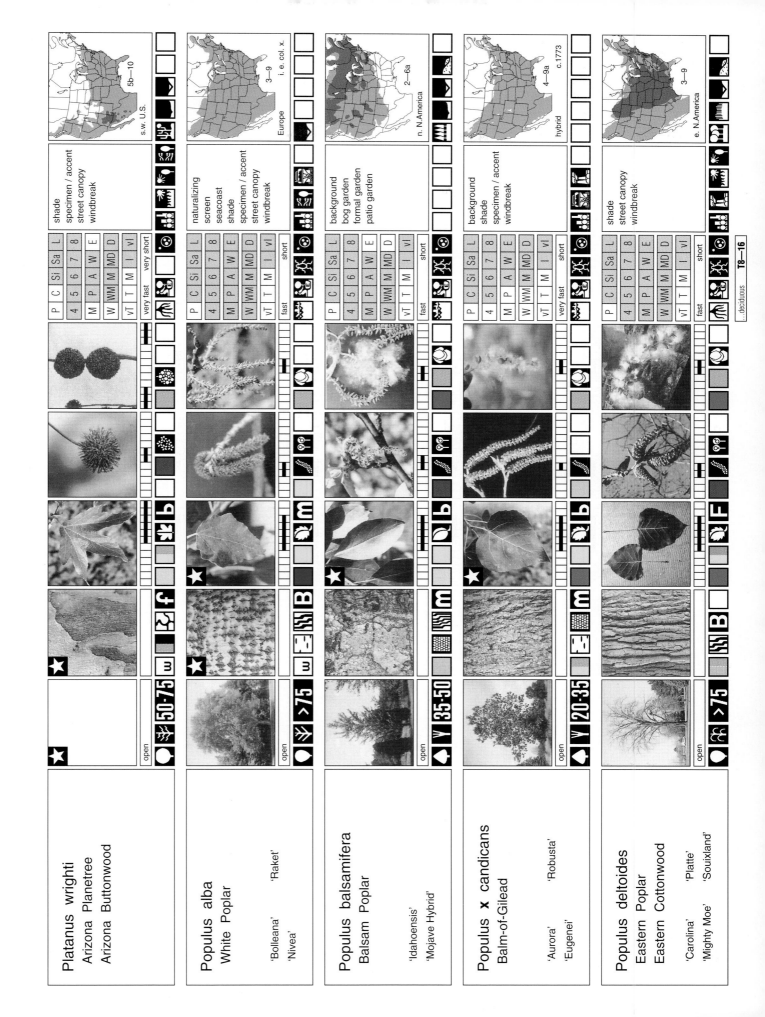

Platanus wrighti
Arizona Planetree
Arizona Buttonwood

P	C	Si	Sa	L
4	5	6	7	8
M	P	A	W	E
W	WM	M	MD	D
vT	T	M	I	vI

very fast · short

5b—10 · s.w. U.S.

shade
specimen / accent
street canopy
windbreak

open · 50-75

Populus alba
White Poplar

'Bolleana' · 'Raket'
'Nivea'

P	C	Si	Sa	L
4	5	6	7	8
M	P	A	W	E
W	WM	M	MD	D
vT	T	M	I	vI

fast · short

3—9 · i. e. col. x. · Europe

naturalizing
screen
seacoast
shade
specimen / accent
street canopy
windbreak

open · >75

Populus balsamifera
Balsam Poplar

'Idahoensis'
'Mojave Hybrid'

P	C	Si	Sa	L
4	5	6	7	8
M	P	A	W	E
W	WM	M	MD	D
vT	T	M	I	vI

fast · short

2—6a · n. N.America

background
bog garden
formal garden
patio garden

open · 35-50

Populus x candicans
Balm-of-Gilead

'Aurora' · 'Robusta'
'Eugenei'

P	C	Si	Sa	L
4	5	6	7	8
M	P	A	W	E
W	WM	M	MD	D
vT	T	M	I	vI

very fast · short

4—9a · c.1773 · hybrid

background
shade
specimen / accent
windbreak

open · 20-35

Populus deltoides
Eastern Poplar
Eastern Cottonwood

'Carolina' · 'Platte'
'Mighty Moe' · 'Souixland'

P	C	Si	Sa	L
4	5	6	7	8
M	P	A	W	E
W	WM	M	MD	D
vT	T	M	I	vI

fast · short

3—9 · e. N.America

shade
street canopy
windbreak

open · >75

...deciduous · **T8—16**

LARGE TREE	FORM	BARK	LEAF	FLOWER	FRUIT	CULTURE	USES	REGION

Populus fremonti
Fremont Cottonwood
Western Cottonwood

'Nevada'
'Texana'

open 35-50 B

FORM: open

CULTURE:
P	C	Si	Sa	L
4	5	6	7	8
M	P	A	W	E
W	WM	M	MD	D
vT	T	M	I	vl
short

USES: shade / street canopy / windbreak

REGION: s.w. U.S. 5—10

Populus grandidentata
Bigtooth Aspen

open 20-35 F

CULTURE:
P	C	Si	Sa	L
4	5	6	7	8
M	P	A	W	E
W	WM	M	MD	D
vT	T	M	I	vl
fast

USES: naturalizing / patio garden / specimen / accent

REGION: e. N.America 2b—7a i.1772

Populus maximowiczi
Japanese Poplar

open 35-50 B

CULTURE:
P	C	Si	Sa	L
4	5	6	7	8
M	P	A	W	E
W	WM	M	MD	D
vT	T	M	I	vl
fast

USES: shade / specimen / accent / windbreak

REGION: Japan (3b)—7b i.1890

Populus nigra 'Italica'
Lombardy Poplar

open 6-12

CULTURE:
P	C	Si	Sa	L
4	5	6	7	8
M	P	A	W	E
W	WM	M	MD	D
vT	T	M	I	vl
fast

USES: formal garden / hedge / barrier / narrow space / seacoast / screen / windbreak

REGION: Eurasia 2—9

Populus sargenti
Plains Poplar
Plains Cottonwood

'Souixland'

open >75 B

CULTURE:
P	C	Si	Sa	L
4	5	6	7	8
M	P	A	W	E
W	WM	M	MD	D
vT	T	M	I	vl
fast

USES: shade / street canopy / windbreak

REGION: c. N.America 3—9a

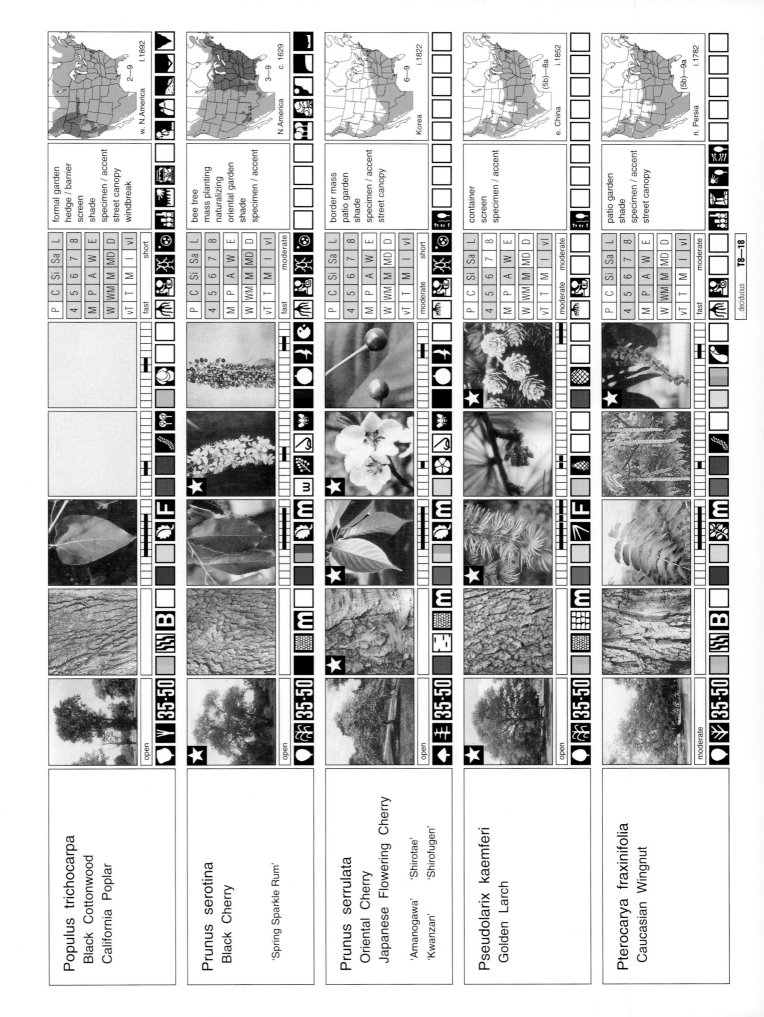

Populus trichocarpa
Black Cottonwood
California Poplar

Prunus serotina
Black Cherry

'Spring Sparkle Rum'

Prunus serrulata
Oriental Cherry
Japanese Flowering Cherry

'Amanogawa'   'Shirotae'
'Kwanzan'   'Shirofugen'

Pseudolarix kaemferi
Golden Larch

Pterocarya fraxinifolia
Caucasian Wingnut

T8—18   ...deciduous

LARGE TREE	FORM	BARK	LEAF	FLOWER	FRUIT	CULTURE	USES	REGION

Pterocarya x rehderiana
Rehder Wingnut

moderate · 35-50

P	C	Si	Sa	L
4	5	6	7	8
M	P	A	W	E
W	WM	M	MD	D
vT	T	M	I	vI

fast · moderate

patio garden
shade
street canopy
specimen / accent

hybrid · (5a)—9a · o.1879

Quercus alba
White Oak

moderate · >75

P	C	Si	Sa	L
4	5	6	7	8
M	P	A	W	E
W	WM	M	MD	D
vT	T	M	I	vI

slow · long

naturalizing
sculptural
seacoast
shade
specimen / accent
street canopy

e. N.America · 4—9 · i.1724

Quercus bicolor
Swamp White Oak

moderate · 50-75

P	C	Si	Sa	L
4	5	6	7	8
M	P	A	W	E
W	WM	M	MD	D
vT	T	M	I	vI

slow · long

bog garden
naturalizing
shade
specimen / accent
street canopy
water garden

e. N.America · (3b)—8 · i.1800

Quercus borealis
syn. Q. rubra
Northern Red Oak

dense · >75

P	C	Si	Sa	L
4	5	6	7	8
M	P	A	W	E
W	WM	M	MD	D
vT	T	M	I	vI

moderate · long

shade
specimen / accent
street canopy

e. N.America · 3—9a · i.1724

Quercus cerris
European Turkey Oak

moderate · 50-75

P	C	Si	Sa	L
4	5	6	7	8
M	P	A	W	E
W	WM	M	MD	D
vT	T	M	I	vI

moderate · moderate

shade
specimen / accent
street canopy

s. Europe · (6b)—9a · i.1735

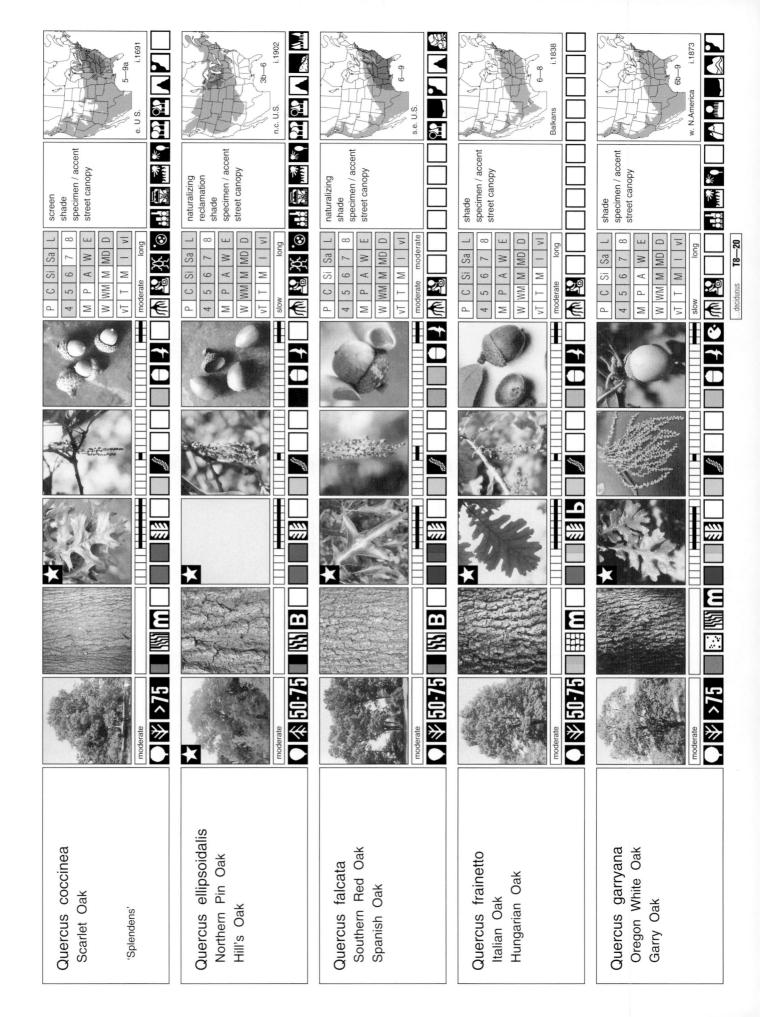

Quercus coccinea
Scarlet Oak

'Splendens'

screen
shade
specimen / accent
street canopy

P	C	Si	Sa	L
4	5	6	7	8
M	P	A	W	E
W	WM	M	MD	D
vT	T	M	I	vI

moderate · long

e. U.S. · 5—9a · i.1691

moderate · >75

Quercus ellipsoidalis
Northern Pin Oak
Hill's Oak

naturalizing
reclamation
shade
specimen / accent
street canopy

P	C	Si	Sa	L
4	5	6	7	8
M	P	A	W	E
W	WM	M	MD	D
vT	T	M	I	vI

slow · long

n.c. U.S. · 3b—6 · i.1902

moderate · 50-75

Quercus falcata
Southern Red Oak
Spanish Oak

naturalizing
shade
specimen / accent
street canopy

P	C	Si	Sa	L
4	5	6	7	8
M	P	A	W	E
W	WM	M	MD	D
vT	T	M	I	vI

slow · long

s.e. U.S. · 6—9 ·

moderate · 50-75

Quercus frainetto
Italian Oak
Hungarian Oak

shade
specimen / accent
street canopy

P	C	Si	Sa	L
4	5	6	7	8
M	P	A	W	E
W	WM	M	MD	D
vT	T	M	I	vI

moderate · moderate

Balkans · 6—8 · i.1838

moderate · 50-75

Quercus garryana
Oregon White Oak
Garry Oak

shade
specimen / accent
street canopy

P	C	Si	Sa	L
4	5	6	7	8
M	P	A	W	E
W	WM	M	MD	D
vT	T	M	I	vI

slow · long

w. N.America · 6b—9 · i.1873

moderate · >75

...deciduous   **T8—20**

LARGE TREE	FORM	BARK	LEAF	FLOWER	FRUIT	CULTURE	USES	REGION

Quercus kelloggi
California Black Oak
Kellogg Oak

- FORM: moderate · 50-75
- CULTURE: P C Si Sa L / 4 5 6 7 8 / M P A W E / W WM M MD D / vT T M I vI · slow · moderate
- USES: shade / specimen / accent / street canopy
- REGION: w. U.S. · 7b–10 · i.1878

Quercus lobata
California White Oak
Valley Oak

- FORM: moderate · >75
- CULTURE: P C Si Sa L / 4 5 6 7 8 / M P A W E / W WM M MD D / vT T M I vI · slow · long
- USES: preservation / sculptural / shade / specimen / accent
- REGION: California · 7b–10 · i.1874

Quercus lyrata
Overcup Oak

- FORM: moderate
- CULTURE: P C Si Sa L / 4 5 6 7 8 / M P A W E / W WM M MD D / vT T M I vI · slow
- USES: shade / specimen / accent
- REGION: e. U.S. · 6–9

Quercus macrocarpa
Bur Oak
'Sweet Idaho'

- FORM: >75
- CULTURE: P C Si Sa L / 4 5 6 7 8 / M P A W E / W WM M MD D / vT T M I vI · slow · long
- USES: fire retardant / naturalizing / sculptural / shade / specimen / accent / street canopy / windbreak
- REGION: e. N. America · 3–9 · i.1811

Quercus nuttalli
Nuttal Oak

- FORM: moderate · 50-75
- CULTURE: P C Si Sa L / 4 5 6 7 8 / M P A W E / W WM M MD D / vT T M I vI · moderate · moderate
- USES: formal garden / naturalizing / screen / shade / specimen / accent
- REGION: s.c. U.S. · 6–9

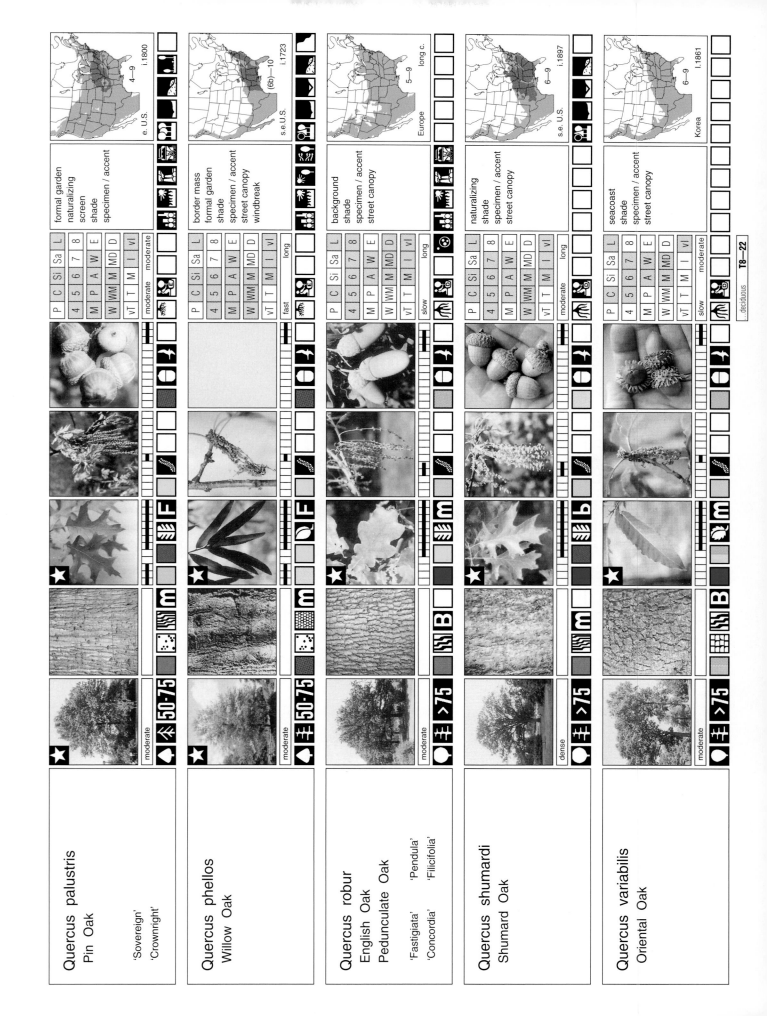

Quercus palustris
Pin Oak

'Sovereign'
'Crownright'

formal garden
naturalizing
screen
shade
specimen / accent

e. U.S.   4—9   i:1800

P	C	Si	Sa	L
4	5	6	7	8
M	P	A	W	E
W	WM	M	MD	D
vT	T	M	I	vl

moderate   moderate

moderate   50-75

Quercus phellos
Willow Oak

border mass
formal garden
shade
specimen / accent
street canopy
windbreak

s.e.U.S.   (6b)—10   i:1723

P	C	Si	Sa	L
4	5	6	7	8
M	P	A	W	E
W	WM	M	MD	D
vT	T	M	I	vl

fast   long

moderate   50-75

Quercus robur
English Oak
Pedunculate Oak

'Fastigiata'   'Pendula'
'Concordia'   'Filicifolia'

background
shade
specimen / accent
street canopy

Europe   5—9   long c.

P	C	Si	Sa	L
4	5	6	7	8
M	P	A	W	E
W	WM	M	MD	D
vT	T	M	I	vl

slow   long

moderate   >75

Quercus shumardi
Shumard Oak

naturalizing
shade
specimen / accent
street canopy

s.e. U.S.   6—9   i:1897

P	C	Si	Sa	L
4	5	6	7	8
M	P	A	W	E
W	WM	M	MD	D
vT	T	M	I	vl

moderate   long

dense   >75

Quercus variabilis
Oriental Oak

seacoast
shade
specimen / accent
street canopy

Korea   6—9   i.1861

P	C	Si	Sa	L
4	5	6	7	8
M	P	A	W	E
W	WM	M	MD	D
vT	T	M	I	vl

slow   moderate

moderate   >75

...deciduous   **T8—22**

LARGE TREE

LARGE TREE	FORM	BARK	LEAF	FLOWER	FRUIT	CULTURE	USES	REGION
Quercus velutina — Black Oak	dense; >75	B				P C Si Sa L / 4 5 6 7 8 / M P A W E / W WM M MD D / vT T M I vl — moderate · moderate	seacoast, shade, specimen / accent, street canopy, windbreak	4—9 · i:1800 · e. U.S.
Robinia pseudoacacia — Black Locust; 'Umbraculifera', 'Frisia'	open; 20-35	B				P C Si Sa L / 4 5 6 7 8 / M P A W E / W WM M MD D / vT T M I vl — fast · short	bee tree, erosion control, narrow space, naturalizing, patio garden, seacoast, specimen / accent, windbreak	4—9a · i:1601 · e.c. U.S.
Salix alba — White Willow; 'Sericea', 'Tristis', 'Vitellina', 'Chermisina'	open; 35-50	B				P C Si Sa L / 4 5 6 7 8 / M P A W E / W WM M MD D / vT T M I vl — fast · short	background, border mass, erosion control, naturalizing, screen, specimen / accent	2—9 · Mediterranean · long c.
Salix fragilis — Crack Willow, Brittle Willow; 'Bullata', Montpelior	open; 35-50	B				P C Si Sa L / 4 5 6 7 8 / M P A W E / W WM M MD D / vT T M I vl — fast · short	background, erosion control, specimen / accent	3—9 · Europe
Salix nigra — Black Willow	open; 35-50	B				P C Si Sa L / 4 5 6 7 8 / M P A W E / W WM M MD D / vT T M I vl — fast · short	erosion control, naturalizing, preservation, shade, screen	3—10 · e. N.America

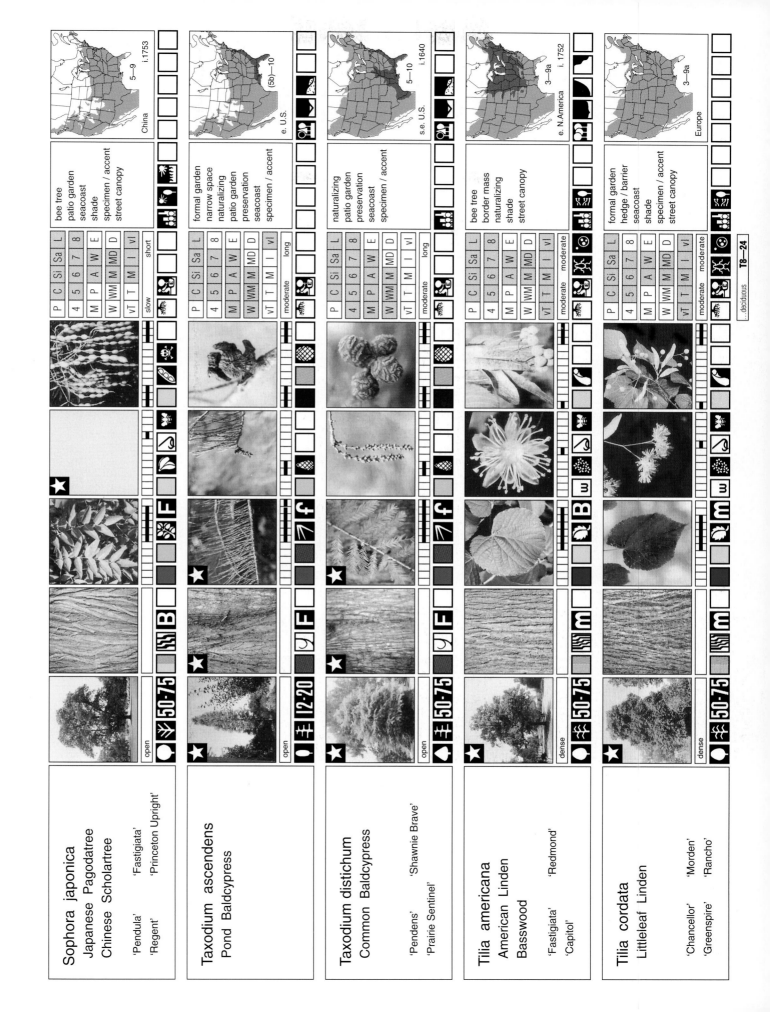

Sophora japonica
Japanese Pagodatree
Chinese Scholartree

'Pendula'   'Fastigiata'
'Regent'   'Princeton Upright'

bee tree
patio garden
seacoast
shade
specimen / accent
street canopy

P	C	Si	Sa	L
4	5	6	7	8
M	P	A	W	E
W	WM	M	MD	D
vT	T	M	I	vI

slow   short

5–9   i.1753
China

Taxodium ascendens
Pond Baldcypress

'Pendens'   'Shawnie Brave'
'Prairie Sentinel'

formal garden
narrow space
naturalizing
patio garden
preservation
seacoast
specimen / accent

P	C	Si	Sa	L
4	5	6	7	8
M	P	A	W	E
W	WM	M	MD	D
vT	T	M	I	vI

moderate   long

(5b)–10   i.1640
e. U.S.

Taxodium distichum
Common Baldcypress

'Pendens'   'Shawnie Brave'
'Prairie Sentinel'

naturalizing
patio garden
preservation
seacoast
specimen / accent

P	C	Si	Sa	L
4	5	6	7	8
M	P	A	W	E
W	WM	M	MD	D
vT	T	M	I	vI

moderate   long

5–10   i.1640
s.e. U.S.

Tilia americana
American Linden
Basswood

'Fastigiata'   'Redmond'
'Capitol'

bee tree
border mass
naturalizing
shade
street canopy

P	C	Si	Sa	L
4	5	6	7	8
M	P	A	W	E
W	WM	M	MD	D
vT	T	M	I	vI

moderate   moderate

3–9a   i. 1752
e. N.America

Tilia cordata
Littleleaf Linden

'Chancellor'   'Morden'
'Greenspire'   'Rancho'

formal garden
hedge / barrier
seacoast
shade
specimen / accent
street canopy

P	C	Si	Sa	L
4	5	6	7	8
M	P	A	W	E
W	WM	M	MD	D
vT	T	M	I	vI

moderate   moderate

3–9a
Europe

...deciduous   **T8—24**

LARGE TREE	FORM	BARK	LEAF	FLOWER	FRUIT	CULTURE	USES	REGION

Tilia x euchlora
European Linden
Crimean Linden

'Redmond'

dense · 50-75

P	C	Si	Sa	L
4	5	6	7	8
M	P	A	W	E
W	WM	M	MD	D
vT	T	M	I	vl

moderate · moderate

Uses: bee tree, formal garden, seacoast, shade, specimen / accent, street canopy

Europe · 7—10 · c.1860

Tilia petiolaris
Silverpendent Linden

dense · 50-75

P	C	Si	Sa	L
4	5	6	7	8
M	P	A	W	E
W	WM	M	MD	D
vT	T	M	I	vl

moderate · moderate

Uses: bee tree, formal garden, shade

s.e. Europe · 6—9a · c.1840

Tilia platyphyllos
Bigleaf Linden

'Pyramidal'
'Rubra'

dense · 50-75

P	C	Si	Sa	L
4	5	6	7	8
M	P	A	W	E
W	WM	M	MD	D
vT	T	M	I	vl

moderate · moderate

Uses: bee tree, border mass, formal garden, shade, specimen / accent, street canopy

Europe · 3—8

Tilia tomentosa
Silver Linden

'Green Mountain'   'Princeton'
'Sterling Silver'

dense · 50-75

P	C	Si	Sa	L
4	5	6	7	8
M	P	A	W	E
W	WM	M	MD	D
vT	T	M	I	vl

moderate · moderate

Uses: bee tree, border mass, formal garden, shade, specimen / accent, street canopy

s.e. Europe · 5—9a · i.1767

Ulmus americana
American Elm

'Augustine'
'Column'

moderate · >75

P	C	Si	Sa	L
4	5	6	7	8
M	P	A	W	E
W	WM	M	MD	D
vT	T	M	I	vl

moderate · moderate

Uses: preservation, shade, specimen / accent, street canopy, windbreak

e. N.America · 2—9 · i.1752

Ulmus carpinifolia
Smoothleaf Elm

'Christine Buiseman'   'Umbraculifera'
'Koopmanii'

Ulmus glabra
Scotch Elm
Wych Elm

'Dumont'
'Klemmer'

Ulmus x hollandica
Dutch Elm
Holland Elm

'Bea Schwartz'   'Urban'
'Groenveldt'

Ulmus parvifolia
Chinese Elm

'Brea'   'Dynasty'
'Drake'   'Prairie Shade'

Ulmus procera
English Elm

'Louis van Houtte'

...deciduous   T8—26

LARGE TREE	FORM	BARK	LEAF	FLOWER	FRUIT	CULTURE	USES	REGION
Ulmus pumila Siberian Elm 'Autumn Gold' 'Dropmore' 'Coolshade' 'Sapparo'	moderate — open >75	B	F			P C Si Sa L 4 5 6 7 8 M P A W E W WM M MD D vT T M I vI fast moderate	hedge seacoast shade street canopy windbreak	2b—9 c.1860 e. Siberia
Ulmus rubra **syn.** U. fulva Slippery Elm Red Elm	moderate >75	B	m			P C Si Sa L 4 5 6 7 8 M P A W E W WM M MD D vT T M I vI moderate short	shade street canopy windbreak	3—9 c.1830 e. N.America
Zelkova serrata Japanese Zelkova 'Village Green' 'Green Vase'	moderate 50-75	F	F			P C Si Sa L 4 5 6 7 8 M P A W E W WM M MD D vT T M I vI moderate moderate	bonsai hedge patio garden seacoast specimen / accent street canopy windbreak	5—8 i.1861 Japan
						P C Si Sa L 4 5 6 7 8 M P A W E W WM M MD D vT T M I vI		
						P C Si Sa L 4 5 6 7 8 M P A W E W WM M MD D vT T M I vI		

MEDIUM TREE	FORM	BARK	LEAF	FLOWER	FRUIT	CULTURE	USES	REGION

Acacia confusa

FORM: 35-50, Open

CULTURE: P C Si Sa L / 4 5 6 7 8 / M P A W E / W WM M MD D / vT T M I vl / short / fast

USES: cut flowers, reclamation, seacoast, shade, specimen / accent

REGION: Philippines, 9–10

Acer barbatum
Florida Maple
Southern Sugar Maple

FORM: 35-50, dense

CULTURE: P C Si Sa L / 4 5 6 7 8 / M P A W E / W WM M MD D / vT T M I vl / moderate

USES: patio garden, shade, specimen / accent, street canopy

REGION: s.e. U.S., 7b–9

Acer buergerianum
Trident Maple

'Goshiki Kaede'

FORM: 20-35, dense

CULTURE: P C Si Sa L / 4 5 6 7 8 / M P A W E / W WM M MD D / vT T M I vl / moderate

USES: bonsai, container, patio garden, shade, seacoast, specimen / accent, street canopy

REGION: China, (5b)–8, i. 1892

Acer campestre
Hedge Maple

'Compactum'
'Queen Elizabeth'

FORM: 35-50, dense

CULTURE: P C Si Sa L / 4 5 6 7 8 / M P A W E / W WM M MD D / vT T M I vl / slow

USES: hedge, patio garden, screen, seacoast, shade, specimen / accent, windbreak

REGION: Europe, 5–8

Acer cappadocium
Coliseum Maple
Cappadocium Maple

'Rubrum'

FORM: 35-50, dense

CULTURE: P C Si Sa L / 4 5 6 7 8 / M P A W E / W WM M MD D / vT T M I vl / moderate / short

USES: formal garden, patio garden, shade, specimen / accent, street canopy

REGION: China, 6–9

Acer davidi
Davids Maple

P	C	Si	Sa	L
4	5	6	7	8
M	P	A	W	E
W	WM	M	MD	D
vT	T	M	I	vl

patio garden
shade
specimen / accent

China 7–9 i. 1902

slow dense 35-50

Acer grandidentatum
Bigtooth Maple
Canyon Maple

P	C	Si	Sa	L
4	5	6	7	8
M	P	A	W	E
W	WM	M	MD	D
vT	T	M	I	vl

patio garden
shade
specimen / accent

e. N.America 5–8

fast short moderate 20-35

Acer lobeli
Lobel Maple

P	C	Si	Sa	L
4	5	6	7	8
M	P	A	W	E
W	WM	M	MD	D
vT	T	M	I	vl

patio garden
shade
specimen / accent

Italy 7–9 i. 1838

slow dense 12-20

Acer macrophyllum
Bigleaf Maple
Oregon Maple

P	C	Si	Sa	L
4	5	6	7	8
M	P	A	W	E
W	WM	M	MD	D
vT	T	M	I	vl

patio garden
sculptural
shade
specimen / accent
street canopy

w. N.America 6–10

fast moderate 35-50

Acer negundo
Common Boxelder
Ash-leaved Maple

'Flamingo'
'Variegatum'

P	C	Si	Sa	L
4	5	6	7	8
M	P	A	W	E
W	WM	M	MD	D
vT	T	M	I	vl

bank erosion
reclamation
screen
shade
windbreak

N.America 2–4

very. fast short open 35-50

...deciduous **T7—2**

MEDIUM TREE	FORM	BARK	LEAF	FLOWER	FRUIT	CULTURE	USES	REGION

Acer nikoense
syn. A. maximowiczianum
Nikko Maple

dense · 20-35

CULTURE:
P	C	Si	Sa	L
4	5	6	7	8
M	P	A	W	E
W	WM	M	MD	D
vT	T	M	I	vI

slow · moderate

USES: patio garden / shade / street canopy

REGION: 5—7a · i.1881 · Japan

Acer opalus
Italian Maple

dense · 35-50

CULTURE:
P	C	Si	Sa	L
4	5	6	7	8
M	P	A	W	E
W	WM	M	MD	D
vT	T	M	I	vI

slow · moderate

USES: formal garden / patio garden / shade

REGION: 6—9 · i.1752 · s. Europe

Acer platanoides
Norway Maple

'Columnare'   'Emerald Queen'
'Crimson King'   'Schwelder'

dense · 35-50

CULTURE:
P	C	Si	Sa	L
4	5	6	7	8
M	P	A	W	E
W	WM	M	MD	D
vT	T	M	I	vI

fast · moderate

USES: patio garden / screen / seacoast / shade / street canopy

REGION: 4—7 · i.col.x. · Europe

Acer truncatum
Shantung Maple
Purpleblow Maple

'Akikaza-Nishiki'
'Mayrii'

dense · 35-50

CULTURE:
P	C	Si	Sa	L
4	5	6	7	8
M	P	A	W	E
W	WM	M	MD	D
vT	T	M	I	vI

slow · moderate

USES: patio garden / shade

REGION: 4—6 · China

Aesculus x carnea
Red Horsechestnut

'Briotii'
'O'neill Red'

dense · 20-35

CULTURE:
P	C	Si	Sa	L
4	5	6	7	8
M	P	A	W	E
W	WM	M	MD	D
vT	T	M	I	vI

slow · moderate

USES: shade / specimen / accent / street canopy

REGION: 5—8 · o. 1858 · hybrid

Aesculus glabra
Ohio Buckeye

P	C	Si	Sa	L
4	5	6	7	8
M	P	A	W	E
W	WM	M	MD	D
vT	T	M	I	vl

slow · moderate

moderate · 35-50

shade
specimen / accent
street canopy
windbreak

3 – 8 · e. U.S.

Aesculus hippocastanum
Common Horsechestnut

'Baumanii'
'Rubra'

P	C	Si	Sa	L
4	5	6	7	8
M	P	A	W	E
W	WM	M	MD	D
vT	T	M	I	vl

slow · moderate

dense · 35-50

shade
specimen / accent
street canopy

4 – 8 · Balkans / Europe

Aesculus turbinata
Japanese Horsechestnut

P	C	Si	Sa	L
4	5	6	7	8
M	P	A	W	E
W	WM	M	MD	D
vT	T	M	I	vl

slow · moderate

moderate · 35-50

shade
specimen / accent
street canopy

6 – 8 · Japan

Ailanthus altissima
Tree-of-heaven Ailanthus

P	C	Si	Sa	L
4	5	6	7	8
M	P	A	W	E
W	WM	M	MD	D
vT	T	M	I	vl

very fast · short

open · 35-50

bank erosion
fragrant leaves
fruit arrangement
reclamation
screen
seacoast
shade
street canopy

i:1784 · 5 – 9a · China

Albizzia lebbeck
Lebbeck Albizzia
Woman's-tongue-tree

P	C	Si	Sa	L
4	5	6	7	8
M	P	A	W	E
W	WM	M	MD	D
vT	T	M	I	vl

fast · short

open · 50-75

fruit arrangement
shade
street canopy

9b – 10 · s.e. Asia

...deciduous

MEDIUM TREE	FORM	BARK	LEAF	FLOWER	FRUIT	CULTURE	USES	REGION

Alnus cordata
Italian Alder

dense 20·35

CULTURE:
P C Si Sa L
4 5 6 7 8
M P A W E
W WM M MD D
vT T M I vl
short / fast

USES:
bank erosion
fruit arrangement
narrow space
reclamation
nitrogen-fixing
seacoast
specimen / accent

REGION:
5 – 7   i:1820
Italy

Alnus glutinosa
European Alder
Black Alder
'Imperialis'

open 20·35

CULTURE:
P C Si Sa L
4 5 6 7 8
M P A W E
W WM M MD D
vT T M I vl
short / fast

USES:
bank erosion
formal garden
narrow space
naturalizing
nitrogen-fixing
reclamation
seacoast
shade

REGION:
4 – 8   i. col. x.
Europe

Alnus incana
Speckled Alder
White Alder
'Pendula'

dense 20·35

CULTURE:
P C Si Sa L
4 5 6 7 8
M P A W E
W WM M MD D
vT T M I vl
slow

USES:
bank erosion
fruit arrangement
narrow space
nitrogen-fixing
reclamation
seacoast
specimen / accent

REGION:
3 – 8
Asia / Europe

Alnus rhombifolia
Sierra Alder
White Alder

dense 20·35

CULTURE:
P C Si Sa L
4 5 6 7 8
M P A W E
W WM M MD D
vT T M I vl
short / fast

USES:
bank erosion
narrow space
nitrogen-fixing
reclamation
seacoast
specimen / accent

REGION:
5 – 9
w. N.America

Amelanchier canadensis
Shadblow Serviceberry
'Prince William'
'Tradition'

open 20·35

CULTURE:
P C Si Sa L
4 5 6 7 8
M P A W E
W WM M MD D
vT T M I vl
moderate / moderate

USES:
border mass
jams, jellies
naturalizing
patio garden
seacoast
specimen / accent

REGION:
3b – 8a
e. N.America

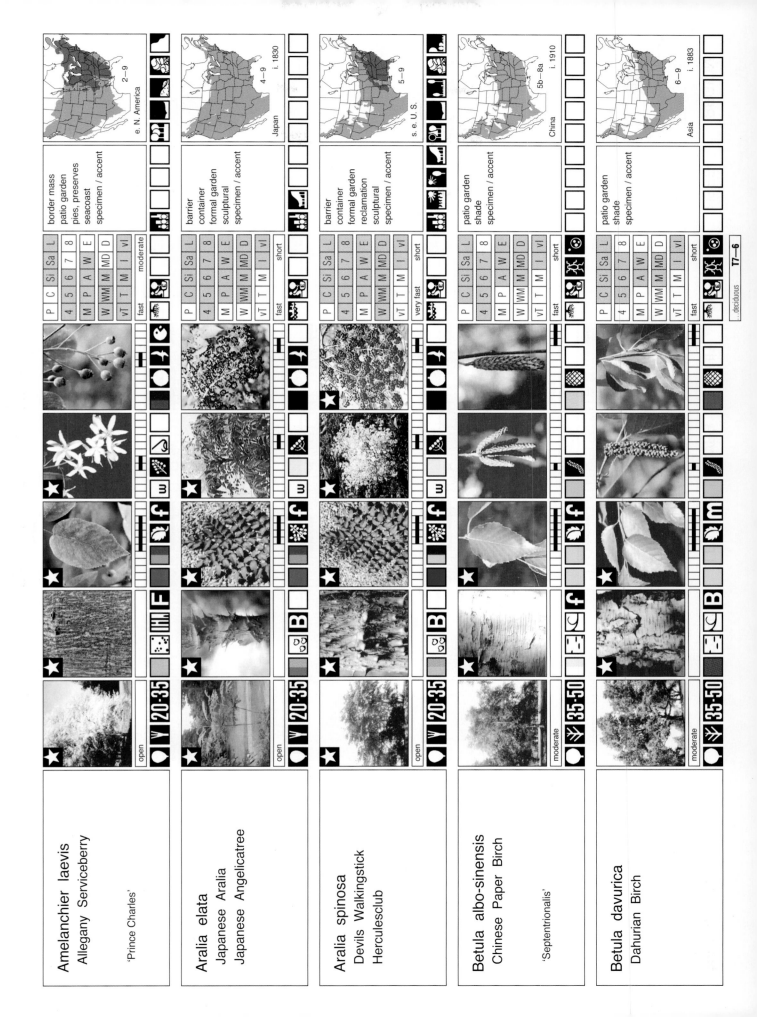

Amelanchier laevis — Allegany Serviceberry — 'Prince Charles'
e. N. America — 2–9
border mass / patio garden / pies, preserves / seacoast / specimen / accent
P C Si Sa L · 4 5 6 7 8 · M P A W E · W WM M MD D · vT T M I vl · moderate · fast · open · 20-35

Aralia elata — Japanese Aralia — Japanese Angelicatree
Japan — 4–9 — i. 1830
barrier / container / formal garden / sculptural / specimen / accent
P C Si Sa L · 4 5 6 7 8 · M P A W E · W WM M MD D · vT T M I vl · short · fast · open · 20-35

Aralia spinosa — Devils Walkingstick — Herculesclub
s. e. U. S. — 5–9
barrier / container / formal garden / reclamation / sculptural / specimen / accent
P C Si Sa L · 4 5 6 7 8 · M P A W E · W WM M MD D · vT T M I vl · short · very fast · open · 20-35

Betula albo-sinensis — Chinese Paper Birch — 'Septentrionalis'
China — 5b–8a — i. 1910
patio garden / shade / specimen / accent
P C Si Sa L · 4 5 6 7 8 · M P A W E · W WM M MD D · vT T M I vl · short · fast · moderate · 35-50

Betula davurica — Dahurian Birch
Asia — 6–9 — i. 1883
patio garden / shade / specimen / accent
P C Si Sa L · 4 5 6 7 8 · M P A W E · W WM M MD D · vT T M I vl · short · fast · moderate · 35-50

...deciduous **T7—6**

MEDIUM TREE	FORM	BARK	LEAF	FLOWER	FRUIT	CULTURE	USES	REGION

Betula ermani
Erman's Birch
Russian Rock Birch

open — 35-50

CULTURE: P C Si Sa L | 4 5 6 7 8 | M P A W E | W WM M MD D | vT T M I vl | fast | short

USES: formal garden / patio garden / shade / specimen / accent

REGION: 5—8 / Manchuria

Betula platyphylla
Manchurian Birch
Japanese White Birch
'Japonica'
'Whitespire'

open — 35-50

CULTURE: P C Si Sa L | 4 5 6 7 8 | M P A W E | W WM M MD D | vT T M I vl | fast | short

USES: formal garden / patio garden / shade / specimen / accent

REGION: 5—7 / Japan / N.China

Betula populifolia
Gray Birch

open — 12-20

CULTURE: P C Si Sa L | 4 5 6 7 8 | M P A W E | W WM M MD D | vT T M I vl | fast | short

USES: formal garden / narrow space / patio garden / reclamation / specimen / accent

REGION: 3—7a / n.e. N.America

Brachychiton discolor
Pink Flametree
Lacebark Bottletree

moderate — 35-50

CULTURE: P C Si Sa L | 4 5 6 7 8 | M P A W E | W WM M MD D | vT T M I vl | slow | long

USES: fruit arrangement / shade / windbreak

REGION: 9—10 / i.1858 / N.Australia

Broussonetia papyrifera
Paper Mulberry
Tapa-cloth-tree

open — 35-50

CULTURE: P C Si Sa L | 4 5 6 7 8 | M P A W E | W WM M MD D | vT T M I vl | moderate | long

USES: sculptural / shade / specimen / accent / windbreak

REGION: 6b—9 / i.1750 / China

Bumelia lanuginosa
Gum Bumelia
Chittamwood

barrier
bog garden
hedge
screen

P	C	Si	Sa	L
4	5	6	7	8
M	P	A	W	E
W	WM	M	MD	D
vT	T	M	I	vl

fast · moderate
open · 20-35
s. e. U.S. · 6b–10

Carpinus betulus
European Hornbeam
'Columnaris' 'Fastigiata'
'Pendula'

hedge
patio garden
screen
sculptural
sheared
specimen / accent

P	C	Si	Sa	L
4	5	6	7	8
M	P	A	W	E
W	WM	M	MD	D
vT	T	M	I	vl

slow · long
dense · 35-50
Europe · 5–7

Carpinus caroliniana
American Hornbeam
Blue Beech

hedge
patio garden
shade
screen
sculptural
specimen / accent

P	C	Si	Sa	L
4	5	6	7	8
M	P	A	W	E
W	WM	M	MD	D
vT	T	M	I	vl

slow · moderate
dense · 35-50
e. U.S. · 3–9

Carpinus japonica
Japanese Hornbeam

container
formal garden
hedge
patio garden
screen
sheared
specimen / accent

P	C	Si	Sa	L
4	5	6	7	8
M	P	A	W	E
W	WM	M	MD	D
vT	T	M	I	vl

slow · moderate
dense · 35-50
Japan · 5b–8 · i.1879

Cassia brewsteri

greenhouse
seacoast
shade
specimen / accent

P	C	Si	Sa	L
4	5	6	7	8
M	P	A	W	E
W	WM	M	MD	D
vT	T	M	I	vl

fast · short
open · 35-50
Australia · 9–10

...deciduous   T7—8

MEDIUM TREE	FORM	BARK	LEAF	FLOWER	FRUIT	CULTURE	USES	REGION

Castanea mollissima
Chinese Chestnut

'Crane'
'Eaton'
'Fords Sweet'
'Norm Higgens'

- dense · 35-50
- CULTURE: P C Si Sa L / 4 5 6 7 8 / M P A W E / W WM M MD D / vT T M I vl / fast · short
- USES: orchard / shade / specimen / accent
- REGION: China · 5–7 · i.1903

Castanea pumila
Allegany Chinquapin

- dense · 35-50
- CULTURE: P C Si Sa L / 4 5 6 7 8 / M P A W E / W WM M MD D / vT T M I vl / moderate · short
- USES: naturalizing / orchard / shade / specimen / accent
- REGION: s. e. U.S. · 5–9

Cedrela sinensis
Chinese Toon

- moderate · 35-50
- CULTURE: P C Si Sa L / 4 5 6 7 8 / M P A W E / W WM M MD D / vT T M I vl / moderate · moderate
- USES: aromatic leaves / fruit arrangements / shade / specimen / accent / street canopy
- REGION: China · 6b–9 · i.1862

Celtis bungeana
Bunge Hackberry

- moderate · 35-50
- CULTURE: P C Si Sa L / 4 5 6 7 8 / M P A W E / W WM M MD D / vT T M I vl / moderate · moderate
- USES: formal garden / patio garden / specimen / accent / street canopy
- REGION: China · 6–9a · i.1862

Celtis reticulata
Netleaf Hackberry
Western Hackberry

- moderate · 35-50
- CULTURE: P C Si Sa L / 4 5 6 7 8 / M P A W E / W WM M MD D / vT T M I vl / slow · short
- USES: shade / specimen / accent / street canopy
- REGION: s.w. N.America · 5–10

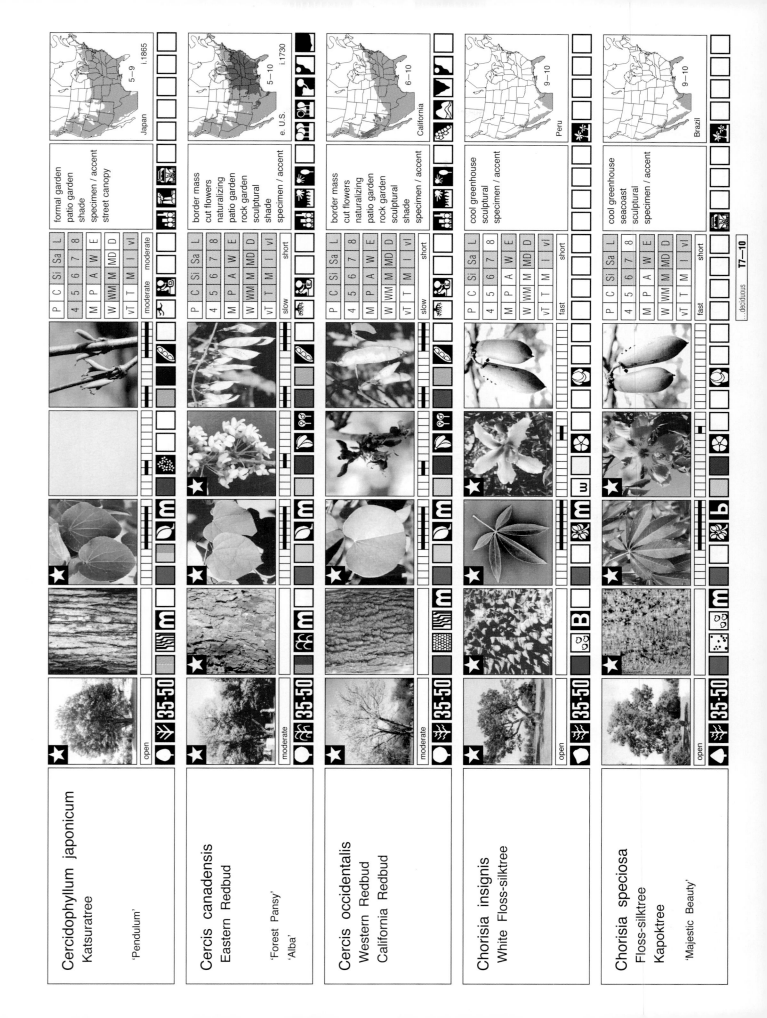

Cercidophyllum japonicum
Katsuratree
'Pendulum'

Cercis canadensis
Eastern Redbud
'Forest Pansy'
'Alba'

Cercis occidentalis
Western Redbud
California Redbud

Chorisia insignis
White Floss-silktree

Chorisia speciosa
Floss-silktree
Kapoktree
'Majestic Beauty'

...deciduous   T7—10

MEDIUM TREE	FORM	BARK	LEAF	FLOWER	FRUIT	CULTURE	USES	REGION

Cladrastis lutea
American Yellowwood

'Rosea'

moderate · 35-50

CULTURE: P C Si Sa L / 4 5 6 7 8 / M P A W E / W WM M MD D / vT T M I vI · moderate moderate

USES: patio garden · preservation · shade · specimen / accent

REGION: s.e. U.S. · 4b—8a · i.1812

Cornus controversa
Giant Dogwood

dense · 35-50

CULTURE: P C Si Sa L / 4 5 6 7 8 / M P A W E / W WM M MD D / vT T M I vI · moderate moderate

USES: border mass · patio garden · preservation · specimen / accent

REGION: China · 6—9a · i.b.1880

Cornus florida
Flowering Dogwood

'Alba'   'First Lady'
'Pendula'   'Rubra'

dense · 35-50

CULTURE: P C Si Sa L / 4 5 6 7 8 / M P A W E / W WM M MD D / vT T M I vI · moderate moderate

USES: border mass · patio garden · sculptural · shade · specimen / accent

REGION: s.e. U.S. · 5b—9a · c.1730

Cornus macrophylla
Largeleaf Dogwood

dense · 35-50

CULTURE: P C Si Sa L / 4 5 6 7 8 / M P A W E / W WM M MD D / vT T M I vI · moderate moderate

USES: border mass · patio garden · sculptural · shade · specimen / accent

REGION: China · 7—8 · i.1827

Couroupita guianensis
Cannonballtree

moderate · 35-50

CULTURE: P C Si Sa L / 4 5 6 7 8 / M P A W E / W WM M MD D / vT T M I vI · fast moderate

USES: curiosity · sculptural · shade · specimen / accent

REGION: Guiana · 10

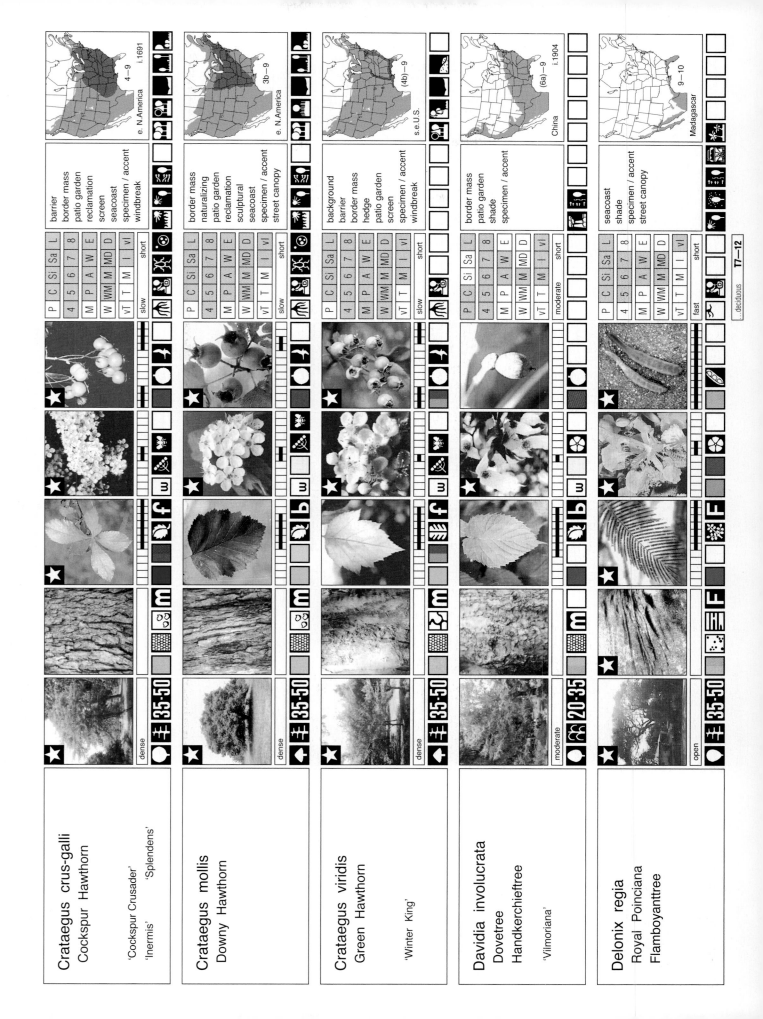

Crataegus crus-galli
Cockspur Hawthorn

'Cockspur Crusader'
'Inermis'   'Splendens'

barrier
border mass
patio garden
reclamation
screen
seacoast
specimen / accent
windbreak

dense   slow   short

4—9   i.1691   e. N.America

Crataegus mollis
Downy Hawthorn

border mass
naturalizing
patio garden
reclamation
sculptural
seacoast
specimen / accent
street canopy

dense   slow   short

3b—9   e. N.America

Crataegus viridis
Green Hawthorn

'Winter King'

background
barrier
border mass
hedge
patio garden
screen
specimen / accent
windbreak

dense   slow   short

(4b)—9   s.e.U.S.

Davidia involucrata
Dovetree
Handkerchieftree

'Vilmoriana'

border mass
patio garden
shade
specimen / accent

moderate   short

(6a)—9   i:1904   China

Delonix regia
Royal Poinciana
Flamboyanttree

seacoast
shade
specimen / accent
street canopy

open   fast   short

9—10   Madagascar

...deciduous   T7—12

MEDIUM TREE

	FORM	BARK	LEAF	FLOWER	FRUIT	CULTURE	USES	REGION

Diospyros kaki
Oriental Persimmon
Japanese Persimmon

'Great Wall' 'Sheng'
'Hachiya'

- FORM: dense — 20·35
- CULTURE: P C Si Sa L / 4 5 6 7 8 / M P A W E / W WM M MD D / vT T M I vl — slow
- USES: container, orchard, patio garden, shade, specimen / accent
- REGION: Korea — 9–10 — i.b.1870

Elaeagnus angustifolia
Russianolive

'King Red'

- FORM: open — 35·50
- CULTURE: P C Si Sa L / 4 5 6 7 8 / M P A W E / W WM M MD D / vT T M I vl — fast
- USES: bank erosion, barrier, border mass, patio garden, reclamation, screen, seacoast, specimen / accent
- REGION: Europe — 2–9 — i. col. x.

Eucalyptus intertexta
Red Gum
Red Box

- FORM: open — 12·20
- CULTURE: P C Si Sa L / 4 5 6 7 8 / M P A W E / W WM M MD D / vT T M I vl — fast
- USES: aromatic leaves, seacoast, shade, specimen / accent, street canopy, windbreak
- REGION: Australia — 9–10

Eucommia ulmoides
Hardy Rubbertree

- FORM: moderate — 35·50
- CULTURE: P C Si Sa L / 4 5 6 7 8 / M P A W E / W WM M MD D / vT T M I vl — moderate
- USES: shade, street canopy
- REGION: China — 6–8 — i.1896

Euonymus nikoensis
Nikko Euonymus

- FORM: moderate — 35·50
- CULTURE: P C Si Sa L / 4 5 6 7 8 / M P A W E / W WM M MD D / vT T M I vl — moderate
- USES: border mass, patio garden, screen, shade, specimen / accent
- REGION: Himalayas / Japan — 6–9

Evodia hupehensis
Hupeh Evodia

patio garden
naturalizing
specimen / accent
street canopy

P	C	Si	Sa	L
4	5	6	7	8
M	P	A	W	E
W	WM	M	MD	D
vI	T	M	I	vI

fast · short

moderate · 35-50

China · 6—8 · i.1908

Fraxinus ornus
Flowering Ash

patio garden
shade
specimen / accent
street canopy

P	C	Si	Sa	L
4	5	6	7	8
M	P	A	W	E
W	WM	M	MD	D
vI	T	M	I	vI

fast · moderate

open · 35-50

s. Europe / w. Asia · 6—8

Fraxinus oxycarpa
'Raywood'

patio garden
seacoast
shade
street canopy
windbreak

P	C	Si	Sa	L
4	5	6	7	8
M	P	A	W	E
W	WM	M	MD	D
vI	T	M	I	vI

fast · moderate

moderate · 20-35

s. Europe / w. Asia · 6—7

Fraxinus velutina
Velvet Ash
Arizona Ash

'Fan-Tex'   'Von Ormi'
glabra

espalier
screen
shade
windbreak

P	C	Si	Sa	L
4	5	6	7	8
M	P	A	W	E
W	WM	M	MD	D
vI	T	M	I	vI

fast · short

moderate · 20-35

s.w. U.S. · 6—10 · i.1891

Griselinia littoralis
Kupuktree

espalier
screen
shade
windbreak

P	C	Si	Sa	L
4	5	6	7	8
M	P	A	W	E
W	WM	M	MD	D
vI	T	M	I	vI

moderate · moderate

dense · 20-35

New Zealand · 9—10

...deciduous   **T7—14**

MEDIUM TREE	FORM	BARK	LEAF	FLOWER	FRUIT	CULTURE	USES	REGION

Halesia carolina
Carolina Silverbell
Snowdrop

FORM: dense — 20-35
CULTURE:
P	C	Si	Sa	L
4	5	6	7	8
M	P	A	W	E
W	WM	M	MD	D
vT	T	M	I	vl
moderate — short
USES: border mass / naturalizing / patio garden / shade / specimen / accent
REGION: s.e. U.S. — 5–10

Halesia monticola
Mountain Silverbell
'Rosea'

FORM: open — 20-35
CULTURE:
P	C	Si	Sa	L
4	5	6	7	8
M	P	A	W	E
W	WM	M	MD	D
vT	T	M	I	vl
moderate — short
USES: border mass / patio garden / shade / specimen / accent
REGION: s.e. U.S. — 5–8   i.1897

Idesia polycarpa
Chinese Idesia
ligeritree

FORM: open — 35-50
CULTURE:
P	C	Si	Sa	L
4	5	6	7	8
M	P	A	W	E
W	WM	M	MD	D
vT	T	M	I	vl
moderate — short
USES: patio garden / shade / specimen / accent
REGION: China / Japan — 7–9   i.1864

Jacaranda acutifolia
syn. J. mimosaefolia
Sharpleaf Jacaranda
'Alba'

FORM: moderate — 35-50
CULTURE:
P	C	Si	Sa	L
4	5	6	7	8
M	P	A	W	E
W	WM	M	MD	D
vT	T	M	I	vl
fast — short
USES: container / fruit arrangements / patio garden / seacoast / shade / street canopy
REGION: Argentina / Brazil — 9b–10

Juglans major
Arizona Black Walnut

FORM: open — 35-50
CULTURE:
P	C	Si	Sa	L
4	5	6	7	8
M	P	A	W	E
W	WM	M	MD	D
vT	T	M	I	vl
fast — moderate
USES: orchard / preservation / shade / windbreak
REGION: s.w. U.S. / Mexico — 6–10   i.1894

P	C	Si	Sa	L
4	5	6	7	8
M	P	A	W	E
W	WM	M	MD	D
vT	T	M	I	vI

open · fast · moderate

35-50

Kalopanax pictus
Castor Aralia

greenhouse
sculptural
shade
specimen / accent
street canopy

5—9 · i.1865 · Japan

P	C	Si	Sa	L
4	5	6	7	8
M	P	A	W	E
W	WM	M	MD	D
vT	T	M	I	vI

moderate · moderate · short

35-50

Koelreuteria paniculata
Panicled Goldraintree

border mass
patio garden
shade
specimen / accent
street canopy

5b—9 · i.1763 · China

P	C	Si	Sa	L
4	5	6	7	8
M	P	A	W	E
W	WM	M	MD	D
vT	T	M	I	vI

open · fast · short

20-35

Larix lyalli
Subalpine Larch

formal garden
specimen / accent

2—5 · i.1904 · w. N.America

P	C	Si	Sa	L
4	5	6	7	8
M	P	A	W	E
W	WM	M	MD	D
vT	T	M	I	vI

dense · slow · short

35-50

Liquidambar formosana
Formosa Sweetgum
Chinese Sweetgum

background
formal garden
shade
specimen / accent
street canopy

7—9 · i.1884 · s. China

P	C	Si	Sa	L
4	5	6	7	8
M	P	A	W	E
W	WM	M	MD	D
vT	T	M	I	vI

moderate · fast · short

20-35

Liriodendron chinense
Chinese Tuliptree

preservation
shade
specimen / accent

7b—9 · i.1901 · China

...deciduous   **T7—16**

MEDIUM TREE	FORM	BARK	LEAF	FLOWER	FRUIT	CULTURE	USES	REGION

Lysiloma latisiliqua
Sabicu Lysiloma
Wild Tamarind

FORM: open · 20-35

CULTURE:
P	C	Si	Sa	L
4	5	6	7	8
M	P	A	W	E
W	WM	M	MD	D
vT	T	M	I	vI
short · fast

USES:
shade
specimen / accent
street canopy

REGION: Cuba / s. Florida · 10

Maclura pomifera
Osageorange
Boxwood

'Park'

FORM: dense · 35-50

CULTURE:
P	C	Si	Sa	L
4	5	6	7	8
M	P	A	W	E
W	WM	M	MD	D
vT	T	M	I	vI
moderate · fast

USES:
background
barrier
hedge
reclamation
shade
street canopy
windbreak

REGION: s.c. U.S. · i.1818 · 5–10

Magnolia dawsoniana
Dawson Magnolia

'Chyverton'
'Clarke'

FORM: dense · 35-50

CULTURE:
P	C	Si	Sa	L
4	5	6	7	8
M	P	A	W	E
W	WM	M	MD	D
vT	T	M	I	vI
moderate · moderate

USES:
border mass
cut flowers
formal garden
patio garden
specimen / accent

REGION: w. China · i.1908 · 7–9

Magnolia denudata
syn. M. heptapeta
Yulan Magnolia

'Purple Eye' 'Swada'
'Wada'

FORM: 35-50

CULTURE:
P	C	Si	Sa	L
4	5	6	7	8
M	P	A	W	E
W	WM	M	MD	D
vT	T	M	I	vI
moderate · moderate

USES:
border mass
cut flowers
patio garden
specimen / accent

REGION: China · i.1789 · 6–9

Magnolia fraseri
Fraser Magnolia

FORM: open · 20-35

CULTURE:
P	C	Si	Sa	L
4	5	6	7	8
M	P	A	W	E
W	WM	M	MD	D
vT	T	M	I	vI
fast · moderate

USES:
border mass
cut flowers
formal garden
specimen / accent

REGION: s.e. U.S. · i.1786 · 5b–9

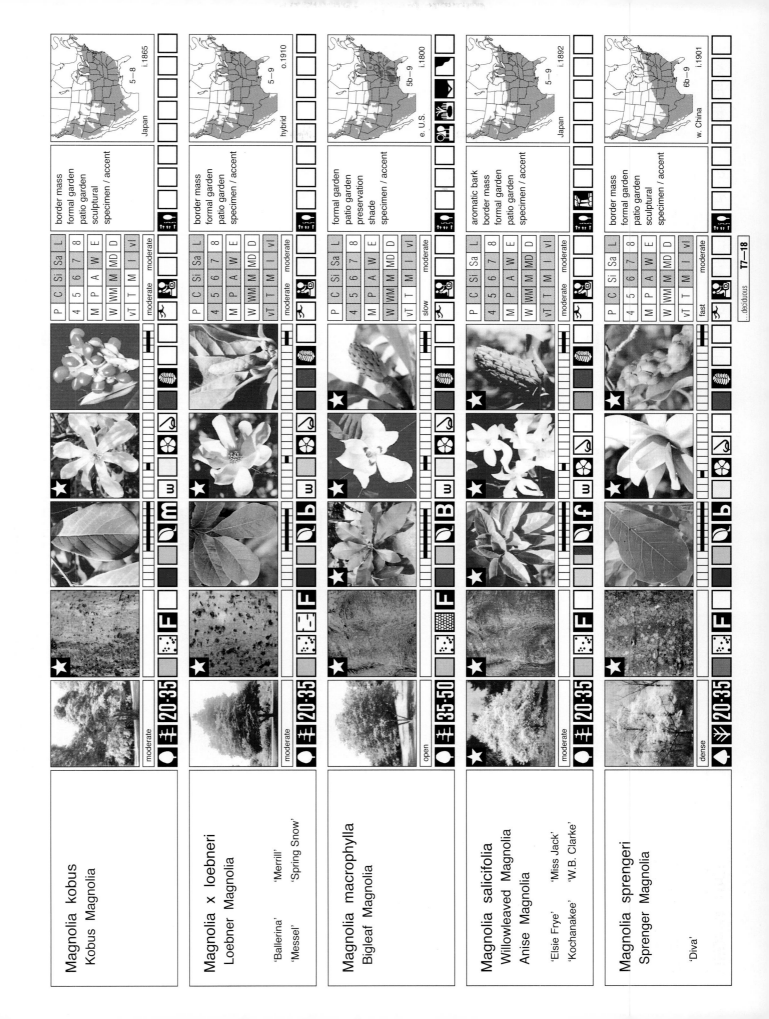

Magnolia kobus — Kobus Magnolia
Japan — i.1865 — 5–8
border mass · formal garden · sculptural · specimen / accent
P C Si Sa L | 4 5 6 7 8 | M P A W E | W WM M MD D | vT T M I vl
moderate moderate
moderate · 20-35

Magnolia x loebneri — Loebner Magnolia
'Ballerina' 'Merrill' 'Messel' 'Spring Snow'
hybrid — o.1910 — 5–9
border mass · formal garden · patio garden · specimen / accent
P C Si Sa L | 4 5 6 7 8 | M P A W E | W WM M MD D | vT T M I vl
moderate moderate
moderate · 20-35

Magnolia macrophylla — Bigleaf Magnolia
e. U.S. — i.1800 — 5b–9
formal garden · patio garden · preservation · shade · specimen / accent
P C Si Sa L | 4 5 6 7 8 | M P A W E | W WM M MD D | vT T M I vl
slow
open · 35-50

Magnolia salicifolia — Willowleaved Magnolia — Anise Magnolia
'Elsie Frye' 'Miss Jack' 'Kochanakee' 'W.B. Clarke'
Japan — i.1892 — 5–9
aromatic bark · border mass · formal garden · patio garden · specimen / accent
P C Si Sa L | 4 5 6 7 8 | M P A W E | W WM M MD D | vT T M I vl
moderate moderate
moderate · 20-35

Magnolia sprengeri — Sprenger Magnolia
'Diva'
w. China — i.1901 — 6b–9
border mass · formal garden · patio garden · sculptural · specimen / accent
P C Si Sa L | 4 5 6 7 8 | M P A W E | W WM M MD D | vT T M I vl
fast moderate
dense · 20-35

...deciduous — T7—18

MEDIUM TREE	FORM	BARK	LEAF	FLOWER	FRUIT	CULTURE	USES	REGION

Magnolia tripetala
Umbrella Magnolia

dense · 20-35
fast · moderate

P	C	Si	Sa	L
4	5	6	7	8
M	P	A	W	E
W	WM	M	MD	D
vT	T	M	I	vl

USES: patio garden, shade, specimen / accent
REGION: s.e. U.S. 4b–9 i.1752

Magnolia × veitchi
Veitch Magnolia

open · 20-35
fast · short

P	C	Si	Sa	L
4	5	6	7	8
M	P	A	W	E
W	WM	M	MD	D
vT	T	M	I	vl

USES: patio garden, shade, specimen / accent
REGION: hybrid 7b–9 o.1907

Malus baccata
Siberian Crabapple
'Columnaris' 'Midwest' 'Jackii' 'Walters'

dense · 35-50
slow · short

P	C	Si	Sa	L
4	5	6	7	8
M	P	A	W	E
W	WM	M	MD	D
vT	T	M	I	vl

USES: jams, jellies, patio garden, screen, shade, specimen / accent, windbreak
REGION: e. Asia 2–7 i.b.1800

Malus 'Dolgo'
Dolgo Crabapple

dense · 20-35
moderate · short

P	C	Si	Sa	L
4	5	6	7	8
M	P	A	W	E
W	WM	M	MD	D
vT	T	M	I	vl

USES: jams, jellies, shade, specimen / accent
REGION: cultivar 3b–7 i.1907

Malus fusca
Oregon Crabapple

dense · 20-35
moderate · short

P	C	Si	Sa	L
4	5	6	7	8
M	P	A	W	E
W	WM	M	MD	D
vT	T	M	I	vl

USES: barrier, jams, jellies, shade, specimen / accent
REGION: w. N. America 6–9 i.1836

Malus 'Oekonomierat Echtermeyer'
Weeping Crabapple

3–8 o.1914
hybrid

oriental garden
patio garden
sculptural
shade
specimen / accent

P	C	Si	Sa	L
4	5	6	7	8
M	P	A	W	E
W	WM	M	MD	D
vT	T	M	I	vl

short

dense 35-50

Malus pumila
Common Apple
Anna Apple

4–9 long c.
Asia

culinary
orchard
pies, sauce
shade

P	C	Si	Sa	L
4	5	6	7	8
M	P	A	W	E
W	WM	M	MD	D
vT	T	M	I	vl

fast short

dense 20-35

Malus 'Rosseau'
Rosseau Crabapple

4–8 o. 1920
hybrid

shade
specimen / accent

P	C	Si	Sa	L
4	5	6	7	8
M	P	A	W	E
W	WM	M	MD	D
vT	T	M	I	vl

moderate short

dense 35-50

Malus 'Sissipuk'
Sissipuk Crabapple

4–8 o. 1920
hybrid

shade
specimen / accent

P	C	Si	Sa	L
4	5	6	7	8
M	P	A	W	E
W	WM	M	MD	D
vT	T	M	I	vl

moderate short

dense 35-50

Malus tschonoski
Tschonoski Crabapple

4b–8 i.1892
Japan

patio garden
specimen / accent

P	C	Si	Sa	L
4	5	6	7	8
M	P	A	W	E
W	WM	M	MD	D
vT	T	M	I	vl

moderate short

dense 20-35

MEDIUM TREE	FORM	BARK	LEAF	FLOWER	FRUIT		USES	REGION

Morus alba
White Mulberry

'Chaparral' 'Pendula'
'Fruitless' 'Tatarica'

...deciduous **T7–21**

P	C	Si	Sa	L
4	5	6	7	8
M	P	A	W	E
W	WM	M	MD	D
vT	T	M	I	vl

fast short

dense 35-50

USES: invasive, jams, jellies, shade, windbreak

REGION: China 4b–7 i. col. x.

Nothofagus oblique
Roble Beech

P	C	Si	Sa	L
4	5	6	7	8
M	P	A	W	E
W	WM	M	MD	D
vT	T	M	I	vl

short

dense 20-35

USES: shade, specimen / accent

REGION: s.w. Chile 7b–9

Ostrya carpinifolia
European Hophornbeam

P	C	Si	Sa	L
4	5	6	7	8
M	P	A	W	E
W	WM	M	MD	D
vT	T	M	I	vl

slow short

dense 35-50

USES: formal garden

REGION: s. Europe 6–9 i.1724

Oxydendrum arboreum
Sourwood
Sorreltree

P	C	Si	Sa	L
4	5	6	7	8
M	P	A	W	E
W	WM	M	MD	D
vT	T	M	I	vl

slow long

moderate 20-35

USES: aromatic leaves, border mass, formal garden, naturalizing, patio garden, specimen / accent, street canopy

REGION: s.e. U.S. (5b)–9 i.1752

Parrotia persica
Persian Parrotia

P	C	Si	Sa	L
4	5	6	7	8
M	P	A	W	E
W	WM	M	MD	D
vT	T	M	I	vl

slow moderate

dense 35-50

USES: seacoast, shade, specimen / accent

REGION: Japan (5b)–9 i.1840

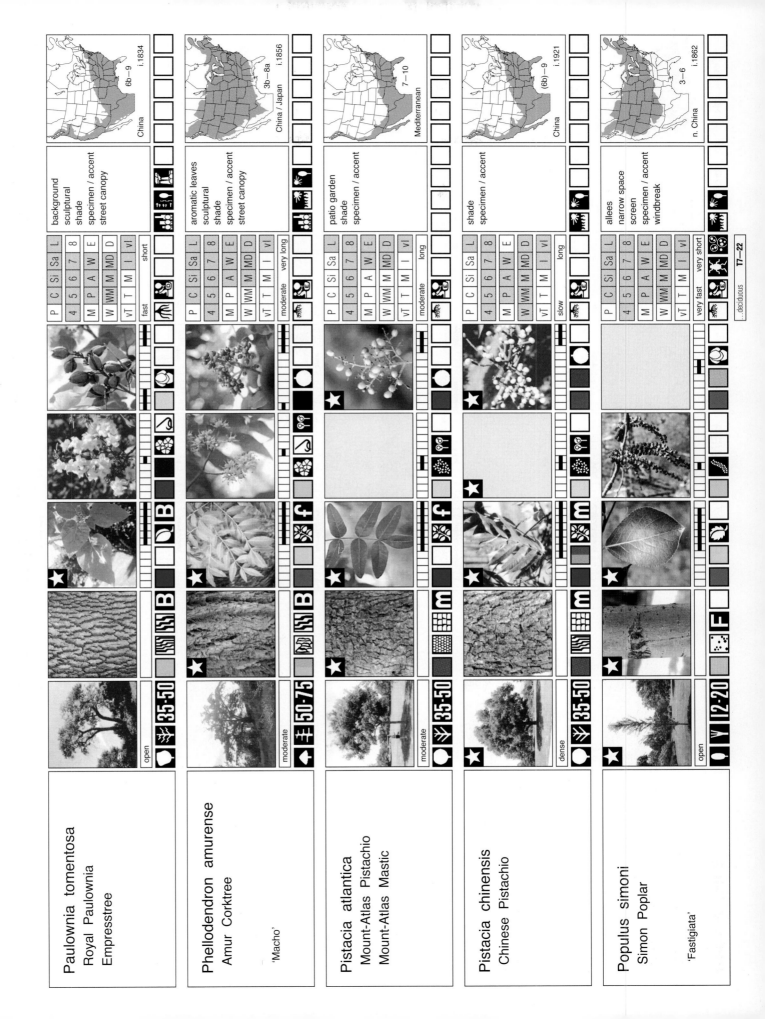

Paulownia tomentosa
Royal Paulownia
Empresstree

background
sculptural
shade
specimen / accent
street canopy

China   6b–9   i:1834

open   35-50   fast   short

Phellodendron amurense
Amur Corktree

'Macho'

aromatic leaves
sculptural
shade
specimen / accent
street canopy

China / Japan   3b–8a   i:1856

moderate   50-75   moderate   very long

Pistacia atlantica
Mount-Atlas Pistachio
Mount-Atlas Mastic

patio garden
shade
specimen / accent

Mediterranean   7–10

moderate   moderate   long

Pistacia chinensis
Chinese Pistachio

shade
specimen / accent

China   (6b)–9   i:1921

dense   35-50   slow   long

Populus simoni
Simon Poplar

'Fastigiata'

allees
narrow space
screen
specimen / accent
windbreak

n. China   3–6   i:1862

open   12-20   very fast   very short

...deciduous   T7–22

MEDIUM TREE	FORM	BARK	LEAF	FLOWER	FRUIT	CULTURE	USES	REGION

Populus tremuloides
Quaking Aspen

'Kiabab'
'Swede'

open — 12-20

CULTURE: P C Si Sa L / 4 5 6 7 8 / M P A W E / W WM M MD D / vT T M I vI / short / fast

USES: allees / border mass / narrow space / naturalizing / patio garden / reclamation / sculptural / specimen / accent

REGION: 2—6 / c.1812 / N America

Prosopis velutina
Velvet Mesquite
Arizona Mesquite

open — 35-50

CULTURE: P C Si Sa L / 4 5 6 7 8 / M P A W E / W WM M MD D / vT T M I vI / short / fast

USES: sculptural / windbreak

REGION: 7—10 / Mexico / s.w. U.S.

Prunus avium
Mazzard Cherry
Sweet Cherry

'Plena'

moderate — 35-50

CULTURE: P C Si Sa L / 4 5 6 7 8 / M P A W E / W WM M MD D / vT T M I vI / short / fast

USES: hedge / jams, jellies, pies / orchard / shade / specimen / accent

REGION: 5—8 / Europe

Prunus maacki
Amur Chokecherry

dense — 20-35

CULTURE: P C Si Sa L / 4 5 6 7 8 / M P A W E / W WM M MD D / vT T M I vI / short / fast

USES: border mass / patio garden / shade / specimen / accent

REGION: 3—7 / i.1878 / Korea / Manchuria

Prunus mahaleb
St. Lucie Cherry
Mahaleb Cherry

moderate — 20-35

CULTURE: P C Si Sa L / 4 5 6 7 8 / M P A W E / W WM M MD D / vT T M I vI / short / fast

USES: border mass / patio garden / shade / specimen / accent

REGION: 6—8 / i.1714 / Europe

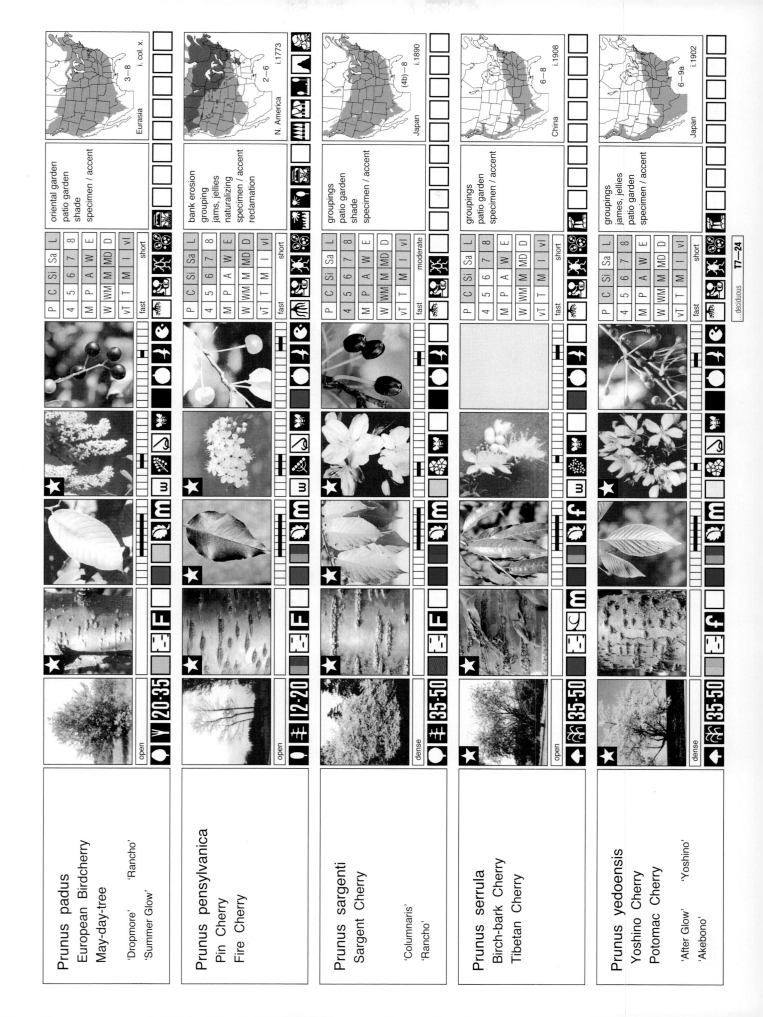

Prunus padus — European Birdcherry — May-day-tree
'Dropmore' 'Rancho' 'Summer Glow'
Eurasia 3–8 i. col. x.
oriental garden / patio garden / shade / specimen / accent
open 20-35

Prunus pensylvanica — Pin Cherry — Fire Cherry
N. America 2–6 i.1773
bank erosion / grouping / jams, jellies / naturalizing / specimen / accent / reclamation
open 12-20

Prunus sargenti — Sargent Cherry
'Columnaris' 'Rancho'
Japan (4b)–8 i.1890
groupings / patio garden / shade / specimen / accent
dense 35-50

Prunus serrula — Birch-bark Cherry — Tibetan Cherry
China 6–8 i.1908
groupings / patio garden / specimen / accent
open 35-50

Prunus yedoensis — Yoshino Cherry — Potomac Cherry
'After Glow' 'Yoshino' 'Akebono'
Japan 6–9a i.1902
groupings / james, jellies / patio garden / specimen / accent
dense 35-50

MEDIUM TREE	FORM	BARK	LEAF	FLOWER	FRUIT	CULTURE	USES	REGION

Pterostyrax hispida
Epauletetree
Fragrant Epauletetree

FORM: open · 35-50

CULTURE: P C Si Sa L · 4 5 6 7 8 · M P A W E · W WM M MD D · vT T M I vI · moderate / short

USES: container · patio garden · shade · specimen / accent

REGION: Japan / China · 6—9 · i:1875

Pyrus ussuriensis
Ussurian Pear
Chinese Pear

FORM: dense · 35-50

CULTURE: P C Si Sa L · 4 5 6 7 8 · M P A W E · W WM M MD D · vT T M I vI · moderate / short

USES: oriental garden · shade · specimen / accent

REGION: Manchuria · 3b—7 · i:1855

Quercus acutissima
Sawtooth Oak

FORM: moderate · 50-75

CULTURE: P C Si Sa L · 4 5 6 7 8 · M P A W E · W WM M MD D · vT T M I vI · moderate / long

USES: sculptural · shade · specimen / accent

REGION: China / Japan · 6—9 · i:1862

Quercus douglasi
Blue Oak

FORM: moderate · 50-75

CULTURE: P C Si Sa L · 4 5 6 7 8 · M P A W E · W WM M MD D · vT T M I vI · slow / long

USES: sculptural · shade · specimen / accent

REGION: California · 7—10

Quercus glandulifera
Glandbearing Oak
Konara Oak

FORM: moderate · 50-75

CULTURE: P C Si Sa L · 4 5 6 7 8 · M P A W E · W WM M MD D · vT T M I vI · slow / long

USES: shade · specimen / accent

REGION: Japan · 5—9 · i:1877

Quercus imbricaria
Shingle Oak

background
border mass
formal garden
patio garden
reclamation
shade
specimen / accent
street canopy

P	C	Si	Sa	L
4	5	6	7	8
M	P	A	W	E
W	WM	M	MD	D
vT	T	M	I	vI

slow · long

dense · 35-50

e. U.S. · 5–8 · i.1786

Quercus marilandica
Blackjack Oak

bank erosion
reclamation
specimen / accent
windbreak

P	C	Si	Sa	L
4	5	6	7	8
M	P	A	W	E
W	WM	M	MD	D
vT	T	M	I	vI

slow · long

moderate · 20-35

e. U.S. · 5b–9 · c.1739

Quercus muehlenbergi
Chinkapin Oak
Yellow Chestnut Oak

patio garden
reclamation
sculptural
shade
specimen / accent

P	C	Si	Sa	L
4	5	6	7	8
M	P	A	W	E
W	WM	M	MD	D
vT	T	M	I	vI

slow · long

moderate · 35-50

e. U.S. · 4b–9 · i.1822

Quercus stellata
Post Oak

reclamation
shade
specimen / accent

P	C	Si	Sa	L
4	5	6	7	8
M	P	A	W	E
W	WM	M	MD	D
vT	T	M	I	vI

slow · long

moderate · 35-50

s.e. U.S. · 5b–9 · i.1819

Rhus typhina
Staghorn Sumac
'Laciniata'

bank erosion
border mass
invasive
naturalizing
reclamation
sculptural
specimen / accent

P	C	Si	Sa	L
4	5	6	7	8
M	P	A	W	E
W	WM	M	MD	D
vT	T	M	I	vI

fast · short

open · 20-35

e. N.America · 3–9 · c.1629

...deciduous   T7–26

...deciduous **T7—27**

MEDIUM TREE	FORM	BARK	LEAF	FLOWER	FRUIT	CULTURE	USES	REGION

Robinia viscosa
Clammy Locust

20-35 · open

CULTURE: P C Si Sa L / 4 5 6 7 8 / M P A W E / W WM M MD D / vT T M I vl / fast short

USES: bank erosion / border mass / naturalizing / reclamation / specimen / accent

REGION: 4b–9a / s.e. U.S. / i.1791

Salix babylonica
Babylon Weeping Willow
Weeping Willow

'Aurea'   'Curley Leaf'
'Crispa'

35-50 · open

CULTURE: P C Si Sa L / 4 5 6 7 8 / M P A W E / W WM M MD D / vT T M I vl / fast short

USES: oriental garden / sculptural / shade / specimen / accent

REGION: 7–10 / Middle East / i.1730

Salix x blanda
Wisconsin Weeping Willow
Weeping Willow

35-50 · open

CULTURE: P C Si Sa L / 4 5 6 7 8 / M P A W E / W WM M MD D / vT T M I vl / fast short

USES: sculptural / shade / specimen / accent

REGION: 5–9 / hybrid / i.b.1830

Salix elaeagnus
Rosemary Willow
Hoary Willow

20-35 · open

CULTURE: P C Si Sa L / 4 5 6 7 8 / M P A W E / W WM M MD D / vT T M I vl / fast short

USES: bank eroison / screen / specimen / accent

REGION: 5–9 / Asia / i.b.1850

Salix matsudana 'Tortuosa'
Contorted Hankow Willow
Corkscrew Willow

20-35 · open

CULTURE: P C Si Sa L / 4 5 6 7 8 / M P A W E / W WM M MD D / vT T M I vl / fast short

USES: patio garden / sculptural / specimen / accent

REGION: 5–9 / hybrid / i.1923

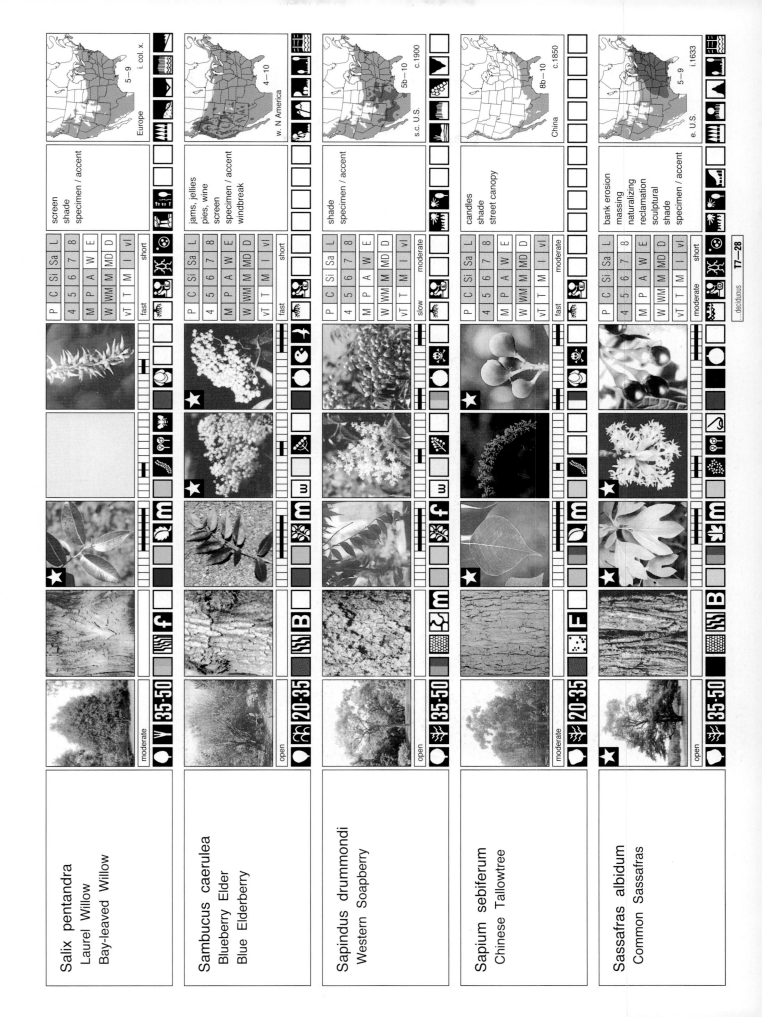

Salix pentandra
Laurel Willow
Bay-leaved Willow

Europe · i. col. x. · 5–9

screen
shade
specimen / accent

P C Si Sa L
4 5 6 7 8
M P A W E
W WM M MD D
vT T M I vl
fast · short
moderate · 35-50

Sambucus caerulea
Blueberry Elder
Blue Elderberry

w. N America · 4–10

jams, jellies
pies, wine
screen
specimen / accent
windbreak

P C Si Sa L
4 5 6 7 8
M P A W E
W WM M MD D
vT T M I vl
fast · short
open · 20-35

Sapindus drummondi
Western Soapberry

s.c. U.S. · 5b–10 · c.1900

shade
specimen / accent

P C Si Sa L
4 5 6 7 8
M P A W E
W WM M MD D
vT T M I vl
slow · moderate
open · 35-50

Sapium sebiferum
Chinese Tallowtree

China · 8b–10 · c.1850

candles
shade
street canopy

P C Si Sa L
4 5 6 7 8
M P A W E
W WM M MD D
vT T M I vl
fast · moderate
moderate · 20-35

Sassafras albidum
Common Sassafras

e. U.S. · 5–9 · i.1633

bank erosion
massing
naturalizing
reclamation
sculptural
shade
specimen / accent

P C Si Sa L
4 5 6 7 8
M P A W E
W WM M MD D
vT T M I vl
moderate · short
open · 35-50

...deciduous   T7—28

MEDIUM TREE	FORM	BARK	LEAF	FLOWER	FRUIT	CULTURE	USES	REGION

Sophora tetraptera
Fourwing Sophora
New Zealand Sophora

open · 35-50

P	C	Si	Sa	L
4	5	6	7	8
M	P	A	W	E
W	WM	M	MD	D
vT	T	M	I	vl
moderate · short

border mass
shade
specimen / accent

New Zealand
9—10 i.1772

Sorbus alnifolia
Korean Mountainash

moderate · 20-35

P	C	Si	Sa	L
4	5	6	7	8
M	P	A	W	E
W	WM	M	MD	D
vT	T	M	I	vl
fast · short

border mass
patio garden
shade
specimen / accent

e. Asia
4—7 i.1892

Sorbus aria
Whitebeam Mountainash
'Lutescens'
'Magnifica'

open · 35-50

P	C	Si	Sa	L
4	5	6	7	8
M	P	A	W	E
W	WM	M	MD	D
vT	T	M	I	vl
fast · short

border mass
patio garden
shade
specimen / accent

Europe
5—7 i.b.1830

Sorbus aucuparia
European Mountainash
Rowan
'Blackhawk'
'Cardinal Royal'

open · 20-35

P	C	Si	Sa	L
4	5	6	7	8
M	P	A	W	E
W	WM	M	MD	D
vT	T	M	I	vl
fast · short

border mass
patio garden
shade
specimen / accent

Eurasia
3b—7 i.col. x.

Sorbus domestica
Servicetree Mountainash

open · 12-20

P	C	Si	Sa	L
4	5	6	7	8
M	P	A	W	E
W	WM	M	MD	D
vT	T	M	I	vl
fast · short

border mass
patio garden
shade
specimen / accent

Mediterranean
4—7 long.c.

Sorbus hupehensis
Hupeh Mountainash

P	C	Si	Sa	L
4	5	6	7	8
M	P	A	W	E
W	WM	M	MD	D
vT	T	M	I	vI

short

fast

border mass
patio garden
shade
specimen / accent

w. China   6—8   i.1910

open   20-35

Stewartia koreana
Korean Stewartia

'Rutger's Gold'

P	C	Si	Sa	L
4	5	6	7	8
M	P	A	W	E
W	WM	M	MD	D
vT	T	M	I	vI

short

patio garden
shade
specimen / accent

Korea   6—8   i.1917

dense   20-35

Stewartia pseudocamellia
Japanese Stewartia

'Cascade'

P	C	Si	Sa	L
4	5	6	7	8
M	P	A	W	E
W	WM	M	MD	D
vT	T	M	I	vI

slow

border mass
patio garden
shade
specimen / accent

Japan   6—8   i.1874

dense   20-35

Syringa reticulata
syn. S. amurensis
japonica

Japanese Tree Lilac

'Ivory Silk'
'Summer Snow'

P	C	Si	Sa	L
4	5	6	7	8
M	P	A	W	E
W	WM	M	MD	D
vT	T	M	I	vI

slow

fast   moderate

border mass
patio garden
sculptural
shade
specimen / accent
street canopy
windbreak

Japan   3—7   i.1876

dense   35-50

Tilia mongolica
Mongolian Linden

P	C	Si	Sa	L
4	5	6	7	8
M	P	A	W	E
W	WM	M	MD	D
vT	T	M	I	vI

moderate   moderate

bee tree
formal garden
shade
specimen / accent

China   3—6   i.1880

dense   35-50

...deciduous   **T7—30**

MEDIUM TREE	FORM	BARK	LEAF	FLOWER	FRUIT	CULTURE	USES	REGION

Tilia oliveri
Oliver Linden

dense
20-35

CULTURE:
P C Si Sa L
4 5 6 7 8
M P A W E
W WM M MD D
vT T M I vl
moderate · moderate

USES: shade · specimen / accent · street canopy

REGION: China · 5–8 · i.1900

Ulmus alata
Winged Elm
Wahoo Elm

moderate
35-50

CULTURE:
P C Si Sa L
4 5 6 7 8
M P A W E
W WM M MD D
vT T M I vl
fast · short

USES: shade · street canopy

REGION: s.e. U.S. · 6–9 · i.1820

Ulmus crassifolia
Cedar Elm

moderate
35-50

CULTURE:
P C Si Sa L
4 5 6 7 8
M P A W E
W WM M MD D
vT T M I vl
fast · short

USES: shade · street canopy

REGION: s.c. U.S. · 7–10

Ulmus thomasi
Cork Elm
Rock Elm

moderate
20-35

CULTURE:
P C Si Sa L
4 5 6 7 8
M P A W E
W WM M MD D
vT T M I vl
fast · short

USES: shade

REGION: e. N.America · 3b–7 · i.1875

CULTURE:
P C Si Sa L
4 5 6 7 8
M P A W E
W WM M MD D
vT T M I vl

SMALL TREE	FORM	BARK	LEAF	FLOWER	FRUIT	CULTURE	USES	REGION
Acacia giraffae **syn**. A. erioloba Giraffe Acacia Camelthorn	open · 20·35					P C Si Sa L 4 5 6 7 8 M P A W E W WM M MD D vT T M l vl slow · long	greenhouse screen windbreak	s. Africa 8b–10
Acacia seyal Seyel Acacia Thirty Thorn	open · 20·35					P C Si Sa L 4 5 6 7 8 M P A W E W WM M MD D vT T M l vl fast · short	greenhouse religious plant windbreak	Egypt / Kenya 8b–10
Acacia smalli **syn**. A. minuta Southwestern Sweet Acacia	open · 20·35					P C Si Sa L 4 5 6 7 8 M P A W E W WM M MD D vT T M l vl fast · short	greenhouse reclamation windbreak	s.w. U.S. 8b–10
Acer capillipes Red Snakebark Maple	open · 20·35					P C Si Sa L 4 5 6 7 8 M P A W E W WM M MD D vT T M l vl slow · moderate	formal garden patio garden shade specimen / accent	Japan 5–9 i.1892
Acer circinatum Vine Maple 'Glen-del' 'Monroe' 'Little Gem'	dense · 20·35					P C Si Sa L 4 5 6 7 8 M P A W E W WM M MD D vT T M l vl moderate · moderate	container espalier patio garden sculptural shade specimen / accent	w. N.America 6–9 i.1826

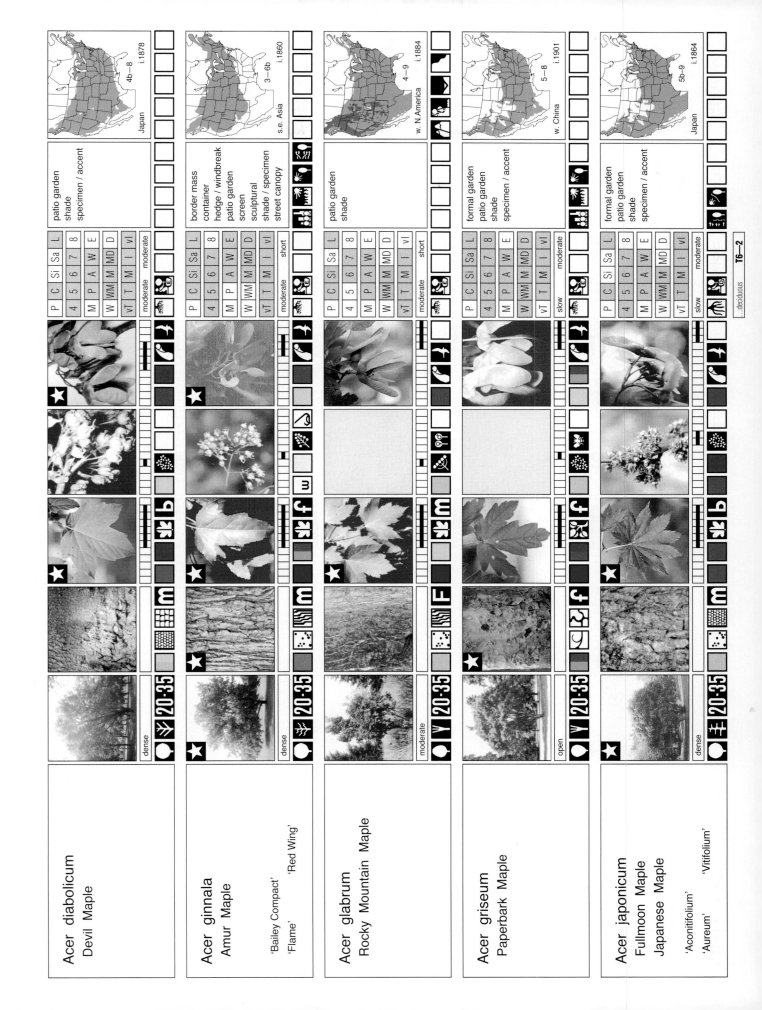

Acer diabolicum
Devil Maple

Acer ginnala
Amur Maple
'Bailey Compact'
'Flame'   'Red Wing'

Acer glabrum
Rocky Mountain Maple

Acer griseum
Paperbark Maple

Acer japonicum
Fullmoon Maple
Japanese Maple
'Aconitifolium'   'Vitifolium'
'Aureum'

Japan
4b–8   i.1878
patio garden
shade
specimen / accent
P C Si Sa L
4 5 6 7 8
M P A W E
W WM M MD D
vT T M I vl
moderate   moderate
dense   20-35

s.e. Asia
3–6b   i.1860
border mass
container
hedge / windbreak
patio garden
screen
sculptural
shade / specimen
street canopy
P C Si Sa L
4 5 6 7 8
M P A W E
W WM M MD D
vT T M I vl
moderate   short
dense   20-35

w. N.America
4–9   i.1884
patio garden
shade
P C Si Sa L
4 5 6 7 8
M P A W E
W WM M MD D
vT T M I vl
moderate   short
moderate   20-35

w. China
5–8   i.1901
formal garden
patio garden
shade
specimen / accent
P C Si Sa L
4 5 6 7 8
M P A W E
W WM M MD D
vT T M I vl
slow   moderate
open   20-35

Japan
5b–9   i.1864
formal garden
patio garden
shade
specimen / accent
P C Si Sa L
4 5 6 7 8
M P A W E
W WM M MD D
vT T M I vl
slow   moderate
dense   20-35

...deciduous   T6—2

SMALL TREE	FORM	BARK	LEAF	FLOWER	FRUIT	CULTURE	USES	REGION

Acer mandshuricum
Manchurian Maple

FORM: open — 20-35
CULTURE:
P	C	Si	Sa	L
4	5	6	7	8
M	P	A	W	E
W	WM	M	MD	D
vT	T	M	I	vl
fast — moderate
USES: patio garden / shade / specimen / accent
REGION: 4b—6 i.1904 Manchuria / Korea

Acer monspessulanum
Montpellier Maple

FORM: dense — 20-35
CULTURE:
P	C	Si	Sa	L
4	5	6	7	8
M	P	A	W	E
W	WM	M	MD	D
vT	T	M	I	vl
slow — moderate
USES: hedge / narrow space / patio garden / shade / street canopy
REGION: 6—9 i.1739 Mediterranean

Acer pensylvanicum
Striped Maple
Moosewood

FORM: open - dense — 20-35
CULTURE:
P	C	Si	Sa	L
4	5	6	7	8
M	P	A	W	E
W	WM	M	MD	D
vT	T	M	I	vl
moderate — moderate
USES: border mass / screen / seacoast / specimen / accent / woodland garden
REGION: 3b—7 i.1755 e. N.America

Acer tataricum
Tatarian Maple

FORM: dense — 20-35
CULTURE:
P	C	Si	Sa	L
4	5	6	7	8
M	P	A	W	E
W	WM	M	MD	D
vT	T	M	I	vl
moderate — short
USES: patio garden / shade / specimen / accent
REGION: 3—6b i.1759 Asia

Acer triflorum
Threeflower Maple

FORM: dense — 20-35
CULTURE:
P	C	Si	Sa	L
4	5	6	7	8
M	P	A	W	E
W	WM	M	MD	D
vT	T	M	I	vl
moderate — short
USES: patio garden / shade / specimen / accent
REGION: 5—8 i.1923 Manchuria / Korea

Aesculus californica
California Buckeye

California   7–10   i.1850

bank erosion
bonsai
fruit arrangement
naturalizing
patio garden
poisonous leaves
seacoast
specimen / accent

P	C	Si	Sa	L
4	5	6	7	8
M	P	A	W	E
W	WM	M	MD	D
vT	T	M	I	vI

long · fast

open · 35-50

Aesculus pavia
Red Buckeye

'Rubra'

e. central U.S.   (5b)–9   i.1711

patio garden
poisonous leaves
sculptural
shade
specimen / accent

P	C	Si	Sa	L
4	5	6	7	8
M	P	A	W	E
W	WM	M	MD	D
vT	T	M	I	vI

short · slow

moderate · 12-20

Albizzia julibrissin
Mimosa
Silktree

'E.H. Wilson'
'Rosea'

China / Iran   6–10   i.1745

container
patio garden
reclamation
seacoast
shade
specimen / accent

P	C	Si	Sa	L
4	5	6	7	8
M	P	A	W	E
W	WM	M	MD	D
vT	T	M	I	vI

short · fast

open · 35-50

Alnus maritima
Seaside Alder

s. central U.S.   6–8   i.1887

nitrogen-fixing
preservation
specimen / accent

P	C	Si	Sa	L
4	5	6	7	8
M	P	A	W	E
W	WM	M	MD	D
vT	T	M	I	vI

short · fast

dense · 20-35

Alnus sinuata
syn. A. sitchensis
Sitka Alder

n.w. U.S.   2–8   i.1902

bank erosion
nitrogen-fixing
reclamation

P	C	Si	Sa	L
4	5	6	7	8
M	P	A	W	E
W	WM	M	MD	D
vT	T	M	I	vI

short · fast

dense · 20-35

...deciduous

SMALL TREE	FORM	BARK	LEAF	FLOWER	FRUIT	CULTURE	USES	REGION

Alnus tenuifolia
Mountain Alder
Thinleaf Alder

moderate · 20·35

CULTURE: P C Si Sa L / 4 5 6 7 8 / M P A W E / W WM M MD D / vT T M I vl — fast / short

USES: bank erosion, nitrogen-fixing, shade, specimen / accent

REGION: w. N.America — 1—6, i.1891

Amelanchier x grandiflora
Apple Serviceberry

'Ballarina'   'Rubescens'
'Cole Select' 'Strata'

dense · 12·20

CULTURE: P C Si Sa L / 4 5 6 7 8 / M P A W E / W WM M MD D / vT T M I vl — moderate / moderate

USES: border mass, patio garden, preserves / pies, shade, specimen / accent

REGION: hybrid — 3b—8, o.1897

Annona cherimola
Cherimoya
Custard Apple

open · 20·35

CULTURE: P C Si Sa L / 4 5 6 7 8 / M P A W E / W WM M MD D / vT T M I vl — fast / short

USES: aromatic leaves, container, espalier, kitchen garden, orchard, patio garden, specimen / accent

REGION: s. America — 10

Annona glabra
Pond Apple

open · 20·35

CULTURE: P C Si Sa L / 4 5 6 7 8 / M P A W E / W WM M MD D / vT T M I vl — fast / short

USES: aromatic leaves, kitchen garden, orchard, preservation, preserves / pies, specimen / accent

REGION: West Indies — 10

Annona squamosa
Sugar Apple

moderate · 20·35

CULTURE: P C Si Sa L / 4 5 6 7 8 / M P A W E / W WM M MD D / vT T M I vl — moderate / short

USES: container, kitchen garden, orchard, specimen / accent

REGION: West Indies — 10

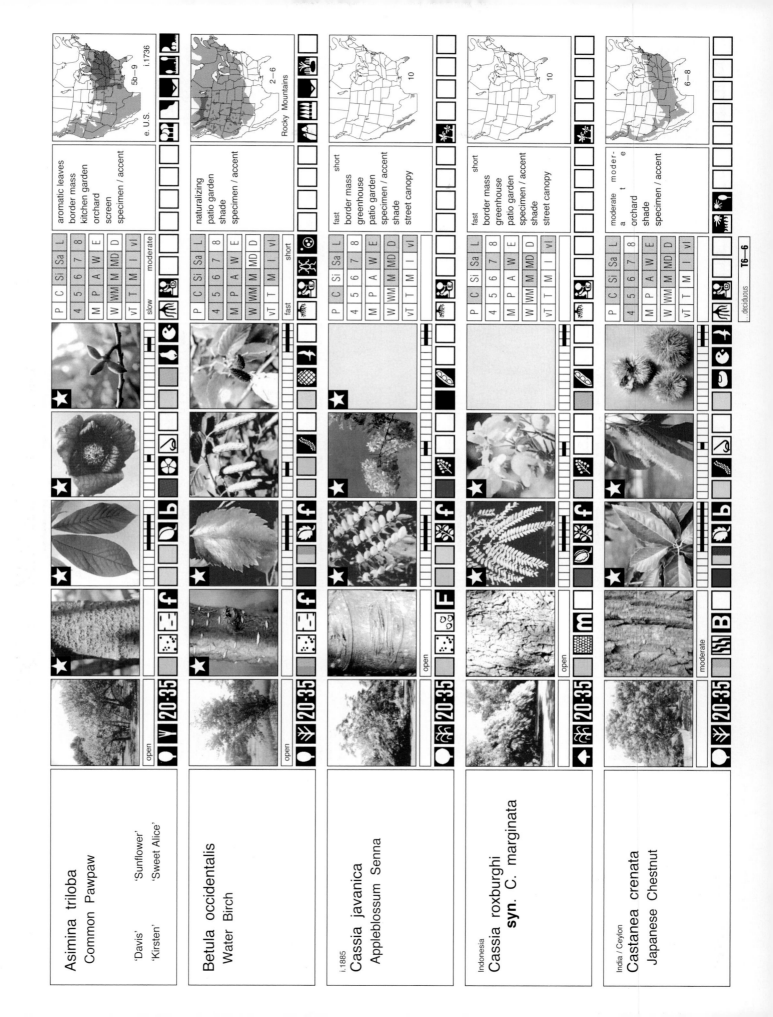

Asimina triloba
Common Pawpaw

'Davis'
'Kirsten'
'Sunflower'
'Sweet Alice'

aromatic leaves
border mass
kitchen garden
orchard
screen
specimen / accent

e. U.S.
5b–9
i.1736

P	C	Si	Sa	L
4	5	6	7	8
M	P	A	W	E
W	WM	M	MD	D
vT	T	M	I	vI

slow   moderate
open

Betula occidentalis
Water Birch

naturalizing
patio garden
shade
specimen / accent

Rocky Mountains
2–6

P	C	Si	Sa	L
4	5	6	7	8
M	P	A	W	E
W	WM	M	MD	D
vT	T	M	I	vI

fast   short
open

Cassia javanica
Appleblossum Senna

i.1885

fast   short
border mass
greenhouse
patio garden
specimen / accent
shade
street canopy

10

P	C	Si	Sa	L
4	5	6	7	8
M	P	A	W	E
W	WM	M	MD	D
vT	T	M	I	vI

open

Cassia roxburghi
syn. C. marginata

Indonesia

fast   short
border mass
greenhouse
patio garden
specimen / accent
shade
street canopy

10

P	C	Si	Sa	L
4	5	6	7	8
M	P	A	W	E
W	WM	M	MD	D
vT	T	M	I	vI

open

Castanea crenata
Japanese Chestnut

India / Ceylon

moderate   moder-
ate
orchard
shade
specimen / accent

6–8

P	C	Si	Sa	L
4	5	6	7	8
M	P	A	W	E
W	WM	M	MD	D
vT	T	M	I	vI

moderate

...deciduous   **T6—6**

SMALL TREE	FORM	BARK	LEAF	FLOWER	FRUIT	CULTURE	USES	REGION

Catalpa ovata
Chinese Catalpa

- FORM: open · 20-35
- CULTURE: P C Si Sa L / 4 5 6 7 8 / M P A W E / W WM M MD D / vT T M I vl / moderate · moderate
- USES: sculptural / shade / specimen / accent
- REGION: 4b—9 · i.1849 · China

Cercis chinensis
Chinese Redbud

'Avondale' 'Nana'

- FORM: moderate · 20-35
- CULTURE: P C Si Sa L / 4 5 6 7 8 / M P A W E / W WM M MD D / vT T M I vl / slow · short
- USES: screen / specimen / accent
- REGION: 6b—10 · i.b.1850 · c China

Cercis siliquastrum
Judastree

- FORM: open · 20-35
- CULTURE: P C Si Sa L / 4 5 6 7 8 / M P A W E / W WM M MD D / vT T M I vl / moderate · short
- USES: patio garden / religious plant / seacoast / shade / specimen / accent
- REGION: 9—10 · i.colonial x · Asia Minor

Chionanthus virginicus
White Fringetree
Old-Man's-Beard

- FORM: dense · 20-35
- CULTURE: P C Si Sa L / 4 5 6 7 8 / M P A W E / W WM M MD D / vT T M I vl / slow · moderate
- USES: border mass / patio garden / shade / specimen / accent / street canopy
- REGION: 5b—10 · i.1736 · e. U.S.

Clethra barbinervis
Japanese Clethra

- FORM: open · 20-35
- CULTURE: P C Si Sa L / 4 5 6 7 8 / M P A W E / W WM M MD D / vT T M I vl / slow · short
- USES: border mass / patio garden / shade / specimen / accent
- REGION: 6—10 · i.1870 · Japan

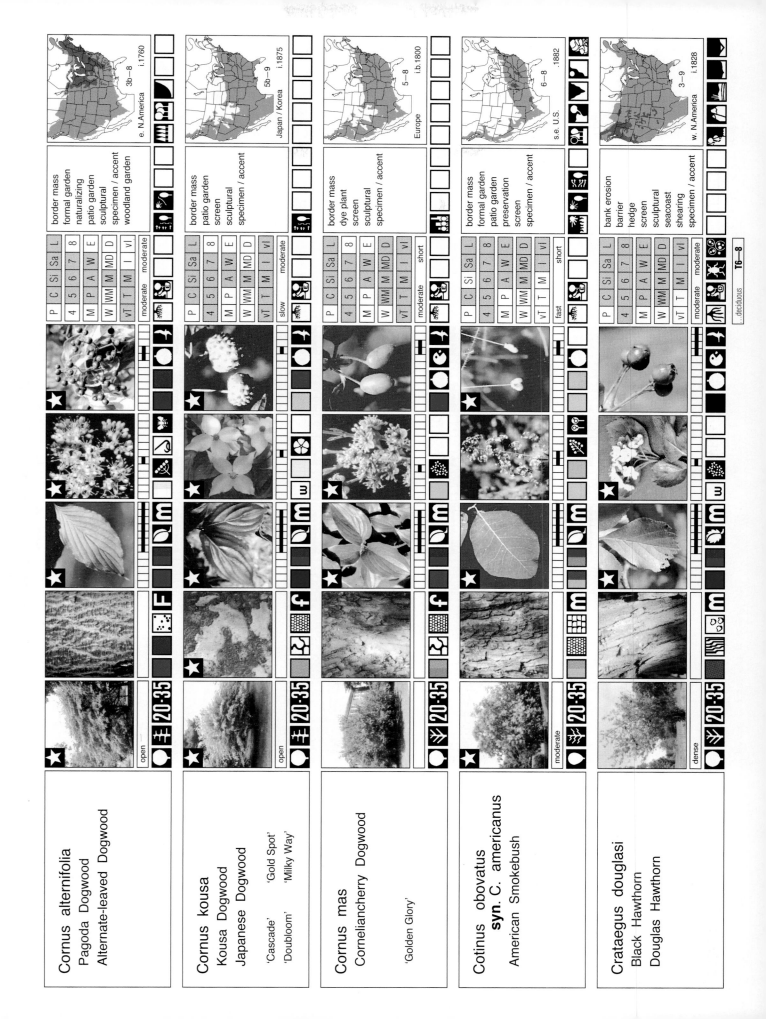

Cornus alternifolia
Pagoda Dogwood
Alternate-leaved Dogwood

e. N.America · 3b–8 · i.1760

border mass · formal garden · naturalizing · patio garden · sculptural · specimen / accent · woodland garden

P C Si Sa L | 4 5 6 7 8 | M P A W E | W WM M MD D | vT T M I vl — moderate · moderate

open · 20-35

Cornus kousa
Kousa Dogwood
Japanese Dogwood
'Cascade'   'Gold Spot'
'Doubloom'   'Milky Way'

Japan / Korea · 5b–9 · i.1875

border mass · patio garden · screen · sculptural · specimen / accent

P C Si Sa L | 4 5 6 7 8 | M P A W E | W WM M MD D | vT T M I vl — slow · moderate

open · 20-35

Cornus mas
Corneliancherry Dogwood
'Golden Glory'

Europe · 5–8 · i.b.1800

border mass · dye plant · screen · sculptural · specimen / accent

P C Si Sa L | 4 5 6 7 8 | M P A W E | W WM M MD D | vT T M I vl — moderate · short

20-35

Cotinus obovatus **syn. C. americanus**
American Smokebush

s.e. U.S. · 6–8 · .1882

border mass · formal garden · patio garden · preservation · screen · specimen / accent

P C Si Sa L | 4 5 6 7 8 | M P A W E | W WM M MD D | vT T M I vl — fast · short

moderate · 20-35

Crataegus douglasi
Black Hawthorn
Douglas Hawthorn

w. N.America · 3–9 · i.1828

bank erosion · barrier · hedge · screen · sculptural · seacoast · shearing · specimen / accent

P C Si Sa L | 4 5 6 7 8 | M P A W E | W WM M MD D | vT T M I vl — moderate · moderate

dense · 20-35

...deciduous   T6—8

SMALL TREE	FORM	BARK	LEAF	FLOWER	FRUIT	CULTURE	USES	REGION

Crataegus laevigata
syn. C. oxyacantha
English Hawthorn

'Autumn Glory'   'Contorta'
'Crimson Cloud'   'Paul II'

- dense
- 20-35
- P C Si Sa L
- 4 5 6 7 8
- M P A W E
- W WM M MD D
- vT T M I vI
- moderate
- barrier
- border mass
- hedge
- patio garden
- screen
- specimen / accent
- street canopy
- Europe
- 5 — 8
- long c.

Crataegus x lavallei
Lavalle Hawthorn

'Carrieri'

- dense
- 20-35
- P C Si Sa L
- 4 5 6 7 8
- M P A W E
- W WM M MD D
- vT T M I vI
- moderate   moderate
- barrier
- formal garden
- patio garden
- seacoast
- specimen / accent
- street canopy
- windbreak
- hybrid
- 4 — 9
- o.1870

Crataegus monogyna
Singleseed Hawthorn
English Hawthorn

'Flexuosa'   'Pendula Rosa'
'Inermis'   'Stricta'

- dense
- 20-35
- P C Si Sa L
- 4 5 6 7 8
- M P A W E
- W WM M MD D
- vT T M I vI
- moderate   moderate
- barrier
- border mass
- hedge
- patio garden
- seacoast
- specimen / accent
- windbreak
- Asia / Mediterranean long c.
- 5 — 7

Crataegus nitida
Glossy Hawthorn

- dense
- 20-35
- P C Si Sa L
- 4 5 6 7 8
- M P A W E
- W WM M MD D
- vT T M I vI
- slow   short
- barrier
- border mass
- hedge
- patio garden
- reclamation
- specimen / accent
- windbreak
- central U.S.
- 5 — 8
- i.1883

Crataegus 'Pauls Scarlet'
Pauls Scarlet Hawthorn

- dense
- 20-35
- P C Si Sa L
- 4 5 6 7 8
- M P A W E
- W WM M MD D
- vT T M I vI
- moderate   m-short
- barrier
- border mass
- patio garden
- screen
- specimen / accent
- street canopy
- cultivar
- 5 — 8
- o.1858

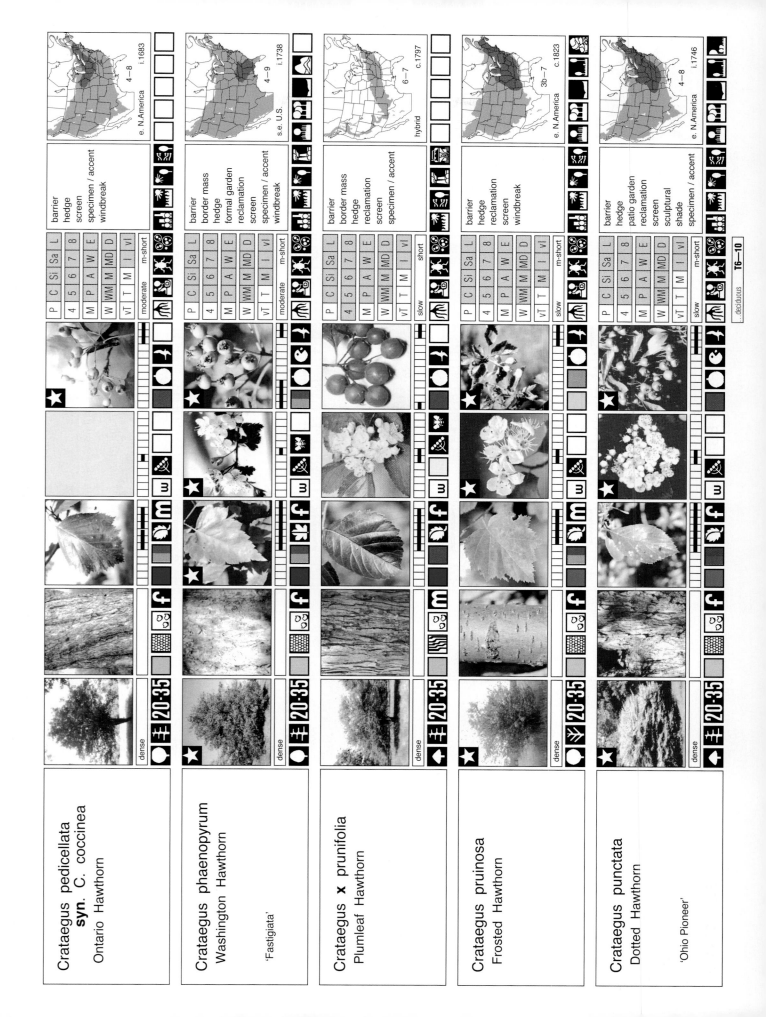

Crataegus pedicellata **syn.** C. coccinea
Ontario Hawthorn

barrier
hedge
screen
specimen / accent
windbreak

P	C	Si	Sa	L
4	5	6	7	8
M	P	A	W	E
W	WM	M	MD	D
vT	T	M	I	vl

moderate · m-short

e. N.America · i.1683 · 4–8

dense · 20-35

Crataegus phaenopyrum
Washington Hawthorn
'Fastigiata'

barrier
border mass
hedge
formal garden
reclamation
screen
specimen / accent
windbreak

P	C	Si	Sa	L
4	5	6	7	8
M	P	A	W	E
W	WM	M	MD	D
vT	T	M	I	vl

moderate · m-short

s.e. U.S. · i.1738 · 4–9

dense · 20-35

Crataegus × prunifolia
Plumleaf Hawthorn

barrier
border mass
hedge
reclamation
screen
specimen / accent

P	C	Si	Sa	L
4	5	6	7	8
M	P	A	W	E
W	WM	M	MD	D
vT	T	M	I	vl

short

hybrid · c.1797 · 6–7

dense · 20-35

Crataegus pruinosa
Frosted Hawthorn

barrier
hedge
reclamation
screen
windbreak

P	C	Si	Sa	L
4	5	6	7	8
M	P	A	W	E
W	WM	M	MD	D
vT	T	M	I	vl

slow · m-short

e. N.America · c.1823 · 3b–7

dense

Crataegus punctata
Dotted Hawthorn
'Ohio Pioneer'

barrier
hedge
patio garden
reclamation
screen
sculptural
shade
specimen / accent

P	C	Si	Sa	L
4	5	6	7	8
M	P	A	W	E
W	WM	M	MD	D
vT	T	M	I	vl

slow · m-short

e. N.America · i.1746 · 4–8

dense · 20-35

...deciduous · T6—10

SMALL TREE	FORM	BARK	LEAF	FLOWER	FRUIT	CULTURE	USES	REGION

Cydonia oblonga
Common Quince

FORM: open — 20-35

CULTURE:
P	C	Si	Sa	L
4	5	6	7	8
M	P	A	W	E
W	WM	M	MD	D
T	M	I	vl
slow — very long

USES:
culinary
jams, jellies
kitchen garden
orchard
patio garden
specimen / accent

REGION:
6 — 9
c. ancient x
w. Asia

Ehretia thyrsiflora
syn. E. acuminata
Heliotrope

FORM: moderate — 35-50

CULTURE:
P	C	Si	Sa	L
4	5	6	7	8
M	P	A	W	E
W	WM	M	MD	D
vl	T	M	I	vl
moderate — short

USES:
shade
specimen / accent

REGION:
5 — 8
i:1900
China / Taiwan

Enkianthus campanulatus
Redvein Enkianthus

'Hollandia Red'
'Red Bells'

FORM: moderate — 20-35

CULTURE:
P	C	Si	Sa	L
4	5	6	7	8
M	P	A	W	E
W	WM	M	MD	D
vT	T	M	I	vl
slow — short

USES:
border mass
container
heath garden
pool garden
rock garden
specimen / accent

REGION:
5b — 8
i.a.1870
Japan

Erythrina caffra
syn. E. constantiana
Kaffirboom Coraltree

FORM: dense — 35-50

CULTURE:
P	C	Si	Sa	L
4	5	6	7	8
M	P	A	W	E
W	WM	M	MD	D
vT	T	M	I	vl
fast — short

USES:
container
greenhouse
seacoast
specimen / accent

REGION:
10
s.e. Africa

Erythrina crista-galli
Cockspur Coraltree
Cry-babytree

FORM: dense — 20-35

CULTURE:
P	C	Si	Sa	L
4	5	6	7	8
M	P	A	W	E
W	WM	M	MD	D
vl	T	M	I	vl
fast — short

USES:
container
greenhouse
seacoast
specimen / accent

REGION:
9 — 10
Argentina / Brazil

Erythrina falcata

P	C	Si	Sa	L
4	5	6	7	8
M	P	A	W	E
W	WM	M	MD	D
vT	T	M	I	vl

container
greenhouse
seacoast
specimen / accent

10

Peru / Bolivia

open
35-50

Eucalyptus lehmani
Lehmann Eucalyptus
Bushy Yate

P	C	Si	Sa	L
4	5	6	7	8
M	P	A	W	E
W	WM	M	MD	D
vT	T	M	I	vl

fast   long

aromatic leaves
patio garden
screen
seacoast
shade
street canopy
windbreak

10

w. Australia

dense
20-35

Euonymus atropurpureus
Eastern Wahoo

P	C	Si	Sa	L
4	5	6	7	8
M	P	A	W	E
W	WM	M	MD	D
vT	T	M	I	vl

moderate   moderate

border mass
patio garden
screen
specimen / accent

3b–8
i.1756

e. N. America

moderate
20-35

Euonymus bungeana
Winterberry Euonymus

'Pendula'

P	C	Si	Sa	L
4	5	6	7	8
M	P	A	W	E
W	WM	M	MD	D
vT	T	M	I	vl

moderate   short

border mass
patio garden
screen
shade
specimen / accent
windbreak

4b–7
i.1902

China

moderate
20-35

Euonymus europaea
European Euonymus
Spindletree

'Aldenhamensis'
'Red Cap'   'Red Cascade'

P	C	Si	Sa	L
4	5	6	7	8
M	P	A	W	E
W	WM	M	MD	D
vT	T	M	I	vl

moderate   short

border mass
patio garden
screen
specimen / accent
windbreak

3b–8
i.1922

Europe / w. Asia

moderate
20-35

...deciduous   T6—12

SMALL TREE	FORM	BARK	LEAF	FLOWER	FRUIT	CULTURE	USES	REGION

Evodia danielli
Korean Evodia

- REGION: Korea · 5b—8 · i.1905
- USES: aromatic leaves / formal garden / patio garden / specimen / accent / street canopy
- CULTURE: P C Si Sa L | 4 5 6 7 8 | M P A W E | W WM M MD D | vT T M I vl | fast | short
- FORM: open · 20-35

Ficus carica
Common Fig
Edible Fig
'Abidjan' 'Asahi'
'Alma' 'Beall'

- REGION: Mediterranean · 7—10 · i.colonial x
- USES: border mass / culinary / container / espalier / jams, jellies / orchard / patio garden / seacoast
- CULTURE: P C Si Sa L | 4 5 6 7 8 | M P A W E | W WM M MD D | vT T M I vl | moderate | short
- FORM: moderate · 20-35

Firmiana simplex
Chinese Parasoltree
Varnishtree

- REGION: Vietnam · (7b)—10 · i.1757
- USES: background / fruit arrangement / patio garden / shade / specimen / accent / street canopy
- CULTURE: P C Si Sa L | 4 5 6 7 8 | M P A W E | W WM M MD D | vT T M I vl | moderate | short
- FORM: dense · 20-35

Forestiera acuminata
syn. F. angustifolia
Texas Forestiera
Swamp Privet

- REGION: s.e. U.S. · 6—9 · i.1812
- USES: border mass / naturalizing / shade
- CULTURE: P C Si Sa L | 4 5 6 7 8 | M P A W E | W WM M MD D | vT T M I vl | fast | short
- FORM: open · 20-35

Franklinia alatamaha
Frankliniatree

- REGION: Extinct in wild · 6b—9 · i.1765
- USES: background / groupings / specimen / accent
- CULTURE: P C Si Sa L | 4 5 6 7 8 | M P A W E | W WM M MD D | vT T M I vl | slow | moderate
- FORM: open · 12-20

Fraxinus holotricha
Balkan Ash

moderate   12-20

P	C	Si	Sa	L
4	5	6	7	8
M	P	A	W	E
W	WM	M	MD	D
vT	T	M	I	vl

fast   short

formal garden
shade
street canopy

6b—8   c.1870
e. Balkans

Fuchsia arborescens
syn. F. syringaeflora
Tree Fuchsia

dense   20-35

P	C	Si	Sa	L
4	5	6	7	8
M	P	A	W	E
W	WM	M	MD	D
vT	T	M	I	vl

fast   short

container
greenhouse
hedge
patio garden
specimen / accent

10   i.1788
Mexico

Hamamelis japonica
Japanese Witchhazel

open   20-35

P	C	Si	Sa	L
4	5	6	7	8
M	P	A	W	E
W	WM	M	MD	D
vT	T	M	I	vl

slow   moderate

border mass
cut flowers
patio garden
sculptural
specimen / accent

5b—9   i.1919
Japan

Hippophae rhamnoides
Common Seabuckthorn

open   12-20

P	C	Si	Sa	L
4	5	6	7	8
M	P	A	W	E
W	WM	M	MD	D
vT	T	M	I	vl

fast   short

bank erosion
barrier
border mass
dune erosion
nitrogen-fixing
patio garden
seacoast
specimen / accent

3—7   i.colonial x
n. China

Hovenia dulcis
Japanese Raisintree

open   20-35

P	C	Si	Sa	L
4	5	6	7	8
M	P	A	W	E
W	WM	M	MD	D
vT	T	M	I	vl

moderate   moderate

shade garden
specimen / accent

6b—8   i.1812
Japan

...deciduous   **T6—14**

SMALL TREE	FORM	BARK	LEAF	FLOWER	FRUIT	CULTURE	USES	REGION
Ilex decidua Deciduous Holly Possumhaw 'Council Fire' 'Warrens Red' 'Pocahontas'	open 12-20					P C Si Sa L 4 5 6 7 8 M P A W E W WM M MD D vT T M I vl moderate short	border mass hedge naturalizing patio garden screen specimen / accent	se. U.S. 5b–9 i.1760
Juglans californica California Black Walnut	moderate 20-35					P C Si Sa L 4 5 6 7 8 M P A W E W WM M MD D vT T M I vl fast	cakes, cookies orchard preservation windbreak	s. California 9–10 c.1889
Juglans microcarpa Texas Walnut River Walnut	moderate 20-35					P C Si Sa L 4 5 6 7 8 M P A W E W WM M MD D vT T M I vl fast	cakes, cookies orchard preservation windbreak	s.w. U.S. 6–9
Koelreuteria elegans Flame Goldraintree	moderate 20-35					P C Si Sa L 4 5 6 7 8 M P A W E W WM M MD D vT T M I vl moderate short	formal garden shade street canopy specimen / accent	Taiwan / Fiji 9–10
Laburnum alpinum Scotch Laburnum	open 12-20					P C Si Sa L 4 5 6 7 8 M P A W E W WM M MD D vT T M I vl fast short	cut flowers espalier formal garden patio garden poisonous leaves specimen / accent	s. Europe 5b–8 c.1596

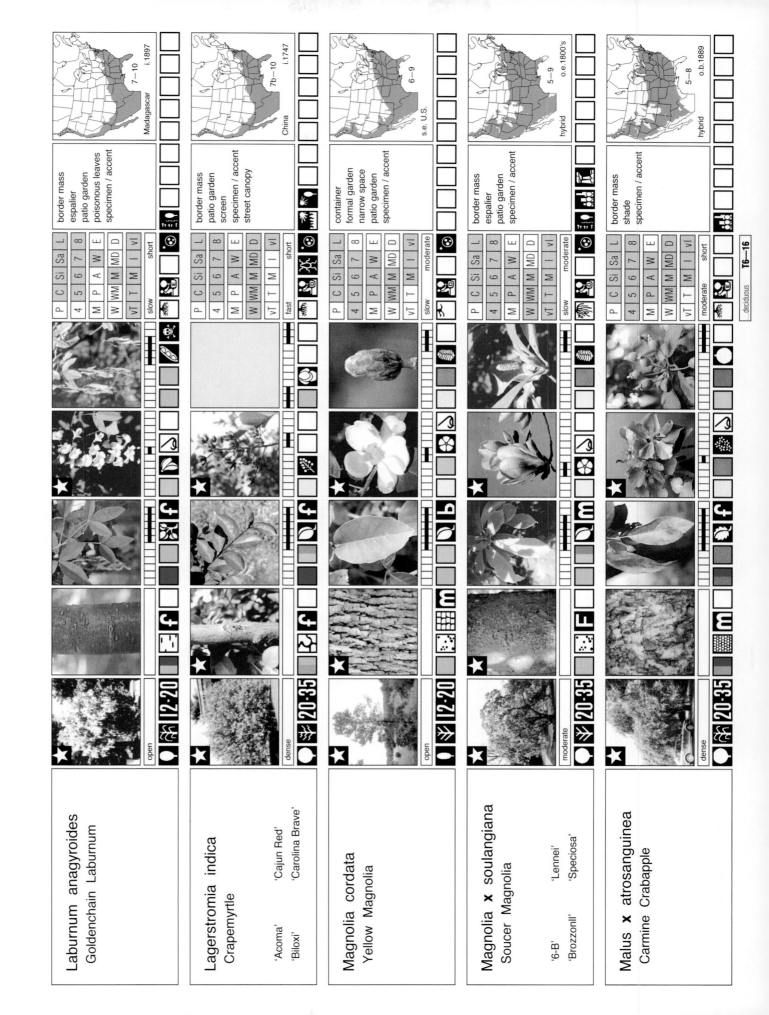

Laburnum anagyroides — Goldenchain Laburnum
Madagascar — i.1897 — 7–10
border mass · espalier · patio garden · poisonous leaves · specimen / accent
slow · open · 12-20

Lagerstromia indica — Crapemyrtle
'Acoma' · 'Cajun Red'
'Biloxi' · 'Carolina Brave'
China — i.1747 — 7b–10
border mass · patio garden · screen · specimen / accent · street canopy
fast · dense · 20-35

Magnolia cordata — Yellow Magnolia
s.e. U.S. — 6–9
container · formal garden · narrow space · patio garden · specimen / accent
slow · open · 12-20

Magnolia x soulangiana — Soucer Magnolia
'6-B' · 'Lennei'
'Brozzonll' · 'Speciosa'
hybrid — o.e.1800's — 5–9
border mass · espalier · patio garden · specimen / accent
slow · moderate · 20-35

Malus x atrosanguinea — Carmine Crabapple
hybrid — o.b.1889 — 5–8
border mass · shade · specimen / accent
moderate · dense · 20-35

...deciduous   T6–16

SMALL TREE	FORM	BARK	LEAF	FLOWER	FRUIT	CULTURE	USES	REGION

Malus 'Blanche Ames'
Blanche Ames Crabapple

'Charlotta'
'Nieuwlandiana'

dense 20-35

P	C	Si	Sa	L
4	5	6	7	8
M	P	A	W	E
W	WM	M	MD	D
vT	T	M	I	vl

moderate short

cut flowers
patio garden
specimen / accent

cultivar   i.1947
4 — 8

Malus coronaria
Wild Sweet Crabapple

dense 20-35

P	C	Si	Sa	L
4	5	6	7	8
M	P	A	W	E
W	WM	M	MD	D
vT	T	M	I	vl

moderate short

cider, jams, jellies
cut flowers
patio garden
specimen / accent

e. N.America   i.1724
5 — 7

Malus 'Dorothea'
Dorothea Crabapple

dense 20-35

P	C	Si	Sa	L
4	5	6	7	8
M	P	A	W	E
W	WM	M	MD	D
vT	T	M	I	vl

moderate short

cut flowers
groupings
specimen / accent

cultivar   o.1897
4 — 8

Malus 'Flame'
Flame Crabapple

dense 12-20

P	C	Si	Sa	L
4	5	6	7	8
M	P	A	W	E
W	WM	M	MD	D
vT	T	M	I	vl

moderate short

formal garden
narrow space
specimen / accent

cultivar   o.1920
5 — 7

Malus floribunda
Japanese Flowering
Crabapple

'Calloway'

dense 20-35

P	C	Si	Sa	L
4	5	6	7	8
M	P	A	W	E
W	WM	M	MD	D
vT	T	M	I	vl

moderate moderate

border mass
jams, jellies
patio garden
sculptural
seacoast
specimen / accent

Japan   i.1862
4b — 8

Malus glabrata
Biltmore Crabapple

background
cut flowers
patio garden
shade
specimen / accent

P	C	Si	Sa	L
4	5	6	7	8
M	P	A	W	E
W	WM	M	MD	D
vT	T	M	I	vl

moderate short

s.e. U.S. 4—8 i.1912

moderate 20-35

Malus 'Gorgeous'
Gorgeous Crabapple

background
cut flowers
patio garden
shade
specimen / accent

P	C	Si	Sa	L
4	5	6	7	8
M	P	A	W	E
W	WM	M	MD	D
vT	T	M	I	vl

moderate short

cultivar 4—8 o.1925

dense 20-35

Malus 'Henry F. Dupont'
Dupont Crabapple

background
cut flowers
patio garden
screen
specimen / accent

P	C	Si	Sa	L
4	5	6	7	8
M	P	A	W	E
W	WM	M	MD	D
vT	T	M	I	vl

moderate short

cultivar 5—7 o.1946

moderate 20-35

Malus hupehensis
Tea Crabapple
Hupeh Crabapple

beverage
edible leaves
patio garden
shade
specimen / accent

P	C	Si	Sa	L
4	5	6	7	8
M	P	A	W	E
W	WM	M	MD	D
vT	T	M	I	vl

moderate short

China 4b—8 i.1900

open 12-20

Malus ioensis
Prairie Crabapple
Iowa Crabapple

'Klehm's'   'Prairie Rose'
'Prairie Crab' 'Prairiefire'

border mass
massing
patio garden
reclamation
specimen / accent
windbreak

P	C	Si	Sa	L
4	5	6	7	8
M	P	A	W	E
W	WM	M	MD	D
vT	T	M	I	vl

moderate short

n.central U.S. 2—9 i.1885

moderate 20-35

...deciduous   **T6—18**

SMALL TREE	FORM	BARK	LEAF	FLOWER	FRUIT	CULTURE	USES	REGION

Malus ioensis 'Plena'
Bechtel Crabapple
Double-flowered Iowa Crab

moderate · 20-35

border mass
cut flowers
patio garden
specimen / accent
windbreak

P	C	Si	Sa	L
4	5	6	7	8
M	P	A	W	E
W	WM	M	MD	D
vT	T	M	I	vl

moderate · short

variety · 2—8 · i:1888

Malus 'Katherine'
Katherine Crabapple

open · 20-35

border mass
cut flowers
patio garden
screen
specimen / accent

P	C	Si	Sa	L
4	5	6	7	8
M	P	A	W	E
W	WM	M	MD	D
vT	T	M	I	vl

moderate · short

cultivar · 4—8 · o.1928

Malus 'Makamik'
Makamik Crabapple

dense · 20-35

border mass
cut flowers
patio garden
screen
sculptural
specimen / accent

P	C	Si	Sa	L
4	5	6	7	8
M	P	A	W	E
W	WM	M	MD	D
vT	T	M	I	vl

moderate · short

cultivar · 4—8 · i:1933

Malus 'Marshall Oyama'
Marshall Oyama Crabapple

open · 12-20

border mass
patio garden
sculptural
specimen / accent

P	C	Si	Sa	L
4	5	6	7	8
M	P	A	W	E
W	WM	M	MD	D
vT	T	M	I	vl

moderate · short

Japan · 5—8 · i:1930

Malus 'Ormiston Roy'
Ormiston Roy Crabapple

moderate · 12-20

border mass
patio garden
sculptural
specimen / accent

P	C	Si	Sa	L
4	5	6	7	8
M	P	A	W	E
W	WM	M	MD	D
vT	T	M	I	vl

moderate · short

cultivar · 4—7 · o.b.1933

Malus 'Prince Georges'
Prince Georges Crabapple

cut flowers
patio garden
shade
specimen / accent

P	C	Si	Sa	L
4	5	6	7	8
M	P	A	W	E
W	WM	M	MD	D
vT	T	M	I	vI

dense · 20-35 · moderate · moderate

cultivar · 4—8 · o.1919

Malus prunifolia
Plumleaf Crabapple
Pearleaf Crabapple

cut flowers
patio garden
screen
shade
windbreak

P	C	Si	Sa	L
4	5	6	7	8
M	P	A	W	E
W	WM	M	MD	D
vT	T	M	I	vI

moderate · 20-35 · moderate · moderate

China · 4—8 · i.1750

Malus x purpurea 'Lemoinei'
Lemoine Crabapple

shade
specimen / accent

P	C	Si	Sa	L
4	5	6	7	8
M	P	A	W	E
W	WM	M	MD	D
vT	T	M	I	vI

moderate · 20-35 · moderate · moderate

hybrid · 4—7 · o.1922

Malus 'Radiant'
Radiant Crabapple

border mass
cut flowers
sculptural
specimen / accent

P	C	Si	Sa	L
4	5	6	7	8
M	P	A	W	E
W	WM	M	MD	D
vT	T	M	I	vI

open · 20-35 · moderate

cultivar · 4—7 · o.1940

Malus x robusta
Cherry Crabapple
'Persicifolia'

cut flowers
jams, jellies
kitchen garden
screen
specimen / accent

P	C	Si	Sa	L
4	5	6	7	8
M	P	A	W	E
W	WM	M	MD	D
vT	T	M	I	vI

dense · 20-35 · fast · moderate

hybrid · 3b—7 · o.a.1815

...deciduous   T6—20

SMALL TREE	FORM	BARK	LEAF	FLOWER	FRUIT	CULTURE	USES	REGION

Malus 'Snowdrift'
Snowdrift Crabapple

- FORM: dense · 20-35
- CULTURE: P C Si Sa L / 4 5 6 7 8 / M P A W E / W WM M MD D / vT T M I vl · moderate
- USES: border mass, formal garden, patio garden, screen, shade, street canopy
- REGION: cultivar · 4—8

Malus spectabilis
Chinese Flowering Crabapple
'Alba'
'Riversii'

- FORM: open · 20-35
- CULTURE: P C Si Sa L / 4 5 6 7 8 / M P A W E / W WM M MD D / vT T M I vl · moderate
- USES: cut flowers, patio garden, sculptural, shade, specimen / accent
- REGION: China · 5—8 · i.1750

Malus sylvestris
Domestic Apple

- FORM: moderate
- CULTURE: P C Si Sa L / 4 5 6 7 8 / M P A W E / W WM M MD D / vT T M I vl · moderate
- USES: allee, bouquet, culinary, hedge, jams, jellies, orchard, shade, specimen / accent
- REGION: Asia Minor · 4—8 · long c.

Malus toringoides
Cutleaf Crabapple
'Macrocarpa'

- FORM: dense · 20-35
- CULTURE: P C Si Sa L / 4 5 6 7 8 / M P A W E / W WM M MD D / vT T M I vl · short
- USES: border mass, patio garden, specimen / accent
- REGION: w. China · 4b—8 · i.1904

Malus x zumi
Zumi Crabapple
'Glen Mills'
'Indian Magic'

- FORM: dense · 20-35
- CULTURE: P C Si Sa L / 4 5 6 7 8 / M P A W E / W WM M MD D / vT T M I vl · short
- USES: cut flowers, patio garden, shade, specimen / accent
- REGION: hybrid · 4—8 · i.1892

Malus x Zumi 'Calocarpa'
Redbud Crabapple

P	C	Si	Sa	L
4 — 8		

cultivar
i.1899

attracts bees
cut flowers
patio garden
screen
shade
specimen / accent

P	C	Si	Sa	L
4	5	6	7	8
M	P	A	W	E
W	WM	M	MD	D
vT	T	M	I	vl

moderate — short

dense
20·35

Mespilus germanica
Medlar

6 — 9

Asia Minor
long c.

orchard
jams, jellies
shade
specimen / accent

P	C	Si	Sa	L
4	5	6	7	8
M	P	A	W	E
W	WM	M	MD	D
vT	T	M	I	vl

slow — long

dense
20·35

Morus nigra
Black Mulberry
Persian Mulberry
'Illinois Everbearing'

8b — 9

w.Asia
c.e. 16th cent.

jams, jellies
jams, jellies
reclamation
windbreak

P	C	Si	Sa	L
4	5	6	7	8
M	P	A	W	E
W	WM	M	MD	D
vT	T	M	I	vl

fast — short

open
20·35

Myoporum laetum
Naio
'Carson II'

10

New Zealand

barrier
hedge
seacoast
windbreak

P	C	Si	Sa	L
4	5	6	7	8
M	P	A	W	E
W	WM	M	MD	D
vT	T	M	I	vl

slow — moderate

dense
12·20

Ostrya virginiana
Eastern Hophornbeam

3b — 9

e. N.America
i.1692

formal garden
naturalizing
sculptural
shade
specimen / accent
street canopy

P	C	Si	Sa	L
4	5	6	7	8
M	P	A	W	E
W	WM	M	MD	D
vT	T	M	I	vl

slow — moderate

dense
20·35

...deciduous   T6—22

SMALL TREE	FORM	BARK	LEAF	FLOWER	FRUIT	CULTURE	USES	REGION

Prosopis glandulosa
Honey Mesquite
Texas Mesquite

open · 20-35

barrier · border mass · naturalizing · specimen / accent

s.w. U.S. · 6—10 · moderate

Prunus americana
American Plum

dense · 20-35

background · border mass · orchard · jams, jellies · reclamation · specimen / accent · windbreak

U.S. · 3—9 · i:1768 · moderate · short

Prunus armeniaca
Apricot

'Morden 604'
'Mandshurica'

open · 20-35

eating, cooking · jams, jellies · orchard · patio garden · seacoast · shade · specimen / accent

China · 5b—9 · i:b1875 · fast · short

Prunus cerasifera
Cherry Plum
Myrobalan Plum

'Thundercloud' 'Nigra'
'Newport' 'Vesuvius'

dense · 20-35

border mass · hedge · jams, jellies · orchard · patio garden · specimen / accent

Asia · 4b—9 · c. 16th cent. · fast · short

Prunus conradinae
Conradina Cherry

dense · 20-35

bank erosion · hedge · screen · sculptural · seacoast · shear · specimen / accent

China · 6b—8 · i:1907 · fast · short

Prunus davidiana
David Peach

cooking, eating
kitchen garden
orchard
patio garden
pies, preserves
specimen / accent

P	C	Si	Sa	L
4	5	6	7	8
M	P	A	W	E
W	WM	M	MD	D
vT	T	M	I	vI

very fast — short

China — 4–8 — i.1865

20–35

Prunus hortulana
Hortulan Plum
Wild Goose Plum

bank erosion
jams, jellies
reclamation
naturalizing
windbreak

P	C	Si	Sa	L
4	5	6	7	8
M	P	A	W	E
W	WM	M	MD	D
vT	T	M	I	vI

fast — short

e. U.S. — 5–7 — c.1890

20–35

Prunus incisa
Fuji Cherry

'Midori'

border mass
cut flowers
patio garden
seacoast
specimen / accent

P	C	Si	Sa	L
4	5	6	7	8
M	P	A	W	E
W	WM	M	MD	D
vT	T	M	I	vI

fast — short

Japan — 6–8 — c.1910

20–35

Prunus mume
Japanese Flowering Plum
Japanese Apricot

'Bonita'   'Kobai'
'Dawn'   'Peggy Clarke'

bonsai
cut flowers
patio garden
specimen / accent

P	C	Si	Sa	L
4	5	6	7	8
M	P	A	W	E
W	WM	M	MD	D
vT	T	M	I	vI

fast — short

Japan — 6b–9 — i.1844

20–35

Prunus persica
Peach

'Alba'   'Rubria'
'Lovell'   'Versicolor'

border mass
container
jams, jellies
orchard
patio garden
screen
specimen / accent

P	C	Si	Sa	L
4	5	6	7	8
M	P	A	W	E
W	WM	M	MD	D
vT	T	M	I	vI

moderate — short

China — 6–9 — i.b.1696

20–35

...deciduous   **T6—24**

SMALL TREE	FORM	BARK	LEAF	FLOWER	FRUIT	CULTURE	USES	REGION

Prunus subhirtella
Higan Cherry
Rosebud Cherry

'Accolade'   'Pendula'
'Autumnalis' 'Rosy Cloud'

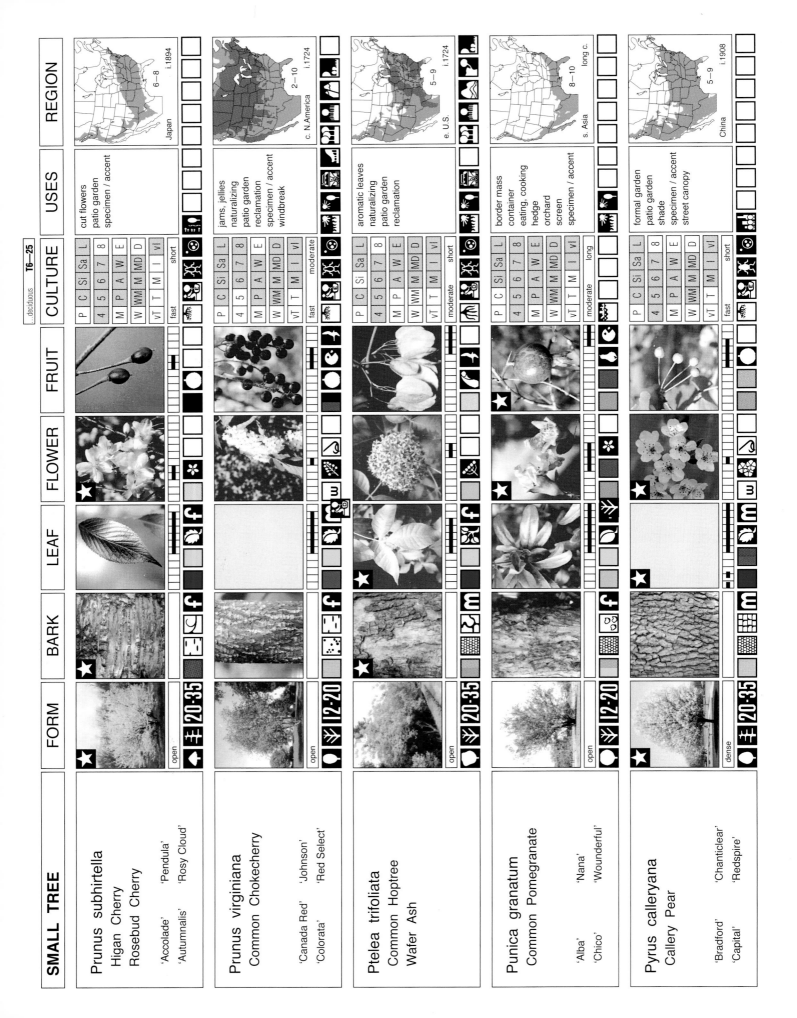

open · 20-35

CULTURE: P C Si Sa L / 4 5 6 7 8 / M P A W E / W WM M MD D / vT T M I vI / fast · short

USES: cut flowers / patio garden / specimen / accent

REGION: Japan · 6–8 · i.1894

Prunus virginiana
Common Chokecherry

'Canada Red'   'Johnson'
'Colorata'   'Red Select'

open · 12-20

CULTURE: P C Si Sa L / 4 5 6 7 8 / M P A W E / W WM M MD D / vT T M I vI / fast · moderate

USES: jams, jellies / naturalizing / patio garden / reclamation / specimen / accent / windbreak

REGION: c. N.America · 2–10 · i.1724

Ptelea trifoliata
Common Hoptree
Wafer Ash

open · 20-35

CULTURE: P C Si Sa L / 4 5 6 7 8 / M P A W E / W WM M MD D / vT T M I vI / moderate · short

USES: aromatic leaves / naturalizing / patio garden / reclamation

REGION: e. U.S. · 5–9 · i.1724

Punica granatum
Common Pomegranate

'Alba'   'Nana'
'Chico'   'Wounderful'

open · 12-20

CULTURE: P C Si Sa L / 4 5 6 7 8 / M P A W E / W WM M MD D / vT T M I vI / moderate · long

USES: border mass / container / eating, cooking / hedge / orchard / screen / specimen / accent

REGION: s. Asia · 8–10 · long c.

Pyrus calleryana
Callery Pear

'Bradford'   'Chanticlear'
'Capital'   'Redspire'

dense · 20-35

CULTURE: P C Si Sa L / 4 5 6 7 8 / M P A W E / W WM M MD D / vT T M I vI / fast · short

USES: formal garden / patio garden / shade / specimen / accent / street canopy

REGION: China · 5–9 · i.1908

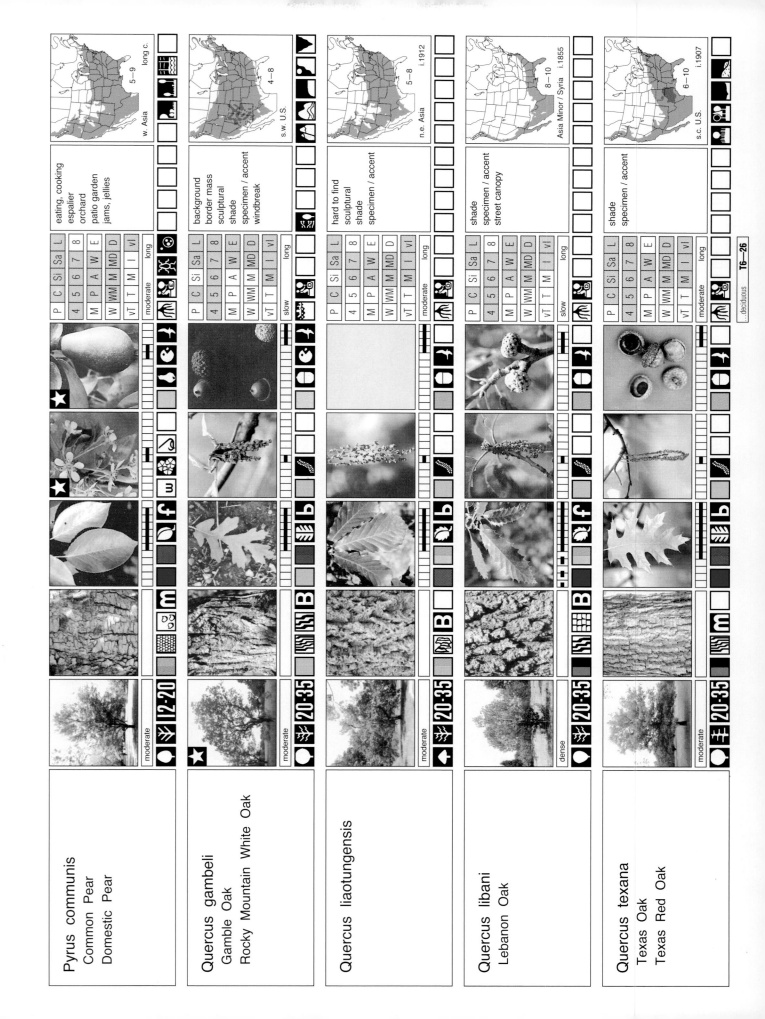

Pyrus communis
Common Pear
Domestic Pear

w. Asia · 5—9 · long c.

eating, cooking
espalier
orchard
patio garden
jams, jellies

moderate · 12-20

Quercus gambeli
Gamble Oak
Rocky Mountain White Oak

s.w. U.S. · 4—8

background
border mass
sculptural
shade
specimen / accent
windbreak

moderate · 20-35

Quercus liaotungensis

n.e. Asia · 5—8 · i.1912

hard to find
sculptural
shade
specimen / accent

moderate · 20-35

Quercus libani
Lebanon Oak

Asia Minor / Syria · 8—10 · i.1855

shade
specimen / accent
street canopy

dense · 20-35

Quercus texana
Texas Oak
Texas Red Oak

s.c. U.S. · 6—10 · i.1907

shade
specimen / accent

moderate · 20-35

...deciduous   T6—26

SMALL TREE	FORM	BARK	LEAF	FLOWER	FRUIT	CULTURE	USES	REGION

Rhamnus cathartica
Common Buckthorn
European Buckthorn

CULTURE: P C Si Sa L / 4 5 6 7 8 / M P A W E / W WM M MD D / vT T M I vl / moderate — moderate — short

USES: background, hedge, medicinal, screen, sheared

REGION: Asia / 3b–6 / long c.

Rhamnus davurica
Dahurian Buckthorn

CULTURE: P C Si Sa L / 4 5 6 7 8 / M P A W E / W WM M MD D / vT T M I vl / fast

USES: hedge, screen, windbreak

REGION: Japan / Korea / 2–6 / i.1817

Rhamnus frangula
Glossy Buckthorn
Alder Buckthorn
'Columnaris'
'Asplenifolia'

CULTURE: P C Si Sa L / 4 5 6 7 8 / M P A W E / W WM M MD D / vT T M I vl / fast

USES: border mass, hedge, narrow space, sheared, screen

REGION: n. Africa / Asia / 4b–8 / long c.

Rhamnus purshiana
Cascara Buckthorn

CULTURE: P C Si Sa L / 4 5 6 7 8 / M P A W E / W WM M MD D / vT T M I vl / fast — moderate

USES: background, hedge, medicinal, screen, sheared

REGION: n. w. U.S. / 5–9 / c.1870

Rhus chinensis
Chinese Sumac
Nutgalltree
'September Beauty'

CULTURE: P C Si Sa L / 4 5 6 7 8 / M P A W E / W WM M MD D / vT T M I vl / fast — short

USES: bank erosion, border mass, large scale mass, naturalizing, road cuts

REGION: Asia / 6–9

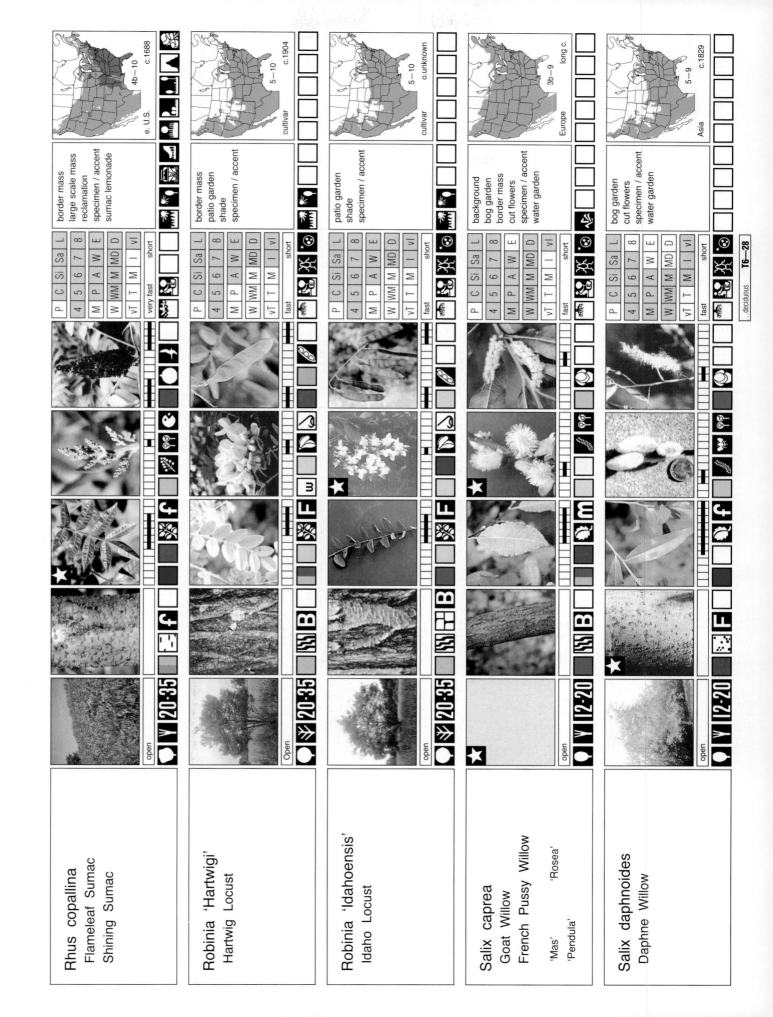

Rhus copallina
Flameleaf Sumac
Shining Sumac

Robinia 'Hartwigi'
Hartwig Locust

Robinia 'Idahoensis'
Idaho Locust

Salix caprea
Goat Willow
French Pussy Willow
'Mas'
'Rosea'
'Pendula'

Salix daphnoides
Daphne Willow

T6—28

SMALL TREE	FORM	BARK	LEAF	FLOWER	FRUIT	CULTURE	USES	REGION

Salix exigua
Coyote Willow
Sandbar Willow
Basket Willow
Narrowleaf Willow

open · 12-20

P	C	Si	Sa	L
4	5	6	7	8
M	P	A	W	E
W	WM	M	MD	D
vT	T	M	I	vl

fast · short

bog garden
naturalizing
water garden

w. N. America
1 – 10   i.1921

Salix sachalinensis
Sakhalin Willow

'Sekka'

moderate · 20-35

P	C	Si	Sa	L
4	5	6	7	8
M	P	A	W	E
W	WM	M	MD	D
vT	T	M	I	vl

fast · short

bog garden
cut flowers
formal garden
specimen / accent
water garden

Japan
5 – 9a

Sambucus mexicana
Mexican Elder
Mexican Elderberry

open · 20-35

P	C	Si	Sa	L
4	5	6	7	8
M	P	A	W	E
W	WM	M	MD	D
vT	T	M	I	vl

fast · short

jams, jellies
kitchen garden
wine
windbreak

Mexico / s.w. U.S.   c.1875
6 – 10

Sambucus nigra
European Elder

open · 20-35

P	C	Si	Sa	L
4	5	6	7	8
M	P	A	W	E
W	WM	M	MD	D
vT	T	M	I	vl

fast · short

beverage
bog garden
jams, jellies
kitchen garden
wine

Mediterranean   c. ancient x
4 – 9a

Sorbus americana
American Mountainash
Dogberry

open · 12-20

P	C	Si	Sa	L
4	5	6	7	8
M	P	A	W	E
W	WM	M	MD	D
vT	T	M	I	vl

slow · short

aromatic bark
groupings
jams, jellies
patio garden
specimen / accent

e. N. America
2 – 7   i.1782

Sorbus decora
Showy Mountainash

n.e. U.S. | 1—5

groupings
jams, jellies
patio garden
specimen / accent

P	C	Si	Sa	L
4	5	6	7	8
M	P	A	W	E
W	WM	M	MD	D
vT	T	M	I	vI

short · moderate

open · 12-20

Sorbus discolor **syn**. S. commixta
Snowberry Mountainash

n. China | 6a—8 · i:1883

groupings
patio garden
specimen / accent

P	C	Si	Sa	L
4	5	6	7	8
M	P	A	W	E
W	WM	M	MD	D
vT	T	M	I	vI

short · moderate

moderate · 12-20

Sorbus **x** hybrida
Oakleaf Mountainash
Hybrid Mountainash

hybrid | 3b—7 · c:1779

groupings
patio garden
specimen / accent

P	C	Si	Sa	L
4	5	6	7	8
M	P	A	W	E
W	WM	M	MD	D
vT	T	M	I	vI

short · moderate

open · 12-20

Stewartia sinensis
Chinese Stewartia

China | 6a—8 · i:1901

patio garden
specimen / accent

P	C	Si	Sa	L
4	5	6	7	8
M	P	A	W	E
W	WM	M	MD	D
vT	T	M	I	vI

slow · moderate

open · 20-35

Styrax japonica
Japanese Snowbell
Japanese Snowdroptree

'Carillon'   'Pendula'
'Kusan'   'Pink Charm'

Japan | (6a)—(9a) · i:1862

patio garden
raised beds
screen
specimen / accent
street canopy

P	C	Si	Sa	L
4	5	6	7	8
M	P	A	W	E
W	WM	M	MD	D
vT	T	M	I	vI

slow · moderate

open · 20-35

...deciduous   T6—30

SMALL TREE	FORM	BARK	LEAF	FLOWER	FRUIT	CULTURE	USES	REGION

Styrax obassia
Fragrant Snowbell

FORM: open · 12·20

CULTURE:
P	C	Si	Sa	L
4	5	6	7	8
M	P	A	W	E
W	WM	M	MD	D
vT	T	M	I	vI
moderate / moderate

USES: border mass · patio garden · street canopy

REGION: Japan · (6a)–8 · i.1879

Symplocos paniculata
Sapphireberry
Sweetleaf

FORM: moderate · 12·20

CULTURE:
P	C	Si	Sa	L
4	5	6	7	8
M	P	A	W	E
W	WM	M	MD	D
vT	T	M	I	vI

USES: aromatic leaves · border mass · screen · specimen / accent

REGION: Himalayas · 6a–8 · i.1875

Ulmus x vegeta
'Camperdowni'
Camperdown Elm

FORM: moderate · 20·35

CULTURE:
P	C	Si	Sa	L
4	5	6	7	8
M	P	A	W	E
W	WM	M	MD	D
vT	T	M	I	vI
moderate / moderate

USES: oriental garden · sculptural · specimen / accent

REGION: hybrid · 4b–9a · c.1850

Ungnadia speciosa
Mexican Buckeye

FORM: moderate · 20·35

CULTURE:
P	C	Si	Sa	L
4	5	6	7	8
M	P	A	W	E
W	WM	M	MD	D
vT	T	M	I	vI
fast / short

USES: background · specimen / accent · windbreak

REGION: Mexico / s.w. U.S. · 7–10 · i.1848

Viburnum lentago
Nannyberry Viburnum

FORM: dense · 20·35

CULTURE:
P	C	Si	Sa	L
4	5	6	7	8
M	P	A	W	E
W	WM	M	MD	D
vT	T	M	I	vI
fast / short

USES: border mass · naturalizing · reclamation · screen · specimen / accent · windbreak

REGION: central U.S. · 2–7 · i.1761

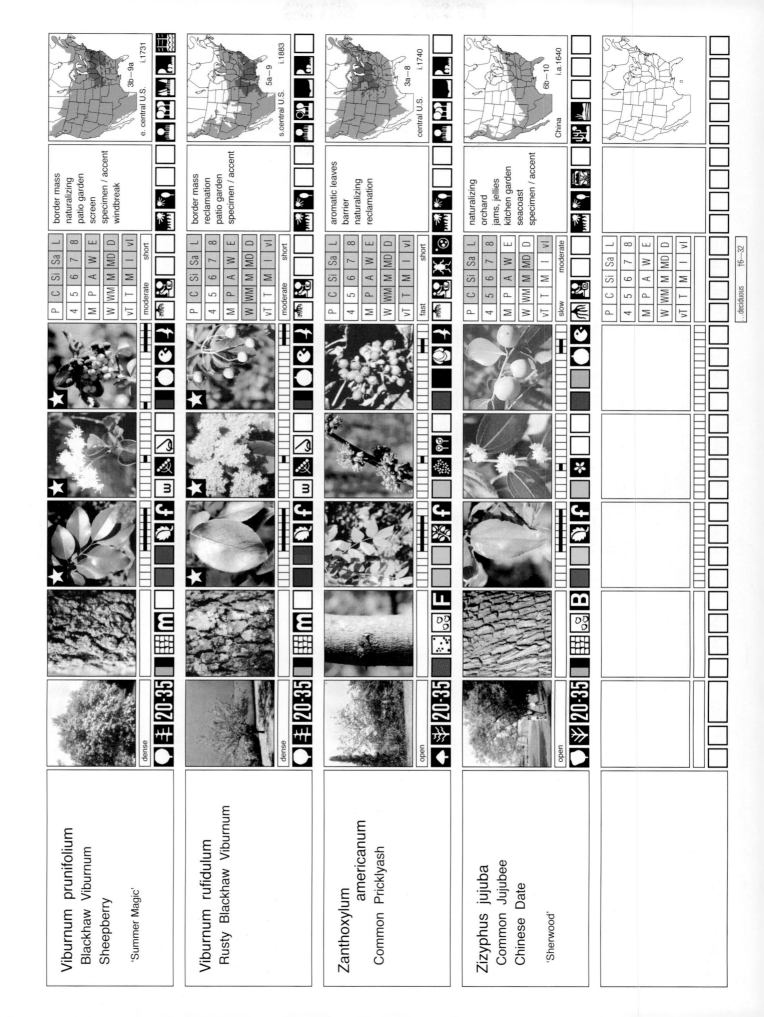

Viburnum prunifolium
Blackhaw Viburnum
Sheepberry
'Summer Magic'

border mass
naturalizing
patio garden
screen
specimen / accent
windbreak

3b–9a   i.1731
e. central U.S.

Viburnum rufidulum
Rusty Blackhaw Viburnum

border mass
reclamation
patio garden
specimen / accent

5a–9   i.1883
s.central U.S.

Zanthoxylum
americanum
Common Pricklyash

aromatic leaves
barrier
naturalizing
reclamation

3a–8   i.1740
central U.S.

Zizyphus jujuba
Common Jujube
Chinese Date
'Sherwood'

naturalizing
orchard
jams, jellies
kitchen garden
seacoast
specimen / accent

6b–10   i.a.1640
China

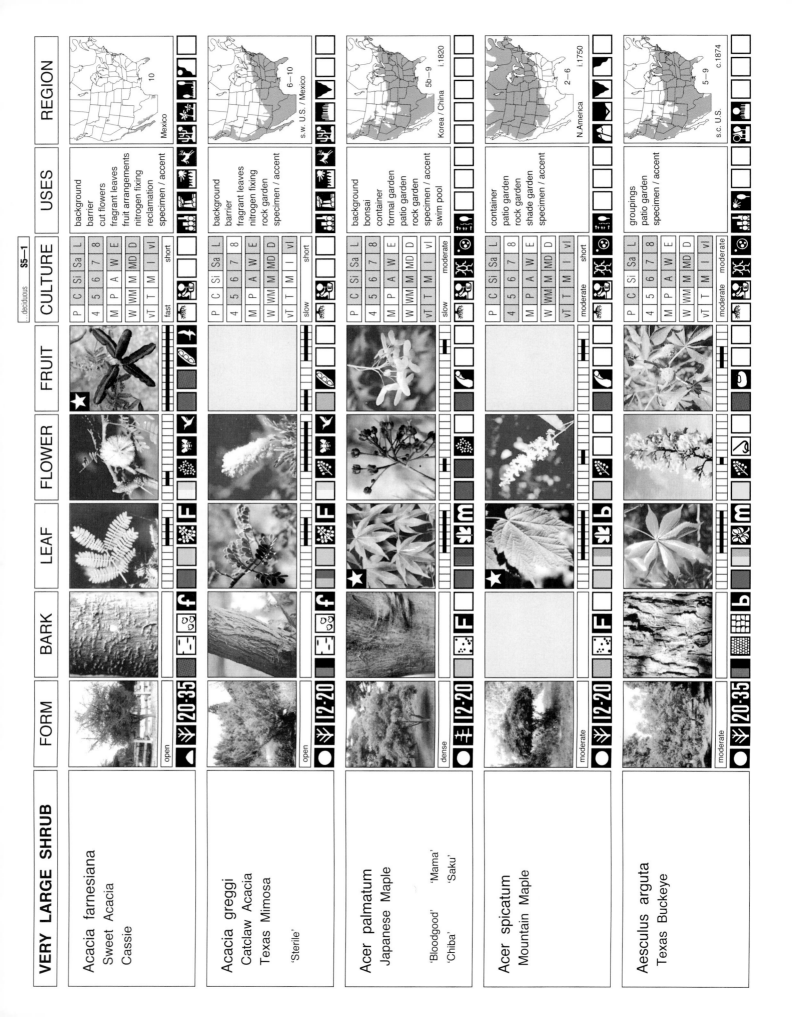

VERY LARGE SHRUB | FORM | BARK | LEAF | FLOWER | FRUIT | CULTURE | USES | REGION

Acacia farnesiana
Sweet Acacia
Cassie

open 20-35

fast short

background
barrier
cut flowers
fragrant leaves
fruit arrangements
nitrogen fixing
reclamation
specimen / accent

Mexico 10

P	C	Si	Sa	L
4	5	6	7	8
M	P	A	W	E
W	WM	M	MD	D
vT	T	M	I	vI

Acacia greggi
Catclaw Acacia
Texas Mimosa
'Sterile'

open 12-20

slow short

background
barrier
fragrant leaves
nitrogen fixing
rock garden
specimen / accent

s.w. U.S. / Mexico 6—10

P	C	Si	Sa	L
4	5	6	7	8
M	P	A	W	E
W	WM	M	MD	D
vT	T	M	I	vI

Acer palmatum
Japanese Maple
'Bloodgood' 'Mama'
'Chiba' 'Saku'

dense 12-20

slow moderate

background
bonsai
container
formal garden
patio garden
rock garden
specimen / accent
swim pool

Korea / China 5b—9 i.1820

P	C	Si	Sa	L
4	5	6	7	8
M	P	A	W	E
W	WM	M	MD	D
vT	T	M	I	vI

Acer spicatum
Mountain Maple

moderate 12-20

moderate short

container
patio garden
rock garden
shade garden
specimen / accent

N.America 2—6 i.1750

P	C	Si	Sa	L
4	5	6	7	8
M	P	A	W	E
W	WM	M	MD	D
vT	T	M	I	vI

Aesculus arguta
Texas Buckeye

moderate 20-35

moderate moderate

groupings
patio garden
specimen / accent

s.c. U.S. 5—9 c.1874

P	C	Si	Sa	L
4	5	6	7	8
M	P	A	W	E
W	WM	M	MD	D
vT	T	M	I	vI

Aesculus sylvatica
Georgia Buckeye
Painted Buckeye

P	C	Si	Sa	L
4	5	6	7	8
M	P	A	W	E
W	WM	M	MD	D
vT	T	M	I	vI

fast · moderate

patio garden
shade garden
specimen / accent
toxic leaves
woodland garden

s.e. U.S. 7–9 i.1905

moderate · 12-20

Alnus serrulata **syn.** A. rugosa
Smooth Alder
Hazel Alder

P	C	Si	Sa	L
4	5	6	7	8
M	P	A	W	E
W	WM	M	MD	D
vT	T	M	I	vI

fast · short

aromatic leaves
bank erosion
bog garden
nitrogen-fixing
screen

e. N.America 3b–9a

open · 12-20

Amelanchier florida
Pacific Serviceberry

P	C	Si	Sa	L
4	5	6	7	8
M	P	A	W	E
W	WM	M	MD	D
vT	T	M	I	vI

moderate · moderate

background
bank erosion
border mass
jams, pies
patio garden
shade garden
specimen / accent
woodland garden

w. N.America 2-7 i.1826

moderate · 12-20

Amelanchier utahensis
Utah Serviceberry
Utah Juneberry

P	C	Si	Sa	L
4	5	6	7	8
M	P	A	W	E
W	WM	M	MD	D
vT	T	M	I	vI

moderate · moderate

background
border mass
jams, pies
patio garden
shade garden
specimen / accent
woodland garden

w.c. U.S. 2-9

moderate · 12-20

Amorpha californica
California Indigobush
California Amorpha

P	C	Si	Sa	L
4	5	6	7	8
M	P	A	W	E
W	WM	M	MD	D
vT	T	M	I	vI

fast · short

aromatic leaves
bank erosion
bog garden
border mass
road cuts

California 8–10

open

...deciduous   S5—2

VERY LARGE SHRUB	FORM	BARK	LEAF	FLOWER	FRUIT	CULTURE	USES	REGION

Amorpha fruticosa
Indigobush Amorpha

CULTURE:
P	C	Si	Sa	L
4	5	6	7	8
M	P	A	W	E
W	WM	M	MD	D
vT	T	M	I	vI
very short · fast

USES:
bog garden
border mass
naturalizing
reclamation
road cuts

REGION: 3b–7a · i.1933 · e. U.S.

FORM: open · 12-20

Amorpha occidentalis
Western Indigobush
Desert Indigobush

CULTURE:
P	C	Si	Sa	L
4	5	6	7	8
M	P	A	W	E
W	WM	M	MD	D
vT	T	M	I	vI
short · fast

USES:
bank erosion
bog garden
naturalizing
road cuts

REGION: 8–10 · i. · e. N.America / Mexico

FORM: open · 12-20

Baccharis halimifolia
Groundselbush
Sea Myrtle
'White Cap'

CULTURE:
P	C	Si	Sa	L
4	5	6	7	8
M	P	A	W	E
W	WM	M	MD	D
vT	T	M	I	vI
short · fast

USES:
bank erosion
border mass
hedge
nitrogen-fixing
reclamation
screen
seacoast
specimen / accent

REGION: (4b)–10 · i.1683 · e. N.America

FORM: moderate · 12-20

Betula pumila
Swamp Birch
Dwarf Birch

CULTURE:
P	C	Si	Sa	L
4	5	6	7	8
M	P	A	W	E
W	WM	M	MD	D
vT	T	M	I	vI
very short · fast

USES:
bog garden
naturalizing
preservation
rock garden
specimen / accent

REGION: 2–6 · i.1762 · e. N.America

FORM: open · 12-20

Buddleia colvillei
Colville Butterflybush

CULTURE:
P	C	Si	Sa	L
4	5	6	7	8
M	P	A	W	E
W	WM	M	MD	D
vT	T	M	I	vI
short · fast

USES:
border mass
container
seacoast
specimen / accent

REGION: 8–9 · i.1849 · Himalayas

FORM: moderate

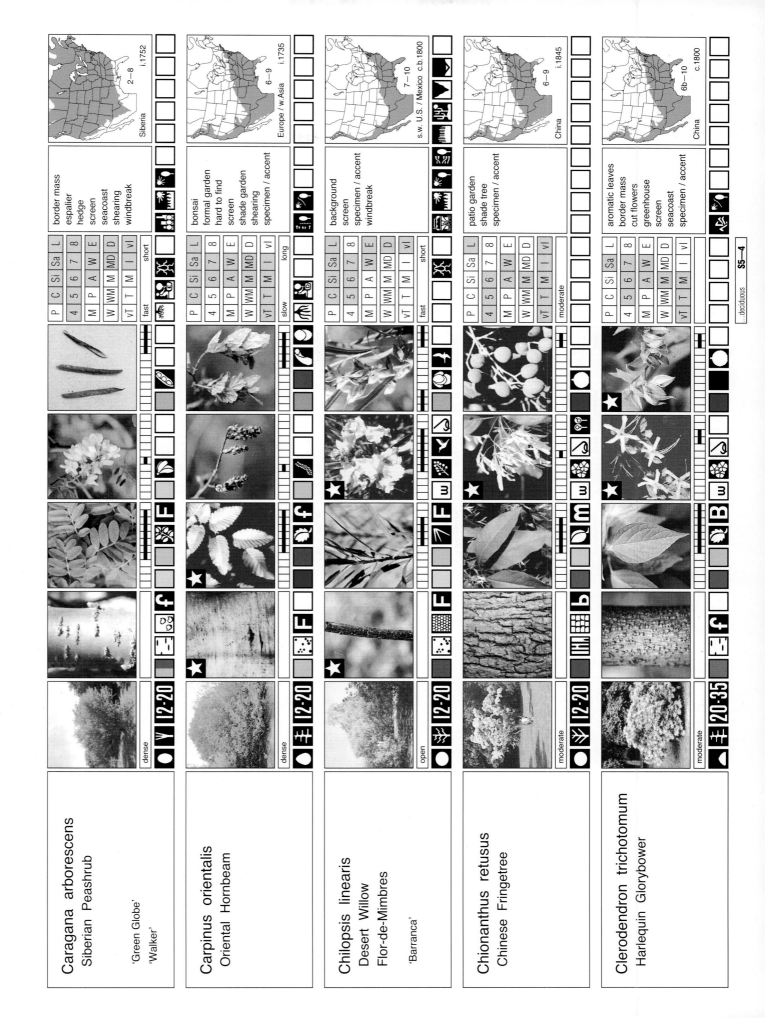

Caragana arborescens
Siberian Peashrub

'Green Globe'
'Walker'

Carpinus orientalis
Oriental Hornbeam

Chilopsis linearis
Desert Willow
Flor-de-Mimbres

'Barranca'

Chionanthus retusus
Chinese Fringetree

Clerodendron trichotomum
Harlequin Glorybower

border mass
espalier
hedge
screen
seacoast
shearing
windbreak

Siberia   2—8   i.1752

bonsai
formal garden
hard to find
screen
shade garden
shearing
specimen / accent

Europe / w.Asia   6—9   i.1735

background
screen
specimen / accent
windbreak

s.w. U.S. / Mexico c.b.1800   7—10

patio garden
shade tree
specimen / accent

China   6—9   i.1845

aromatic leaves
border mass
cut flowers
greenhouse
screen
seacoast
specimen / accent

China   6b—10   c.1800

P	C	Si	Sa	L
4	5	6	7	8
M	P	A	W	E
W	WM	M	MD	D
vT	T	M	I	vI

short   fast   dense   12-20

long   slow   dense   12-20

short   fast   open   12-20

moderate   moderate   12-20

moderate   moderate   20-35

...deciduous   S5—4

VERY LARGE SHRUB	FORM	BARK	LEAF	FLOWER	FRUIT	CULTURE	USES	REGION

Clethra acuminata
Cinnamon Clethra

- FORM: moderate, 12-20
- CULTURE: P C Si Sa L / 4 5 6 7 8 / M P A W E / W WM M MD D / vT T M I vI / short / slow
- USES: patio garden, rock garden, shade garden, specimen / accent, woodland garden
- REGION: s.e. U.S. / 6–10 / i.1806

Colutea arborescens
Bladder Senna

- FORM: moderate, 12-20
- CULTURE: P C Si Sa L / 4 5 6 7 8 / M P A W E / W WM M MD D / vT T M I vI / short / fast
- USES: background, border mass, hedge, screen, seacoast
- REGION: Europe / 6–9 / i.1570

Cornus officinalis
Japanese Corneliancherry
Japanese Cornel

- FORM: dense, 12-20
- CULTURE: P C Si Sa L / 4 5 6 7 8 / M P A W E / W WM M MD D / vT T M I vI / short / moderate
- USES: border mass, patio garden, shade garden, shade tree, specimen / accent
- REGION: Japan / Korea / 5–8a / i.1877

Corylopsis glabrescens
Fragrant Winterhazel

- FORM: dense, 12-20
- CULTURE: P C Si Sa L / 4 5 6 7 8 / M P A W E / W WM M MD D / vT T M I vI / short / moderate
- USES: cut flowers, screen, specimen / accent
- REGION: Japan / 5b–9 / i.1905

Corylopsis sinensis
Chinese Winterhazel

- FORM: dense, 12-20
- CULTURE: P C Si Sa L / 4 5 6 7 8 / M P A W E / W WM M MD D / vT T M I vI / short / moderate
- USES: cut flowers, espalier, specimen / accent
- REGION: China / 6–9 / i.1901

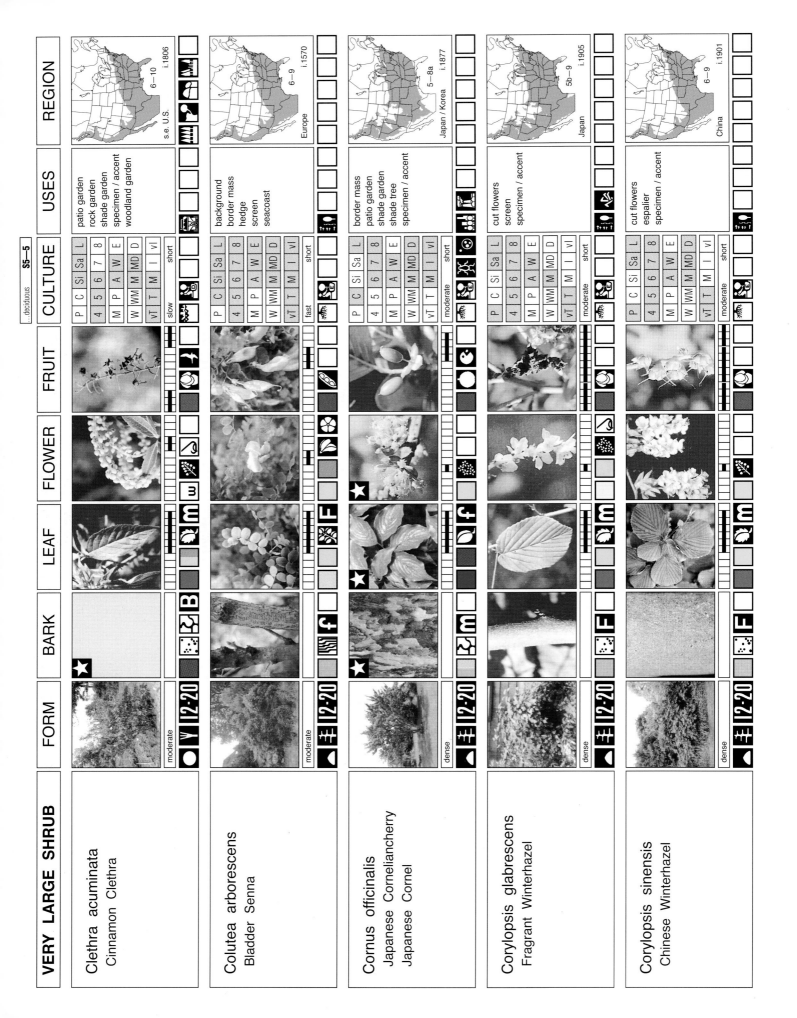

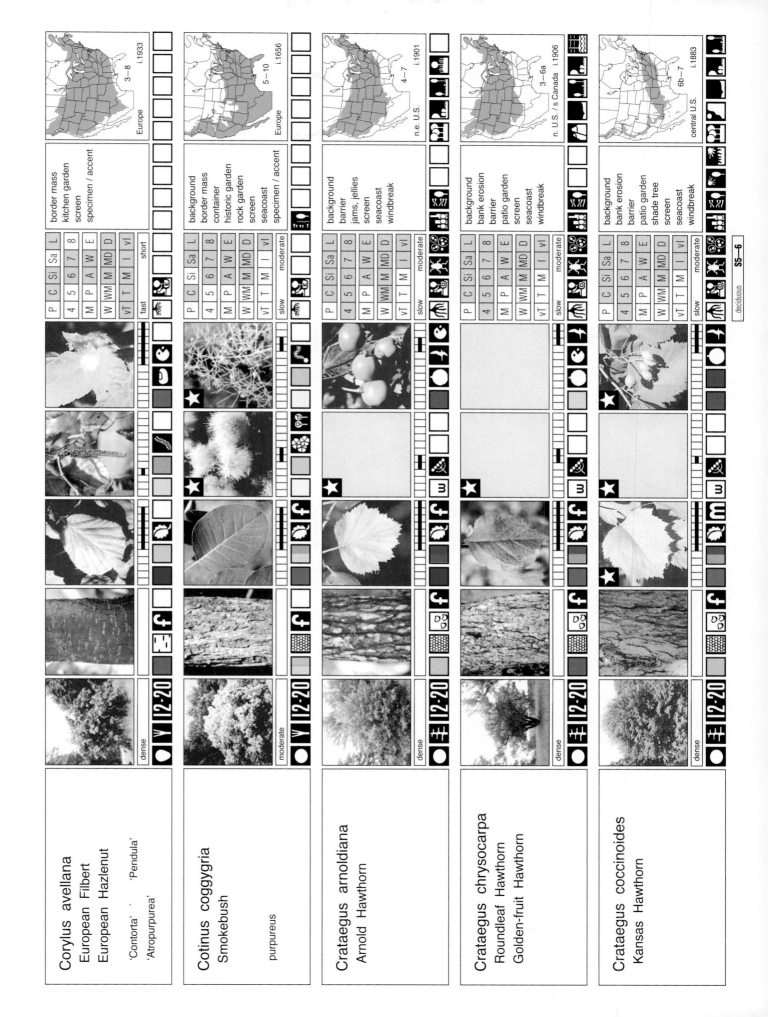

Corylus avellana
European Filbert
European Hazlenut

'Contorta'   'Pendula'
'Atropurpurea'

P	C	Si	Sa	L
4	5	6	7	8
M		P	A	W	E
W	WM	M	MD	D
vT	T	M	I	vl

border mass
kitchen garden
screen
specimen / accent

fast   short

Europe   3–8   i.1933

dense   12-20

Cotinus coggygria
Smokebush

purpureus

P	C	Si	Sa	L
4	5	6	7	8
M	P	A	W	E
W	WM	M	MD	D
vT	T	M	I	vl

background
border mass
container
historic garden
rock garden
screen
seacoast
specimen / accent

slow   moderate

Europe   5–10   i.1656

moderate   12-20

Crataegus arnoldiana
Arnold Hawthorn

P	C	Si	Sa	L
4	5	6	7	8
M	P	A	W	E
W	WM	M	MD	D
vT	T	M	I	vl

background
barrier
jams, jellies
screen
seacoast
windbreak

slow   moderate

n.e. U.S.   4–7   i.1901

dense   12-20

Crataegus chrysocarpa
Roundleaf Hawthorn
Golden-fruit Hawthorn

P	C	Si	Sa	L
4	5	6	7	8
M	P	A	W	E
W	WM	M	MD	D
vT	T	M	I	vl

background
bank erosion
barrier
patio garden
screen
seacoast
windbreak

slow   moderate

n. U.S. / s Canada   3–6a   i.1906

dense   12-20

Crataegus coccinoides
Kansas Hawthorn

P	C	Si	Sa	L
4	5	6	7	8
M	P	A	W	E
W	WM	M	MD	D
vT	T	M	I	vl

background
bank erosion
barrier
patio garden
shade tree
screen
seacoast
windbreak

slow   moderate

central U.S.   6b–7   i.1883

dense   12-20

...deciduous   **S5–6**

VERY LARGE SHRUB

	FORM	BARK	LEAF	FLOWER	FRUIT	CULTURE	USES	REGION

Crataegus erythropoda
syn. C. cerronis

Cerro Hawthorn

- CULTURE: P C Si Sa L / 4 5 6 7 8 / M P A W E / W WM M MD D / vT T M I vl / slow — moderate
- USES: background, barrier, patio garden, screen, specimen / accent, windbreak
- REGION: 3–7 — w. U.S.
- FORM: dense — 12-20

Crataegus pinnatifida

Chinese Hawthorn

- CULTURE: P C Si Sa L / 4 5 6 7 8 / M P A W E / W WM M MD D / vT T M I vl / slow — moderate
- USES: background, barrier, patio garden, screen, specimen / accent, windbreak
- REGION: 3b–7a c.1860 — China
- FORM: dense — 12-20

Crataegus succulenta

Fleshy Hawthorn

- CULTURE: P C Si Sa L / 4 5 6 7 8 / M P A W E / W WM M MD D / vT T M I vl / slow — moderate
- USES: barrier, hedge, screen, specimen / accent, windbreak
- REGION: 3–7 c.1830 — e. N.America
- FORM: dense — 12-20

Cydonia sinensis

Chinese Quince

- CULTURE: P C Si Sa L / 4 5 6 7 8 / M P A W E / W WM M MD D / vT T M I vl / moderate — long
- USES: border mass, culinary, espalier, hedge, jams, jellies, pies, kitchen garden, sculpture
- REGION: 5–8 i.1800 — China
- FORM: open — 12-20

Cyrilla racemiflora

Black Titi
American Cyrilla

- CULTURE: P C Si Sa L / 4 5 6 7 8 / M P A W E / W WM M MD D / vT T M I vl / moderate — short
- USES: bank erosion, bog garden, seacoast, specimen / accent
- REGION: 6–9 i.1756 — s.e. U.S.
- FORM: moderate — 12-20

Decaisnea fargesi
Chinese Decaisnea

P	C	Si	Sa	L
4	5	6	7	8
M	P	A	W	E
W	WM	M	MD	D
vT	T	M	I	VI

slow — short

open — 6-12

China — 7–9 — i.1895

novelty
sculptural
specimen / accent

Dipelta floribunda
Rosy Dipelta

P	C	Si	Sa	L
4	5	6	7	8
M	P	A	W	E
W	WM	M	MD	D
vT	T	M	I	VI

fast — short

open — 12-20

China — 6–9 — i.1902

border mass
screen
specimen / accent

Elaeagnus umbellata
Autumn Elaeagnus

'Cardinal' 'Titan'
'Jazbo'

P	C	Si	Sa	L
4	5	6	7	8
M	P	A	W	E
W	WM	M	MD	D
vT	T	M	I	VI

moderate — short

dense — 12-20

China — 4–9a — i.1830

background
bank erosion
barrier
hedge
screen
seacoast
specimen / accent
windbreak

Euonymus latifolia
Broadleaf Euonymus

P	C	Si	Sa	L
4	5	6	7	8
M	P	A	W	E
W	WM	M	MD	D
vT	T	M	I	VI

moderate — moderate

open-moderate — 12-20

Europe — 6b–9 — i.1730

background
hedge
screen
specimen / accent

Euonymus sanguinea

P	C	Si	Sa	L
4	5	6	7	8
M	P	A	W	E
W	WM	M	MD	D
vT	T	M	I	VI

moderate — moderate

dense — 12-21

China — 6b–9 — i.1900

background
hedge
screen

...deciduous

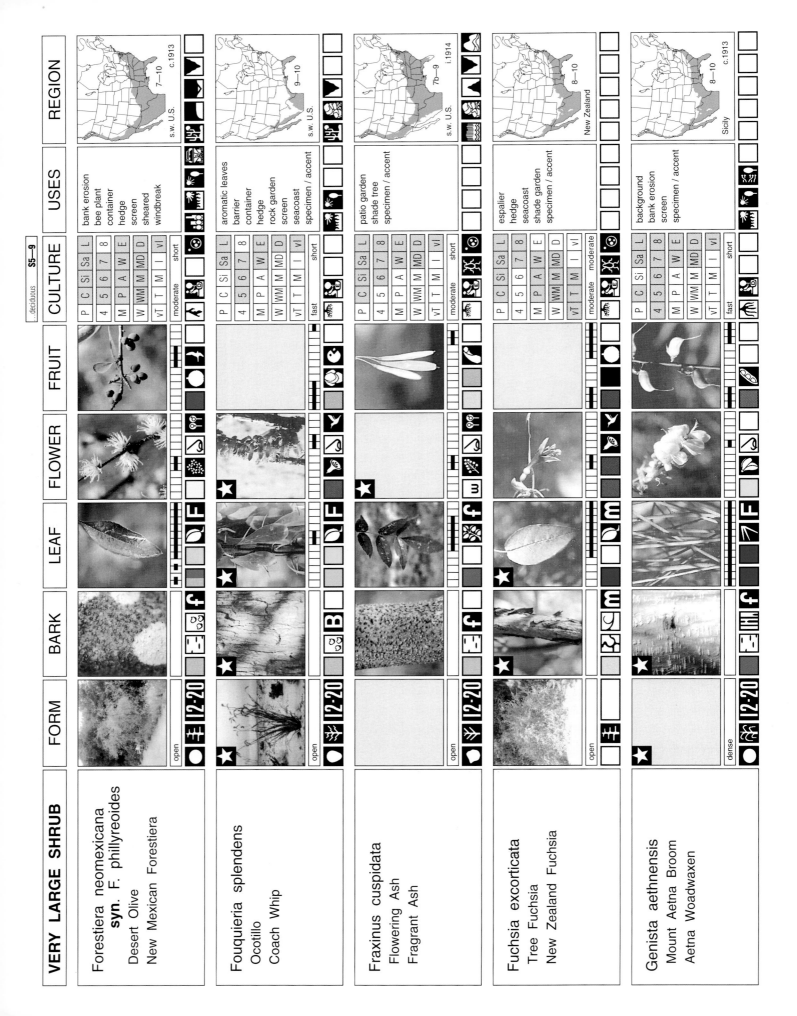

VERY LARGE SHRUB	FORM	BARK	LEAF	FLOWER	FRUIT	CULTURE	USES	REGION

Forestiera neomexicana syn. F. phillyreoides
Desert Olive
New Mexican Forestiera

Uses: bank erosion · bee plant · container · hedge · screen · sheared · windbreak
Culture: P C Si Sa L · 4 5 6 7 8 · M P A W E · W WM M MD D · vT T M I vI · moderate · short
Region: s.w. U.S. · 7–10 · c.1913
Form: open · 12-20

Fouquieria splendens
Ocotillo
Coach Whip

Uses: aromatic leaves · barrier · container · hedge · rock garden · screen · seacoast · specimen / accent
Culture: P C Si Sa L · 4 5 6 7 8 · M P A W E · W WM M MD D · vT T M I vI · fast · short
Region: s.w. U.S. · 9–10
Form: open · 12-20

Fraxinus cuspidata
Flowering Ash
Fragrant Ash

Uses: patio garden · shade tree · specimen / accent
Culture: P C Si Sa L · 4 5 6 7 8 · M P A W E · W WM M MD D · vT T M I vI · moderate · short
Region: s.w. U.S. · 7b–9 · i.1914
Form: open · 12-20

Fuchsia excorticata
Tree Fuchsia
New Zealand Fuchsia

Uses: espalier · hedge · seacoast · shade garden · specimen / accent
Culture: P C Si Sa L · 4 5 6 7 8 · M P A W E · W WM M MD D · vT T M I vI · moderate · moderate
Region: New Zealand · 8–10
Form: open

Genista aethnensis
Mount Aetna Broom
Aetna Woadwaxen

Uses: background · bank erosion · screen · specimen / accent
Culture: P C Si Sa L · 4 5 6 7 8 · M P A W E · W WM M MD D · vT T M I vI · fast · short
Region: Sicily · 8–10 · c.1913
Form: dense

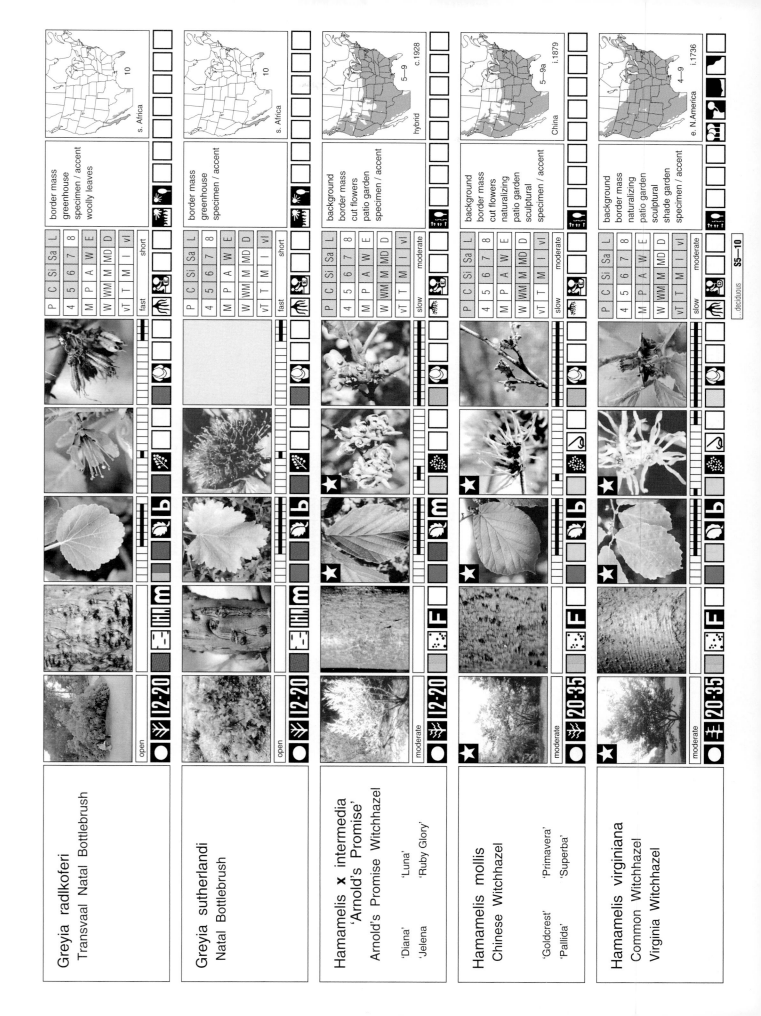

Greyia radlkoferi
Transvaal Natal Bottlebrush

border mass
greenhouse
specimen / accent
woolly leaves

s. Africa — 10

P	C	Si	Sa	L
4	5	6	7	8
M	P	A	W	E
W	WM	M	MD	D
vT	T	M	I	vl

fast — short

open — 12-20

Greyia sutherlandi
Natal Bottlebrush

border mass
greenhouse
specimen / accent

s. Africa — 10

P	C	Si	Sa	L
4	5	6	7	8
M	P	A	W	E
W	WM	M	MD	D
vT	T	M	I	vl

fast — short

open — 12-20

Hamamelis x intermedia
'Arnold's Promise'
Arnold's Promise Witchhazel

'Diana'   'Luna'
'Jelena'   'Ruby Glory'

hybrid — c.1928 — 5—9

P	C	Si	Sa	L
4	5	6	7	8
M	P	A	W	E
W	WM	M	MD	D
vT	T	M	I	vl

slow — moderate

moderate — 12-20

Hamamelis mollis
Chinese Witchhazel

'Goldcrest'   'Primavera'
'Pallida'   'Superba'

China — i.1879 — 5—9a

background
border mass
cut flowers
naturalizing
patio garden
sculptural
specimen / accent

P	C	Si	Sa	L
4	5	6	7	8
M	P	A	W	E
W	WM	M	MD	D
vT	T	M	I	vl

slow — moderate

moderate — 20-35

Hamamelis virginiana
Common Witchhazel
Virginia Witchhazel

e. N.America — i.1736 — 4—9

background
border mass
naturalizing
patio garden
sculptural
shade garden
specimen / accent

P	C	Si	Sa	L
4	5	6	7	8
M	P	A	W	E
W	WM	M	MD	D
vT	T	M	I	vl

slow — moderate

moderate — 20-35

...deciduous   **S5—10**

VERY LARGE SHRUB	FORM	BARK	LEAF	FLOWER	FRUIT	CULTURE	USES	REGION

Hemiptelea davidi

David Hemiptelea

dense — 12-20

CULTURE:
P C Si Sa L
4 5 6 7 8
M P A W E
W WM M MD D
vT T M I vl
moderate · moderate

USES:
background
hedge
screen
specimen / accent

REGION: Asia · 6—9 · c.1908

Hibiscus syriacus

Rose-of-Sharon
Shrub Althaea

'Ardens'   'Red Heart'
'Diana'   'Rubis'

dense — 6-12

CULTURE:
P C Si Sa L
4 5 6 7 8
M P A W E
W WM M MD D
vT T M I vl
moderate · short

USES:
border mass
container
espalier
hedge
patio garden
screen
seacoast
specimen / accent

REGION: India · 5b—9 · i.b.1790

Hydrangea paniculata

Panicle Hydrangea

'Floribunda'   'Tardiva'
'Grandiflora'

moderate — 20-35

CULTURE:
P C Si Sa L
4 5 6 7 8
M P A W E
W WM M MD D
vT T M I vl
fast

USES:
hedge
poisonous leaves
seacoast
specimen / accent

REGION: Japan · 4—8a · i.1861

Ilex serrata

Japanese Winterberry
Finetooth Holly

'Bonfire'
'Subtilis Ohwi'

dense — 12-20

CULTURE:
P C Si Sa L
4 5 6 7 8
M P A W E
W WM M MD D
vT T M I vl
slow · short

USES:
border mass
fruit arrangement
patio garden
screen
shade garden
shade tree
specimen / accent

REGION: Japan · 6—9 · i.1893

Laburnum watereri

Golden Chaintree
Waterer Laburnum

'Vossii'
'Vossii Pendula'

open — 6-12

CULTURE:
P C Si Sa L
4 5 6 7 8
M P A W E
W WM M MD D
vT T M I vl
fast · short

USES:
container
espalier
greenhouse
nitrogen-fixing
poisonous leaves
specimen / accent

REGION: hybrid · 6—9 · o.b.1864

Leitneria floridana
Corkwood

s.e. U.S. 6—10 i.1894

bank erosion
preservation
screen
seacoast

P	C	Si	Sa	L
4	5	6	7	8
M	P	A	W	E
W	WM	M	MD	D
vT	T	M	I	vl

moderate · short

open · 12-20

Ligustrum amurense
Amur Privet

'River North'

China 4—8a i.1860

barrier
hedge
screen
seacoast
shearing
windbreak

P	C	Si	Sa	L
4	5	6	7	8
M	P	A	W	E
W	WM	M	MD	D
vT	T	M	I	vl

fast · short

dense · 12-20

Ligustrum × ibolium
Ibolium Privet

'Midas'
'Variegatum'

hybrid 5b—8 o.1910

barrier
hedge
screen
shearing
windbreak

P	C	Si	Sa	L
4	5	6	7	8
M	P	A	W	E
W	WM	M	MD	D
vT	T	M	I	vl

fast · short

dense · 12-20

Ligustrum vulgare
European Privet

'Cheyenne'   'Lodense'
'Lavrifolium'

Europe 4—8a long c.

barrier
hedge
screen
seacoast
shearing
windbreak

P	C	Si	Sa	L
4	5	6	7	8
M	P	A	W	E
W	WM	M	MD	D
vT	T	M	I	vl

fast · short

dense · 12-20

Lindera benzoin
Common Spicebush

e. N.America (5a)—9 i.1683

aromatic property
cut flowers
fruit arrangement
medicinal
naturalizing
sculptural
specimen / accent
woodland garden

P	C	Si	Sa	L
4	5	6	7	8
M	P	A	W	E
W	WM	M	MD	D
vT	T	M	I	vl

slow · short

open · 12-20

...deciduous

VERY LARGE SHRUB	FORM	BARK	LEAF	FLOWER	FRUIT	CULTURE	USES	REGION

Lindera obtusiloba
Japanese Spicebush

podocarpa
'Rem Red'

moderate · 12-20

CULTURE: P C Si Sa L · 4 5 6 7 8 · M P A W E · W WM M MD D · vT T M I vl · slow · short

USES: aromatic bark · aromatic leaves · cut flowers · fruit arrangements · sculptural · specimen / accent · woodland garden

REGION: China · 6—9 · i.1880

Lonicera maacki
Amur Honeysuckle

dense · 12-20

CULTURE: P C Si Sa L · 4 5 6 7 8 · M P A W E · W WM MD D · vT T M I vl · fast · short

USES: background · border mass · hedge · screen · specimen / accent · windbreak

REGION: Korea · 3—8 · i.1880

Lonicera tatarica
Tatarian Honeysuckle

'Alba'   'Hack's Red'
'Arnold's Red' 'Rosea'

dense · 12-20

CULTURE: P C Si Sa L · 4 5 6 7 8 · M P A W E · W WM MD D · vT T M I vl · fast · short

USES: background · border mass · hedge · screen · seacoast · windbreak

REGION: Russia · 3—8 · i.1752

Maackia amurensis
Amur Maackia

'Buergeri'

open · 12-20

CULTURE: P C Si Sa L · 4 5 6 7 8 · M P A W E · W WM M MD D · vT T M I vl · slow · short

USES: background · preservation · shade tree · specimen / accent

REGION: Manchuria · 5—8 · i.1864

Magnolia stellata
Star Magnolia

'Centennial' 'Rosea'
'King Rose'   'Royal Star'

dense · 12-20

CULTURE: P C Si Sa L · 4 5 6 7 8 · M P A W E · W WM M MD D · vT T M I vl · slow · moderate

USES: border mass · formal garden · patio garden · sculptural · specimen / accent

REGION: Japan · 5—8 · i.1862

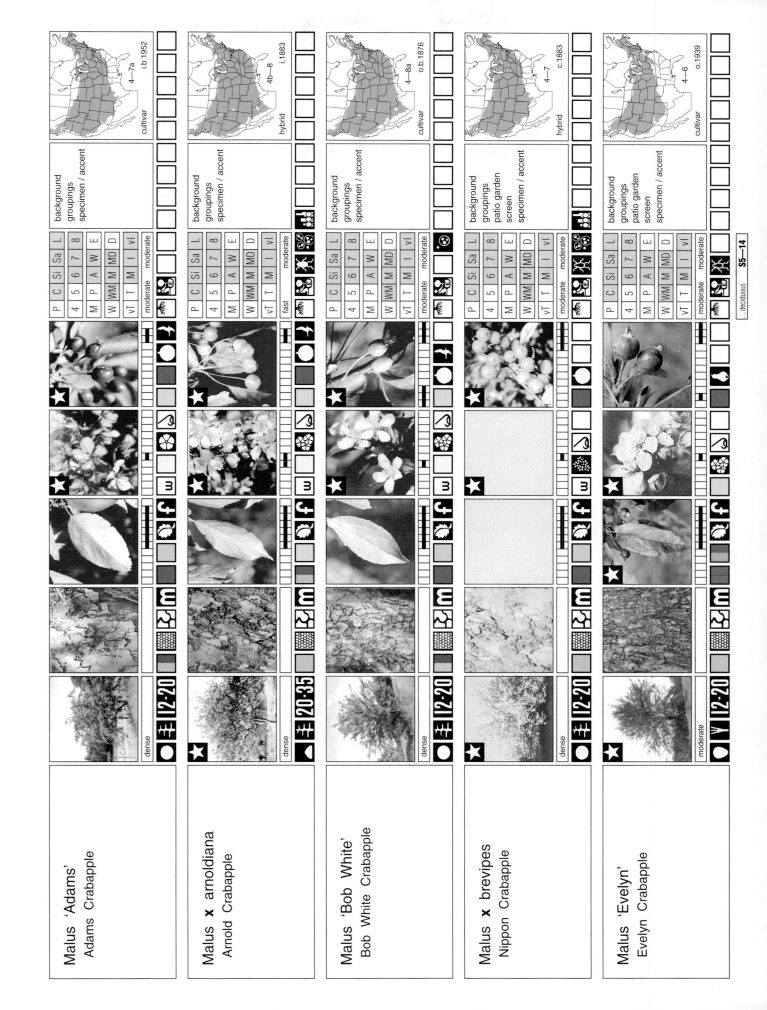

Malus 'Adams'
Adams Crabapple

Malus x arnoldiana
Arnold Crabapple

Malus 'Bob White'
Bob White Crabapple

Malus x brevipes
Nippon Crabapple

Malus 'Evelyn'
Evelyn Crabapple

...deciduous   **S5—14**

VERY LARGE SHRUB	FORM	BARK	LEAF	FLOWER	FRUIT	CULTURE	USES	REGION

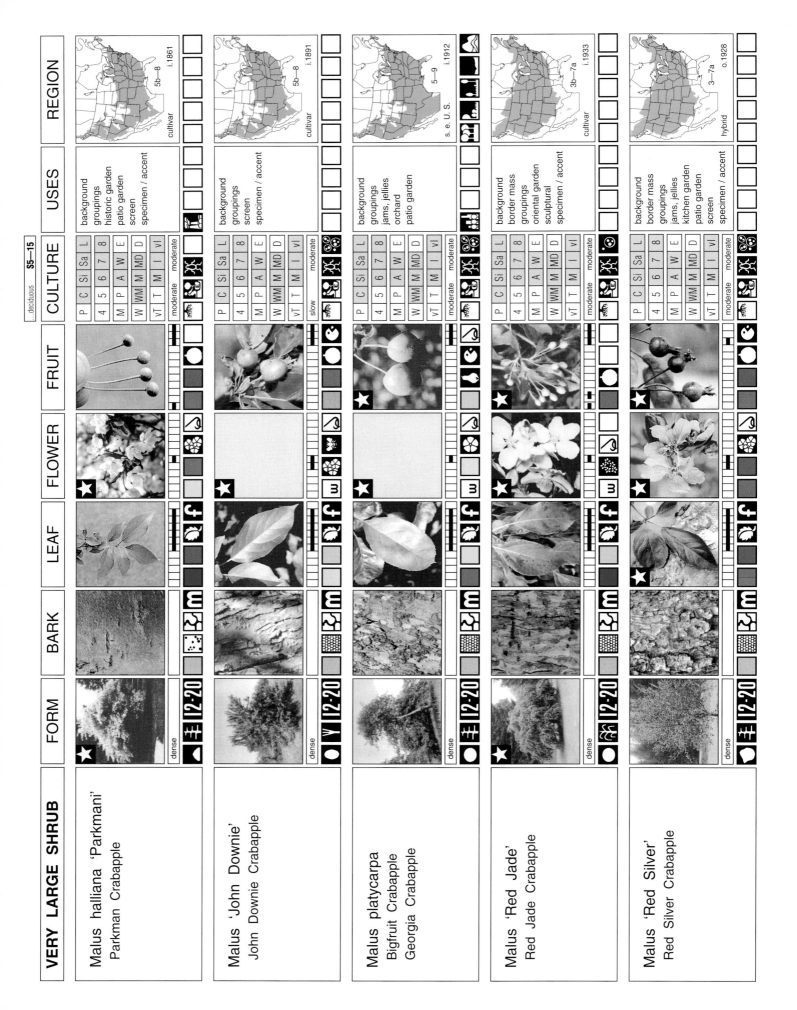

Malus halliana 'Parkmani'
Parkman Crabapple

background
groupings
historic garden
patio garden
screen
specimen / accent

5b—8 i.1861
cultivar

Malus 'John Downie'
John Downie Crabapple

background
groupings
screen
specimen / accent

5b—8 i.1891
cultivar

Malus platycarpa
Bigfruit Crabapple
Georgia Crabapple

background
groupings
jams, jellies
orchard
patio garden

5—9 i.1912
s. e. U. S.

Malus 'Red Jade'
Red Jade Crabapple

background
border mass
groupings
oriental garden
sculptural
specimen / accent

3b—7a i.1933
cultivar

Malus 'Red Silver'
Red Silver Crabapple

background
border mass
groupings
jams, jellies
kitchen garden
patio garden
screen
specimen / accent

3—7a o.1928
hybrid

Malus × scheideckeri — Scheidecker Crabapple

P	C	Si	Sa	L
4	5	6	7	8
M	P	A	W	E
W	WM	M	MD	D
vT	T	M	I	vl

moderate · moderate

background
border mass
groupings
patio garden
screen
specimen / accent

hybrid · 5—8 · o.b.1988

dense · 12-20

Malus 'Tanner' — Tanner Crabapple

P	C	Si	Sa	L
4	5	6	7	8
M	P	A	W	E
W	WM	M	MD	D
vT	T	M	I	vl

moderate · moderate

border mass
groupings
patio garden
screen
specimen / accent

cultivar · 4b—7 · i.b.1931

dense · 12-20

Malus 'Van Eseltine' — Van Eseltine Crabapple

P	C	Si	Sa	L
4	5	6	7	8
M	P	A	W	E
W	WM	M	MD	D
vT	T	M	I	vl

moderate · moderate

border mass
groupings
formal garden
narrow space
patio garden
specimen / accent

cultivar · 4b—7a · i:1938

moderate · 12-20

Malus 'Winter Gold' — Winter Gold Crabapple

P	C	Si	Sa	L
4	5	6	7	8
M	P	A	W	E
W	WM	M	MD	D
vT	T	M	I	vl

moderate · moderate

border mass
groupings
patio garden
screen
specimen / accent

cultivar · 4b—7 · i.b.1950

dense · 12-20

Melaleuca nesophila — Pink Melaleuca — Western Tea Myrtle

P	C	Si	Sa	L
4	5	6	7	8
M	P	A	W	E
W	WM	M	MD	D
vT	T	M	I	vl

fast · short

bank erosion
hedge
screen
sculpture
seacoast
shearing
specimen / accent

Australia · 9—10

open · 12-20

...deciduous · **S5—16**

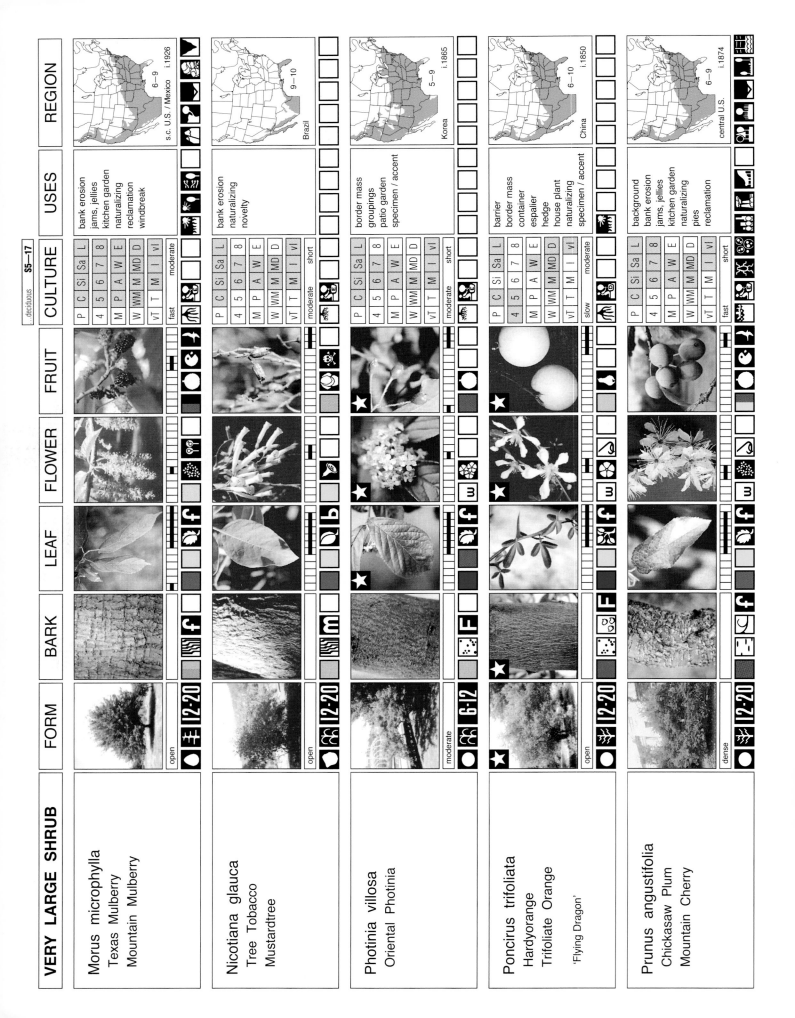

VERY LARGE SHRUB	FORM	BARK	LEAF	FLOWER	FRUIT	CULTURE	USES	REGION

Morus microphylla
Texas Mulberry
Mountain Mulberry

open 12-20

CULTURE:
P	C	Si	Sa	L
4	5	6	7	8
M	P	A	W	E
W	WM	M	MD	D
vT	T	M	I	vI
fast

USES: bank erosion, jams, jellies, kitchen garden, naturalizing, reclamation, windbreak

REGION: s.c. U.S. / Mexico 6—9 i.1926

Nicotiana glauca
Tree Tobacco
Mustardtree

open 12-20

CULTURE:
P	C	Si	Sa	L
4	5	6	7	8
M	P	A	W	E
W	WM	M	MD	D
vT	T	M	I	vI
moderate

USES: bank erosion, naturalizing, novelty

REGION: Brazil 9—10

Photinia villosa
Oriental Photinia

moderate 6-12

CULTURE:
P	C	Si	Sa	L
4	5	6	7	8
M	P	A	W	E
W	WM	M	MD	D
vT	T	M	I	vI
moderate

USES: border mass, groupings, patio garden, specimen / accent

REGION: Korea 5—9 i.1865

Poncirus trifoliata
Hardyorange
Trifoliate Orange
'Flying Dragon'

open 12-20

CULTURE:
P	C	Si	Sa	L
4	5	6	7	8
M	P	A	W	E
W	WM	M	MD	D
vT	T	M	I	vI
slow

USES: barrier, border mass, container, espalier, hedge, house plant, naturalizing, specimen / accent

REGION: China 6—10 i.1850

Prunus angustifolia
Chickasaw Plum
Mountain Cherry

dense 12-20

CULTURE:
P	C	Si	Sa	L
4	5	6	7	8
M	P	A	W	E
W	WM	M	MD	D
vT	T	M	I	vI
fast

USES: background, bank erosion, jams, jellies, kitchen garden, naturalizing, pies, reclamation

REGION: central U.S. 6—9 i.1874

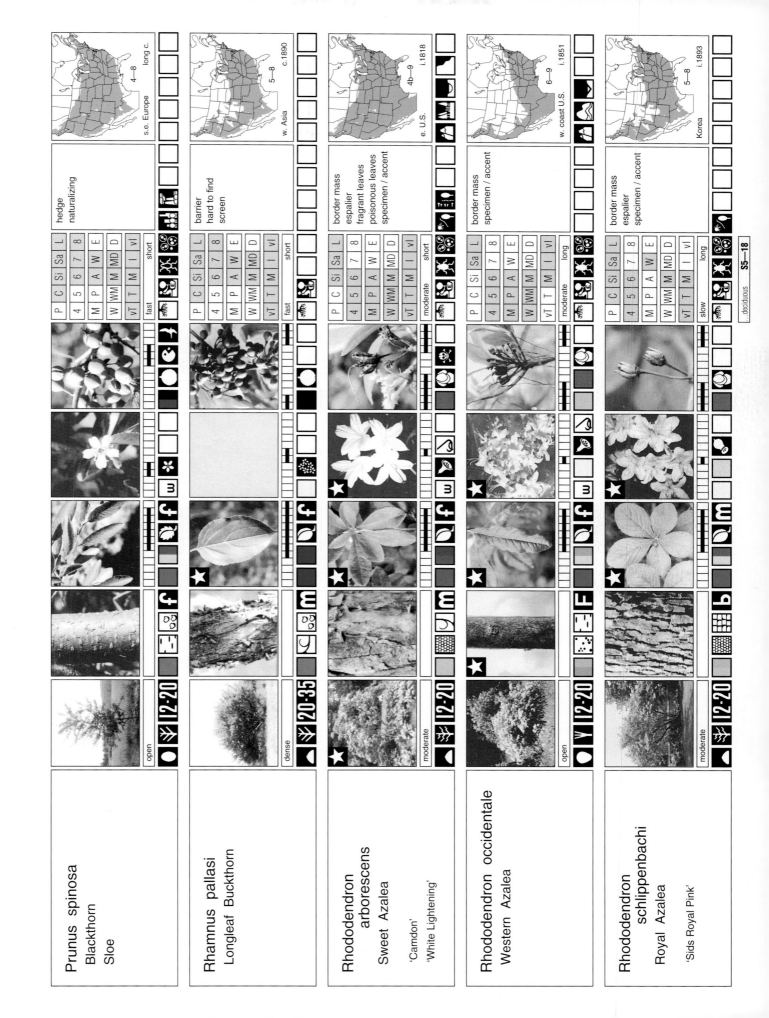

Prunus spinosa
Blackthorn
Sloe

s.e. Europe   4—8   long c.

hedge
naturalizing

P	C	Si	Sa	L
4	5	6	7	8
M	P	A	W	E
W	WM	M	MD	D
vT	T	M	I	vl

fast   short

open   12-20

Rhamnus pallasi
Longleaf Buckthorn

w. Asia   5—8   c.1890

barrier
hard to find
screen

P	C	Si	Sa	L
4	5	6	7	8
M	P	A	W	E
W	WM	M	MD	D
vT	T	M	I	vl

fast   short

dense   20-35

Rhododendron arborescens
Sweet Azalea

'Camdon'
'White Lightening'

e. U.S.   4b—9   i.1818

border mass
espalier
fragrant leaves
poisonous leaves
specimen / accent

P	C	Si	Sa	L
4	5	6	7	8
M	P	A	W	E
W	WM	M	MD	D
vT	T	M	I	vl

moderate   short

moderate   12-20

Rhododendron occidentale
Western Azalea

w. coast U.S.   6—9   i.1851

border mass
specimen / accent

P	C	Si	Sa	L
4	5	6	7	8
M	P	A	W	E
W	WM	M	MD	D
vT	T	M	I	vl

moderate   long

open   12-20

Rhododendron schlippenbachi
Royal Azalea

'Sids Royal Pink'

Korea   5—8   i.1893

border mass
espalier
specimen / accent

P	C	Si	Sa	L
4	5	6	7	8
M	P	A	W	E
W	WM	M	MD	D
vT	T	M	I	vl

slow   long

moderate   12-20

...deciduous   **S5—18**

VERY LARGE SHRUB	FORM	BARK	LEAF	FLOWER	FRUIT	CULTURE	USES	REGION

Rhododendron vaseyi
Pinkshell Azalea

'Alba'

open · 6-12

P	C	Si	Sa	L
4	5	6	7	8
M	P	A	W	E
W	WM	M	MD	D
vT	T	M	I	vl

moderate · moderate

USES: border mass, espalier, groupings, poisonous leaves, sculptural, specimen / accent

REGION: s.e. U.S. · 5—8 · i.1880

Rhus glabra
Smooth Sumac
Scarlet Sumac

'Lacineata'   'Cismontana'
'Mordens'

open · 20-35

P	C	Si	Sa	L
4	5	6	7	8
M	P	A	W	E
W	WM	M	MD	D
vT	T	M	I	vl

fast · short

USES: bank erosion, border mass, naturalizing, reclamation, road cuts, screen, seacoast, sculptural

REGION: N.America · 3—8 · c.1620

Rosa helenae
Helen rose

'Rosea'

moderate · 12-20

P	C	Si	Sa	L
4	5	6	7	8
M	P	A	W	E
W	WM	M	MD	D
vT	T	M	I	vl

fast · short

USES: barrier, border mass, screen, specimen / accent

REGION: China · 5—8 · i.1907

Salix discolor
Pussy Willow

open · 6-12

P	C	Si	Sa	L
4	5	6	7	8
M	P	A	W	E
W	WM	M	MD	D
vT	T	M	I	vl

very fast · very short

USES: bog garden, colonial garden, cut flowers, screen, specimen / accent, water garden

REGION: e. N.America · 2—8 · i.1811

Salix interior
Sandbar Willow

open · 20-35

P	C	Si	Sa	L
4	5	6	7	8
M	P	A	W	E
W	WM	M	MD	D
vT	T	M	I	vl

very-fast · very short

USES: bank erosion, bog garden, naturalizing, reclamation, water garden

REGION: N.America · 1—8

P C Si Sa L				
4 5 6 7 8				
M P A W E				
W WM M MD D				
vT T M I vl				

Salix lucida
Shining Willow

bank erosion
bog garden
edible leaves
water garden

e. N.America   c.1830

| P C Si Sa L |
| 4 5 6 7 8 |
| M P A W E |
| W WM M MD D |
| vT T M I vl |
very fast   very short

open   12-20

Sambucus callicarpa
Pacific Red Elder

border mass
poisonous leaves
shade garden
specimen / accent
wild garden
woodland garden

w. coast U.S.   i.a.1900

| P C Si Sa L |
| 4 5 6 7 8 |
| M P A W E |
| W WM M MD D |
| vT T M I vl |
very fast   very short

open   6-12

Sambucus pubens
Scarlet Elder
American Red Elder

border mass
poisonous leaves
shade garden
specimen / accent
wild garden
woodland garden

N.America   i.1812

| P C Si Sa L |
| 4 5 6 7 8 |
| M P A W E |
| W WM M MD D |
| vT T M I vl |
very fast   very short

open   6-12

Sorbus scopulina
Greene Mountainash

groupings
patio garden
specimen / accent

w. N.America   i.1917

| P C Si Sa L |
| 4 5 6 7 8 |
| M P A W E |
| W WM M MD D |
| vT T M I vl |
fast   very short

open   6-12

Sorbus tianshanica
Turkestan Mountainash

'Red Cascade'

groupings
patio garden
specimen / accent

Turkestan   i.1895

| P C Si Sa L |
| 4 5 6 7 8 |
| M P A W E |
| W WM M MD D |
| vT T M I vl |
fast   very short

open   6-12

...deciduous

VERY LARGE SHRUB

	FORM	BARK	LEAF	FLOWER	FRUIT	CULTURE	USES	REGION

Staphylea holocarpa
Chinese Bladderwart

- moderate — 12-20

CULTURE:
P	C	Si	Sa	L
4	5	6	7	8
M	P	A	W	E
W	WM	M	MD	D
vT	T	M	I	vl

moderate / short

USES:
border mass
screen
seacoast
specimen / accent

REGION: 6—8 i.1908 — China

Stewartia ovata
Mountain Stewartia

grandifolia

- open — 12-20

CULTURE:
P	C	Si	Sa	L
4	5	6	7	8
M	P	A	W	E
W	WM	M	MD	D
vT	T	M	I	vl

slow / short

USES:
border mass
groupings
patio garden
preservation
sculptural
specimen / accent

REGION: 6b—8 c.1800 — s.e. U.S.

Styrax americanus
syn. S. rothomagensis
American Snowbell

pulverulentus

- moderate — 6-12

CULTURE:
P	C	Si	Sa	L
4	5	6	7	8
M	P	A	W	E
W	WM	M	MD	D
vT	T	M	I	vl

moderate / short

USES:
bog garden
border mass
patio garden
preservation
screen
specimen / accent
water garden

REGION: 6b—9 i.1765 — s.e. U.S.

Syringa x chinensis
Chinese Lilac

alba
'Suageana'

- dense — 6-12

CULTURE:
P	C	Si	Sa	L
4	5	6	7	8
M	P	A	W	E
W	WM	M	MD	D
vT	T	M	I	vl

fast / short

USES:
background
border mass
cut flowers
hedge
screen
seacoast
windbreak

REGION: 4—8a c.1777 — hybrid

Syringa x prestoniae
Preston Lilac

'Donald Wyman'   'Nocturne'
'Hiawatha'   'Royalty'

- dense — 12-20

CULTURE:
P	C	Si	Sa	L
4	5	6	7	8
M	P	A	W	E
W	WM	M	MD	D
vT	T	M	I	vl

fast / short

USES:
background
border mass
cut flowers
hedge
screen
windbreak

REGION: 2b—7 i.1950 — hybrid

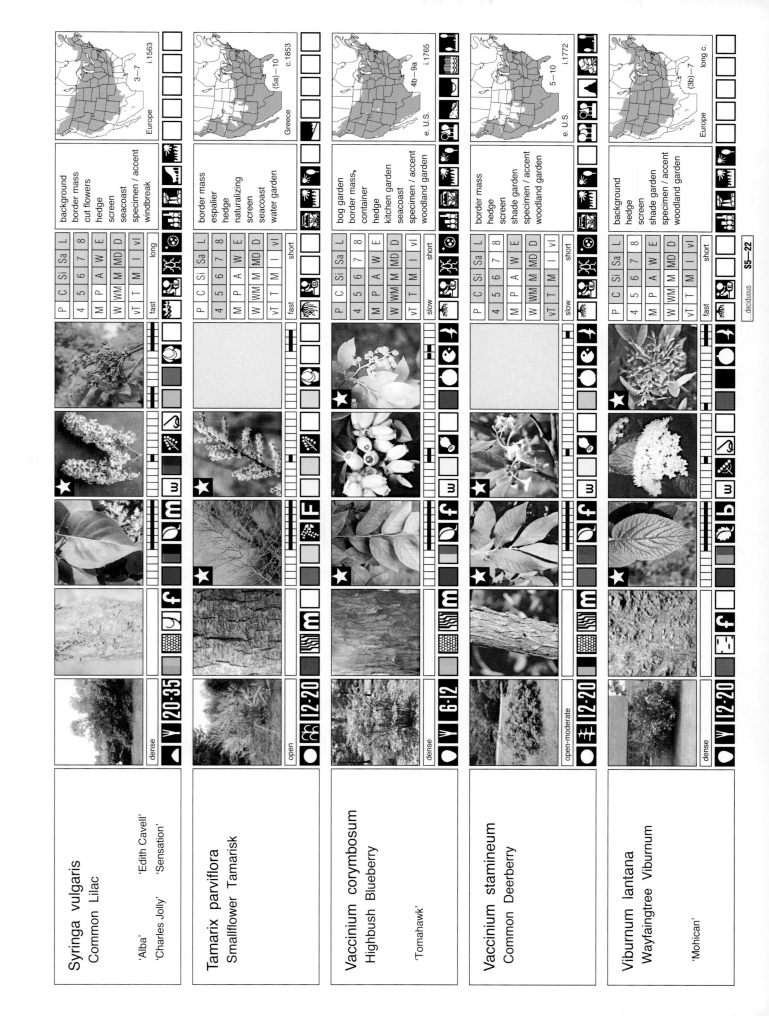

Syringa vulgaris
Common Lilac

'Alba'   'Edith Cavell'
'Charles Jolly'   'Sensation'

background
border mass
cut flowers
hedge
screen
seacoast
specimen / accent
windbreak

Europe   i.1563   3–7   dense   20-35

Tamarix parviflora
Smallflower Tamarisk

border mass
espalier
hedge
naturalizing
screen
seacoast
water garden

Greece   c.1853   (5a)–10   open   12-20

Vaccinium corymbosum
Highbush Blueberry

'Tomahawk'

bog garden
border mass
container
hedge
kitchen garden
seacoast
specimen / accent
woodland garden

e. U.S.   i.1765   4b–9a   dense   6-12

Vaccinium stamineum
Common Deerberry

border mass
hedge
screen
shade garden
specimen / accent
woodland garden

e. U.S.   i.1772   5–10   open-moderate   12-20

Viburnum lantana
Wayfaringtree Viburnum

'Mohican'

background
hedge
screen
shade garden
specimen / accent
woodland garden

Europe   long c.   (3b)–7   dense   12-20

VERY LARGE SHRUB	FORM	BARK	LEAF	FLOWER	FRUIT	CULTURE	USES	REGION

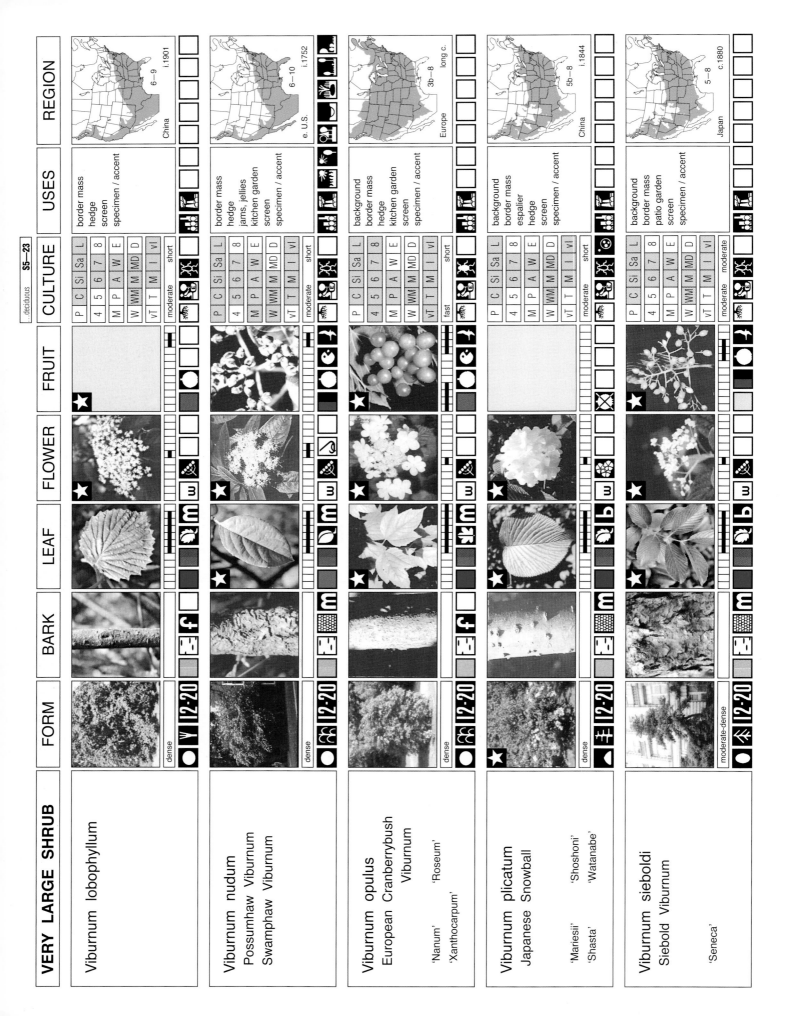

Viburnum lobophyllum

dense · 12-20

P	C	Si	Sa	L
4	5	6	7	8
M	P	A	W	E
W	WM	M	MD	D
vT	T	M	I	vl

moderate – short

border mass
hedge
screen
specimen / accent

6—9 i.1901
China

Viburnum nudum
Possumhaw Viburnum
Swamphaw Viburnum

dense · 12-20

P	C	Si	Sa	L
4	5	6	7	8
M	P	A	W	E
W	WM	M	MD	D
vT	T	M	I	vl

moderate – short

border mass
hedge
jams, jellies
kitchen garden
screen
specimen / accent

6—10 i.1752
e. U.S.

Viburnum opulus
European Cranberrybush
Viburnum

'Nanum'
'Xanthocarpum'

dense · 12-20

P	C	Si	Sa	L
4	5	6	7	8
M	P	A	W	E
W	WM	M	MD	D
vT	T	M	I	vl

fast – short

background
border mass
hedge
kitchen garden
screen
specimen / accent

3b—8 long c.
Europe

Viburnum plicatum
Japanese Snowball

'Mariesii'
'Shasta'
'Shoshoni'
'Watanabe'

dense · 12-20

P	C	Si	Sa	L
4	5	6	7	8
M	P	A	W	E
W	WM	M	MD	D
vT	T	M	I	vl

moderate – short

background
border mass
espalier
hedge
screen
specimen / accent

5b—8 i.1844
China

Viburnum sieboldi
Siebold Viburnum

'Seneca'

moderate-dense · 12-20

P	C	Si	Sa	L
4	5	6	7	8
M	P	A	W	E
W	WM	M	MD	D
vT	T	M	I	vl

moderate – moderate

background
border mass
patio garden
screen
specimen / accent

5—8 c.1880
Japan

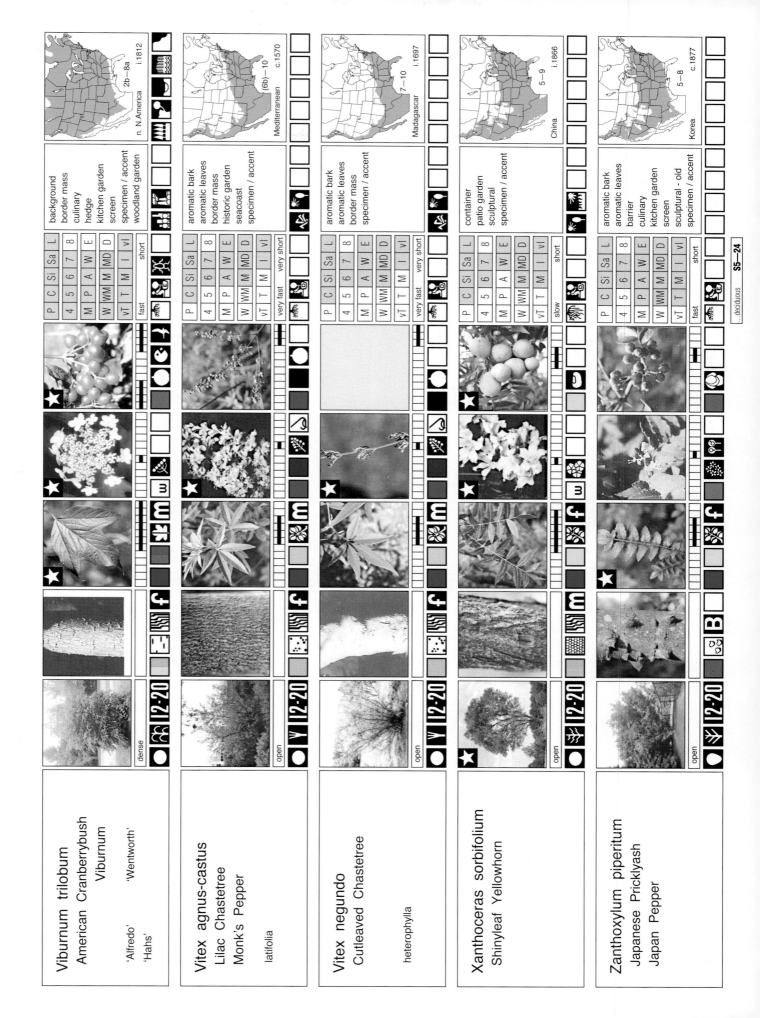

Viburnum trilobum
American Cranberrybush
Viburnum

'Alfredo'   'Wentworth'
'Hans'

P	C	Si	Sa	L
4	5	6	7	8
M	P	A	E
W	WM	M	MD	D
vT	T	M	I	vl

background
border mass
culinary
hedge
kitchen garden
screen
specimen / accent
woodland garden

2b–8a   i.1812
n. N.America

dense   12-20   fast   short

Vitex agnus-castus
Lilac Chastetree
Monk's Pepper

latifolia

P	C	Si	Sa	L
4	5	6	7	8
M	P	A	W	E
W	WM	M	MD	D
vT	T	M	I	vl

aromatic bark
aromatic leaves
border mass
historic garden
seacoast
specimen / accent

(6b)–10   c.1570
Mediterranean

open   12-20   very fast   very short

Vitex negundo
Cutleaved Chastetree

heterophylla

P	C	Si	Sa	L
4	5	6	7	8
M	P	A	W	E
W	WM	M	MD	D
vT	T	M	I	vl

aromatic bark
aromatic leaves
border mass
specimen / accent

7–10   i.1697
Madagascar

open   12-20   very fast   very short

Xanthoceras sorbifolium
Shinyleaf Yellowhorn

P	C	Si	Sa	L
4	5	6	7	8
M	P	A	W	E
W	WM	M	MD	D
vT	T	M	I	vl

container
patio garden
sculptural
specimen / accent

5–9   i.1866
China

open   12-20   slow   short

Zanthoxylum piperitum
Japanese Pricklyash
Japan Pepper

P	C	Si	Sa	L
4	5	6	7	8
M	P	A	W	E
W	WM	M	MD	D
vT	T	M	I	vl

aromatic bark
aromatic leaves
barrier
culinary
kitchen garden
screen
sculptural - old
specimen / accent

5–8   c.1877
Korea

open   12-20   fast   short

VERY LARGE SHRUB

FORM	BARK	LEAF	FLOWER	FRUIT	CULTURE	USES	REGION

Zanthoxylum simulans
Flatspine Pricklyash

FORM: open, 20-35

CULTURE:
P C Si Sa L
4 5 6 7 8
M P A W E
W WM M MD D
vT T M I vl
fast / short

USES:
aromatic bark
aromatic leaves
barrier
screen
sculptural - old
specimen / accent

REGION: China, 5—8, i:1869

LARGE SHRUB

	FORM	BARK	LEAF	FLOWER	FRUIT	CULTURE	USES	REGION

Acacia cardiophylla
Wyalong Acacia

open 6-12

CULTURE:
P C Si Sa L
4 5 6 7 8
M P A W E
W WM M MD D
vT T M I vI
fast / short

USES: cut flowers, fruit arrangement, reclamation

REGION: 8—10, Australia

Acanthopanax sieboldianus
Fiveleaved Aralia

open 6-12

CULTURE:
P C Si Sa L
4 5 6 7 8
M P A W E
W WM M MD D
vT T M I vI
moderate / short

USES: bank erosion, barrier, hedge, historic garden, screen, sheared

REGION: 4—9a, i.1859, Japan

Aesculus parviflora
Bottlebrush Buckeye
Sweet Buckeye
serotina

moderate 12-20

CULTURE:
P C Si Sa L
4 5 6 7 8
M P A W E
W WM M MD D
vT T M I vI
slow / short

USES: border mass, poisonous leaves, sculptural, specimen / accent

REGION: 5—9a, i.1781, s. U.S.

Aloysia triphylla
Lemon Verbena

open 6-12

CULTURE:
P C Si Sa L
4 5 6 7 8
M P A W E
W WM M MD D
vT T M I vI
fast / short

USES: container, culinary, drinks, greenhouse, herb garden, kitchen garden, leaf arrangements, potpourri

REGION: 8—10, i.1784, Chile

Amelanchier alnifolia
Saskatoon Serviceberry
'Honeywood' 'Regent'
'Northline' 'Smokey'

moderate 6-12

CULTURE:
P C Si Sa L
4 5 6 7 8
M P A W E
W WM M MD D
vT T M I vI
fast / short

USES: bank erosion, jams, jellies, low maintenance, naturalizing, rock garden

REGION: 3b—9a, i.1918, w. U.S.

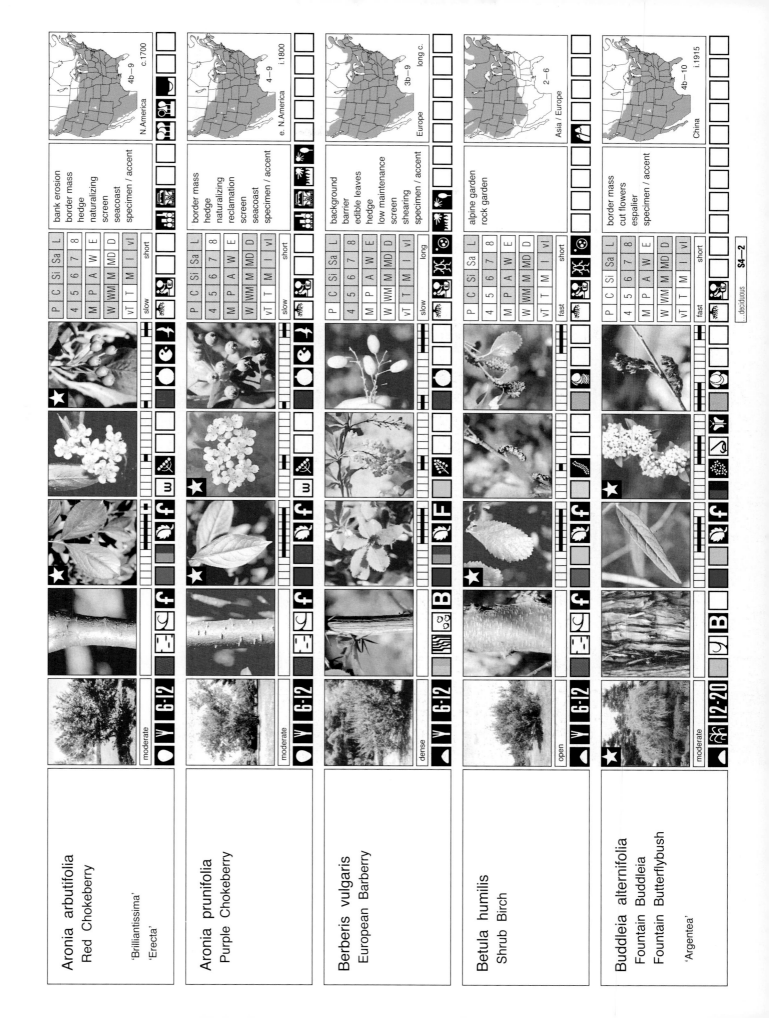

Aronia arbutifolia
Red Chokeberry
'Brilliantissima'
'Erecta'

bank erosion
border mass
hedge
naturalizing
screen
seacoast
specimen / accent

N.America   4b–9   c.1700

Aronia prunifolia
Purple Chokeberry

border mass
hedge
naturalizing
reclamation
screen
seacoast
specimen / accent

e. N.America   4–9   i.1800

Berberis vulgaris
European Barberry

background
barrier
edible leaves
hedge
low maintenance
screen
shearing
specimen / accent

Europe   3b–9   long c.

Betula humilis
Shrub Birch

alpine garden
rock garden

Asia / Europe   2–6

Buddleia alternifolia
Fountain Buddleia
Fountain Butterflybush
'Argentea'

border mass
cut flowers
espalier
specimen / accent

China   4b–10   i.1915

...deciduous   **S4—2**

LARGE SHRUB	FORM	BARK	LEAF	FLOWER	FRUIT	CULTURE	USES	REGION

Buddleia fallowiana
Fallow's Butterflybush
'Lochinch'

open · fast
CULTURE: P C Si Sa L / 4 5 6 7 8 / M P A W E / W WM M MD D / vT T M I vl / short
USES: border mass / hedge / seacoast / specimen / accent
REGION: 8—9 / c.1921 / China

Callicarpa bodinieri
Bodinier Beautyberry
'Profusion'

dense · fast
CULTURE: P C Si Sa L / 4 5 6 7 8 / M P A W E / W WM M MD D / vT T M I vl / short
USES: border mass / hedge / screen / specimen / accent
REGION: 6—8 / c.1900 / China

Calycanthus fertilis
Pale Sweetshrub

moderate · moderate
CULTURE: P C Si Sa L / 4 5 6 7 8 / M P A W E / W WM M MD D / vT T M I vl / short
USES: background / historic garden / specimen / accent
REGION: 5b—9a / i.1806 / e. U.S.

Calycanthus floridus
Common Sweetshrub
Carolina Allspice
'Athens'

moderate · moderate
CULTURE: P C Si Sa L / 4 5 6 7 8 / M P A W E / W WM M MD D / vT T M I vl / short
USES: aromatic leaves / background / border mass / historic garden / specimen / accent
REGION: 5a—9 / i.1726 / e. U.S.

Calycanthus occidentalis
California Sweetshrub
California Allspice

moderate · moderate
CULTURE: P C Si Sa L / 4 5 6 7 8 / M P A W E / W WM M MD D / vT T M I vl / short
USES: aromatic leaves / background / border mass / screen / specimen / accent
REGION: 6—9 / i.1831 / California

Caragana aurantiaca		
Dwarf Peashrub		

hedge
screen
shearing
specimen / accent
windbreak

P	C	Si	Sa	L
4	5	6	7	8
M	P	A	W	E
W	WM	M	MD	D
vT	T	M	I	vl

fast · short

6-12 · open

Siberia · i.1887 · 2–6

Caragana frutex		
Russian Peashrub		
'Globosa'		

bank erosion
hedge
shearing
windbreak

P	C	Si	Sa	L
4	5	6	7	8
M	P	A	W	E
W	WM	M	MD	D
vT	T	M	I	vl

fast · moderate

12-20 · open

Siberia · i.1752 · 2–8

Cephalanthus occidentalis		
Buttonbush		
Honeyballs		
californica		

bee shrub
naturalizing
poisonous leaves
specimen / accent

P	C	Si	Sa	L
4	5	6	7	8
M	P	A	W	E
W	WM	M	MD	D
vT	T	M	I	vl

fast · short

6-12 · open

N.America · i.1735 · 4–9

Chaenomeles speciosa **syn.** C. lagenaria		
Common Floweringquince		
'Cameo'	'Rubra'	
'Nivalis'	'Spit Fire'	

barrier
border mass
cut flowers
espalier
hedge
seacoast
shearing

P	C	Si	Sa	L
4	5	6	7	8
M	P	A	W	E
W	WM	M	MD	D
vT	T	M	I	vl

fast · moderate

6-12 · dense

China · i.1796 · 4b–9

Chimonanthus praecox		
Wintersweet		

border mass
cut flowers
screen
specimen / accent

P	C	Si	Sa	L
4	5	6	7	8
M	P	A	W	E
W	WM	M	MD	D
vT	T	M	I	vl

slow · moderate

6-12 · open

China · i.1766 · 7–9

...deciduous   S4–4

LARGE SHRUB

	FORM	BARK	LEAF	FLOWER	FRUIT	CULTURE	USES	REGION

Clethra alnifolia
Sweet Pepperbush
Summersweet

'Paniculata'   'Rosea'
'Pink Spire'

FORM: dense · 12-20

CULTURE:
P	C	Si	Sa	L
4	5	6	7	8
M	P	A	W	E
W	WM	M	MD	D
vT	T	M	I	vI

moderate · short

USES:
bank erosion
border mass
screen
seacoast
specimen / accent

REGION: e. U.S. · 4—9 · i.1731

Cornus amomum
Silky Dogwood

FORM: moderate · 12-20

CULTURE:
P	C	Si	Sa	L
4	5	6	7	8
M	P	A	W	E
W	WM	M	MD	D
vT	T	M	I	vI

fast

USES:
bank erosion
border mass
naturalizing
reclamation
screen

REGION: e. N.America · 4—9 · i.1683

Cornus paucinervis
Littleleaf Dogwood

FORM: dense · 6-12

CULTURE:
P	C	Si	Sa	L
4	5	6	7	8
M	P	A	W	E
W	WM	M	MD	D
vT	T	M	I	vI

moderate · short

USES:
bank erosion
border mass
hedge
screen

REGION: China · 4—8 · i.1907

Cornus racemosa
Gray Dogwood
Panicled Dogwood

'Heaven Sent'

FORM: dense · 6-12

CULTURE:
P	C	Si	Sa	L
4	5	6	7	8
M	P	A	W	E
W	WM	M	MD	D
vT	T	M	I	vI

moderate · short

USES:
bank erosion
border mass
hedge
naturalizing
reclamation
screen
shearing
windbreak

REGION: e. U.S. · 3b—7 · i.1758

Cornus rugosa
Roundleaved Dogwood

FORM: moderate · 6-12

CULTURE:
P	C	Si	Sa	L
4	5	6	7	8
M	P	A	W	E
W	WM	M	MD	D
vT	T	M	I	vI

moderate · short

USES:
preservation
shade garden
specimen / accent
woodland garden

REGION: Mexico · 4—10 · i.1874

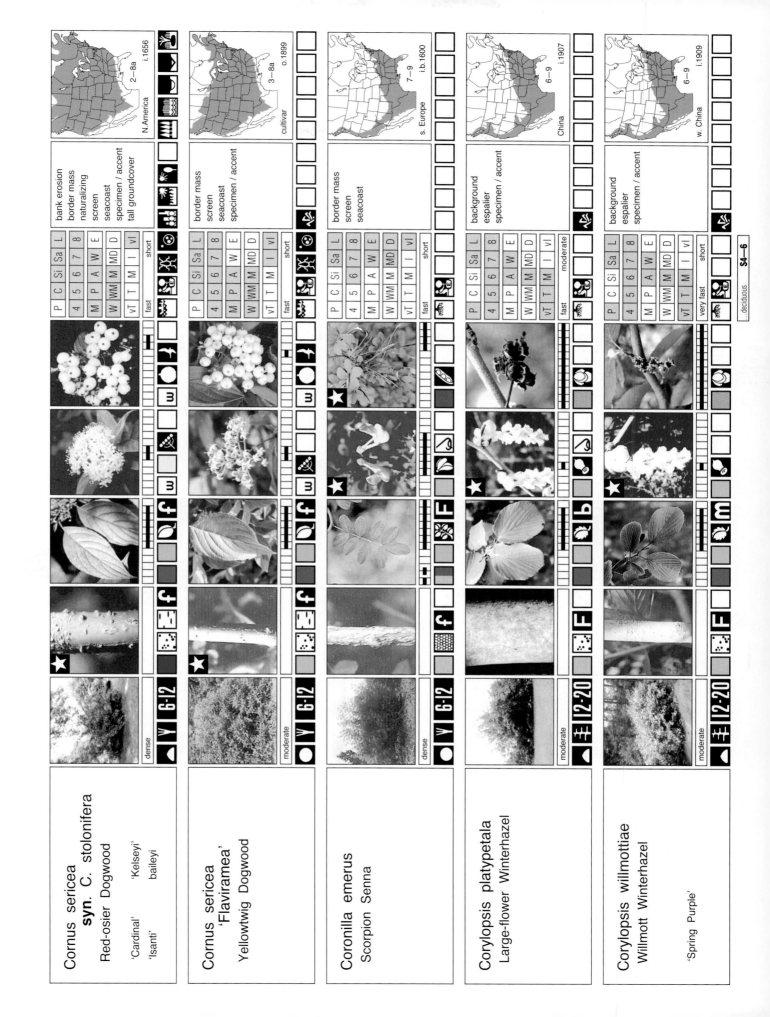

Cornus sericea syn. C. stolonifera — Red-osier Dogwood
'Cardinal' 'Kelseyi' 'Isanti' baileyi
N. America — 2–8a — i.1656
bank erosion / border mass / naturalizing / screen / seacoast / specimen / accent / tall groundcover
dense — 6-12
P C Si Sa L — 4 5 6 7 8 — M P A W E — W WM M MD D — vT T M I vl — fast — short

Cornus sericea 'Flaviramea' — Yellowtwig Dogwood
cultivar — 3–8a — o.1899
border mass / screen / seacoast / specimen / accent
moderate — 6-12
P C Si Sa L — 4 5 6 7 8 — M P A W E — W WM M MD D — vT T M I vl — fast — short

Coronilla emerus — Scorpion Senna
s. Europe — 7–9 — i.b.1600
border mass / screen / seacoast
dense — 6-12
P C Si Sa L — 4 5 6 7 8 — M P A W E — W WM M MD D — vT T M I vl — fast — short

Corylopsis platypetala — Large-flower Winterhazel
China — 6–9 — i.1907
background / espalier / specimen / accent
moderate — 12-20
P C Si Sa L — 4 5 6 7 8 — M P A W E — W WM M MD D — vT T M I vl — fast — moderate

Corylopsis willmottiae — Willmott Winterhazel
'Spring Purple'
w. China — 6–9 — i.1909
background / espalier / specimen / accent
moderate — 12-20
P C Si Sa L — 4 5 6 7 8 — M P A W E — W WM M MD D — vT T M I vl — very fast — short

...deciduous   S4–6

LARGE SHRUB	FORM	BARK	LEAF	FLOWER	FRUIT	CULTURE	USES	REGION

Corylus americana
American Filbert
American Hazelnut

- FORM: dense, 6-12
- CULTURE: P C Si Sa L / 4 5 6 7 8 / M P A W E / W WM M MD D / vT T M I vI — fast — 3—8 — i:1798
- USES: border mass / kitchen garden / naturalizing / reclamation / shade garden
- REGION: e. N.America

Corylus cornuta
Beaked Filbert
Beaked Hazelnut

- FORM: dense, 6-12
- CULTURE: P C Si Sa L / 4 5 6 7 8 / M P A W E / W WM M MD D / vT T M I vI — moderate short — 2b—8 — i:1745
- USES: border mass / kitchen garden / naturalizing / reclamation / shade garden
- REGION: n. N.America

Cotoneaster acutifolia
Peking Cotoneaster
'Nana'

- FORM: dense, 6-12
- CULTURE: P C Si Sa L / 4 5 6 7 8 / M P A W E / W WM M MD D / vT T M I vI — slow — 2—6 — i:1900
- USES: border mass / hedge / screen / seacoast / windbreak
- REGION: n. China

Cotoneaster foveolata
Glossy Cotoneaster

- FORM: dense, 6-12
- CULTURE: P C Si Sa L / 4 5 6 7 8 / M P A W E / W WM M MD D / vT T M I vI — moderate short — 5—7 — i:1908
- USES: border mass / hedge / screen / seacoast / windbreak
- REGION: China

Cotoneaster lucida
Hedge Cotoneaster

- FORM: dense, 6-12
- CULTURE: P C Si Sa L / 4 5 6 7 8 / M P A W E / W WM M MD D / vT T M I vI — moderate moderate — 2b—7 — i:1804
- USES: border mass / hedge / preservation / screen / seacoast / shearing / specimen / accent / windbreak
- REGION: Asia / Siberia

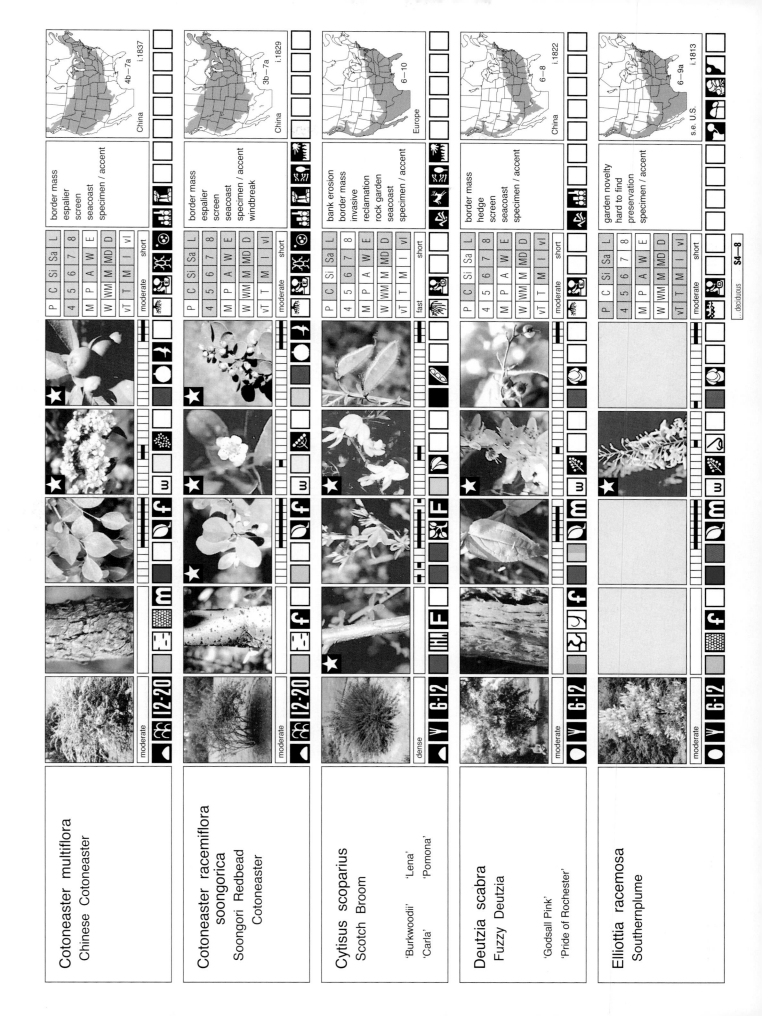

Cotoneaster multiflora
Chinese Cotoneaster

'Burkwoodii'　'Lena'
'Carla'　'Pomona'

China
4b–7a
i.1837

border mass
espalier
screen
specimen / accent

moderate | 12-20

P	C	Si	Sa	L
4	5	6	7	8
M	P	A	W	E
W	WM	M	MD	D
vT	T	M	I	vl

moderate short

Cotoneaster racemiflora soongorica
Soongori Redbead Cotoneaster

China
3b–7a
i.1829

border mass
espalier
screen
seacoast
specimen / accent
windbreak

moderate | 12-20

P	C	Si	Sa	L
4	5	6	7	8
M	P	A	W	E
W	WM	M	MD	D
vT	T	M	I	vl

moderate short

Cytisus scoparius
Scotch Broom

Europe
6–10

bank erosion
border mass
invasive
reclamation
rock garden
seacoast
specimen / accent

dense | 6-12

P	C	Si	Sa	L
4	5	6	7	8
M	P	A	W	E
W	WM	M	MD	D
vT	T	M	I	vl

fast short

Deutzia scabra
Fuzzy Deutzia

'Godsall Pink'
'Pride of Rochester'

China
6–8
i.1822

border mass
hedge
screen
seacoast
specimen / accent

moderate | 6-12

P	C	Si	Sa	L
4	5	6	7	8
M	P	A	W	E
W	WM	M	MD	D
vT	T	M	I	vl

moderate short

Elliottia racemosa
Southernplume

s.e. U.S.
6–9a
i.1813

garden novelty
hard to find
preservation
specimen / accent

moderate | 6-12

P	C	Si	Sa	L
4	5	6	7	8
M	P	A	W	E
W	WM	M	MD	D
vT	T	M	I	vl

moderate short

...deciduous　**S4—8**

LARGE SHRUB	FORM	BARK	LEAF	FLOWER	FRUIT	CULTURE	USES	REGION

Euonymus alatus
Winged Euonymus
Winged Spindletree

'Compacta'   'Tures'
'Nordine'

dense 12-20

- CULTURE: P C Si Sa L / 4 5 6 7 8 / M P A W E / W WM M MD D / vT T M I vl / moderate — moderate
- USES: background, barrier, border mass, container, hedge / screen, patio garden, sheared, specimen / accent
- REGION: Asia 3b—8a i.1860

Euonymus americana
Strawberrybush Euonymus
Bursting-heart

open 6-12

- CULTURE: P C Si Sa L / 4 5 6 7 8 / M P A W E / W WM M MD D / vT T M I vl / moderate — short
- USES: background, border mass, naturalizing, preservation
- REGION: e. U.S. (5b)—9 c.i.1683

Euonymus sachalinensis
Sakhalin Euonymus

moderate 6-12

- CULTURE: P C Si Sa L / 4 5 6 7 8 / M P A W E / W WM M MD D / vT T M I vl / moderate — moderate
- USES: border mass, screen, seacoast
- REGION: n.e. Asia 6—9 i.1892

Euonymus yedoensis
Yeddo Euonymus

moderate

- CULTURE: P C Si Sa L / 4 5 6 7 8 / M P A W E / W WM M MD D / vT T M I vl / slow — moderate
- USES: border mass, screen, specimen / accent, windbreak
- REGION: Japan 4—8 i.1865

Exochorda giraldi
Redbud Pearlbush

'Wilsonii'

dense 6-12

- CULTURE: P C Si Sa L / 4 5 6 7 8 / M P A W E / W WM M MD D / vT T M I vl / fast — short
- USES: small groupings, specimen / accent, windbreak
- REGION: China 6—9 i.1907

Exochorda x macrantha
Hybrid Pearlbush

'The Bride'

border mass
patio garden
screen
small groupings
specimen / accent

hybrid   5–9   i.1900

moderate   6·12   fast   short

P C Si Sa L | 4 5 6 7 8 | M P A W E | W WM M MD D | vT T M I vl

Exochorda racemosa
Common Pearlbush

border mass
hedge
screen
specimen / accent

China   5–9   i.1844

moderate   12·20   fast   short

P C Si Sa L | 4 5 6 7 8 | M P A W E | W WM M MD D | vT T M I vl

Fontanesia fortunei
Fortune Fontanesia

'Titan'

hedge
screen
shearing

China   5b–8   i.1845

open   6·12   fast   short

P C Si Sa L | 4 5 6 7 8 | M P A W E | W WM M MD D | vT T M I vl

Fontanesia phillyreoides
Syrianprivet Fontenisia

hedge
screen
shearing

Syria   7b–10   i.1787

open   fast   short

P C Si Sa L | 4 5 6 7 8 | M P A W E | W WM M MD D | vT T M I vl

Forsythia 'Beatrix Farrand'
Beatrix Farrand Forsythia

cut flowers
espalier
hedge
screen
seacoast
specimen / accent

cultivar   5–9   i.1944

open   6·12   fast   short

P C Si Sa L | 4 5 6 7 8 | M P A W E | W WM M MD D | vT T M I vl

LARGE SHRUB	FORM	BARK	LEAF	FLOWER	FRUIT	CULTURE	USES	REGION

Forsythia 'Spring Glory'
Spring Glory Forsythia

- FORM: moderate · 6-12
- CULTURE:
P	C	Si	Sa	L
4	5	6	7	8
M	P	A	W	E
W	WM	M	MD	D
vT	T	M	I	vI
  fast · short
- USES: cut flowers / espalier / hedge / screen / seacoast / specimen / accent
- REGION: cultivar · 5—8 · i.1930

Forsythia suspensa
Weeping Forsythia
'Sieboldii'

- FORM: moderate · 12-20
- CULTURE:
P	C	Si	Sa	L
4	5	6	7	8
M	P	A	W	E
W	WM	M	MD	D
vT	T	M	I	vI
  fast · short
- USES: above wall / bank erosion / climbing vine / cut flowers / hedge / reclamation / seacoast / specimen / accent
- REGION: Japan · 5—8 · i.1833

Fothergilla major
Large Fothergilla
Witchalder

- FORM: dense · 6-12
- CULTURE:
P	C	Si	Sa	L
4	5	6	7	8
M	P	A	W	E
W	WM	M	MD	D
vT	T	M	I	vI
  slow · short
- USES: aromatic leaves / naturalizing / shade garden / specimen / accent
- REGION: s.e. U.S. · (5b)—9 · i.1780

Hamamelis vernalis
Vernal Witchhazel
'Christmas Cheer'
'Rubra'   'Sandra'

- FORM: dense · 6-12
- CULTURE:
P	C	Si	Sa	L
4	5	6	7	8
M	P	A	W	E
W	WM	M	MD	D
vT	T	M	I	vI
  fast · short
- USES: background / border mass / hedge / screen
- REGION: s.c. U.S. · 4—9 · i.1908

Holodiscus discolor
Rockspirea
Creambush

- FORM: open · 12-20
- CULTURE:
P	C	Si	Sa	L
4	5	6	7	8
M	P	A	W	E
W	WM	M	MD	D
vT	T	M	I	vI
  fast · short
- USES: background / border mass / hedge / seacoast / specimen / accent
- REGION: w. N. America · 6—9 · i.1827

Hypericum canariense — Canary Island Spirea

7–10

Canary Islands

hard to find
hedge
screen
specimen / accent

P	C	Si	Sa	L
4	5	6	7	8
M	P	A	W	E
W	WM	M	MD	D
vT	T	M	I	vI

moderate · short

open · 6·12

Ilex laevigata — Smooth Winterberry

4b–8 i.1812

e. U.S.

bog garden
border mass
fruit arrangements
seacoast
specimen / accent

P	C	Si	Sa	L
4	5	6	7	8
M	P	A	W	E
W	WM	M	MD	D
vT	T	M	I	vI

moderate · short

moderate · 6·12

Ilex verticillata — Common Winterberry / Michigan Holly

'Aurantiaca'   'Sunset'
'Compacta'   'Winter Red'

3b–9 i.1736

N. America

bog garden
border mass
fruit arrangements
seacoast
specimen / accent

P	C	Si	Sa	L
4	5	6	7	8
M	P	A	W	E
W	WM	M	MD	D
vT	T	M	I	vI

slow · short

moderate · 6·12

Jasminum nudiflorum — Winter Jasmine

'Aureo Variegata'
'Variegata'

6–9b i.1844

China

above wall
bank erosion
border mass
espalier
greenhouse
hedge
low maintanence
seacoast

P	C	Si	Sa	L
4	5	6	7	8
M	P	A	W	E
W	WM	M	MD	D
vT	T	M	I	vI

fast · short

open · 6·12

Kolkwitzia amabilis — Beautybush

'Pink Cloud'

5a–8 i.1901

China

border mass
container
hedge
screen
seacoast
specimen / accent
windbreak

P	C	Si	Sa	L
4	5	6	7	8
M	P	A	W	E
W	WM	M	MD	D
vT	T	M	I	vI

fast · moderate

dense · 6·12

...deciduous   **S4—12**

LARGE SHRUB	FORM	BARK	LEAF	FLOWER	FRUIT	CULTURE	USES	REGION

Lespedeza bicolor
Shrub Bushclover

CULTURE: P C Si Sa L / 4 5 6 7 8 / M P A W E / W WM M MD D / vT T M I vl / very fast — short

USES: background, nitrogen-fixing

REGION: 5–7 · China · i.1856

FORM: open · 6-12

Lespedeza maximowiczi
Japanese Bushclover
Maximowicz Bushclover

CULTURE: P C Si Sa L / 4 5 6 7 8 / M P A W E / W WM M MD D / vT T M I vl / very fast — short

USES: background, nitrogen-fixing

REGION: 6–8a · Korea · i.1917

FORM: open · 6-12

Lespedeza thunbergi
Thunberg Bushclover
Thunberg Lespedeza
'Alba'
'Albiflora'

CULTURE: P C Si Sa L / 4 5 6 7 8 / M P A W E / W WM M MD D / vT T M I vl / very fast — short

USES: background, nitrogen-fixing

REGION: 6–8a · Japan · i.1837

FORM: open · 6-12

Leucothoe racemosa
Sweetbells Leucothoe
Fetterbush

CULTURE: P C Si Sa L / 4 5 6 7 8 / M P A W E / W WM M MD D / vT T M I vl / moderate — moderate

USES: bank erosion, border mass, cut flowers, dried flowers, naturalizing, poisonous leaves, rock garden, specimen / accent

REGION: 6–9a · e. U.S. · i.1736

FORM: moderate · 12-20

Ligustrum obtusifolium
Border Privet
regelianum
'Variegatum'

CULTURE: P C Si Sa L / 4 5 6 7 8 / M P A W E / W WM M MD D / vT T M I vl / fast — short

USES: background, bank erosion, barrier, hedge, screen, shearing, specimen / accent

REGION: 4b–8a · Japan · i.1860

FORM: dense · 6-12

Lonicera x amoena
Gotha Honeysuckle

hybrid
i.1892
4b–8a

P	C	Si	Sa	L
4	5	6	7	8
M	P	A	W	E
W	WM	M	MD	D
vT	T	M	I	vI

background
hedge
screen
shearing

short
fast
dense
6-12

Lonicera 'Clavey's Dwarf'
Clavey's Dwarf Honeysuckle

cultivar
3b–8a

P	C	Si	Sa	L
4	5	6	7	8
M	P	A	W	E
W	WM	M	MD	D
vT	T	M	I	vI

background
hedge
screen
shearing

short
fast
dense
6-12

Lonicera korolkowi
Blueleaf Honeysuckle
'Zabelii'

Turkestan
i.1880
5 –8a

P	C	Si	Sa	L
4	5	6	7	8
M	P	A	W	E
W	WM	M	MD	D
vT	T	M	I	vI

background
border mass
hedge
screen
seacoast
shearing
specimen / accent

short
fast
open
6-12

Lonicera syringantha
Lilac Honeysuckle

China
i.1890
5 –8a

P	C	Si	Sa	L
4	5	6	7	8
M	P	A	W	E
W	WM	M	MD	D
vT	T	M	I	vI

background
hedge
screen
seacoast
shearing

short
fast
open
6-12

Lyonia ligustrina
He-Huckleberry
Maleberry

e. U.S.
i.1748
4 –9

P	C	Si	Sa	L
4	5	6	7	8
M	P	A	W	E
W	WM	M	MD	D
vT	T	M	I	vI

aquatic garden
bog garden
poisonous leaves
seacoast

short
moderate
...deciduous
open
6-12

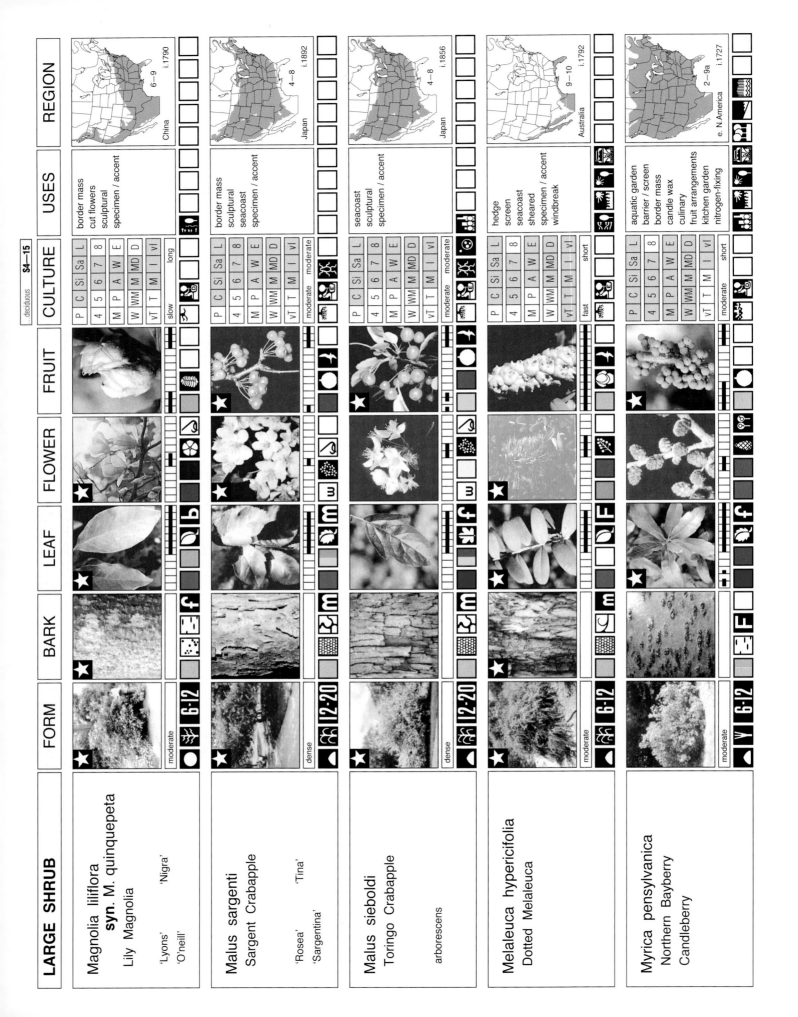

LARGE SHRUB	FORM	BARK	LEAF	FLOWER	FRUIT	CULTURE	USES	REGION

Magnolia liliflora
syn. M. quinquepeta
Lily Magnolia

'Lyons'   'Nigra'
'O'neill'

moderate 6-12

P	C	Si	Sa	L
4	5	6	7	8
M	P	A	W	E
W	WM	M	MD	D
vT	T	M	I	vl

slow   long

border mass
cut flowers
sculptural
specimen / accent

China   6–9   i.1790

Malus sargenti
Sargent Crabapple

'Rosea'   'Tina'
'Sargentina'

dense 12-20

P	C	Si	Sa	L
4	5	6	7	8
M	P	A	W	E
W	WM	M	MD	D
vT	T	M	I	vl

moderate

border mass
sculptural
seacoast
specimen / accent

Japan   4–8   i.1892

Malus sieboldi
Toringo Crabapple

arborescens

dense 12-20

P	C	Si	Sa	L
4	5	6	7	8
M	P	A	W	E
W	WM	M	MD	D
vT	T	M	I	vl

moderate

seacoast
sculptural
specimen / accent

Japan   4–8   i.1856

Melaleuca hypericifolia
Dotted Melaleuca

moderate 6-12

P	C	Si	Sa	L
4	5	6	7	8
M	P	A	W	E
W	WM	M	MD	D
vT	T	M	I	vl

fast   short

hedge
screen
seacoast
sheared
specimen / accent
windbreak

Australia   9–10   i.1792

Myrica pensylvanica
Northern Bayberry
Candleberry

moderate 6-12

P	C	Si	Sa	L
4	5	6	7	8
M	P	A	W	E
W	WM	M	MD	D
vT	T	M	I	vl

moderate   short

aquatic garden
barrier / screen
border mass
candle wax
culinary
fruit arrangements
kitchen garden
nitrogen-fixing

e. N.America   2–9a   i.1727

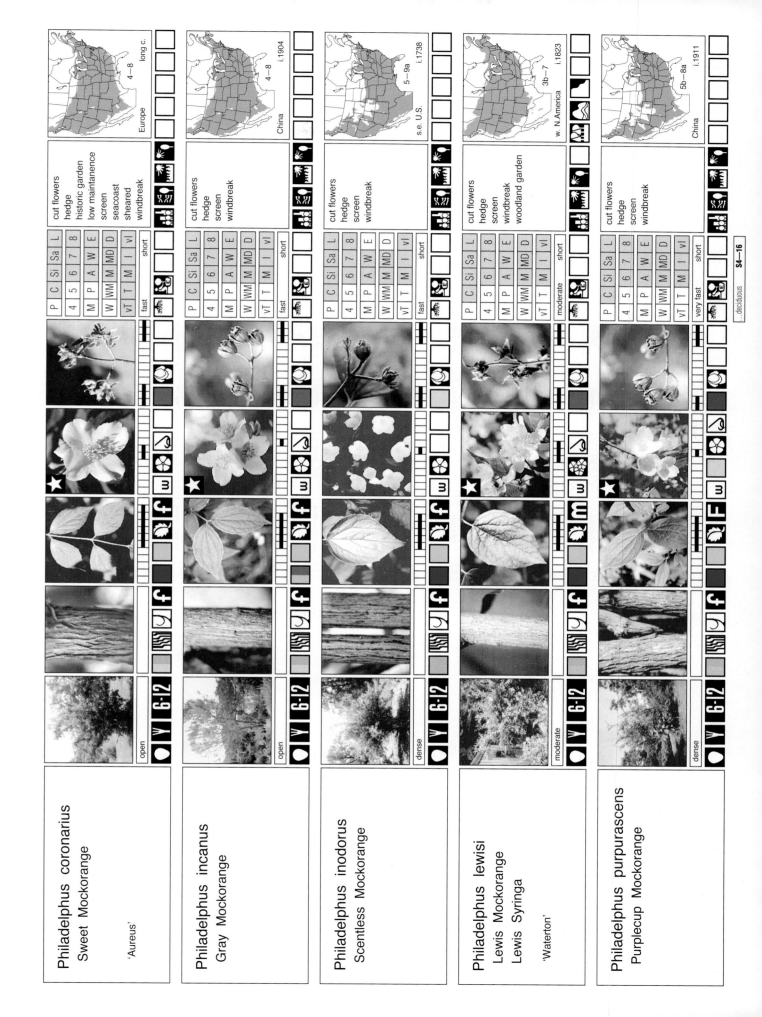

Philadelphus coronarius
Sweet Mockorange
'Aureus'

P	C	Si	Sa	L
4	5	6	7	8
M	P	A	W	E
W	WM	M	MD	D
vT	T	M	I	vl

short
fast
open

cut flowers
hedge
historic garden
low maintenance
screen
seacoast
sheared
windbreak

Europe   4—8   long c.

Philadelphus incanus
Gray Mockorange

P	C	Si	Sa	L
4	5	6	7	8
M	P	A	W	E
W	WM	M	MD	D
vT	T	M	I	vl

short
fast
open

cut flowers
hedge
screen
windbreak

China   4—8   i.1904

Philadelphus inodorus
Scentless Mockorange

P	C	Si	Sa	L
4	5	6	7	8
M	P	A	W	E
W	WM	M	MD	D
vT	T	M	I	vl

short
fast
dense

cut flowers
hedge
screen
windbreak

s.e. U.S.   5—9a   i.1738

Philadelphus lewisi
Lewis Mockorange
Lewis Syringa
'Waterton'

P	C	Si	Sa	L
4	5	6	7	8
M	P	A	W	E
W	WM	M	MD	D
vT	T	M	I	vl

short
moderate
moderate

cut flowers
hedge
screen
windbreak
woodland garden

w. N.America   3b—7   i.1823

Philadelphus purpurascens
Purplecup Mockorange

P	C	Si	Sa	L
4	5	6	7	8
M	P	A	W	E
W	WM	M	MD	D
vT	T	M	I	vl

short
very fast
dense

cut flowers
hedge
screen
windbreak

China   5b—8a   i.1911

...deciduous   S4—16

LARGE SHRUB	FORM	BARK	LEAF	FLOWER	FRUIT	CULTURE	USES	REGION

Philadelphus schrenki
Schrenk Mockorange

dense · 6-12

P	C	Si	Sa	L
4	5	6	7	8
M	P	A	W	E
W	WM	M	MD	D
vT	T	M	I	vl

fast · short

cut flowers
hedge
screen
windbreak

3—7a · i.1874
Korea

Philadelphus x virginalis
Virginalis Mockorange

'Natchez'   'Virginal'

dense · 6-12

P	C	Si	Sa	L
4	5	6	7	8
M	P	A	W	E
W	WM	M	MD	D
vT	T	M	I	vl

fast · short

cut flowers
hedge
screen
seacoast
windbreak

4b—9 · i.1910
hybrid

Physocarpus capitatus
Pacific Ninebark
Western Ninebark

dense · 6-12

P	C	Si	Sa	L
4	5	6	7	8
M	P	A	W	E
W	WM	M	MD	D
vT	T	M	I	vl

fast · short

bank erosion
border mass
hedge
naturalizing
screen

4—8 · i.1827
w. N.America

Physocarpus opulifolius
Common Ninebark

'Aureus'   'Luteus'
'Darts Gold'   'Nanus'

dense · 6-12

P	C	Si	Sa	L
4	5	6	7	8
M	P	A	W	E
W	WM	M	MD	D
vT	T	M	I	vl

fast · short

bank erosion
border mass
hedge
naturalizing
screen
windbreak

2—8 · i.1687
central U.S.

Polygonum cuspidatum
Japanese Fleeceflower
Japanese Knotweed

'Compactum'   'Spectabile'

dense · 12-20

P	C	Si	Sa	L
4	5	6	7	8
M	P	A	W	E
W	WM	M	MD	D
vT	T	M	I	vl

very fast · very short

bank erosion
border mass
naturalizing

4b—9a · i.
Japan

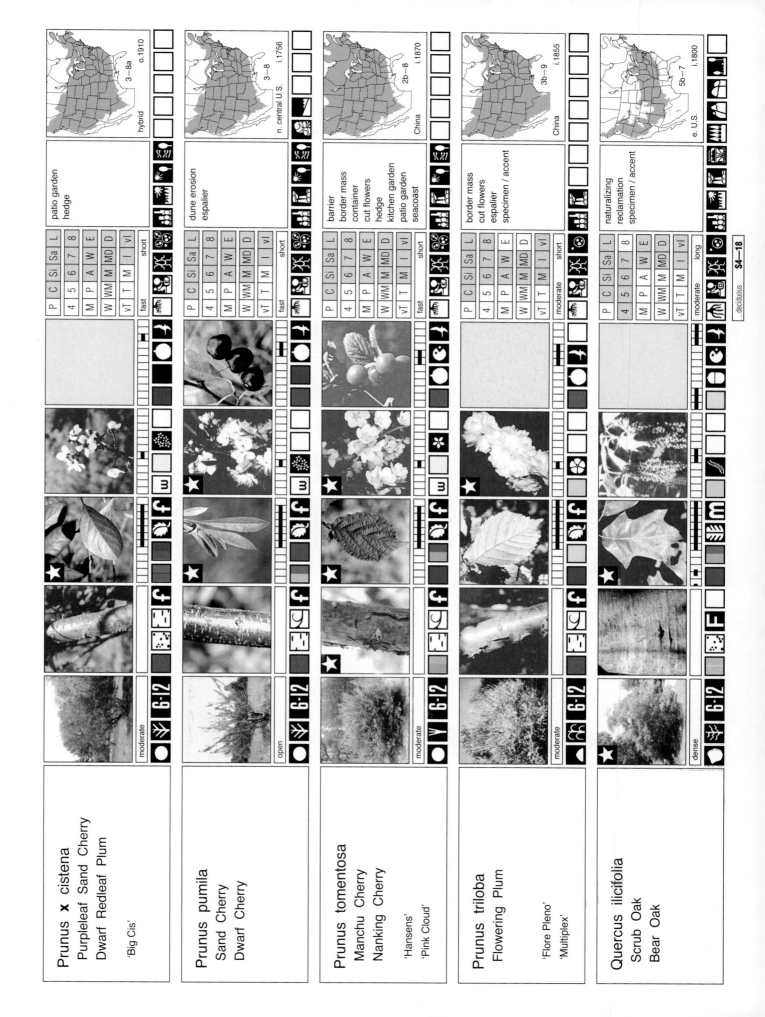

Prunus x cistena
Purpleleaf Sand Cherry
Dwarf Redleaf Plum

'Big Cis'

3–8a   o.1910
hybrid

patio garden
hedge

P	C	Si	Sa	L
4	5	6	7	8
M	P	A	W	E
W	WM	M	MD	D
vT	T	M	I	vI

fast   short

moderate   6·12

Prunus pumila
Sand Cherry
Dwarf Cherry

3–8   i.1756
n. central U.S.

dune erosion
espalier

P	C	Si	Sa	L
4	5	6	7	8
M	P	A	W	E
W	WM	M	MD	D
vT	T	M	I	vI

fast   short

open   6·12

Prunus tomentosa
Manchu Cherry
Nanking Cherry

'Hansens'
'Pink Cloud'

2b–8   i.1870
China

barrier
border mass
container
cut flowers
hedge
kitchen garden
patio garden
seacoast

P	C	Si	Sa	L
4	5	6	7	8
M	P	A	W	E
W	WM	M	MD	D
vT	T	M	I	vI

fast   short

moderate   6·12

Prunus triloba
Flowering Plum

'Flore Pleno'
'Multiplex'

3b–9   i.1855
China

border mass
cut flowers
espalier
specimen / accent

P	C	Si	Sa	L
4	5	6	7	8
M	P	A	W	E
W	WM	M	MD	D
vT	T	M	I	vI

moderate   short

moderate   6·12

Quercus ilicifolia
Scrub Oak
Bear Oak

5b–7   i.1800
e. U.S.

naturalizing
reclamation
specimen / accent

P	C	Si	Sa	L
4	5	6	7	8
M	P	A	W	E
W	WM	M	MD	D
vT	T	M	I	vI

moderate   long

dense   6·12

...deciduous   S4—18

LARGE SHRUB	FORM	BARK	LEAF	FLOWER	FRUIT	CULTURE	USES	REGION

Rhododendron bakeri
Cumberland Azalea

- moderate
- 6-12
- CULTURE: P C Si Sa L / 4 5 6 7 8 / M P A W E / W WM M MD D / vT T M I vl / moderate — long
- USES: border mass / espalier / poisonous leaves / sculptural / specimen / accent
- REGION: (5a)–8 / s.e. U.S.

Rhododendron calendulaceum
Flame Azalea

- moderate
- 6-12
- CULTURE: P C Si Sa L / 4 5 6 7 8 / M P A W E / W WM M MD D / vT T M I vl / moderate — long
- USES: border mass / espalier / poisonous leaves / sculptural / specimen / accent
- REGION: 5–9 / i.1806 / s.e. U.S.

Rhododendron 'Exbury Hybrids'
Exbury Hybrid Azaleas

- moderate
- 6-12
- CULTURE: P C Si Sa L / 4 5 6 7 8 / M P A W E / W WM M MD D / vT T M I vl / moderate — long
- USES: border mass / sculptural / specimen / accent
- REGION: 5–9 / hybrid

Rhododendron x gandavense
Ghent Azalea

- moderate
- 6-12
- CULTURE: P C Si Sa L / 4 5 6 7 8 / M P A W E / W WM M MD D / vT T M I vl / moderate — long
- USES: border mass / sculptural / specimen / accent
- REGION: 5–7 / i.b.1850 / hybrid

Rhododendron luteum syn. R. flavum
Pontic Azalea
'Batumi Gold'

- moderate
- 6-12
- CULTURE: P C Si Sa L / 4 5 6 7 8 / M P A W E / W WM M MD D / vT T M I vl / moderate — long
- USES: border mass / espalier / sculptural / specimen / accent
- REGION: 6b–8 / i 1793 / Caucasus

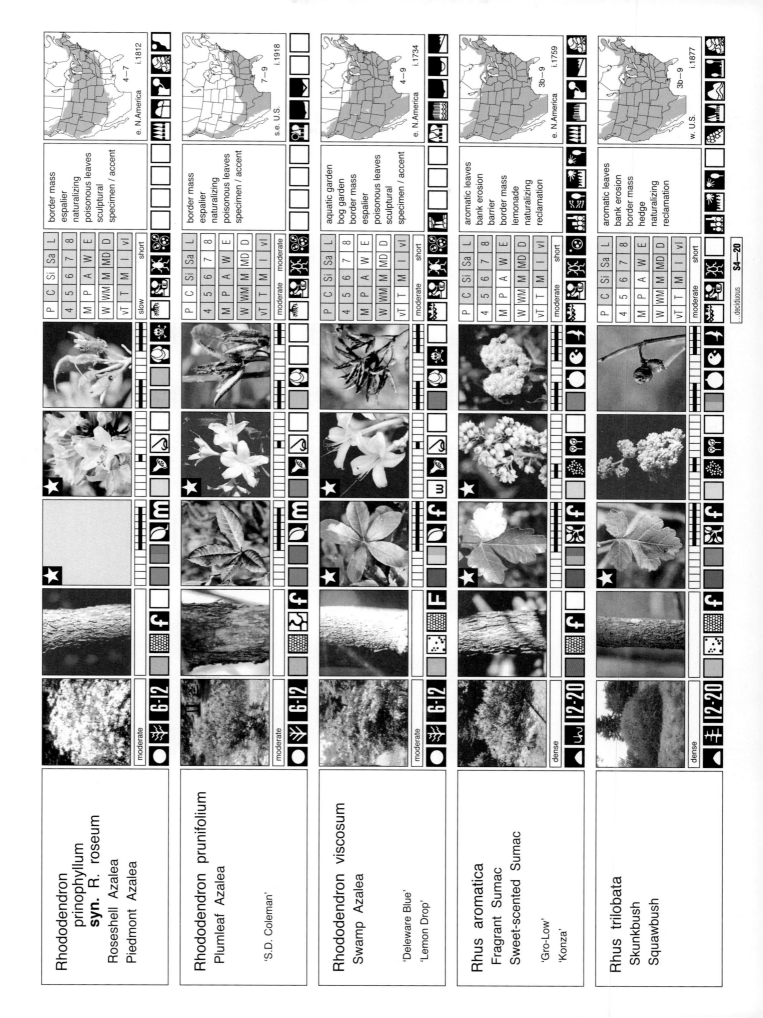

Rhododendron
prinophyllum
syn. R. roseum

Roseshell Azalea
Piedmont Azalea

border mass
espalier
naturalizing
poisonous leaves
sculptural
specimen / accent

P C Si Sa L
4 5 6 7 8
M P A W E
W WM M MD D
vT T M I vl

slow   short

e. N.America   4–7   i.1812

moderate   6-12

Rhododendron prunifolium

Plumleaf Azalea

'S.D. Coleman'

border mass
espalier
naturalizing
poisonous leaves
specimen / accent

P C Si Sa L
4 5 6 7 8
M P A W E
W WM M MD D
vT T M I vl

moderate   moderate

s.e. U.S.   7–9   i.1918

moderate   6-12

Rhododendron viscosum

Swamp Azalea

'Deleware Blue'
'Lemon Drop'

aquatic garden
bog garden
border mass
espalier
poisonous leaves
sculptural
specimen / accent

P C Si Sa L
4 5 6 7 8
M P A W E
W WM M MD D
vT T M I vl

moderate   short

e. N.America   4–9   i.1734

moderate   6-12

Rhus aromatica

Fragrant Sumac
Sweet-scented Sumac

'Gro-Low'
'Konza'

aromatic leaves
bank erosion
barrier
border mass
lemonade
naturalizing
reclamation

P C Si Sa L
4 5 6 7 8
M P A W E
W WM M MD D
vT T M I vl

moderate   short

e. N.America   3b–9   i.1759

dense   12-20

Rhus trilobata

Skunkbush
Squawbush

aromatic leaves
bank erosion
border mass
hedge
naturalizing
reclamation

P C Si Sa L
4 5 6 7 8
M P A W E
W WM M MD D
vT T M I vl

moderate   short

w. U.S.   3b–9   i.1877

dense   12-20

| LARGE SHRUB | FORM | BARK | LEAF | FLOWER | FRUIT | CULTURE | USES | REGION |

Ribes sanguineum
Red Flowering Currant
Winter Currant

'King Edward VII'
"White Icicle"

open   6-12

P C Si Sa L
4 5 6 7 8
M P A W E
W WM M MD D
vT T M I vl
fast   very short

aromatic leaves
border mass
fragrant flowers
hedge
kitchen garden
seacoast
specimen / accent

6—8   i.1826
w. N.America

Romneya coulteri
California Tree Poppy
Matilija Poppy

open   6-12

P C Si Sa L
4 5 6 7 8
M P A W E
W WM M MD D
vT T M I vl
fast   short

bank erosion
barrier
border mass
hedge
naturalizing
screen

8—10   i.1875
s. California

Rosa californica
California Rose

'Plena'

moderate   6-12

P C Si Sa L
4 5 6 7 8
M P A W E
W WM M MD D
vT T M I vl
fast   short

bank erosion
barrier
border mass
hedge
naturalizing
screen

5—8   c.1878
w. U.S.

Rosa canina
Dog Rose
Brier Rose

moderate   6-12

P C Si Sa L
4 5 6 7 8
M P A W E
W WM M MD D
vT T M I vl
fast   short

barrier
border mass
hedge
naturalizing
screen
seacoast

5—9
Europe

Rosa foetida
Austrian Brier Rose

'Persiana'
"Bicolor"

moderate   6-12

P C Si Sa L
4 5 6 7 8
M P A W E
W WM M MD D
vT T M I vl
fast   short

barrier
border mass
colonial gardens
historic gardens
screen

3—10   c.b.1500
s.w. Asia

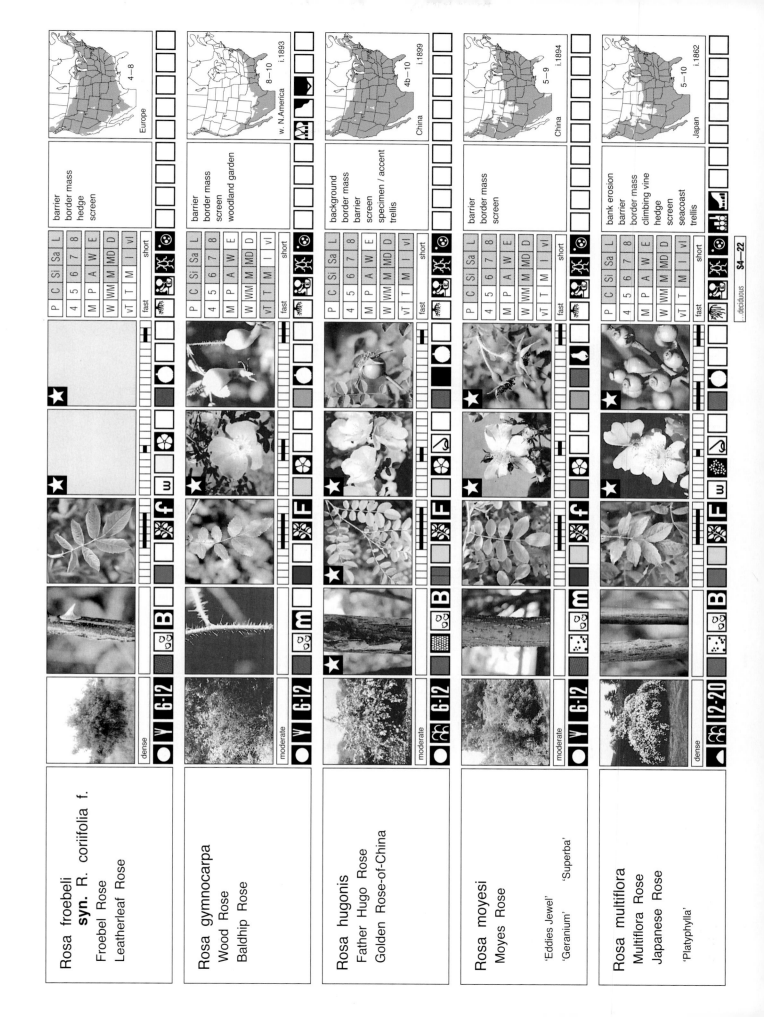

Rosa froebeli syn. R. coriifolia f.
Froebel Rose
Leatherleaf Rose

Europe 4—8

barrier
border mass
hedge
screen

Rosa gymnocarpa
Wood Rose
Baldhip Rose

w. N.America 8—10 i.1893

barrier
border mass
screen
woodland garden

Rosa hugonis
Father Hugo Rose
Golden Rose-of-China

China 4b—10 i.1899

background
border mass
barrier
screen
specimen / accent
trellis

Rosa moyesi
Moyes Rose
'Eddies Jewel'
'Geranium'   'Superba'

China 5—9 i.1894

barrier
border mass
screen

Rosa multiflora
Multiflora Rose
Japanese Rose
'Platyphylla'

Japan 5—10 i.1862

bank erosion
barrier
border mass
climbing vine
hedge
screen
seacoast
trellis

...deciduous **S4—22**

LARGE SHRUB	FORM	BARK	LEAF	FLOWER	FRUIT	CULTURE	USES	REGION
Rosa omeiensis Omei Rose	dense 6-12					P C Si Sa L 4 5 6 7 8 M P A W E W WM M MD D vT T M I vl fast short	barrier border mass kitchen garden screen	China 5 – 9 i:1901
Rosa primula Primrose Rose	dense 6-12					P C Si Sa L 4 5 6 7 8 M P A W E W WM M MD D vT T M I vl fast short	bank erosion barrier border mass screen	Turkey 4b–8a i:1910
Rosa roxburghi Roxburgh Rose Chestnut Rose	moderate 6-12					P C Si Sa L 4 5 6 7 8 M P A W E W WM M MD D vT T M I vl fast short	bank erosion barrier border mass screen	China 6b–9 i:1814
Rosa setigera Prairie Rose Climbing Rose	dense 6-12					P C Si Sa L 4 5 6 7 8 M P A W E W WM M MD D vT T M I vl fast short	above wall bank erosion barrier climbing vine hedge naturalizing reclamation screen	e. U.S. 4b–9 i.1810
Rubus alleghaniensis Allegany Blackberry	open 6-12					P C Si Sa L 4 5 6 7 8 M P A W E W WM M MD D vT T M I vl very fast very short	bank erosion barrier espalier kitchen garden naturalizing tall groundcover	e. U.S. 3b–10 c.1905

Rubus occidentalis
Blackcap Raspberry

bank erosion
barrier
espalier
kitchen garden
naturalizing
reclamation
tall groundcover

P	C	Si	Sa	L
4	5	6	7	8
M	P	A	W	E
W	WM	M	MD	D
vT	T	M	I	vl

fast · very short
open

3—8a · c.1696 · n.e. U.S.

Salix fargesi
Farges Willow

bog garden
seacoast

P	C	Si	Sa	L
4	5	6	7	8
M	P	A	W	E
W	WM	M	MD	D
vT	T	M	I	vl

moderate · short
moderate

6—8 · i.1911 · China

Salix humilis
Prairie Willow

background
border mass
edible leaves
seacoast
specimen / accent

P	C	Si	Sa	L
4	5	6	7	8
M	P	A	W	E
W	WM	M	MD	D
vT	T	M	I	vl

slow · short
moderate

2—9 · i.1876 · e. N.America

Salix purpurea
Purpleosier Willow
Basket Willow

'Gracilis' 'Pendula'
'Streamco'

background
basket weaving
bog garden
kitchen garden
specimen / accent

P	C	Si	Sa	L
4	5	6	7	8
M	P	A	W	E
W	WM	M	MD	D
vT	T	M	I	vl

moderate · short
dense

4—10 · i.1897 · Madagascar

Sambucus canadensis
American Elder
American Elderberry

'Adams' 'Nova'
'Aurea'' 'York'

aquatic garden
background
bank erosion
container
hedge
jams, jellies, wine
kitchen garden
reclamation

P	C	Si	Sa	L
4	5	6	7	8
M	P	A	W	E
W	WM	M	MD	D
vT	T	M	I	vl

fast · very short
open

3—9 · i.1761 · e. N.America

LARGE SHRUB	FORM	BARK	LEAF	FLOWER	FRUIT	CULTURE	USES	REGION

Sambucus racemosa
European Red Elder
Red Elderberry
'Plumosa Aurea'
'Arborescens'

open · 6-12

P	C	Si	Sa	L
4	5	6	7	8
M	P	A	W	E
W	WM	M	MD	D
vT	T	M	I	vI

fast · very short

bank erosion
bog garden
hedge
jams, jellies
screen
seacoast
specimen / accent
water garden

Europe · 3–7 · c.b.1600

Shepherdia argentea
Silver Bufflaloberry
'Commutata'

open · 12-20

P	C	Si	Sa	L
4	5	6	7	8
M	P	A	W	E
W	WM	M	MD	D
vT	T	M	I	vI

moderate · long

barrier
hedge
seacoast
windbreak

c N.America · 2–7 · i.1818

Sophora davidi syn. S. viciifolia
Vetch Sophora

open · 12-20

P	C	Si	Sa	L
4	5	6	7	8
M	P	A	W	E
W	WM	M	MD	D
vT	T	M	I	vI

moderate · moderate

bank erosion
barrier
specimen / accent

China · 6–9 · i.1897

Sorbaria aitchisoni
Kashmir False Spirea

moderate · 6-12

P	C	Si	Sa	L
4	5	6	7	8
M	P	A	W	E
W	WM	M	MD	D
vT	T	M	I	vI

fast · short

bank erosion
border mass
hedge
screen
shade garden
water garden
woodland garden

Afghanistan · 6–8 · i.1895

Sorbaria assurgens

moderate · 6-12

P	C	Si	Sa	L
4	5	6	7	8
M	P	A	W	E
W	WM	M	MD	D
vT	T	M	I	vI

fast · short

bank erosion
border mass
hedge
screen
shade garden
water garden
woodland garden

China · 5–8 · i.1896

Spiraea canescens — Hoary Spirea

Himalayas | 3–7 | i.1837

border mass · hedge · screen · seacoast · specimen / accent

moderate · fast · short · 6·12

P	C	Si	Sa	L
4	5	6	7	8
M	P	A	W	E
W	WM	M	MD	D
vT	T	M	I	vl

Spiraea x vanhouttei — Vanhoutte Spirea

hybrid | 3b–9 | o.1862

barrier · border mass · hedge · screen · seacoast · specimen / accent · windbreak

dense · fast · short · 6·12

P	C	Si	Sa	L
4	5	6	7	8
M	P	A	W	E
W	WM	M	MD	D
vT	T	M	I	vl

Spiraea veitchi — Veitch Spirea

China | 5b–9 | i.1900

background · border mass · hedge · screen · seacoast · specimen / accent · windbreak

dense · fast · short · 6·12

P	C	Si	Sa	L
4	5	6	7	8
M	P	A	W	E
W	WM	M	MD	D
vT	T	M	I	vl

Spiraea wilsoni — Wilson Spirea

China | 6–9 | i.1900

background · border mass · hedge · seacoast · screen · specimen / accent · windbreak

moderate · fast · short · 6·12

P	C	Si	Sa	L
4	5	6	7	8
M	P	A	W	E
W	WM	M	MD	D
vT	T	M	I	vl

Stachyurus praecox

Japan | 7–10 | i.1864

border mass · specimen / accent

open · slow · short · 6·12

P	C	Si	Sa	L
4	5	6	7	8
M	P	A	W	E
W	WM	M	MD	D
vT	T	M	I	vl

...deciduous

LARGE SHRUB

FORM	BARK	LEAF	FLOWER	FRUIT	CULTURE	USES	REGION

Staphylea bolanderi — Sierra Bladdernut

- CULTURE: P C Si Sa L / 4 5 6 7 8 / M P A W E / W WM M MD D / vT T M I vl — fast / short
- USES: border mass, preservation, screen, wild garden, woodland garden
- REGION: w. U.S. / 8–9 / i.1879
- FORM: moderate / 6-12

Staphylea colchica — Colchis Bladdernut

- CULTURE: P C Si Sa L / 4 5 6 7 8 / M P A W E / W WM M MD D / vT T M I vl — moderate / short
- USES: border mass, screen, specimen / accent, wild garden, woodland garden
- REGION: Caucasus / 6–8 / i.1850
- FORM: moderate / 6-12

Staphylea trifolia — American Bladdernut

- CULTURE: P C Si Sa L / 4 5 6 7 8 / M P A W E / W WM M MD D / vT T M I vl — moderate / short
- USES: border mass, screen, specimen / accent, wild garden, woodland garden
- REGION: e. U.S. / 4–7 / c.1640
- FORM: moderate / 6-12

Styrax wilsoni — Chinese Snowbell

- CULTURE: P C Si Sa L / 4 5 6 7 8 / M P A W E / W WM M MD D / vT T M I vl — moderate / short
- USES: border mass, screen, specimen / accent
- REGION: China / 6–8 / i.1908
- FORM: dense / 12-20

Symphoricarpos microphyllus — Pink Snowberry

- CULTURE: P C Si Sa L / 4 5 6 7 8 / M P A W E / W WM M MD D / vT T M I vl — fast / short
- USES: above wall, bank erosion, fruit arrangements, seacoast, specimen / accent
- REGION: Mexico / 4–8 / i.1910
- FORM: dense / 6-12

Symphoricarpos rivularis
syn. S. albus laevigatus
Waxberry

w. N.America · i.1817 · 4—7

above wall / bank erosion / fruit arrangements / seacoast / specimen / accent

P	C	Si	Sa	L
4	5	6	7	8
M	P	A	W	E
W	WM	M	MD	D
vT	T	M	I	vI

fast · very short

dense · 12-20

Syringa × josiflexa
'Pallida'

hybrid · c.1938 · (2b)—7

background / border mass / cut flowers / hedge / screen / specimen / accent / windbreak

P	C	Si	Sa	L
4	5	6	7	8
M	P	A	W	E
W	WM	M	MD	D
vT	T	M	I	vI

moderate · moderate

dense · 6-12

Syringa josikaea
Hungarian Lilac

Hungary · i.1830 · 2b—7

background / border mass / cut flowers / hedge / screen / shearing / windbreak

P	C	Si	Sa	L
4	5	6	7	8
M	P	A	W	E
W	WM	M	MD	D
vT	T	M	I	vI

moderate · moderate

dense · 6-12

Syringa oblata dilatata
Korean Early Lilac

Korea · i.1917 · 4—7

background / border mass / cut flowers / hedge / screen / specimen / accent / windbreak

P	C	Si	Sa	L
4	5	6	7	8
M	P	A	W	E
W	WM	M	MD	D
vT	T	M	I	vI

long · moderate

dense · 6-12

Syringa patula
Manchurian Lilac
'Miss Kim'

Korea · 3—7

background / border mass / cut flowers / hedge / screen / standard / windbreak

P	C	Si	Sa	L
4	5	6	7	8
M	P	A	W	E
W	WM	M	MD	D
vT	T	M	I	vI

moderate · moderate

...deciduous S4—28

..deciduous **S4—29**

LARGE SHRUB	FORM	BARK	LEAF	FLOWER	FRUIT	CULTURE	USES	REGION

Syringa potanini
Potanin Lilac

dense

CULTURE:
P C Si Sa L
4 5 6 7 8
M P A W E
W WM M MD D
vT T M I vl
moderate · moderate

USES:
background
border mass
cut flowers
hedge
screen

REGION: China · 6–7 · i.1905

Syringa reflexa
Nodding Lilac

dense

CULTURE:
P C Si Sa L
4 5 6 7 8
M P A W E
W WM M MD D
vT T M I vl
moderate · moderate

USES:
background
border mass
cut flowers
hedge
seacoast
screen
specimen / accent
windbreak

REGION: China · 5–7 · i.1904

Syringa x swegiflexa
Swegiflexa Lilac
Pink Pearl Lilac
'James McFarland'

dense

CULTURE:
P C Si Sa L
4 5 6 7 8
M P A W E
W WM M MD D
vT T M I vl
moderate · moderate

USES:
background
border mass
cut flowers
hedge
screen
specimen / accent
windbreak

REGION: hybrid · 5b–7 · o.1934

Syringa villosa
Late Lilac

dense

CULTURE:
P C Si Sa L
4 5 6 7 8
M P A W E
W WM M MD D
vT T M I vl
moderate · moderate

USES:
background
border mass
cut flowers
hedge
screen
specimen / accent
windbreak

REGION: China · 3–7 · i.1882

Vaccinium parvifolium
Red Whortleberry
Red Huckleberry

open

CULTURE:
P C Si Sa L
4 5 6 7 8
M P A W E
W WM M MD D
vT T M I vl
slow · short

USES:
cut flowers
hedge
jams, pies
kitchen garden

REGION: w. N.America · 5–8 · i.1881

Viburnum alnifolium
Hobblebush Viburnum

border mass
shade garden
specimen / accent
woodland garden

P	C	Si	Sa	L
4	5	6	7	8
M	P	A	W	E
W	WM	M	MD	D
vT	T	M	I	vl

moderate / short

dense

e. N.America   i.1820   3b–6

6-12

Viburnum bitchiuense
Yeddo Viburnum

border mass
hedge
screen
specimen / accent

P	C	Si	Sa	L
4	5	6	7	8
M	P	A	W	E
W	WM	M	MD	D
vT	T	M	I	vl

slow / short

open

Japan   i.1911   4b–8a

6-12

Viburnum x bodnantense
'Dawn'

border mass
hedge
screen
specimen / accent

P	C	Si	Sa	L
4	5	6	7	8
M	P	A	W	E
W	WM	M	MD	D
vT	T	M	I	vl

fast / short

open

hybrid   o.1935   (6b)–10

6-12

Viburnum x carlcephalum
Fragrant Snowball

border mass
espalier
hedge
screen
specimen / accent

P	C	Si	Sa	L
4	5	6	7	8
M	P	A	W	E
W	WM	M	MD	D
vT	T	M	I	vl

moderate / short

moderate

hybrid   o.1930   5–8

6-12

Viburnum dentatum
Arrowwood Viburnum

bog garden
border mass
hedge
naturalizing
screen
seacoast
shade garden
woodland garden

P	C	Si	Sa	L
4	5	6	7	8
M	P	A	W	E
W	WM	M	MD	D
vT	T	M	I	vl

moderate / short

dense

e. N.America   i.1735   4–9

6-12

LARGE SHRUB	FORM	BARK	LEAF	FLOWER	FRUIT	CULTURE	USES	REGION

Viburnum dilatatum
Linden Viburnum

'Erie'
'Oneida'

- FORM: dense 12-20
- CULTURE:

P	C	Si	Sa	L
4	5	6	7	8
M	P	A	W	E
W	WM	M	MD	D
vT	T	M	I	vl

moderate / short

- USES: border mass, hedge, screen, specimen / accent
- REGION: Japan, 5—8, i.1845

Viburnum ellipticum
Oregon Viburnum

- FORM: moderate 6-12
- CULTURE:

P	C	Si	Sa	L
4	5	6	7	8
M	P	A	W	E
W	WM	M	MD	D
vT	T	M	I	vl

fast / short

- USES: border mass, hedge, naturalizing, screen, shade garden, woodland garden
- REGION: n.w. U.S., 4—8, i.1908

Viburnum farreri
syn. V. fragrans
Fragrant Viburnum

'Bowles'
'Nanum'

- FORM: open 6-12
- CULTURE:

P	C	Si	Sa	L
4	5	6	7	8
M	P	A	W	E
W	WM	M	MD	D
vT	T	M	I	vl

fast / short

- USES: border mass, hedge, screen, specimen / accent
- REGION: China, 5—10, i.1910

Viburnum x juddi
Judd Viburnum

- FORM: dense 12-20
- CULTURE:

P	C	Si	Sa	L
4	5	6	7	8
M	P	A	W	E
W	WM	M	MD	D
vT	T	M	I	vl

fast / short

- USES: background, border mass, hedge, screen, specimen / accent
- REGION: hybrid, 4b—8, o.1920

Viburnum plicatum
      tomentosum
Doublefile Viburnum

'Casade'   'Shasta'
'Mariesii'   'Watanabe'

- FORM: moderate 12-20
- CULTURE:

P	C	Si	Sa	L
4	5	6	7	8
M	P	A	W	E
W	WM	M	MD	D
vT	T	M	I	vl

moderate / short

- USES: border mass, patio garden, screen, sculptural, specimen / accent
- REGION: Japan / China, (5b)—8, i.1865

Viburnum sargenti
Sargent Viburnum
Sargent Cranberrybush
'Onandago'
'Susquehanna'

Asia
(3b)—8
i.1892

border mass
hedge
kitchen garden
screen
specimen / accent
woodland garden

P	C	Si	Sa	L
4	5	6	7	8
M	P	A	W	E
W	WM	M	MD	D
vT	T	M	I	vl

moderate   short

moderate

6-12

Viburnum setigerum
Tea Viburnum
'Aurantiacum'

China
(5b)—8
i.1901

border mass
hedge
kitchen garden
screen
specimen / accent

P	C	Si	Sa	L
4	5	6	7	8
M	P	A	W	E
W	WM	M	MD	D
vT	T	M	I	vl

moderate   short

open

6-12

Viburnum trilobum
'Compactum'
Compact Cranberrybush
Viburnum

cultivar
3—8a

border mass
formal garden
hedge
kitchen garden
screen
shade garden
shearing
specimen / accent

P	C	Si	Sa	L
4	5	6	7	8
M	P	A	W	E
W	WM	M	MD	D
vT	T	M	I	vl

fast   short

dense

6-12

Viburnum wrighti
Wright Viburnum

Japan
(5b)—8
i.1892

border mass
hedge
screen
specimen / accent

P	C	Si	Sa	L
4	5	6	7	8
M	P	A	W	E
W	WM	M	MD	D
vT	T	M	I	vl

moderate   short

moderate-open

6-12

Weigela florida
Old-fashioned Weigela
'Pink Delight'   'Vanidek'
'Rosea'   'Variegata'

Korea
(4b)—9a
i.1845

background
border mass
colonial garden
historic garden
pool garden
screen

P	C	Si	Sa	L
4	5	6	7	8
M	P	A	W	E
W	WM	M	MD	D
vT	T	M	I	vl

fast   very short

moderate

6-12

...deciduous

S4—32

LARGE SHRUB	FORM	BARK	LEAF	FLOWER	FRUIT	CULTURE	USES	REGION
Wigandia caracasana Caracas Wigandia	 open 6-12	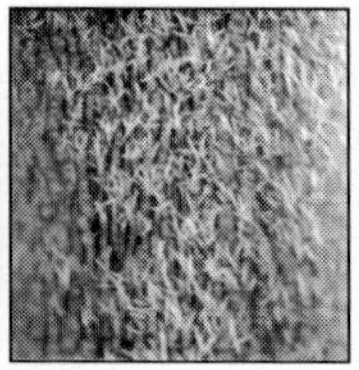				P C Si Sa L 4 5 6 7 8 M P A W E W WM M MD D vT T M I vl very fast very short	specimen / accent	
						P C Si Sa L 4 5 6 7 8 M P A W E W WM M MD D vT T M I vl		
						P C Si Sa L 4 5 6 7 8 M P A W E W WM M MD D vT T M I vl		
						P C Si Sa L 4 5 6 7 8 M P A W E W WM M MD D vT T M I vl		
						P C Si Sa L 4 5 6 7 8 M P A W E W WM M MD D vT T M I vl		

MEDIUM SHRUB	FORM	BARK	LEAF	FLOWER	FRUIT	CULTURE	USES	REGION

Abelia chinensis
Chinese Abelia

	P	C	Si	Sa	L
	4	5	6	7	8
	M	P	A	W	E
	W	WM	M	MD	D
	vT	T	M	I	vl

dense · 3-6 · fast

bank erosion
border mass
container
hedge
seacoast
specimen / accent

China · 8–10 · c.1844

Abelia schumanni
Schumann Abelia

	P	C	Si	Sa	L
	4	5	6	7	8
	M	P	A	W	E
	W	WM	M	MD	D
	vT	T	M	I	vl

dense · 3-6 · fast

bank erosion
border mass
container
hedge
seacoast
specimen / accent

central China · 7–9 · i.1910

Abeliophllum distichum
Korean Abelialeaf
White Forsythia

	P	C	Si	Sa	L
	4	5	6	7	8
	M	P	A	W	E
	W	WM	M	MD	D
	vT	T	M	I	vl

dense · 3-6

border edge
cut flowers
hedge
seacoast
specimen / accent

Korea · 5–8 · i.1924

Adina rubella

	P	C	Si	Sa	L
	4	5	6	7	8
	M	P	A	W	E
	W	WM	M	MD	D
	vT	T	M	I	vl

moderate

specimen / accent

s. China · 6b–9a

Amelanchier sanguinea
Roundleaved Serviceberry

	P	C	Si	Sa	L
	4	5	6	7	8
	M	P	A	W	E
	W	WM	M	MD	D
	vT	T	M	I	vl

dense · 6-12 · moderate · short

bank erosion
border mass
hedge
specimen / accent
reclamation
windbreak

n. U.S. · 4–8 · i.1824

Amelanchier stolonifera
Running Serviceberry

n. U.S. 4–8a i.1883

bank erosion
border mass
groundcover
low maintenance
reclamation

moderate / short

dense

6-12

P	C	Si	Sa	L
4	5	6	7	8
M	P	A	W	E
W	WM	M	MD	D
vT	T	M	I	vl

Aronia melanocarpa
Black Chokeberry
'Elata'

n. U.S. 3b–7 i.1700

bank erosion
border mass
groundcover
naturalizing
low maintenance
reclamation

slow / short

open

3-6

P	C	Si	Sa	L
4	5	6	7	8
M	P	A	W	E
W	WM	M	MD	D
vT	T	M	I	vl

Artemisia absinthium
Absinthe
Common Wormwood
'Huntington Gardens'
'Lambrook Silver'

n.e. U.S. 4–8 long c.

aromatic leaves
border mass
dried flowers
edging
herb garden
kitchen garden
medicinal
seacoast

fast / very short

open

3-6

P	C	Si	Sa	L
4	5	6	7	8
M	P	A	W	E
W	WM	M	MD	D
vT	T	M	I	vl

Artemisia californica
California Sagebrush
'Canyon Grey'

California 4–10

aromatic leaves
bank erosion
border edging
border mass
naturalizing

fast / very short

open

3-6

P	C	Si	Sa	L
4	5	6	7	8
M	P	A	W	E
W	WM	M	MD	D
vT	T	M	I	vl

Artemisia lactiflora
White Mugwort

China 4–8

aromatic leaves
border edge
border mass
naturalizing

fast / very short

open

3-6

P	C	Si	Sa	L
4	5	6	7	8
M	P	A	W	E
W	WM	M	MD	D
vT	T	M	I	vl

...deciduous S3–2

MEDIUM SHRUB	FORM	BARK	LEAF	FLOWER	FRUIT	CULTURE	USES	REGION

Artemisia pontica
Roman Wormwood

FORM: open · 3-6
CULTURE: P C Si Sa L / 4 5 6 7 8 / M P A W E / W WM M MD D / vT T M I vl · fast · very short
USES: aromatic leaves · border edging · border mass · herb garden · kitchen garden
REGION: s.e. Europe · 4—8 · c.1810

Berberis beaniana
Bean's Barberry

FORM: dense · 3-6
CULTURE: P C Si Sa L / 4 5 6 7 8 / M P A W E / W WM M MD D / vT T M I vl · fast · short
USES: bank erosion · barrier · border mass · hedge · specimen / accent
REGION: w. China · 6—9 · i.1904

Berberis gilgiana
Wildfire Barberry

FORM: dense · 3-6
CULTURE: P C Si Sa L / 4 5 6 7 8 / M P A W E / W WM M MD D / vT T M I vl · fast · short
USES: bank erosion · barrier · border mass · hedge · specimen / accent
REGION: China · 5—8a · i.1910

Berberis koreana
Korean Barberry

FORM: dense · 3-6
CULTURE: P C Si Sa L / 4 5 6 7 8 / M P A W E / W WM M MD D / vT T M I vl · fast · short
USES: barrier · border mass · hedge · specimen / accent
REGION: Korea · 4—(8a) · i.1905

Berberis thunbergi
Japanese Barberry

'Aurea'   Rosy Glow'
'Erecta'

FORM: dense · 3-6
CULTURE: P C Si Sa L / 4 5 6 7 8 / M P A W E / W WM M MD D / vT T M I vl · fast · short
USES: bank erosion · barrier · border mass · hedge · seacoast · specimen / accent
REGION: Japan · 4—9 · i.1883

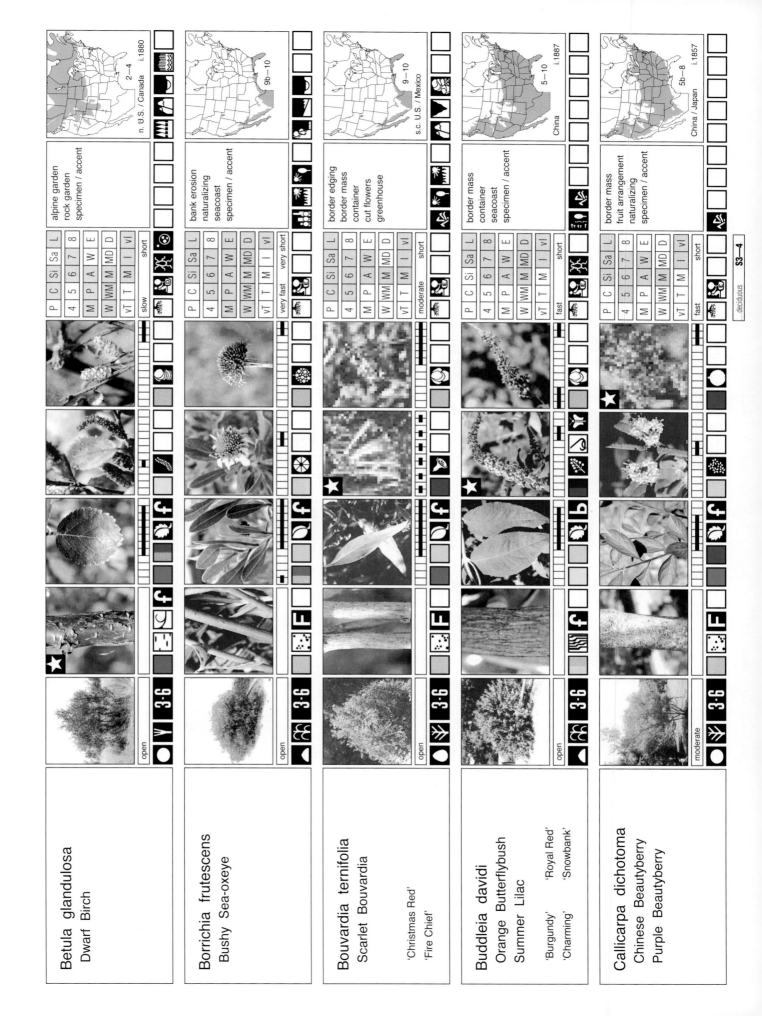

Betula glandulosa — Dwarf Birch

alpine garden / rock garden / specimen / accent

n. U.S. / Canada   i.1880   2–4

P	C	Si	Sa	L
4	5	6	7	8
M	P	A	W	E
W	WM	M	MD	D
vT	T	M	I	vI

slow / short

open — 3·6

Borrichia frutescens — Bushy Sea-oxeye

bank erosion / naturalizing / seacoast / specimen / accent

9b–10

P	C	Si	Sa	L
4	5	6	7	8
M	P	A	W	E
W	WM	M	MD	D
vT	T	M	I	vI

very fast / very short

open — 3·6

Bouvardia ternifolia — Scarlet Bouvardia

'Christmas Red'
'Fire Chief'

border edging / border mass / container / cut flowers / greenhouse

s.c. U.S. / Mexico   9–10

P	C	Si	Sa	L
4	5	6	7	8
M	P	A	W	E
W	WM	M	MD	D
vT	T	M	I	vI

moderate / short

open — 3·6

Buddleia davidi — Orange Butterflybush / Summer Lilac

'Burgundy'   'Royal Red'
'Charming'   'Snowbank'

border mass / container / seacoast / specimen / accent

China   i.1887   5–10

P	C	Si	Sa	L
4	5	6	7	8
M	P	A	W	E
W	WM	M	MD	D
vT	T	M	I	vI

fast / short

open — 3·6

Callicarpa dichotoma — Chinese Beautyberry / Purple Beautyberry

border mass / fruit arrangement / naturalizing / specimen / accent

China / Japan   i.1857   5b–8

P	C	Si	Sa	L
4	5	6	7	8
M	P	A	W	E
W	WM	M	MD	D
vT	T	M	I	vI

fast / short

moderate — 3·6

...deciduous   S3—4

MEDIUM SHRUB	FORM	BARK	LEAF	FLOWER	FRUIT	CULTURE	USES	REGION

Callicarpa japonica
Japanese Beautyberry
'Leucocarpa'

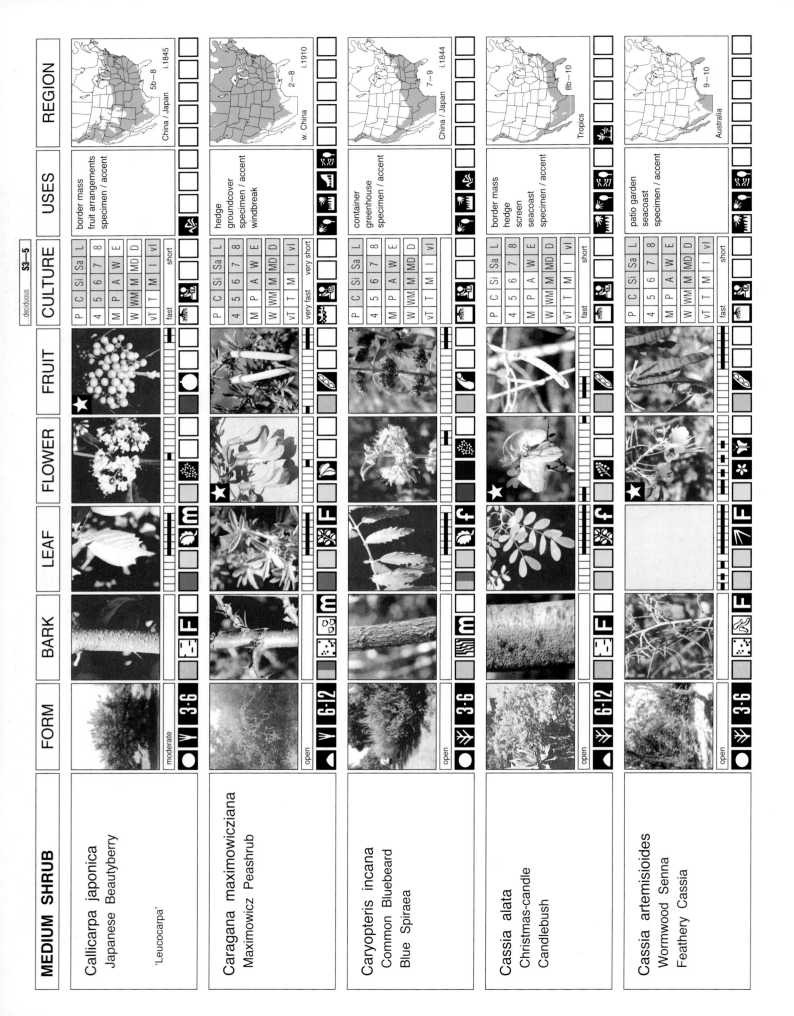

FORM: moderate 3-6

CULTURE:
P	C	Si	Sa	L
4	5	6	7	8
M	P	A	W	E
W	WM	M	MD	D
vT	T	M	I	vI
fast short

USES: border mass / fruit arrangements / specimen / accent

REGION: China / Japan 5b—8 i.1845

Caragana maximowicziana
Maximowicz Peashrub

FORM: open 6-12

CULTURE:
P	C	Si	Sa	L
4	5	6	7	8
M	P	A	W	E
W	WM	M	MD	D
vT	T	M	I	vI
very fast very short

USES: hedge / groundcover / specimen / accent / windbreak

REGION: w. China 2—8 i.1910

Caryopteris incana
Common Bluebeard
Blue Spiraea

FORM: open 3-6

CULTURE:
P	C	Si	Sa	L
4	5	6	7	8
M	P	A	W	E
W	WM	M	MD	D
vT	T	M	I	vI

USES: container / greenhouse / specimen / accent

REGION: China / Japan 7—9 i.1844

Cassia alata
Christmas-candle
Candlebush

FORM: open 6-12

CULTURE:
P	C	Si	Sa	L
4	5	6	7	8
M	P	A	W	E
W	WM	M	MD	D
vT	T	M	I	vI
fast short

USES: border mass / hedge / screen / seacoast / specimen / accent

REGION: Tropics 8b—10

Cassia artemisioides
Wormwood Senna
Feathery Cassia

FORM: open 3-6

CULTURE:
P	C	Si	Sa	L
4	5	6	7	8
M	P	A	W	E
W	WM	M	MD	D
vT	T	M	I	vI
fast short

USES: patio garden / seacoast / specimen / accent

REGION: Australia 9—10

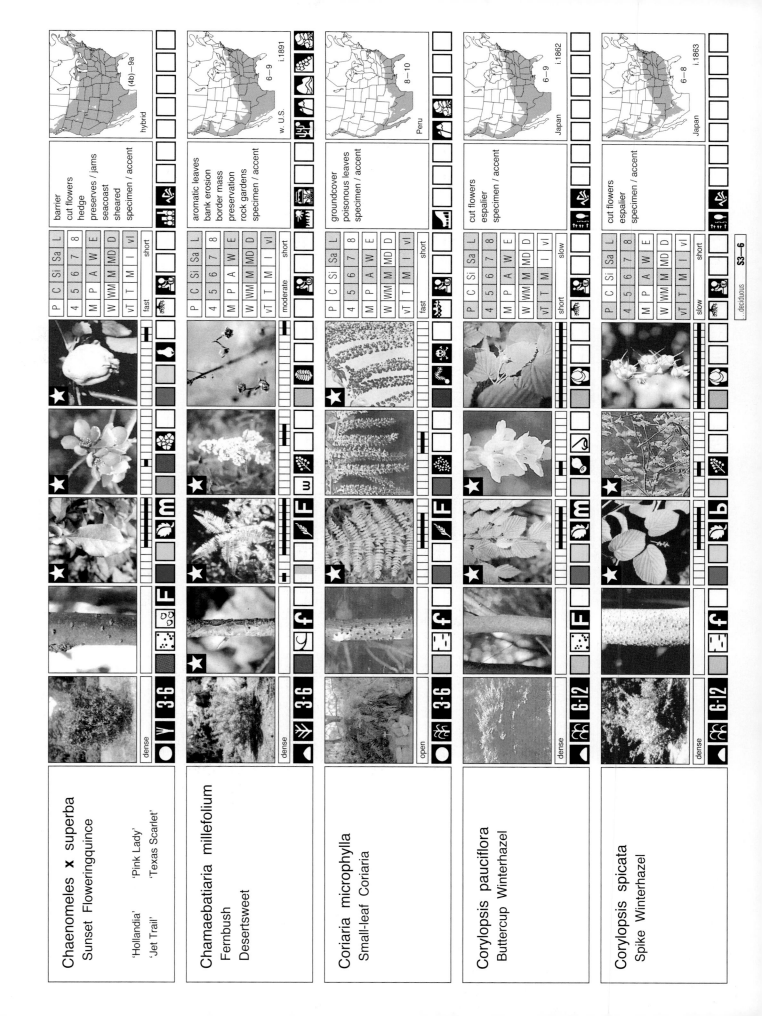

Chaenomeles **x** superba
Sunset Floweringquince

'Hollandia'   'Pink Lady'
'Jet Trail'   'Texas Scarlet'

barrier
cut flowers
hedge
preserves / jams
seacoast
sheared
specimen / accent

hybrid   (4b)—9a

Chamaebatiaria millefolium
Fernbush
Desertsweet

aromatic leaves
bank erosion
border mass
preservation
rock gardens
specimen / accent

w. U.S.   6—9   i.1891

Coriaria microphylla
Small-leaf Coriaria

groundcover
poisonous leaves
specimen / accent

Peru   8—10

Corylopsis pauciflora
Buttercup Winterhazel

cut flowers
espalier
specimen / accent

Japan   6—9   i.1862

Corylopsis spicata
Spike Winterhazel

cut flowers
espalier
specimen / accent

Japan   6—8   i.1863

...deciduous   S3—6

MEDIUM SHRUB | FORM | BARK | LEAF | FLOWER | FRUIT | CULTURE | USES | REGION

Corylopsis veitchiana — Veitch Winterhazel

- FORM: moderate, 3–6
- USES: espalier; specimen / accent
- REGION: w. China; 6–9a; i.1900

Cotoneaster dielsiana — Diel's Cotoneaster
'Major'

- FORM: open, 6–12
- CULTURE: moderate
- USES: bank erosion; espalier; hedge; seacoast; specimen / accent
- REGION: w. China; 6–8; i.1900

Cotoneaster divaricata — Spreading Cotoneaster

- FORM: dense, 6–12
- CULTURE: short
- USES: bank erosion; border mass; espalier; hedge; screen; seacoast; specimen / accent
- REGION: China; 5–8; i.1904

Cotoneaster integerrimus — European Cotoneaster

- FORM: open, 6–12
- CULTURE: moderate, short
- USES: bank erosion; border mass; espalier; hedge; screen; seacoast; specimen / accent
- REGION: n. Europe; 6–9; i.1783

Cotoneaster zabeli — Cherryberry Cotoneaster

- FORM: open, 6–12
- CULTURE: moderate, short
- USES: bank erosion; border mass; espalier; hedge; screen; seacoast; specimen / accent; woolly leaves
- REGION: China; 5–7; i.1907

CULTURE legend (per card):
P C Si Sa L / 4 5 6 7 8 / M P A W E / W WM M MD D / vT T M I vl

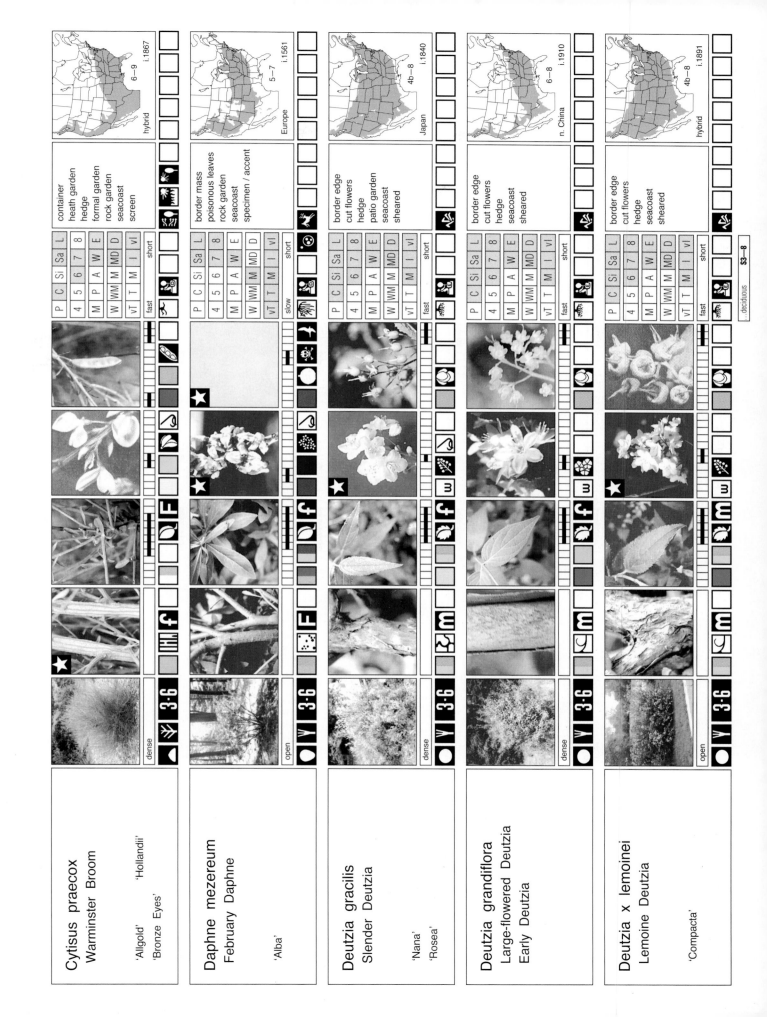

Cytisus praecox — Warminster Broom
'Allgold' 'Hollandii'
'Bronze Eyes'

hybrid i.1867 6–9

container
heath garden
hedge
formal garden
rock garden
seacoast
screen

P	C	Si	Sa	L
4	5	6	7	8
M	P	A	W	E
W	WM	M	MD	D
vT	T	M	I	vI

fast short
dense
3-6

Daphne mezereum — February Daphne
'Alba'

Europe i.1561 5–7

border mass
poisonous leaves
rock garden
seacoast
specimen / accent

P	C	Si	Sa	L
4	5	6	7	8
M	P	A	W	E
W	WM	M	MD	D
vT	T	M	I	vI

slow short
open
3-6

Deutzia gracilis — Slender Deutzia
'Nana'
'Rosea'

Japan i.1840 4b–8

border edge
cut flowers
hedge
patio garden
seacoast
sheared

P	C	Si	Sa	L
4	5	6	7	8
M	P	A	W	E
W	WM	M	MD	D
vT	T	M	I	vI

fast short
dense
3-6

Deutzia grandiflora — Large-flowered Deutzia
Early Deutzia

n. China i.1910 6–8

border edge
cut flowers
hedge
seacoast
sheared

P	C	Si	Sa	L
4	5	6	7	8
M	P	A	W	E
W	WM	M	MD	D
vT	T	M	I	vI

fast short
dense
3-6

Deutzia x lemoinei — Lemoine Deutzia
'Compacta'

hybrid i.1891 4b–8

border edge
cut flowers
hedge
seacoast
sheared

P	C	Si	Sa	L
4	5	6	7	8
M	P	A	W	E
W	WM	M	MD	D
vT	T	M	I	vI

fast short
open
3-6

...deciduous   S3—8

MEDIUM SHRUB

MEDIUM SHRUB	FORM	BARK	LEAF	FLOWER	FRUIT	CULTURE	USES	REGION
Deutzia parviflora Mongolian Deutzia	dense · 3-6					P C Si Sa L / 4 5 6 7 8 / M P A W E / W WM M MD D / vT T M I vl · fast / short	border edge, cut flowers, hedge, seacoast, sheared	Korea · 4b—8a · i:1883
Deutzia x rosea Rosepanicle Deutzia Rose Deutzia 'Carminea' 'Eximia'	moderate · 3-6					P C Si Sa L / 4 5 6 7 8 / M P A W E / W WM M MD D / vT T M I vl · fast / short	border edge, cut flowers, hedge, seacoast, sheared	hybrid · 5—8
Dirca palustris Atlantic Leatherwood Moosewood	dense · 3-6					P C Si Sa L / 4 5 6 7 8 / M P A W E / W WM M MD D / vT T M I vl · slow / short	sculptural, specimen / accent	e. U.S. · 4—8a · i.1750
Elaeagnus multiflorus Cherry Elaeagnus Gumi	dense · 6-12					P C Si Sa L / 4 5 6 7 8 / M P A W E / W WM M MD D / vT T M I vl · fast / short	background mass, bank erosion, barrier, hedge, roadside, seacoast, specimen / accent, windbreak	China / Japan · 5—9 · i.1862
Elsholtzia stauntoni Staunton Elsholtzia Mintshrub	dense · 3-6					P C Si Sa L / 4 5 6 7 8 / M P A W E / W WM M MD D / vT T M I vl · fast / short	aromatic leaves, border mass, container, seacoast	n. China · 5—7a · i.1909

P	C	Si	Sa	L
4	5	6	7	8
M	P	A	W	E
W	WM	M	MD	D
vT	T	M	I	vl

Enkianthus perulatus
White Enkianthus

Japan i.1859 6–9

container
specimen / accent

slow moderate

dense 6-12

P	C	Si	Sa	L
4	5	6	7	8
M	P	A	W	E
W	WM	M	MD	D
vT	T	M	I	vl

Fallugia paradoxa
Apache Plume

s.w. U.S. 6–9

background
bank erosion
hedge
screen
sheared
specimen / accent
windbreak
woolly leaves

moderate moderate

dense 3-6

P	C	Si	Sa	L
4	5	6	7	8
M	P	A	W	E
W	WM	M	MD	D
vT	T	M	I	vl

Fendlera rupicola
Cliff Fendlerbush

s. central U.S. 5–8

border mass
preservation
specimen / accent

moderate moderate

open 3-6

P	C	Si	Sa	L
4	5	6	7	8
M	P	A	W	E
W	WM	M	MD	D
vT	T	M	I	vl

Forsythia ovata
Early Forsythia
Korean Forsythia

'Ottawa'
'Tetragold'

Korea (4b)–7a i.1918

bank erosion
border mass
hedge
seacoast
specimen / accent

fast short

dense 6-12

P	C	Si	Sa	L
4	5	6	7	8
M	P	A	W	E
W	WM	M	MD	D
vT	T	M	I	vl

Fothergilla monticola
Alabama Fothergilla

s. U.S. (5b)–9 i.1889

naturalizing
shade garden
specimen / accent
woodland garden

slow short

moderate 6-12

...deciduous **S3—10**

MEDIUM SHRUB	FORM	BARK	LEAF	FLOWER	FRUIT	CULTURE	USES	REGION

Halimodendron
halodendron
Siberian Salttree

open | 6-12

CULTURE: P C Si Sa L · 4 5 6 7 8 · M P A W E · W WM M MD D · vT T M I vl · fast · short
USES: barrier · seacoast · woolly leaves
REGION: Turkey · 3–6 · i.1779

Holodiscus dumosus
Rockspiraea
Mountainspray

open | 6-12

CULTURE: P C Si Sa L · 4 5 6 7 8 · M P A W E · W WM M MD D · vT T M I vl · fast · short
USES: background · border mass · hedge · seacoast · specimen / accent
REGION: w. U.S. · 5–7 · i.1879

Hydrangea arborescens
Smooth Hydrangea
Sevenbark
'Annabelle'
radiata

open | 3-6

CULTURE: P C Si Sa L · 4 5 6 7 8 · M P A W E · W WM M MD D · vT T M I vl · fast · very short
USES: border mass · cut flowers · hedge · poisonous leaves · seacoast · specimen / accent
REGION: e. U.S. · 4–9a · i.1736

Hydrangea arborescens 'Grandiflora'
Snowhill Hydrangea
Hills-of-Snow

open | 3-6

CULTURE: P C Si Sa L · 4 5 6 7 8 · M P A W E · W WM M MD D · vT T M I vl · fast · short
USES: border mass · cut flowers · hedge · poisonous leaves · seacoast · specimen / accent
REGION: cultivar · 4–9 · c.b.1900

Hydrangea aspera
Roughleaved Hydrangea
'Robusta'
sargentiana

open | 3-6

CULTURE: P C Si Sa L · 4 5 6 7 8 · M P A W E · W WM M MD D · vT T M I vl · slow · short
USES: container · cut flowers · poisonous leaves · seacoast
REGION: w. China · 7–9 · i.1907

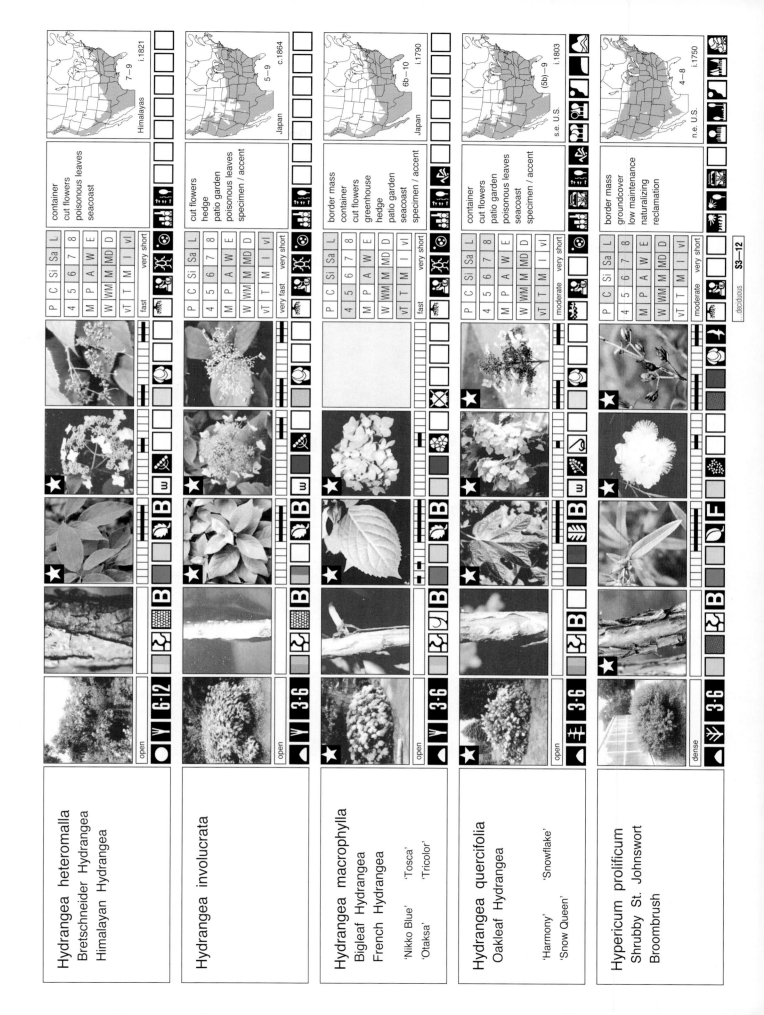

Hydrangea heteromalla
Bretschneider Hydrangea
Himalayan Hydrangea

Himalayas — 7–9 — i.1821

container
cut flowers
poisonous leaves
seacoast

P	C	Si	Sa	L
4	5	6	7	8
M	P	A	W	E
W	WM	M	MD	D
vT	T	M	I	vl

fast — very short

open — 6·12

Hydrangea involucrata

Japan — 5–9 — c.1864

cut flowers
hedge
patio garden
poisonous leaves
specimen / accent

P	C	Si	Sa	L
4	5	6	7	8
M	P	A	W	E
W	WM	M	MD	D
vT	T	M	I	vl

very fast — very short

open — 3·6

Hydrangea macrophylla
Bigleaf Hydrangea
French Hydrangea

'Nikko Blue'   'Tosca'
'Otaksa'   'Tricolor'

Japan — 6b–10 — i.1790

border mass
container
cut flowers
greenhouse
hedge
patio garden
seacoast
specimen / accent

P	C	Si	Sa	L
4	5	6	7	8
M	P	A	W	E
W	WM	M	MD	D
vT	T	M	I	vl

very fast — very short

open — 3·6

Hydrangea quercifolia
Oakleaf Hydrangea

'Harmony'   'Snowflake'
'Snow Queen'

s.e. U.S. — (5b)–9 — i.1803

container
cut flowers
patio garden
poisonous leaves
seacoast
specimen / accent

P	C	Si	Sa	L
4	5	6	7	8
M	P	A	W	E
W	WM	M	MD	D
vT	T	M	I	vl

fast — moderate   very short

open — 3·6

Hypericum prolificum
Shrubby St. Johnswort
Broombrush

n.e. U.S. — 4–8 — i.1750

border mass
groundcover
low maintenance
naturalizing
reclamation

P	C	Si	Sa	L
4	5	6	7	8
M	P	A	W	E
W	WM	M	MD	D
vT	T	M	I	vl

moderate — very short

dense — 3·6

MEDIUM SHRUB	FORM	BARK	LEAF	FLOWER	FRUIT	CULTURE	USES	REGION

Hyptis emoryi
Desert Lavender
Bee Sage

USES: aromatic leaves, naturalizing, reclamation, woolly leaves

CULTURE: P C Si Sa L / 4 5 6 7 8 / M P A W E / W WM M MD D / vT T M I vI — very fast / very short

FORM: open — 6-12

REGION: s.w. U.S. — 9–10 — i.1874

Indigofera amblyantha
Pink Indigo

USES: hedge

CULTURE: P C Si Sa L / 4 5 6 7 8 / M P A W E / W WM M MD D / vT T M I vI — fast / short

FORM: open — 3-6

REGION: China — 5–9 — i.1908

Itea virginica
Virginia Sweetspire

'Henry's Garnet'

USES: aromatic leaves, border mass, naturalizing, screen, seacoast, specimen / accent

CULTURE: P C Si Sa L / 4 5 6 7 8 / M P A W E / W WM M MD D / vT T M I vI — slow / very short

FORM: dense — 6-12

REGION: e. U.S. — 5b–9 — i.1774

Jasminum beesianum
Bees Jasmine
Pink Jasmine

USES: climbing vine, container, fence, greenhouse, groundcover, hedge

CULTURE: P C Si Sa L / 4 5 6 7 8 / M P A W E / W WM M MD D / vT T M I vI — very fast / short

FORM: open — 3-6

REGION: w. China — 7–10 — i.1906

Kerria japonica
Japanese Rose
Japanese Kerria

'Picta'   'Shannon'
'Pleniflora' 'Variegata'

USES: border mass, groundcover, seacoast, screen, specimen / accent, woodland garden

CULTURE: P C Si Sa L / 4 5 6 7 8 / M P A W E / W WM M MD D / vT T M I vI — fast / short

FORM: dense — 6-12

REGION: China / Japan — 5–9 — i.1834

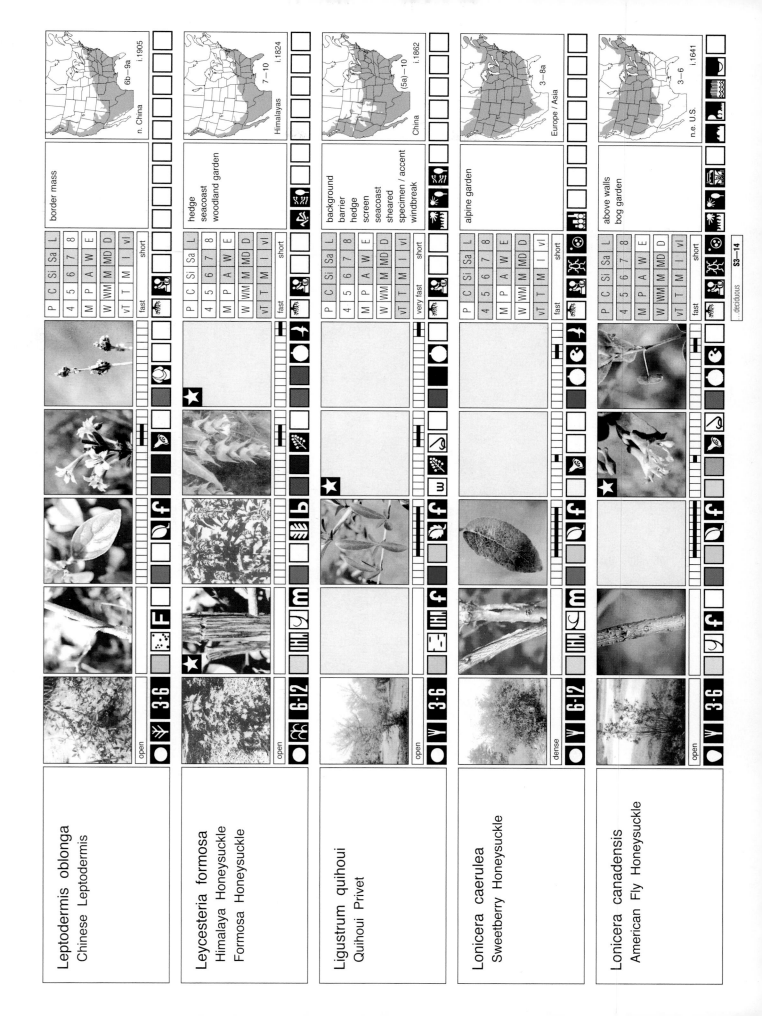

Leptodermis oblonga
Chinese Leptodermis

border mass

n. China
6b–9a   i.1905

Leycesteria formosa
Himalaya Honeysuckle
Formosa Honeysuckle

hedge
seacoast
woodland garden

Himalayas
7–10   i.1824

Ligustrum quihoui
Quihoui Privet

background
barrier
hedge
screen
seacoast
sheared
specimen / accent
windbreak

China
(5a)–10   i.1862

Lonicera caerulea
Sweetberry Honeysuckle

alpine garden

Europe / Asia
3–8a

Lonicera canadensis
American Fly Honeysuckle

above walls
bog garden

n.e. U.S.
3–6   i.1641

...deciduous   S3–14

MEDIUM SHRUB	FORM	BARK	LEAF	FLOWER	FRUIT	CULTURE	USES	REGION

Lonicera morrowi
Morrow Honeysuckle

'Xanthocarpa'

dense · 6-12

P	C	Si	Sa	L
4	5	6	7	8
M	P	A	W	E
W	WM	M	MD	D
vT	T	M	I	vI

fast · short

background
border mass
hedge
screen
seacoast

Japan · (4b)—8 · i.1875

Lonicera quinquelocularis
Mistletoe Honeysuckle

dense · 6-12

P	C	Si	Sa	L
4	5	6	7	8
M	P	A	W	E
W	WM	M	MD	D
vT	T	M	I	vI

fast · short

background
border mass
hedge
screen

Himalayas · 5—9 · i.1840

Lonicera xylosteum
European Fly Honeysuckle

'Emerald Mound'
'Clavey'

dense · 6-12

P	C	Si	Sa	L
4	5	6	7	8
M	P	A	W	E
W	WM	M	MD	D
vT	T	M	I	vI

fast · short

background
border mass
hedge
screen
specimen / accent

Europe / Siberian · long c. · 3b—9

Lupinus albifrons
Whiteface Lupine
Silver Lupine

dense

P	C	Si	Sa	L
4	5	6	7	8
M	P	A	W	E
W	WM	M	MD	D
vT	T	M	I	vI

very fast · very short

bank erosion
border mass
espalier
naturalizing
nitrogen-fixing
rock garden
seacoast
specimen / accent

California · 8—10

Lyonia mariana
Staggerbush Lyonia
Staggerbush

open · 3-6

P	C	Si	Sa	L
4	5	6	7	8
M	P	A	W	E
W	WM	M	MD	D
vT	T	M	I	vI

slow · short

bog garden
border mass
poisonous leaves
seacoast

e. U.S. · 5—9 · i.1736

Magnolia **x** thompsoniana
Thompson Magnolia

'Urbana'

hybrid
7–10
i.1808

groupings
specimen / accent

P	C	Si	Sa	L
4	5	6	7	8
M	P	A	W	E
W	WM	M	MD	D
vT	T	M	I	vI

fast — short

open

6·12

Melaleuca erubescens

Australia
9–10

hedge
screen
seacoast

P	C	Si	Sa	L
4	5	6	7	8
M	P	A	W	E
W	WM	M	MD	D
vT	T	M	I	vI

very fast — short

open

3·6

Mimulus aurantiacus
syn. Diplacus glutinosus
Orangebush Monkeyflower
Sticky Monkeyflower

w. U.S.
7–10

above wall
container
greenhouse
seacoast

P	C	Si	Sa	L
4	5	6	7	8
M	P	A	W	E
W	WM	M	MD	D
vT	T	M	I	vI

fast — short

open

3·6

Myrica gale
Sweet Gale
Bog Myrtle

n. N.America
1–8a
i.1750

aromatic leaves
aquatic garden
bank erosion
bog garden
fruit arrangement
kitchen garden
seacoast

P	C	Si	Sa	L
4	5	6	7	8
M	P	A	W	E
W	WM	M	MD	D
vT	T	M	I	vI

slow — short

moderate

6·12

Neillia sinensis
Chinese Neillia

China
6–9
i.1901

border mass
hedge
screen

P	C	Si	Sa	L
4	5	6	7	8
M	P	A	W	E
W	WM	M	MD	D
vT	T	M	I	vI

moderate — short

dense

3·6

...deciduous
S3—16

MEDIUM SHRUB	FORM	BARK	LEAF	FLOWER	FRUIT	CULTURE	USES	REGION

Neviusia alabamensis
Snowwreath

FORM: dense
CULTURE: P C Si Sa L / (4) 5 6 7 8 / M P A W E / W WM M MD D / vT T M I vl / moderate short
USES: border mass / preservation / specimen / accent
REGION: s.e. U.S. / (4b)—8 / i.1860

Paeonia delavayi
Delavay Tree Peony

FORM: open
CULTURE: P C Si Sa L / 4 5 6 7 8 / M P A W E / W WM M MD D / vT T M I vl / fast short
USES: sculptural / specimen / accent
REGION: w. China / 5b—8 / i.1908

Paeonia lutea
Tibetan Tree Peony
Golden Tree Peony

FORM: open
CULTURE: P C Si Sa L / 4 5 6 7 8 / M P A W E / W WM M MD D / vT T M I vl / fast short
USES: sculptural / specimen / accent
REGION: w. China / (5b)—8a / i.1886

Paeonia suffruticosa
Mountain Tree Peony
Chinese Tree Peony
'Rocks Variety'

FORM: open
CULTURE: P C Si Sa L / 4 5 6 7 8 / M P A W E / W WM M MD D / vT T M I vl / fast short
USES: sculptural / specimen / accent
REGION: China / (5b)—8a / i.1800

Philadelphus x lemoinei
Lemoine Mockorange

'Belle Etoile' 'Erectus'
'Enchantment' 'Sylvaine'

FORM: dense
CULTURE: P C Si Sa L / 4 5 6 7 8 / M P A W E / W WM M MD D / vT T M I vl / fast short
USES: hedge / screen / seacoast / windbreak
REGION: hybrid / 4b—8a / o.1884

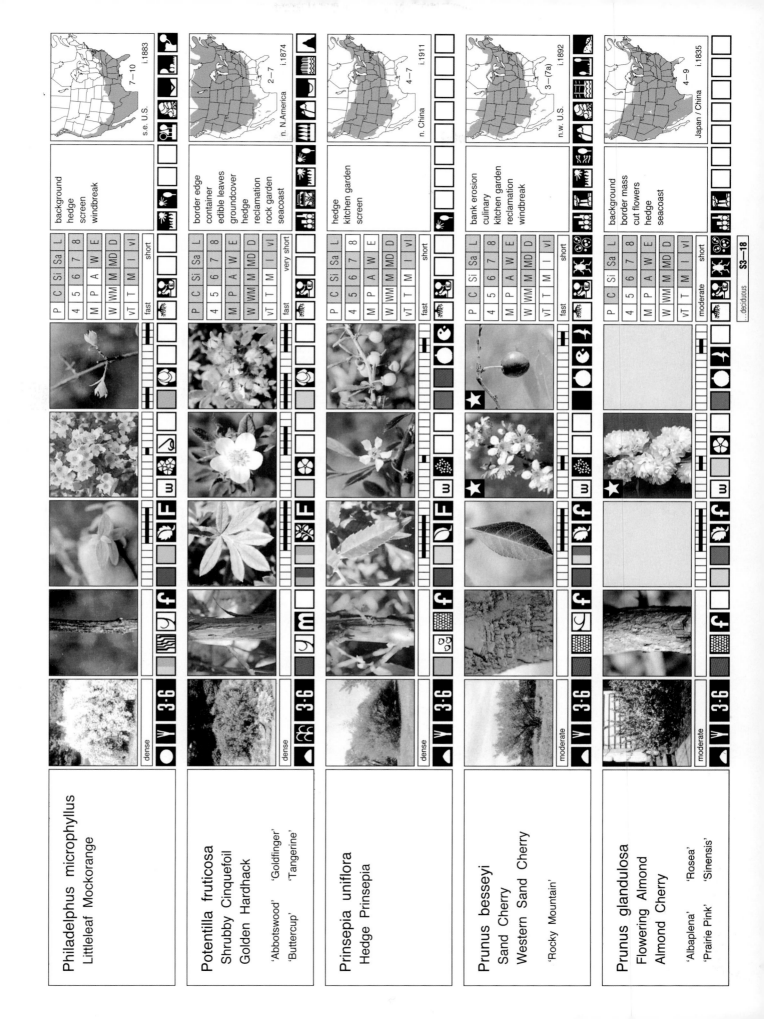

Philadelphus microphyllus
Littleleaf Mockorange
7–10   i.1883   s.e. U.S.

background
hedge
screen
windbreak

P C Si Sa L
4 5 6 7 8
M P A W E
W WM M MD D
vT T M I vI
short
fast
dense   3·6

Potentilla fruticosa
Shrubby Cinquefoil
Golden Hardhack
2–7   i.1874   n. N.America

'Abbotswood'   'Goldfinger'
'Buttercup'   'Tangerine'

border edge
container
edible leaves
groundcover
hedge
reclamation
rock garden
seacoast

P C Si Sa L
4 5 6 7 8
M P A W E
W WM M MD D
vT T M I vI   very short
fast
dense   3·6

Prinsepia uniflora
Hedge Prinsepia
4–7   i.1911   n. China

hedge
kitchen garden
screen

P C Si Sa L
4 5 6 7 8
M P A W E
W WM M MD D
vT T M I vI
fast
dense   3·6

Prunus besseyi
Sand Cherry
Western Sand Cherry
3–(7a)   i.1892   n.w. U.S.

'Rocky Mountain'

bank erosion
culinary
kitchen garden
reclamation
windbreak

P C Si Sa L
4 5 6 7 8
M P A W E
W WM M MD D
vT T M I vI   short
fast
moderate   3·6

Prunus glandulosa
Flowering Almond
Almond Cherry
4–9   i.1835   Japan / China

'Albaplena'   'Rosea'
'Prairie Pink'   'Sinensis'

background
border mass
cut flowers
hedge
seacoast

P C Si Sa L
4 5 6 7 8
M P A W E
W WM M MD D
vT T M I vI   short
moderate
moderate   3·6

. deciduous   **S3—18**

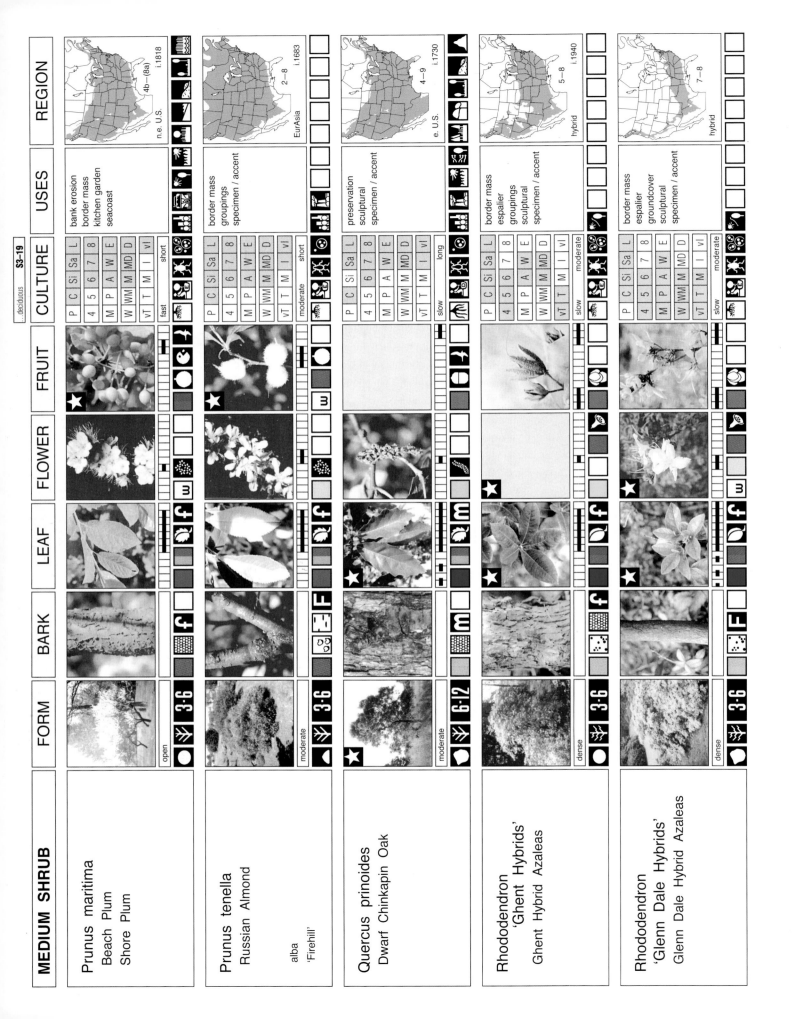

MEDIUM SHRUB	FORM	BARK	LEAF	FLOWER	FRUIT	CULTURE	USES	REGION
Prunus maritima Beach Plum Shore Plum	open · 3·6					P C Si Sa L / 4 5 6 7 8 / M P A W E / W WM M MD D / vT T M I vl — fast, short	bank erosion, border mass, kitchen garden, seacoast	n.e. U.S. · 4b–(8a) · i.1818
Prunus tenella Russian Almond — alba — 'Firehill'	moderate · 3·6					P C Si Sa L / 4 5 6 7 8 / M P A W E / W WM M MD D / vT T M I vl — moderate, short	border mass, groupings, specimen / accent	EurAsia · 2–8 · i.1683
Quercus prinoides Dwarf Chinkapin Oak	moderate · 6·12					P C Si Sa L / 4 5 6 7 8 / M P A W E / W WM M MD D / vT T M I vl — slow, long	preservation, sculptural, specimen / accent	e. U.S. · 4–9 · i.1730
Rhododendron 'Ghent Hybrids' Ghent Hybrid Azaleas	dense · 3·6					P C Si Sa L / 4 5 6 7 8 / M P A W E / W WM M MD D / vT T M I vl — slow, moderate	border mass, espalier, groupings, sculptural, specimen / accent	hybrid · 5–8 · i.1940
Rhododendron 'Glenn Dale Hybrids' Glenn Dale Hybrid Azaleas	dense · 3·6					P C Si Sa L / 4 5 6 7 8 / M P A W E / W WM M MD D / vT T M I vl — slow, moderate	border mass, espalier, groundcover, sculptural, specimen / accent	hybrid · 7–8

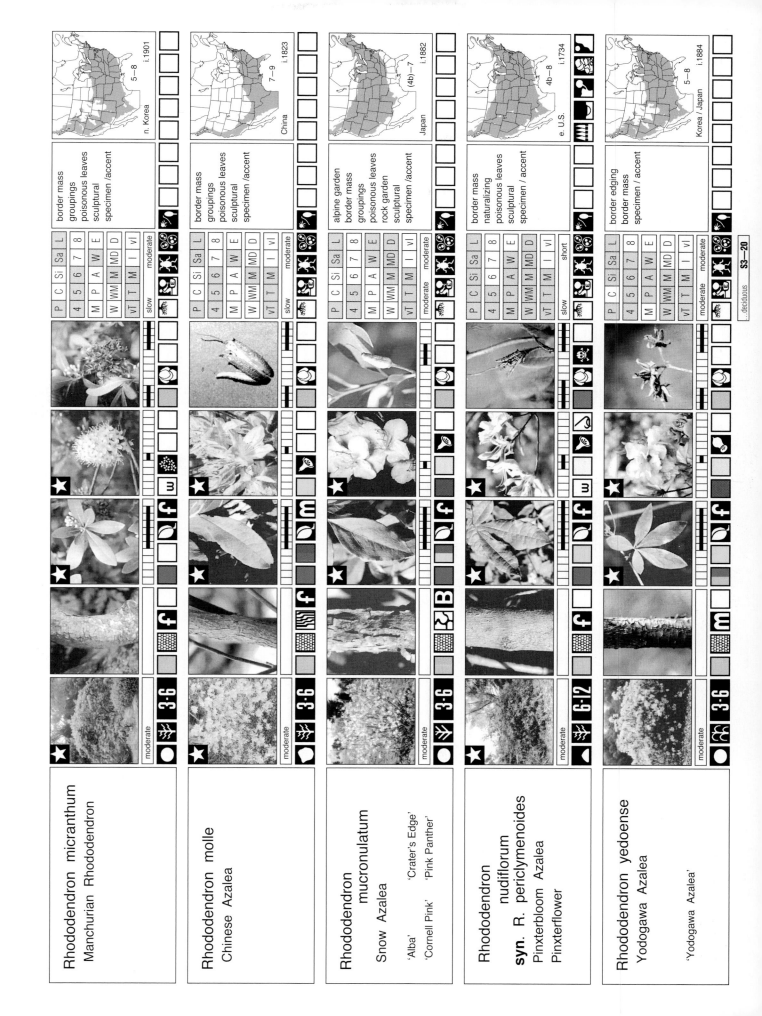

Rhododendron micranthum
Manchurian Rhododendron

n. Korea
5–8
i.1901

border mass
groupings
poisonous leaves
sculptural
specimen /accent

P	C	Si	Sa	L
4	5	6	7	8
M	P	A	W	E
W	WM	M	MD	D
vT	T	M	I	vI

slow · moderate

3·6

moderate

Rhododendron molle
Chinese Azalea

China
7–9
i.1823

border mass
groupings
poisonous leaves
sculptural
specimen /accent

P	C	Si	Sa	L
4	5	6	7	8
M	P	A	W	E
W	WM	M	MD	D
vT	T	M	I	vI

slow · moderate

3·6

moderate

Rhododendron mucronulatum
Snow Azalea

'Alba'   'Crater's Edge'
'Cornell Pink' 'Pink Panther'

Japan
(4b)–7
i.1882

alpine garden
border mass
groupings
poisonous leaves
rock garden
sculptural
specimen /accent

P	C	Si	Sa	L
4	5	6	7	8
M	P	A	W	E
W	WM	M	MD	D
vT	T	M	I	vI

moderate · moderate

3·6

moderate

Rhododendron nudiflorum
syn. R. periclymenoides
Pinxterbloom Azalea
Pinxterflower

e. US.
4b–8
i.1734

border mass
naturalizing
poisonous leaves
sculptural
specimen /accent

P	C	Si	Sa	L
4	5	6	7	8
M	P	A	W	E
W	WM	M	MD	D
vT	T	M	I	vI

slow · short

6·12

moderate

Rhododendron yedoense
Yodogawa Azalea

'Yodogawa Azalea'

Korea . Japan
5–8
i.1884

border edging
border mass
specimen / accent

P	C	Si	Sa	L
4	5	6	7	8
M	P	A	W	E
W	WM	M	MD	D
vT	T	M	I	vI

moderate · moderate

3·6

moderate

MEDIUM SHRUB	FORM	BARK	LEAF	FLOWER	FRUIT	CULTURE	USES	REGION

Rhodotypos scandens
Black Jetbead

- dense · 3·6
- CULTURE: P C Si Sa L / 4 5 7 8 / M P A W E / W WM M MD D / vT T M I vl — moderate · short
- USES: border mass / sculptural / specimen / accent
- REGION: Japan / China · 5 – 8 · i.1866

Ribes alpinum
Alpine Currant
Mountain Currant
'Europa'   'Schmidt'
'Green Mound'

- dense · 3·6
- CULTURE: P C Si Sa L / 4 5 6 7 8 / M P A W E / W WM M MD D / vT T M I vl — moderate · very short
- USES: alpine garden / bank erosion / border edging / border mass / hedge / rock garden / shearing
- REGION: Europe · 3 – 7 · i.1588

Ribes americanum
American Black Currant

- open · 3·6
- CULTURE: P C Si Sa L / 4 5 6 7 8 / M P A W E / W WM M MD D / vT T M I vl — moderate · very short
- USES: bog garden / kitchen garden
- REGION: U.S. · 3 – 6 · i.1729

Ribes aureum
Western Golden Currant
Buffalo Currant
'Gwen's Buffalo'

- dense · 3·6
- CULTURE: P C Si Sa L / 4 5 6 7 8 / M P A W E / W WM M MD D / vT T M I vl — fast · very short
- USES: bank erosion / border mass / hedge / kitchen garden / reclamation / screen / specimen / accent
- REGION: w. U.S. · 3b – 7 · i.1806

Ribes cereum
White-flowered Currant
Wax Currant

- dense · 3·6
- CULTURE: P C Si Sa L / 4 5 6 7 8 / M P A W E / W WM M MD D / vT T M I vl — fast · very short
- USES: aromatic leaves / bank erosion / border mass / hedge / reclamation / screen
- REGION: w. U.S · 5 – 8 · i.1827.

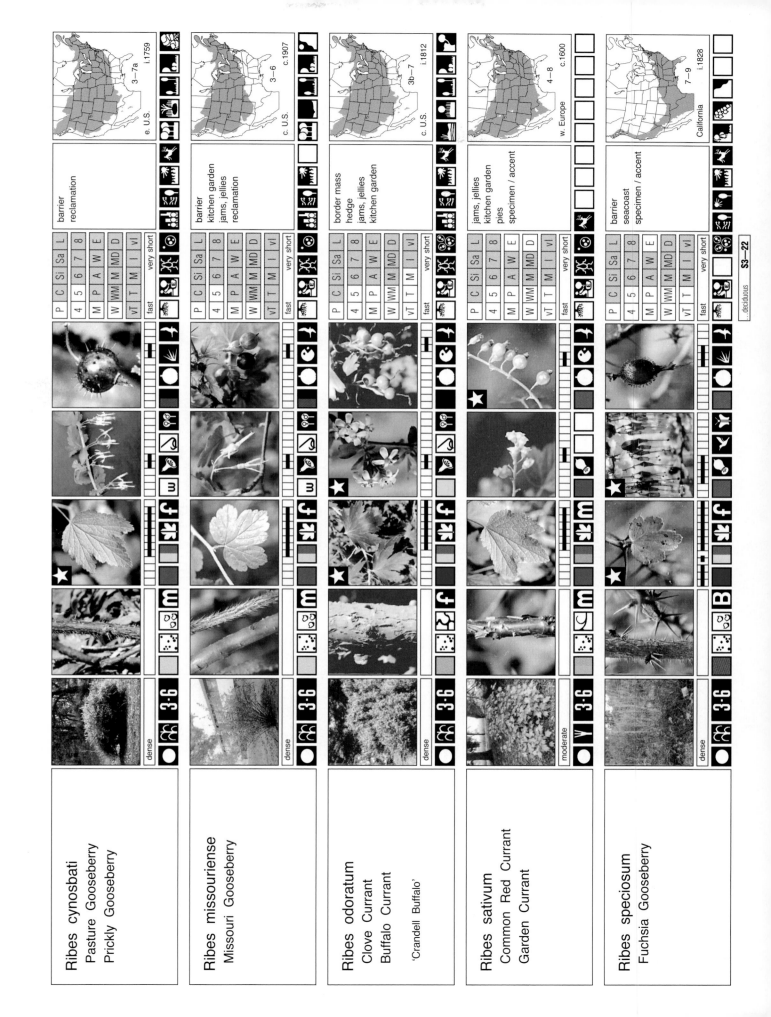

Ribes cynosbati
Pasture Gooseberry
Prickly Gooseberry

barrier
reclamation

e. U.S.   3–7a   i.1759

P	C	Si	Sa	L
4	5	6	7	8
M	P	A	W	E
W	WM	M	MD	D
vT	T	M	I	vI

fast   very short   dense   3-6

Ribes missouriense
Missouri Gooseberry

barrier
kitchen garden
jams, jellies
reclamation

c. U.S.   3–6   c.1907

P	C	Si	Sa	L
4	5	6	7	8
M	P	A	W	E
W	WM	M	MD	D
vT	T	M	I	vI

fast   very short   dense   3-6

Ribes odoratum
Clove Currant
Buffalo Currant
'Crandell Buffalo'

border mass
hedge
jams, jellies
kitchen garden

c. U.S.   3b–7   i.1812

P	C	Si	Sa	L
4	5	6	7	8
M	P	A	W	E
W	WM	M	MD	D
vT	T	M	I	vI

fast   very short   dense   3-6

Ribes sativum
Common Red Currant
Garden Currant

jams, jellies
kitchen garden
pies
specimen / accent

w. Europe   4–8   c.1600

P	C	Si	Sa	L
4	5	6	7	8
M	P	A	W	E
W	WM	M	MD	D
vT	T	M	I	vI

fast   very short   moderate   3-6

Ribes speciosum
Fuchsia Gooseberry

barrier
seacoast
specimen / accent

California   7–9   i.1828

P	C	Si	Sa	L
4	5	6	7	8
M	P	A	W	E
W	WM	M	MD	D
vT	T	M	I	vI

fast   very short   dense   3-6

...deciduous   S3—22

MEDIUM SHRUB	FORM	BARK	LEAF	FLOWER	FRUIT	CULTURE	USES	REGION

Robinia hispida
Moss Locust
Roseacacia Locust

open · 6-12

P	C	Si	Sa	L
4	5	6	7	8
M	P	A	W	E
W	WM	M	MD	D
vT	T	M	I	vI

very fast · short

USES: bank erosion, border mass, naturalizing, nitrogen-fixing, poisonous leaves, reclamation, specimen / accent, tall groundcover

REGION: e. U.S. · 4—10 · i.1743

Rosa alba
Cottage Rose

open-dense · 3-6

P	C	Si	Sa	L
4	5	6	7	8
M	P	A	W	E
W	WM	M	MD	D
vT	T	M	I	vI

fast · short

USES: barrier, border mass, colonial garden, groupings, hedge

REGION: hybrid · 4—9 · c.b.1600

Rosa amblyotis
Kamtchatka Rose
Erectprickle Rose

open-dense · 3-6

P	C	Si	Sa	L
4	5	6	7	8
M	P	A	W	E
W	WM	M	MD	D
vT	T	M	I	vI

fast · short

USES: barrier, border mass, groupings, hedge, specimen / accent

REGION: Kamtchatka · 2—6 · c.1917

Rosa blanda
Meadow Rose
Smooth Rose

open-dense · 6-12

P	C	Si	Sa	L
4	5	6	7	8
M	P	A	W	E
W	WM	M	MD	D
vT	T	M	I	vI

fast · short

USES: barrier, boder mass, groupings, hedge

REGION: e. U.S. · (2b)—6 · i.1773

Rosa x centifolia
Cabbage Rose
Holland Rose

moderate · 3-6

P	C	Si	Sa	L
4	5	6	7	8
M	P	A	W	E
W	WM	M	MD	D
vT	T	M	I	vI

fast · short

USES: barrier, border mass, groupings, hedge, specimen / accent

REGION: Europe / Caucasus · 5b—9a · long c.

Rosa gallica
French Rose
Red Rose

Europe · 5—9 · long c.

bank erosion
barrier
fragrant leaves
hedge
naturalizing

P	C	Si	Sa	L
4	5	6	7	8
M	P	A	W	E
W	WM	M	MD	D
vT	T	M	I	vl

short · fast · dense · 3-6

Rosa x harisoni
Harison's Yellow Rose

hybrid · 4—8a · o.1830

barrier
container
seacoast
specimen / accent

P	C	Si	Sa	L
4	5	6	7	8
M	P	A	W	E
W	WM	M	MD	D
vT	T	M	I	vl

short · fast · open-dense · 3-6

Rosa palustris
Swamp Rose

'Plena'

e. U.S. · 4—8 · i.1726

bank erosion
barrier
bog garden

P	C	Si	Sa	L
4	5	6	7	8
M	P	A	W	E
W	WM	M	MD	D
vT	T	M	I	vl

short · fast · open-dense · 3-6

Rosa pendulina
Alpine Rose
Drophip Rose

s. Europe · 5—9 · i.1789

alpine garden
bank erosion
barrier
naturalizing
rock garden
specimen / accent
tall groundcover

P	C	Si	Sa	L
4	5	6	7	8
M	P	A	W	E
W	WM	M	MD	D
vT	T	M	I	vl

short · fast · dense · 3-6

Rosa pomifera syn. R. villosa
Apple Rose

s. Europe · 4b—9a · i.1771

bank erosion
barrier
culinary
fragrant leaves
jams, jellies
kitchen garden
specimen / accent
tall groundcover

P	C	Si	Sa	L
4	5	6	7	8
M	P	A	W	E
W	WM	M	MD	D
vT	T	M	I	vl

short · fast · dense · 3-6

MEDIUM SHRUB

	FORM	BARK	LEAF	FLOWER	FRUIT	CULTURE	USES	REGION
Rosa rubrifolia — Redleaf Rose	dense / 6-12					P C Si Sa L / 4 5 6 7 8 / M P A W E / W WM M MD D / vT T M I vl; fast; short	barrier, border mass, floral arrangement, hedge, screen	c. Europe; 2b–8a; i.1814
Rosa rugosa — Rugosa Rose, Turkestan Rose ('Big John' 'Magnifica', 'Dart'd Dash' 'Topaz')	open-moderate / 3-6					P C Si Sa L / 4 5 6 7 8 / M P A W E / W WM M MD D / vT T M I vl; fast; short	bank erosion, barrier, border edging, culinary, hedge, jams, jellies, kitchen gardens, seacoast	Korea; 3–7; i.1796
Rosa virginiana — Virginia Rose ('Plena')	dense / 6-12					P C Si Sa L / 4 5 6 7 8 / M P A W E / W WM M MD D / vT T M I vl; fast; short	accent, bank erosion, barrier, goundcover, hedge, naturalizing, seacoast	e. U.S.; (4b)–7; i.1800
Rubus idaeus — European Red Raspberry	open / 6-12					P C Si Sa L / 4 5 6 7 8 / M P A W E / W WM M MD D / vT T M I vl; very fast; very short	bank erosion, barrier, border mass, jams, jellies, kitchen garden, naturalizing, pies, tall groundcover	EurAsia; 3–7; long c.
Rubus odoratus — Flowering Raspberry, Fragrant Thimbleberry	moderate / 6-12					P C Si Sa L / 4 5 6 7 8 / M P A W E / W WM M MD D / vT T M I vl; fast; very short	bank erosion, border mass, naturalizing, shade garden, specimen / accent, woodland garden	e. U.S.; 4–7; i.1770

Rubus parviflorus
Western Thimbleberry
Salmonberry

N.America
4b–7a
i.1927

moderate
6-12

bank erosion
border mass
naturalizing
shade garden
specimen / accent
tall groundcover
woodland garden

P	C	Si	Sa	L
4	5	6	7	8
M	P	A	W	E
W	WM	M	MD	D
vT	T	M	I	vI

fast   short

Shepherdia canadensis
Russet Buffaloberry

N.America
2b–6
i.1759

open
6-12

culinary
jams, jellies
hedge
kitchen garden
nitrogen-fixing
seacoast
windbreak

P	C	Si	Sa	L
4	5	6	7	8
M	P	A	W	E
W	WM	M	MD	D
vT	T	M	I	vI

moderate   short

Solanum rantonneti
syn. S. lycianthes
Blue Potatobush
Paraguay Nightshade
'Royal Robe'

Paraguay
9–10

open

climbing vine
container
greenhouse
groundcover
standards

P	C	Si	Sa	L
4	5	6	7	8
M	P	A	W	E
W	WM	M	MD	D
vT	T	M	I	vI

fast

Sorbaria sorbifolia
Ural Falsespirea

Asia
3–8
i.1759

open
6-12

border mass
naturalizing
water garden

P	C	Si	Sa	L
4	5	6	7	8
M	P	A	W	E
W	WM	M	MD	D
vT	T	M	I	vI

fast   short

Spiraea **x** arguta
Garland Spirea
'Compacta'
'Graciosa'

hybrid
3–9a
c.1884

dense
3-6

border edging
border mass
hedge
seacoast
specimen / accent

P	C	Si	Sa	L
4	5	6	7	8
M	P	A	W	E
W	WM	M	MD	D
vT	T	M	I	vI

moderate

...deciduous

MEDIUM SHRUB	FORM	BARK	LEAF	FLOWER	FRUIT	CULTURE	USES	REGION
Spiraea chamaedrifolia Germander Spirea	moderate · 6-12	F				P C Si Sa L · 4 5 6 7 8 · M P A W E · W WM M MD D · vT T M I vl fast / short	bank erosion hedge historic garden naturalizing tall groundcover	5–9 c.1789 n.e. Asia
Spiraea douglasi Douglas Spirea Western Spirea	dense · 6-12	F				P C Si Sa L · 4 5 6 7 8 · M P A W E · W WM M MD D · vT T M I vl fast / short	bank erosion hedge naturalizing seacoast tall groundcover water garden	3b–8 i.1827 w. N.America
Spiraea japonica Japanese Spirea 'Alpina' 'Gold Mound' 'Coccinea' 'Shirobana'	dense · 3-6	F				P C Si Sa L · 4 5 6 7 8 · M P A W E · W WM M MD D · vT T M I vl fast / short	background hedge naturalizing screen seacoast	5–9 c.1870 Asia
Spiraea latifolia Broadleaf Meadowsweet Spirea	dense · 6-12	F				P C Si Sa L · 4 5 6 7 8 · M P A W E · W WM M MD D · vT T M I vl fast / short	bog garden naturalizing tall groundcover water garden	3b–9a c.1789 e. U.S.
Spiraea menziesi Menzies Spirea	dense · 6-12	F				P C Si Sa L · 4 5 6 7 8 · M P A W E · W WM M MD D · vT T M I vl fast / short	background hedge naturalizing screen tall groundcover	3–8a i.1838 w. U.S.

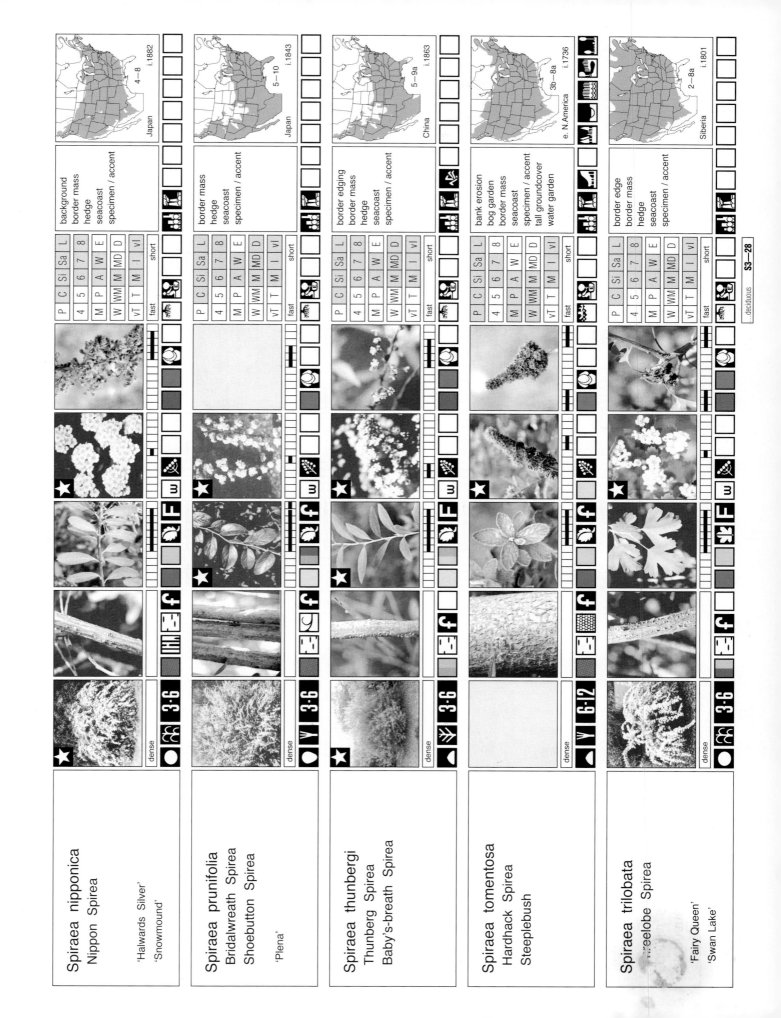

Spiraea nipponica
Nippon Spirea
'Halwards Silver'
'Snowmound'

Japan · i.1882 · 4–8

background
border mass
hedge
seacoast
specimen / accent

P	C	Si	Sa	L
4	5	6	7	8
M	P	A	W	E
W	WM	M	MD	D
vT	T	M	I	vI

fast · short · dense · 3·6

Spiraea prunifolia
Bridalwreath Spirea
Shoebutton Spirea
'Plena'

Japan · i.1843 · 5–10

border mass
hedge
seacoast
specimen / accent

P	C	Si	Sa	L
4	5	6	7	8
M	P	A	W	E
W	WM	M	MD	D
vT	T	M	I	vI

fast · short · dense · 3·6

Spiraea thunbergi
Thunberg Spirea
Baby's-breath Spirea

China · i.1863 · 5–9a

border edging
border mass
hedge
seacoast
specimen / accent

P	C	Si	Sa	L
4	5	6	7	8
M	P	A	W	E
W	WM	M	MD	D
vT	T	M	I	vI

fast · short · dense · 3·6

Spiraea tomentosa
Hardhack Spirea
Steeplebush

e. N.America · i.1736 · 3b–8a

bank erosion
bog garden
border mass
seacoast
specimen / accent
tall groundcover
water garden

P	C	Si	Sa	L
4	5	6	7	8
M	P	A	W	E
W	WM	M	MD	D
vT	T	M	I	vI

fast · short · dense · 6·12

Spiraea trilobata
Threelobe Spirea
'Fairy Queen'
'Swan Lake'

Siberia · i.1801 · 2–8a

border edge
border mass
hedge
seacoast
specimen / accent

P	C	Si	Sa	L
4	5	6	7	8
M	P	A	W	E
W	WM	M	MD	D
vT	T	M	I	vI

fast · short · dense · 3·6

...deciduous · S3—28

MEDIUM SHRUB	FORM	BARK	LEAF	FLOWER	FRUIT	CULTURE	USES	REGION

..deciduous **S3–29**

Stephanandra incisa — Cutleaf Stephanandra — 'Crispa', 'Crispifolia Nana'
- FORM: dense, 3-6
- CULTURE: P C Si Sa L / 4 5 6 7 8 / M P A W E / W WM M MD D / vT T M I vl — short — fast
- USES: bank erosion, border edging, border mass, hedge, seacoast, shearing
- REGION: Japan / Korea, 5–8, i.1872

Stephanandra tanakae — Tanaka Stephanandra
- FORM: dense, 3-6
- CULTURE: P C Si Sa L / 4 5 6 7 8 / M P A W E / W WM M MD D / vT T M I vl — short — fast
- USES: border edging, border mass, hedge, shearing
- REGION: Japan, 6–8, i.1893

Symphoricarpos albus — Common Snowberry — 'Jewell'
- FORM: moderate, 3-6
- CULTURE: P C Si Sa L / 4 5 6 7 8 / M P A W E / W WM M MD D / vT T M I vl — very short — moderate
- USES: bank erosion, groundcover, seacoast, shade garden, specimen / accent, tall groundcover, woodland garden
- REGION: N.America, 2–6, i.1879

Symphoricarpos occidentalis — Western Snowberry — Wolfberry
- FORM: dense, 6-12
- CULTURE: P C Si Sa L / 4 5 6 7 8 / M P A W E / W WM M MD D / vT T M I vl — very short — fast
- USES: bank erosion, groundcover, hedge, reclamation, seacoast, specimen / accent, tall groundcover
- REGION: w. U.S., 2–5, c.1880

Symphoricarpos oreophilus **syn.** S. rotundifolius — Mountain Snowberry
- FORM: moderate, 3-6
- CULTURE: P C Si Sa L / 4 5 6 7 8 / M P A W E / W WM M MD D / vT T M I vl — very short — fast
- USES: bank erosion, groundcover, hedge, shearing, specimen / accent, wild garden, woodland garden
- REGION: w. U.S., 2–5, i.1894

Syringa laciniata — Cutleaf Lilac

China — i.1614 — 5–9a

Uses: background, barrier, cut flowers, hedge, screen, specimen / accent

P	C	Si	Sa	L
4	5	6	7	8
M	P	A	W	E
W	WM	M	MD	D
vT	T	M	I	vI

moderate — long

moderate — 3-6

Syringa meyeri — Meyer's Lilac

'Palibin'

China — i.1908 — 4–7

Uses: background, barrier, cut flowers, hedge, screen, specimen /accent

P	C	Si	Sa	L
4	5	6	7	8
M	P	A	W	E
W	WM	M	MD	D
vT	T	M	I	vI

slow — long

dense — 3-6

Syringa microphylla — Littleleaf Lilac

'Superba'

China — i.1910 — 5–7

Uses: background, barrier, cut flowers, hedge, screen, seacoast

P	C	Si	Sa	L
4	5	6	7	8
M	P	A	W	E
W	WM	M	MD	D
vT	T	M	I	vI

slow — long

dense — 6-12

Syringa x persica — Persian Lilac

'Laciniata'
'Purple Dark'

hybrid — i.1613 — 4b–9a

Uses: background, barrier, cut flowers, hedge, screen, seacoast

P	C	Si	Sa	L
4	5	6	7	8
M	P	A	W	E
W	WM	M	MD	D
vT	T	M	I	vI

moderate — long

dense — 3-6

Viburnum acerifolium — Mapleleaf Viburnum

e. N.America — i.1736 — 3b–9a

Uses: bog garden, border mass, hedge, naturalizing, shade garden, screen, woodland garden

P	C	Si	Sa	L
4	5	6	7	8
M	P	A	W	E
W	WM	M	MD	D
vT	T	M	I	vI

slow — short

moderate — 3-6

MEDIUM SHRUB	FORM	BARK	LEAF	FLOWER	FRUIT	CULTURE	USES	REGION

Viburnum carlesi
Koreanspice Viburnum

'Aurora'
'Compactum'

dense — 6-12

CULTURE:
P C Si Sa L
4 5 6 7 8
M P A W E
W WM M MD D
vT T M I vl
moderate — moderate

USES:
border mass
grouping
hedge
patio garden
screen
specimen / accent
windbreak

REGION:
Korea — 4b—8a — i.1902

Viburnum cassinoides
Witherod Viburnum

moderate — 3-6

CULTURE:
P C Si Sa L
4 5 6 7 8
M P A W E
W WM M MD D
vT T M I vl
moderate — short

USES:
bog garden
border mass
hedge
naturalizing
patio garden
screen
specimen / accent
woodland garden

REGION:
e. N.America — 3b—7a — 1761

Viburnum opulus
'Compactum'
Compact European
Cranberrybush

dense — 3-6

CULTURE:
P C Si Sa L
4 5 6 7 8
M P A W E
W WM M MD D
vT T M I vl
fast — short

USES:
background
border edge
border mass
hedge
screen
specimen / accent

REGION:
cultivar — 4—8

Viburnum rafinesquianum
Downy Arrowwood Viburnum
Rafinesque Viburnum

dense — 3-6

CULTURE:
P C Si Sa L
4 5 6 7 8
M P A W E
W WM M MD D
vT T M I vl
fast — short

USES:
hedge
screen
shade garden
woodland garden

REGION:
N.America — 3—8a — c.1883

Viburnum veitchi
Veitch Viburnum
Vetter Viburnum

dense — 3-6

CULTURE:
P C Si Sa L
4 5 6 7 8
M P A W E
W WM M MD D
vT T M I vl
moderate — short

USES:
border mass
hedge
screen
shade garden
specimen / accent
woodland garden

REGION:
China — 5—8 — i.1901

Weigela praecox
Early Weigela

(4b)—9a
c.1894
Korea

border mass
grouping
specimen /accent
water garden

P	C	Si	Sa	L
4	5	6	7	8
M	P	A	W	E
W	WM	M	MD	D
vT	T	M	I	vl

very short
fast
open
3-6

SMALL SHRUB	FORM	BARK	LEAF	FLOWER	FRUIT	CULTURE	USES	REGION

Acalypha californica
California Copperleaf

open | 1-3

CULTURE: P C Si Sa L / 4 5 6 7 8 / M P A W E / W WM M MD D / vT T M I vl / fast short

USES: bank erosion, container, hedge, preservation

REGION: California / 9—10

Adolphia californica
California Adolphia

open | 6-12

CULTURE: P C Si Sa L / 4 5 6 7 8 / M P A W E / W WM M MD D / vT T M I vl / fast short

USES: bank erosion, barrier, border mass

REGION: California / 9—10

Amorpha canescens
Leadplant Amorpha
Leadplant

open | 1-3

CULTURE: P C Si Sa L / 4 5 6 7 8 / M P A W E / W WM M MD D / vT T M I vl / moderate short

USES: border mass, nitrogen-fixing, preservation, restoration, rock garden, specimen / accent

REGION: central U.S. / 3—9 / i.1812

Artemisia pycnocephala
Sandhill Sage
Coast Sagebrush

open | 3-6

CULTURE: P C Si Sa L / 4 5 6 7 8 / M P A W E / W WM M MD D / vT T M I vl / fast very short

USES: bank erosion, border mass, dried flowers, naturalizing, seacoast

REGION: w. coast U.S. / 4—10

Artemisia stelleriana
Beach Wormwood
Dusty Miller

open | 1-3

CULTURE: P C Si Sa L / 4 5 6 7 8 / M P A W E / W WM M MD D / vT T M I vl / fast short

USES: border edging, border mass, groundcover, herb garden, seacoast

REGION: n.e. U.S. / 3—8 / c.1870

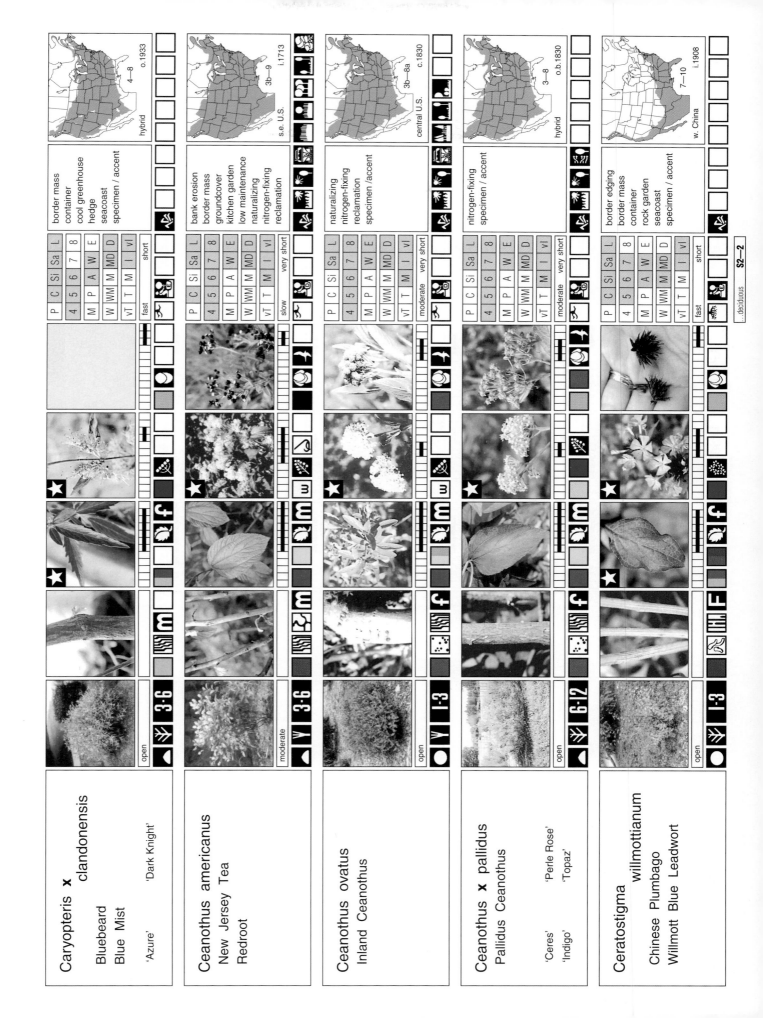

Caryopteris **x** clandonensis

Bluebeard
Blue Mist

'Azure'   'Dark Knight'

hybrid   4—8   o.1933

border mass
container
cool greenhouse
hedge
seacoast
specimen / accent

P C Si Sa L
4 5 6 7 8
M P A W E
W WM M MD D
vT T M I vI
fast   short

open   3·6

Ceanothus americanus

New Jersey Tea
Redroot

s.e. U.S.   3b—9   i.1713

bank erosion
border mass
groundcover
kitchen garden
low maintenance
naturalizing
nitrogen-fixing
reclamation

P C Si Sa L
4 5 6 7 8
M P A W E
W WM M MD D
vT T M I vI
slow   very short

moderate   3·6

Ceanothus ovatus

Inland Ceanothus

central U.S.   3b—8a   c.1830

naturalizing
nitrogen-fixing
reclamation
specimen /accent

P C Si Sa L
4 5 6 7 8
M P A W E
W WM M MD D
vT T M I vI
moderate   very short

open   1·3

Ceanothus **x** pallidus

Pallidus Ceanothus

'Ceres'   'Perle Rose'
'Indigo'   'Topaz'

hybrid   3—8   o.b.1830

nitrogen-fixing
specimen / accent

P C Si Sa L
4 5 6 7 8
M P A W E
W WM M MD D
vT T M I vI
moderate   very short

open   6·12

Ceratostigma willmottianum

Chinese Plumbago
Willmott Blue Leadwort

w. China   7—10   i.1908

border edging
border mass
container
rock garden
seacoast
specimen / accent

P C Si Sa L
4 5 6 7 8
M P A W E
W WM M MD D
vT T M I vI
fast   short

open   1·3

...deciduous   **S2—2**

SMALL SHRUB	FORM	BARK	LEAF	FLOWER	FRUIT	CULTURE	USES	REGION

Chaenomeles japonica
Japanese Floweringquince

'Coles Red'   'Minerva'
'Mavlei'   'Super Red'

dense

CULTURE: P C Si Sa L | 4 5 6 7 8 | M P A W E | W WM M MD D | vT T M I vl | very fast | short

USES: barrier, bonsai, border edging, fresh cut flowers, seacoast, specimen / accent

REGION: Japan   i.1869   4b—9a

Clematis heracleifolia
Fragrant Tube Clematis

'Davidiana'

open

CULTURE: P C Si Sa L | 4 5 6 7 8 | M P A W E | W WM M MD D | vT T M I vl | very fast | short

USES: border mass, flower bed, specimen / accent

REGION: n. China   i.1837   4—9

Clematis integrifolia
Solitary Clematis

open

CULTURE: P C Si Sa L | 4 5 6 7 8 | M P A W E | W WM M MD D | vT T M I vl | very fast | short

USES: border mass, flower bed, specimen / accent

REGION: Asia / Europe   3—9

Comptonia peregrina
Sweetfern

open

CULTURE: P C Si Sa L | 4 5 6 7 8 | M P A W E | W WM M MD D | vT T M I vl | slow | short

USES: bank erosion, groundcover, naturalizing, nitrogen-fixing, reclamation, seacoast

REGION: e. U.S.   i.1714   2—8a

Cornus sericea 'Kelseyi'
Kelsey's Dwarf Dogwood

moderate

CULTURE: P C Si Sa L | 4 5 6 7 8 | M P A W E | W WM M MD D | vT T M I vl | moderate | short

USES: border mass, border edging, groundcover, rock garden

REGION: cultivar   3—8a

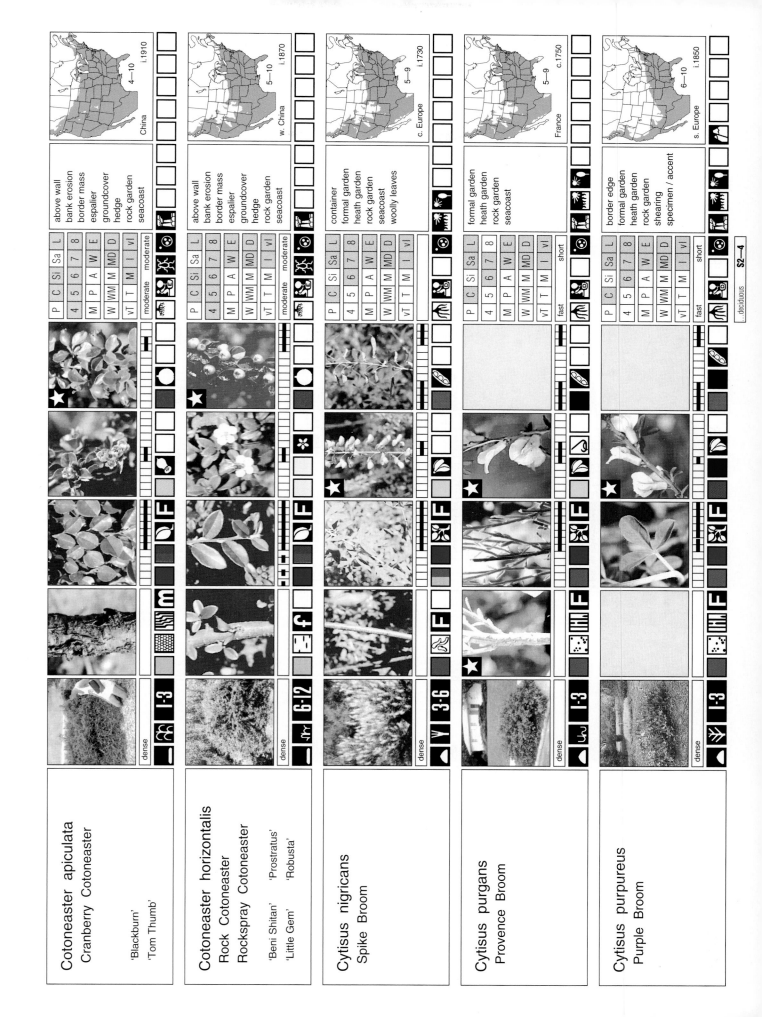

Cotoneaster apiculata
Cranberry Cotoneaster

'Blackburn'
'Tom Thumb'

above wall
bank erosion
border mass
espalier
groundcover
hedge
rock garden
seacoast

P	C	Si	Sa	L
4	5	6	7	8
M	P	A	W	E
W	WM	M	MD	D
vT	T	M	I	vI

moderate

dense

1-3

China   4—10   i.1910

Cotoneaster horizontalis
Rock Cotoneaster
Rockspray Cotoneaster

'Beni Shitan'   'Prostratus'
'Little Gem'   'Robusta'

above wall
bank erosion
border mass
espalier
groundcover
hedge
rock garden
seacoast

P	C	Si	Sa	L
4	5	6	7	8
M	P	A	W	E
W	WM	M	MD	D
vT	T	M	I	vI

moderate

dense

6-12

w. China   5—10   i.1870

Cytisus nigricans
Spike Broom

container
formal garden
heath garden
rock garden
seacoast
woolly leaves

P	C	Si	Sa	L
4	5	6	7	8
M	P	A	W	E
W	WM	M	MD	D
vT	T	M	I	vI

dense

3-6

c. Europe   5—9   i.1730

Cytisus purgans
Provence Broom

formal garden
heath garden
rock garden
seacoast

P	C	Si	Sa	L
4	5	6	7	8
M	P	A	W	E
W	WM	M	MD	D
vT	T	M	I	vI

fast   short

dense

1-3

France   5—9   c.1750

Cytisus purpureus
Purple Broom

border edge
formal garden
heath garden
rock garden
shearing
specimen / accent

P	C	Si	Sa	L
4	5	6	7	8
M	P	A	W	E
W	WM	M	MD	D
vT	T	M	I	vI

fast   short

dense

1-3

s. Europe   6—10   i.1850

...deciduous   S2—4

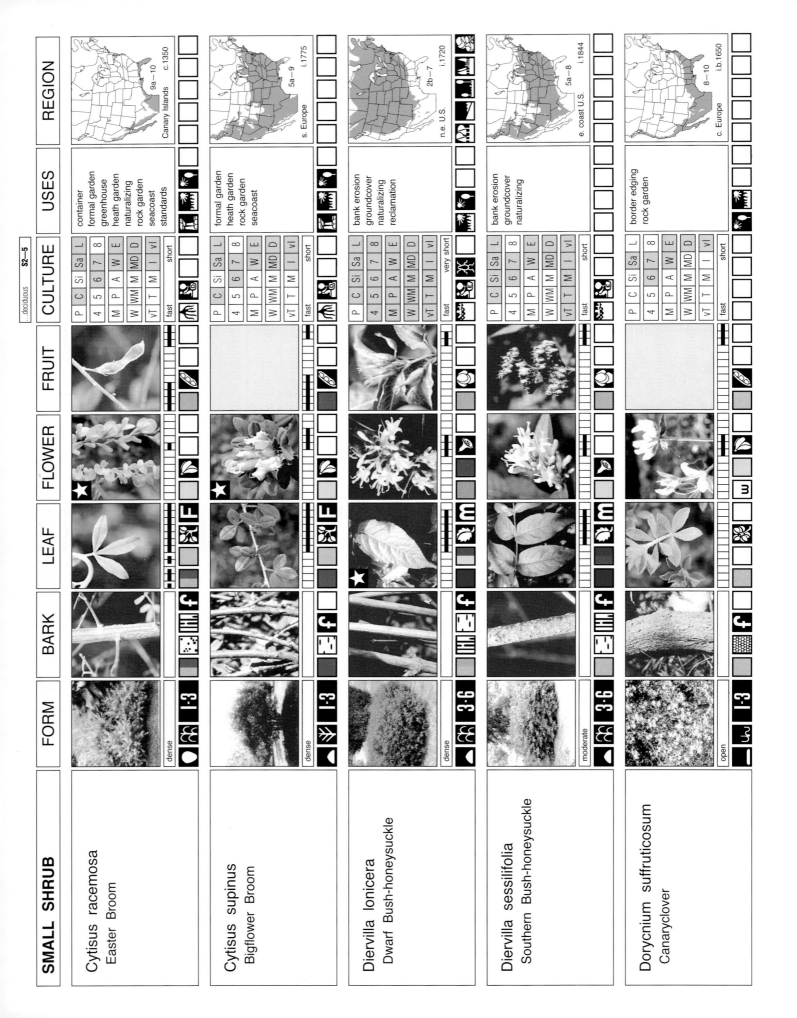

SMALL SHRUB

	FORM	BARK	LEAF	FLOWER	FRUIT	CULTURE	USES	REGION

Cytisus racemosa — Easter Broom
- Form: dense · 1-3
- Culture: P C Si Sa L / 4 5 6 7 8 / M P A W E / W WM M MD D / vT T M I vl — fast / short
- Uses: container, formal garden, greenhouse, heath garden, naturalizing, rock garden, seacoast, standards
- Region: Canary Islands · 9a–10 · c.1350

Cytisus supinus — Bigflower Broom
- Form: dense · 1-3
- Culture: P C Si Sa L / 4 5 6 7 8 / M P A W E / W WM M MD D / vT T M I vl — fast / short
- Uses: formal garden, heath garden, rock garden, seacoast
- Region: s. Europe · 5a–9 · i.1775

Diervilla lonicera — Dwarf Bush-honeysuckle
- Form: dense · 3-6
- Culture: P C Si Sa L / 4 5 6 7 8 / M P A W E / W WM M MD D / vT T M I vl — fast / very short
- Uses: bank erosion, groundcover, naturalizing, reclamation
- Region: n.e. U.S. · 2b–7 · i.1720

Diervilla sessilifolia — Southern Bush-honeysuckle
- Form: moderate · 3-6
- Culture: P C Si Sa L / 4 5 6 7 8 / M P A W E / W WM M MD D / vT T M I vl — fast / short
- Uses: bank erosion, groundcover, naturalizing
- Region: e. coast U.S. · 5a–8 · i.1844

Dorycnium suffruticosum — Canaryclover
- Form: open · 1-3
- Culture: P C Si Sa L / 4 5 6 7 8 / M P A W E / W WM M MD D / vT T M I vl — fast / short
- Uses: border edging, rock garden
- Region: c. Europe · 8–10 · i.b.1650

Forsythia 'Arnold Dwarf'
Arnold's Dwarf Forsythia

'Bronxensis'

bank erosion
barrier
groundcover

hybrid — o.1941 — 5–9

P	C	Si	Sa	L
4	5	6	7	8
M	P	A	W	E
W	WM	M	MD	D
vT	T	M	I	vI

fast · short

open · 3–6

Forsythia viridissima
Greenstem Forsythia

Korea — o.1939 — 5–8a

P	C	Si	Sa	L
4	5	6	7	8
M	P	A	W	E
W	WM	M	MD	D
vT	T	M	I	vI

bank erosion
border mass

slow · short

moderate · 1–3

Fothergilla gardenii
Dwarf Fothergilla
Witch Alder

'Blue Mist'
'Jane Platt'

aromatic leaves
border mass
naturalizing
specimen / accent

s.e. U.S. — i.1765 — (5b)–9

P	C	Si	Sa	L
4	5	6	7	8
M	P	A	W	E
W	WM	M	MD	D
vT	T	M	I	vI

slow · short

moderate · 1–3

Gaylussacia baccata
Black Huckleberry

bank erosion
naturalizing
rock garden

n.e. U.S. — i.1772 — 3–7

P	C	Si	Sa	L
4	5	6	7	8
M	P	A	W	E
W	WM	M	MD	D
vT	T	M	I	vI

very fast · short

open · 1–3

Genista germanica
German Woadwaxen

bank erosion
border mass
container
groundcover
patio garden
rock garden

Europe / Russia — c.1588 — 5–7

P	C	Si	Sa	L
4	5	6	7	8
M	P	A	W	E
W	WM	M	MD	D
vT	T	M	I	vI

moderate · short

dense · 1–3

…deciduous S2—6

SMALL SHRUB	FORM	BARK	LEAF	FLOWER	FRUIT	CULTURE	USES	REGION

Genista lydia — Lydia Woodwaxen

CULTURE: P C Si Sa L / 4 5 6 7 8 / M P A W E / W WM M MD D / vT T M I VI — moderate — dense
USES: bank erosion, container, groundcover, patio garden, rock garden, seacoast
REGION: e. Balkans, i.1926, 6—9

Genista radiata

CULTURE: P C Si Sa L / 4 5 6 7 8 / M P A W E / W WM M MD D / vT T M I VI — moderate — dense
USES: bank erosion, container, groundcover, patio garden, rock garden
REGION: s. Europe, i.1758, 3—8

Genista tinctoria — Dyer's Greenweed, Dyer's Broom — 'Plena', 'Royal Gold'

CULTURE: P C Si Sa L / 4 5 6 7 8 / M P A W E / W WM M MD D / vT T M I VI — moderate — dense
USES: bank erosion, container, dye plant, groundcover, rock garden, seacoast
REGION: Europe, c.1789, 2—8a

Helianthemum scoparium — Rush Rose, Bush Frostwort

CULTURE: P C Si Sa L / 4 5 6 7 8 / M P A W E / W WM M MD D / vT T M I VI — very fast — open
USES: bank erosion, border edging, flower bed, rock garden
REGION: California, 10

Helichrysum bracteatum — Strawflower, Everlasting — 'Dragon Hill', 'Monstrosum'

CULTURE: P C Si Sa L / 4 5 6 7 8 / M P A W E / W WM M MD D / vT T M I VI — fast — open
USES: container, cut flowers, flower bed, rock garden, window box
REGION: Australia, 9b—10

Hypericum androsaemum
Tutsan St. Johnswort

e. Europe 6—9 c.1600

bank erosion
border mass
container
fragrant leaves
groundcover
naturalizing
seacoast
woodland garden

P	C	Si	Sa	L
4	5	6	7	8
M	P	A	W	E
W	WM	M	MD	D
vT	T	M	I	vl

very short   fast

open   1-3

Hypericum frondosum
Golden St. Johnswort
'Sunburst'

s.e. U.S. 6—9a c.1776

bank erosion
border mass
container
groundcover
hedge

P	C	Si	Sa	L
4	5	6	7	8
M	P	A	W	E
W	WM	M	MD	D
vT	T	M	I	vl

very short   slow

open   3-6

Hypericum Kalmianum
Kalm St. Johnswort

n.e. U.S./Canada 4—8 i.1759

bank erosion
border mass
container
hedge
preservation

P	C	Si	Sa	L
4	5	6	7	8
M	P	A	W	E
W	WM	M	MD	D
vT	T	M	I	vl

very short   slow

open   1-3

Hypericum uralum
Ural St. Johnswort

Himalayas 3—6 i.1820

bank erosion
border edging
border mass
groundcover

P	C	Si	Sa	L
4	5	6	7	8
M	P	A	W	E
W	WM	M	MD	D
vT	T	M	I	vl

moderate   short

open   1-3

Indigofera kirilowi
Kirilow Indigo
'Coreana'

n. Korea 5—7 i.1899

bank erosion
border mass
groundcover
rock garden

P	C	Si	Sa	L
4	5	6	7	8
M	P	A	W	E
W	WM	M	MD	D
vT	T	M	I	vl

fast   short   ...deciduous

open   1-3

SMALL SHRUB	FORM	BARK	LEAF	FLOWER	FRUIT	CULTURE	USES	REGION

Linum perenne
Perrenial Blue Flax

'Alba'   'Sapphire'
'Diamond'   'Sky Blue'

- FORM: open, 1-3
- CULTURE: P C Si Sa L / 4 5 6 7 8 / M P A W E / W WM M MD D / vT T M I vl / fast / very short
- USES: border edge, container, flower bed, greenhouse, perennial border, rock garden
- REGION: 5–8, Europe

Lonicera alpigena nana
Alps Honeysuckle

- FORM: open, 1-3
- CULTURE: P C Si Sa L / 4 5 6 7 8 / M P A W E / W WM M MD D / vT T M I vl / fast / short
- USES: alpine garden, border mass, ground cover, rock garden
- REGION: 4b–8, c.1500, Europe

Lonicera involucrata
Twinberry
Bearberry Honeysuckle

- FORM: open, 6-12
- CULTURE: P C Si Sa L / 4 5 6 7 8 / M P A W E / W WM M MD D / vT T M I vl / fast / short
- USES: bank erosion, border mass, ground cover, rock garden
- REGION: 8–10, i.1824, w. U.S.

Lonicera microphylla
Littleleaf Honeysuckle

- FORM: moderate, 3-6
- CULTURE: P C Si Sa L / 4 5 6 7 8 / M P A W E / W WM M MD D / vT T M I vl / fast / short
- USES: border edge, border mass
- REGION: 6–9, i.1818, central Asia

Menziesia ciliicalyx syn. M. tubiflora
Mock Azalea

- FORM: open, 1-3
- CULTURE: P C Si Sa L / 4 5 6 7 8 / M P A W E / W WM M MD D / vT T M I vl / slow / short
- USES: alpine garden, rock garden
- REGION: 5b–9, i.1915, Japan

Potentilla gracilis
Northern Cinquefoil

alpine garden
rock garden
seacoast

P	C	Si	Sa	L
4	5	6	7	8
M	P	A	W	E
W	WM	M	MD	D
vT	T	M	I	vl

very fast | very short

dense | I-3

Potentilla simplex
Old Field Cinquefoil
Barren-strawberry

low maintenance
rock garden
seacoast

P	C	Si	Sa	L
4	5	6	7	8
M	P	A	W	E
W	WM	M	MD	D
vT	T	M	I	vl

fast | short

dense | I-3

Potentilla 'Snowflake
Coronation'

border edge
border mass

P	C	Si	Sa	L
4	5	6	7	8
M	P	A	W	E
W	WM	M	MD	D
vT	T	M	I	vl

fast | short

dense | I-3

Prostanthera nivea
Snowy Mintbush

container
espalier
fragrant leaves
hedge
seacoast
specimen / accent

P	C	Si	Sa	L
4	5	6	7	8
M	P	A	W	E
W	WM	M	MD	D
vT	T	M	I	vl

moderate | short

open | I-3

Rhamnus saxatilis
Rock Buckthorn

alpine garden
barrier
rock garden
shade garden

P	C	Si	Sa	L
4	5	6	7	8
M	P	A	W	E
W	WM	M	MD	D
vT	T	M	I	vl

slow | moderate

dense | I-3

...deciduous

SMALL SHRUB	FORM	BARK	LEAF	FLOWER	FRUIT	CULTURE	USES	REGION

Rhododendron atlanticum
Coast Azalea
'Choptank'
'Marydel'

moderate · 1-3 · | P C Si Sa L / 4 5 6 7 8 / M P A W E / W WM M MD D / vT T M I vl / moderate · long

border mass, container, oriental garden, seacoast, shade garden, woodland garden

n.e. U.S. · 5–9a · i.1916

Rhododendron canadense
Rhodora

open · 3-6 · | P C Si Sa L / 4 5 6 7 8 / M P A W E / W WM M MD D / vT T M I vl · moderate · long

alpine garden, border mass, naturalizing, rock garden, shade garden, woodland garden

n.e. U.S. · 2–5 · i.1767

Rhododendron kaempferi
Torch Azalea

moderate · 3-6 · | P C Si Sa L / 4 5 6 7 8 / M P A W E / W WM M MD D / vT T M I vl · moderate · long

border mass, container, oriental garden, patio garden, shade garden, woodland garden

Japan · 5b–9a · i.1844

Rosa arkansana
Arkansas Rose

open · 1-3 · | P C Si Sa L / 4 5 6 7 8 / M P A W E / W WM M MD D / vT T M I vl · fast · short

barrier, border mass, groundcover, perennial border

c. U.S. · 2–5 · c.1917

Rosa carolina
Carolina Rose
Pasture Rose

moderate · 3-6 · | P C Si Sa L / 4 5 6 7 8 / M P A W E / W WM M MD D / vT T M I vl · fast · short

bank erosion, barrier, border mass, naturalizing, perennial border, tall groundcover

e.c. U.S. · 5–8 · c.1826

Rosa nitida — Shining Rose

- bank erosion
- barrier
- border mass
- naturalizing
- seacoast

P	C	Si	Sa	L
4	5	6	7	8
M	P	A	W	E
W	WM	M	MD	D
vT	T	M	I	vI

moderate · fast · short

3·6

n.e. U.S. · 4–6 · i.1807

Rosa spinosissima **syn.** R. pimpinellifolia — Scotch Rose / Burnet Rose / 'Petite Pink'

- bank erosion
- barrier
- border mass
- naturalizing
- seacoast

P	C	Si	Sa	L
4	5	6	7	8
M	P	A	W	E
W	WM	M	MD	D
vT	T	M	I	vI

moderate · fast · short

3·6

Mediterranean · 5–8a · c.1600

Rubus laciniatus — Cutleaf Blackberry

- bank erosion
- barrier
- groundcover

P	C	Si	Sa	L
4	5	6	7	8
M	P	A	W	E
W	WM	M	MD	D
vT	T	M	I	vI

open · fast · very short

3·6

Europe · 5–7 · o.1770

Salix purpurea nana — Dwarf Purpleosier Willow

- basket weaving
- groundcover
- hedge
- kitchen garden
- sheared
- specimen / accent

P	C	Si	Sa	L
4	5	6	7	8
M	P	A	W	E
W	WM	M	MD	D
vT	T	M	I	vI

dense · fast · short

1·3

Europe · 4–9

Spiraea alba — Narrowleaf Meadowsweet / Spirea / Meadowsweet

- bog garden
- groundcover
- naturalizing
- pool garden
- wild garden

P	C	Si	Sa	L
4	5	6	7	8
M	P	A	W	E
W	WM	M	MD	D
vT	T	M	I	vI

open · fast · very short

3·6

e. U.S. · 3–9a

...deciduous **S2–12**

SMALL SHRUB	FORM	BARK	LEAF	FLOWER	FRUIT	CULTURE	USES	REGION

Spiraea albiflora
Japanese White Spirea

open · 3-6

border mass
hedge
seacoast
specimen / accent

P C Si Sa L
4 5 6 7 8
M P A W E
W WM M MD D
vT T M I vl
fast · very short

Japan · i.1868 · 4—9

Spiraea bullata
Crispleaf Spirea

open · 3-6

border mass
hedge
specimen / accent

P C Si Sa L
4 5 6 7 8
M P A W E
W WM M MD D
vT T M I vl
fast · very short

Japan · c.1881 · 6—10

Spiraea x bumalda
Bumalda Spirea

'Coccinea'   'Goldenflame'
'Froebelii'   'Norman'

open · 3-6

border mass
container
hedge
rock garden
seacoast
specimen / accent

P C Si Sa L
4 5 6 7 8
M P A W E
W WM M MD D
vT T M I vl
fast · very short

hybrid · c.1890 · (3b)—9a

Spiraea cantoniensis
syn. S. reevesiana
Reeve's Spirea

'Flora Plena'
'Lanceata'

moderate · 3-6

border mass
hedge
seacoast
specimen / accent

P C Si Sa L
4 5 6 7 8
M P A W E
W WM M MD D
vT T M I vl
moderate · short

China · i.1824 · 7—9

Symphoricarpos x
chenaulti
Chenault Coralberry

'Hancock'

moderate · 1-3

above wall
bank erosion
barrier
border mass
groundcover
seacoast

P C Si Sa L
4 5 6 7 8
M P A W E
W WM M MD D
vT T M I vl
fast · very short

hybrid · o.1910 · 5—8

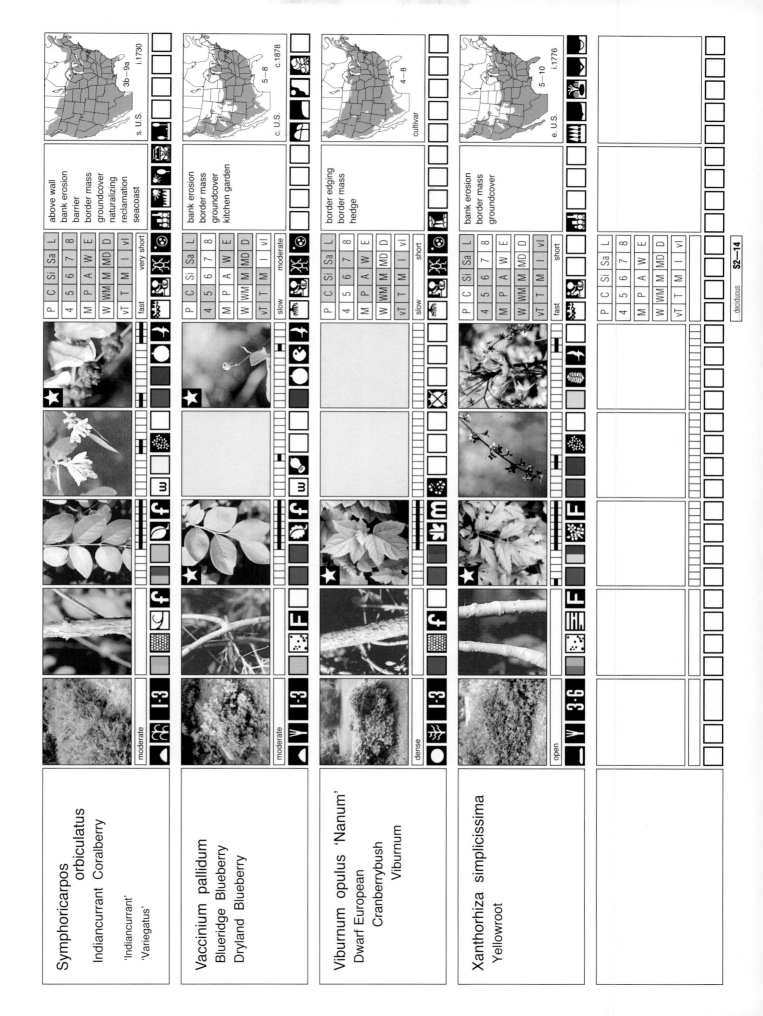

Symphoricarpos orbiculatus
Indiancurrant Coralberry
'Indiancurrant'
'Variegatus'

s. U.S. — 3b–9a — i.1730

above wall
bank erosion
barrier
border mass
groundcover
naturalizing
reclamation
seacoast

P	C	Si	Sa	L
4	5	6	7	8
M	P	A	W	E
W	WM	M	MD	D
vT	T	M	I	vl

fast — very short
moderate
moderate — 1-3

Vaccinium pallidum
Blueridge Blueberry
Dryland Blueberry

c. U.S. — 5–8 — c.1878

bank erosion
border mass
groundcover
kitchen garden

P	C	Si	Sa	L
4	5	6	7	8
M	P	A	W	E
W	WM	M	MD	D
vT	T	M	I	vl

slow — moderate
moderate
moderate — 1-3

Viburnum opulus 'Nanum'
Dwarf European
Cranberrybush
Viburnum

cultivar — 4–8

border edging
border mass
hedge

P	C	Si	Sa	L
4	5	6	7	8
M	P	A	W	E
W	WM	M	MD	D
vT	T	M	I	vl

slow — short
dense — 1-3

Xanthorhiza simplicissima
Yellowroot

e. U.S. — 5–10 — i.1776

bank erosion
border mass
groundcover

P	C	Si	Sa	L
4	5	6	7	8
M	P	A	W	E
W	WM	M	MD	D
vT	T	M	I	vl

fast — short
open — 3-6

P	C	Si	Sa	L
4	5	6	7	8
M	P	A	W	E
W	WM	M	MD	D
vT	T	M	I	vl

...deciduous

VERY SMALL SHRUB	FORM	BARK	LEAF	FLOWER	FRUIT	CULTURE	USES	REGION

Amorpha nana
Fragrant Falseindigo
Dwarfindigo Amorpha

open

P	C	Si	Sa	L
4	5	6	7	8
M	P	A	W	E
W	WM	M	MD	D
vT	T	M	I	vI

moderate · very short

nitrogen-fixing

c. N.America
3a—9   i:1811

Chaenomeles japonica alpina
Alpine Floweringquince

dense

P	C	Si	Sa	L
4	5	6	7	8
M	P	A	W	E
W	WM	M	MD	D
vT	T	M	I	vI

moderate · short

alpine garden
bank erosion
barrier
flower arranging
groundcover
rock garden
specimen / accent

Japan
3—6

Cotoneaster adpressa
Creeping Cotoneaster

dense

P	C	Si	Sa	L
4	5	6	7	8
M	P	A	W	E
W	WM	M	MD	D
vT	T	M	I	vI

very slow · moderate

bank erosion
bonsai
container
espalier
groundcover
rock garden
seacoast

w. China
(4b)—8   i:1896

Cytisus albus
Portuguese Broom

dense

P	C	Si	Sa	L
4	5	6	7	8
M	P	A	W	E
W	WM	M	MD	D
vT	T	M	I	vI

fast · short

bank erosion
container
formal garden
groundcover
rock garden
seacoast

e. Europe
6—10   i:1806

Cytisus x kewensis
Kew Broom

dense

P	C	Si	Sa	L
4	5	6	7	8
M	P	A	W	E
W	WM	M	MD	D
vT	T	M	I	vI

fast · short

above wall
bank erosion
groundcover
rock garden
seacoast
specimen / accent

hybrid
6b—10   o.1891

Daphne alpina — Alpine Daphne

alpine garden
border edging
rock garden
woolly leaves

P	C	Si	Sa	L
4	5	6	7	8
M	P	A	W	E
W	WM	M	MD	D
vT	T	M	I	vI

moderate · short
dense

5–7 · c.1759 · c. U.S.
I-3

Fuchsia procumbens — Trailing Fuchsia

above wall
bank erosion
container
groundcover
hanging basket
seacoast

P	C	Si	Sa	L
4	5	6	7	8
M	P	A	W	E
W	WM	M	MD	D
vT	T	M	I	vI

fast · short
dense

8a–10 · i.1854 · New Zealand
3-6

Genista pilosa — Silkyleaf Woadwaxen

'Goldilocks'
'Vancouver Gold'

bank erosion
container
groundcover
rock garden
seacoast

P	C	Si	Sa	L
4	5	6	7	8
M	P	A	W	E
W	WM	M	MD	D
vT	T	M	I	vI

fast · short
dense

5b–9a · i.1789 · Europe
3-6

Genista sagittalis — Arrow Broom · Winged Broom

bank erosion
border mass
container
groundcover
patio garden
rock garden
seacoast

P	C	Si	Sa	L
4	5	6	7	8
M	P	A	W	E
W	WM	M	MD	D
vT	T	M	I	vI

fast · short
dense

3—8 · i.1588 · Europe
3-6

Hypericum buckleyi — Blue Ridge St. Johnswort · Buckley St. Johnswort

bank erosion
groundcover
preservation
rock garden

P	C	Si	Sa	L
4	5	6	7	8
M	P	A	W	E
W	WM	M	MD	D
vT	T	M	I	vI

fast · short
dense

6—8 · e. U.S.
I-3

VERY SMALL SHRUB	FORM	BARK	LEAF	FLOWER	FRUIT	CULTURE	USES	REGION

Hypericum olympicum
Olympic St. Johnswort
uniflorum

- FORM: dense, 3·6
- CULTURE: P C Si Sa L / 4 5 6 7 8 / M P A W E / W WM M MD D / vT T M I vI — fast, short
- USES: bank erosion, groundcover, rock garden
- REGION: Asia Minor / Syria, 6—8

Indigofera incarnata
syn. I. decora
Chinese Indigo
'Alba'

- FORM: open, 3·6
- CULTURE: P C Si Sa L / 4 5 6 7 8 / M P A W E / W WM M MD D / vT T M I vI — fast, short
- USES: bank erosion, groundcover, rock garden, preservation
- REGION: China, 6—8, i:1846

Pachysandra procumbens
Alleghany Spurge
Alleghany Pachysandra

- FORM: dense, <1
- CULTURE: P C Si Sa L / 4 5 6 7 8 / M P A W E / W WM M MD D / vT T M I vI — moderate
- USES: groundcover, rock garden, specimen / accent, wild garden, woodland garden
- REGION: s.e. U.S., 4—7, i:1800

Salix arctica
Arctic Willow

- FORM: moderate, 1·3
- CULTURE: P C Si Sa L / 4 5 6 7 8 / M P A W E / W WM M MD D / vT T M I vI — slow, long
- USES: alpine garden, border mass, groundcover, rock garden
- REGION: N.America, 1—4

Salix repens
Creeping Willow
Rosemary Willow
argentea
'Boyd's Pendula'

- FORM: moderate, 1·3
- CULTURE: P C Si Sa L / 4 5 6 7 8 / M P A W E / W WM M MD D / vT T M I vI — slow, long
- USES: alpine garden, border mass, groundcover, rock garden, specimen / accent
- REGION: n. Europe, 3—9

Salix uva-ursi
Bearberry Willow

1—4 i.1890
n. N.America

alpine garden
groundcover
rock garden

P	C	Si	Sa	L
4	5	6	7	8
M	P	A	W	E
W	WM	M	MD	D
vT	T	M	I	vl

very slow — long

moderate

Spiraea decumbens
Prostrate Spirea
Decumbent Spirea

4—8 i.1830
n. Italy

bank erosion
rock garden
seacoast

P	C	Si	Sa	L
4	5	6	7	8
M	P	A	W	E
W	WM	M	MD	D
vT	T	M	I	vl

very fast — short

open

Symphoricarpos mollis
Creeping Snowberry
Spreading Snowberry

3b—8
California

bank erosion
groundcover
rock garden

P	C	Si	Sa	L
4	5	6	7	8
M	P	A	W	E
W	WM	M	MD	D
vT	T	M	I	vl

fast — short

moderate

..deciduous   S1—4

TALL VINE	FORM	BARK	LEAF	FLOWER	FRUIT	CULTURE	USES	REGION

Actinidia arguta
Bower Actinidia
Yang-Tao

'Akin #3'
'Ananasnaja'

open | 20-35

CULTURE: P C Si Sa L / 4 5 6 7 8 / M P A W E / W WM M MD D / vT T M I vl / short / very fast

USES:
arbor
fence
pergola
screen
shade arbor
trellis

REGION: 4b–8 c.1874 w. Asia

Antigonon leptopus
Mexican Creeper
Coralvine

'Flava'

open | 35-50

CULTURE: P C Si Sa L / 4 5 6 7 8 / M P A W E / W WM M MD D / vT T M I vl / short / very fast

USES:
arbor
container
cut flowers
fence
screening

REGION: 8b–10 Mexico

Campsis radicans
Common Trumpetcreeper
Trumpetvine

'Crimson Trumpet'

moderate | 20-35

CULTURE: P C Si Sa L / 4 5 6 7 8 / M P A W E / W WM M MD D / vT T M I vl / long / very fast

USES:
arbors
building walls
fence
pergola
pillars
trellis

REGION: 4b–10 i.1640 e. central U.S.

Congea tomentosa
Shower Orchid
Woolly Congea

moderate | 20-35

CULTURE: P C Si Sa L / 4 5 6 7 8 / M P A W E / W WM M MD D / vT T M I vl / short / fast

USES:
arbor
climbing vine
cut flowers
dried flowers
flower decorations
greenhouse
woolly leaves

REGION: 10 Burma

Parthenocissus quinquefolia
Virginia Creeper
American Ivy

'Engelmannii'

dense | 35-50

CULTURE: P C Si Sa L / 4 5 6 7 8 / M P A W E / W WM M MD D / vT T M I vl / long / very fast

USES:
arbors
buildings
groundcover
pergola
pillars
walls

REGION: 3b–10 i.1629 e. central U.S.

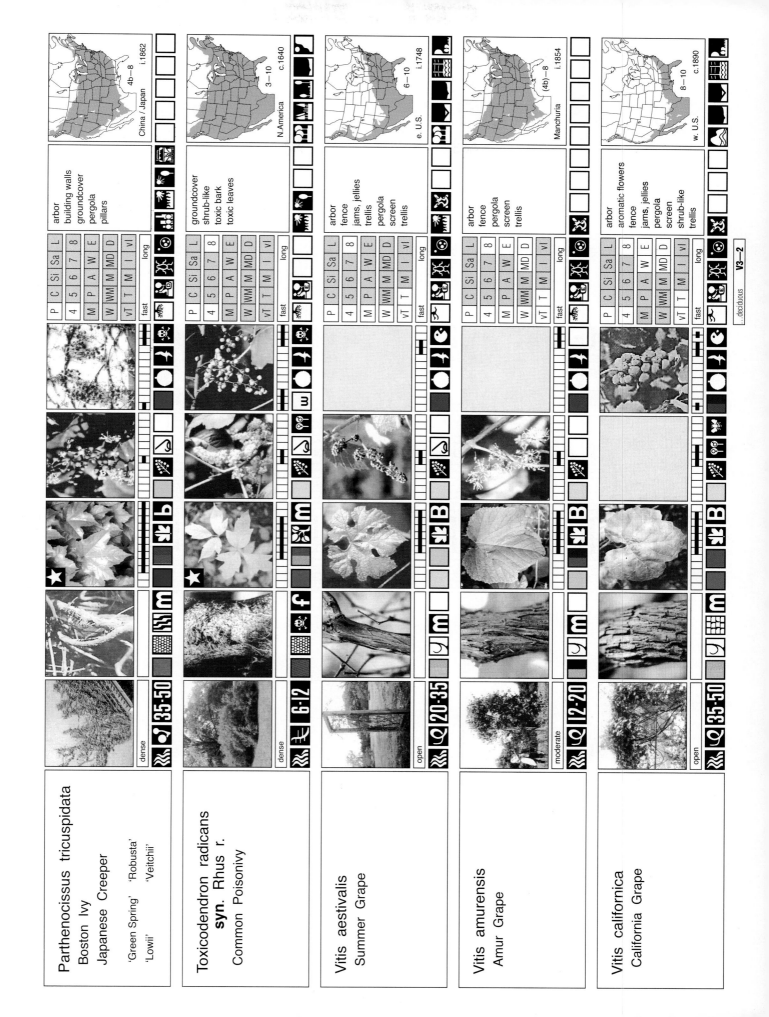

Parthenocissus tricuspidata

Boston Ivy

Japanese Creeper

'Green Spring' 'Robusta'

'Lowii' 'Veitchii'

China / Japan i.1862 4b–8

arbor
building walls
groundcover
pergola
pillars

P	C	Si	Sa	L
4	5	6	7	8
M	P	A	W	E
W	WM	M	MD	D
vT	T	M	I	vI

fast   long

dense   35-50

Toxicodendron radicans

syn. Rhus r.

Common Poisonivy

N.America c.1640 3–10

groundcover
shrub-like
toxic bark
toxic leaves

P	C	Si	Sa	L
4	5	6	7	8
M	P	A	W	E
W	WM	M	MD	D
vT	T	M	I	vI

fast   long

dense   6-12

Vitis aestivalis

Summer Grape

e. U.S. i.1748 6–10

arbor
fence
jams, jellies
trellis
pergola
screen
trellis

P	C	Si	Sa	L
4	5	6	7	8
M	P	A	W	E
W	WM	M	MD	D
vT	T	M	I	vI

fast   long

open   20-35

Vitis amurensis

Amur Grape

Manchuria i.1854 (4b)–8

arbor
fence
pergola
screen
trellis

P	C	Si	Sa	L
4	5	6	7	8
M	P	A	W	E
W	WM	M	MD	D
vT	T	M	I	vI

fast   long

moderate   12-20

Vitis californica

California Grape

w. U.S. c.1890 8–10

arbor
aromatic flowers
fence
jams, jellies
pergola
screen
shrub-like
trellis

P	C	Si	Sa	L
4	5	6	7	8
M	P	A	W	E
W	WM	M	MD	D
vT	T	M	I	vI

fast   long

open   35-50

...deciduous   **V3—2**

	FORM	BARK	LEAF	FLOWER	FRUIT	CULTURE	USES	REGION

Vitis riparia
Riverbank Grape
Frost Grape

- FORM: open — 20·35
- CULTURE: P C Si Sa L / 4 5 6 7 8 / M P A W E / W WM M MD D / vT T M I vl — fast — long
- USES: arbor / bank erosion / jams, jellies / naturalizing / pergola / screen
- REGION: c. N America — 3–8 — i.1556

Vitis vinifera
Wine Grape
European Grape

'Chardonnay' 'Merlot'
'Gewurztraminer'

- FORM: open — 12·20
- CULTURE: P C Si Sa L / 4 5 6 7 8 / M P A W E / W WM M MD D / vT T M I vl — fast — long
- USES: arbor / bank erosion / beverage / fence / screen / historic gardens / jams, jellies / seacoast
- REGION: Caucasian — 6–9 — long c.

Vitis vulpina
Frost Grape
Winter Grape

- FORM: open — 20·35
- CULTURE: P C Si Sa L / 4 5 6 7 8 / M P A W E / W WM M MD D / vT T M I vl — fast — long
- USES: arbor / bank erosion / jams, jellies / naturalizing / pergola / tree trunks / trellis / walls/fence/screen
- REGION: c. U.S. — 6–10 — 1806

Wisteria frutescens
American Wisteria

- FORM: open — 20·35
- CULTURE: P C Si Sa L / 4 5 6 7 8 / M P A W E / W WM M MD D / vT T M I vl — slow — short
- USES: above wall / arbor / pergola / pillar, post / seacoast / trellis
- REGION: s. U.S. — 7b–10 — i.1724

Wisteria sinensis
Chinese Wisteria

'Alba' 'Plena'
'Caroline' 'Rosea'

- FORM: open — 20·35
- CULTURE: P C Si Sa L / 4 5 6 7 8 / M P A W E / W WM M MD D / vT T M I vl — moderate — moderate
- USES: above wall / arbor / pergola / container / greenhouse / seacoast / standard / trellis / wall cover
- REGION: China — 6–10 — i.1816

MEDIUM VINE	FORM	BARK	LEAF	FLOWER	FRUIT	CULTURE	USES	REGION

Actinidia callosa

FORM: open, 12-20

CULTURE: P C Si Sa L / 4 5 6 7 8 / M P A W E / W WM M MD D / vT T M I vl / fast / short

USES: arbor, fence, pergola, screen, trellis, walls

REGION: India, c.1836, 7–10

Actinidia chinensis
Chinese Gooseberry
Kiwi
'Tomuri'
'Vincent'

FORM: open, 20-35

CULTURE: P C Si Sa L / 4 5 6 7 8 / M P A W E / W WM M MD D / vT T M I vl / fast / short

USES: arbor, fence, kitchen garden, orchard, pergola, screen, seacoast, trellis

REGION: China, i.1900, 7b–10

Actinidia polygama
Silvervine

FORM: open, 12-20

CULTURE: P C Si Sa L / 4 5 6 7 8 / M P A W E / W WM M MD D / vT T M I vl / fast / moderate

USES: arbor, fence, kitchen garden, pergola, screen, trellis

REGION: Japan, i.1861, 4b–8

Akebia trifoliata
Threeleaf Akebia

FORM: moderate, 12-20

CULTURE: P C Si Sa L / 4 5 6 7 8 / M P A W E / W WM M MD D / vT T M I vl / fast / short

USES: arbor, background, container, groundcover, pergola, seacoast, trellis, walls / fence

REGION: Japan / China, i.1895, 4b–9

Ampelopsis brevipedunculata
Porcelainberry
Turquoiseberry
'Elegans'   'Variegata'

FORM: open, 12-20

CULTURE: P C Si Sa L / 4 5 6 7 8 / M P A W E / W WM M MD D / vT T M I vl / moderate / short

USES: container, parapets, pergola, rock garden, screen, shade arbor, specimen / accent

REGION: Korea, c.1870, 5–9

Ampelopsis cordata
Heartleaf Ampelopsis

s.e. U.S. 5–9 i.1803

P	C	Si	Sa	L
4	5	6	7	8
M	P	A	W	E
W	WM	M	MD	D
vT	T	M	I	vl

arbor
groundcover
screen
shrub-like
tree trunk

fast · short · open · 20-35

Ampelopsis humulifolia
Hop Ampelopsis

n. China 7–10 i.1868

P	C	Si	Sa	L
4	5	6	7	8
M	P	A	W	E
W	WM	M	MD	D
vT	T	M	I	vl

arbor
groundcover
screen
shrub-like
trellis

fast · short · open · 12-20

Aristolochia californica
California Dutchmanspipe

w. U.S. 7–10 i.1877

P	C	Si	Sa	L
4	5	6	7	8
M	P	A	W	E
W	WM	M	MD	D
vT	T	M	I	vl

accent
arbor
container
pergola
screen
trellis

fast · short · dense · 12-20

Aristolochia durior
Common Dutchmanspipe
Pipe Vine

central U.S. 4b–7 i.1783

P	C	Si	Sa	L
4	5	6	7	8
M	P	A	W	E
W	WM	M	MD	D
vT	T	M	I	vl

container
pergola
screen
shade arbor
texture accent
trellis

fast · short · dense · 12-20

Campsis x tagliabuana
Hybrid Trumpetvine

'Madame Galen'

hybrid 5b–10 c.1889

P	C	Si	Sa	L
4	5	6	7	8
M	P	A	W	E
W	WM	M	MD	D
vT	T	M	I	vl

arbor
fence
pillar
screen
seacoast
shrub-like
specimen / accent

fast · moderate · moderate · 20-35

...deciduous **V2—2**

MEDIUM VINE	FORM	BARK	LEAF	FLOWER	FRUIT	CULTURE	USES	REGION

Celastrus orbiculatus
Oriental Bittersweet

'Indian Brave'
'Indian Maiden'

P	C	Si	Sa	L
4	5	6	7	8
M	P	A	W	E
W	WM	M	MD	D
vT	T	M	I	vl

moderate

bank erosion
house decoration
rock garden
screen
shade arbor
shrub-like
specimen / accent
trellis

Japan / China   i.1860   5—9

Celastrus scandens
American Bittersweet

P	C	Si	Sa	L
4	5	6	7	8
M	P	A	W	E
W	WM	M	MD	D
vT	T	M	I	vl

moderate

bank erosion
house decoration
rock garden
screen
seacoast
shrub-like
specimen / accent
trellis

c. N.America   i.1736   3b—8

Clematis apiifolia
October Clematis

P	C	Si	Sa	L
4	5	6	7	8
M	P	A	W	E
W	WM	M	MD	D
vT	T	M	I	vl

fast   short

arbor
pillar, post
screen
specimen / accent
trellis

Japan   i.a.1863   4—9

Clematis montana
Anemone Clematis

'Alba'   'Marjorie'
'Elizabeth' 'Tetrarose'

P	C	Si	Sa	L
4	5	6	7	8
M	P	A	W	E
W	WM	M	MD	D
vT	T	M	I	vl

fast   short

arbor
rock wall
screen
specimen / accent
trellis

China / Himalayas   i.1831   6—9

Clematis paniculata
syn. C. dioscoreifolia
Sweetautumn Clematis
Japanese Clematis

P	C	Si	Sa	L
4	5	6	7	8
M	P	A	W	E
W	WM	M	MD	D
vT	T	M	I	vl

moderate   short

rock garden
screen
shade arbor
specimen / accent
trellis

New Zealand   i.1840   4b—8

Clematis virginiana
Virgin's Bower

bank erosion
fence
reclamation
naturalizing
trellis
woodland garden

P	C	Si	Sa	L
4	5	6	7	8
M	P	A	W	E
W	WM	M	MD	D
vT	T	M	I	vl

fast — very short

e. N.America
3b—8   i.1767

open   6-12

Clematis vitalba
Travelers Joy
Old-Man's-Beard

bank erosion
trellis
woodland garden

P	C	Si	Sa	L
4	5	6	7	8
M	P	A	W	E
W	WM	M	MD	D
vT	T	M	I	vl

fast — short

Asia
10   i.b.1820

open   12-20

Cocculus carolinus
Carolina Moonseed
Snailseed
Coralbeads

rock garden
trellis
wire fence

P	C	Si	Sa	L
4	5	6	7	8
M	P	A	W	E
W	WM	M	MD	D
vT	T	M	I	vl

very fast — very short

s.e. U.S.
6—9   i.1759

open   6-12

Decumaria barbara
Climbing Hydrangea
Woodvamp

arbor
bog garden
building walls
groundcover

P	C	Si	Sa	L
4	5	6	7	8
M	P	A	W	E
W	WM	M	MD	D
vT	T	M	I	vl

moderate — moderate

s.e. U.S.
7b—9   i.1785

moderate   20-35

Hydrangea anomala petiolaris
Climbing Hydrangea

bank erosion
building walls
groundcover
seacoast
shrub-like
tree trunk
walls

P	C	Si	Sa	L
4	5	6	7	8
M	P	A	W	E
W	WM	M	MD	D
vT	T	M	I	vl

slow — long

Japan
5—(8a)   i.1839

moderate   20-35

…deciduous   V2—4

MEDIUM VINE	FORM	BARK	LEAF	FLOWER	FRUIT	CULTURE	USES	REGION

Lonicera caprifolium
Sweet Honeysuckle
Italian Woodbine

'Goldflame'

open · 12-20

CULTURE:
P C Si Sa L
4 5 6 7 8
M P A W E
W WM M MD D
vT T M I vl
fast · short

USES:
border edging
border mass
cottage garden
fence
groundcover
trellis
wire

REGION:
Europe
4–7 · i.b.1850

Lonicera x heckrotti
Everblooming Honeysuckle
Coral Honeysuckle

dense · 12-20

CULTURE:
P C Si Sa L
4 5 6 7 8
M P A W E
W WM M MD D
vT T M I vl
fast · short

USES:
cool greenhouse
gazebo
pillar
trellis
wire

REGION:
hybrid
4–9 · o.b.1895

Lonicera periclymenum
Woodbine Honeysuckle

'Belgiea'

dense · 12-20

CULTURE:
P C Si Sa L
4 5 6 7 8
M P A W E
W WM M MD D
vT T M I vl
fast · short

USES:
border mass
cottage garden
fence
groundcover
trellis
woodland garden

REGION:
Mediterranean
5b–9 · long c.

Parthenocissus henryana
Silvervein Creeper

'Silvervein Creeper'

dense · 20-35

CULTURE:
P C Si Sa L
4 5 6 7 8
M P A W E
W WM M MD D
vT T M I vl
fast · long

USES:
arbor
building walls
groundcover
pergola
pillars
walls

REGION:
China
7b–10 · i.1900

Philadelphus mexicanus
Mexican Mockorange
Evergreen Mockorange

dense · 6-12

CULTURE:
P C Si Sa L
4 5 6 7 8
M P A W E
W WM M MD D
vT T M I vl
fast · short

USES:
climbing vine
fence
hard to find
rare in cultivation
trellis

REGION:
Mexico
8–10 · c.1842

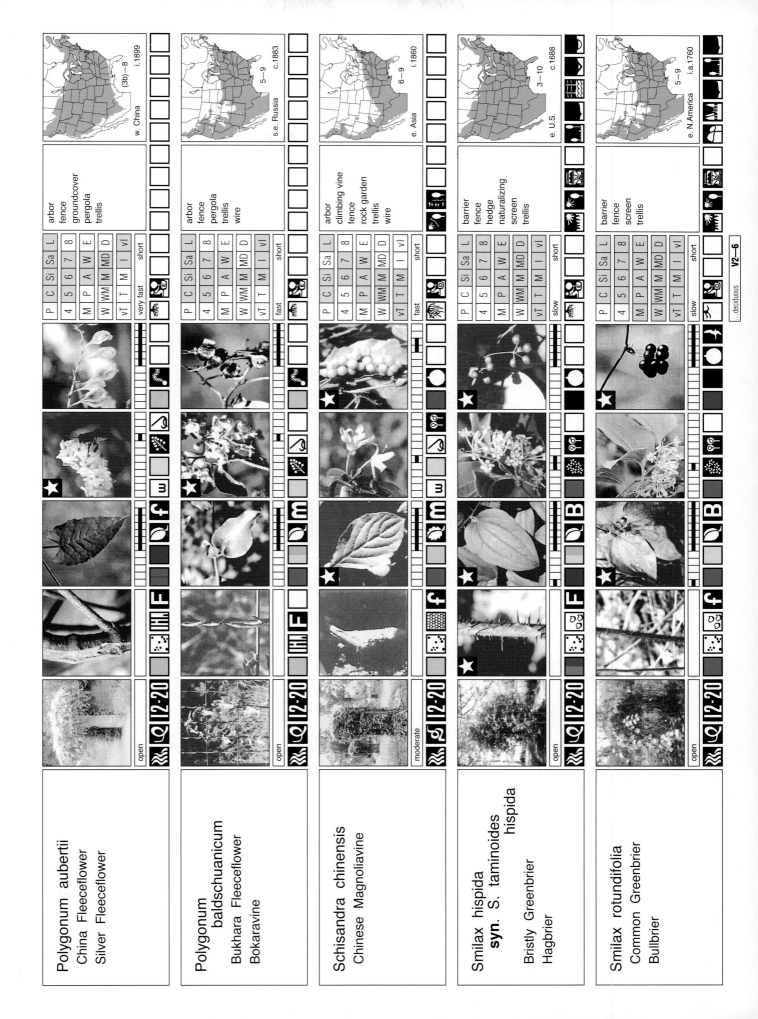

Polygonum aubertii
China Fleeceflower
Silver Fleeceflower

Polygonum baldschuanicum
Bukhara Fleeceflower
Bokaravine

Schisandra chinensis
Chinese Magnoliavine

Smilax hispida **syn.** S. taminoides hispida
Bristly Greenbrier
Hagbrier

Smilax rotundifolia
Common Greenbrier
Bullbrier

w. China   i.1899   (3b)—8
s.e. Russia   c.1883   5—9
e. Asia   i.1860   6—9
e. U.S.   c.1688   3—10
e. N.America   i.a.1760   5—9

arbor
fence
groundcover
pergola
trellis

arbor
fence
pergola
trellis
wire

arbor
climbing vine
fence
rock garden
trellis
wire

barrier
fence
hedge
naturalizing
screen
trellis

barrier
fence
screen
trellis

very fast   short
fast   short
fast   short
slow   short
slow   short

open
open
moderate
open
open

P C Si Sa L
4 5 6 7 8
M P A W E
W WM M MD D
vT T M I vl

MEDIUM VINE	FORM	BARK	LEAF	FLOWER	FRUIT	CULTURE	USES	REGION

Solanum wendlandi
Costa Rican Nightshade

open — 12·20

P	C	Si	Sa	L
4	5	6	7	8
M	P	A	W	E
W	WM	M	MD	D
vT	T	M	I	vl

slow / short

containers
greenhouse
pillars
poles
trellis
wires

Costa Rica   10

Tripterygium regeli
Regel's Threewingnut
Tripterygium

dense — 12·20

P	C	Si	Sa	L
4	5	6	7	8
M	P	A	W	E
W	WM	M	MD	D
vT	T	M	I	vl

fast / short

climbing vine
fence
trellis
wall

Japan   5–8   i.1905

Vigna caracalla
Snailflower
Corkscrewflower

open — 12·20

P	C	Si	Sa
4	5	6	7	8
M	P	A	W	E
W	WM	M	MD	D
vT	T	M	I	vl

fast / short

container
greenhouse
house plant
naturalizing
specimen / accent
trellis

S. America   9–10

Vitis coignetiae
Crimson Gloryvine
Gloryvine

moderate — 12·20

P	C	Si	Sa	L
4	5	6	7	8
M	P	A	W	E
W	WM	M	MD	D
vT	T	M	I	vl

very fast / moderate

arbor
fence
groundcover
pergola
trellis

Japan   5b–9   c.1875

Vitis labrusca
Fox Grape
Skunk Grape

'Concord'
'Catawba'

moderate — 20·35

P	C	Si	Sa	L
4	5	6	7	8
M	P	A	W	E
W	WM	M	MD	D
vT	T	M	I	vl

fast / long

arbor
beverage
fence
jams, jellies
kitchen garden
naturalizing
pergola
trellis

e. U.S.   4b–7   i.1656

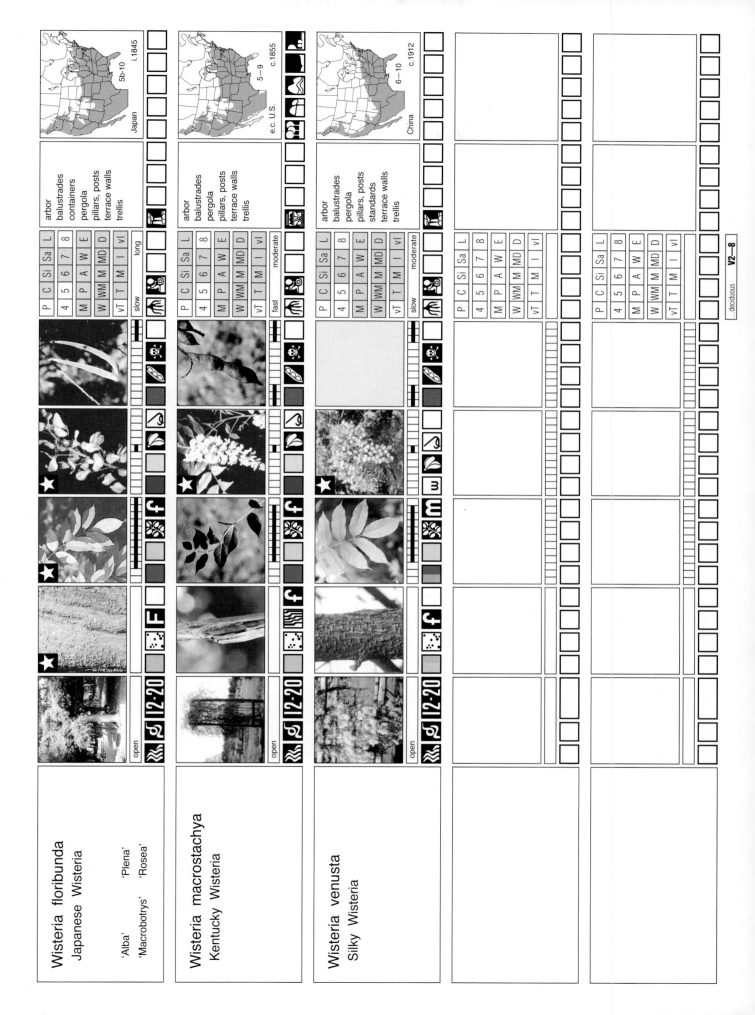

Wisteria floribunda
Japanese Wisteria

'Alba'   'Plena'
'Macrobotrys' 'Rosea'

Wisteria macrostachya
Kentucky Wisteria

Wisteria venusta
Silky Wisteria

Japan — 5b-10 — i.1845
e.c. U.S. — 5–9 — c.1855
China — 6–10 — c.1912

arbor
balustrades
containers
pergola
pillars, posts
terrace walls
trellis

arbor
balustrades
pergola
pillars, posts
terrace walls
trellis

arbor
balustrades
pergola
pillars, posts
standards
terrace walls
trellis

P C Si Sa L
4 5 6 7 8
M P A W E
W WM M MD D
vT T M I vl

long   slow   open   12·20
fast   moderate   open   12·20
slow   moderate   open   12·20

LOW VINE	FORM	BARK	LEAF	FLOWER	FRUIT	CULTURE	USES	REGION

Actinidia kolomikta
Kolomikta Actinidia
Kolomikta Kiwi

'Arctic Beauty'
'Krupnopladnaya'

FORM: moderate · 12-20
CULTURE: P C Si Sa L / 4 5 6 7 8 / M P A W E / W WM M MD D / vT T M I vl · fast
USES: arbor, fence, kitchen garden, pergola, screen, shrub-like, walls
REGION: Manchuria · 4b–8 · i.1855

Ampelopsis megalophylla
Spikenard Ampelopsis

FORM: open · 12-20
CULTURE: P C Si Sa L / 4 5 6 7 8 / M P A W E / W WM M MD D / vT T M I vl · fast · moderate
USES: arbors, low walls, pergola, pillars
REGION: China · 6–10 · i.1894

Asarina scandens
syn. Maurandya s.

FORM: open · 6-12
CULTURE: P C Si Sa L / 4 5 6 7 8 / M P A W E / W WM M MD D / vT T M I vl · very short
USES: container, fence, greenhouse, groundcover, trellis, wire
REGION: Mexico · 9–10

Campsis grandiflora
syn. C. chinensis
Chinese Trumpetcreeper
Chinese Trumpetflower

FORM: open · 6-12
CULTURE: P C Si Sa L / 4 5 6 7 8 / M P A W E / W WM M MD D / vT T M I vl · fast · short
USES: arbor, fence, pillar, screen, seacoast, shrub-like, specimen / accent
REGION: China · 7b–9 · i.1800

Clematis alpina
Alpine Clematis

'Columbine'   'Ruby'
'Pamela Jack'   'White Moth'

FORM: open · 6-12
CULTURE: P C Si Sa L / 4 5 6 7 8 / M P A W E / W WM M MD D / vT T M I vl · fast · very short
USES: alpine garden, groundcover, poisonous leaves, rock garden
REGION: Eurasia · 6b–8 · i.1753

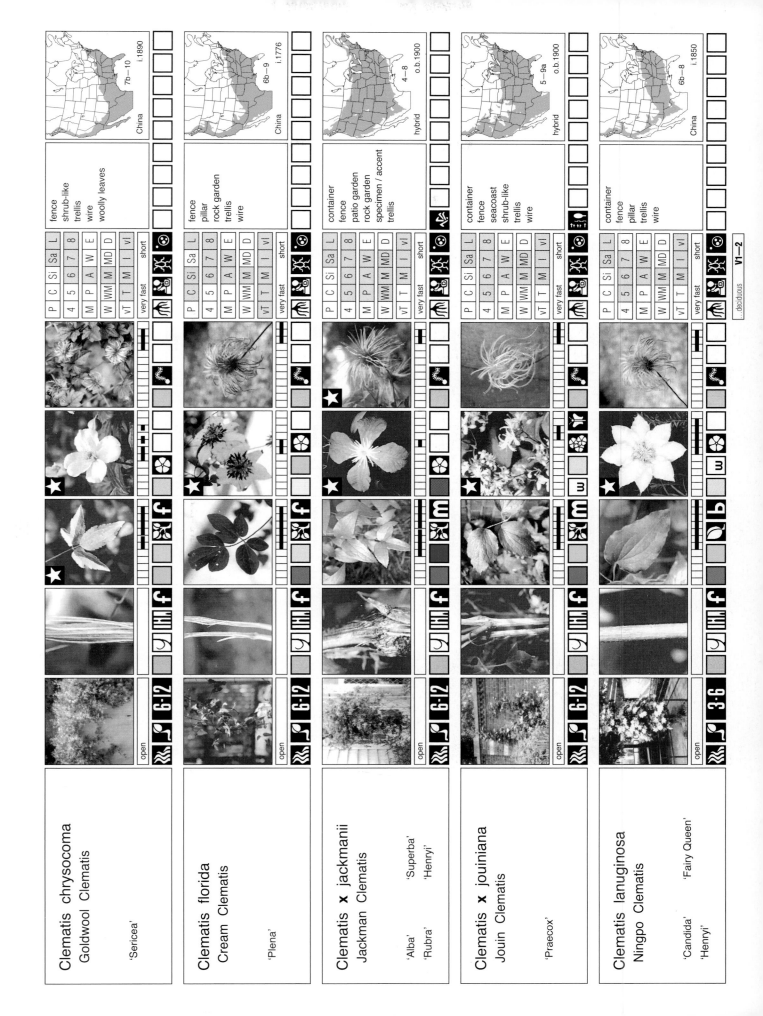

Clematis chrysocoma — Goldwool Clematis — 'Sericea'
China — 7b–10 — i.1890
fence, shrub-like, trellis, wire, woolly leaves

Clematis florida — Cream Clematis — 'Plena'
China — 6b–9 — i.1776
fence, pillar, rock garden, trellis, wire

Clematis × jackmanii — Jackman Clematis — 'Alba', 'Superba', 'Rubra', 'Henryi'
hybrid — 4–8 — o.b.1900
container, fence, patio garden, rock garden, specimen / accent, trellis

Clematis × jouiniana — Jouin Clematis — 'Praecox'
hybrid — 5–9a — o.b.1900
container, fence, seacoast, shrub-like, trellis, wire

Clematis lanuginosa — Ningpo Clematis — 'Candida', 'Fairy Queen', 'Henryi'
China — 6b–8 — i.1850
container, fence, pillar, trellis, wire

...deciduous   **V1–2**

LOW VINE	FORM	BARK	LEAF	FLOWER	FRUIT	CULTURE	USES	REGION

Clematis macropetala
Downy Clematis
Bigpetal Clematis

'Pink'   'Snowbird'
'Markham's Pink'

CULTURE: P C Si Sa L / 4 5 6 7 8 / M P A W E / W WM M MD D / vT T M I vl / short

REGION: 3b–7   China / Siberia   i:1910

USES: container / fence / rock garden / seacoast / specimen / accent / trellis / wire

open   6-12

Clematis patens
Lilac Clematis

'Fortunei'   'Standishii'
'Grandiflora'

CULTURE: P C Si Sa L / 4 5 6 7 8 / M P A W E / W WM M MD D / vT T M I vl / short

REGION: 6b–8   China   i:1836

USES: fence / specimen / accent / trellis / wire

open   6-12

Clematis tangutica
Golden Clematis

'Aurolin'

CULTURE: P C Si Sa L / 4 5 6 7 8 / M P A W E / W WM M MD D / vT T M I vl / short

REGION: 2b–8   Mongolia   c.1890

USES: fence / specimen / accent / trellis / wire

open   6-12

Clematis texensis
Scarlet Clematis
Texas Clematis

'Duchess of Albany'
'Gravetye Beauty'

CULTURE: P C Si Sa L / 4 5 6 7 8 / M P A W E / W WM M MD D / vT T M I vl / short

REGION: 4b–8   s.c. U.S. / Mexico   i.b.1878

USES: container / fence / seacoast / screen / specimen / accent / trellis / wire

open   6-12

Clematis versicolor
Leather Flower
Manycolor Clematis

CULTURE: P C Si Sa L / 4 5 6 7 8 / M P A W E / W WM M MD D / vT T M I vl / short

REGION: 5–8   e. U.S.

USES: fence / rock garden / trellis / wire

open

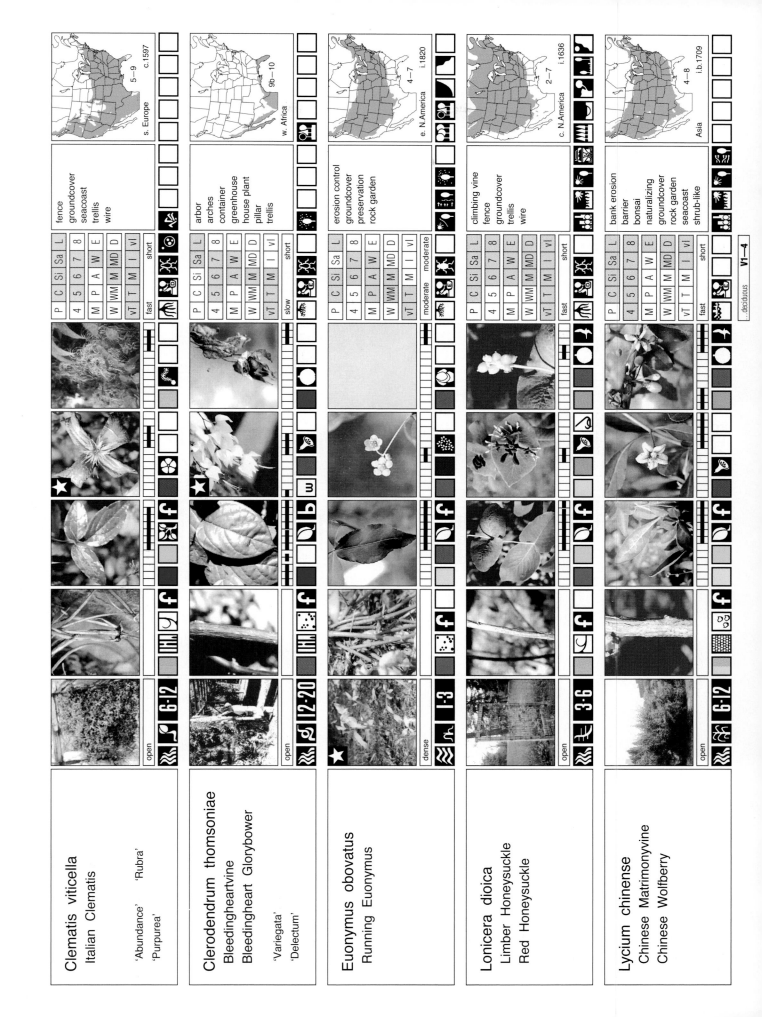

Clematis viticella
Italian Clematis

'Abundance'   'Rubra'
'Purpurea'

fence
groundcover
seacoast
trellis
wire

s. Europe   c.1597
5–9

Clerodendrum thomsoniae
Bleedingheartvine
Bleedingheart Glorybower

'Variegata'
'Delectum'

arbor
arches
container
greenhouse
house plant
pillar
trellis

w. Africa
9b–10

Euonymus obovatus
Running Euonymus

erosion control
groundcover
preservation
rock garden

e. N.America   i.1820
4–7

Lonicera dioica
Limber Honeysuckle
Red Honeysuckle

climbing vine
fence
groundcover
trellis
wire

c. N.America   i.1636
2–7

Lycium chinense
Chinese Matrimonyvine
Chinese Wolfberry

bank erosion
barrier
bonsai
naturalizing
groundcover
rock garden
seacoast
shrub-like

Asia   i.b.1709
4–8

...deciduous   **V1—4**

LOW VINE

...deciduous V1—5

LOW VINE	FORM	BARK	LEAF	FLOWER	FRUIT	CULTURE	USES	REGION

Lycium halimifolium — Common Matrimonyvine
- FORM: dense, 6-12
- CULTURE: P C Si Sa L / 4 5 6 7 8 / M P A W E / W WM M MD D / vT T M I vl — very short, fast
- USES: bank erosion, barrier, climbing vine, groundcover, rock garden, seacoast, shrub-like, trellis
- REGION: Asia, 5—9, long c.

Menispermum canadense — Common Moonseed / Yellow Parilla
- FORM: open, 6-12
- CULTURE: very fast, very short
- USES: fence, groundcover, specimen / accent, trellis
- REGION: n. N.America, 4—9, c.1646

Parthenocissus inserta — Thicket Creeper / Woodbine
- FORM: open, 20-35
- CULTURE: very fast, very short
- USES: bank erosion, climbing vine, rock garden
- REGION: c. N.America, 3b—10, c.b.1800

Periploca sepium — Chinese Silkvine
- FORM: open, 6-12
- CULTURE: moderate, fast, short
- USES: bank erosion, fence, trellis, wire
- REGION: China, 4—9, i.1905

Toxicodendron diversilobum — **syn.** Rhus t. / Pacific Poisonoak
- FORM: moderate, 12-20
- CULTURE: fast, moderate
- USES: climbing vine, poisonous, post, tree trunk
- REGION: w. N.America, 6—10, c.1845

Evergreen master file

LARGE TREE	FORM	BARK	LEAF	FLOWER	FRUIT	CULTURE	USES	REGION

Abies alba
Silver Fir

dense   12·20

fast   long

P	C	Si	Sa	L
4	5	6	7	8
M	P	A	W	E
W	WM	M	MD	D
vT	T	M	I	vI

background
barrier
border mass
formal garden
mass planting
specimen / accent

Europe   5—7   i.1603

Abies amabilis
Cascade Fir
Pacific Silver Fir

dense   20·35

slow   long

P	C	Si	Sa	L
4	5	6	7	8
M	P	A	W	E
W	WM	M	MD	D
vT	T	M	I	vI

background
barrier
border mass
formal garden
mass planting
specimen / accent
seacoast

w. N.America   6—8   i.1830

Abies bracteata
Bristlecone Fir
Santa Lucia Fir

dense   12·20

slow   long

P	C	Si	Sa	L
4	5	6	7	8
M	P	A	W	E
W	WM	M	MD	D
vT	T	M	I	vI

background
barrier
border mass
formal garden
mass planting
preservation
specimen / accent

California   7—9   i.1852

Abies cephalonica
Greek Fir

dense   20·35

slow   long

P	C	Si	Sa	L
4	5	6	7	8
M	P	A	W	E
W	WM	M	MD	D
vT	T	M	I	vI

background
barrier
border mass
formal garden
mass planting
specimen / accent

Greece   6b—8a   i.1824

Abies concolor
White Fir

dense   20·35

slow   very long

P	C	Si	Sa	L
4	5	6	7	8
M	P	A	W	E
W	WM	M	MD	D
vT	T	M	I	vI

barrier
border mass
formal garden
mass planting
specimen / accent
windbreak

w. U.S.   4—8   i.1873

Abies veitchi
Veitch Fir

background
barrier
border mass
formal garden
deer proof
mass planting
specimen / accent

P	C	Si	Sa	L
4	5	6	7	8
M	P	A	W	E
W	WM	M	MD	D
vT	T	M	I	vI

short
fast

Japan 3b–(6b) i:1879

dense 20-35

Aleurites moluccana
syn. Rhus vernicifolia
Candlenut Tree
Varnish Tree

raw fruit — toxic
shade

P	C	Si	Sa	L
4	5	6	7	8
M	P	A	W	E
W	WM	M	MD	D
vT	T	M	I	vI

short
fast

Malaysia 10

open 50-75

Araucaria araucana
Monkeypuzzletree
Chilean Pine

container
formal garden
greenhouse
house plant
sculptural
seacoast
specimen / accent

P	C	Si	Sa	L
4	5	6	7	8
M	P	A	W	E
W	WM	M	MD	D
vT	T	M	I	vI

long
moderate

Chile 8–10 i.1795

moderate 35-50

Araucaria bidwilli
Bunya Bunya
Bunya Pine

container
formal garden
greenhouse
pool garden
seacoast
shade
specimen / accent

P	C	Si	Sa	L
4	5	6	7	8
M	P	A	W	E
W	WM	M	MD	D
vT	T	M	I	vI

long
slow

Australia 9–10 i.1843

dense-open 35-50

Araucaria cunninghami
Hoop Pine
Cunningham Araucaria

container
formal garden
sculptural
specimen / accent

P	C	Si	Sa	L
4	5	6	7	8
M	P	A	W	E
W	WM	M	MD	D
vT	T	M	I	vI

long
slow

e. Australia 9–10

moderate 20-35

...evergreen **T8—4**

LARGE TREE

LARGE TREE	FORM	BARK	LEAF	FLOWER	FRUIT	CULTURE	USES	REGION

Araucaria heterophylla **syn.** A excelsa
Norfolk Island Pine
'Magestic Beauty'

- FORM: open — 12-20
- CULTURE: P C Si Sa L / 4 5 6 7 8 / M P A W E / W WM M MD D / vT T M I vl — moderate / long
- USES: container, formal garden, greenhouse, house plant, narrow space, patio garden, pool garden, sculptural
- REGION: Norfolk Island — 10

Athrotaxis selaginoides
King William Pine

- FORM: dense — 50-75
- CULTURE: P C Si Sa L / 4 5 6 7 8 / M P A W E / W WM M MD D / vT T M I vl — moderate / moderate
- USES: background, formal garden, screen, specimen / accent
- REGION: Tasmania — 10 i.1857

Calocedrus decurrens **syn.** Libocedrus d.
California Insense Cedar

- FORM: dense — 12-20
- CULTURE: P C Si Sa L / 4 5 6 7 8 / M P A W E / W WM M MD D / vT T M I vl — very slow / long
- USES: bonsai, formal garden, narrow space, screen, seacoast, specimen / accent, windbreak
- REGION: w. U.S. — (6a)—9a i.1853

Caryota urens
Toddy Fishtailpalm
Wine Fishtailpalm
Sago Fishtailpalm

- FORM: open — 20-35
- CULTURE: P C Si Sa L / 4 5 6 7 8 / M P A W E / W WM M MD D / vT T M I vl — fast / moderate
- USES: container, beverages, greenhouse, screen, sculptural, specimen / accent
- REGION: India — 10

Casuarina cunninghamiana
Australian Pine
River SheOak

- FORM: open — 20-35
- CULTURE: P C Si Sa L / 4 5 6 7 8 / M P A W E / W WM M MD D / vT T M I vl — fast / short
- USES: bank erosion, canopy tree, friut arrangement, seacoast, screen, shade, specimen / accent
- REGION: e. Australia — 10

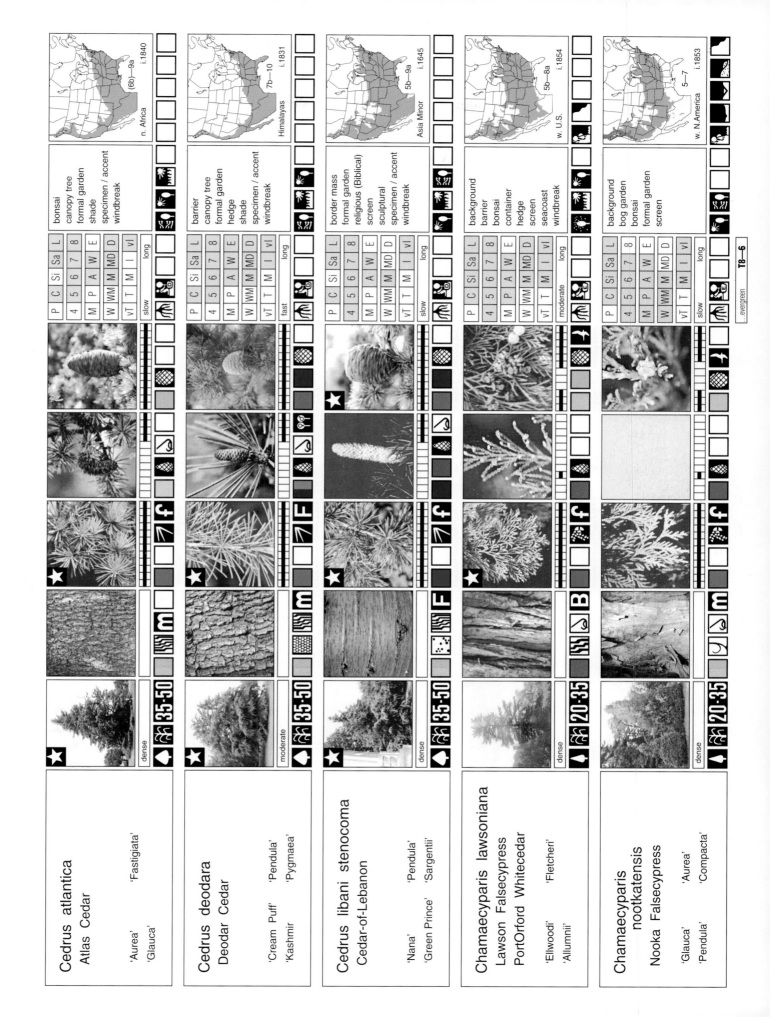

Cedrus atlantica — Atlas Cedar
'Aurea' 'Fastigiata' 'Glauca'

Uses: bonsai, canopy tree, formal garden, shade, specimen / accent, windbreak

P	C	Si	Sa	L
4	5	6	7	8
M	P	A	W	E
W	WM	M	MD	D
vT	T	M	I	vl

slow — long
35-50, dense

n. Africa, (6b)–9a, i.1840

Cedrus deodara — Deodar Cedar
'Cream Puff' 'Pendula' 'Kashmir' 'Pygmaea'

Uses: barrier, canopy tree, formal garden, hedge, shade, specimen / accent, windbreak

P	C	Si	Sa	L
4	5	6	7	8
M	P	A	W	E
W	WM	M	MD	D
vT	T	M	I	vl

fast — long
35-50, moderate

Himalayas, 7b–10, i.1831

Cedrus libani stenocoma — Cedar-of-Lebanon
'Nana' 'Pendula' 'Green Prince' 'Sargentii'

Uses: border mass, formal garden, religious (Biblical), screen, sculptural, specimen / accent, windbreak

P	C	Si	Sa	L
4	5	6	7	8
M	P	A	W	E
W	WM	M	MD	D
vT	T	M	I	vl

slow — long
35-50, dense

Asia Minor, 5b–9a, i.1645

Chamaecyparis lawsoniana — Lawson Falsecypress / PortOrford Whitecedar
'Ellwoodi' 'Fletcheri' 'Allumnii'

Uses: background, barrier, bonsai, container, hedge, screen, seacoast, windbreak

P	C	Si	Sa	L
4	5	6	7	8
M	P	A	W	E
W	WM	M	MD	D
vT	T	M	I	vl

moderate — long
20-35, dense

w. U.S., 5b–8a, i.1854

Chamaecyparis nootkatensis — Nooka Falsecypress
'Glauca' 'Aurea' 'Pendula' 'Compacta'

Uses: background, bog garden, bonsai, formal garden, screen

P	C	Si	Sa	L
4	5	6	7	8
M	P	A	W	E
W	WM	M	MD	D
vT	T	M	I	vl

slow — long
20-35, dense

w. N.America, 5–7, i.1853

LARGE TREE	FORM	BARK	LEAF	FLOWER	FRUIT	CULTURE	USES	REGION

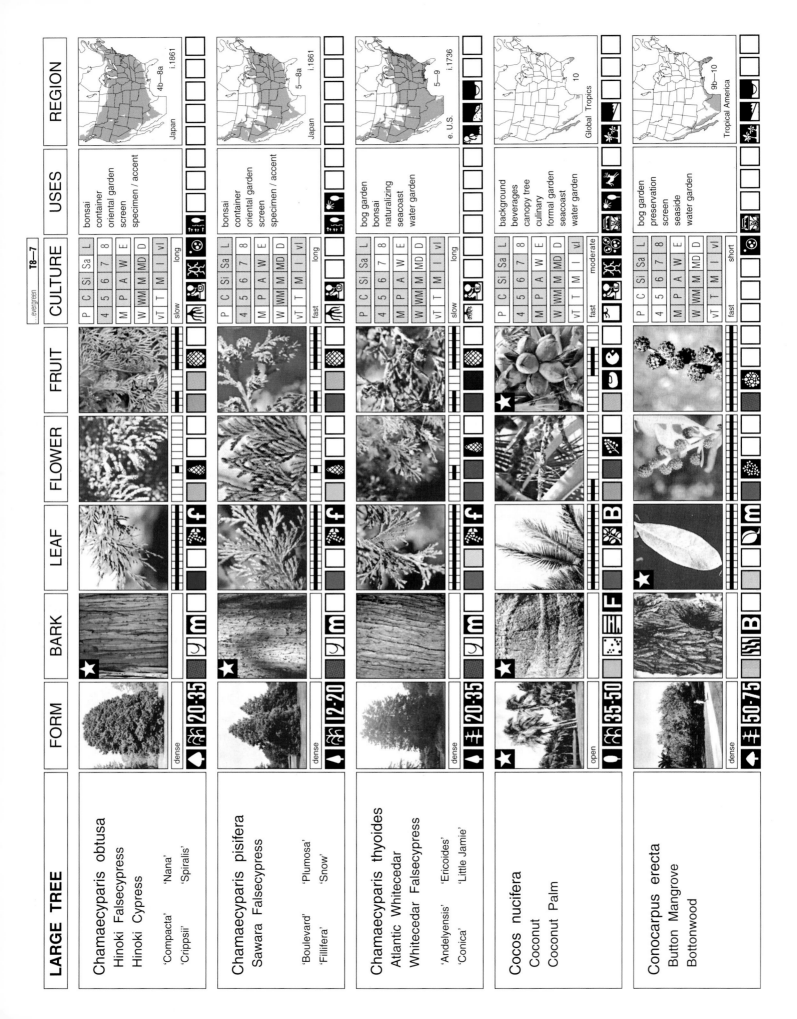

Chamaecyparis obtusa
Hinoki Falsecypress
Hinoki Cypress

'Compacta' 'Nana'
'Crippsii' 'Spiralis'

dense · 20-35

CULTURE: P C Si Sa L · 4 5 6 7 8 · M P A W E · W WM M MD D · vT T M I vI · slow — long

USES: bonsai / container / oriental garden / screen / specimen / accent

REGION: 4b—8a · i.1861 · Japan

Chamaecyparis pisifera
Sawara Falsecypress

'Boulevard' 'Plumosa'
'Fillifera' 'Snow'

dense · 12-20

CULTURE: P C Si Sa L · 4 5 6 7 8 · M P A W E · W WM M MD D · vT T M I vI · fast — long

USES: bonsai / container / oriental garden / screen / specimen / accent

REGION: 5—8a · i.1861 · Japan

Chamaecyparis thyoides
Atlantic Whitecedar
Whitecedar Falsecypress

'Andelyensis' 'Ericoides'
'Conica' 'Little Jamie'

dense · 20-35

CULTURE: P C Si Sa L · 4 5 6 7 8 · M P A W E · W WM M MD D · vT T M I vI · slow — long

USES: bog garden / bonsai / naturalizing / seacoast / water garden

REGION: 5—9 · i.1736 · e. U.S.

Cocos nucifera
Coconut
Coconut Palm

open · 35-50

CULTURE: P C Si Sa L · 4 5 6 7 8 · M P A W E · W WM M MD D · vT T M I vI · fast — moderate

USES: background / beverages / canopy tree / culinary / formal garden / seacoast / water garden

REGION: 10 · Global Tropics

Conocarpus erecta
Button Mangrove
Bottonwood

dense · 50-75

CULTURE: P C Si Sa L · 4 5 6 7 8 · M P A W E · W WM M MD D · vT T M I vI · fast — short

USES: bog garden / preservation / screen / seaside / water garden

REGION: 9b—10 · Tropical America

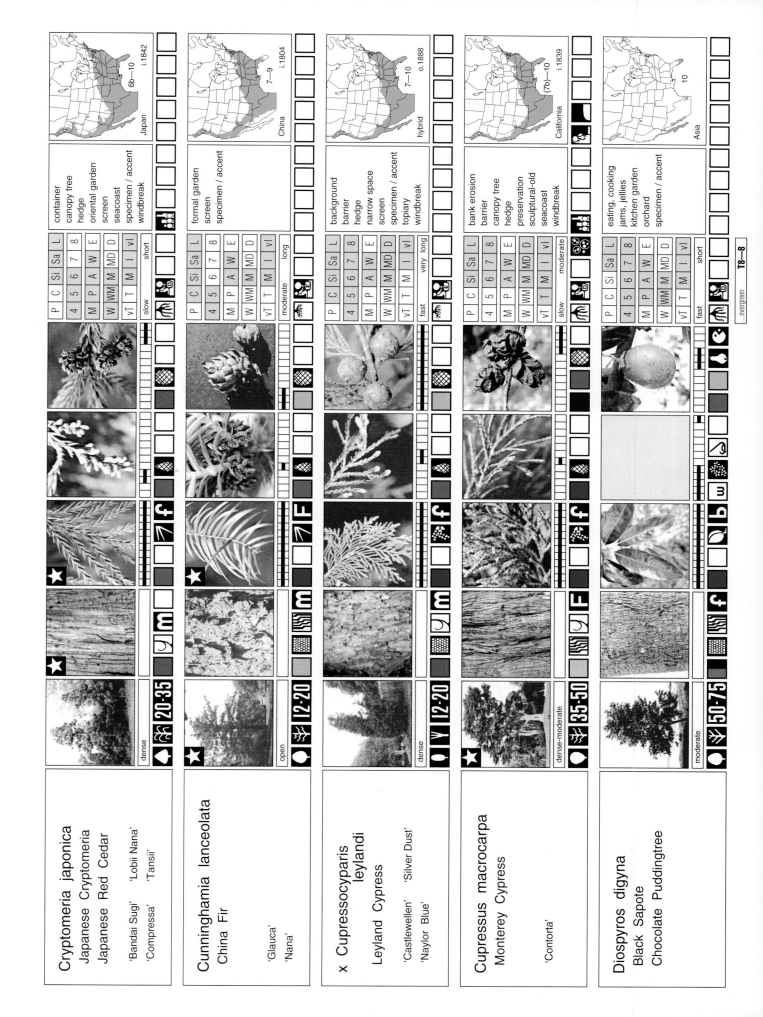

Cryptomeria japonica
Japanese Cryptomeria
Japanese Red Cedar
'Bandai Sugi'   'Lobii Nana'
'Compressa'   'Tansii'

container / canopy tree / hedge / oriental garden / screen / seacoast / specimen / accent / windbreak

Japan   6b–10   i.1842

20-35   dense   short

P C Si Sa L / 4 5 6 7 8 / M P A W E / W WM M MD D / vT T M I vI

Cunninghamia lanceolata
China Fir
'Glauca'
'Nana'

formal garden / screen / specimen / accent

China   7–9   i.1804

12-20   open   moderate — long

P C Si Sa L / 4 5 6 7 8 / M P A W E / W WM M MD D / vT T M I vI

---

x Cupressocyparis leylandi
Leyland Cypress
'Castlewellen'   'Silver Dust'
'Naylor Blue'

background / barrier / hedge / narrow space / screen / specimen / accent / topiary / windbreak

hybrid   7–10   o.1888

12-20   dense   fast — very long

P C Si Sa L / 4 5 6 7 8 / M P A W E / W WM M MD D / vT T M I vI

Cupressus macrocarpa
Monterey Cypress
'Contorta'

bank erosion / barrier / canopy tree / hedge / preservation / sculptural-old / seacoast / windbreak

California   (7b)–10   i.1839

35-50   dense-moderate   slow — moderate

P C Si Sa L / 4 5 6 7 8 / M P A W E / W WM M MD D / vT T M I vI

Diospyros digyna
Black Sapote
Chocolate Puddingtree

eating, cooking / jams, jellies / kitchen garden / orchard / specimen / accent

Asia   10

50-75   moderate   fast — short   ...evergreen

P C Si Sa L / 4 5 6 7 8 / M P A W E / W WM M MD D / vT T M I vI

LARGE TREE	FORM	BARK	LEAF	FLOWER	FRUIT	CULTURE	USES	REGION

Eucalyptus camaldulensis
Red Gum
Longbeak Eucalyptus

- FORM: open · 35-50
- CULTURE: P C Si Sa L / 4 5 6 7 8 / M P A W E / W WM M MD D / vT T M I vl / fast · moderate
- USES: bank erosion, bee tree, canopy tree, screen, seacoast, shade, specimen / accent
- REGION: 8—10 · Australia

Eucalyptus globulus
Blue Gum
Tasmanian Blue Eucalyptus
'Compacta'

- FORM: open · 35-50
- CULTURE: P C Si Sa L / 4 5 6 7 8 / M P A W E / W WM M MD D / vT T M I vl / fast · moderate
- USES: bank erosion, canopy tree, leaf arrangements, screen, shade, specimen / accent, windbreak
- REGION: 9—10 · c.1829 · Australia

Eucalyptus gunni
Cider Gum
Cider Eucalyptus

- FORM: open · 35-50
- CULTURE: P C Si Sa L / 4 5 6 7 8 / M P A W E / W WM M MD D / vT T M I vl / fast · moderate
- USES: canopy tree, leaf arrangements, screen, seacoast, specimen / accent, windbreak
- REGION: 7b—10 · Australia

Ficus benghalensis
Banyon Fig

- FORM: moderate · 50-75
- CULTURE: P C Si Sa L / 4 5 6 7 8 / M P A W E / W WM M MD D / vT T M I vl / long
- USES: bog garden, sculptural, shade, specimen / accent, street tree, water garden
- REGION: 10 · India

Fraxinus uhdei
Evergreen Ash
Shamel Ash
'Majestic Beauty'

- FORM: moderate · 35-50
- CULTURE: P C Si Sa L / 4 5 6 7 8 / M P A W E / W WM M MD D / vT T M I vl / fast · short
- USES: background, canopy tree, shade, street tree
- REGION: 9—10 · Mexico / California

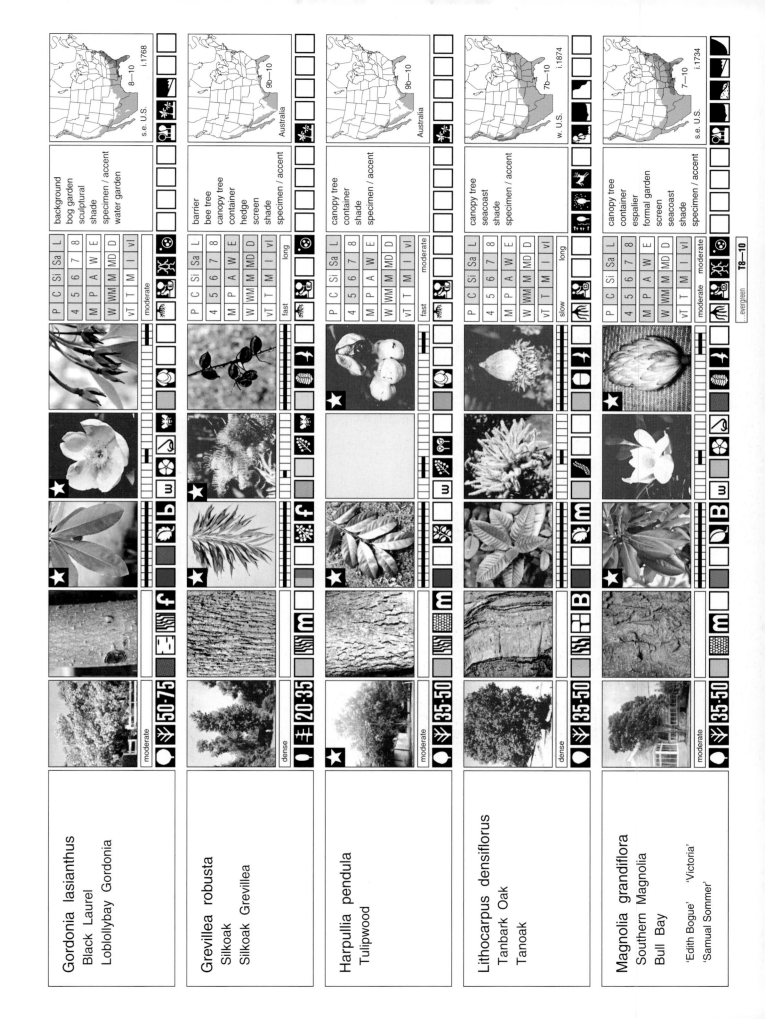

Gordonia lasianthus
Black Laurel
Loblollybay Gordonia

s.e. U.S. · 8—10 · i.1768

background
bog garden
sculptural
shade
specimen / accent
water garden

P C Si Sa L · 4 5 6 7 8 · M P A W E · W WM M MD D · vT T M I Vl
moderate · moderate · 50-75

Grevillea robusta
Silkoak
Silkoak Grevillea

Australia · 9b—10

barrier
bee tree
canopy tree
container
hedge
screen
shade
specimen / accent

P C Si Sa L · 4 5 6 7 8 · M P A W E · W WM M MD D · vT T M I Vl
long · dense · fast · 20-35

Harpullia pendula
Tulipwood

Australia · 9b—10

canopy tree
container
shade
specimen / accent

P C Si Sa L · 4 5 6 7 8 · M P A W E · W WM M MD D · vT T M I Vl
moderate · moderate · fast · 35-50

Lithocarpus densiflorus
Tanbark Oak
Tanoak

w. U.S. · 7b—10 · i.1874

canopy tree
seacoast
shade
specimen / accent

P C Si Sa L · 4 5 6 7 8 · M P A W E · W WM M MD D · vT T M I Vl
long · dense · slow · 35-50

Magnolia grandiflora
Southern Magnolia
Bull Bay

'Edith Bogue'   'Victoria'
'Samual Sommer'

s.e. U.S. · 7—10 · i.1734

canopy tree
container
espalier
formal garden
screen
seacoast
shade
specimen / accent

P C Si Sa L · 4 5 6 7 8 · M P A W E · W WM M MD D · vT T M I Vl
moderate · moderate · moderate · 35-50

...evergreen   **T8—10**

LARGE TREE	FORM	BARK	LEAF	FLOWER	FRUIT	CULTURE	USES	REGION

Melaleuca leucadendron
Cajeputtree
Paperbarktree

FORM: open-moderate · 20-35

CULTURE:
P C Si Sa L
4 5 6 7 8
M P A W E
W WM M MD D
vT T M I vl
fast

USES:
bank erosion
canopy tree
hedge
inovasive
patio garden
seacoast
shade
specimen / accent

REGION: 9b—10 · Australia

Michelia doltsopa
Himalayan Magnolia

FORM: moderate · 20-35

CULTURE:
P C Si Sa L
4 5 6 7 8
M P A W E
W WM M MD D
vT T M I vl
moderate · short

USES:
groupings
patio garden
specimen / accent

REGION: 6—8 · Himalayas

Phyllostachys bambosoides
Giant Timber Bamboo
Japanese Timber Bamboo

'White Crookstem'

FORM: dense · 20-35

CULTURE:
P C Si Sa L
4 5 6 7 8
M P A W E
W WM M MD D
vT T M I vl
fast · short

USES:
background
forestry
hedge
oriental garden
rarely flowers
screen
specimen / accent

REGION: 8—10 · Japan

Phyllostachys pubescens
Moso Bamboo

FORM: dense · 35-50

CULTURE:
P C Si Sa L
4 5 6 7 8
M P A W E
W WM M MD D
vT T M I vl
fast · short

USES:
background
hedge
oriental garden
rarely flowers
screen
specimen / accent

REGION: 8—10 · China

Picea abies
Norway Spruce

'Little Gem'   'Nidiformis'
'Maxwellii'   'Repens'

FORM: dense · 20-35

CULTURE:
P C Si Sa L
4 5 6 7 8
M P A W E
W WM M MD D
vT T M I vl
moderate · long

USES:
background
bonsai
border mass
hedge
screen
specimen / accent
windbreak

REGION: 3—8a · n. Europe · i.e.col.x.

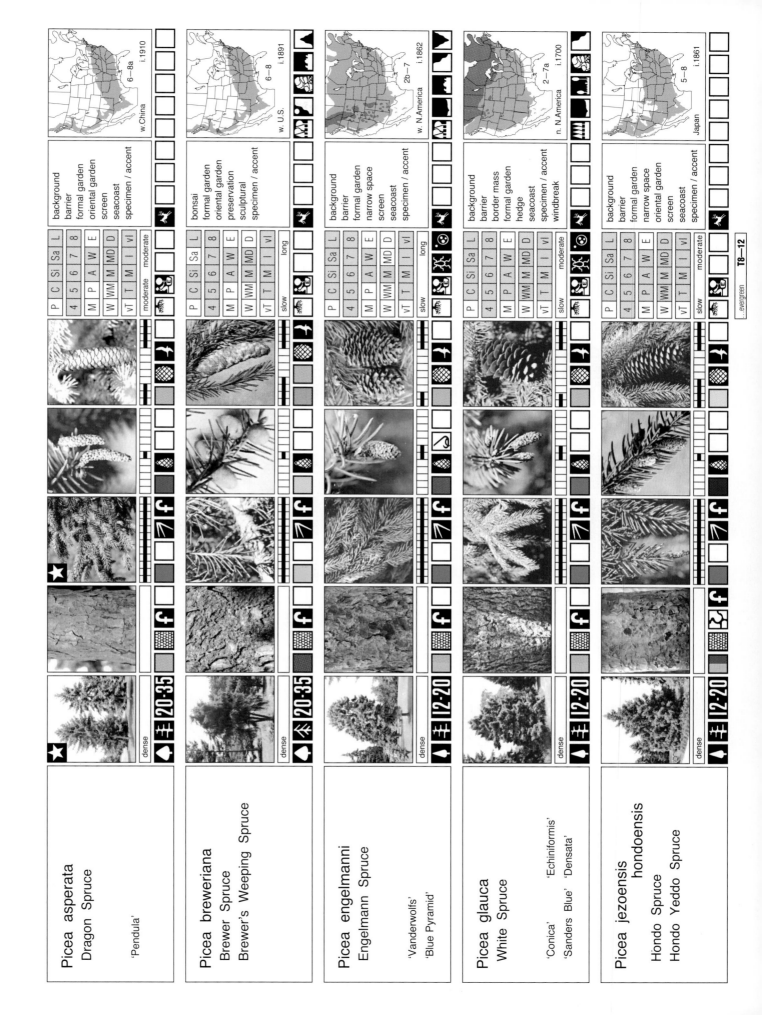

Picea asperata — Dragon Spruce — 'Pendula'
w.China — 6–8a — i.1910
background / barrier / formal garden / oriental garden / screen / seacoast / specimen / accent
20-35 — dense — moderate

Picea breweriana — Brewer Spruce — Brewer's Weeping Spruce
w. U.S. — 6–8 — i.1891
bonsai / formal garden / oriental garden / preservation / sculptural / specimen / accent
20-35 — dense — moderate — long

Picea engelmanni — Engelmann Spruce — 'Vanderwolfs' 'Blue Pyramid'
w. N.America — 2b–7 — i.1862
background / barrier / formal garden / narrow space / screen / seacoast / specimen / accent
12-20 — dense — slow — long

Picea glauca — White Spruce — 'Conica' 'Echiniformis' 'Sanders Blue' 'Densata'
n. N.America — 2–7a — i.1700
background / barrier / border mass / formal garden / hedge / seacoast / specimen / accent / windbreak
12-20 — dense — slow — moderate

Picea jezoensis hondoensis — Hondo Spruce — Hondo Yeddo Spruce
Japan — 5–8 — i.1861
background / barrier / formal garden / narrow space / oriental garden / screen / seacoast / specimen / accent
12-20 — dense — slow — moderate

...evergreen T8—12

LARGE TREE	FORM	BARK	LEAF	FLOWER	FRUIT	CULTURE	USES	REGION

Picea koyamai
Koyama Spruce

'Nana'
'Pendula'

dense | 12·20

CULTURE:
P C Si Sa L
4 5 6 7 8
M P A W E
W WM M MD D
vT T M I vl
slow

USES:
background
bonsai
formal garden
narrow space
oriental garden
screen
specimen / accent

REGION: Japan 5–8 i.1914

Picea omorika
Serbian Spruce

'Nana'
'Pendula'

dense | 20·35

CULTURE:
P C Si Sa L
4 5 6 7 8
M P A W E
W WM M MD D
vT T M I vl
moderate   long

USES:
background
barrier
bonsai
formal garden
narrow space
screen
specimen / accent
windbreak

REGION: s.e. Europe 4b–8a i.1889

Picea orientalis
Oriental Spruce

'Gowdy'   'Nana'
'Aurea Compacta'

dense | 20·35

CULTURE:
P C Si Sa L
4 5 6 7 8
M P A W E
W WM M MD D
vT T M I vl
slow

USES:
background
barrier
bonsai
formal garden
oriental garden
rock garden
specimen / accent

REGION: Asia Minor 5–8a i.1839

Picea pungens
Colorado Spruce

'Bakeri'   'Hoopsii'
'Fat Albert'   'Koster'

dense | 20·35

CULTURE:
P C Si Sa L
4 5 6 7 8
M P A W E
W WM M MD D
vT T M I vl
slow   long

USES:
background
barrier
border mass
bonsai
formal garden
hedge
specimen / accent
windbreak

REGION: w. U.S. 2b–7 i.1862

Picea pungens glauca
Colorado Blue Spruce

'Globosa'

dense | 20·35

CULTURE:
P C Si Sa L
4 5 6 7 8
M P A W E
W WM M MD D
vT T M I vl
slow   long

USES:
background
barrier
bonsai
formal garden
screen
seacoast
specimen / accent
windbreak

REGION: variety 3–6a

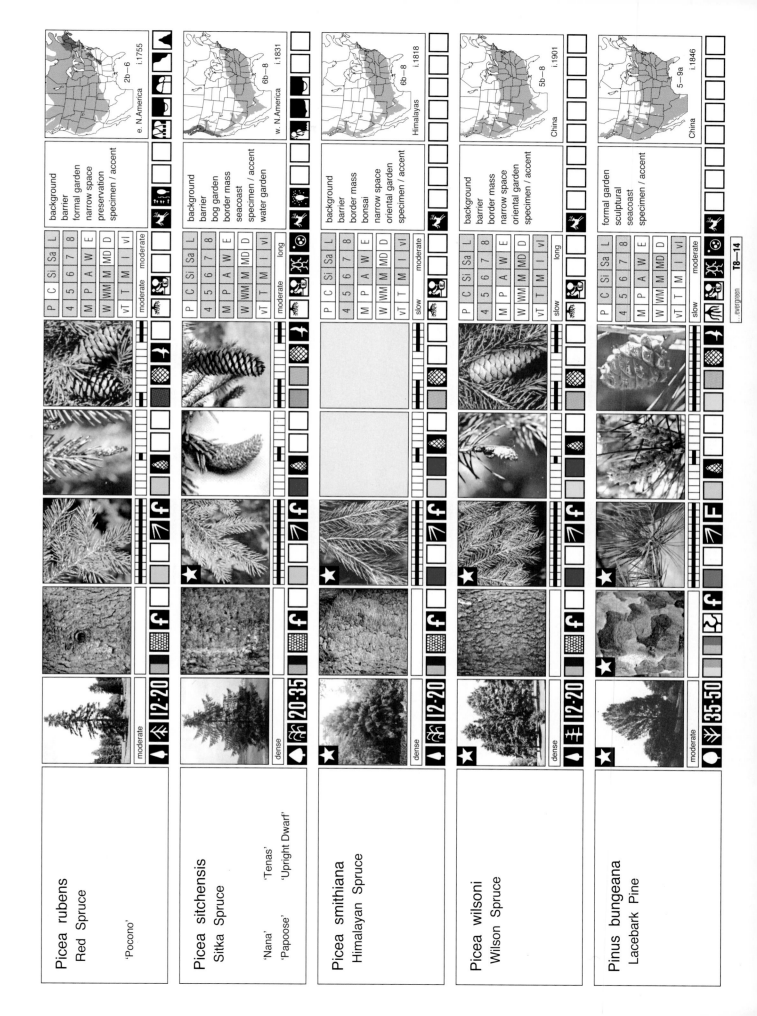

Picea rubens
Red Spruce
'Pocono'

e. N.America   2b–6   i.1755

background
barrier
formal garden
narrow space
preservation
specimen / accent

P | C | Si | Sa | L
4 | 5 | 6 | 7 | 8
M | P | A | W | E
W | WM | M | MD | D
vT | T | M | I | vl

moderate | moderate

moderate   12-20

Picea sitchensis
Sitka Spruce
'Nana' 'Tenas'
'Papoose' 'Upright Dwarf'

w. N.America   6b–8   i.1831

background
barrier
bog garden
border mass
seacoast
specimen / accent
water garden

P | C | Si | Sa | L
4 | 5 | 6 | 7 | 8
M | P | A | W | E
W | WM | M | MD | D
vT | T | M | I | vl

moderate | long

dense   20-35

Picea smithiana
Himalayan Spruce

Himalayas   6b–8   i.1818

background
barrier
border mass
bonsai
narrow space
oriental garden
specimen / accent

P | C | Si | Sa | L
4 | 5 | 6 | 7 | 8
M | P | A | W | E
W | WM | M | MD | D
vT | T | M | I | vl

slow | moderate

dense   12-20

Picea wilsoni
Wilson Spruce

China   5b–8   i.1901

background
barrier
border mass
narrow space
oriental garden
specimen / accent

P | C | Si | Sa | L
4 | 5 | 6 | 7 | 8
M | P | A | W | E
W | WM | M | MD | D
vT | T | M | I | vl

slow | long

dense   12-20

Picea bungeana
Lacebark Pine

China   5–9a   i.1846

formal garden
sculptural
seacoast
specimen / accent

P | C | Si | Sa | L
4 | 5 | 6 | 7 | 8
M | P | A | W | E
W | WM | M | MD | D
vT | T | M | I | vl

slow | moderate

moderate   35-50

...evergreen   T8–14

LARGE TREE	FORM	BARK	LEAF	FLOWER	FRUIT	CULTURE	USES	REGION

Pinus contorta latifolia
Lodgepole Pine

moderate · 12-20

CULTURE: P C Si Sa L / 4 5 6 7 8 / M P A W E / W WM M MD D / vT T M I vl — fast / short

USES: bank erosion, naturalizing, reclamation, rock garden, windbreak

REGION: w. N. America — 2b—8a i.1853

Pinus coulteri
Coulter Pine

moderate · 35-50

CULTURE: P C Si Sa L / 4 5 6 7 8 / M P A W E / W WM M MD D / vT T M I vl — slow / long

USES: background, barrier, border mass, screen, specimen / accent, windbreak

REGION: California — 7b—9 i.1832

Pinus densiflora
Japanese Red Pine

'Globosa'   "Oculus Draconis"
'Pendula'   'Umbraculifera'

moderate · 50-75

CULTURE: P C Si Sa L / 4 5 6 7 8 / M P A W E / W WM M MD D / vT T M I vl — moderate / moderate

USES: bonsai, border mass, oriental garden, sculptural, specimen / accent, windbreak

REGION: Japan — (5a)—7 i.1852

Pinus echinata
Shortleaf Pine
Southern Yellow Pine

moderate · 50-75

CULTURE: P C Si Sa L / 4 5 6 7 8 / M P A W E / W WM M MD D / vT T M I vl — fast / moderate

USES: background, forestry, shade, specimen / accent, windbreak

REGION: e. N.America — 6—9a i.1739

Pinus elliotti
Slash Pine

moderate · 50-75

CULTURE: P C Si Sa L / 4 5 6 7 8 / M P A W E / W WM M MD D / vT T M I vl — fast / short

USES: background, bank erosion, canopy tree, reclamation, restoration, sculptural, shade, specimen / accent

REGION: s.e. N.America — 8b—10

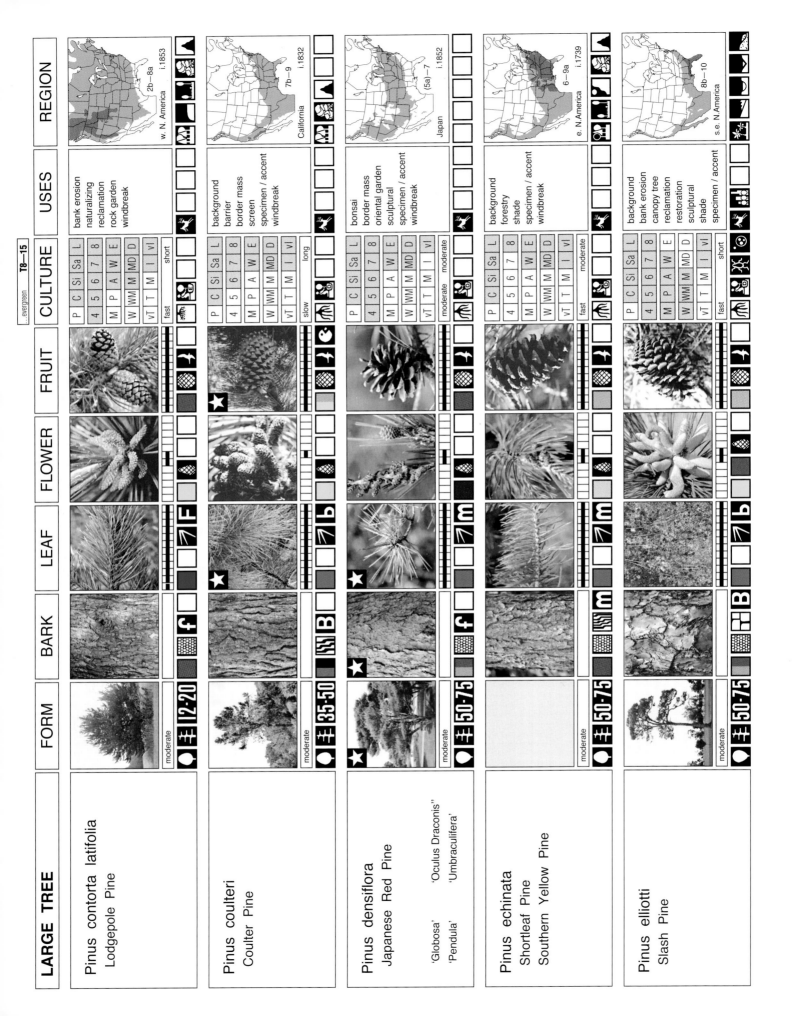

Pinus griffithi
Himalayan White Pine
Bhutan Pine

moderate 35-50

P	C	Si	Sa	L
4	5	6	7	8
M		P	A	E
W		WM	M	MD	D
vT		T	M	I	vl

fast   moderate

background
barrier
canopy tree
screen
sculptural
shade
specimen / accent

Himalayas   5b–9a   i.1827

Pinus jeffreyi
Jeffrey Pine

moderate 35-50

P	C	Si	Sa	L
4	5	6	7	8
M		P	A	E
W		WM	M	MD	D
vT		T	M	I	vl

fast   very long

background
barrier
bonsai
screen
sculptural
shade
specimen / accent
windbreak

w. N.America   6–9   i.1853

Pinus koraiensis
Korean Pine

'Dragon Eye'   'Jack Corbet'
'Glauca'

moderate 50-75

P	C	Si	Sa	L
4	5	6	7	8
M		P	A	E
W		WM	M	MD	D
vT		T	M	I	vl

slow   long

background
canopy tree
oriental garden
patio garden
screen
sculptural
shade
specimen / accent

Japan   3b–8a   i.1861

Pinus lambertiana
Sugar Pine

moderate 35-50

P	C	Si	Sa	L
4	5	6	7	8
M		P	A	E
W		WM	M	MD	D
vT		T	M	I	vl

fast   long

background
forestry
large cones
sculptural
shade
specimen / accent

w.N.America   6b–8a   i.1827

Pinus monticola
Western White Pine

'Pygmaea'
'Rigby's Weeping'

moderate 35-50

P	C	Si	Sa	L
4	5	6	7	8
M		P	A	E
W		WM	M	MD	D
vT		T	M	I	vl

moderate   long

background
barrier
border mass
forestry
screen
sculptural
shade

w. N.America   5–(7b)   i.1831

...evergreen   **T8—16**

LARGE TREE	FORM	BARK	LEAF	FLOWER	FRUIT	CULTURE	USES	REGION

Pinus nigra
Austrian Pine

'Globosa'   "Pyramidalis"
'Hornibrookiana' 'Pygmaea'

- moderate
- 50-75
- CULTURE:
  - P C Si Sa L
  - 4 5 6 7 8
  - M P A W E
  - W WM M MD D
  - vT T M I vl
  - moderate ... moderate
- USES:
  - background
  - border mass
  - canopy tree
  - screen
  - seacoast
  - shade
  - windbreak
- REGION: 4—8a   i.1759   s.e. Europe

Pinus palustris
Longleaf Pine
Southern Yellow Pine

- moderate
- 50-75
- CULTURE:
  - P C Si Sa L
  - 4 5 6 7 8
  - M P A W E
  - W WM M MD D
  - vT T M I vl
  - slow ... moderate
- USES:
  - background
  - border mass
  - forestry
  - shade
  - specimen / accent
  - windbreak
- REGION: 7b—10   i.1730   s.e. N.America

Pinus peuce
Balkan Pine
Macedonian Pine

'Nana'

- moderate
- 20-35
- CULTURE:
  - P C Si Sa L
  - 4 5 6 7 8
  - M P A W E
  - W WM M MD D
  - vT T M I vl
  - fast ... moderate
- USES:
  - background
  - barrier
  - formal garden
  - screen
  - shade
  - specimen / accent
  - windbreak
- REGION: 5—9a   i.1863   Balkans

Pinus pinaster
Maritime Pine
Cluster Pine

- moderate
- 20-35
- CULTURE:
  - P C Si Sa L
  - 4 5 6 7 8
  - M P A W E
  - W WM M MD D
  - vT T M I vl
  - fast ... short
- USES:
  - bank erosion
  - seacoast
  - sculptural
  - shade
  - specimen / accent
  - windbreak
- REGION: 7b—9a   c.16th c.   n. Africa

Pinus pinea
Italian Stone Pine
Umbrella Pine

- dense
- 50-75
- CULTURE:
  - P C Si Sa L
  - 4 5 6 7 8
  - M P A W E
  - W WM M MD D
  - vT T M I vl
  - moderate ... moderate
- USES:
  - bank erosion
  - canopy tree
  - sculptural
  - shade
  - specimen / accent
  - windbreak
- REGION: 8—10   Mediterranean

Pinus ponderosa
Ponderosa Pine
Western Yellow Pine

w. N.America   3b—8a   i.1826

background
barrier
border mass
shade
specimen / accent
windbreak

P	C	Si	Sa	L
4	5	6	7	8
M	P	A	W	E
W	WM	M	MD	D
vT	T	M	I	vI

moderate   long

moderate   35-50

Pinus radiata
Monterey Pine

California   7b—10   i.1833

background
bank erosion
hedge
preservation
screen
seacoast
shade
specimen / accent

P	C	Si	Sa	L
4	5	6	7	8
M	P	A	W	E
W	WM	M	MD	D
vT	T	M	I	vI

fast   short

open-moderate   35-50

Pinus resinosa
Red Pine

n.e. N.America   3—6   c.1736

background
barrier
border mass
hedge
seacoast
shade
windbreak

P	C	Si	Sa	L
4	5	6	7	8
M	P	A	W	E
W	WM	M	MD	D
vT	T	M	I	vI

moderate   moderate

moderate   35-50

Pinus rigida
Pitch Pine

'Sherman Eddy'

e. N.America   4b—7a   c.1759

background
border mass
naturalizing
sculptural
shade
seacoast
windbreak

P	C	Si	Sa	L
4	5	6	7	8
M	P	A	W	E
W	WM	M	MD	D
vT	T	M	I	vI

fast   short

moderate   35-50

Pinus strobus
Eastern White Pine

'Fastigiata'   'Pendula'
'Nana'   'Umbraculifera'

e. N.America   3—9a   c.16th c.

background
border mass
hedge
screen
sculptural
seacoast
shade
specimen / accent

P	C	Si	Sa	L
4	5	6	7	8
M	P	A	W	E
W	WM	M	MD	D
vT	T	M	I	vI

slow   long

moderate   35-50

LARGE TREE

FORM	BARK	LEAF	FLOWER	FRUIT	CULTURE	USES	REGION

Pinus sylvestris — Scotch Pine
'Beauoronensis' 'Repens'
'Fastigiata' 'Watereri'

CULTURE: P C Si Sa L / 4 5 6 7 8 / M P A W E / W WM M MD D / vT T M I vl — moderate / fast / moderate
USES: background, border mass, sculptural, seacoast, shade, specimen / accent, windbreak
REGION: 2b–8 / n. Europe / col. x.
FORM: 50-75

Pinus taeda — Loblolly Pine / Bull Pine

CULTURE: P C Si Sa L / 4 5 6 7 8 / M P A W E / W WM M MD D / vT T M I vl — moderate / fast / long
USES: border mass, canopy tree, forestry, naturalizing, seacoast, shade, specimen / accent, windbreak
REGION: 6b–9a / e. N.America / i.1741
FORM: 50-75

Pinus thunbergiana — Japanese Black Pine
'Pygmaea' 'Yatsubusa'
'Thunderhead'

CULTURE: P C Si Sa L / 4 5 6 7 8 / M P A W E / W WM M MD D / vT T M I vl — moderate / fast / slow
USES: bonsai, border mass, container, formal garden, seacoast, screen, sculptural, windbreak
REGION: 5b–9a / Japan / i.1855
FORM: 35-50

Podocarpus totara — Totara Pine / Mahogany Pine

CULTURE: P C Si Sa L / 4 5 6 7 8 / M P A W E / W WM M MD D / vT T M I vl — dense / slow / moderate
USES: background, barrier, formal garden, greenhouse, hedge, screen, specimen / accent
REGION: 9–10 / New Zealand
FORM: 35-50

Pouteria sapota — Sapota / Marmalade Plum

CULTURE: P C Si Sa L / 4 5 6 7 8 / M P A W E / W WM M MD D / vT T M I vl — moderate / fast / short
USES: jellies, jams, orchard, shade, specimen / accent
REGION: 10 / c. America
FORM: 50-75

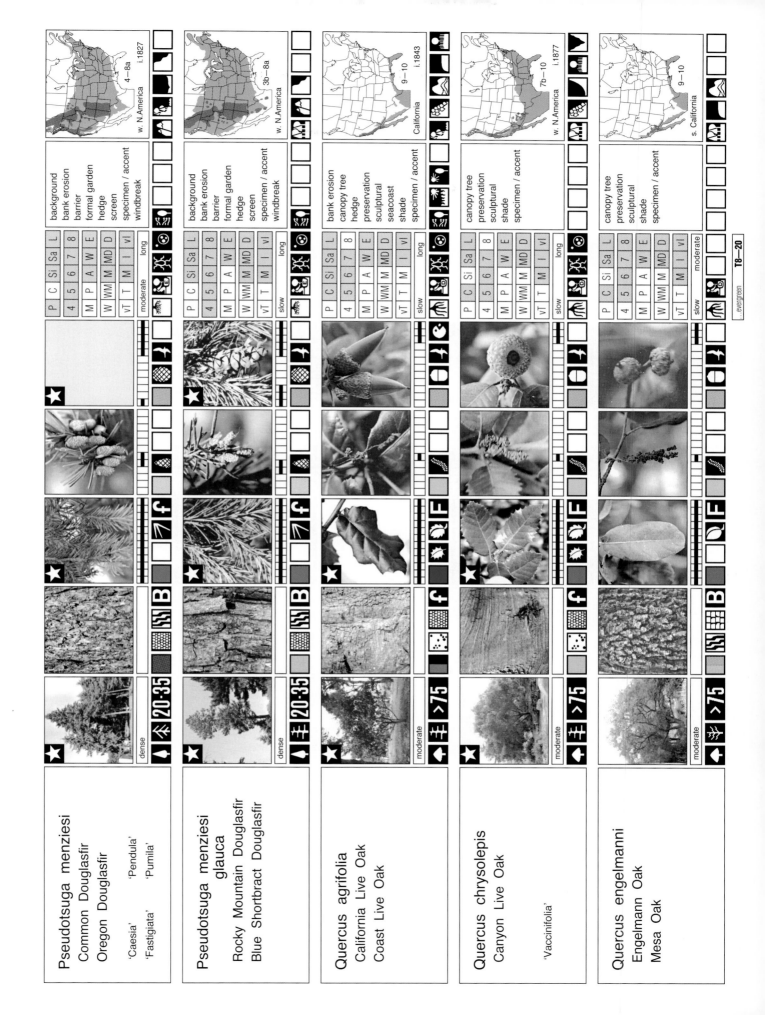

Pseudotsuga menziesi
Common Douglasfir
Oregon Douglasfir

'Caesia'   'Pendula'
'Fastigiata'   'Pumila'

w. N.America   4–8a   i.1827

background
bank erosion
barrier
formal garden
hedge
screen
specimen / accent
windbreak

dense   20-35

moderate   long

Pseudotsuga menziesi glauca
Rocky Mountain Douglasfir
Blue Shortbract Douglasfir

w. N.America   3b–8a

background
bank erosion
barrier
formal garden
hedge
screen
specimen / accent
windbreak

dense   20-35

slow   long

Quercus agrifolia
California Live Oak
Coast Live Oak

California   9–10   i.1843

bank erosion
canopy tree
hedge
preservation
sculptural
seacoast
shade
specimen / accent

moderate   >75

slow   long

Quercus chrysolepis
Canyon Live Oak

'Vaccinifolia'

w. N.America   7b–10   i.1877

canopy tree
preservation
sculptural
shade
specimen / accent

moderate   >75

slow   long

Quercus engelmanni
Engelmann Oak
Mesa Oak

s. California   9–10

canopy tree
preservation
sculptural
shade
specimen / accent

moderate   >75

slow   moderate

...evergreen   **T8—20**

LARGE TREE	FORM	BARK	LEAF	FLOWER	FRUIT	CULTURE	USES	REGION

Quercus laurifolia
Laurel Oak

dense >75

P	C	Si	Sa	L
4	5	6	7	8
M	P	A	W	E
W	WM	M	MD	D
vT	T	M	I	vl
fast short

USES: bog garden / canopy tree / sculptural / shade / specimen / accent / water garden

REGION: 7b–10 i.1786 e. N.America

Quercus suber
Cork Oak

moderate >75

P	C	Si	Sa	L
4	5	6	7	8
M	P	A	W	E
W	WM	M	MD	D
vT	T	M	I	vl
moderate very long

USES: canopy tree / oriental garden / patio garden / sculptural / seacoast / shade / specimen / accent

REGION: 7b–10 i.col.x. Mediterranean

Quercus virginiana
Southern Live Oak

moderate >75

P	C	Si	Sa	L
4	5	6	7	8
M	P	A	W	E
W	WM	M	MD	D
vT	T	M	I	vl
moderate very long

USES: canopy tree / preservation / sculptural / seacoast / shade / specimen / accent

REGION: (8a)–10 i.1739 s.e. N.America

Quercus wislizeni
Interior Live Oak

moderate >75

P	C	Si	Sa	L
4	5	6	7	8
M	P	A	W	E
W	WM	M	MD	D
vT	T	M	I	vl
slow very long

USES: canopy tree / sculptural / shade / preservation / specimen / accent

REGION: 7–10 i.1874 California

Roystonea regia
Cuban Royalpalm
Royal Palm

open 20-35

P	C	Si	Sa	L
4	5	6	7	8
M	P	A	W	E
W	WM	M	MD	D
vT	T	M	I	vl
fast short

USES: border mass / canopy tree / container / greenhouse / narrow space / patio garden / seacoast / specimen / accent

REGION: 10 Cuba

Sabal palmetto
Cabbage Palmetto

bog garden
canopy tree
container
narrow space
patio garden
preservation
seacoast
specimen / accent

P	C	Si	Sa	L
4	5	6	7	8
M	P	A	W	E
W	WM	M	MD	D
vT	T	M	I	vI

moderate / moderate

s.e. U.S. / Caribbean
8–10

open
12-20

Sciadopitys verticillata
Umbrella Pine

background
bonsai
container
formal garden
leaf arrangements
screen
specimen / accent

P	C	Si	Sa	L
4	5	6	7	8
M	P	A	W	E
W	WM	M	MD	D
vT	T	M	I	vI

slow / long

Japan
(6a) – 8   i.1853

dense
35-50

Sequoia sempervirens
Coast Redwood

background
formal garden
hedge
preservation
screen
seacoast
shade

P	C	Si	Sa	L
4	5	6	7	8
M	P	A	W	E
W	WM	M	MD	D
vT	T	M	I	vI

slow / very long

California
7 – 9a   i.1840

dense
35-50

Sequoiadendron giganteum
Giant Sequoia
Big Tree
'Pendula'

novelty
preservation
screen
sculpture-old
seacoast
specimen / accent

P	C	Si	Sa	L
4	5	6	7	8
M	P	A	W	E
W	WM	M	MD	D
vT	T	M	I	vI

fast / very long

California
6b – 10   i.1853

dense
35-50

Spathodea campanulata
African Tuliptree
Bell Flambeautree

canopy tree
sculptural
seacoast
shade
specimen / accent

P	C	Si	Sa	L
4	5	6	7	8
M	P	A	W	E
W	WM	M	MD	D
vT	T	M	I	vI

fast / moderate

Tropical Africa
10

...evergreen

open - moderate
50-75

T8—22

LARGE TREE	FORM	BARK	LEAF	FLOWER	FRUIT	CULTURE	USES	REGION

Syagrus orinocensis
Cococita Palm
Coquito

- FORM: open, 20-35
- CULTURE: P C Si Sa L / 4 5 6 7 8 / M P A W E / W WM M MD D / vT T M I vl — moderate
- USES: bog garden, container, greenhouse, pool garden, sculptural, specimen / accent, water garden
- REGION: Venezuela, 8–10

Thuja plicata
Western Red Cedar
Giant Arborvitae
'Atrovirens' 'Hillerii'
'Elegantissima' 'Stoneham Gold'

- FORM: dense, 20-35
- CULTURE: P C Si Sa L / 4 5 6 7 8 / M P A W E / W WM M MD D / vT T M I vl — fast, very long
- USES: background, bog garden, bonsai, formal garden, hedge, screen, seacoast, windbreak
- REGION: w. N. America, 5–9, i:1853

Thuja standishi
Japanese Arborvitae

- FORM: dense, 20-35
- CULTURE: P C Si Sa L / 4 5 6 7 8 / M P A W E / W WM M MD D / vT T M I vl — fast, very long
- USES: background, barrier, bonsai, formal garden, hedge, oriental garden, screen
- REGION: Japan, 6b–10, i:1860

Thujopsis dolabrata
Hiba Cedar
Deerhorn Cedar
'Nana'

- FORM: dense
- CULTURE: P C Si Sa L / 4 5 6 7 8 / M P A W E / W WM M MD D / vT T M I vl — fast, long
- USES: background, barrier, bonsai, formal garden, hedge, screen
- REGION: Japan, 10, i:1853

Tsuga canadensis
Eastern Hemlock
Canada Hemlock
'Coles Prostrate' 'Jeddeloh'
'Hussii' 'Sargentii'

- FORM: dense, 20-35
- CULTURE: P C Si Sa L / 4 5 6 7 8 / M P A W E / W WM M MD D / vT T M I vl — slow, long
- USES: background, barrier, border mass, container, formal garden, hedge, screen, specimen / accent
- REGION: e. N. America, 3–8, i.b.1730

Tsuga heterophylla
Western Hemlock

w. N.America

6b–8 | i:1851

P	C	Si	Sa	L
4	5	6	7	8
M	P	A	W	E
W	WM	M	MD	D
vT	T	M	I	vI

moderate — long

open

20-35

background
barrier
hedge
screen
specimen / accent
windbreak

Tsuga mertensiana
Mountain Hemlock

'Elizabeth'
'Vans Prostrate'

w. N.America

6–8 | i:1854

P	C	Si	Sa	L
4	5	6	7	8
M	P	A	W	E
W	WM	M	MD	D
vT	T	M	I	vI

slow — long

open

20-35

background
bonsai
container
formal garden
hedge
rock garden
screen
specimen / accent

Umbellularia californica
California Laurel
Oregon Myrtle
Pepperwood

California

8–10 | i:1829

P	C	Si	Sa	L
4	5	6	7	8
M	P	A	W	E
W	WM	M	MD	D
vT	T	M	I	vI

fast — moderate

open-moderate

20-35

background
canopy tree
formal garden
hedge
patio garden
seacoast
screen

Veitchia joannis
Joannis Palm

Fiji Islands

10

P	C	Si	Sa	L
4	5	6	7	8
M	P	A	W	E
W	WM	M	MD	D
vT	T	M	I	vI

fast — moderate

open

20-35

canopy tree
narrow space
pool garden
sculptural
specimen / accent
water garden

Washingtonia robusta
Mexican Fan Palm
Thread Palm

Mexico

8b–10

P	C	Si	Sa	L
4	5	6	7	8
M	P	A	W	E
W	WM	M	MD	D
vT	T	M	I	vI

fast — long

open

20-35

canopy tree
container
preservation
seacoast
specimen / accent

...evergreen   T8–24

MEDIUM TREE	FORM	BARK	LEAF	FLOWER	FRUIT	CULTURE	USES	REGION

Abies balsamea
Balsam Fir

'Globosa' 'Hudsonia'
'Nana'

FORM: dense 12-20

CULTURE:
P	C	Si	Sa	L
4	5	6	7	8
M	P	A	W	E
W	WM	M	MD	D
vT	T	M	I	vI

slow/mod   mod/short

USES:
background
barrier
Christmas tree
formal garden
medicinal
screen
seacoast
topiary

REGION: N.America   2–5a   i.1696

Abies fraseri
Fraser Fir
Southern Balsam Fir

FORM: dense 12-20

CULTURE:
P	C	Si	Sa	L
4	5	6	7	8
M	P	A	W	E
W	WM	M	MD	D
vT	T	M	I	vI

moderate

USES:
background
barrier
Christmas tree
formal garden
screen
specimen / accent
topiary

REGION: e. U.S.   5–7a   i.1811

Abies koreana
Korean Fir

'Aurea'
'Blue Cone'

FORM: dense 12-20

CULTURE:
P	C	Si	Sa	L
4	5	6	7	8
M	P	A	W	E
W	WM	M	MD	D
vT	T	M	I	vI

moderate   short

USES:
background
barrier
formal garden
screen
specimen / accent
topiary

REGION: Korea   4b–7a   i.1918

Acacia dealbata
Silver Wattle
Silver Acacia

FORM: open 20-35

CULTURE:
P	C	Si	Sa	L
4	5	6	7	8
M	P	A	W	E
W	WM	M	MD	D
vT	T	M	I	vI

fast   short

USES:
background
cut flowers
fruit arrangements
reclamation
seacoast
specimen / accent
street tree

REGION: Australia   8b–10   i.1820

Acacia melanoxylon
Black Acacia
Blackwood Acacia

FORM: open 20-35

CULTURE:
P	C	Si	Sa	L
4	5	6	7	8
M	P	A	W	E
W	WM	M	MD	D
vT	T	M	I	vI

fast   short

USES:
background
cut flowers
deer proof
fruit arrangements
hedge
screen
shearing
street tree

REGION: Tasmania   8b–10   i.1808

Acer oblongum
Evergreen Maple

oriental garden
patio garden
shade
specimen / accent

Himalayas   7–10   i.1824

P	C	Si	Sa	L
4	5	6	7	8
M	P	A	W	E
W	WM	M	MD	D
vT	T	M	I	vI

slow   moderate

dense   20-35

Agonis flexuosa
Pepperminttree
Australian Willow Myrtle

background
canopy tree
cool greenhouse
espalier
patio garden
seacoast
shade
specimen / accent

Australia   10   i.1886

P	C	Si	Sa	L
4	5	6	7	8
M	P	A	W	E
W	WM	M	MD	D
vT	T	M	I	vI

moderate   short

open   35-50

Agonis juniperiana
Juniper Myrtle
Australian Cedar

container
cool greenhouse
espalier
cut flowers
screen
sculptural
shade

Australia   10

P	C	Si	Sa	L
4	5	6	7	8
M	P	A	W	E
W	WM	M	MD	D
vT	T	M	I	vI

fast   short

open   12-20

Araucaria angustifolia
Brazilian Pine

background
formal garden
sculptural
seacoast
specimen / accent

Brazil   10

P	C	Si	Sa	L
4	5	6	7	8
M	P	A	W	E
W	WM	M	MD	D
vT	T	M	I	vI

moderate   long

moderate   20-35

Arbutus menziesi
Pacific Madrone

background
orchard
preservation
sculptural
specimen / accent

w. N. America   7b–9   i.1827

P	C	Si	Sa	L
4	5	6	7	8
M	P	A	W	E
W	WM	M	MD	D
vT	T	M	I	vI

moderate   moderate

open   35-50

...evergreen   **T7–2**

MEDIUM TREE	FORM	BARK	LEAF	FLOWER	FRUIT	CULTURE	USES	REGION

Athrotaxis laxifolia
Summit Cedar

- FORM: dense · 20-35
- CULTURE: P C Si Sa L / 4 5 6 7 8 / M P A W E / W WM M MD D / vT T M I vl / slow · very long
- USES: hard to find / novelty / specimen / accent
- REGION: Tasmania · 9–10 · i:1857

Bambusa oldhami
Giant Timber Bamboo
Oldham Bamboo

- FORM: dense · 35-50
- CULTURE: P C Si Sa L / 4 5 6 7 8 / M P A W E / W WM M MD D / vT T M I vl / fast · long
- USES: background / greenhouse / hedge / screen / specimen / accent
- REGION: Taiwan · 10

Banksia serrata
Saw Banksia

- FORM: moderate · 20-35
- CULTURE: P C Si Sa L / 4 5 6 7 8 / M P A W E / W WM M MD D / vT T M I vl / slow · short
- USES: background / cut flowers / seacoast / specimen /accent
- REGION: Australia · 10

Brachychiton acerifolia
Australian Flametree
Flame Bottletree

- FORM: dense · 20-35
- CULTURE: P C Si Sa L / 4 5 6 7 8 / M P A W E / W WM M MD D / vT T M I vl / short · long
- USES: background / fruit arrangements / shade / specimen / accent / street tree
- REGION: Australia · 9–10

Brachychiton populneum
Bottletree
Kurrajong Bottletree

- FORM: dense · 20-35
- CULTURE: P C Si Sa L / 4 5 6 7 8 / M P A W E / W WM M MD D / vT T M I vl / fast · long
- USES: background / canopy tree / fruit arrangements / screen / seacoast / shade / shearing / specimen / accent
- REGION: Australia · 10 · i:1824

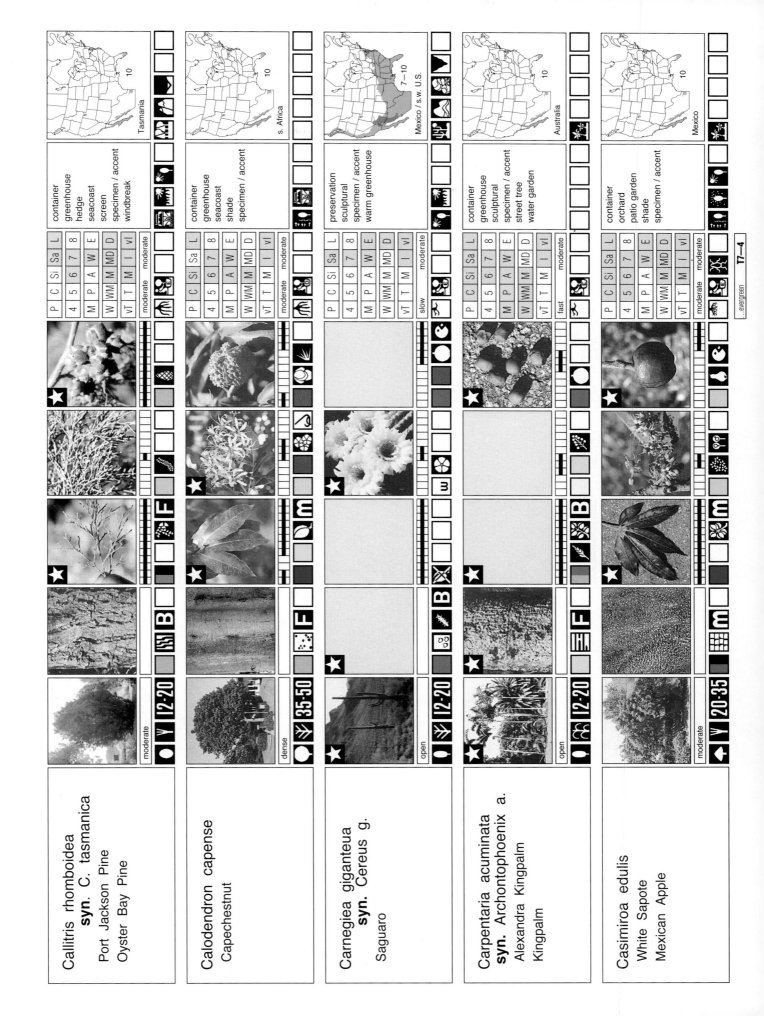

Callitris rhomboidea
syn. C. tasmanica
Port Jackson Pine
Oyster Bay Pine

container
greenhouse
hedge
seacoast
screen
specimen / accent
windbreak

Tasmania 10

moderate 12-20 moderate moderate

P C Si Sa L
4 5 6 7 8
M P A W E
W WM M MD D
vT T M I vI

Calodendron capense
Capechestnut

container
greenhouse
seacoast
shade
specimen / accent

s. Africa 10

dense 35-50 moderate moderate

P C Si Sa L
4 5 6 7 8
M P A W E
W WM M MD D
vT T M I vI

Carnegiea giganteua
syn. Cereus g.
Saguaro

preservation
sculptural
specimen / accent
warm greenhouse

Mexico / s.w. U.S. 7–10

open 12-20 slow moderate

P C Si Sa L
4 5 6 7 8
M P A W E
W WM M MD D
vT T M I vI

Carpentaria acuminata
syn. Archontophoenix a.
Alexandra Kingpalm
Kingpalm

container
greenhouse
sculptural
specimen / accent
street tree
water garden

Australia 10

open 12-20 fast moderate

P C Si Sa L
4 5 6 7 8
M P A W E
W WM M MD D
vT T M I vI

Casimiroa edulis
White Sapote
Mexican Apple

container
orchard
patio garden
shade
specimen / accent

Mexico 10

moderate 20-35 moderate moderate

P C Si Sa L
4 5 6 7 8
M P A W E
W WM M MD D
vT T M I vI

...evergreen   T7—4

MEDIUM TREE

	FORM	BARK	LEAF	FLOWER	FRUIT	CULTURE	USES	REGION

Ceratonia siliqua
Carob
St. Johnsbread

dense — 35-50

CULTURE:
P C Si Sa L
4 5 6 7 8
M P A W E
W WM M MD D
vT T M I vl
slow · moderate · long

USES:
canopy tree
fire retardant
hedge
patio garden
religious plant
screen
seacoast
shade

REGION: Mediterranean 9–10 i.1854

Cercocarpus ledifolius
Curleaf Mountainmahogany

open — 35-50

CULTURE:
P C Si Sa L
4 5 6 7 8
M P A W E
W WM M MD D
vT T M I vl
moderate · long

USES:
espalier
hedge
reclamation
sculptural
seacoast
specimen / accent

REGION: w. U.S. 4–10 i.1879

Cereus peruvianus
Peruvian Apple

open — 20-35

CULTURE:
P C Si Sa L
4 5 6 7 8
M P A W E
W WM M MD D
vT T M I vl
fast · long

USES:
background
container
greenhouse
novelty
sculptural
specimen / accent

REGION: s.e. S.America 10

Chiranthodendron pentadactylon
Monkey Handtree
Mexican Handtree

moderate — 35-50

CULTURE:
P C Si Sa L
4 5 6 7 8
M P A W E
W WM M MD D
vT T M I vl
fast · moderate

USES:
curiosity
novelty
religious plant
shade
specimen / accent

REGION: Mexico 10

Chrysophyllum cainito
Starapple
Cainito Starapple

open — 35-50

CULTURE:
P C Si Sa L
4 5 6 7 8
M P A W E
W WM M MD D
vT T M I vl
slow · moderate

USES:
fruit salads
kitchen garden
orchard
patio garden
specimen / accent

REGION: Tropical America 10b

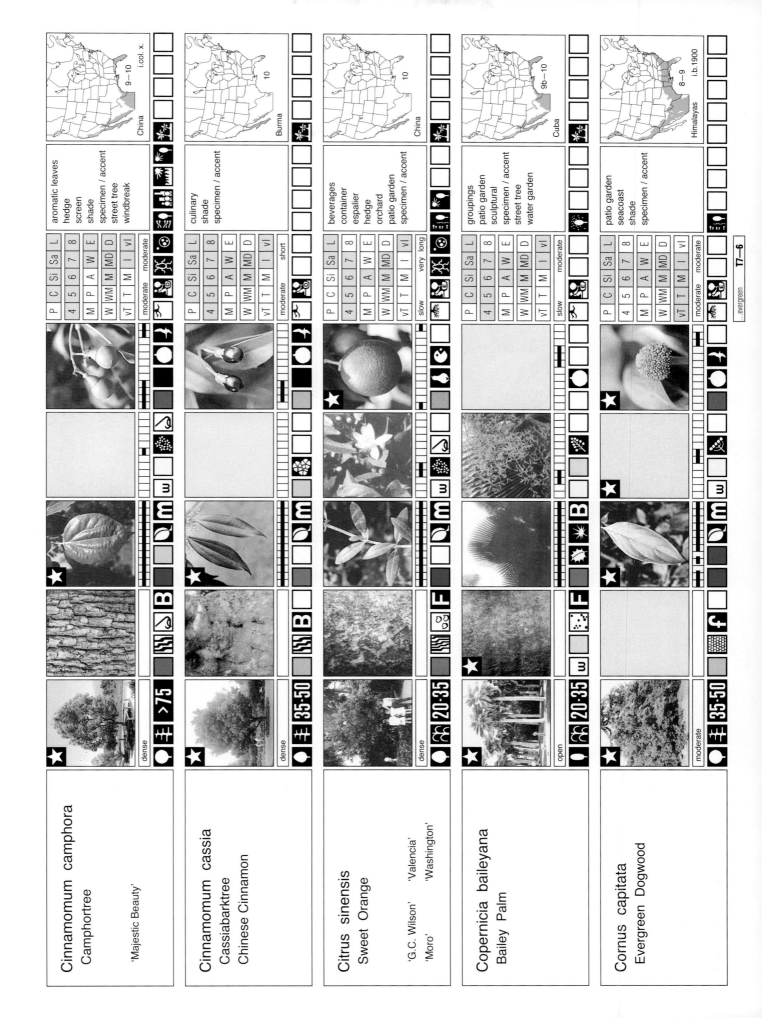

Cinnamomum camphora
Camphortree
'Majestic Beauty'

China — 9–10 — i.col. x.

dense — >75

aromatic leaves
hedge
screen
shade
specimen / accent
street tree
windbreak

P C Si Sa L / 4 5 6 7 8 / M P A W E / W WM M MD D / vT T M l vl — moderate

---

Cinnamomum cassia
Cassiabarktree
Chinese Cinnamon

Burma — 10

dense — 35-50

culinary
shade
specimen / accent

P C Si Sa L / 4 5 6 7 8 / M P A W E / W WM M MD D / vT T M l vl — moderate / short

---

Citrus sinensis
Sweet Orange

'G.C. Wilson'   'Valencia'
'Moro'   'Washington'

China — 10

dense — 20-35

beverages
container
espalier
hedge
orchard
patio garden
specimen / accent

P C Si Sa L / 4 5 6 7 8 / M P A W E / W WM M MD D / vT T M l vl — very long / slow

---

Copernicia baileyana
Bailey Palm

Cuba — 9b–10

open — 20-35

groupings
patio garden
sculptural
specimen / accent
street tree
water garden

P C Si Sa L / 4 5 6 7 8 / M P A W E / W WM M MD D / vT T M l vl — slow

---

Cornus capitata
Evergreen Dogwood

Himalayas — 8–9 — i.b.1900

moderate — 35-50

patio garden
seacoast
shade
specimen / accent

P C Si Sa L / 4 5 6 7 8 / M P A W E / W WM M MD D / vT T M l vl — moderate / moderate

...evergreen   **T7—6**

MEDIUM TREE	FORM	BARK	LEAF	FLOWER	FRUIT	CULTURE	USES	REGION

Cupressus goveniana
Gowen Cypress

dense · 20-35

CULTURE: P C Si Sa L / 4 5 6 7 8 / M P A W E / W WM M MD D / vT T M I vl — slow / long

USES: background, barrier, hedge, preservation, screen, shearing, windbreak

REGION: California · 9–10 · i.1846

Cupressus guadalupensis
Guadalupe Cypress
Tecate Cypress

dense · 20-35

CULTURE: P C Si Sa L / 4 5 6 7 8 / M P A W E / W WM M MD D / vT T M I vl — fast / long

USES: background, barrier, hedge, preservation, screen, shearing, windbreak

REGION: Guadalupe / U.S · 9–10 · i.1880

Cupressus macnabiana
MacNab Cypress

dense · 35-50

CULTURE: P C Si Sa L / 4 5 6 7 8 / M P A W E / W WM M MD D / vT T M I vl — fast / long

USES: background, barrier, hedge, preservation, screen, shearing, windbreak

REGION: California · 7–10 · i.1854

Cyathea medullaris
syn. Sphaeropteris m.
Black Treefern
Saga Fern

open · 20-35

CULTURE: P C Si Sa L / 4 5 6 7 8 / M P A W E / W WM M MD D / vT T M I vl — fast / short

USES: container, cool greenhouse, pool garden, sculptural, specimen / accent

REGION: New Zealand · 10

Erythea armata
syn. Brahea a.
Blue Fan Palm
Mexican Blue Palm

moderate · 12-20

CULTURE: P C Si Sa L / 4 5 6 7 8 / M P A W E / W WM M MD D / vT T M I vl — slow / moderate

USES: pool garden, specimen / accent, water garden

REGION: Mexico · 10

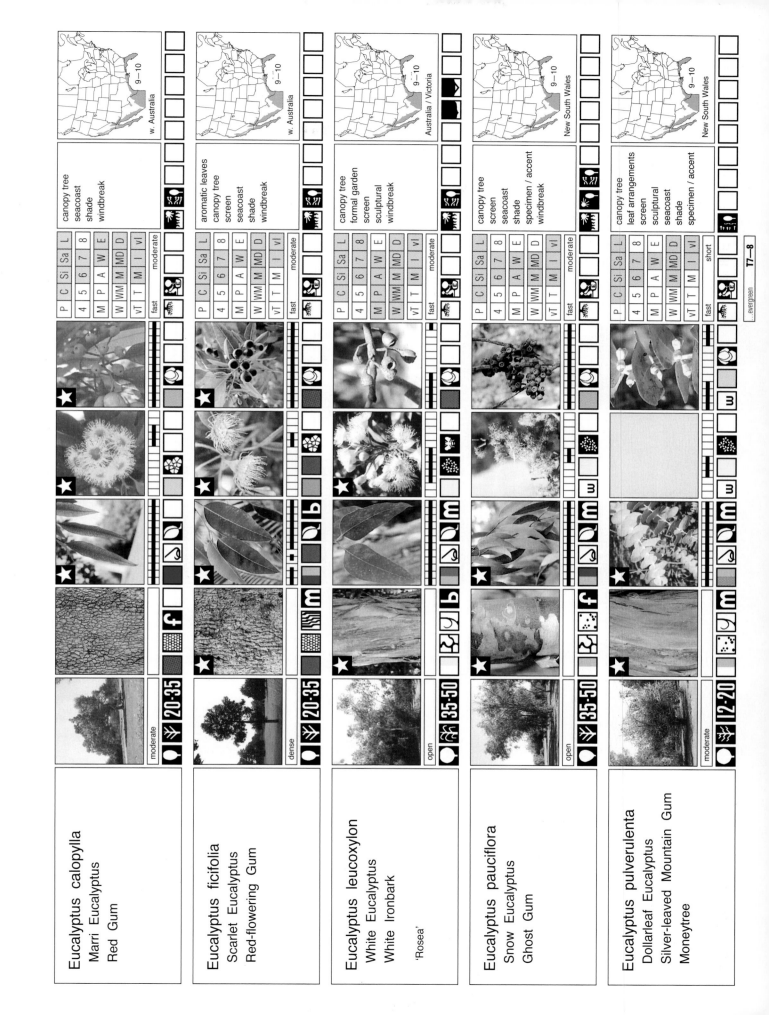

Eucalyptus calopylla
Marri Eucalyptus
Red Gum

canopy tree
seacoast
shade
windbreak

W. Australia
9—10

moderate
20-35

fast
moderate

Eucalyptus ficifolia
Scarlet Eucalyptus
Red-flowering Gum

aromatic leaves
canopy tree
screen
seacoast
shade
windbreak

W. Australia
9—10

dense
20-35

fast
moderate

Eucalyptus leucoxylon
White Eucalyptus
White Ironbark

'Rosea'

canopy tree
formal garden
screen
sculptural
windbreak

Australia / Victoria
9—10

open
35-50

fast
moderate

Eucalyptus pauciflora
Snow Eucalyptus
Ghost Gum

canopy tree
screen
seacoast
shade
specimen / accent
windbreak

New South Wales
9—10

open
35-50

fast
moderate

Eucalyptus pulverulenta
Dollarleaf Eucalyptus
Silver-leaved Mountain Gum
Moneytree

canopy tree
leaf arrangements
screen
sculptural
seacoast
shade
specimen / accent

New South Wales
9—10

moderate
12-20

fast
short

evergreen

T7—8

MEDIUM TREE	FORM	BARK	LEAF	FLOWER	FRUIT	CULTURE	USES	REGION

Eucalyptus sideroxylon
Mugga Eucalyptus
Red Ironbark
'Rosea'

- FORM: open · 35-50
- CULTURE: P C Si Sa L · 4 5 6 7 8 · M P A W E · W WM M MD D · vT T M I vl · fast · moderate
- USES: aromatic leaves, canopy tree, screen, shade, seacoast, specimen / accent, windbreak
- REGION: 9–10 · New South Wales

Ficus benjamina
Benjamin Fig
Weeping Laurel
Small-leaved Rubberplant
'Major'   'Variegata'

- FORM: moderate · 50-75
- CULTURE: P C Si Sa L · 4 5 6 7 8 · M P A W E · W WM M MD D · vT T M I vl · fast · moderate
- USES: canopy tree, container, espalier, greenhouse, hedge, house plant, patio garden, screen
- REGION: 10 · India

Ficus lyrata
Fiddleleaf Fig

- FORM: open · 35-50
- CULTURE: P C Si Sa L · 4 5 6 7 8 · M P A W E · W WM M MD D · vT T M I vl · moderate · short
- USES: container, greenhouse, house plant, patio garden, pool garden, specimen / accent
- REGION: 10 · Tropical America

Ficus macrophylla
Moretonbay Fig

- FORM: moderate · >75
- CULTURE: P C Si Sa L · 4 5 6 7 8 · M P A W E · W WM M MD D · vT T M I vl · fast · moderate
- USES: canopy tree, container, sculptural, shade, specimen / accent
- REGION: 9–10 · i.b.1877 · e. Australia

Geijera parviflora
Australian Willow
Wilga

- FORM: open · 20-35
- CULTURE: P C Si Sa L · 4 5 6 7 8 · M P A W E · W WM M MD D · vT T M I vl · moderate · short
- USES: canopy tree, container, edible leaves, patio garden, shade, shelterbelt, specimen / accent
- REGION: 8–10 · e. Australia

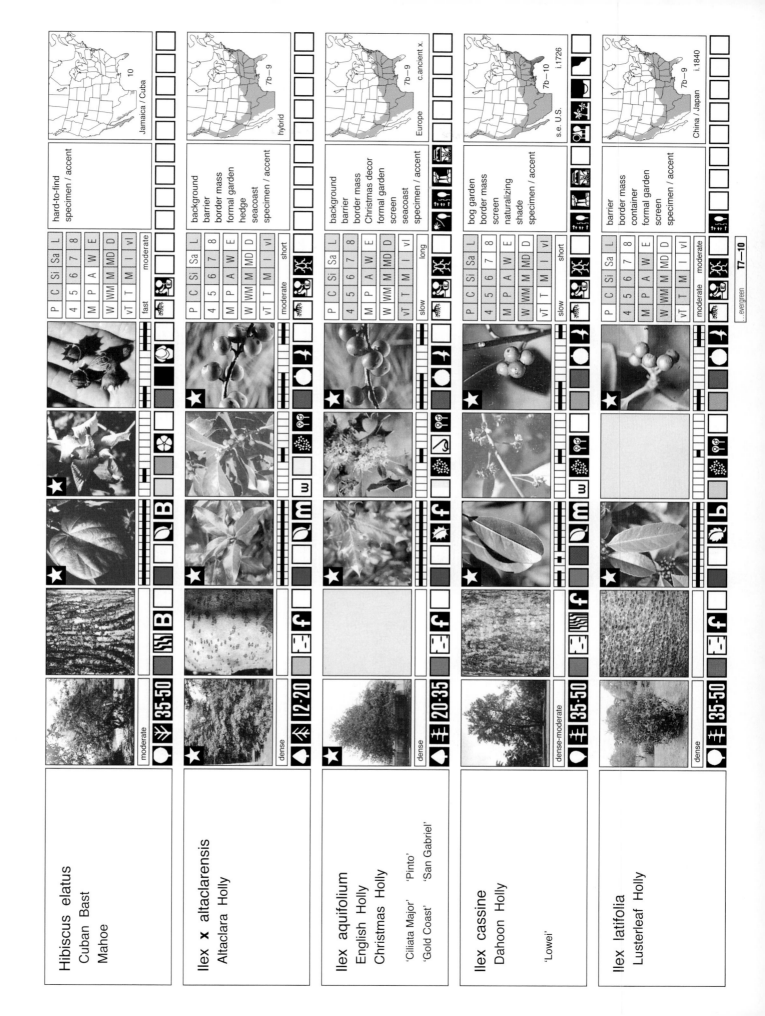

Hibiscus elatus — Cuban Bast — Mahoe

- Jamaica / Cuba
- 10
- hard-to-find
- specimen / accent
- P C Si Sa L / 4 5 6 7 8 / M P A W E / W WM M MD D / vT T M I vI
- fast — moderate
- moderate
- 35-50

Ilex x altaclarensis — Altaclara Holly
'Ciliata Major' 'Gold Coast'

- hybrid
- 7b–9
- background / barrier / border mass / formal garden / hedge / seacoast / specimen / accent
- P C Si Sa L / 4 5 6 7 8 / M P A W E / W WM M MD D / vT T M I vI
- moderate — short
- dense
- 12-20

Ilex aquifolium — English Holly — Christmas Holly
'Pinto' 'San Gabriel'

- Europe
- c.ancient x.
- 7b–9
- background / barrier / border mass / Christmas decor / formal garden / screen / seacoast / specimen / accent
- P C Si Sa L / 4 5 6 7 8 / M P A W E / W WM M MD D / vT T M I vI
- slow — long
- dense
- 20-35

Ilex cassine — Dahoon Holly
'Lowei'

- s.e. U.S.
- 7b–10
- i.1726
- bog garden / border mass / screen / naturalizing / shade / specimen / accent
- P C Si Sa L / 4 5 6 7 8 / M P A W E / W WM M MD D / vT T M I vI
- slow — short
- dense-moderate
- 35-50

Ilex latifolia — Lusterleaf Holly

- China / Japan
- 7b–9
- i.1840
- barrier / border mass / container / formal garden / screen / specimen / accent
- P C Si Sa L / 4 5 6 7 8 / M P A W E / W WM M MD D / vT T M I vI
- moderate — moderate
- dense
- 35-50

...evergreen **T7–10**

MEDIUM TREE	FORM	BARK	LEAF	FLOWER	FRUIT	CULTURE	USES	REGION

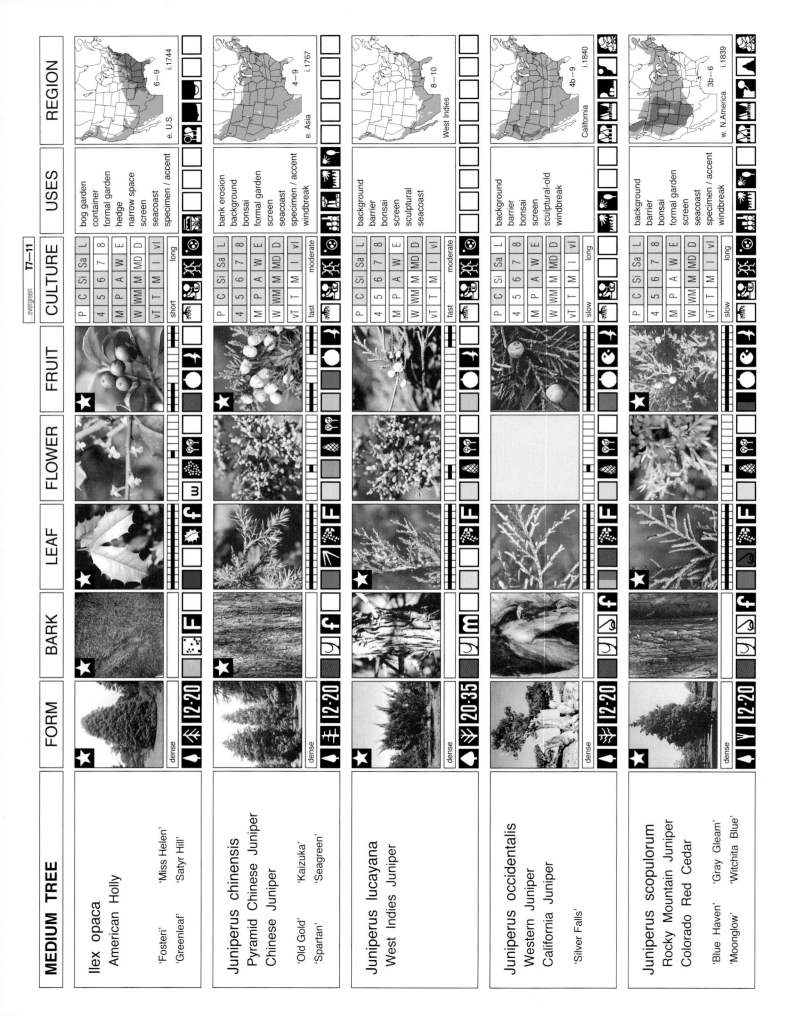

Ilex opaca
American Holly

'Fosteri' 'Miss Helen'
'Greenleaf' 'Satyr Hill'

dense · 12-20

P C Si Sa L
4 5 6 7 8
M P A W E
W WM M MD D
vT T M I vl
short · long

bog garden
container
formal garden
hedge
narrow space
screen
seacoast
specimen / accent

6—9 i.1744 e. U.S.

Juniperus chinensis
Pyramid Chinese Juniper
Chinese Juniper

'Old Gold' 'Kaizuka'
'Spartan' 'Seagreen'

dense · 12-20

P C Si Sa L
4 5 6 7 8
M P A W E
W WM M MD D
vT T M I vl
fast · moderate

bank erosion
background
bonsai
formal garden
screen
seacoast
specimen / accent
windbreak

4—9 i.1767 e. Asia

Juniperus lucayana
West Indies Juniper

dense · 20-35

P C Si Sa L
4 5 6 7 8
M P A W E
W WM M MD D
vT T M I vl
fast · moderate

background
barrier
bonsai
screen
sculptural
seacoast

8—10 West Indies

Juniperus occidentalis
Western Juniper
California Juniper

'Silver Falls'

dense · 12-20

P C Si Sa L
4 5 6 7 8
M P A W E
W WM M MD D
vT T M I vl
slow · long

background
barrier
bonsai
screen
sculptural-old
windbreak

4b—9 i.1840 California

Juniperus scopulorum
Rocky Mountain Juniper
Colorado Red Cedar

'Blue Haven' 'Gray Gleam'
'Moonglow' 'Witchita Blue'

dense · 12-20

P C Si Sa L
4 5 6 7 8
M P A W E
W WM M MD D
vT T M I vl
slow · long

background
barrier
bonsai
formal garden
screen
seacoast
specimen / accent
windbreak

3b—6 i.1839 w. N.America

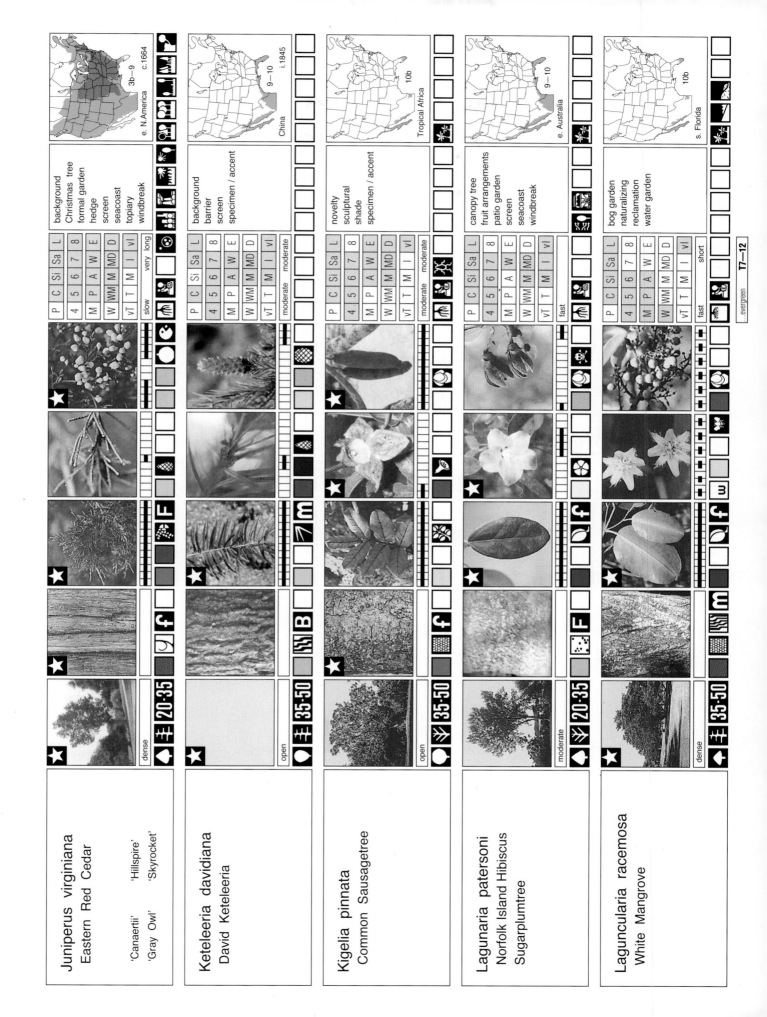

Juniperus virginiana
Eastern Red Cedar

'Canaertii'   'Hillspire'
'Gray Owl'   'Skyrocket'

background
Christmas tree
formal garden
hedge
screen
seacoast
topiary
windbreak

e. N.America   3b–9   c.1664

P	C	Si	Sa	L
4	5	6	7	8
M	P	A	W	E
W	WM	M	MD	D
vT	T	M	I	vI

slow   very long

dense   20-35

Keteleeria davidiana
David Keteleeria

background
barrier
screen
specimen / accent

e. N.America   9–10   i.1845

P	C	Si	Sa	L
4	5	6	7	8
M	P	A	W	E
W	WM	M	MD	D
vT	T	M	I	vI

moderate   moderate

open   35-50

Kigelia pinnata
Common Sausagetree

novelty
sculptural
shade
specimen / accent

China   10b

P	C	Si	Sa	L
4	5	6	7	8
M	P	A	W	E
W	WM	M	MD	D
vT	T	M	I	vI

moderate   moderate

open   35-50

Lagunaria patersoni
Norfolk Island Hibiscus
Sugarplumtree

canopy tree
fruit arrangements
patio garden
screen
seacoast
windbreak

Tropical Africa   10b

P	C	Si	Sa	L
4	5	6	7	8
M	P	A	W	E
W	WM	M	MD	D
vT	T	M	I	vI

fast

moderate   20-35

Laguncularia racemosa
White Mangrove

bog garden
naturalizing
reclamation
water garden

e. Australia   9–10

P	C	Si	Sa	L
4	5	6	7	8
M	P	A	W	E
W	WM	M	MD	D
vT	T	M	I	vI

fast   short

dense   35-50

s. Florida   10b

...evergreen   **T7–12**

MEDIUM TREE	FORM	BARK	LEAF	FLOWER	FRUIT	CULTURE	USES	REGION

Latania verschaffelti
Yellow Latin Palm

'Carolina Glory'
'Compactum'   'Jackfrost'

open   2-20

CULTURE: P C Si Sa L / 4 5 6 7 8 / M P A W E / W WM M MD D / vT T M I vl — fast / moderate

USES: background, groupings, sculptural, seacoast, specimen / accent, water garden

REGION: Rodriguez / Mascarene Is.   10

Ligustrum lucidum
Glossy Privet
Chinese Privet

'Carolina Glory'
'Compactum'   'Jackfrost'

moderate-dense   35-50

CULTURE: P C Si Sa L / 4 5 6 7 8 / M P A W E / W WM M MD D / vT T M I vl — fast / short

USES: canopy tree, container, hedge, patio garden, screen, windbreak

REGION: China / Korea   7b–10   i.1794

Litchi chinensis
Lychee
Litchinut

'Brewster'   'Kaimana'
'Graff'   'Kwai Mi'

moderate   35-50

CULTURE: P C Si Sa L / 4 5 6 7 8 / M P A W E / W WM M MD D / vT T M I vl — slow / moderate

USES: background, orchard, patio garden, shade

REGION: s. China   9b–10

Livistona chinensis
Chinese Fanpalm
Chinese Fountainpalm

open   20-35

CULTURE: P C Si Sa L / 4 5 6 7 8 / M P A W E / W WM M MD D / vT T M I vl — slow / moderate

USES: background, container, groupings, seacoast, patio garden, specimen / accent, water garden

REGION: s. Japan / China   9b–10

Lyonothamnus floribundus
Catalina Ironwood
Catalina Lyontree

moderate   20-35

CULTURE: P C Si Sa L / 4 5 6 7 8 / M P A W E / W WM M MD D / vT T M I vl — moderate / long

USES: formal garden, hedge, patio garden, seacoast, shade, specimen / accent

REGION: Channel Islands   9–10   i.1900

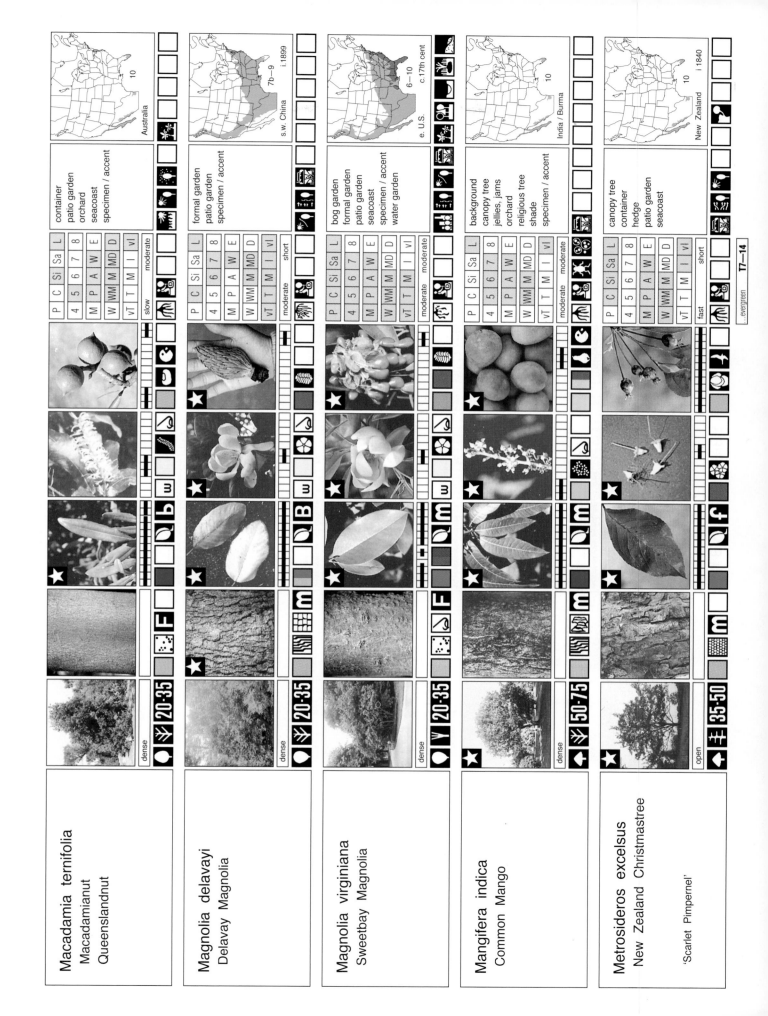

Macadamia ternifolia
Macadamianut
Queenslandnut

container
patio garden
orchard
seacoast
specimen / accent

Australia
10

P C Si Sa L
4 5 6 7 8
M P A W E
W WM M MD D
vT T M I vl

slow
moderate

dense
20-35

Magnolia delavayi
Delavay Magnolia

formal garden
patio garden
specimen / accent

s.w. China
7b–9
i.1899

P C Si Sa L
4 5 6 7 8
M P A W E
W WM M MD D
vT T M I vl

moderate
short

dense
20-35

Magnolia virginiana
Sweetbay Magnolia

bog garden
formal garden
patio garden
seacoast
specimen / accent
water garden

e. U.S.
6—10
c.17th cent

P C Si Sa L
4 5 6 7 8
M P A W E
W WM M MD D
vT T M I vl

moderate
moderate

dense
20-35

Mangifera indica
Common Mango

background
canopy tree
jellies, jams
orchard
religious tree
shade
specimen / accent

India / Burma
10

P C Si Sa L
4 5 6 7 8
M P A W E
W WM M MD D
vT T M I vl

moderate
moderate

dense
50-75

Metrosideros excelsus
New Zealand Christmastree

'Scarlet Pimpernel'

canopy tree
container
hedge
patio garden
seacoast

New Zealand
10
i 1840

P C Si Sa L
4 5 6 7 8
M P A W E
W WM M MD D
vT T M I vl

fast
short

...evergreen   T7—14

open
35-50

MEDIUM TREE	FORM	BARK	LEAF	FLOWER	FRUIT	CULTURE	USES	REGION

Montezuma speciosissima
syn. Thespesia
grandiflora

Maga

moderate · 35-50

P	C	Si	Sa	L
4	5	6	7	8
M	P	A	W	E
W	WM	M	MD	D
vT	T	M	I	vI

slow · long

canopy tree
shade
specimen / accent

Puerto Rico · 10

Nothofagus dombeyi
Southern Beech

moderate-dense · 20-35

P	C	Si	Sa	L
4	5	6	7	8
M	P	A	W	E
W	WM	M	MD	D
vT	T	M	I	vI

slow · moderate

novelty
shade
specimen / accent

Argentina / Chile · 7b–9 · i.1916

Nothofagus obliqua
Roble Beech

moderate-dense · 20-35

P	C	Si	Sa	L
4	5	6	7	8
M	P	A	W	E
W	WM	M	MD	D
vT	T	M	I	vI

slow · moderate

novelty
shade
specimen / accent

s.w. Chile · 8–9 · i.1849

Persea americana
American Avocado
Alligator Pear

'Fuerta'   'Hass'
'Gwen'   'Sharwil'

moderate · 20-35

P	C	Si	Sa	L
4	5	6	7	8
M	P	A	W	E
W	WM	M	MD	D
vT	T	M	I	vI

moderate · moderate

container
orchard
patio garden
sculptural
shade
specimen / accent

Central America · 10

Persea borbonia
Redbay
Florida Mahogony

dense · 20-35

P	C	Si	Sa	L
4	5	6	7	8
M	P	A	W	E
W	WM	M	MD	D
vT	T	M	I	vI

fast · short

bog garden
seacoast
shade
specimen / accent
water garden

s.e. U.S. · 8–10 · i.1739

Phoenix canariensis
Canary Islands Date Palm
Canary Date

P	C	Si	Sa	L
4	5	6	7	8
M	P	A	W	E
W	WM	M	MD	D
vT	T	M	I	vI

slow   moderate

background
canopy tree
formal garden
pool garden
sculptural
seacoast
specimen / accent
water garden

9–10
Canary Islands

moderate   35-50

Phoenix dactylifera
Date Palm
Date

P	C	Si	Sa	L
4	5	6	7	8
M	P	A	W	E
W	WM	M	MD	D
vT	T	M	I	vI

slow   moderate

canopy tree
orchard
seacoast
sculptural
specimen / accent
sugar

9–10
Arabia / n.Africa

moderate   20-35

Photinia serrulata
Chinese Photinia

P	C	Si	Sa	L
4	5	6	7	8
M	P	A	W	E
W	WM	M	MD	D
vT	T	M	I	vI

fast   short

border mass
hedge
patio garden
screen
specimen / accent

7b–10   i.1804
China

dense   20-35

Phyllostachys viridus
Kou-chiku

'Robert Young'

P	C	Si	Sa	L
4	5	6	7	8
M	P	A	W	E
W	WM	M	MD	D
vT	T	M	I	vI

fast   long

bank erosion
barrier
greenhouse
naturalizing
oriental garden
rarely flowers

8–10   i.1846
China

open   12-20

Picea mariana
Black Spruce
Bog Spruce

'Corbet'
'Golden'   'Nana'

P	C	Si	Sa	L
4	5	6	7	8
M	P	A	W	E
W	WM	M	MD	D
vT	T	M	I	vI

slow   short

bog garden
formal garden
narrow space
seacoast
water garden
windbreak

1b–6   c.1700
n. N.America

moderate   12-20

...evergreen   T7—16

MEDIUM TREE	FORM	BARK	LEAF	FLOWER	FRUIT	CULTURE	USES	REGION

Picea mariana 'Doumeti'
Doumet Spruce

- FORM: 20-35 · dense
- CULTURE: P C Si Sa L / 4 5 6 7 8 / M P A W E / W WM M MD D / vT T M I vl · slow · short
- USES: background, barrier, bonsai, formal garden, screen, seacoast
- REGION: hybrid · 2–6 · c.1850

Pinus aristata
Bristlecone Pine

- FORM: 12-20 · dense
- CULTURE: P C Si Sa L / 4 5 6 7 8 / M P A W E / W WM M MD D / vT T M I vl · very slow · very long
- USES: barrier, container, edible leaves, espalier, formal garden, seacoast, specimen / accent, windbreak
- REGION: w. U.S. · 4–7a · i.1863

Pinus banksiana
Jack Pine

'Uncle Foggy'   'Nana'
'Fastigiata'   'Schoodic'

- FORM: 20-35 · open
- CULTURE: P C Si Sa L / 4 5 6 7 8 / M P A W E / W WM M MD D / vT T M I vl · fast · short
- USES: background, barrier, reclamation, screen, seacoast, windbreak
- REGION: n.e. N.America · 2–6a · c.1783

Pinus cembra
Swiss Stone Pine

'Broom'   'Nana'
'Compacta'   'Siberica'

- FORM: 20-35 · moderate
- CULTURE: P C Si Sa L / 4 5 6 7 8 / M P A W E / W WM M MD D / vT T M I vl · very slow · long
- USES: background, bonsai, border mass, formal garden, patio garden, screen, specimen / accent, windbreak
- REGION: Europe · 3b–7 · i.b.1875

Pinus flexilis
Limber Pine

'Glauca'   'Reflexa'
'Pendula'

- FORM: 20-35 · moderate
- CULTURE: P C Si Sa L / 4 5 6 7 8 / M P A W E / W WM M MD D / vT T M I vl · slow · long
- USES: background, bonsai, border mass, reclamation, screen, sheared, specimen / accent, windbreak
- REGION: w. N.America · 3–7 · i.1851

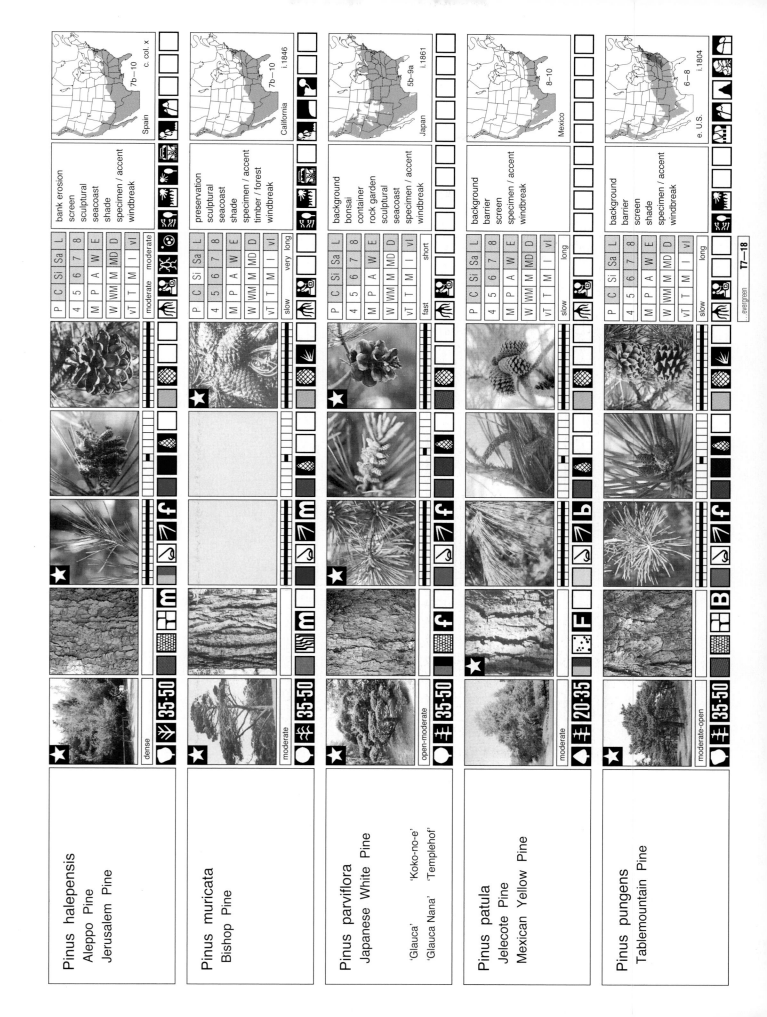

Pinus halepensis — Aleppo Pine, Jerusalem Pine
uses: bank erosion · screen · sculptural · seacoast · shade · specimen / accent · windbreak
Spain · 7b–10 · c. col. x · dense · 35-50 · moderate moderate

Pinus muricata — Bishop Pine
uses: preservation · sculptural · seacoast · shade · specimen / forest · timber / forest · windbreak
California · i.1846 · 7b–10 · slow long · moderate · 35-50

Pinus parviflora — Japanese White Pine
'Glauca' 'Koko-no-e'
'Glauca Nana' 'Templehof'
uses: background · bonsai · container · rock garden · sculptural · seacoast · specimen / accent · windbreak
Japan · i.1861 · 5b–9a · short fast · open-moderate · 35-50

Pinus patula — Jelecote Pine, Mexican Yellow Pine
uses: background · barrier · screen · specimen / accent · windbreak
Mexico · 8–10 · long slow · moderate · 20-35

Pinus pungens — Tablemountain Pine
uses: background · barrier · screen · shade · specimen / accent · windbreak
e. U.S. · i.1804 · 6–8 · long slow · moderate-open · 35-50

...evergreen   T7—18

MEDIUM TREE

	FORM	BARK	LEAF	FLOWER	FRUIT	CULTURE	USES	REGION

Pinus sabiniana
Digger Pine

- FORM: open-moderate, 35-50
- CULTURE: P C Si Sa L / 4 5 6 7 8 / M P A W E / W WM M MD D / vT T M I vI — fast, long
- USES: background, barrier, screen, shade, specimen / accent, windbreak
- REGION: California, 6–10, i.1832

Pinus torreyana
Torrey Pine

- FORM: moderate, 35-50
- CULTURE: P C Si Sa L / 4 5 6 7 8 / M P A W E / W WM M MD D / vT T M I vI — fast, moderate
- USES: background, preservation, screen, seacoast, shade, specimen / accent, windbreak
- REGION: s. California, 7b–10, i.1853

Pithecellobium flexicaule
Texas Ebony
Ebony Blackhead

- FORM: open, 35-50
- CULTURE: P C Si Sa L / 4 5 6 7 8 / M P A W E / W WM M MD D / vT T M I vI — slow, long
- USES: barrier, patio garden, screen, sculptural, shade, specimen / accent
- REGION: n.Mexico / s.Texas, 9–10

Pittosporum eugenioides
Tarata Pittosporum
Lemonwood
'Platinum'

- FORM: moderate, 20-35
- CULTURE: P C Si Sa L / 4 5 6 7 8 / M P A W E / W WM M MD D / vT T M I vI — very fast, short
- USES: background, border mass, canopy tree, container, hedge, screen, shade, specimen / accent
- REGION: New Zealand, 9–10

Pittosporum rhombifolium
Diamondleaf Pittosporum
Queensland Pittosporum

- FORM: moderate, 20-35
- CULTURE: P C Si Sa L / 4 5 6 7 8 / M P A W E / W WM M MD D / vT T M I vI — slow, moderate
- USES: background, border mass, canopy tree, hedge, patio garden, screen, shade, specimen / accent
- REGION: e. Australia, 10

Pittosporum truncatum

P	C	Si	Sa	L
4	5	6	7	8
M	P	A	W	E
W	WM	M	MD	D
vT	T	M	I	vI

fast — moderate

background
border mass
canopy tree
shade
specimen / accent

9b–10

moderate · 20-35

Podocarpus andinus
Andes Podocarpus
Plum Fir

P	C	Si	Sa	L
4	5	6	7	8
M	P	A	W	E
W	WM	M	MD	D
vT	T	M	I	vI

slow — moderate

container
espalier
formal garden
hedge
patio garden
screen
specimen / accent

7b–10
i.1860
Chile

dense-moderate · 20-35

Podocarpus henkeli
Longleaved Yellowwood

P	C	Si	Sa	L
4	5	6	7	8
M	P	A	W	E
W	WM	M	MD	D
vT	T	M	I	vI

slow — moderate

container
espalier
formal garden
hedge
patio garden
screen
specimen / accent

10
s. Africa

dense · 20-35

Podocarpus macrophyllus
Yew Podocarpus
Yew Pine

'Buddhist Pink'

P	C	Si	Sa	L
4	5	6	7	8
M	P	A	W	E
W	WM	M	MD	D
vT	T	M	I	vI

slow — very long

background
border mass
container
espalier
hedge
house plant
screen
topiary

7b–10
i.1804
Japan

dense · 20-35

Prunus lyoni
Catalina Cherry

P	C	Si	Sa	L
4	5	6	7	8
M	P	A	W	E
W	WM	M	MD	D
vT	T	M	I	vI

fast — short

canopy tree
hedge
patio garden
preservation
screen
sheared

8–10
Channel Islands

dense · 20-35

MEDIUM TREE	FORM	BARK	LEAF	FLOWER	FRUIT	CULTURE	USES	REGION
Quercus arizonica Arizona White Oak	moderate 35-50					P C Si Sa L 4 5 6 7 8 M P A W E W WM M MD D vT T M I vl slow — moderate	sculptural-old shade specimen / accent	s.w. U.S. 6–10
Quillaja saponaria Soapbarktree	open 20-35					P C Si Sa L 4 5 6 7 8 M P A W E W WM M MD D vT T M I vl fast — short	hedge screen sheared	Chile 8–10 i.1832
Rhododendron arboreum Tree Rhododendron 'Barto White' 'Sir Charles Lemon'	moderate 20-35					P C Si Sa L 4 5 6 7 8 M P A W E W WM M MD D vT T M I vl slow — moderate	background border mass groupings patio garden shade specimen / accent	Himalayas 6b–8 i.1810
Schinus molle California Peppertree Peruvian Peppertree	moderate 35-50					P C Si Sa L 4 5 6 7 8 M P A W E W WM M MD D vT T M I vl moderate — short	background canopy tree fruit arrangements seacoast shade specimen / accent	Peru 9–10
Syzygium cumini Java Plum Jambu	dense 20-35					P C Si Sa L 4 5 6 7 8 M P A W E W WM M MD D vT T M I vl slow — short	hedge kitchen garden screen orchard	India 10

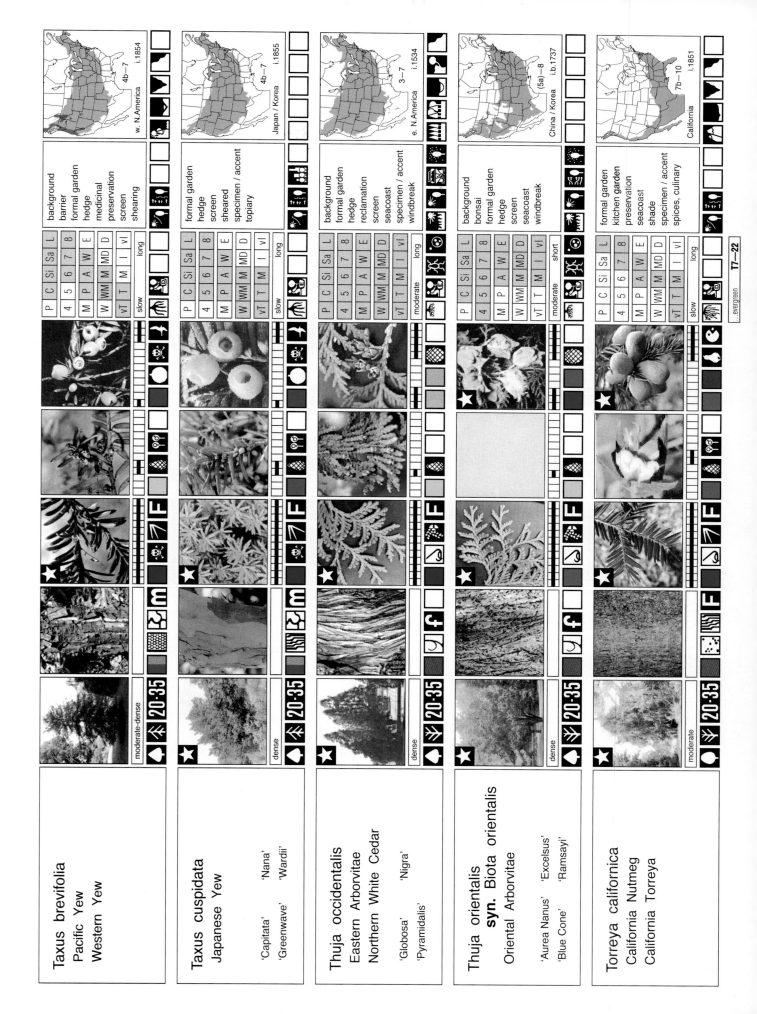

Taxus brevifolia
Pacific Yew
Western Yew

'Capitata' 'Nana'
'Greenwave' 'Wardii'

background
barrier
formal garden
hedge
medicinal
preservation
screen
shearing

P	C	Si	Sa	L
4	5	6	7	8
M	P	A	W	E
W	WM	M	MD	D
vT	T	M	I	vl

long · slow

4b–7 · i.1854 · w. N.America

moderate-dense · 20-35

Taxus cuspidata
Japanese Yew

formal garden
hedge
screen
sheared
specimen / accent
topiary

P	C	Si	Sa	L
4	5	6	7	8
M	P	A	W	E
W	WM	M	MD	D
vT	T	M	I	vl

long · slow

4b–7 · i.1855 · Japan / Korea

dense · 20-35

Thuja occidentalis
Eastern Arborvitae
Northern White Cedar

'Globosa' 'Nigra'
'Pyramidalis'

background
formal garden
hedge
reclamation
screen
seacoast
specimen / accent
windbreak

P	C	Si	Sa	L
4	5	6	7	8
M	P	A	W	E
W	WM	M	MD	D
vT	T	M	I	vl

long · moderate

3–7 · i.1534 · e. N.America

dense · 20-35

Thuja orientalis **syn.** Biota orientalis
Oriental Arborvitae

'Aurea Nanus' 'Excelsus'
'Blue Cone' 'Ramsayi'

background
bonsai
formal garden
hedge
screen
seacoast
windbreak

P	C	Si	Sa	L
4	5	6	7	8
M	P	A	W	E
W	WM	M	MD	D
vT	T	M	I	vl

short · moderate

(5a)–8 · i.b.1737 · China / Korea

dense · 20-35

Torreya californica
California Nutmeg
California Torreya

formal garden
kitchen garden
preservation
seacoast
shade
specimen / accent
spices, culinary

P	C	Si	Sa	L
4	5	6	7	8
M	P	A	W	E
W	WM	M	MD	D
vT	T	M	I	vl

long · slow

7b–10 · i.1851 · California

moderate · 20-35

MEDIUM TREE	FORM	BARK	LEAF	FLOWER	FRUIT	CULTURE	USES	REGION
Torreya taxifolia Florida Torreya	moderate 20-35					P C Si Sa L 4 5 6 7 8 M P A W E W WM M MD D vT T M I vl slow moderate	formal garden novelty preservation shade specimen / accent	8–10 i.1840 Florida
Tsuga caroliniana Carolina Hemlock 'Arnold Pyramid' 'Labar's Weeping'	dense 20-35					P C Si Sa L 4 5 6 7 8 M P A W E W WM M MD D vT T M I vl slow long	background barrier formal garden hedge preservation screen specimen / accent windbreak	(5a)–(8a) i.1881 s.e. U.S.
Tsuga diversifolia Japanese Hemlock	dense 20-35					P C Si Sa L 4 5 6 7 8 M P A W E W WM M MD D vT T M I vl moderate long	background barrier formal garden hedge oriental garden screen specimen / accent	(5a)–8a i.1861 Japan
Washingtonia filifera California Washingtonia Washington Palm	open 20-35					P C Si Sa L 4 5 6 7 8 M P A W E W WM M MD D vT T M I vl fast moderate	canopy tree preservation sculptural specimen / accent water garden	9–10 s.w. U.S.

SMALL TREE	FORM	BARK	LEAF	FLOWER	FRUIT	CULTURE	USES	REGION

Acacia baileyana
Bailey Acacia
Golden Mimosa

'Purpurea'

open · 20-35

CULTURE:
P	C	Si	Sa	L
4	5	6	7	8
M	P	A	W	E
W	WM	M	MD	D
vT	T	M	I	vI
fast · short

USES: border mass, canopy tree, cut flowers, fruit arrangements, nitrogen-fixing, seacoast, specimen / accent, windbreak

REGION: 9–10 i.1888 s.e. Australia

Acacia floribunda
Gossamer Acacia

open · 20-35

CULTURE:
P	C	Si	Sa	L
4	5	6	7	8
M	P	A	W	E
W	WM	M	MD	D
vT	T	M	I	vI
fast · short

USES: canopy tree, screen, seacoast, windbreak

REGION: 8–10 Australia

Acacia longifolia
Sydney Golden Wattle
Sydney Acacia

open · 20-35

CULTURE:
P	C	Si	Sa	L
4	5	6	7	8
M	P	A	W	E
W	WM	M	MD	D
vT	T	M	I	vI
very fast · short

USES: bank erosion, greenhouse, hedge, screen, seacoast, specimen / accent, windbreak

REGION: 8–10 i.1792 e. Australia

Acacia pendula
Weeping Acacia
Weeping Myall

open

CULTURE:
P	C	Si	Sa	L
4	5	6	7	8
M	P	A	W	E
W	WM	M	MD	D
vT	T	M	I	vI
slow · short

USES: espalier, greenhouse, nitrogen-fixing, patio garden, seacoast, shade, specimen / accent

REGION: 10 e. Australia

Acacia saligna
Blueleaf Acacia
Golden Wreath Acacia
Weeping Acacia

moderate · 20-35

CULTURE:
P	C	Si	Sa	L
4	5	6	7	8
M	P	A	W	E
W	WM	M	MD	D
vT	T	M	I	vI
very fast · short

USES: background, barrier, border mass, hedge, espalier, screen, seacoast, sheared

REGION: 8–10 w. Australia

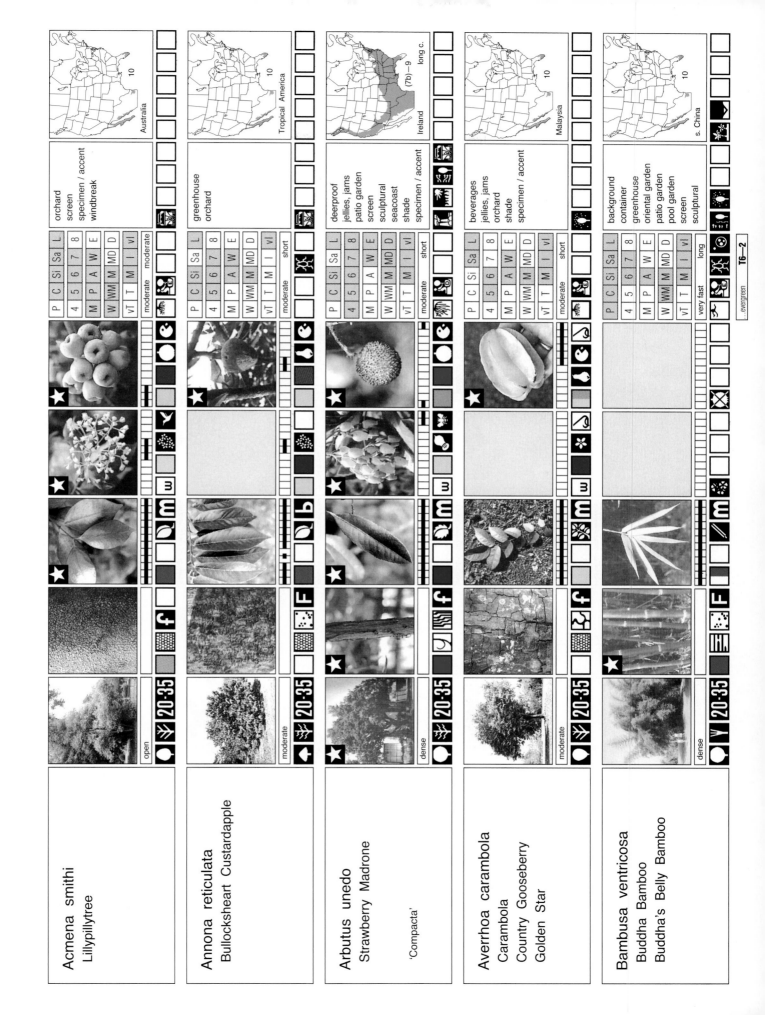

Acmena smithi
Lillypillytree

orchard
screen
specimen / accent
windbreak

Australia 10

P	C	Si	Sa	L
4	5	6	7	8
M	P	A	W	E
W	WM	M	MD	D
vT	T	M	I	vI

moderate / moderate

open 20-35

Annona reticulata
Bullocksheart Custardapple

greenhouse
orchard

Tropical America 10

P	C	Si	Sa	L
4	5	6	7	8
M	P	A	W	E
W	WM	M	MD	D
vT	T	M	I	vI

moderate / short

moderate 20-35

Arbutus unedo
Strawberry Madrone
'Compacta'

deerproof
jellies, jams
patio garden
screen
sculptural
seacoast
shade
specimen / accent

Ireland (7b)—9 long c.

P	C	Si	Sa	L
4	5	6	7	8
M	P	A	W	E
W	WM	M	MD	D
vT	T	M	I	vI

moderate / short

dense 20-35

Averrhoa carambola
Carambola
Country Gooseberry
Golden Star

beverages
jellies, jams
orchard
shade
specimen / accent

Malaysia 10

P	C	Si	Sa	L
4	5	6	7	8
M	P	A	W	E
W	WM	M	MD	D
vT	T	M	I	vI

moderate / short

moderate 20-35

Bambusa ventricosa
Buddha Bamboo
Buddha's Belly Bamboo

background
container
greenhouse
oriental garden
patio garden
pool garden
screen
sculptural

s. China 10

P	C	Si	Sa	L
4	5	6	7	8
M	P	A	W	E
W	WM	M	MD	D
vT	T	M	I	vI

very fast / long

dense 20-35

…evergreen

T6—2

SMALL TREE	FORM	BARK	LEAF	FLOWER	FRUIT	CULTURE	USES	REGION

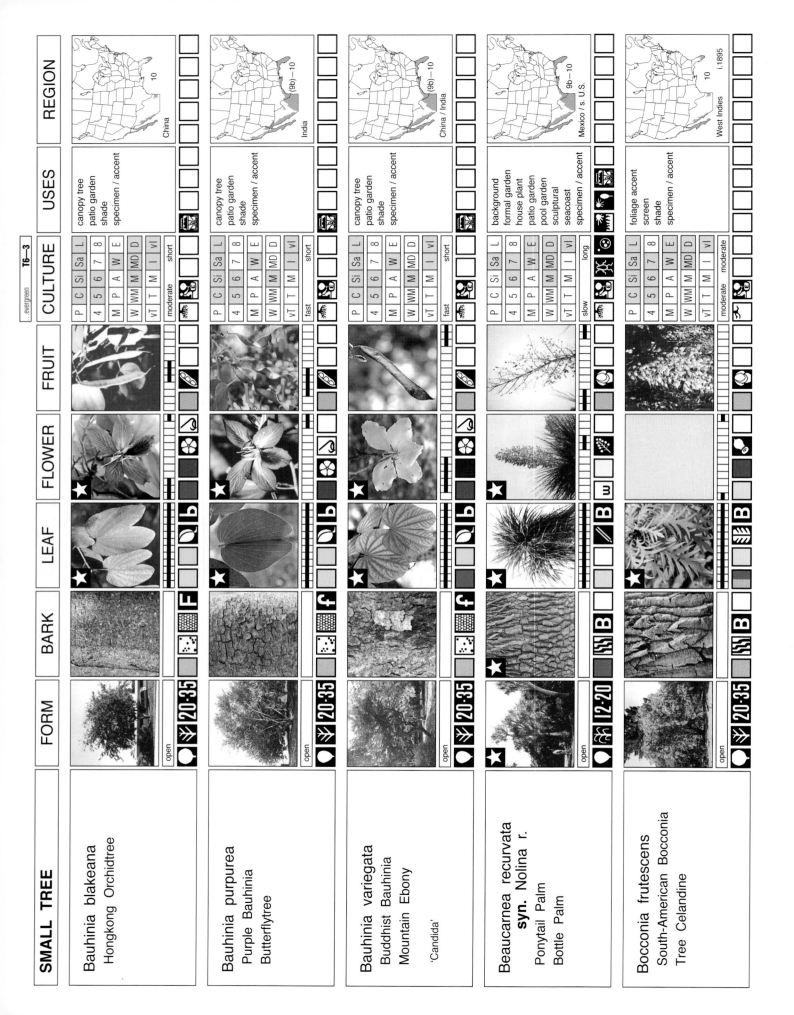

Bauhinia blakeana
Hongkong Orchidtree

open · 20-35

P C Si Sa L
4 5 6 7 8
M P A W E
W WM M MD D
vT T M I vl
moderate · short

canopy tree
patio garden
shade
specimen / accent

China · 10

Bauhinia purpurea
Purple Bauhinia
Butterflytree

open · 20-35

P C Si Sa L
4 5 6 7 8
M P A W E
W WM M MD D
vT T M I vl
fast · short

canopy tree
patio garden
shade
specimen / accent

India · (9b)–10

Bauhinia variegata
Buddhist Bauhinia
Mountain Ebony
'Candida'

open · 20-35

P C Si Sa L
4 5 6 7 8
M P A W E
W WM M MD D
vT T M I vl
fast · short

canopy tree
patio garden
shade
specimen / accent

China / India · (9b)–10

Beaucarnea recurvata
syn. Nolina r.
Ponytail Palm
Bottle Palm

open · 12-20

P C Si Sa L
4 5 6 7 8
M P A W E
W WM M MD D
vT T M I vl
slow · long

background
formal garden
house plant
patio garden
pool garden
sculptural
seacoast
specimen / accent

Mexico / s. U.S. · 9b–10

Bocconia frutescens
South-American Bocconia
Tree Celandine

open · 20-35

P C Si Sa L
4 5 6 7 8
M P A W E
W WM M MD D
vT T M I vl
moderate · moderate

foliage accent
screen
shade
specimen / accent

West Indies · 10 · i. 1895

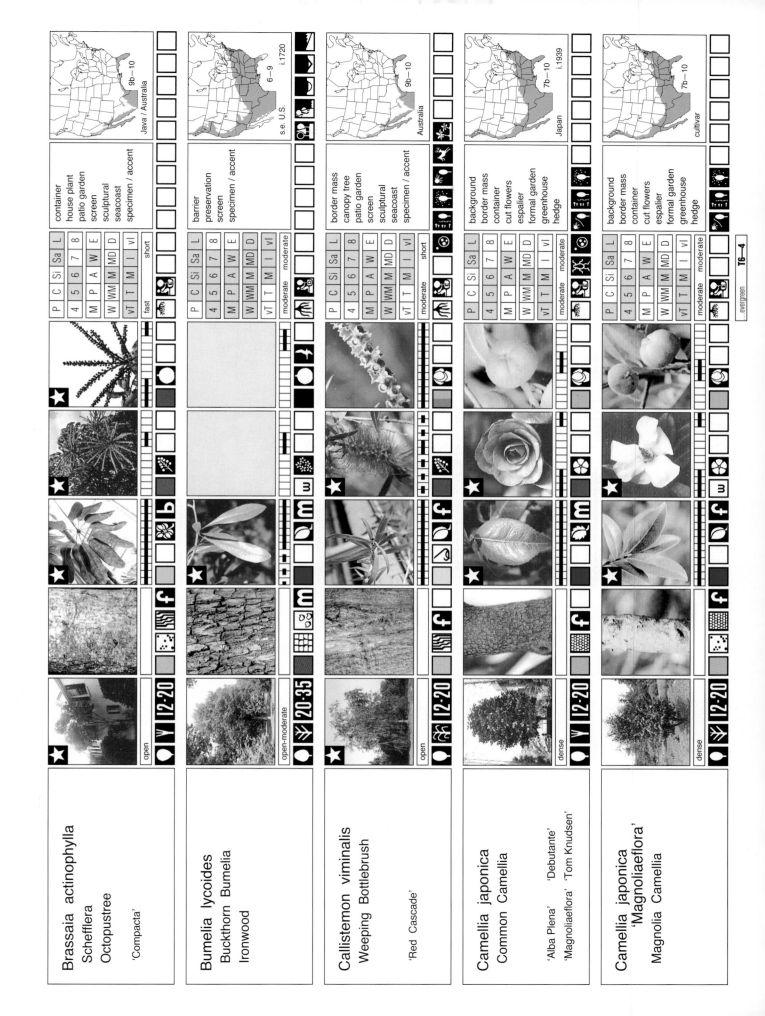

Brassaia actinophylla
Schefflera
Octopustree
'Compacta'

Java / Australia — 9b–10

container · house plant · patio garden · screen · sculptural · seacoast · specimen / accent

P C Si Sa L | 4 5 6 7 8 | M P A W E | W WM M MD D | vT T M I vl
short · fast · open · 12-20

Bumelia lycoides
Buckthorn Bumelia
Ironwood

s.e. U.S. — 6–9 — i.1720

barrier · preservation · screen · specimen / accent

P C Si Sa L | 4 5 6 7 8 | M P A W E | W WM M MD D | vT T M I vl
moderate · moderate · open-moderate · 20-35

Callistemon viminalis
Weeping Bottlebrush
'Red Cascade'

Australia — 9b–10

border mass · canopy tree · patio garden · screen · sculptural · seacoast · specimen / accent

P C Si Sa L | 4 5 6 7 8 | M P A W E | W WM M MD D | vT T M I vl
moderate · short · open · 12-20

Camellia japonica
Common Camellia
'Alba Plena'   'Debutante'
'Magnoliaeflora'   'Tom Knudsen'

Japan — 7b–10 — i.1939

background · border mass · container · cut flowers · espalier · formal garden · greenhouse · hedge

P C Si Sa L | 4 5 6 7 8 | M P A W E | W WM M MD D | vT T M I vl
moderate · moderate · dense · 12-20

Camellia japonica 'Magnoliaeflora'
Magnolia Camellia

cultivar — 7b–10

background · border mass · container · cut flowers · espalier · formal garden · greenhouse · hedge

P C Si Sa L | 4 5 6 7 8 | M P A W E | W WM M MD D | vT T M I vl
moderate · moderate · dense · 12-20

...evergreen   **T6—4**

SMALL TREE	FORM	BARK	LEAF	FLOWER	FRUIT	CULTURE	USES	REGION

Camellia sinensis
Tea

- FORM: dense — 12-20
- CULTURE: P C Si Sa L / 4 5 6 7 8 / M P A W E / W WM M MD D / vT T M I vl — slow
- USES: border mass, container, cut flowers, espalier, formal garden, greenhouse, hedge, patio garden
- REGION: China — 9–10, i.a.1770

Carica papaya
Papaya
Melontree
'Kapoho'   'Sunset'
'Solo'   'Waimanalo'

- FORM: open — 12-20
- CULTURE: P C Si Sa L / 4 5 6 7 8 / M P A W E / W WM M MD D / vT T M I vl — fast
- USES: beverages, culinary, greenhouse, jellies, jams, orchard
- REGION: Mexico — 10

Cassia excelsa
Crown-of-Gold

- FORM: open — 20-35
- CULTURE: P C Si Sa L / 4 5 6 7 8 / M P A W E / W WM M MD D / vT T M I vl — fast, short
- USES: canopy tree, patio garden, specimen / accent
- REGION: Argentina — 10

Cassia leptophylla
Gold Medalliontree

- FORM: open — 20-35
- CULTURE: P C Si Sa L / 4 5 6 7 8 / M P A W E / W WM M MD D / vT T M I vl — fast, short
- USES: canopy tree, patio garden, specimen / accent
- REGION: s.e. Brazil — 10

Casuarina torulosa
Forest Beefwood
Rose SheOak

- FORM: dense-open — 12-20
- CULTURE: P C Si Sa L / 4 5 6 7 8 / M P A W E / W WM M MD D / vT T M I vl — moderate
- USES: canopy tree, patio garden, seacoast, specimen / accent
- REGION: e. Australia — 10

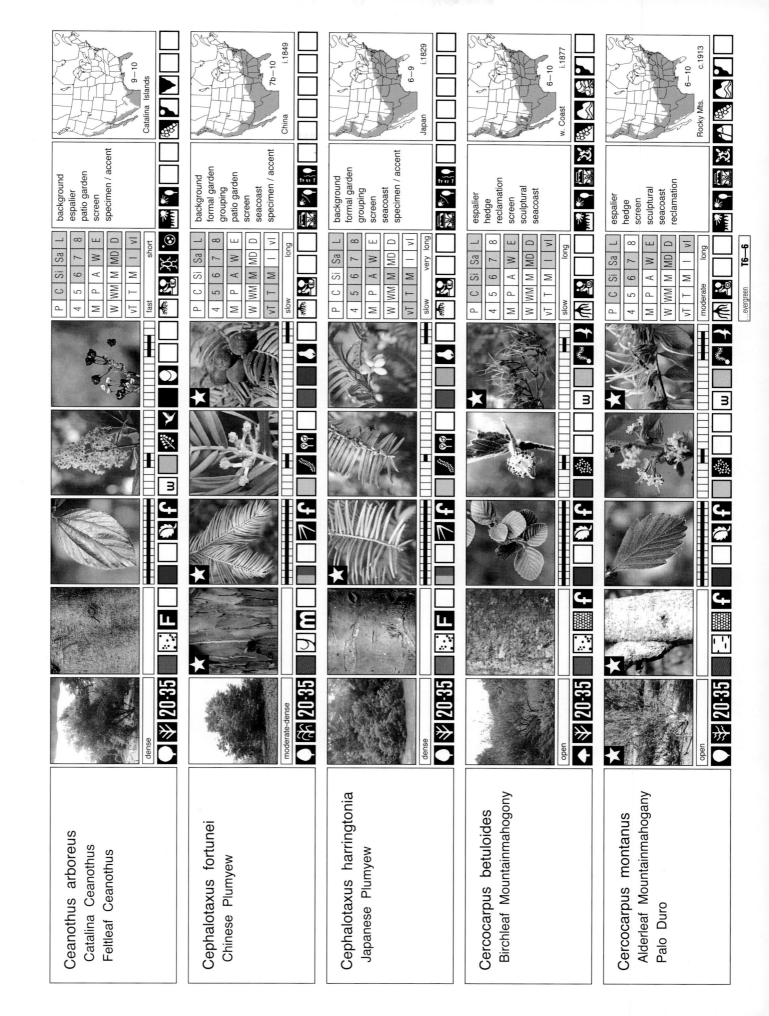

Ceanothus arboreus
Catalina Ceanothus
Feltleaf Ceanothus

9–10
Catalina Islands

background
espalier
patio garden
screen
specimen / accent

fast — short
dense
20·35

Cephalotaxus fortunei
Chinese Plumyew

7b–10
i.1849
China

background
formal garden
grouping
patio garden
screen
seacoast
specimen / accent

slow — long
moderate-dense
20·35

Cephalotaxus harringtonia
Japanese Plumyew

6–9
i.1829
Japan

background
formal garden
grouping
screen
seacoast
specimen / accent

slow — very long
dense
20·35

Cercocarpus betuloides
Birchleaf Mountainmahogany

6–10
i.1877
w. Coast

espalier
hedge
reclamation
screen
sculptural
seacoast

slow — long
open
20·35

Cercocarpus montanus
Alderleaf Mountainmahogany
Palo Duro

6–10
c.1913
Rocky Mts.

espalier
hedge
screen
sculptural
seacoast
reclamation

moderate — long
open
20·35

...evergreen   **T6–6**

SMALL TREE	FORM	BARK	LEAF	FLOWER	FRUIT	CULTURE	USES	REGION

Cercocarpus traskiae
Catalina Mountainmahogony

open — 20-35 — slow — long

CULTURE: P C Si Sa L / 4 5 6 7 8 / M P A W E / W WM M MD D / vT T M I vl

USES: espalier, hedge, preservation, reclamation, screen, sculptural, seacoast

REGION: 9–10 — Santa Catalina Islands

Chamaecyparis pisifera 'Plumosa'
Plumed Sawara Cypress

dense — 12-20 — moderate — long

CULTURE: P C Si Sa L / 4 5 6 7 8 / M P A W E / W WM M MD D / vT T M I vl

USES: aromatic foliage, background, bonsai, formal garden, hedge, narrow space, screen

REGION: 5–8 — i:1861 — cultivar

Chrysobalanus icaco
Coco Plum
Icaco

moderate — 20-35 — moderate — short

CULTURE: P C Si Sa L / 4 5 6 7 8 / M P A W E / W WM M MD D / vT T M I vl

USES: bank erosion, jams, jellies, kitchen garden, reclamation, screen, specimen / accent, water garden

REGION: 10 — S. America / Florida

Cinnamomum glanduliferum
Nepal Camphortree

moderate — 35-50 — fast — short

CULTURE: P C Si Sa L / 4 5 6 7 8 / M P A W E / W WM M MD D / vT T M I vl

USES: patio garden, shade, specimen / accent

REGION: 10 — Himalayas

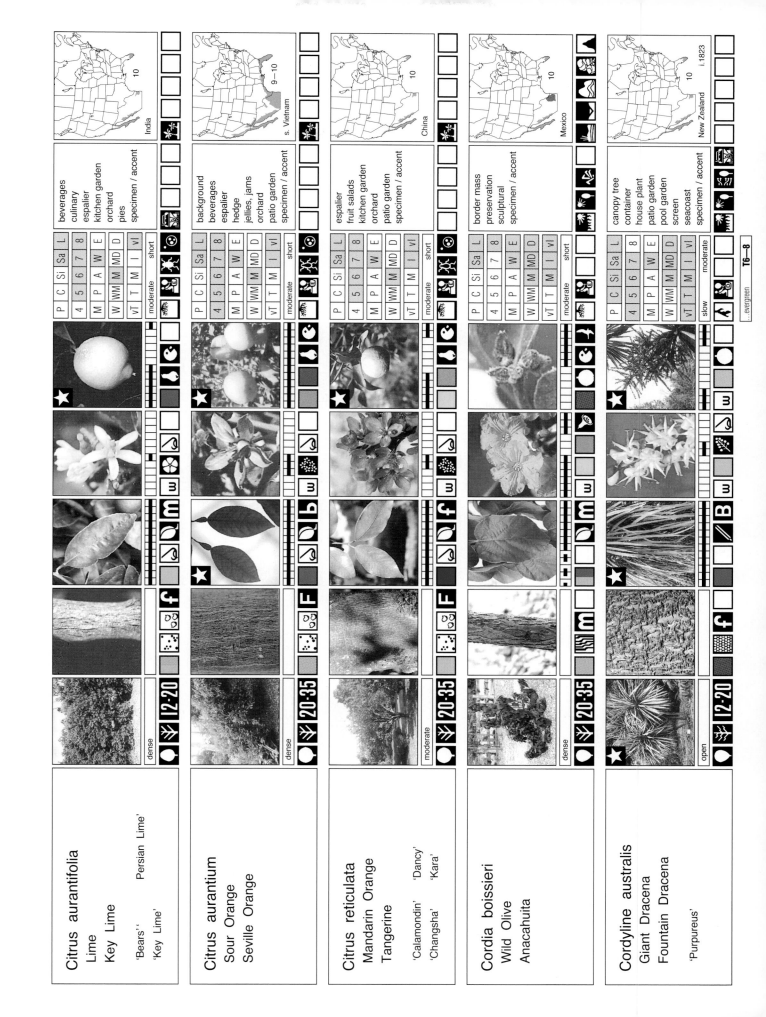

Citrus aurantifolia
Lime
Key Lime
'Bears''   Persian Lime
'Key Lime'

India   10

beverages
culinary
espalier
kitchen garden
orchard
pies
specimen / accent

P	C	Si	Sa	L
4	5	6	7	8
M	P	A	W	E
W	WM	M	MD	D
vT	T	M	l	vl

short

dense   12-20

Citrus aurantium
Sour Orange
Seville Orange

s. Vietnam   9 – 10

background
beverages
espalier
hedge
jellies, jams
orchard
patio garden
specimen / accent

P	C	Si	Sa	L
4	5	6	7	8
M	P	A	W	E
W	WM	M	MD	D
vT	T	M	l	vl

short

dense   20-35

Citrus reticulata
Mandarin Orange
Tangerine
'Calamondin'   'Dancy'
'Changsha'   'Kara'

China   10

espalier
fruit salads
kitchen garden
orchard
patio garden
specimen / accent

P	C	Si	Sa	L
4	5	6	7	8
M	P	A	W	E
W	WM	M	MD	D
vT	T	M	l	vl

short

moderate   20-35

Cordia boissieri
Wild Olive
Anacahuita

Mexico   10

border mass
preservation
sculptural
specimen / accent

P	C	Si	Sa	L
4	5	6	7	8
M	P	A	W	E
W	WM	M	MD	D
vT	T	M	l	vl

short

dense   20-35

Cordyline australis
Giant Dracena
Fountain Dracena
'Purpureus'

New Zealand   i.1823   10

canopy tree
container
house plant
patio garden
pool garden
screen
seacoast
specimen / accent

P	C	Si	Sa	L
4	5	6	7	8
M	P	A	W	E
W	WM	M	MD	D
vT	T	M	l	vl

moderate

slow

open   12-20

SMALL TREE	FORM	BARK	LEAF	FLOWER	FRUIT	CULTURE	USES	REGION

Corynocarpus laevigata
New Zealand Laurel
New Zealand Karakanut

- FORM: moderate / 12-20
- CULTURE: P C Si Sa L / 5 6 7 8 / M P A W E / W WM M MD D / vT T M I vl / slow — moderate
- USES: background, container, hedge, house plant, screen, seeds poisonous, shade
- REGION: 10 / New Zealand / i.1823

Cupressus bakeri
Modoc Cypress
Siskiyou Cypress

- FORM: open-dense / 12-20
- CULTURE: P C Si Sa L / 4 5 6 7 8 / M P A W E / W WM M MD D / vT T M I vl / slow — long
- USES: background, formal garden, hedge, narrow space, preservation, screen
- REGION: 6b—9a / n. California / c.1930

Dombeya cacuminum

- FORM: moderate / 12-20
- CULTURE: P C Si Sa L / 4 5 6 7 8 / M P A W E / W WM M MD D / vT T M I vl / fast — short
- USES: hard-to-find, patio garden, shade, shade garden, specimen / accent
- REGION: 10 / Madagascar

Drimys winteri
Wintersbark Drimys

- FORM: open -moderate / 6-12
- CULTURE: P C Si Sa L / 4 5 6 7 8 / M P A W E / W WM M MD D / vT T M I vl / fast — short
- USES: border mass, container, screen, seacoast, specimen / accent
- REGION: 9—10 / Chile / i.1827

Eriobotrya japonica
Loquat
Japanese Plum
'Gold Nugget'

- FORM: open -moderate / 20-35
- CULTURE: P C Si Sa L / 4 5 6 7 8 / M P A W E / W WM M MD D / vT T M I vl / moderate — short
- USES: border mass, container, espalier, leaf arrangements, orchard, patio garden, screen, seacoast
- REGION: 8—10 / China / i.1784

Escallonia herrerae

- patio garden
- shade
- specimen / accent

8–10

P C Si Sa L | 4 5 6 7 8 | M P A W E | W WM M MD D | vT T M I vI
slow | moderate

open | 12-20

Eucalyptus erythrocorys
Red-cap Gum
Illyarie Eucalyprus

- cut flowers
- leaf arrangement
- patio garden
- screen
- seacoast
- shade
- specimen / accent
- windbreak

w. Australia | 9–10

P C Si Sa L | 4 5 6 7 8 | M P A W E | W WM M MD D | vT T M I vI
slow | very long

open | 12-20

Eucalyptus perriniana
Spinning Gum
Roundleaved Snow Gum

- canopy tree
- cut flowers
- leaf arrangements
- screen
- seacoast
- shade
- specimen / accent
- windbreak

Tasmania | 9–10

P C Si Sa L | 4 5 6 7 8 | M P A W E | W WM M MD D | vT T M I vI
fast | moderate

moderate | 12-20

Eucalyptus stellulata
Black Sally
Blacksally Eucalyptus

- cut flowers
- leaf arrangement
- patio garden
- screen
- seacoast
- shade
- specimen / accent
- windbreak

Australia | 8–10

P C Si Sa L | 4 5 6 7 8 | M P A W E | W WM M MD D | vT T M I vI
fast | moderate

open | 12-20

Eucryphia lucida
Tasmanian Leatherwood

- background
- screen
- shade
- specimen / accent

Tasmania | 9–10

P C Si Sa L | 4 5 6 7 8 | M P A W E | W WM M MD D | vT T M I vI
moderate | short

...evergreen   T6–10

open | 20-35

SMALL TREE	FORM	BARK	LEAF	FLOWER	FRUIT	CULTURE	USES	REGION

Fortunella margarita
Nagami Kumquat
'Nagami'
'Sun Stripe'

- FORM: open-moderate — 12-20
- CULTURE: P C Si Sa L / 4 5 6 7 8 / M P A W E / W WM M MD D / vT T M I vI — short / moderate
- USES: container, espalier, jellies, jams, kitchen garden, orchard, patio garden, screen, specimen / accent
- REGION: 9–10, s.e. China

Fremontodendron californicum
Common Flannelbush
California Fremontia
'California Glory'
'Pacific Sunset HYB'

- FORM: open — 20-35
- CULTURE: P C Si Sa L / 4 5 6 7 8 / M P A W E / W WM M MD D / vT T M I vI — very long / slow
- USES: background, bank erosion, hedge, preservation, screen, seacoast, specimen / accent
- REGION: 7–10, i.1851, s.w. N.America

Fremontodendron mexicanum
Southern Flannelbush
Mexican Fremontia
San Diago Fremontia

- FORM: open — 20-35
- CULTURE: P C Si Sa L / 4 5 6 7 8 / M P A W E / W WM M MD D / vT T M I vI — short / fast
- USES: background, bank erosion, hedge, preservation, screen, specimen / accent
- REGION: 8–10, i.1926, California / Baja

Garrya elliptica
Wavyleaf Silktassel
Coast Silktassel
'Evie'
'James's Roof'

- FORM: moderate — 20-35
- CULTURE: P C Si Sa L / 4 5 6 7 8 / M P A W E / W WM M MD D / vT T M I vI — moderate / fast
- USES: background, bank erosion, hedge, screen, specimen / accent
- REGION: 9–10, i.1828, w. Coast

Guajacum officinale
Lignumvitae

- FORM: moderate — 20-35
- CULTURE: P C Si Sa L / 4 5 6 7 8 / M P A W E / W WM M MD D / vT T M I vI — moderate / moderate
- USES: medicinal, seacoast, shade, specimen / accent
- REGION: 10, Panama

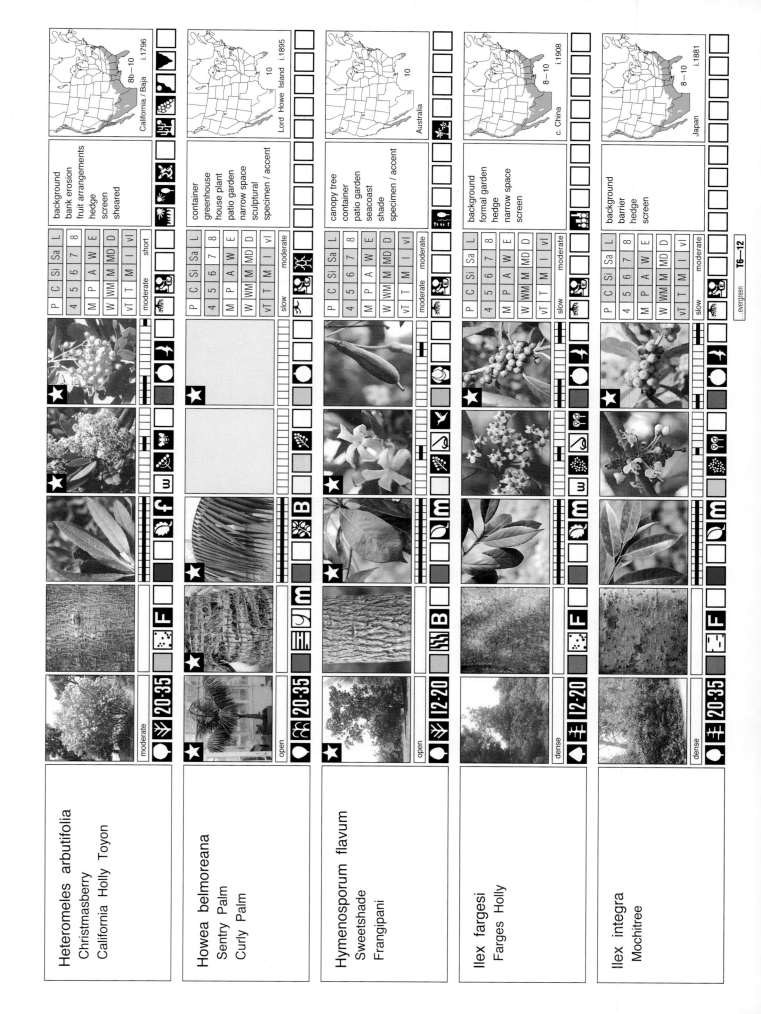

Heteromeles arbutifolia
Christmasberry
California Holly Toyon

background
bank erosion
fruit arrangements
hedge
screen
sheared

8b–10 i.1796
California / Baja

Howea belmoreana
Sentry Palm
Curly Palm

container
greenhouse
house plant
patio garden
narrow space
sculptural
specimen / accent

10 i.1895
Lord Howe Island

Hymenosporum flavum
Sweetshade
Frangipani

canopy tree
container
patio garden
seacoast
shade
specimen / accent

10
Australia

Ilex fargesi
Farges Holly

background
formal garden
hedge
narrow space
screen

8–10 i.1908
c. China

Ilex integra
Mochitree

background
barrier
hedge
screen

8–10 i.1881
Japan

...evergreen   **T6–12**

SMALL TREE	FORM	BARK	LEAF	FLOWER	FRUIT	CULTURE	USES	REGION

Ilex perado
Azores Holly
Madeira Holly

dense — 12-20

CULTURE: P C Si Sa L / 4 5 6 7 8 / M P A W E / W WM M MD D / vT T M I vl / slow — long

USES: background, barrier, border mass, formal garden, hedge, narrow space, screen

REGION: Canary Islands — 8—10 — c.1760

Ilex pernyi
Perny Holly
'Compacta'

dense — 12-20

CULTURE: P C Si Sa L / 4 5 6 7 8 / M P A W E / W WM M MD D / vT T M I vl / moderate

USES: background, barrier, border mass, patio garden, screen, specimen / accent

REGION: China — 6b—9a — i:1900

Juniperus californica
California Juniper

dense — 20-35

CULTURE: P C Si Sa L / 4 5 6 7 8 / M P A W E / W WM M MD D / vT T M I vl / slow — long

USES: aromatic bark, background, barrier, bonsai, naturalizing, screen, windbreak

REGION: California — 6—10 — i.1853

Juniperus osteosperma
Utah Juniper

dense — 20-35

CULTURE: P C Si Sa L / 4 5 6 7 8 / M P A W E / W WM M MD D / vT T M I vl / very slow — long

USES: aromatic bark, background, barrier, bonsai, naturalizing, screen, windbreak

REGION: w. N.America — 4—9

Juniperus recurva
Drooping Juniper
Himalayan Juniper

moderate — 20-35

CULTURE: P C Si Sa L / 4 5 6 7 8 / M P A W E / W WM M MD D / vT T M I vl / slow — long

USES: background, barrier, bonsai, formal garden, oriental garden, screen, specimen / accent, windbreak

REGION: Himalayas — 7b—10 — i.1822

Juniperus rigida
Needle Juniper
'Pendula'

Japan
i.1861
4—8

background
barrier
bonsai
formal garden
screen
windbreak

P	C	Si	Sa	L
4	5	6	7	8
M	P	A	W	E
W	WM	M	MD	D
vT	T	M	I	vI

slow · long

open · 12-20

Laurus nobilis
Sweetbay
Grecian Laurel

Mediterranean · i.col.x.
(7b)—10

background
container
culinary
hedge
herb garden
patio garden
sculptural
topiary

P	C	Si	Sa	L
4	5	6	7	8
M	P	A	W	E
W	WM	M	MD	D
vT	T	M	I	vI

slow · moderate

dense · 12-20

Leucadendron argenteum
Silver Leucadendron
Silvertree

s. Africa
10

container
greenhouse
rock garden
seacoast

P	C	Si	Sa	L
4	5	6	7	8
M	P	A	W	E
W	WM	M	MD	D
vT	T	M	I	vI

fast · short

open · 12-20

Maytenus boaria
Chile Mayten

Chile
8b—10 · i.1822

cut flowers
hedge
house
patio garden
raised bed
screen
seacoast
shade

P	C	Si	Sa	L
4	5	6	7	8
M	P	A	W	E
W	WM	M	MD	D
vT	T	M	I	vI

moderate · short

moderate · 20-35

Melaleuca armillaris
Drooping Melaleuca
Bracelet Honeymyrtle

s.e. Australia
10

oriental garden
screen
seacoast
shade
sheared
specimen / accent
windbreak

P	C	Si	Sa	L
4	5	6	7	8
M	P	A	W	E
W	WM	M	MD	D
vT	T	M	I	vI

fast · short

open · 20-35

..evergreen   T6—14

SMALL TREE	FORM	BARK	LEAF	FLOWER	FRUIT	CULTURE	USES	REGION

Melaleuca linariifolia
Snow-in-Summer
Flaxleaf Paperbark

moderate · 20-35

P	C	Si	Sa	L
4	5	6	7	8
M	P	A	W	E
W	WM	M	MD	D
vT	T	M	I	vl

fast · short

background
canopy tree
hedge
screen
seacoast
shade
specimen / accent
windbreak

Australia · 9–10

Melaleuca styphelioides
Prickly Melaleuca

moderate · 12-20

P	C	Si	Sa	L
4	5	6	7	8
M	P	A	W	E
W	WM	M	MD	D
vT	T	M	I	vl

fast · short

canopy tree
hedge
patio garden
screen
seacoast
specimen / accent
windbreak

Australia · 9–10

Metrosideros kermadecensis
Irontree

dense · 20-35

P	C	Si	Sa	L
4	5	6	7	8
M	P	A	W	E
W	WM	M	MD	D
vT	T	M	I	vl

fast · short

background
container
greenhouse
oriental garden
patio garden
pool garden
screen
sculptural

New Zealand · 9–10

Musa ensete
Abyssinian Banana

open · 12-20

P	C	Si	Sa	L
4	5	6	7	8
M	P	A	W	E
W	WM	M	MD	D
vT	T	M	I	vl

fast · very short

greenhouse
container
specimen / accent

Abyssinia · 10

Myrciaria cauliflora
Jaboticaba

moderate · 12-20

P	C	Si	Sa	L
4	5	6	7	8
M	P	A	W	E
W	WM	M	MD	D
vT	T	M	I	vl

slow · short

background
container
espalier
formal garden
jellies, jams
orchard
patio garden

s. Brazil · 10

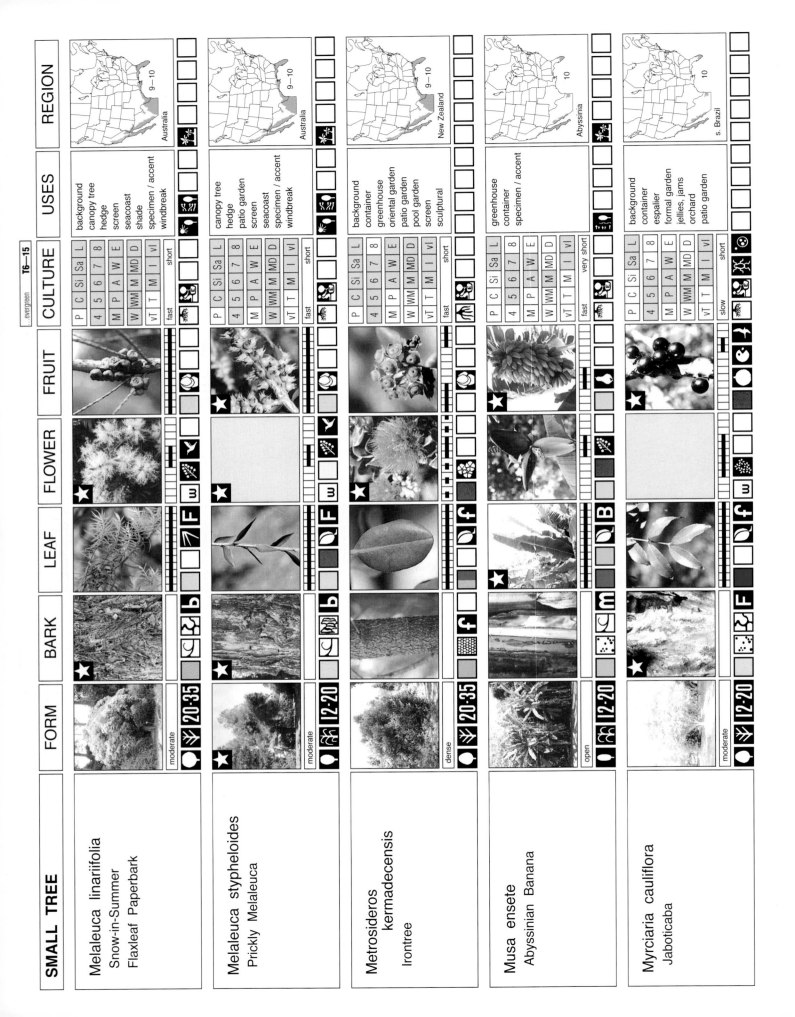

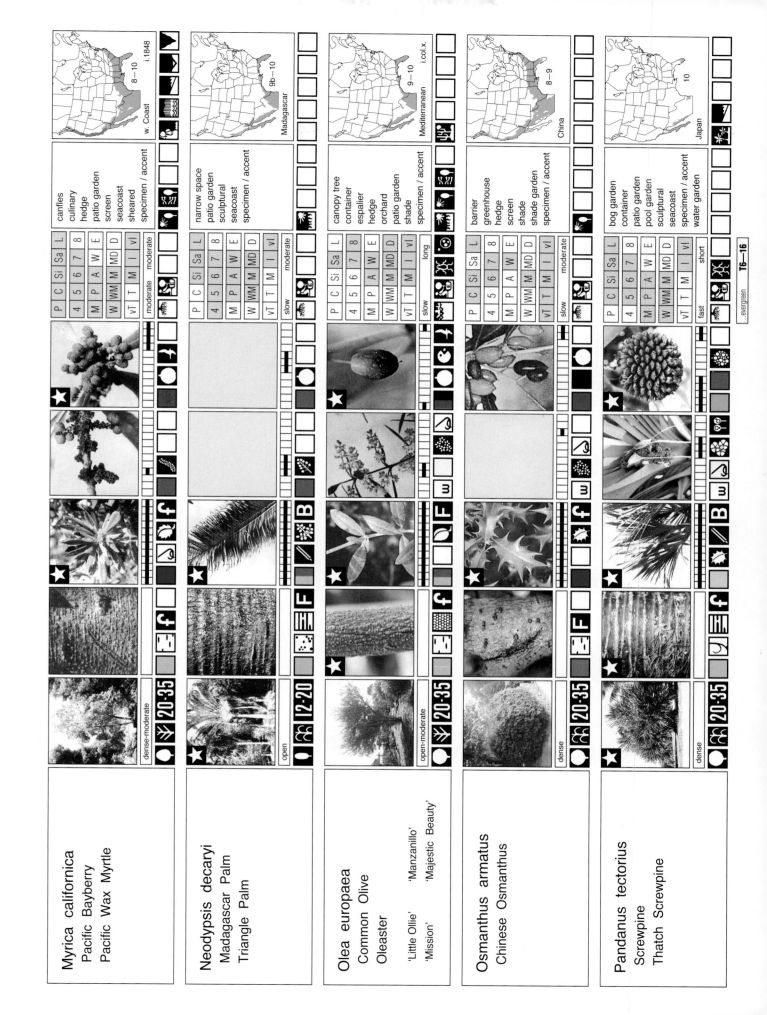

Myrica californica
Pacific Bayberry
Pacific Wax Myrtle

w. Coast   i.1848   8–10

candles
culinary
hedge
patio garden
screen
seacoast
sheared
specimen / accent

P	C	Si	Sa	L
4	5	6	7	8
M	P	A	W	E
W	WM	M	MD	D
vT	T	M	I	vI

moderate   moderate

dense-moderate   20-35

Neodypsis decaryi
Madagascar Palm
Triangle Palm

Madagascar   9b–10

narrow space
patio garden
sculptural
seacoast
specimen / accent

P	C	Si	Sa	L
4	5	6	7	8
M	P	A	W	E
W	WM	M	MD	D
vT	T	M	I	vI

slow   moderate

open   12-20

Olea europaea
Common Olive
Oleaster

'Little Ollie'   'Manzanillo'
'Mission'   'Majestic Beauty'

Mediterranean   i.col.x.   9–10

canopy tree
container
espalier
hedge
orchard
patio garden
shade
specimen / accent

P	C	Si	Sa	L
4	5	6	7	8
M	P	A	W	E
W	WM	M	MD	D
vT	T	M	I	vI

slow   long

open-moderate   20-35

Osmanthus armatus
Chinese Osmanthus

China   8–9

barrier
greenhouse
hedge
screen
shade
shade garden
specimen / accent

P	C	Si	Sa	L
4	5	6	7	8
M	P	A	W	E
W	WM	M	MD	D
vT	T	M	I	vI

slow   moderate

dense   20-35

Pandanus tectorius
Screwpine
Thatch Screwpine

Japan   10

bog garden
container
patio garden
pool garden
sculptural
seacoast
specimen / accent
water garden

P	C	Si	Sa	L
4	5	6	7	8
M	P	A	W	E
W	WM	M	MD	D
vT	T	M	I	vI

fast   short

dense   20-35

...evergreen   **T6–16**

SMALL TREE	FORM	BARK	LEAF	FLOWER	FRUIT	CULTURE	USES	REGION

Parkinsonia aculeata
Mexican Palo Verde
Jerusalemthorn

FORM: open — 20-35

CULTURE:
P	C	Si	Sa	L
4	5	6	7	8
M	P	A	W	E
W	WM	M	MD	D
vT	T	M	I	vl
short / fast

USES: background, barrier, cut flowers, naturalizing, screen, sculptural, seacoast, specimen / accent

REGION: 9—10 Mexico

Paurotis wrighti
syn. Acoelorraphe a.
Everglades Palm
Saw Cabbage Palm

FORM: open — 6-12

CULTURE:
P	C	Si	Sa	L
4	5	6	7	8
M	P	A	W	E
W	WM	M	MD	D
vT	T	M	I	vl
moderate / slow

USES: border mass, container, formal garden, house plant, pool garden, preservation, shade garden, water garden

REGION: 9b—10 Caribbean Islands

Peltophorum africanum
African Peltophorum

FORM: moderate — 35-50

CULTURE:
P	C	Si	Sa	L
4	5	6	7	8
M	P	A	W	E
W	WM	M	MD	D
vT	T	M	I	vl
short / fast

USES: hard-to-find, shade

REGION: 9b—10 Africa

Phillyrea latifolia
Tree Phillyrea

FORM: dense — 20-35

CULTURE:
P	C	Si	Sa	L
4	5	6	7	8
M	P	A	W	E
W	WM	M	MD	D
vT	T	M	I	vl
short / slow

USES: background, screen

REGION: 8—10 s. Europe

Phoenix reclinata
Senegal Date Palm
Cape Palm

FORM: dense — 20-35

CULTURE:
P	C	Si	Sa	L
4	5	6	7	8
M	P	A	W	E
W	WM	M	MD	D
vT	T	M	I	vl
moderate / fast

USES: patio garden, pool garden, sculptural, seacoast, specimen / accent, water garden

REGION: 9—10 Africa

Phyllostachys aureosulcata
Yellowgroove Bamboo

dense | 20-35

P	C	Si	Sa	L
4	5	6	7	8
M	P	A	W	E
W	WM	M	MD	D
vT	T	M	I	vI

fast | short

aromatic shoots
background
bank erosion
edible shoots
oriental garden
reclamation
screen

7b–10
China

Phyllostachys nigra
Black Bamboo

'Bory'
'Henon'

dense | 20-35

P	C	Si	Sa	L
4	5	6	7	8
M	P	A	W	E
W	WM	M	MD	D
vT	T	M	I	vI

fast | short

background
bank erosion
barrier
oriental garden
rarely fruits
reclamation
screen

8–10
China

Picea glauca densata
Blackhills Spruce

dense | 12-20

P	C	Si	Sa	L
4	5	6	7	8
M	P	A	W	E
W	WM	M	MD	D
vT	T	M	I	vI

slow | long

background
bonsai
border mass
hedge
narrow space
reclamation
windbreak

2–7a
c. United States

Pinus cembroides
Mexican Pinyon Pine

moderate | 20-35

P	C	Si	Sa	L
4	5	6	7	8
M	P	A	W	E
W	WM	M	MD	D
vT	T	M	I	vI

slow | long

background
edible seeds
naturalizing
reclamation
specimen / accent
windbreak

7b–10
Mexico / Texas

Pinus contorta
Shore Pine
Beach Pine

'Murrayana'
'Spaan's Dwarf'

moderate | 12-20

P	C	Si	Sa	L
4	5	6	7	8
M	P	A	W	E
W	WM	M	MD	D
vT	T	M	I	vI

fast | short

container
patio garden
reclamation
sculptural
seacoast
specimen / accent
windbreak

7b–9
i.1831
w. Coast

...evergreen   T6—18

SMALL TREE	FORM	BARK	LEAF	FLOWER	FRUIT	CULTURE	USES	REGION

Pinus edulis
Colorado Pinyon Pine
Two-needle Pinyon Pine

moderate 20-35

P	C	Si	Sa	L
4	5	6	7	8
M	P	A	W	E
W	WM	M	MD	D
vT	T	M	I	vI

slow   long

USES: background, Christmas trees, container, edible seeds, rock garden, screen, seacoast, windbreak

REGION: s.w. U.S.   4–8

Pinus monophylla
Singleleaf Pinyon Pine

moderate 20-35

P	C	Si	Sa	L
4	5	6	7	8
M	P	A	W	E
W	WM	M	MD	D
vT	T	M	I	vI

slow   very long

USES: background, bonsai, edible seeds, naturalizing, rock garden, screen, windbreak

REGION: w. N.America   4–10   i.1848

Pinus serotina
Pond Pine
Pocosin Pine

open 20-35

P	C	Si	Sa	L
4	5	6	7	8
M	P	A	W	E
W	WM	M	MD	D
vT	T	M	I	vI

fast   short

USES: background, bank erosion, bog garden, border mass, naturalizing, reclamation, screen, water garden

REGION: s.e. U.S.   7-9

Pinus virginiana
Virginia Pine
'Nashawena'
'Wates Golden'

moderate 35-50

P	C	Si	Sa	L
4	5	6	7	8
M	P	A	W	E
W	WM	M	MD	D
vT	T	M	I	vI

slow   short

USES: background, border mass, naturalizing, reclamation, rocky barrens, screen, specimen / accent, windbreak

REGION: e.U.S.   5b–9a   i.1739

Pittosporum bicolor
Banyalla Pittosporum

moderate 20-35

P	C	Si	Sa	L
4	5	6	7	8
M	P	A	W	E
W	WM	M	MD	D
vT	T	M	I	vI

moderate   moderate

USES: background, border mass, bonsai, fruit arrangement, hedge, patio garden, screen, specimen / accent

REGION: 9b–10

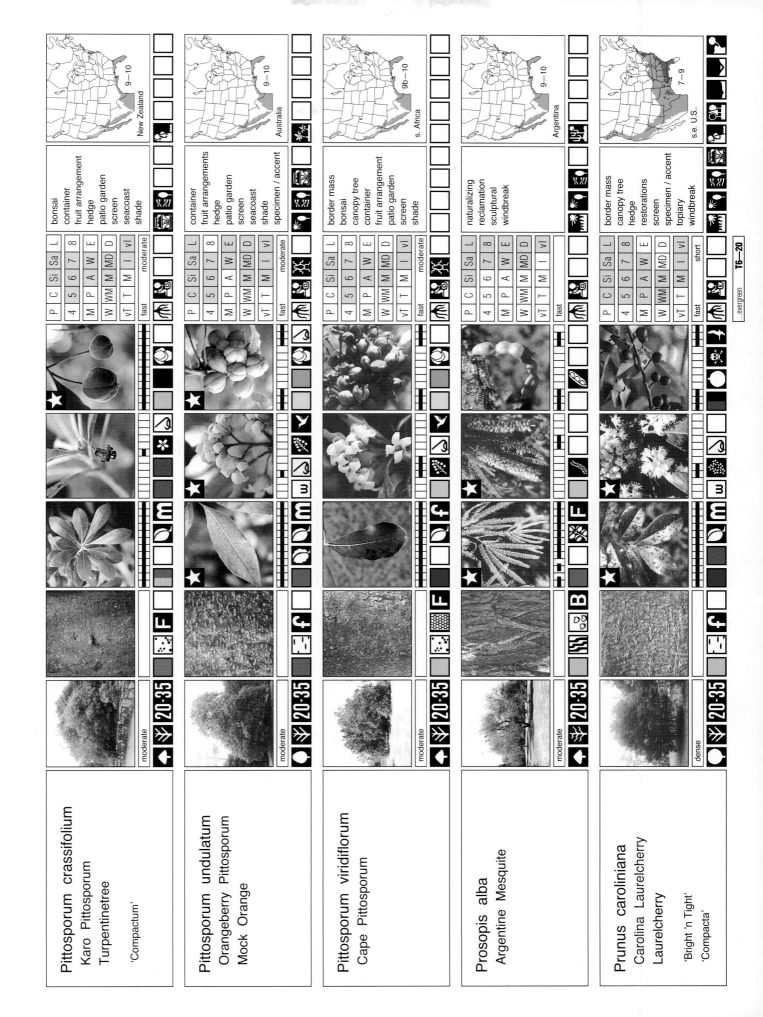

Pittosporum crassifolium
Karo Pittosporum
Turpentinetree
'Compactum'

container
fruit arrangement
hedge
patio garden
screen
seacoast
shade

New Zealand
9–10

Pittosporum undulatum
Orangeberry Pittosporum
Mock Orange

container
fruit arrangements
hedge
patio garden
screen
seacoast
shade
specimen / accent

Australia
9–10

Pittosporum viridiflorum
Cape Pittosporum

border mass
bonsai
canopy tree
container
fruit arrangement
patio garden
screen
shade

s. Africa
9b–10

Prosopis alba
Argentine Mesquite

naturalizing
reclamation
sculptural
windbreak

Argentina
9–10

Prunus caroliniana
Carolina Laurelcherry
Laurelcherry
'Bright 'n Tight'
'Compacta'

border mass
canopy tree
hedge
restorations
screen
specimen / accent
topiary
windbreak

s.e. U.S.
7–9

...evergreen   T6—20

SMALL TREE	FORM	BARK	LEAF	FLOWER	FRUIT	CULTURE	USES	REGION

Prunus lusitanica
Portugese Laurelcherry
Portugal Laurel
'Lucidum'

dense · 20-35

CULTURE: P C Si Sa L · 4 5 6 7 8 · M P A W E · W WM M MD D · vT T M I vI · moderate — short

USES: background · canopy tree · formal garden · patio garden · screen · specimen / accent

REGION: Spain / Portugal · 7b–10 · i.1648

Psidium littorale
syn. P. cattleianum
Cattley Guava
Strawberry Guava

moderate · 20-35

CULTURE: P C Si Sa L · 4 5 6 7 8 · M P A W E · W WM M MD D · vT T M I vI · moderate — short

USES: barrier · hedge · jellies, jams · kitchen garden · orchard · specimen / accent

REGION: C. America / Brazil · 10

Radermachia sinica
Glory Asiabelltree

moderate · 20-35

CULTURE: P C Si Sa L · 4 5 6 7 8 · M P A W E · W WM M MD D · vT T M I vI · fast

USES: container · groupings · house plant · shade · specimen / accent

REGION: China · 10

Ravenala madagascariensis
Travelers Palm

open · 20-35

CULTURE: P C Si Sa L · 4 5 6 7 8 · M P A W E · W WM M MD D · vT T M I vI · moderate — moderate

USES: background · container · greenhouse · formal garden · narrow space · sculptural · seacoast · specimen / accent

REGION: Madagascar · 10

Rhododendron maximum
Rosebay Rhododendron
'Prides Pink' 'Roseum'
"Lady Clementine Mitford"

dense · 20-35

CULTURE: P C Si Sa L · 4 5 6 7 8 · M P A W E · W WM M MD D · vT T M I vI · moderate — moderate

USES: background · border mass · groupings · naturalizing · screen · specimen / accent

REGION: e.Coast · (3b)–7 · i.1736

Rhus integrifolia
Lemonade Sumac

P	C	Si	Sa	L
4	5	6	7	8
M	P	A	W	E
W	WM	M	MD	D
vT	T	M	I	vl

fast · short

background
beverages
espalier
hedge
screen
seacoast
sheared
windbreak

9—10 · Mexico / California.

20-35 · open

Rhus laurina syn. Malosma l.
Laurel Sumac

P	C	Si	Sa	L
4	5	6	7	8
M	P	A	W	E
W	WM	M	MD	D
vT	T	M	I	vl

fast · short

aromatic leaves
background
bank erosion
espalier
hedge
screen
sheared
windbreak

9—10 · Mexico / California

20-35 · moderate

Schinus latifolia
Chilean Peppertree

P	C	Si	Sa	L
4	5	6	7	8
M	P	A	W	E
W	WM	M	MD	D
vT	T	M	I	vl

fast · short

container
patio garden
pool garden
sculptural
shade
specimen / accent

9—10 · Chile

20-35 · open

Schinus terebinthifolia
Brazilian Peppertree
Christmasberry

P	C	Si	Sa	L
4	5	6	7	8
M	P	A	W	E
W	WM	M	MD	D
vT	T	M	I	vl

moderate · moderate

canopy tree
Christmas wreath
fruit arrangements
container
patio garden
pool garden
seacoast
shade

9—10 · Brazil

35-50 · open

Stenocarpus sinuatus
Wheel-of-fire
Tall Firewheeltree

P	C	Si	Sa	L
4	5	6	7	8
M	P	A	W	E
W	WM	M	MD	D
vT	T	M	I	vl

slow · moderate

container
house plant
patio garden
pool garden
shade

10 · Australia

12-20 · dense

...evergreen   T6—22

SMALL TREE	FORM	BARK	LEAF	FLOWER	FRUIT	CULTURE	USES	REGION

Syzygium paniculata
syn. Eugenia p. australis
Brushcherry Eugenia
Magenta Lilly Pilly
'Globulus'   'Teenie Genie'

- Form: moderate · 12-20
- Culture: P C Si Sa L / 4 5 6 7 8 / M P A W E / W WM M MD D / vT T M I vl · fast · short
- Uses: background, container, jams, jellies, kitchen garden, orchard, screen
- Region: Australia · 9–10

Syzygium uniflora
syn. Eugenia u.
Surinam Cherry
Pitanga

- Form: dense · 12-20
- Culture: P C Si Sa L / 4 5 6 7 8 / M P A W E / W WM M MD D / vT T M I vl · fast · short
- Uses: background, container, hedge, jams, jellies, kitchen garden, orchard, screen
- Region: Tropical Brazil · 10

Taxus baccata
English Yew
'Repandens'
'Standishii'

- Form: dense · 20-35
- Culture: P C Si Sa L / 4 5 6 7 8 / M P A W E / W WM M MD D / vT T M I vl · slow · very long
- Uses: background, bonsai, border mass, hedge, screen, seacoast, specimen / accent, topiary
- Region: Europe · 6b–8a · early colonial.

Torreya nucifera
Japanese Torreya

- Form: dense · 12-20
- Culture: P C Si Sa L / 4 5 6 7 8 / M P A W E / W WM M MD D / vT T M I vl · slow · long
- Uses: background, border mass, formal garden, patio garden, preservation, screen
- Region: Japan · (6b)–8a · i.a. 1860

Trachycarpus fortunei
Fortunes Palm
Windmill Palm

- Form: moderate · 6-12
- Culture: P C Si Sa L / 4 5 6 7 8 / M P A W E / W WM M MD D / vT T M I vl · slow · moderate
- Uses: canopy tree, container, house plant, patio garden, seacoast, specimen / accent
- Region: n. Burma · 8b–10

Tristania laurina
Kanooka Tristania
Watergum

Australia 10

background
container
formal garden
patio garden
screen
specimen / accent
water garden

P	C	Si	Sa	L
4	5	6	7	8
M	P	A	W	E
W	WM	M	MD	D
vT	T	M	I	vI

slow   short

moderate   20-35

Xylosma senticosa
syn. X. japonica
Shiny Xylosma

'Compactum'

China 9–10

container
espalier
hedge

P	C	Si	Sa	L
4	5	6	7	8
M	P	A	W	E
W	WM	M	MD	D
vT	T	M	I	vI

slow   moderate

dense   20-35

Yucca brevifolia
Joshuatree Yucca

s.w. U.S. 6–10

container
groupings
novelty
preservation
sculptural
specimen / accent

P	C	Si	Sa	L
4	5	6	7	8
M	P	A	W	E
W	WM	M	MD	D
vT	T	M	I	vI

slow   long

open   12-20

Yucca elephantipes
Giant Yucca
Bulbstem Yucca
Spineless Yucca

Guatemala 9b–10

container
groupings
novelty
preservation
sculptural
specimen / accent

P	C	Si	Sa	L
4	5	6	7	8
M	P	A	W	E
W	WM	M	MD	D
vT	T	M	I	vI

fast   long

open   12-20

P	C	Si	Sa	L
4	5	6	7	8
M	P	A	W	E
W	WM	M	MD	D
vT	T	M	I	vI

…evergreen

VERY LARGE SHRUB

	FORM	BARK	LEAF	FLOWER	FRUIT	CULTURE	USES	REGION

Acacia cyclopis
Coastal Acacia
Cyclops Acacia

- FORM: dense — 20-35
- CULTURE: P C Si Sa L / 4 5 6 7 8 / M P A W E / W WM M MD D / vT T M I vl — fast
- USES: background, border mass, deerproof, fruit arrangements, nitrogen-fixing, screen, seacoast, sheared
- REGION: 8b–10 — Australia

Acacia pycnantha
Golden Acacia
Golden Wattle

- FORM: open — 12-20
- CULTURE: P C Si Sa L / 4 5 6 7 8 / M P A W E / W WM M MD D / vT T M I vl — fast
- USES: cut flowers, deerproof, greenhouse, nitrogen-fixing, screen, seacoast, specimen / accent, wildlife habitat
- REGION: 8–10 — Australia

Adenostoma sparsifolium
Ribbonwood
Redshanks

- FORM: open — 12-20
- CULTURE: P C Si Sa L / 4 5 6 7 8 / M P A W E / W WM M MD D / vT T M I vl — fast
- USES: background, bank erosion, naturalizing, reclamation, specimen / accent
- REGION: 8b–10 — s. California

Alpinia purpurata
Red Shellflower

- FORM: open — 12-20
- CULTURE: P C Si Sa L / 4 5 6 7 8 / M P A W E / W WM M MD D / vT T M I vl — fast
- USES: border mass, container, greenhouse, groupings, naturalizing, screen, specimen / accent
- REGION: 9–10 — Polynesia

Arctostaphylos glauca
Bigberry Manzanita

- FORM: moderate — 12-20
- CULTURE: P C Si Sa L / 4 5 6 7 8 / M P A W E / W WM M MD D / vT T M I vl — fast
- USES: background, bank erosion, naturalizing, screen, specimen / accent
- REGION: 8–10 — s. California

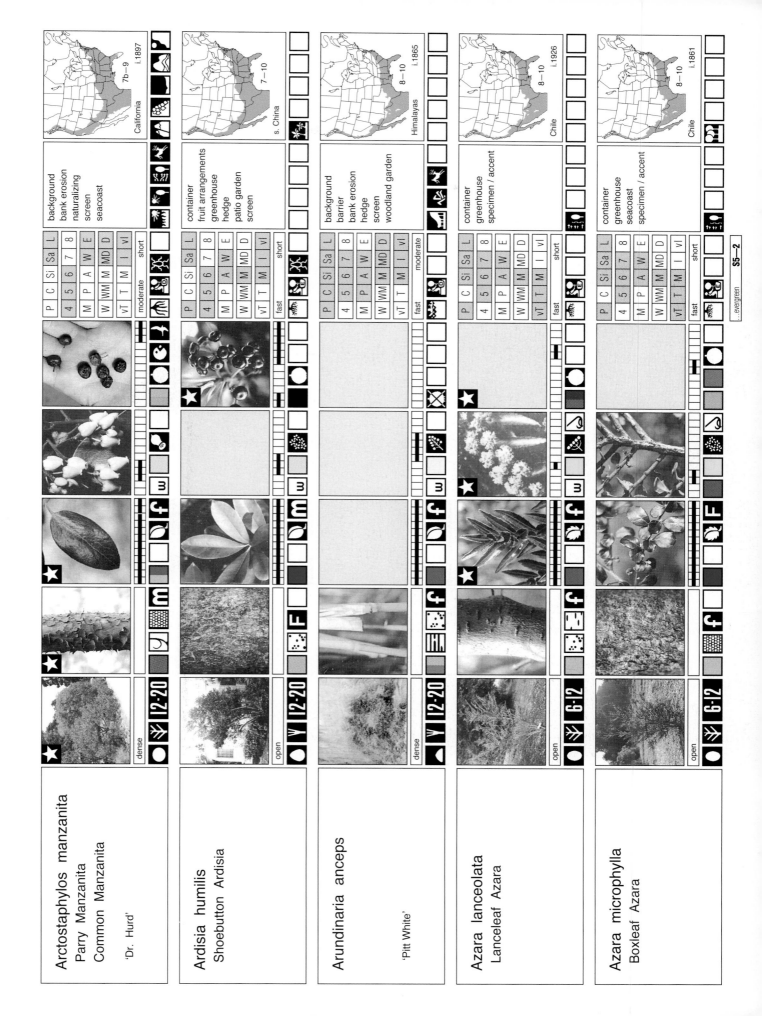

Arctostaphylos manzanita
Parry Manzanita
Common Manzanita

'Dr. Hurd'

California   i.1897   7b–9

background
bank erosion
naturalizing
screen
seacoast

P	C	Si	Sa	L
4	5	6	7	8
M	P	A	W	E
W	WM	M	MD	D
		vT	T	vl

moderate   short

dense   12-20

Ardisia humilis
Shoebutton Ardisia

s. China   7–10

container
fruit arrangements
greenhouse
hedge
patio garden
screen

P	C	Si	Sa	L
4	5	6	7	8
M	P	A	W	E
W	WM	M	MD	D
		vT	T	vl

fast   short

open   12-20

Arundinaria anceps

'Pitt White'

Himalayas   i.1865   8–10

background
barrier
bank erosion
hedge
screen
woodland garden

P	C	Si	Sa	L
4	5	6	7	8
M	P	A	W	E
W	WM	M	MD	D
		vT	T	

moderate   fast

dense   12-20

Azara lanceolata
Lanceleaf Azara

Chile   i.1926   8–10

container
greenhouse
specimen / accent

P	C	Si	Sa	L
4	5	6	7	8
M	P	A	W	E
W	WM	M	MD	D
vT	T	I	M	vl

fast   short

open   6-12

Azara microphylla
Boxleaf Azara

Chile   i.1861   8–10

container
greenhouse
seacoast
specimen / accent

P	C	Si	Sa	L
4	5	6	7	8
M	P	A	W	E
W	WM	M	MD	D
vT	T	I	M	vl

fast   short

open   6-12

...evergreen

S5—2

VERY LARGE SHRUB	FORM	BARK	LEAF	FLOWER	FRUIT	CULTURE	USES	REGION

Azara petiolaris
Golden Azara

CULTURE: P C Si Sa L · 4 5 6 7 8 · M P A W E · W WM M MD D · vT T M I vl · fast · short
USES: container / greenhouse / specimen / accent
REGION: 8–10 · i.1859 · Chile
FORM: dense · 12·20

Bixa orellana
Lipstick Tree
Annatto

CULTURE: P C Si Sa L · 4 5 6 7 8 · M P A W E · W WM M MD D · vT T M I vl · fast · short
USES: border mass / dye plant / fruit arrangements / medicinal / specimen / accent
REGION: 9b–10
FORM: moderate · 12·20

Brachyglottis repanda

CULTURE: P C Si Sa L · 4 5 6 7 8 · M P A W E · W WM M MD D · vT T M I vl · moderate · short
USES: container / fragrant flowers / seacoast / specimen / accent / windbreak
REGION: 9–10 · New Zealand
FORM: open · 12·20

Brugmansia x candida
syn. Datura **x** c.
Thornapple
Angel's Trumpet
'Double White'

CULTURE: P C Si Sa L · 4 5 6 7 8 · M P A W E · W WM M MD D · vT T M I vl · fast · moderate
USES: border mass / container / greenhouse / screen / specimen / accent
REGION: 9–10 · hybrid
FORM: dense · 12·20

Brugmansia suaveolens
syn. Datura s.
Angeltears

CULTURE: P C Si Sa L · 4 5 6 7 8 · M P A W E · W WM M MD D · vT T M I vl · fast · moderate
USES: border mass / container / greenhouse / screen / specimen / accent
REGION: 10
FORM: dense · 12·20

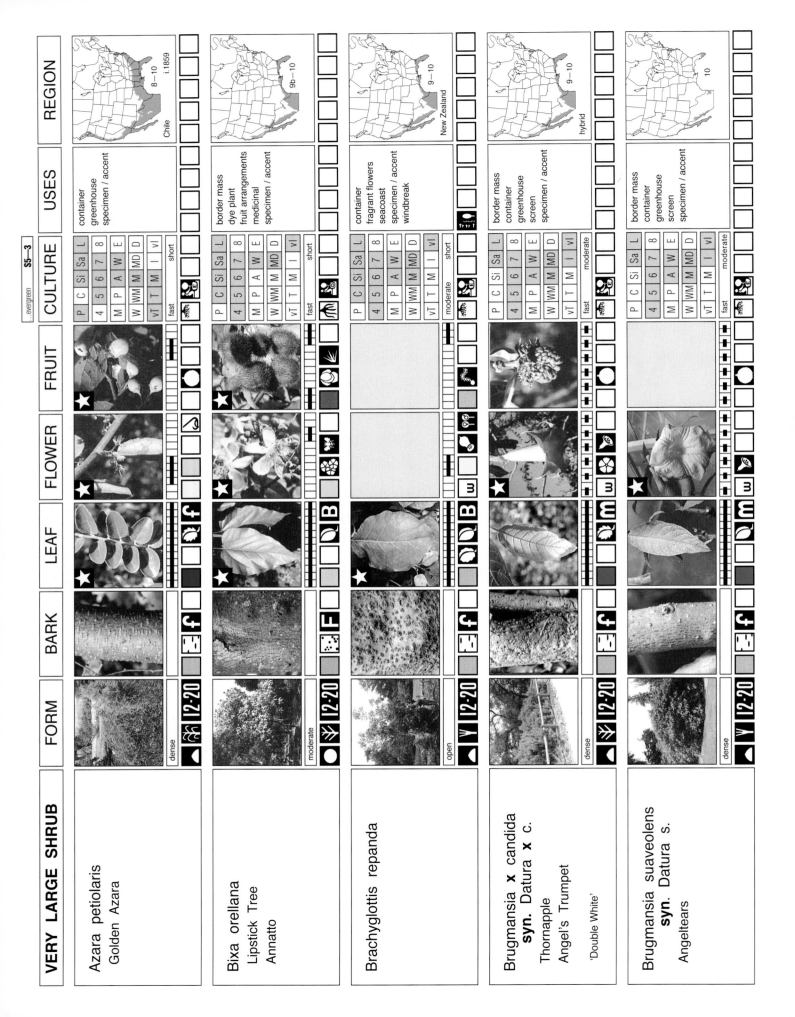

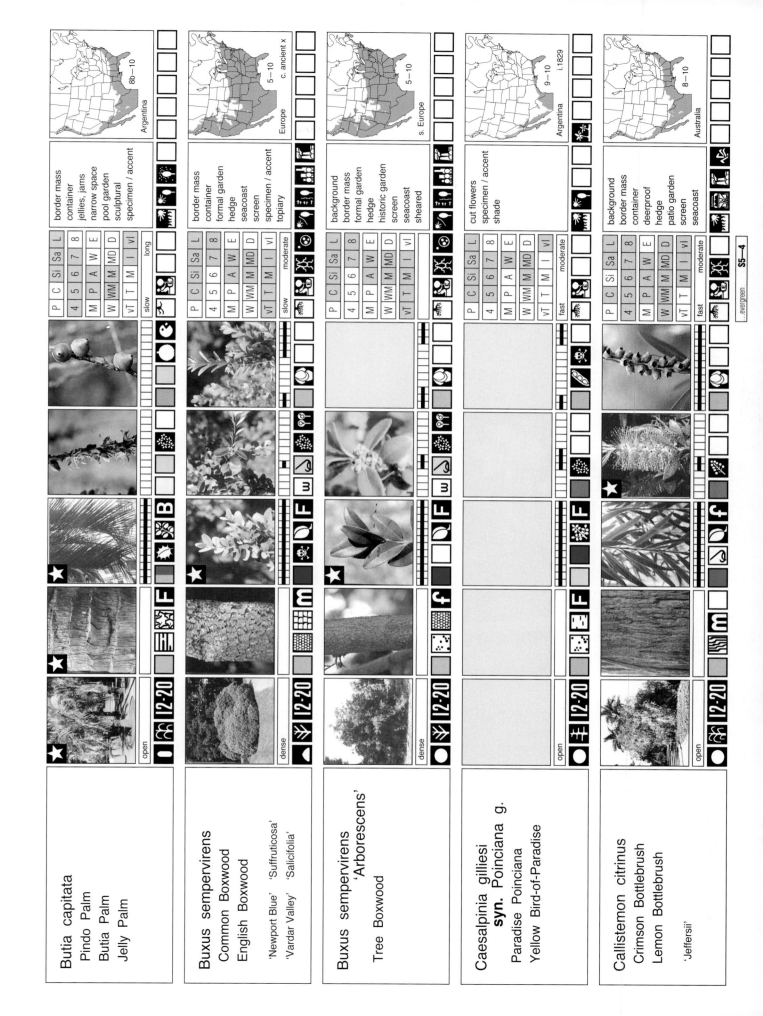

Butia capitata
Pindo Palm
Butia Palm
Jelly Palm

border mass
container
jellies, jams
narrow space
pool garden
sculptural
specimen / accent

P C Si Sa L
4 5 6 7 8
M P A W E
W WM M MD D
vT T M I vI

slow · long
open · 12-20
Argentina · 8b–10

Buxus sempervirens
Common Boxwood
English Boxwood
'Newport Blue' 'Suffruticosa'
'Vardar Valley' 'Salicifolia'

border mass
container
formal garden
hedge
seacoast
screen
specimen / accent
topiary

P C Si Sa L
4 5 6 7 8
M P A W E
W WM M MD D
vT T M I vI

slow · moderate
dense · 12-20
Europe · 5–10 · c. ancient x

Buxus sempervirens 'Arborescens'
Tree Boxwood

background
border mass
formal garden
hedge
historic garden
screen
seacoast
sheared

P C Si Sa L
4 5 6 7 8
M P A W E
W WM M MD D
vT T M I vI

dense · 12-20
s. Europe · 5–10

Caesalpinia gilliesi
syn. Poinciana g.
Paradise Poinciana
Yellow Bird-of-Paradise

cut flowers
specimen / accent
shade

P C Si Sa L
4 5 6 7 8
M P A W E
W WM M MD D
vT T M I vI

fast · moderate
open · 12-20
Argentina · 9–10 · i.1829

Callistemon citrinus
Crimson Bottlebrush
Lemon Bottlebrush
'Jeffersii'

background
border mass
container
deerproof
hedge
patio garden
screen
seacoast

P C Si Sa L
4 5 6 7 8
M P A W E
W WM M MD D
vT T M I vI

fast · moderate
open · 12-20
Australia · 8–10

...evergreen   S5–4

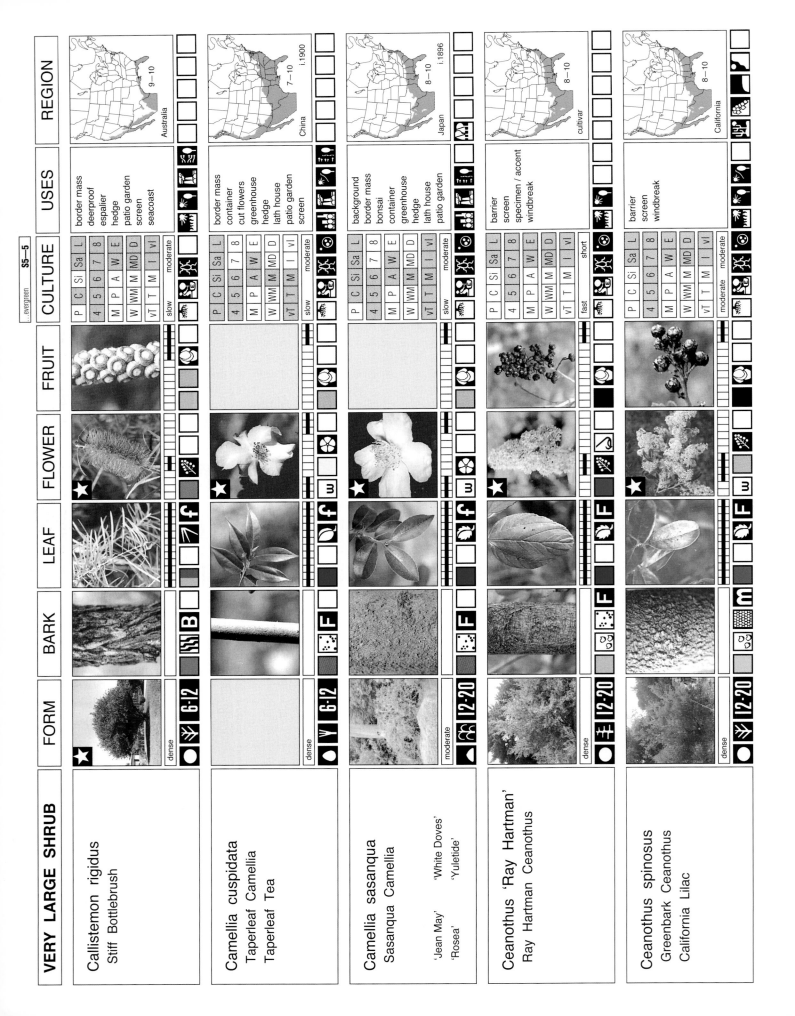

VERY LARGE SHRUB	FORM	BARK	LEAF	FLOWER	FRUIT	CULTURE	USES	REGION

Callistemon rigidus
Stiff Bottlebrush

CULTURE: P C Si Sa L / 4 5 6 7 8 / M P A W E / W WM M MD D / vT T M I vl — slow, moderate

USES: border mass, deerproof, espalier, hedge, patio garden, screen, seacoast

REGION: Australia — 9–10

FORM: dense — 6-12

Camellia cuspidata
Taperleaf Camellia
Taperleaf Tea

CULTURE: P C Si Sa L / 4 5 6 7 8 / M P A W E / W WM M MD D / vT T M I vl — slow

USES: border mass, container, cut flowers, greenhouse, hedge, lath house, patio garden, screen

REGION: China — 7–10, i.1900

FORM: dense — 6-12

Camellia sasanqua
Sasanqua Camellia

'Jean May'   'White Doves'
'Rosea'   'Yuletide'

CULTURE: P C Si Sa L / 4 5 6 7 8 / M P A W E / W WM M MD D / vT T M I vl — slow, moderate

USES: background, border mass, bonsai, container, greenhouse, hedge, lath house, patio garden

REGION: Japan — 8–10, i.1896

FORM: moderate — 12-20

Ceanothus 'Ray Hartman'
Ray Hartman Ceanothus

CULTURE: P C Si Sa L / 4 5 6 7 8 / M P A W E / W WM M MD D / vT T M I vl — fast, short

USES: barrier, screen, specimen / accent, windbreak

REGION: cultivar — 8–10

FORM: dense — 12-20

Ceanothus spinosus
Greenbark Ceanothus
California Lilac

CULTURE: P C Si Sa L / 4 5 6 7 8 / M P A W E / W WM M MD D / vT T M I vl — moderate, moderate

USES: barrier, screen, windbreak

REGION: California — 8–10

FORM: dense — 12-20

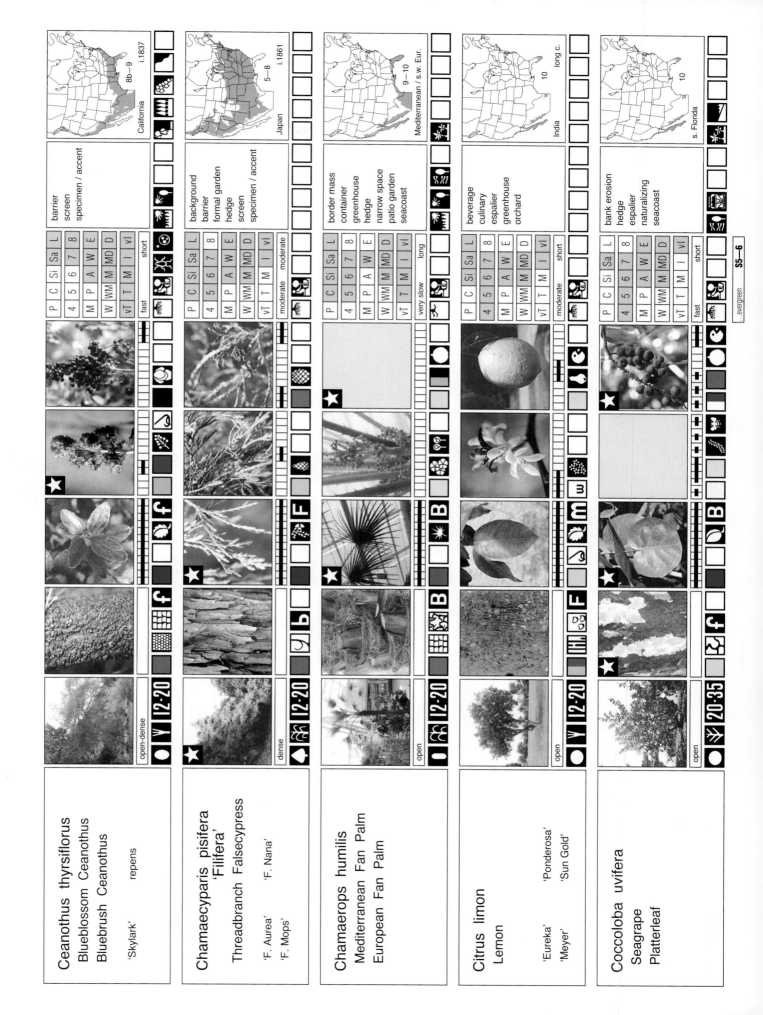

Ceanothus thyrsiflorus
Blueblossom Ceanothus
Bluebrush Ceanothus
'Skylark'   repens

barrier
screen
specimen / accent

California   i.1837   8b–9

Chamaecyparis pisifera 'Filifera'
Threadbranch Falsecypress
'F. Aurea'   'F. Nana'
'F. Mops'

background
barrier
formal garden
hedge
screen
specimen / accent

Japan   5–8   i.1861

Chamaerops humilis
Mediterranean Fan Palm
European Fan Palm

border mass
container
greenhouse
hedge
narrow space
patio garden
seacoast

Mediterranean / s.w. Eur.   9–10

Citrus limon
Lemon
'Eureka'   'Ponderosa'
'Meyer'   'Sun Gold'

beverage
culinary
espalier
greenhouse
orchard

India   10   long c.

Coccoloba uvifera
Seagrape
Platterleaf

bank erosion
hedge
espalier
naturalizing
seacoast

s. Florida   10

...evergreen   S5–6

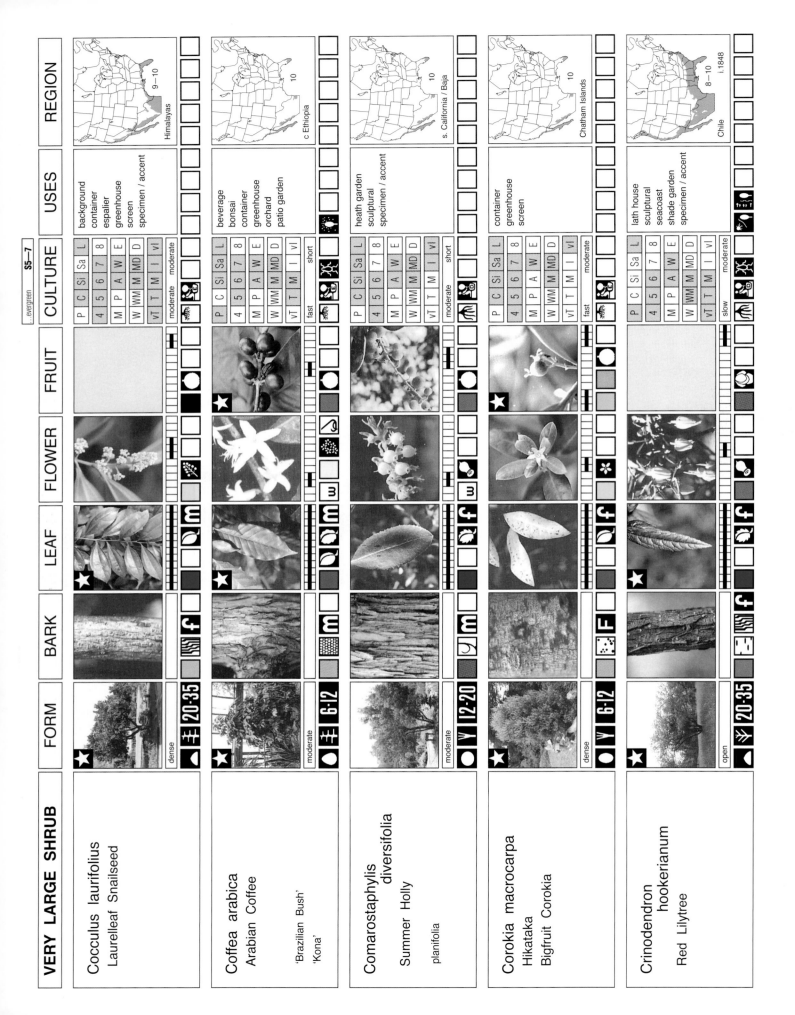

...evergreen **S5—7**

VERY LARGE SHRUB	FORM	BARK	LEAF	FLOWER	FRUIT	CULTURE	USES	REGION

Cocculus laurifolius — Laurelleaf Snailseed
- Form: dense, 20-35
- Culture: P C Si Sa L | 4 5 6 7 8 | M P A W E | W WM M MD D | vT T M I vl | moderate moderate
- Uses: background, container, espalier, greenhouse, screen, specimen / accent
- Region: Himalayas 9–10

Coffea arabica — Arabian Coffee — 'Brazilian Bush', 'Kona'
- Form: moderate, 6-12
- Culture: P C Si Sa L | 4 5 6 7 8 | M P A W E | W WM M MD D | vT T M I vl | fast short
- Uses: beverage, bonsai, container, greenhouse, orchard, patio garden
- Region: c Ethiopia 10

Comarostaphylis diversifolia — Summer Holly — planifolia
- Form: moderate, 12-20
- Culture: P C Si Sa L | 4 5 6 7 8 | M P A W E | W WM M MD D | vT T M I vl | moderate short
- Uses: heath garden, sculptural, specimen / accent
- Region: s. California / Baja 10

Corokia macrocarpa — Hikataka, Bigfruit Corokia
- Form: dense, 6-12
- Culture: P C Si Sa L | 4 5 6 7 8 | M P A W E | W WM M MD D | vT T M I vl | fast moderate
- Uses: container, greenhouse, screen
- Region: Chatham Islands 10

Crinodendron hookerianum — Red Lilytree
- Form: open, 20-35
- Culture: P C Si Sa L | 4 5 6 7 8 | M P A W E | W WM M MD D | vT T M I vl | slow moderate
- Uses: lath house, sculptural, seacoast, shade garden, specimen / accent
- Region: Chile 8–10 i:1848

Cupressus sargenti — Sargent Cypress

California 8–10

P	C	Si	Sa	L
4	5	6	7	8
M	P	A	W	E
W	WM	M	MD	D
vT	T	M	I	vl

fast — long

background
barrier
hedge
preservation
screen
shearing

dense · 12-20

Cycas revoluta — Sago Palm

Java 9–10

P	C	Si	Sa	L
4	5	6	7	8
M	P	A	W	E
W	WM	M	MD	D
vT	T	M	I	vl

slow — long

border mass
container
greenhouse
house plant
leaf arrangements
patio garden
screen
specimen / accent

moderate · 6-12

Dendromecon 'Harfordi' — Island Bushpoppy

Santa Cruz Islands 8–10

P	C	Si	Sa	L
4	5	6	7	8
M	P	A	W	E
W	WM	M	MD	D
vT	T	M	I	vl

slow — moderate

background
naturalizing
preservation
screen
seacoast

open · 12-20

Dovyalis caffra — Kei Apple / Umkokola

s. Africa 10

P	C	Si	Sa	L
4	5	6	7	8
M	P	A	W	E
W	WM	M	MD	D
vT	T	M	I	vl

slow — short

barrier
hedge
jellies, jams
kitchen garden
orchard
sculptural

dense · 12-20

Dracaena draco — Dragontree / Dragon Dracaena

Canary Islands 10

P	C	Si	Sa	L
4	5	6	7	8
M	P	A	W	E
W	WM	M	MD	D
vT	T	M	I	vl

slow — very long

greenhouse
house plant
sculptural
specimen / accent

open · 12-20

...evergreen

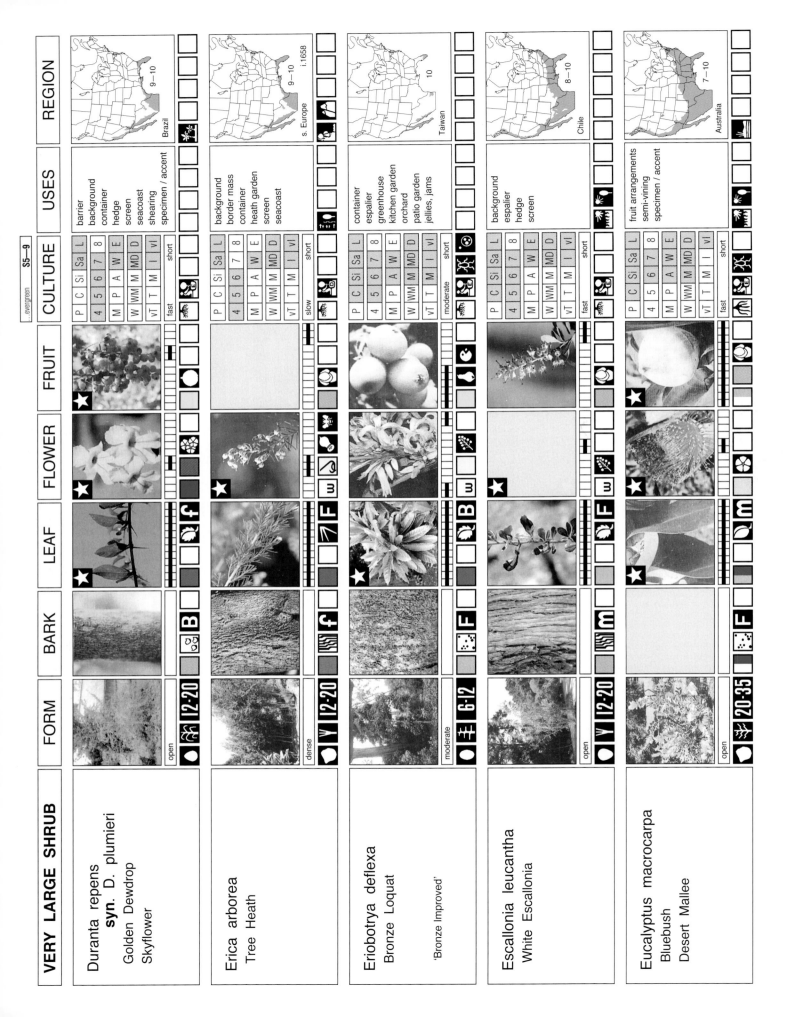

VERY LARGE SHRUB	FORM	BARK	LEAF	FLOWER	FRUIT	CULTURE	USES	REGION

Duranta repens
syn. D. plumieri
Golden Dewdrop
Skyflower

open — 12-20

CULTURE: P C Si Sa L / 4 5 6 7 8 / M P A W E / W WM M MD D / vT T M I vl / fast / short

USES: barrier, background, container, hedge, screen, seacoast, shearing, specimen / accent

REGION: Brazil — 9–10

Erica arborea
Tree Heath

dense — 12-20

CULTURE: P C Si Sa L / 4 5 6 7 8 / M P A W E / W WM M MD D / vT T M I vl / slow / short

USES: background, border mass, container, heath garden, screen, seacoast

REGION: s. Europe — 9–10   i:1658

Eriobotrya deflexa
Bronze Loquat
'Bronze Improved'

moderate — 6-12

CULTURE: P C Si Sa L / 4 5 6 7 8 / M P A W E / W WM M MD D / vT T M I vl / moderate / short

USES: container, espalier, greenhouse, kitchen garden, orchard, patio garden, jellies, jams

REGION: Taiwan — 10

Escallonia leucantha
White Escallonia

open — 12-20

CULTURE: P C Si Sa L / 4 5 6 7 8 / M P A W E / W WM M MD D / vT T M I vl / fast / short

USES: background, espalier, hedge, screen

REGION: Chile — 8–10

Eucalyptus macrocarpa
Bluebush
Desert Mallee

open — 20-35

CULTURE: P C Si Sa L / 4 5 6 7 8 / M P A W E / W WM M MD D / vT T M I vl / fast / short

USES: fruit arrangements, semi-vining, specimen / accent

REGION: Australia — 7–10

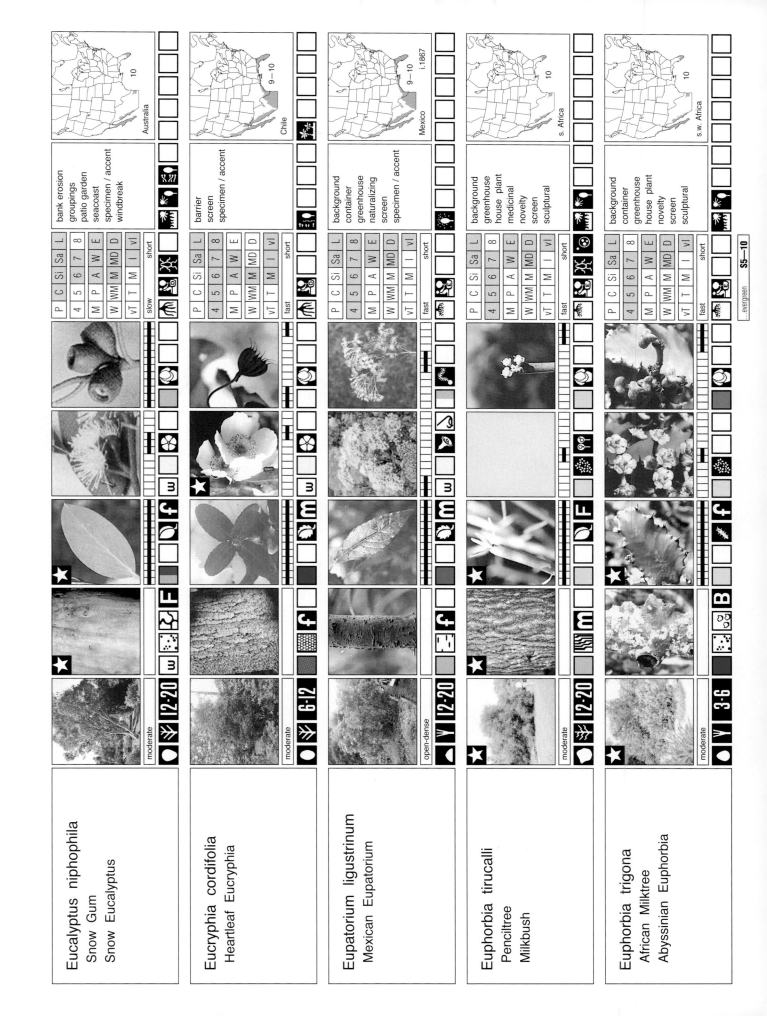

Eucalyptus niphophila
Snow Gum
Snow Eucalyptus

Australia · 10

bank erosion
groupings
patio garden
seacoast
specimen / accent
windbreak

P C Si Sa L · 4 5 6 7 8 · M P A W E · W WM M MD D · vT T M I vl

slow · short · moderate · 12-20

Eucryphia cordifolia
Heartleaf Eucryphia

Chile · 9–10

barrier
screen
specimen / accent

P C Si Sa L · 4 5 6 7 8 · M P A W E · W WM M MD D · vT T M I vl

fast · short · moderate · 6-12

Eupatorium ligustrinum
Mexican Eupatorium

Mexico · 9–10 · i.1867

background
container
greenhouse
naturalizing
screen
specimen / accent

P C Si Sa L · 4 5 6 7 8 · M P A W E · W WM M MD D · vT T M I vl

fast · short · open-dense · 12-20

Euphorbia tirucalli
Penciltree
Milkbush

s. Africa · 10

background
greenhouse
house plant
medicinal
novelty
screen
sculptural

P C Si Sa L · 4 5 6 7 8 · M P A W E · W WM M MD D · vT T M I vl

fast · short · moderate · 12-20

Euphorbia trigona
African Milktree
Abyssinian Euphorbia

s.w. Africa · 10

background
container
greenhouse
house plant
novelty
screen
sculptural

P C Si Sa L · 4 5 6 7 8 · M P A W E · W WM M MD D · vT T M I vl

fast · short · moderate · 3-6

...evergreen

VERY LARGE SHRUB	FORM	BARK	LEAF	FLOWER	FRUIT	CULTURE	USES	REGION

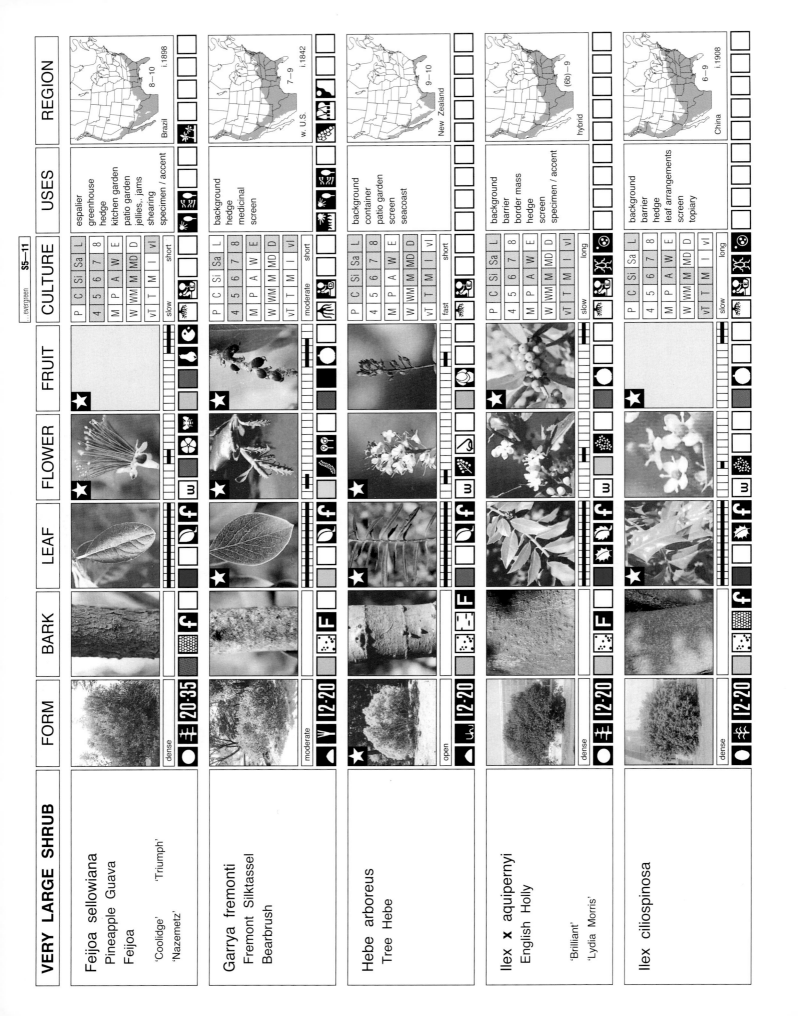

Feijoa sellowiana
Pineapple Guava
Feijoa
'Coolidge'   'Triumph'
'Nazemetz'

dense   20-35

CULTURE: P C Si Sa L / 4 5 6 7 8 / M P A W E / W WM M MD D / vT T M I vl / slow

USES: espalier / greenhouse / hedge / kitchen garden / patio garden / jellies.. jams / shearing / specimen / accent

REGION: Brazil   8–10   i.1898

Garrya fremonti
Fremont Silktassel
Bearbrush

moderate   12-20

CULTURE: P C Si Sa L / 4 5 6 7 8 / M P A W E / W WM M MD D / vT T M I vl / moderate   short

USES: background / hedge / medicinal / screen

REGION: w. U.S.   7–9   i.1842

Hebe arboreus
Tree Hebe

open   12-20

CULTURE: P C Si Sa L / 4 5 6 7 8 / M P A W E / W WM M MD D / vT T M I vl / fast   short

USES: background / container / patio garden / screen / seacoast

REGION: New Zealand   9–10

Ilex x aquipernyi
English Holly

'Brilliant'
'Lydia Morris'

dense   12-20

CULTURE: P C Si Sa L / 4 5 6 7 8 / M P A W E / W WM M MD D / vT T M I vl / slow   long

USES: background / barrier / border mass / hedge / screen / specimen / accent

REGION: hybrid   (6b)–9

Ilex ciliospinosa

dense   12-20

CULTURE: P C Si Sa L / 4 5 6 7 8 / M P A W E / W WM M MD D / vT T M I vl / slow   long

USES: background / barrier / hedge / leaf arrangements / screen / topiary

REGION: China   6–9   i.1908

Ilex cornuta 'Burfordi' Burford Holly	background barrier border mass fruit arrangements espalier hedge screen shearing	P C Si Sa L / 4 5 6 7 8 / M P A W E / W WM M MD D / vT T M I vI / slow moderate	cultivar o.1895 / 7–9
'B. Nana' 'B. Willowleaf'		dense / 12-20	

Ilex pedunculosa Longstalk Holly	background formal garden fruit arrangements hedge screen	P C Si Sa L / 4 5 6 7 8 / M P A W E / W WM M MD D / vT T M I vI / moderate long	Japan i.1893 / 6–9
		dense / 12-20	

Jacquinia armillaris **syn.** J. barbasco Barbasco Armed Jacquinia	background screen seacoast shade garden specimen / accent	P C Si Sa L / 4 5 6 7 8 / M P A W E / W WM M MD D / vT T M I vI / fast short	w.Indies 10
		dense / 12-20	

Jacquinia aurantiaca	background screen seacoast specimen / accent	P C Si Sa L / 4 5 6 7 8 / M P A W E / W WM M MD D / vT T M I vI / fast short	Mexico 10
		moderate / 12-20	

Juniperus chinensis 'Columnaris' Blue Column Juniper	background barrier formal garden hedge narrow space screen specimen / accent	P C Si Sa L / 4 5 6 7 8 / M P A W E / W WM M MD D / vT T M I vI / fast moderate	China i.1905 / 4–8
		dense / 6-12	

...evergreen **S5—12**

VERY LARGE SHRUB	FORM	BARK	LEAF	FLOWER	FRUIT	CULTURE	USES	REGION

Juniperus chinensis 'Hetzi'

Hetz Blue Juniper

'H. Columnaris'   'H. Viridis'
'H. Glauca'

FORM: dense, 12-20

CULTURE:
P C Si Sa L
4 5 6 7 8
M P A W E
W WM M MD D
vT T M I vI
fast — moderate

USES: background, barrier, bonsai, hedge, screen, specimen / accent, windbreak

REGION: 4—8, i.1937, cultivar

Juniperus chinensis 'Keteleeri'

Keteleer Juniper

FORM: dense, 6-12

CULTURE:
P C Si Sa L
4 5 6 7 8
M P A W E
W WM M MD D
vT T M I vI
slow — moderate

USES: background, barrier, bonsai, hedge, screen, windbreak

REGION: 4—8, c.1910, cultivar

Juniperus sabina 'Von Ehron'

Von Ehron Juniper

FORM: dense, 20-35

CULTURE:
P C Si Sa L
4 5 6 7 8
M P A W E
W WM M MD D
vT T M I vI
slow — moderate

USES: background, barrier, bonsai, hedge, screen, sculptural - old, windbreak

REGION: 4—8, c.1912, cultivar

Juniperus virginiana 'Hilli'

Hillspire Juniper

Hill Dundee

FORM: dense, 6-12

CULTURE:
P C Si Sa L
4 5 6 7 8
M P A W E
W WM M MD D
vT T M I vI
fast — moderate

USES: background, barrier, formal garden, hedge, narrow space, screen

REGION: 4—8, c.1932, cultivar

Kalmia latifolia

Mountain Laurel

Calicobush

'Bullseye'   'Fresca'
'Carousel'   'Ostbo Red'

FORM: moderate, 12-20

CULTURE:
P C Si Sa L
4 5 6 7 8
M P A W E
W WM M MD D
vT T M I vI
slow — m-short

USES: container, bog garden, border mass, naturalizing, patio garden, poisonous leaves, sculptural, specimen / accent

REGION: 5—9, i.1734, e. N.America

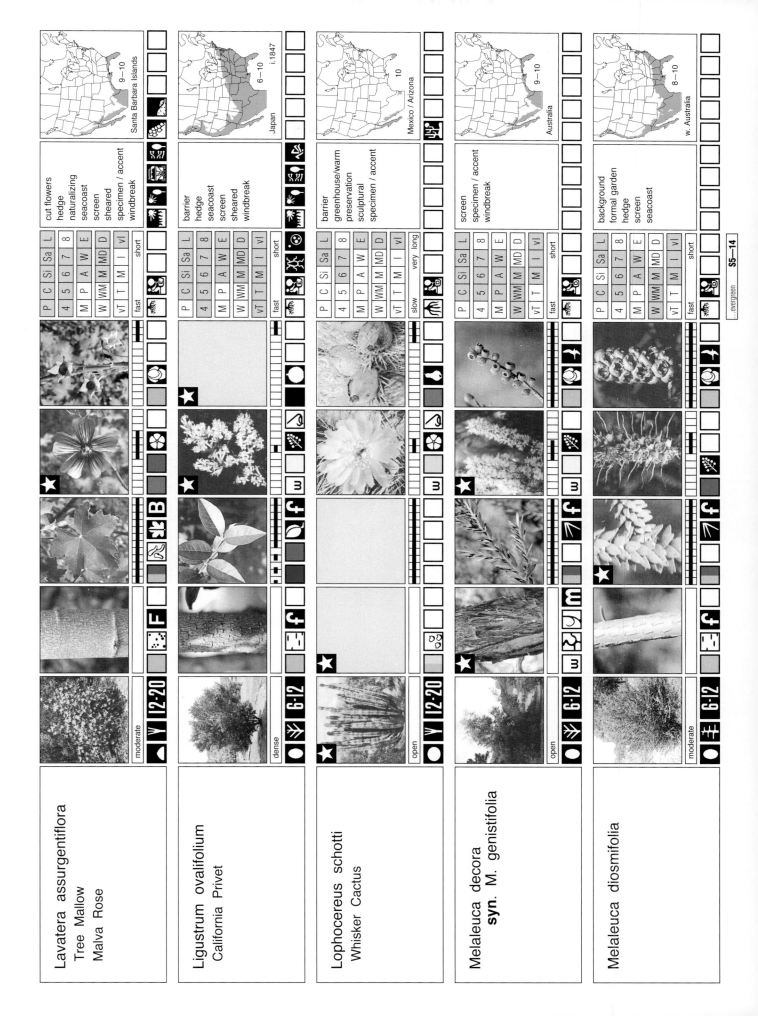

Lavatera assurgentiflora
Tree Mallow
Malva Rose

Santa Barbara Islands | 9–10

cut flowers
hedge
naturalizing
seacoast
screen
sheared
specimen / accent
windbreak

P	C	Si	Sa	L
4	5	6	7	8
M	P	A	W	E
W	WM	M	MD	D
vT	T	M	I	vl

fast   short
moderate   12·20

Ligustrum ovalifolium
California Privet

Japan | 6–10 | i.1847

barrier
hedge
seacoast
screen
sheared
windbreak

P	C	Si	Sa	L
4	5	6	7	8
M	P	A	W	E
W	WM	M	MD	D
vT	T	M	I	vl

fast   short
dense   6·12

Lophocereus schotti
Whisker Cactus

Mexico / Arizona | 10

barrier
greenhouse/warm
preservation
sculptural
specimen / accent

P	C	Si	Sa	L
4	5	6	7	8
M	P	A	W	E
W	WM	M	MD	D
vT	T	M	I	vl

slow   very long
open   12·20

Melaleuca decora **syn**. M. genistifolia

Australia | 9–10

screen
specimen / accent
windbreak

P	C	Si	Sa	L
4	5	6	7	8
M	P	A	W	E
W	WM	M	MD	D
vT	T	M	I	vl

fast   short
open   6·12

Melaleuca diosmifolia

w. Australia | 8–10

background
formal garden
hedge
screen
seacoast

P	C	Si	Sa	L
4	5	6	7	8
M	P	A	W	E
W	WM	M	MD	D
vT	T	M	I	vl

fast   short
moderate   6·12

...evergreen

VERY LARGE SHRUB	FORM	BARK	LEAF	FLOWER	FRUIT	CULTURE	USES	REGION

Melaleuca ericifolia
Heath Melaleuca
Swamp Paperbark

open — 20-35

fast — short

P	C	Si	Sa	L
4	5	6	7	8
M	P	A	W	E
W	WM	M	MD	D
vT	T	M	I	vI

background
container
hedge
screen
seacoast
water garden

Australia 9—10

Michelia figo
Bananashrub

'Port Wine'
'Stubbs Purple'

dense — 12-20

slow — long

P	C	Si	Sa	L
4	5	6	7	8
M	P	A	W	E
W	WM	M	MD	D
vT	T	M	I	vI

espalier
hedge
patio garden
specimen / accent

China 8—10   i.1850

Montanoa hibiscifolia
Christmas-daisy
Christmas-cosmos

moderate — 12-20

fast — short

P	C	Si	Sa	L
4	5	6	7	8
M	P	A	W	E
W	WM	M	MD	D
vT	T	M	I	vI

background
border mass
container
greenhouse
screen
specimen / accent

Guatemala 10

Murraya paniculata
Common Jasmine
Orange Jasmine

dense — 12-20

fast — short

P	C	Si	Sa	L
4	5	6	7	8
M	P	A	W	E
W	WM	M	MD	D
vT	T	M	I	vI

background
container
greenhouse
hedge
patio garden
screen
specimen / accent

India 9b—10

Musa x paradisiaca
Edible Banana
Plantain Banana

'Ae Ae Green'
'Mysore'

open — 12-20

fast — very short

P	C	Si	Sa	L
4	5	6	7	8
M	P	A	W	E
W	WM	M	MD	D
vT	T	M	I	vI

background
border mass
fruit salad
greenhouse
orchard
sculptural
specimen / accent

hybrid 10

Myrica cerifera
Southern Bayberry

'Evergreen'

background
bank erosion
bog garden
hedge
naturalizing
seacoast
water garden

P C Si Sa L
4 5 6 7 8
M P A W E
W WM M MD D
vT T M I vl
fast short

dense

e. U.S.
7–10
i.1669

Myrsine australis
Cape Myrtle
African Boxwood

background
container
hedge
house plant
leaf arrangements
screen
topiary

P C Si Sa L
4 5 6 7 8
M P A W E
W WM M MD D
vT T M I vl
slow long

dense

s. Africa
9–10
i.1691

Nerium oleander
Common Oleander

'Hardy Pink'   'Petite Pink'
'Hardy Red'   'Ruby Lace'

background
border mass
container
fruit arrangements
greenhouse
hedge
patio garden
windbreak

P C Si Sa L
4 5 6 7 8
M P A W E
W WM M MD D
vT T M I vl
fast short

dense

Mediterranean
8–10
i.1596

Nopalea cochenillifera
Cochinealplant

barrier
dye plant
greenhouse/warm
sculptural
specimen / accent

P C Si Sa L
4 5 6 7 8
M P A W E
W WM M MD D
vT T M I vl
slow long

open

Jamaica
10

Notospartium glabrescens
Pink Broom
Southern Broom

border mass
preservation
screen
specimen / accent

P C Si Sa L
4 5 6 7 8
M P A W E
W WM M MD D
vT T M I vl
fast short

open

New Zealand
8–10
i.1930

S5–16

...evergreen

VERY LARGE SHRUB

	FORM	BARK	LEAF	FLOWER	FRUIT	CULTURE	USES	REGION

Olearia paniculata
Akiraho Daisybush

- FORM: dense — 12·20
- CULTURE: P C Si Sa L / 4 5 6 7 8 / M P A W E / W WM M MD D / vT T M I vI — fast — short
- USES: background / hedge / seacoast / screen / specimen / accent
- REGION: 10 — New Zealand — i.1816

Opuntia brasiliensis
Beavertail Pricklypear

- FORM: open — 12·20
- CULTURE: P C Si Sa L / 4 5 6 7 8 / M P A W E / W WM M MD D / vT T M I vI — slow — long
- USES: barrier / sculptural / specimen / accent
- REGION: 10 — Brazil

Opuntia ficus-indica
Indian Fig
Spineless Cactus

- FORM: dense — 12·20
- CULTURE: P C Si Sa L / 4 5 6 7 8 / M P A W E / W WM M MD D / vT T M I vI — moderate — long
- USES: barrier / sculptural / specimen / accent
- REGION: 9–10 — unknown

Opuntia fulgida
Jumping Cholla

- FORM: open — 6·12
- CULTURE: P C Si Sa L / 4 5 6 7 8 / M P A W E / W WM M MD D / vT T M I vI — slow — long
- USES: barrier / sculptural / specimen / accent
- REGION: 7–10 — Mexico

Photinia x fraseri
Fraser Photinia

'Indian Princess'
'Red Robin'

- FORM: moderate — 12·20
- CULTURE: P C Si Sa L / 4 5 6 7 8 / M P A W E / W WM M MD D / vT T M I vI — moderate — short
- USES: background / espalier / hedge / screen / specimen / accent
- REGION: 7–10 — hybrid

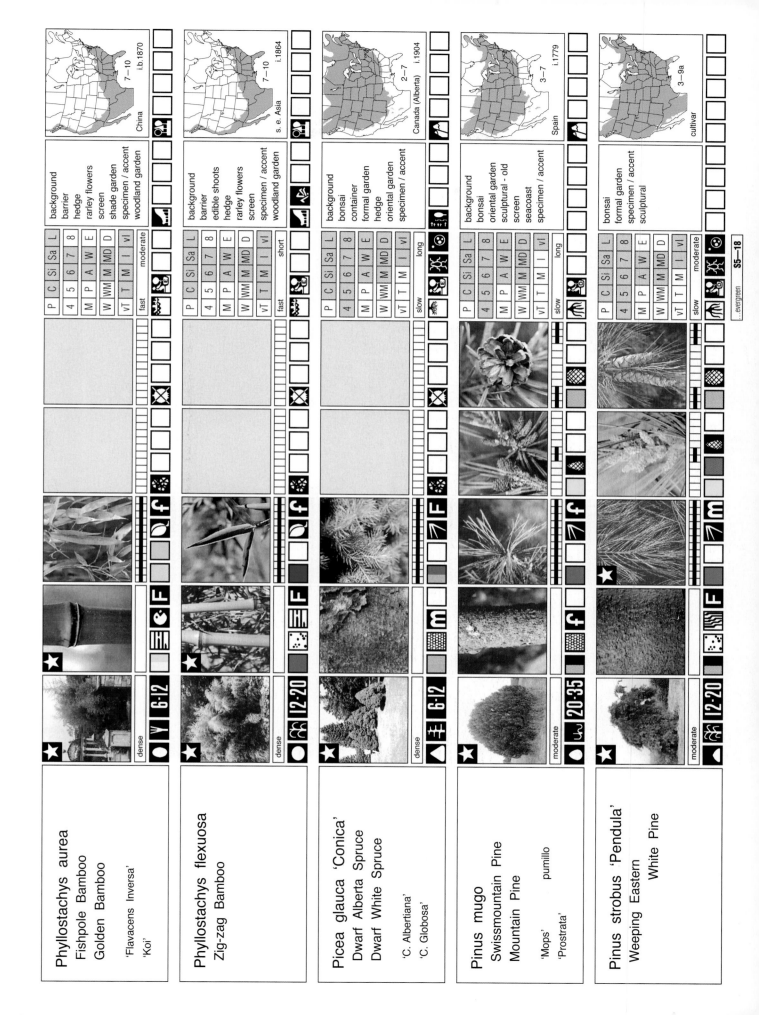

Phyllostachys aurea
Fishpole Bamboo
Golden Bamboo
'Flavacens Inversa'
"Koi'

background / barrier / hedge / rarely flowers / screen / shade garden / specimen / accent / woodland garden

P C Si Sa L · 4 5 6 7 8 · M P A W E · W WM M MD D · vT T M I vl · moderate
fast · dense · 6-12
China · 7–10 · i.b.1870

Phyllostachys flexuosa
Zig-zag Bamboo

background / barrier / edible shoots / hedge / rarely flowers / screen / specimen / accent / woodland garden

P C Si Sa L · 4 5 6 7 8 · M P A W E · W WM M MD D · vT T M I vl · short
fast · dense · 12-20
s. e. Asia · 7–10 · i.1864

Picea glauca 'Conica'
Dwarf Alberta Spruce
Dwarf White Spruce
'C. Albertiana'
'C. Globosa'

background / bonsai / container / formal garden / hedge / oriental garden / specimen / accent

P C Si Sa L · 4 5 6 7 8 · M P A W E · W WM M MD D · vT T M I vl · long
slow · dense · 6-12
Canada (Alberta) · 2–7 · i.1904

Pinus mugo
Swissmountain Pine
Mountain Pine
'Mops'
pumilio
'Prostrata'

background / bonsai / oriental garden / sculptural - old / screen / seacoast / specimen / accent

P C Si Sa L · 4 5 6 7 8 · M P A W E · W WM M MD D · vT T M I vl · long
slow · moderate · 20-35
Spain · 3–7 · i.1779

Pinus strobus 'Pendula'
Weeping Eastern White Pine

bonsai / formal garden / specimen / accent / sculptural

P C Si Sa L · 4 5 6 7 8 · M P A W E · W WM M MD D · vT T M I vl · moderate
...evergreen · slow · moderate · 12-20
cultivar · 3–9a

S5—18

VERY LARGE SHRUB	FORM	BARK	LEAF	FLOWER	FRUIT	CULTURE	USES	REGION

Plumeria obtusa
Singapore Plumeria
Bluntlobe Frangipani

open · 12-20

CULTURE: P C Si Sa L / 4 5 6 7 8 / M P A W E / W WM M MD D / vT T M I vl / moderate · moderate

USES: container / cut flowers / medicinal / religious plant / seacoast / specimen / accent

REGION: s. e. Asia · 10

Plumeria rubra
Nosegay Frangipani

open · 12-20

CULTURE: P C Si Sa L / 4 5 6 7 8 / M P A W E / W WM M MD D / vT T M I vl / moderate · moderate

USES: container / cut flowers / greenhouse / house plant / medicinal / religious plant / seacoast / specimen / accent

REGION: s. e. Asia · 10

Prunus ilicifolia
Hollyleaf Cherry
Evergreen Cherry

dense · 35-50

CULTURE: P C Si Sa L / 4 5 6 7 8 / M P A W E / W WM M MD D / vT T M I vl / slow · long

USES: background / hedge / naturalizing / screen / shade / shearing / specimen / accent

REGION: California · 8-10

Prunus laurocerasus
Laurel Cherry
English Laurel
'Portugal' 'Schipkaesis'
'Ottoluyken' 'Zabeliana'

dense · 12-20

CULTURE: P C Si Sa L / 4 5 6 7 8 / M P A W E / W WM M MD D / vT T M I vl / fast · moderate

USES: background / hedge / seacoast / naturalizing / screen / shade / shearing

REGION: Europe · 7-10 · i.1576

Rhamnus californica
California Buckthorn
Coffeeberry
'Eve Case' 'Little Sur'
'Seaview Improved'

dense · 12-20

CULTURE: P C Si Sa L / 4 5 6 7 8 / M P A W E / W WM M MD D / vT T M I vl / moderate · moderate

USES: background / bank erosion / hedge / screen / specimen / accent

REGION: w. N.America · 6b-10 · i.1861

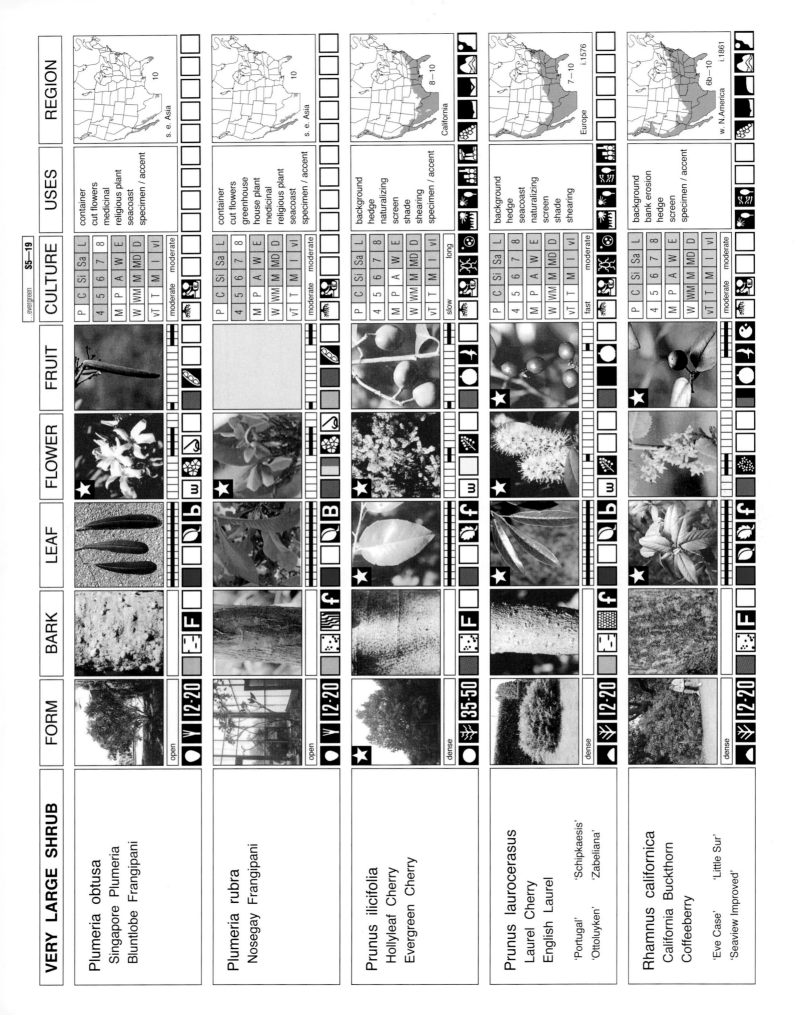

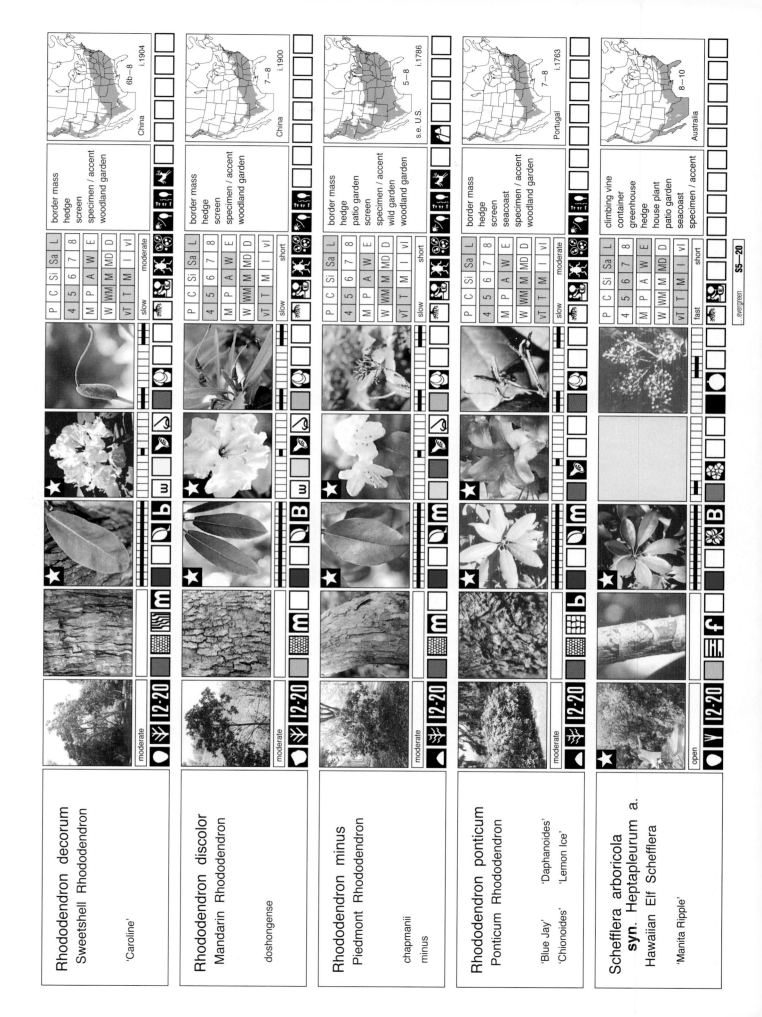

Rhododendron decorum
Sweetshell Rhododendron

'Caroline'

China   6b–8   i.1904

border mass
hedge
screen
specimen / accent
woodland garden

Rhododendron discolor
Mandarin Rhododendron

doshongense

China   7–8   i.1900

border mass
hedge
screen
specimen / accent
woodland garden

Rhododendron minus
Piedmont Rhododendron

chapmanii
minus

s.e. U.S.   5–8   i.1786

border mass
hedge
patio garden
screen
specimen / accent
wild garden
woodland garden

Rhododendron ponticum
Ponticum Rhododendron

'Blue Jay'   'Daphanoides'
'Chionoides'   'Lemon Ice'

Portugal   7–8   i.1763

border mass
hedge
screen
seacoast
specimen / accent
woodland garden

Schefflera arboricola **syn.** Heptapleurum a.
Hawaiian Elf Schefflera

'Manita Ripple'

Australia   8–10

climbing vine
container
greenhouse
hedge
house plant
patio garden
seacoast
specimen / accent

S5—20

VERY LARGE SHRUB	FORM	BARK	LEAF	FLOWER	FRUIT	CULTURE	USES	REGION

Schinus lentiscifolia
Pinkberry Peppertree

open

P	C	Si	Sa	L
4	5	6	7	8
M	P	A	W	E
W	WM	M	MD	D
vT	T	M	I	vI

moderate · moderate

fruit arrangements
specimen / accent
windbreak

Brazil · 10

Semiarundinaria fastuosa
Narihira Bamboo
Narihira Cane

dense

P	C	Si	Sa	L
4	5	6	7	8
M	P	A	W	E
W	WM	M	MD	D
vT	T	M	I	vI

fast · long

background
hedge
oriental garden
pool garden
screen
specimen / accent
windbreak
woodland garden

Japan · i.1892 · 7–10

Sinarundinaria nitida
Fountain Bamboo
Glossyleaf Chinacane

dense

P	C	Si	Sa	L
4	5	6	7	8
M	P	A	W	E
W	WM	M	MD	D
vT	T	M	I	vI

fast · moderate

background
container
hedge
oriental garden
pool garden
rarley flowers
screen
specimen / accent

China · c.1889 · 7–10

Solanum crispum
Chilean Potatotree

moderate

P	C	Si	Sa	L
4	5	6	7	8
M	P	A	W	E
W	WM	M	MD	D
vT	T	M	I	vI

fast · short

background
border mass
container
greenhouse
hedge
screen
specimen / accent

Peru · i.1830 · 9–10

Sparmannia africana
African Linden
African Hemp
'Variegata'

dense

P	C	Si	Sa	L
4	5	6	7	8
M	P	A	W	E
W	WM	M	MD	D
vT	T	M	I	vI

fast · short

border mass
container
greenhouse
house plant
pool garden
screen

s. Africa · i.1790 · 9–10

Sphaeropteris cooperi
syn. Cyathea c.
Australian Tree Fern

P	C	Si	Sa	L		border mass
4	5	6	7	8		container
M	P	A	W	E		greenhouse
W	WM	M	MD	D		groupings
vT	T	M	I	vI		house plant
						sculptural
						specimen / accent
						water garden

open ● 12-20 fast short

Australia 10

Stranvaesia davidiana
Chinese Stranvaesia

P	C	Si	Sa	L		background
4	5	6	7	8		fruit arrangement
M	P	A	W	E		screen
W	WM	M	MD	D		seacoast
vT	T	M	I	vI		specimen / accent

moderate 20-35

China i.1917 7–10

Strelitzia nicolai
White Bird-of-Paradise

P	C	Si	Sa	L		border mass
4	5	6	7	8		cut flowers
M	P	A	W	E		greenhouse
W	WM	M	MD	D		groupings
vT	T	M	I	vI		patio garden
						sculptural
						specimen / accent

moderate-open ● 12-20 fast short

10

Taxus cuspidata 'Capitata'
Upright Japanese Yew

P	C	Si	Sa	L		background
4	5	6	7	8		formal garden
M	P	A	W	E		hedge
W	WM	M	MD	D		screen
vT	T	M	I	vI		seacoast
						shade garden
						specimen / accent

dense 12-20 slow long

cultivar 4–7

Taxus x media
Anglojapanese Yew
Intermediate Yew

P	C	Si	Sa	L		background
4	5	6	7	8		formal garden
M	P	A	W	E		hedge
W	WM	M	MD	D		screen
vT	T	M	I	vI		shade garden
						sheared
						topiary

dense 12-20 slow long

'Mooni'
'Nigra'

hybrid o.a1900 4–7

...evergreen

S5—22

VERY LARGE SHRUB	FORM	BARK	LEAF	FLOWER	FRUIT	CULTURE	USES	REGION

Taxus x media 'Hicksi'
Hicks Anglojapanese Yew
Hicks Intermediate Yew

6-12 · dense

P	C	Si	Sa	L
4	5	6	7	8
M	P	A	W	E
W	WM	M	MD	D
vT	T	M	I	vI

slow · moderate

background
formal garden
hedge
screen
seacoast
shade garden
sheared
topiary

cultivar · 5 – 8 · c.1900

Tecoma stans
Florida Yellowtrumpet
Yellowbells

12-20 · dense

P	C	Si	Sa	L
4	5	6	7	8
M	P	A	W	E
W	WM	M	MD	D
vT	T	M	I	vI

fast · short

border mass
groupings
patio garden
rock garden
screen
specimen / accent

w. Indies / s. Florida · 9 – 10

Tetrapanax papyriferum
Ricepaperplant

20-35 · moderate

P	C	Si	Sa	L
4	5	6	7	8
M	P	A	W	E
W	WM	M	MD	D
vT	T	M	I	vI

fast · short

container
greenhouse
naturalizing
patio garden
screen

Formosa · 9 – 10

Tibouchina urvilleana
Princessflower
Purple Glorybush

12-20 · open

P	C	Si	Sa	L
4	5	6	7	8
M	P	A	W	E
W	WM	M	MD	D
vT	T	M	I	vI

fast · short

container
greenhouse
naturalizing
pillar
semi-vining
wires

Brazil · 10

Tupidanthus calyptratus

12-20 · open

P	C	Si	Sa	L
4	5	6	7	8
M	P	A	W	E
W	WM	M	MD	D
vT	T	M	I	vI

fast · short

climbing vine
container
greenhouse
house plant
patio garden
pool garden

Cambodia · 10

Vauquelinia californica
Arizona Rosewood
Torrey Vauquelinia

background
screen
windbreak

Arizona
8–10

Viburnum macrocephalum
Chinese Viburnum
Chinese Snowball
'Sterile'

background
border mass
cut flowers
espalier
screen
specimen / accent

China
7–10   i.1844

Viburnum odoratissimum
Sweet Viburnum

background
border mass
historic garden
screen
specimen / accent

India
8b–10   i.1818

Viburnum **x** rhytidophylloides
Lantanaphyllum Viburnum
'Alleghany'
'Willowwood'

background
border mass
screen
specimen / accent

hybrid
5b–8   c.1927

Xylosma congestum
syn. X. senticosa
Shiny Xylosma
'Compactum'

background
barrier
container
espalier
hedge
screen
shearing
specimen / accent

China
9–10

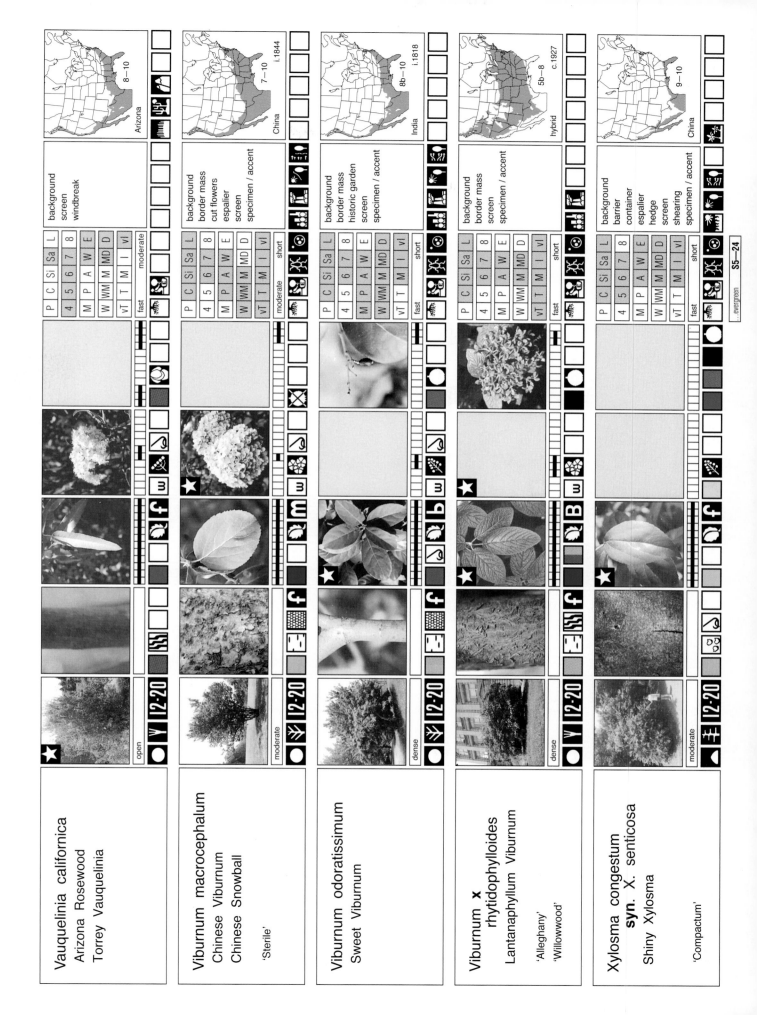

VERY LARGE SHRUB	FORM	BARK	LEAF	FLOWER	FRUIT	CULTURE	USES	REGION

Yucca elata
Soaptree Yucca

- dense
- 6-12

CULTURE: P C Si Sa L / 4 5 6 7 8 / M P A W E / W WM M MD D / vT T M I vl / slow / long

USES: barrier, border mass, container, sculptural, soap, specimen / accent

REGION: 8—10, s.w. U.S.

Yucca schidigera
Mohave Yucca

- dense
- 3-6

CULTURE: P C Si Sa L / 4 5 6 7 8 / M P A W E / W WM M MD D / vT T M I vl / slow / long

USES: barrier, border mass, container, sculptural, soap, specimen / accent

REGION: 8—10, s.w. U.S.

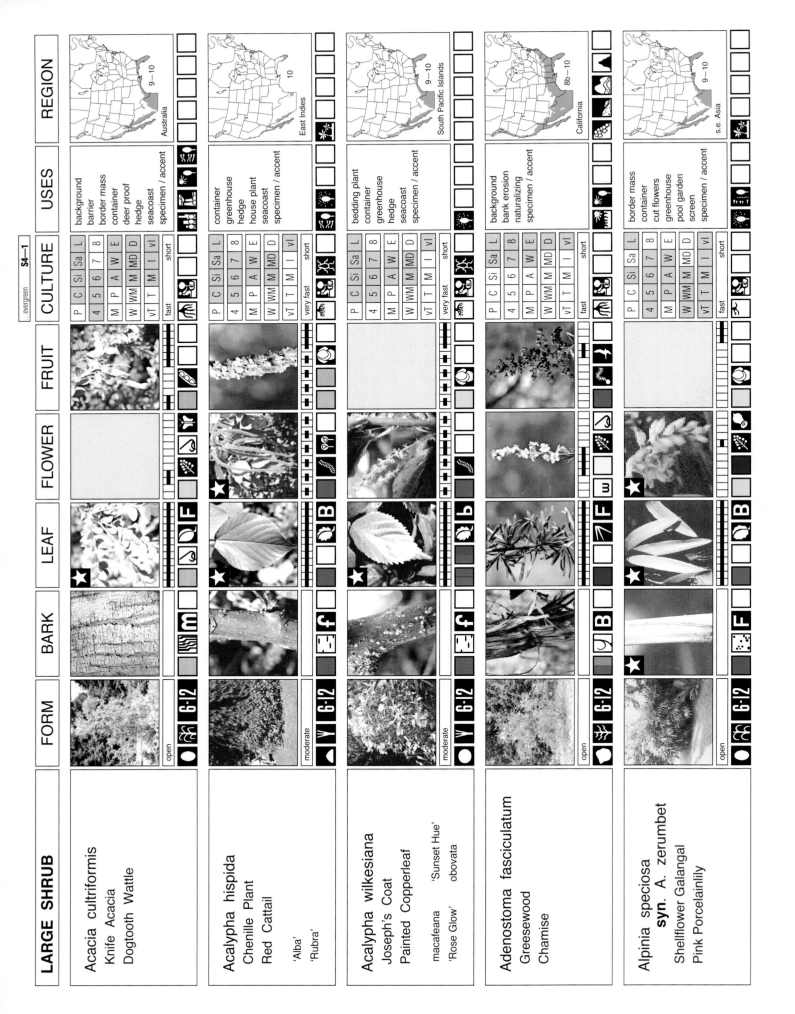

LARGE SHRUB	FORM	BARK	LEAF	FLOWER	FRUIT	CULTURE	USES	REGION

Acacia cultriformis
Knife Acacia
Dogtooth Wattle

- CULTURE: P C Si Sa L / 4 5 6 7 8 / M P A W E / W WM M MD D / vT T M I vl — fast / short
- USES: background, barrier, border mass, container, deer proof, hedge, seacoast, specimen / accent
- REGION: Australia 9–10
- FORM: open 6-12

Acalypha hispida
Chenille Plant
Red Cattail
'Alba'
'Rubra'

- CULTURE: P C Si Sa L / 4 5 6 7 8 / M P A W E / W WM M MD D / vT T M I vl — very fast / short
- USES: container, greenhouse, hedge, house plant, seacoast, specimen / accent
- REGION: East Indies 10
- FORM: moderate 6-12

Acalypha wilkesiana
Joseph's Coat
Painted Copperleaf
macafeana   'Sunset Hue'
'Rose Glow'   obovata

- CULTURE: P C Si Sa L / 4 5 6 7 8 / M P A W E / W WM M MD D / vT T M I vl — very fast / short
- USES: bedding plant, container, greenhouse, hedge, seacoast, specimen / accent
- REGION: South Pacific Islands 9–10
- FORM: moderate 6-12

Adenostoma fasciculatum
Greesewood
Chamise

- CULTURE: P C Si Sa L / 4 5 6 7 8 / M P A W E / W WM M MD D / vT T M I vl — fast / short
- USES: background, bank erosion, naturalizing, specimen / accent
- REGION: California 8b–10
- FORM: open 6-12

Alpinia speciosa syn. A. zerumbet
Shellflower Galangal
Pink Porcelainlily

- CULTURE: P C Si Sa L / 4 5 6 7 8 / M P A W E / W WM M MD D / vT T M I vl — fast / short
- USES: border mass, container, cut flowers, greenhouse, pool garden, screen, specimen / accent
- REGION: s.e. Asia 9–10
- FORM: open 6-12

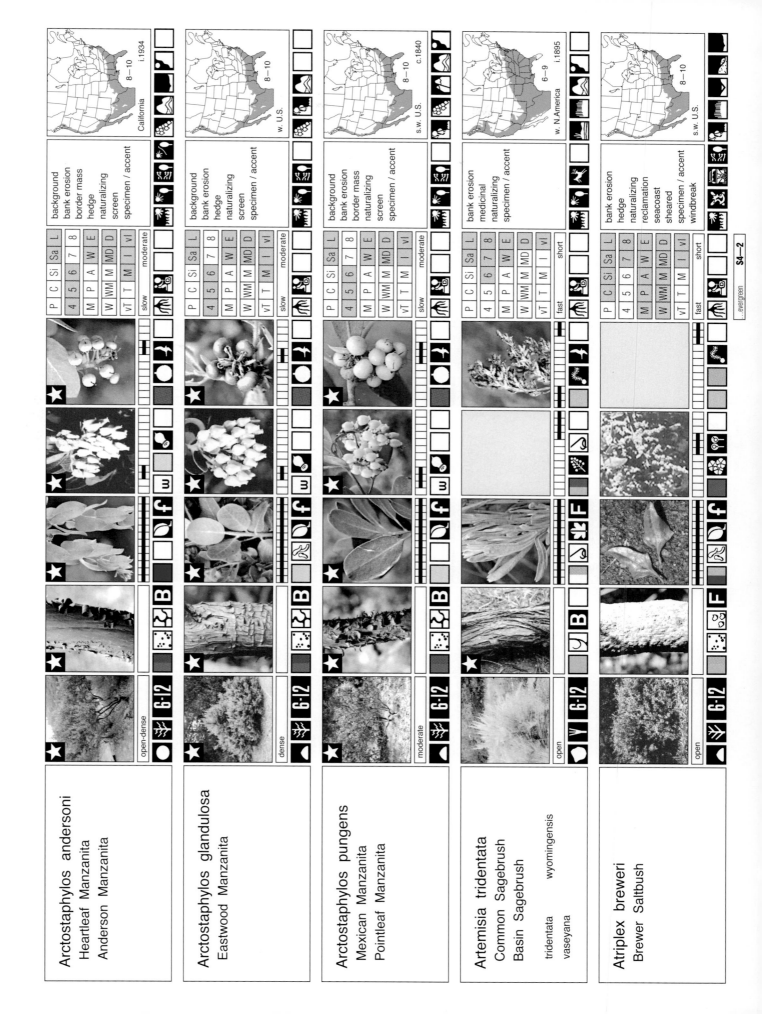

Arctostaphylos andersoni — Heartleaf Manzanita, Anderson Manzanita
California — i.1934 — 8–10
background, bank erosion, border mass, hedge, naturalizing, screen, specimen / accent

Arctostaphylos glandulosa — Eastwood Manzanita
w. U.S. — 8–10
background, bank erosion, hedge, naturalizing, screen, specimen / accent

Arctostaphylos pungens — Mexican Manzanita, Pointleaf Manzanita
s.w. U.S. — c.1840 — 8–10
background, bank erosion, border mass, naturalizing, screen, specimen / accent

Artemisia tridentata — Common Sagebrush, Basin Sagebrush
tridentata   wyomingensis
vaseyana
w. N.America — i.1895 — 6–9
bank erosion, medicinal, naturalizing, specimen / accent

Atriplex breweri — Brewer Saltbush
s.w. U.S. — 8–10
bank erosion, hedge, naturalizing, reclamation, seacoast, sheared, specimen / accent, windbreak

…evergreen   S4—2

LARGE SHRUB	FORM	BARK	LEAF	FLOWER	FRUIT	CULTURE	USES	REGION

Atriplex lentiformis
Quailbrush
Big Saltbush

CULTURE: P C Si Sa L / 4 5 6 7 8 / M P A W E / W WM M MD D / vT T M I vl / fast · short
USES: border mass / hedge / naturalizing / reclamation / windbreak
REGION: s.w. U.S. · 8–10
FORM: dense

Aucuba japonica
Japanese Aucuba
Japanese Laurel
'Gold Dust'   'Picturata'
'Nana'   'Variegata'

CULTURE: P C Si Sa L / 4 5 6 7 8 / M P A W E / W WM M MD D / vT T M I vl / slow · moderate
USES: border mass / background / container / greenhouse / hedge / house plant / patio garden / seacoast
REGION: Japan · 7–10 · i.1861
FORM: dense · 12-20

Azara serrata

CULTURE: P C Si Sa L / 4 5 6 7 8 / M P A W E / W WM M MD D / vT T M I vl / fast · short
USES: border edge / container / cool greenhouse / espalier / seacoast / specimen / accent
REGION: Chile · 8–10
FORM: dense · 6-12

Baccharis viminea
Mulefat

CULTURE: P C Si Sa L / 4 5 6 7 8 / M P A W E / W WM M MD D / vT T M I vl / moderate · moderate
USES: bank erosion / naturalizing / nitrogen-fixing / reclamation
REGION: California · 8–10
FORM: open · 6-12

Baeckea virgata
Heath Myrtle

CULTURE: P C Si Sa L / 4 5 6 7 8 / M P A W E / W WM M MD D / vT T M I vl / slow · moderate
USES: cut flowers / greenhouse / heath garden / specimen / accent
REGION: e. Australia · 9–10
FORM: open · 6-12

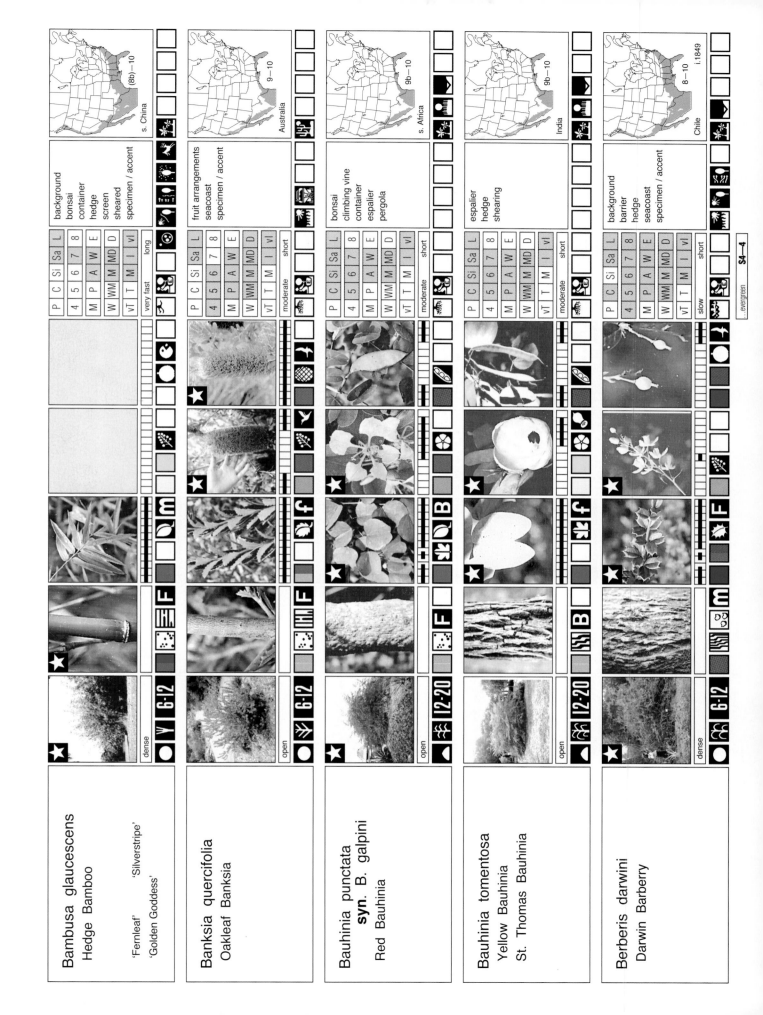

Bambusa glaucescens
Hedge Bamboo

'Fernleaf'   'Silverstripe'
'Golden Goddess'

s. China

background
bonsai
container
hedge
screen
sheared
specimen / accent

P	C	Si	Sa	L
4	5	6	7	8
M	P	A	W	E
W	WM	M	MD	D
vT	T	M	I	vI

very fast   long

dense

6-12

Banksia quercifolia
Oakleaf Banksia

Australia

fruit arrangements
seacoast
specimen / accent

P	C	Si	Sa	L
4	5	6	7	8
M	P	A	W	E
W	WM	M	MD	D
vT	T	M	I	vI

moderate   short

9—10

open

6-12

Bauhinia punctata syn. B. galpini
Red Bauhinia

s. Africa

bonsai
climbing vine
container
espalier
pergola

P	C	Si	Sa	L
4	5	6	7	8
M	P	A	W	E
W	WM	M	MD	D
vT	T	M	I	vI

moderate   short

9b—10

open

12-20

Bauhinia tomentosa
Yellow Bauhinia
St. Thomas Bauhinia

India

espalier
hedge
shearing

P	C	Si	Sa	L
4	5	6	7	8
M	P	A	W	E
W	WM	M	MD	D
vT	T	M	I	vI

moderate   short

9b—10

open

12-20

Berberis darwini
Darwin Barberry

Chile

background
barrier
hedge
seacoast
specimen / accent

P	C	Si	Sa	L
4	5	6	7	8
M	P	A	W	E
W	WM	M	MD	D
vT	T	M	I	vI

slow   short

8—10   i.1849

dense

6-12

...evergreen

S4—4

LARGE SHRUB

	FORM	BARK	LEAF	FLOWER	FRUIT	CULTURE	USES	REGION

Berberis x stenophylla
Rosemary Barbery

'Corallina Compacta'
'Nana Compacta'

dense | 6-12

CULTURE: P C Si Sa L / 4 5 6 7 8 / M P A W E / W WM M MD D / vT T M I vl
fast | short

USES: background, bank erosion, barrier, hedge, seacoast, specimen / accent

REGION: hybrid | (6b) — 9 | i.1864

Brugmansia sanguinea
Scarlet Angel's Trumpet

flava

open | 6-12

CULTURE: P C Si Sa L / 4 5 6 7 8 / M P A W E / W WM M MD D / vT T M I vl
fast | moderate

USES: container, greenhouse, hard-to-find, house plant, specimen / accent

REGION: Peru | 9 — 10

Brunfelsia australis
Paraguay Jasmine

dense | 6-12

CULTURE: P C Si Sa L / 4 5 6 7 8 / M P A W E / W WM M MD D / vT T M I vl
fast | short

USES: container, greenhouse

REGION: Argentina | 9 — 10

Brunfelsia grandiflora
Bigflower Jasmine

dense | 6-12

CULTURE: P C Si Sa L / 4 5 6 7 8 / M P A W E / W WM M MD D / vT T M I vl
fast | short

USES: container, greenhouse

REGION: n. S.America | 9 — 10

Brunfelsia pauciflora
'Floribunda'
Yesterday-today-and-
tomorrow

dense | 6-12

CULTURE: P C Si Sa L / 4 5 6 7 8 / M P A W E / W WM M MD D / vT T M I vl
fast | short

USES: container, greenhouse

REGION: cultivar | 9 — 10

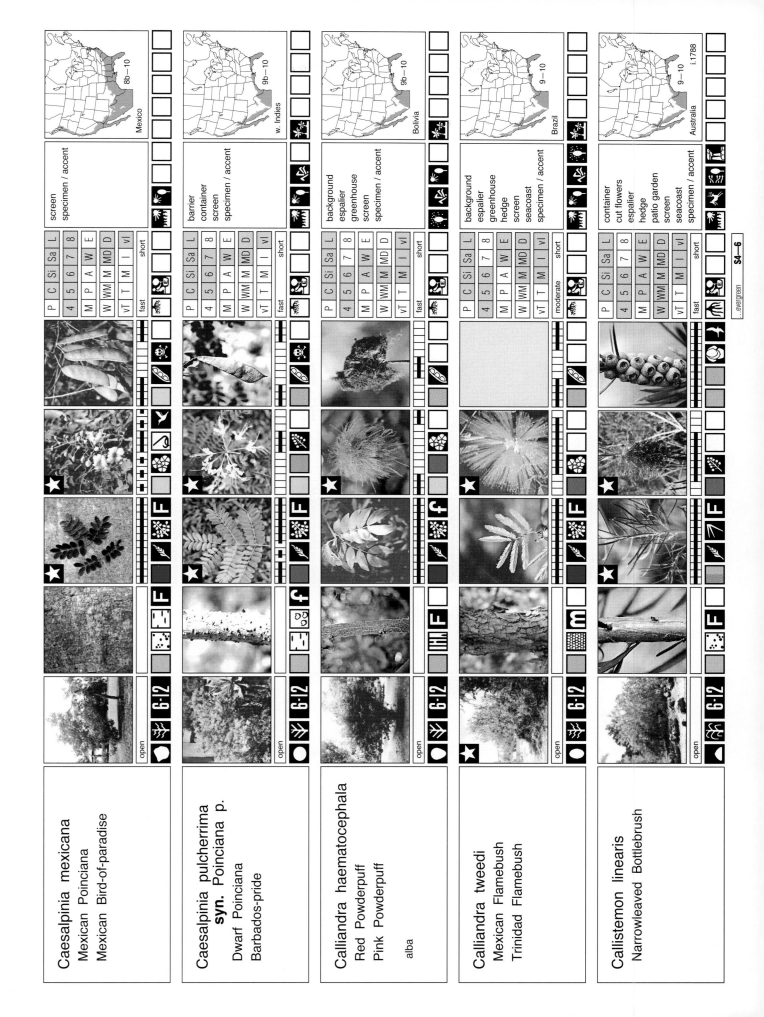

Caesalpinia mexicana
Mexican Poinciana
Mexican Bird-of-paradise

Mexico
8b—10

screen
specimen / accent

P C Si Sa L
4 5 6 7 8
M P A W E
W WM M MD D
vT T M I vI
fast short

Caesalpinia pulcherrima
syn. Poinciana p.
Dwarf Poinciana
Barbados-pride

w. Indies
9b—10

barrier
container
screen
specimen / accent

P C Si Sa L
4 5 6 7 8
M P A W E
W WM M MD D
vT T M I vI
fast short

Calliandra haematocephala
Red Powderpuff
Pink Powderpuff

alba

Bolivia
9b—10

background
espalier
greenhouse
screen
specimen / accent

P C Si Sa L
4 5 6 7 8
M P A W E
W WM M MD D
vT T M I vI
fast short

Calliandra tweedi
Mexican Flamebush
Trinidad Flamebush

Brazil
9—10

background
espalier
greenhouse
hedge
screen
seacoast
specimen / accent

P C Si Sa L
4 5 6 7 8
M P A W E
W WM M MD D
vT T M I vI
moderate short

Callistemon linearis
Narrowleaved Bottlebrush

Australia
9—10
i:1788

container
cut flowers
espalier
hedge
patio garden
screen
seacoast
specimen / accent

P C Si Sa L
4 5 6 7 8
M P A W E
W WM M MD D
vT T M I vI
fast short

...evergreen

S4—6

LARGE SHRUB	FORM	BARK	LEAF	FLOWER	FRUIT	CULTURE	USES	REGION

Callistemon pallidus

open | 6-12

CULTURE: P C Si Sa L / 4 5 6 7 8 / M P A W E / W WM M MD D / vT T M I vI

USES: background, espalier, greenhouse, hedge, patio garden, screen, seacoast

REGION: Tasmania 8-10

Callistemon speciosus
Showy Bottlebrush

open | 6-12 | fast

CULTURE: P C Si Sa L / 4 5 6 7 8 / M P A W E / W WM M MD D / vT T M I vI

USES: container, cut flowers, espalier, greenhouse, hedge, screen, seacoast

REGION: w. Australia i.1823 9-10

Camellia saluenensis
'Appleblossom'

dense | 6-12 | fast | moderate

CULTURE: P C Si Sa L / 4 5 6 7 8 / M P A W E / W WM M MD D / vT T M I vI

USES: border mass, container, espalier, greenhouse, hedge, lath house, shade garden, specimen / accent

REGION: China i.1917 7-9

Carissa grandiflora
syn. C. macrocarpa
Natalplum Carissa

dense | 12-20 | moderate

CULTURE: P C Si Sa L / 4 5 6 7 8 / M P A W E / W WM M MD D / vT T M I vI

USES: barrier, culinary, formal garden, greenhouse, house plant, kitchen garden, screen, seacoast

REGION: s. Africa 9-10

Cassinia vauvilliersi

dense | 6-12 | fast | short

CULTURE: P C Si Sa L / 4 5 6 7 8 / M P A W E / W WM M MD D / vT T M I vI

USES: seacoast

REGION: New Zealand 8-10

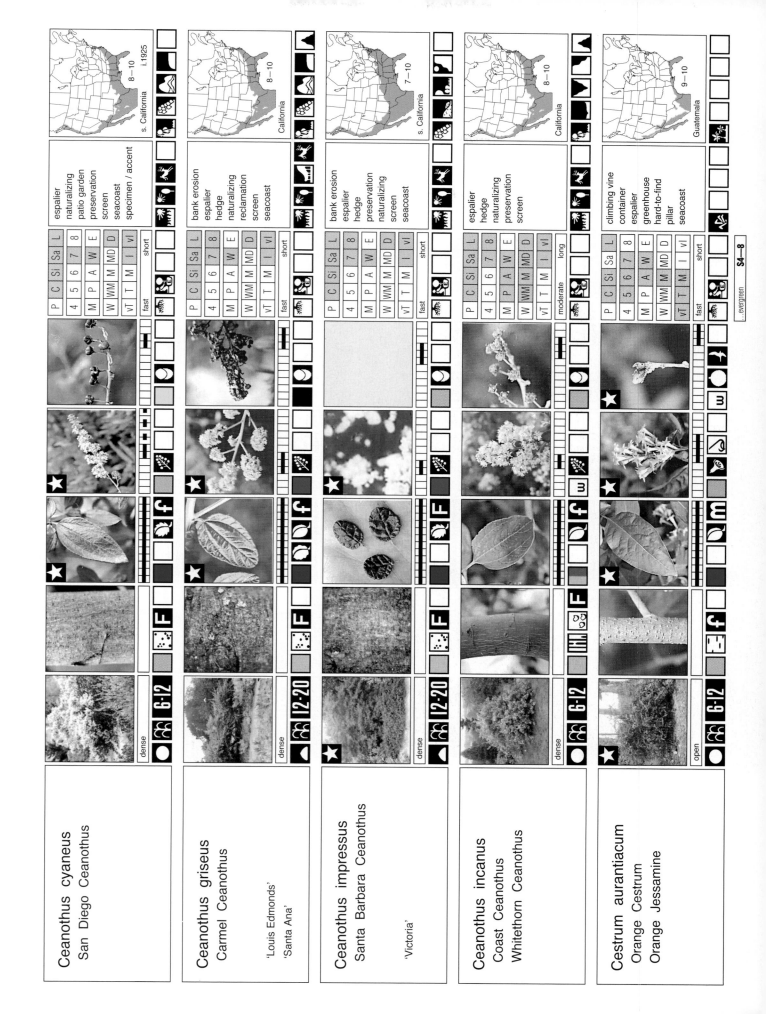

Ceanothus cyaneus — San Diego Ceanothus
espalier / naturalizing / patio garden / preservation / screen / seacoast / specimen / accent
s. California 8–10 i:1925
dense 6-12
fast short
P C Si Sa L | 4 5 6 7 8 | M P A W E | W WM M MD D | vT T M I vI

Ceanothus griseus — Carmel Ceanothus
'Louis Edmonds' / 'Santa Ana'
bank erosion / espalier / hedge / naturalizing / reclamation / screen / seacoast
California 8–10
dense 12-20
fast short
P C Si Sa L | 4 5 6 7 8 | M P A W E | W WM M MD D | vT T M I vI

Ceanothus impressus — Santa Barbara Ceanothus
'Victoria'
bank erosion / espalier / hedge / preservation / naturalizing / screen / seacoast
s. California 7–10
dense 12-20
fast short
P C Si Sa L | 4 5 6 7 8 | M P A W E | W WM M MD D | vT T M I vI

Ceanothus incanus — Coast Ceanothus / Whitethorn Ceanothus
espalier / hedge / naturalizing / preservation / screen
California 8–10
dense 6-12
moderate long
P C Si Sa L | 4 5 6 7 8 | M P A W E | W WM M MD D | vT T M I vI

Cestrum aurantiacum — Orange Cestrum / Orange Jessamine
climbing vine / container / espalier / greenhouse / hard-to-find / pillar / seacoast
Guatemala 9–10
open 6-12
fast short
P C Si Sa L | 4 5 6 7 8 | M P A W E | W WM M MD D | vT T M I vI

...evergreen S4—8

LARGE SHRUB	FORM	BARK	LEAF	FLOWER	FRUIT	CULTURE	USES	REGION

Cestrum elegans
Red Cestrum
Purple Jessamine

moderate

P	C	Si	Sa	L
4	5	6	7	8
M	P	A	W	E
W	WM	M	MD	D
vT	T	M	I	vI

fast · short

USES: climbing vine, container, espalier, greenhouse, pillar

REGION: Mexico · 8–10

Cestrum nocturnum
Nightblooming Cestrum
Night Jessamine

moderate

P	C	Si	Sa	L
4	5	6	7	8
M	P	A	W	E
W	WM	M	MD	D
vT	T	M	I	vI

fast · short

USES: container, espalier, greenhouse, seacoast

REGION: w. Indies · 9–10

Cestrum parqui
Chilean Cestrum
Willowleaved Jessamine

moderate

P	C	Si	Sa	L
4	5	6	7	8
M	P	A	W	E
W	WM	M	MD	D
vT	T	M	I	vI

fast · short

USES: container, espalier, greenhouse, seacoast

REGION: Chile · i.1787 · 8–10

Chamaecyparis obtusa
'Lycopodiodes'
Clubmoss Falsecypress

open-dense

P	C	Si	Sa	L
4	5	6	7	8
M	P	A	W	E
W	WM	M	MD	D
vT	T	M	I	vI

slow · moderate

USES: bonsai, border edge, container, formal garden, rock garden, specimen / accent

REGION: cultivar · i.1861 · 5–8

Chamaecyparis pisifera
'Boulevard'
Boulevard Falsecypress

dense

P	C	Si	Sa	L
4	5	6	7	8
M	P	A	W	E
W	WM	M	MD	D
vT	T	M	I	vI

slow · moderate

USES: container, formal garden, rock garden, specimen / accent

REGION: cultivar · o.1934 · 5–9

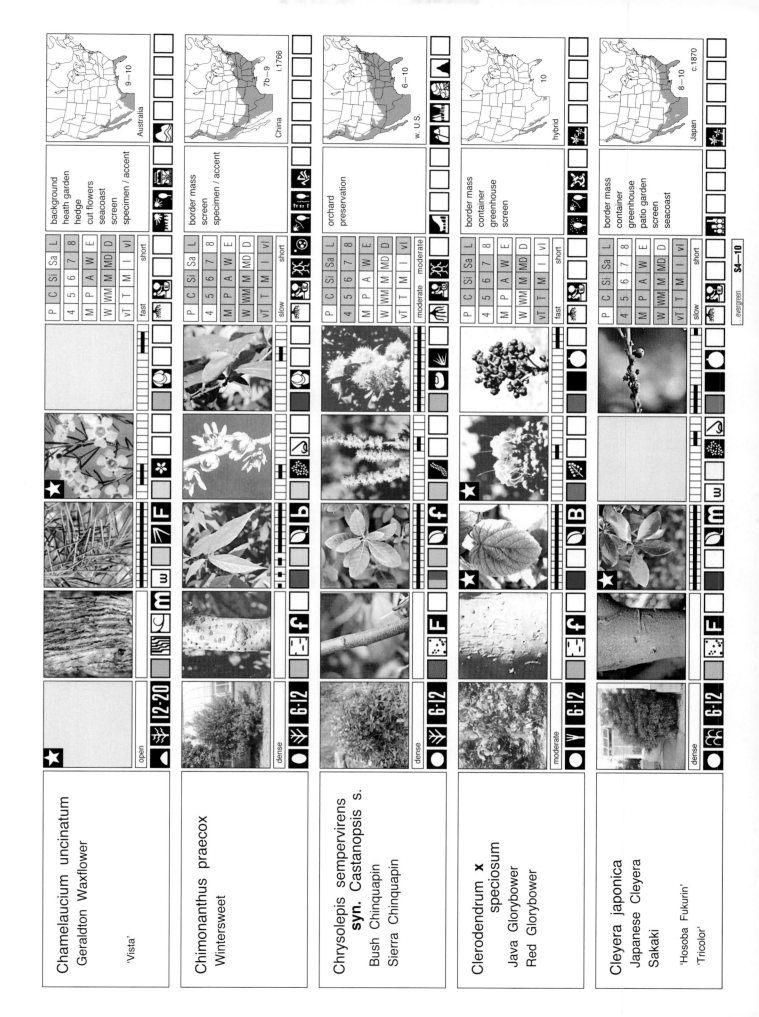

Chamelaucium uncinatum
Geraldton Waxflower

'Vista'

background
heath garden
hedge
cut flowers
seacoast
screen
specimen / accent

P	C	Si	Sa	L
4	5	6	7	8
M	P	A	W	E
W	WM	M	MD	D
vT	T	M	I	vI

fast · short

open 12-20

Australia 9–10

Chimonanthus praecox
Wintersweet

border mass
screen
specimen / accent

P	C	Si	Sa	L
4	5	6	7	8
M	P	A	W	E
W	WM	M	MD	D
vT	T	M	I	vI

slow · short

dense 6-12

China 7b–9 i:1766

Chrysolepis sempervirens
syn. Castanopsis s.

Bush Chinquapin
Sierra Chinquapin

orchard
preservation

P	C	Si	Sa	L
4	5	6	7	8
M	P	A	W	E
W	WM	M	MD	D
vT	T	M	I	vI

moderate · moderate

dense 6-12

w. U.S. 6–10

Clerodendrum x
speciosum

Java Glorybower
Red Glorybower

border mass
container
greenhouse
screen

P	C	Si	Sa	L
4	5	6	7	8
M	P	A	W	E
W	WM	M	MD	D
vT	T	M	I	vI

fast · short

moderate 6-12

hybrid 10

Cleyera japonica
Japanese Cleyera
Sakaki

'Hosoba Fukurin'
'Tricolor'

border mass
container
greenhouse
patio garden
screen
seacoast

P	C	Si	Sa	L
4	5	6	7	8
M	P	A	W	E
W	WM	M	MD	D
vT	T	M	I	vI

slow · short

dense 6-12

Japan 8–10 c.1870

…evergreen **S4—10**

LARGE SHRUB	FORM	BARK	LEAF	FLOWER	FRUIT	CULTURE	USES	REGION

Colletia cruciata
Anchorplant
open   6-12

greenhouse
novelty
sculptural

Uraguay
7–10   i.1824

Cotoneaster francheti
Franchet Cotoneaster
cinerascens
open   6-12

background
bank erosion
espalier
hedge
screen
seacoast
spacimen / accent

China
6–8a   i.1895

Cotoneaster lacteus
Parney Cotoneaster
Red Clusterberry
parneyi
dense   6-12

background
bank erosion
espalier
hedge
screen
sculptural
seacoast
specimen / accent

China
6b–9a   i.1913

Cotoneaster rotundifolia
Redbox Cotoneaster
'prestratus'
dense   6-12

background
bank erosion
espalier
hedge
screen
seacoast
specimen / accent

Himalayas
7–8   i.1825

Cotoneaster salicifolia
Willowleaf Cotoneaster
'Emerald Carpet'   'Repens'
'Repandens'   'Scarlet Leader'
dense   12-20

background
espalier
formal garden
hedge
screen
seacoast
specimen / accent

China
6–9   i.1908

CULTURE codes (repeated per row):
P C Si Sa L
4 5 6 7 8
M P A W E
W WM M MD D
vT T M I vI
short / fast / slow

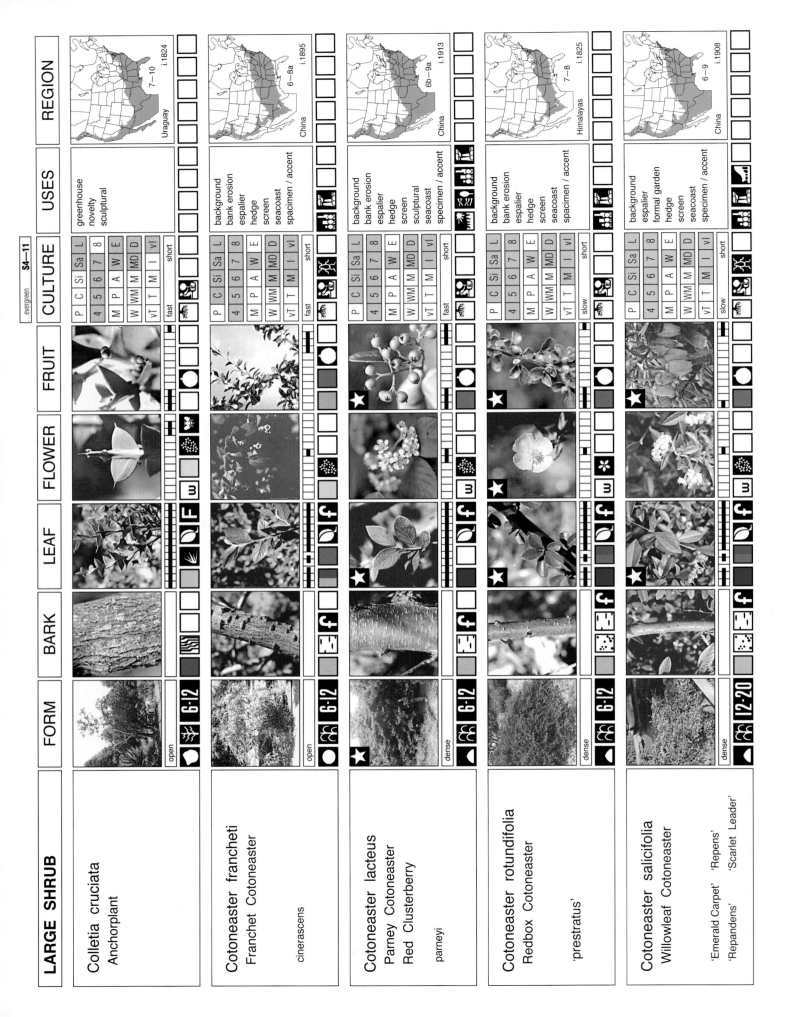

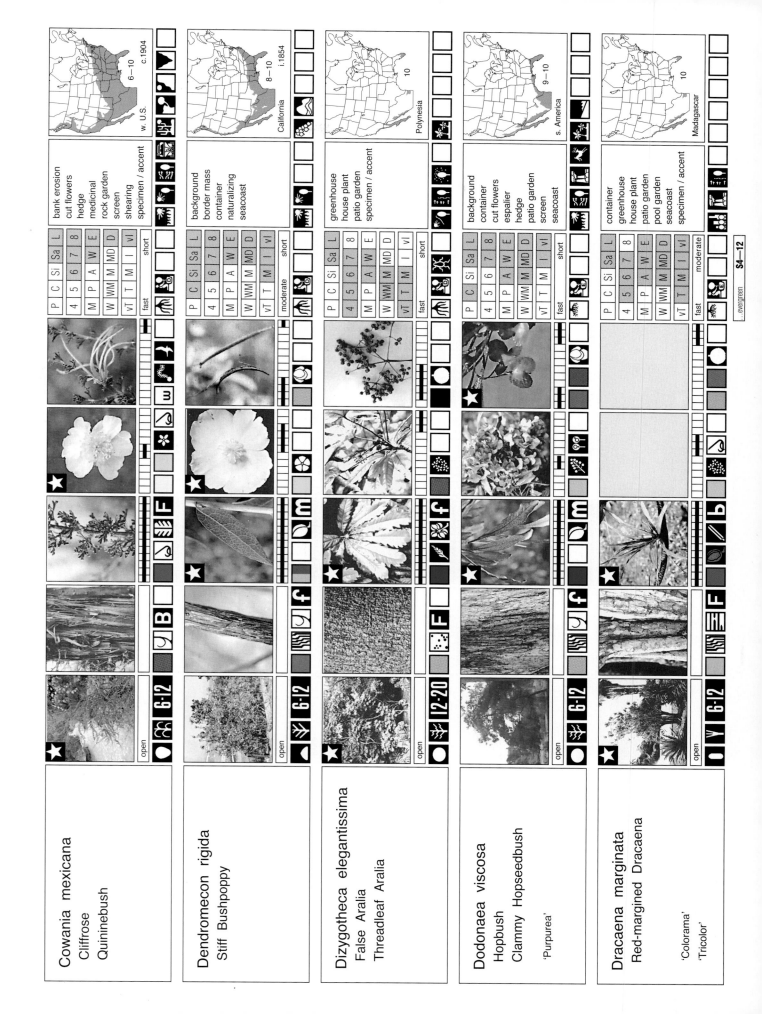

Cowania mexicana
Cliffrose
Quininebush

bank erosion
cut flowers
hedge
medicinal
rock garden
screen
shearing
specimen / accent

w. U.S.   6—10   c.1904

Dendromecon rigida
Stiff Bushpoppy

background
border mass
container
naturalizing
seacoast

California   8—10   i.1854

Dizygotheca elegantissima
False Aralia
Threadleaf Aralia
'Purpurea'

greenhouse
house plant
patio garden
specimen / accent

Polynesia   10

Dodonaea viscosa
Hopbush
Clammy Hopseedbush

background
container
cut flowers
espalier
hedge
patio garden
screen
seacoast

s. America   9—10

Dracaena marginata
Red-margined Dracaena
'Colorama'
'Tricolor'

container
greenhouse
house plant
patio garden
pool garden
seacoast
specimen / accent

Madagascar   10

S4—12

LARGE SHRUB	FORM	BARK	LEAF	FLOWER	FRUIT	CULTURE	USES	REGION

Duranta stenostachya
Brazilian Skyflower

open — 6-12

CULTURE:
P C Si Sa L
4 5 6 7 8
M P A W E
W WM M MD D
vT T M I vl
fast / short

USES: screen

REGION: Brazil — 10

Elaeagnus × ebbingei
Ebbing Elaeagnus
Ebbing Silverberry

'Gilt Edge'

dense — 6-12

CULTURE:
P C Si Sa L
4 5 6 7 8
M P A W E
W WM M MD D
vT T M I vl
fast / short

USES:
background
barrier
culinary
espalier
hedge
screen
seacoast
windbreak

REGION: hybrid — 6–9 — o.b.1939

Elaeagnus pungens
Thorny Elaeagnus

'Fruitlandii'   'Rotundifolia'
'Reflexa'   'Variegata'

dense — 6-12

CULTURE:
P C Si Sa L
4 5 6 7 8
M P A W E
W WM M MD D
vT T M I vl
fast / short

USES:
background
bank erosion
border mass
bonsai
container
hedge
screen
seacoast

REGION: Japan — 7–10 — i.1830

Erica australis
Spanish Heath
Southern Heath

moderate — 6-12

CULTURE:
P C Si Sa L
4 5 6 7 8
M P A W E
W WM M MD D
vT T M I vl
slow / shirt

USES:
background
container
patio garden
screen
seacoast

REGION: Spain — 7b–10

Eriogonum giganteum
St. Catherine's Lace

formosum

moderate — 12-20

CULTURE:
P C Si Sa L
4 5 6 7 8
M P A W E
W WM M MD D
vT T M I vl
moderate / long

USES:
bank erosion
cut flowers
naturalizing
patio garden
preservation
specimen / accent

REGION: Santa Catalina Island — 9–10

Escallonia bifida
White Escallonia

Brazil — 8b–10

background
espalier
hedge
screen
seacoast
shearing
windbreak

P	C	Si	Sa	L
4	5	6	7	8
M	P	A	E
W	WM	M	MD	D
vT	T	M	I	vl

long · fast · dense · 12-20

Escallonia myrtilloides
Myrtle Escallonia

Chile — 8–10

background
hedge
screen
shearing
wildbreak

P	C	Si	Sa	L
4	5	6	7	8
M	P	A	E
W	WM	M	MD	D
vT	T	M	I	vl

short · fast · dense · 6-12

Escallonia rubra
Red Escallonia

Chile — 7b–10   i.1827

background
espalier
hedge
seacoast
shearing
screen
windbreak

P	C	Si	Sa	L
4	5	6	7	8
M	P	A	E
W	WM	M	MD	D
vT	T	M	I	vl

short · fast · moderate · 6-12

Eucalyptus x rhodantha
Rose Mallee

hybrid — 8–10

container
espalier
fruit arrangement
leaf arrangement
sculptural
specimen / accent

P	C	Si	Sa	L
4	5	6	7	8
M	P	A	E
W	WM	M	MD	D
vT	T	M	I	vl

moderate · fast · open · 6-12

Eucalyptus tetraptera
Squarefruit Mallee
Fourwing Mallee

Australia — 9–10

bank erosion
fruit arrangement
leaf arrangement
seacoast

P	C	Si	Sa	L
4	5	6	7	8
M	P	A	E
W	WM	M	MD	D
vT	T	M	I	vl

moderate · fast · open · 6-12

...evergreen

LARGE SHRUB	FORM	BARK	LEAF	FLOWER	FRUIT	CULTURE	USES	REGION

Euphorbia leucocephala

Pascuita

CULTURE:
P C Si Sa L
4 5 6 7 8
M P A W E
W WM M MD D
vT T M I vI
fast / short

USES: cut flowers

REGION: 9–10 Mexico

Euphorbia pulcherrima

Poinsettia

Christmas-flower

'Brilliant'   'Jingle Bell'
'Gutbier Hybrid' 'Marble'

CULTURE:
P C Si Sa L
4 5 6 7 8
M P A W E
W WM M MD D
vT T M I vI
fast / short

USES: container, greenhouse, hedge, house plant, patio garden, rock garden, seacoast

REGION: 9b–10 Mexico

Fabiana imbricata

Peru Falseheath

CULTURE:
P C Si Sa L
4 5 6 7 8
M P A W E
W WM M MD D
vT T M I vI

USES: container, rock garden, seacoast

REGION: 9–10 i.1838 Chile

Fatsia japonica

Paperplant

Japanese Fatsia

CULTURE:
P C Si Sa L
4 5 6 7 8
M P A W E
W WM M MD D
vT T M I vI

USES: border mass, container, espalier, house plant, patio garden, seacoast, specimen / accent

REGION: (7b)–10 i.1838 Japan

Gardenia thunbergi

Starry Gardenia

Katjiepiering

CULTURE:
P C Si Sa L
4 5 6 7 8
M P A W E
W WM M MD D
vT T M I vI
slow / moderate

USES: border mass, espalier, cut flowers, greenhouse, specimen / accent

REGION: 9–10 s. Africa

Graptophyllum pictum
Caricatureplant

New Guinea (9b)–10

container
greenhouse
seacoast
specimen / accent

P	C	Si	Sa	L
4	5	6	7	8
M	P	A	W	E
W	WM	M	MD	D
vT	T	M	I	vI

short

open

6-12

Grewia biloba
Chinese Grewia
Himalayan Grewia

China c.1890

bank erosion
espalier
hedge
screen
sheared

P	C	Si	Sa	L
4	5	6	7	8
M	P	A	W	E
W	WM	M	MD	D
vT	T	M	I	vI

fast short

dense

6-12

Grewia occidentalis
Lavender Starflower

Africa 8–10

bank erosion
espalier
hedge
screen
sheared
trellis

P	C	Si	Sa	L
4	5	6	7	8
M	P	A	W	E
W	WM	M	MD	D
vT	T	M	I	vI

fast short

dense

6-12

Hakea elliptica
Ovalfruit Hakea

w. Australia 9–10

background
border mass
seacoast
specimen / accent

P	C	Si	Sa	L
4	5	6	7	8
M	P	A	W	E
W	WM	M	MD	D
vT	T	M	I	vI

fast short

dense

6-12

Hebe elliptica syn. H. deccusata

New Zealand 8–10

'Autumnglory'
'Bluegem'

container
patio garden
seacoast

P	C	Si	Sa	L
4	5	6	7	8
M	P	A	W	E
W	WM	M	MD	D
vT	T	M	I	vI

fast short

dense

6-12

…evergreen

LARGE SHRUB	FORM	BARK	LEAF	FLOWER	FRUIT	CULTURE	USES	REGION

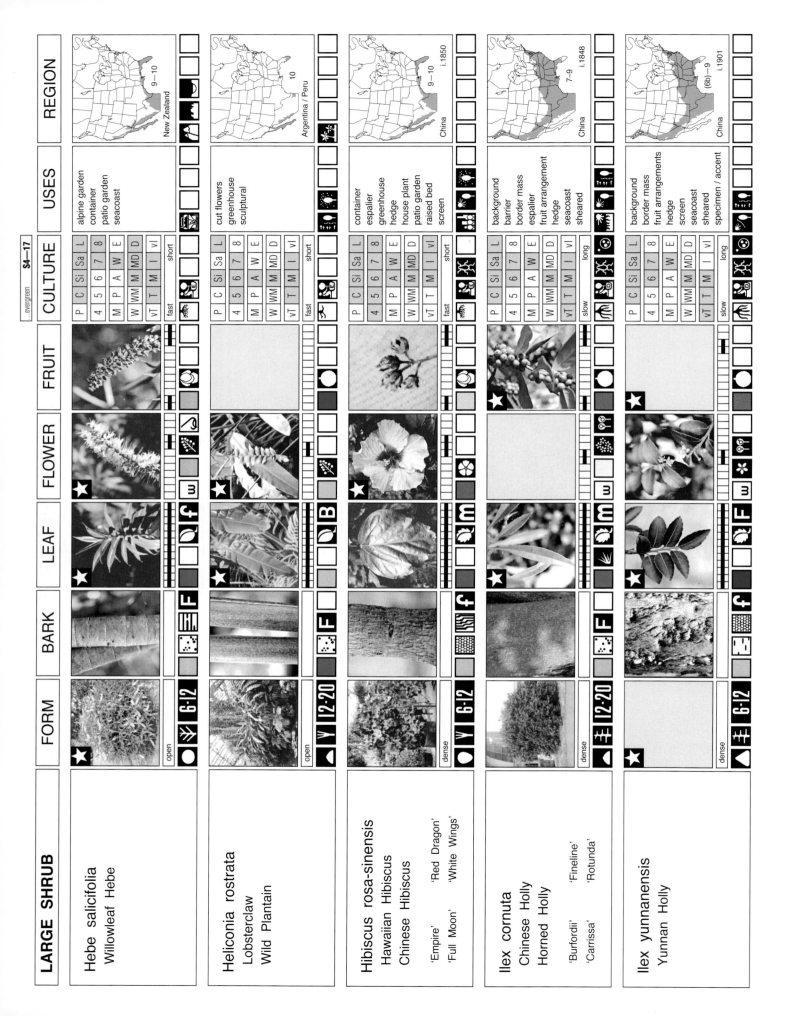

Hebe salicifolia
Willowleaf Hebe

CULTURE: P C Si Sa L / 4 5 6 7 8 / M P A W E / W WM M MD D / vT T M I vl — fast

USES: alpine garden, container, patio garden, seacoast

REGION: New Zealand 9—10

Heliconia rostrata
Lobsterclaw
Wild Plantain

CULTURE: P C Si Sa L / 4 5 6 7 8 / M P A W E / W WM M MD D / vT T M I vl — fast

USES: cut flowers, greenhouse, sculptural

REGION: Argentina / Peru 10

Hibiscus rosa-sinensis
Hawaiian Hibiscus
Chinese Hibiscus

'Empire'   'Red Dragon'
'Full Moon'   'White Wings'

CULTURE: P C Si Sa L / 4 5 6 7 8 / M P A W E / W WM M MD D / vT T M I vl — fast

USES: container, espalier, greenhouse, hedge, house plant, patio garden, raised bed, screen

REGION: China 9—10 i.1850

Ilex cornuta
Chinese Holly
Horned Holly

'Burfordii'   'Fineline'
'Carrissa'   'Rotunda'

CULTURE: P C Si Sa L / 4 5 6 7 8 / M P A W E / W WM M MD D / vT T M I vl — slow long

USES: background, barrier, border mass, espalier, fruit arrangement, hedge, seacoast, sheared

REGION: China 7—9 i.1848

Ilex yunnanensis
Yunnan Holly

CULTURE: P C Si Sa L / 4 5 6 7 8 / M P A W E / W WM M MD D / vT T M I vl — slow long

USES: background, border mass, fruit arrangements, hedge, screen, seacoast, sheared, specimen / accent

REGION: China (6b)—9 i.1901

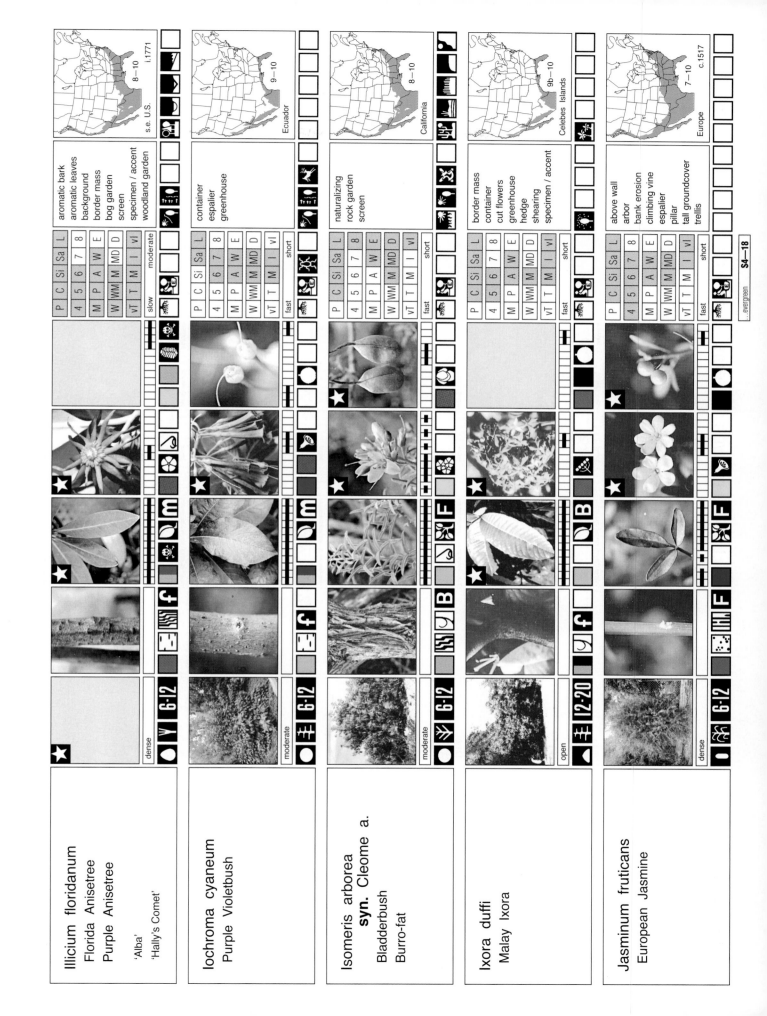

Illicium floridanum
Florida Anisetree
Purple Anisetree
'Alba'
'Hally's Comet'

aromatic bark · aromatic leaves · background · border mass · bog garden · screen · specimen / accent · woodland garden

s.e. U.S. · 8–10 · i.1771

dense · slow

P C Si Sa L / 4 5 6 7 8 / M P A W E / W WM M MD D / vT T M I vI
moderate

6-12

Iochroma cyaneum
Purple Violetbush

container · espalier · greenhouse

Ecuador · 9–10

moderate · fast · short

P C Si Sa L / 4 5 6 7 8 / M P A W E / W WM M MD D / vT T M I vI

6-12

Isomeris arborea
syn. Cleome a.
Bladderbush
Burro-fat

naturalizing · rock garden · screen

California · 8–10

moderate · fast · short

P C Si Sa L / 4 5 6 7 8 / M P A W E / W WM M MD D / vT T M I vI

6-12

Ixora duffi
Malay Ixora

border mass · container · cut flowers · greenhouse · hedge · shearing · specimen / accent

Celebes Islands · 9b–10

open · fast · short

P C Si Sa L / 4 5 6 7 8 / M P A W E / W WM M MD D / vT T M I vI

12-20

Jasminum fruticans
European Jasmine

above wall · arbor · bank erosion · climbing vine · espalier · pillar · tall groundcover · trellis

Europe · 7–10 · c.1517

dense · fast · short

P C Si Sa L / 4 5 6 7 8 / M P A W E / W WM M MD D / vT T M I vI

6-12

...evergreen   **S4—18**

LARGE SHRUB	FORM	BARK	LEAF	FLOWER	FRUIT	CULTURE	USES	REGION

Juniperus chinensis 'Blue Cloud'
Blue Cloud Juniper

- CULTURE: P C Si Sa L / 4 5 6 7 8 / M P A W E / W WM M MD D / vT T M I vl — moderate — fast — dense
- USES: barrier, bonsai, background, screen
- REGION: China, 4–8, c.1955
- FORM: 12–20

Juniperus chinensis 'Maney'
Maney Juniper

- CULTURE: P C Si Sa L / 4 5 6 7 8 / M P A W E / W WM M MD D / vT T M I vl — moderate — fast — dense
- USES: background, barrier, bonsai, border mass, screen
- REGION: cultivar, 3b–8, c.1948
- FORM: 12–20

Juniperus chinensis 'Pfitzeriana'
Pfitzer Juniper

'P. Curea'   'P. Glauca'
'P. Compacta'   'P. Kallay'

- CULTURE: P C Si Sa L / 4 5 6 7 8 / M P A W E / W WM M MD D / vT T M I vl — moderate — fast — dense
- USES: background, barrier, bonsai, border mass, screen
- REGION: cultivar, 4–9, i.1866
- FORM: 12–20

Juniperus communis
Common Juniper

'Berkshire'   'Effusa'
'Compressa'   'Hibernica'

- CULTURE: P C Si Sa L / 4 5 6 7 8 / M P A W E / W WM M MD D / vT T M I vl — slow — long — moderate
- USES: background, bank erosion, barrier, reclamation, rock garden, seacoast, specimen / accent, tall groundcover
- REGION: N. America / Eurasia, 2–8
- FORM: 12–20

Juniperus sabina
Savin Juniper

'Arcadia'   'Buffalo'
'Broadmoor'   'Skandia'

- CULTURE: P C Si Sa L / 4 5 6 7 8 / M P A W E / W WM M MD D / vT T M I vl — slow — long — dense
- USES: aromatic leaves, barrier, border mass, container, hedge, seacoast, specimen / accent, tall groundcover
- REGION: Europe, 3b–(9a), c.1812
- FORM: 12–20

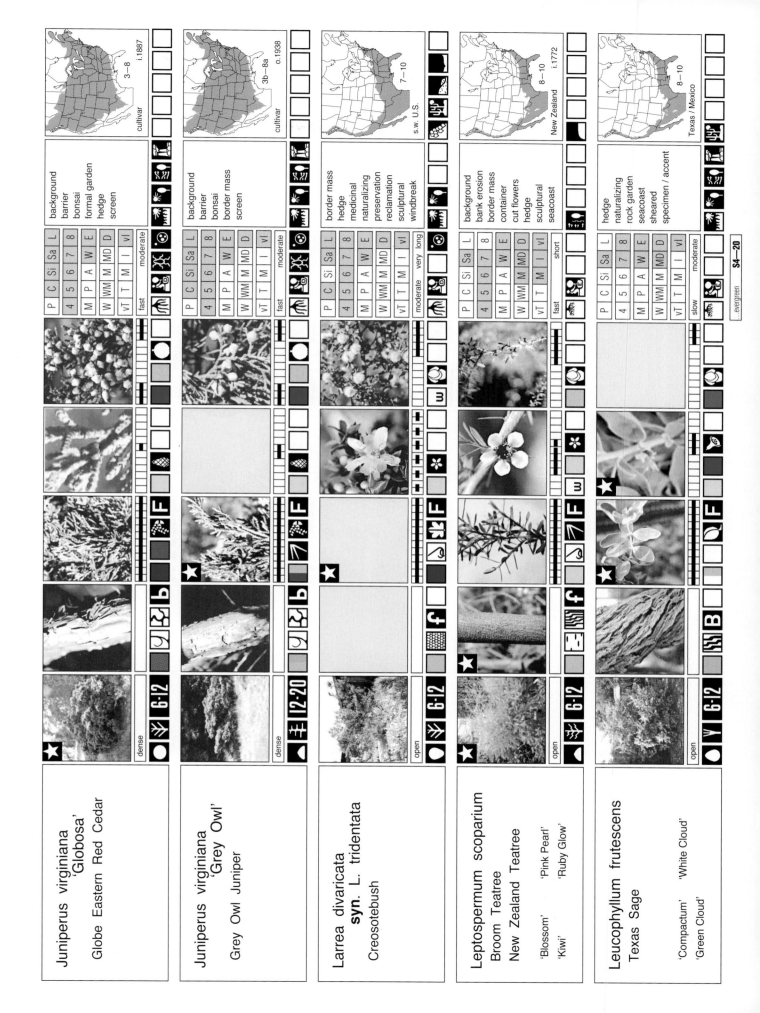

Juniperus virginiana 'Globosa'
Globe Eastern Red Cedar

3–8 i.1887 cultivar

background
barrier
bonsai
formal garden
hedge
screen

P	C	Si	Sa	L
4	5	6	7	8
M	P	A	W	E
W	WM	M	MD	D
vT	T	M	I	vI

fast moderate dense 6-12

Juniperus virginiana 'Grey Owl'
Grey Owl Juniper

3b–8a o.1938 cultivar

background
barrier
bonsai
border mass
screen

P	C	Si	Sa	L
4	5	6	7	8
M	P	A	W	E
W	WM	M	MD	D
vT	T	M	I	vI

fast moderate dense 12-20

Larrea divaricata **syn.** L. tridentata
Creosotebush

7–10 s.w. U.S.

border mass
hedge
medicinal
naturalizing
preservation
reclamation
sculptural
windbreak

P	C	Si	Sa	L
4	5	6	7	8
M	P	A	W	E
W	WM	M	MD	D
vT	T	M	I	vI

moderate very long open 6-12

Leptospermum scoparium
Broom Teatree
New Zealand Teatree

8–10 i.1772 New Zealand

'Blossom'   'Pink Pearl'
'Kiwi'   'Ruby Glow'

background
bank erosion
border mass
container
cut flowers
hedge
sculptural
seacoast

P	C	Si	Sa	L
4	5	6	7	8
M	P	A	W	E
W	WM	M	MD	D
vT	T	M	I	vI

fast short open 6-12

Leucophyllum frutescens
Texas Sage

8–10 Texas / Mexico

'Compactum'   'White Cloud'
'Green Cloud'

hedge
naturalizing
rock garden
seacoast
sheared
specimen / accent

P	C	Si	Sa	L
4	5	6	7	8
M	P	A	W	E
W	WM	M	MD	D
vT	T	M	I	vI

slow moderate open 6-12

...evergreen **S4—20**

LARGE SHRUB	FORM	BARK	LEAF	FLOWER	FRUIT	CULTURE	USES	REGION

Leucospermum reflexum
Rocket Pincushion

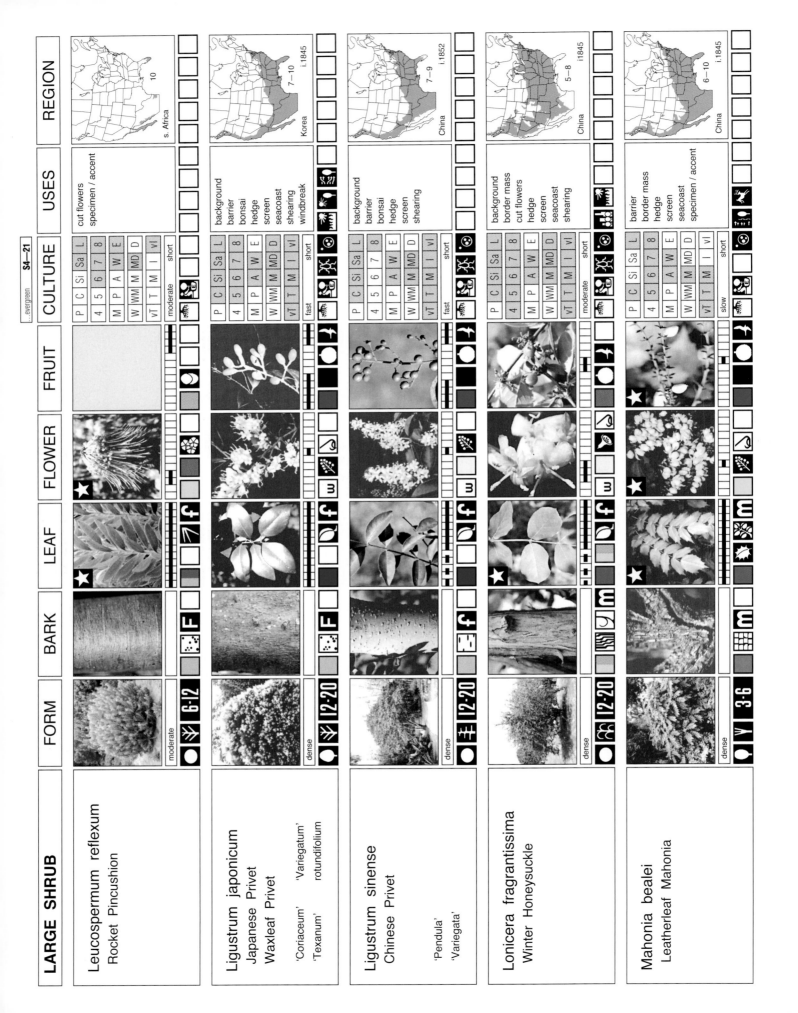

moderate   6-12

P	C	Si	Sa	L
4	5	6	7	8
M	P	A	W	E
W	WM	M	MD	D
vT	T	M	I	vI

moderate   short

cut flowers
specimen / accent

s. Africa   10

Ligustrum japonicum
Japanese Privet
Waxleaf Privet

'Coriaceum'   'Variegatum'
'Texanum'   rotundifolium

dense   12-20

P	C	Si	Sa	L
4	5	6	7	8
M	P	A	W	E
W	WM	M	MD	D
vT	T	M	I	vI

fast   short

background
barrier
bonsai
hedge
screen
seacoast
shearing
windbreak

Korea   7–10   i.1845

Ligustrum sinense
Chinese Privet

'Pendula'
'Variegata'

dense   12-20

P	C	Si	Sa	L
4	5	6	7	8
M	P	A	W	E
W	WM	M	MD	D
vT	T	M	I	vI

fast   short

background
barrier
bonsai
hedge
screen
shearing

China   7–9   i.1852

Lonicera fragrantissima
Winter Honeysuckle

dense   12-20

P	C	Si	Sa	L
4	5	6	7	8
M	P	A	W	E
W	WM	M	MD	D
vT	T	M	I	vI

moderate   short

background
border mass
cut flowers
hedge
screen
seacoast
shearing

China   5–8   i1845

Mahonia bealei
Leatherleaf Mahonia

dense   3-6

P	C	Si	Sa	L
4	5	6	7	8
M	P	A	W	E
W	WM	M	MD	D
vT	T	M	I	vI

slow   short

barrier
border mass
hedge
screen
seacoast
specimen / accent

China   6–10   i.1845

Mahonia japonica
Japanese Mahonia

barrier
border mass
hedge
screen
seacoast
specimen / accent

P	C	Si	Sa	L
4	5	6	7	8
M	P	A	W	E
W	WM	M	MD	D
vT	T	M	I	vl

slow
short
dense
6-12
Taiwan (6b)–9

Malvaviscus arboreus
South American Waxmallow
Giant Turk's Cap

drummondii
mexicanus

bedding plant
border mass
container
hedge
naturalizing
seacoast
tall groundcover

P	C	Si	Sa	L
4	5	6	7	8
M	P	A	W	E
W	WM	M	MD	D
vT	T	M	I	vl

fast
short
open
6-12
Mexico 9–10

Melaleuca decussata
Lilac Melaleuca

hedge
screen
seacoast
specimen / accent

P	C	Si	Sa	L
4	5	6	7	8
M	P	A	W	E
W	WM	M	MD	D
vT	T	M	I	vl

fast
short
dense
12-20
Australia 9–10

Melaleuca elliptica

hedge
screen
sculptural
specimen / accent
windbreak

P	C	Si	Sa	L
4	5	6	7	8
M	P	A	W	E
W	WM	M	MD	D
vT	T	M	I	vl

fast
short
moderate
6-12
Australia 9–10

Melastoma candidum

border mass
container
hedge
screen
specimen / accent

P	C	Si	Sa	L
4	5	6	7	8
M	P	A	W	E
W	WM	M	MD	D
vT	T	M	I	vl

moderate
short
dense
6-12
China 10

...evergreen   **S4—22**

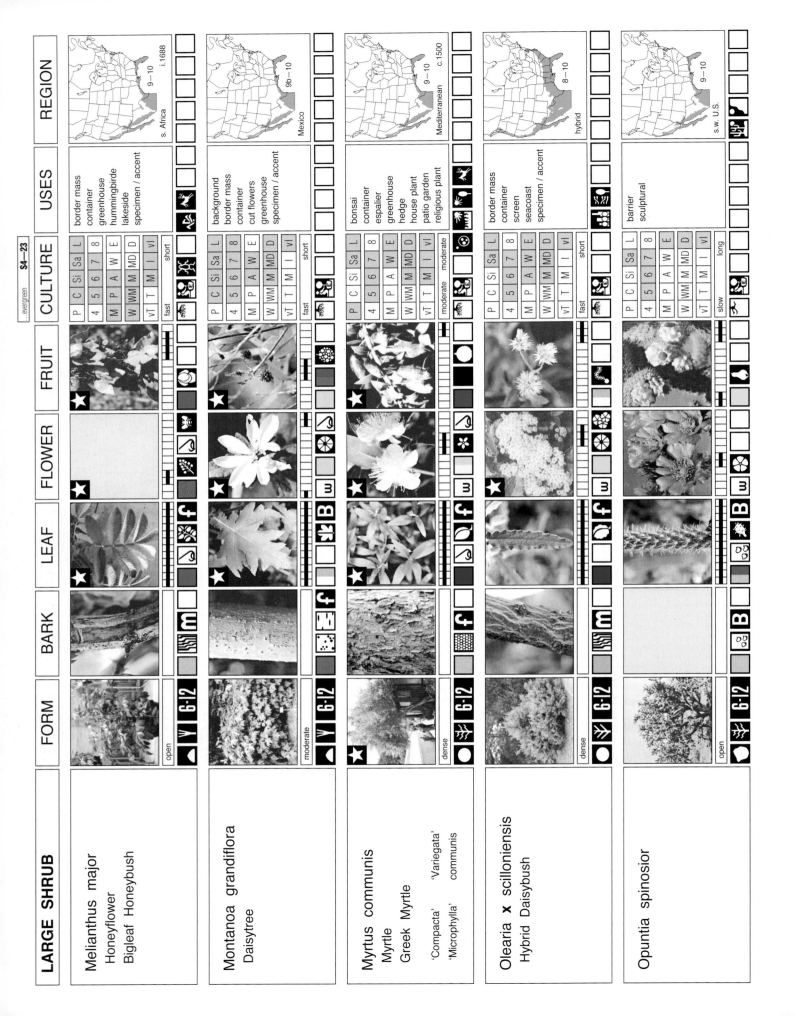

LARGE SHRUB	FORM	BARK	LEAF	FLOWER	FRUIT	CULTURE	USES	REGION

Melianthus major
Honeyflower
Bigleaf Honeybush

open · 6-12

Culture: P C Si Sa L / 4 5 6 7 8 / M P A W E / W WM M MD D / vT T M I vl · fast · short

Uses: border mass, container, greenhouse, hummingbird, lakeside, specimen / accent

Region: s. Africa · 9–10 · i.1688

Montanoa grandiflora
Daisytree

moderate · 6-12

Culture: P C Si Sa L / 4 5 6 7 8 / M P A W E / W WM M MD D / vT T M I vl · fast · short

Uses: background, border mass, container, cut flowers, greenhouse, specimen / accent

Region: Mexico · 9b–10

Myrtus communis
Myrtle
Greek Myrtle
'Compacta' 'Variegata'
'Microphylla' communis

dense · 6-12

Culture: P C Si Sa L / 4 5 6 7 8 / M P A W E / W WM M MD D / vT T M I vl · moderate · moderate

Uses: bonsai, container, espalier, greenhouse, hedge, house plant, patio garden, religious plant

Region: Mediterranean · 9–10 · c.1500

Olearia x scilloniensis
Hybrid Daisybush

dense · 6-12

Culture: P C Si Sa L / 4 5 6 7 8 / M P A W E / W WM M MD D / vT T M I vl · fast · short

Uses: border mass, container, screen, seacoast, specimen / accent

Region: hybrid · 8–10

Opuntia spinosior

open · 6-12

Culture: P C Si Sa L / 4 5 6 7 8 / M P A W E / W WM M MD D / vT T M I vl · slow · long

Uses: barrier, sculptural

Region: s.w. U.S. · 9–10

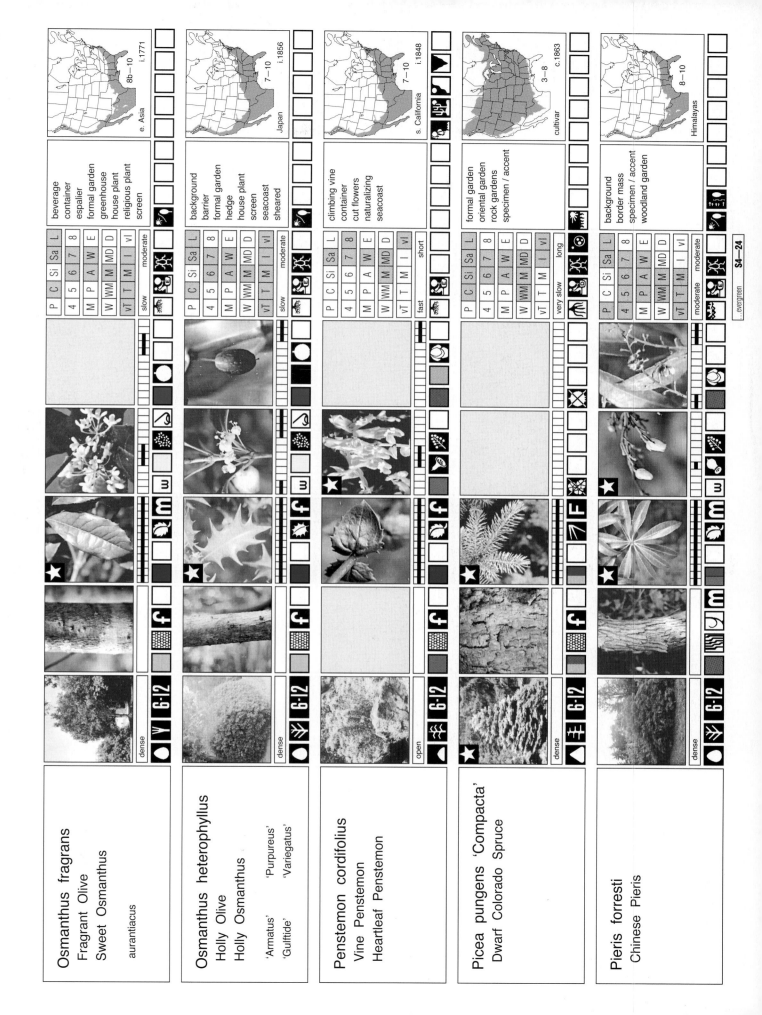

Osmanthus fragrans
Fragrant Olive
Sweet Osmanthus

aurantiacus

8b–10 i.1771 e. Asia

beverage
container
espalier
formal garden
greenhouse
house plant
religious plant
screen

P C Si Sa L
4 5 6 7 8
M P A W E
W WM M MD D
vT T M I vI
slow moderate
dense

Osmanthus heterophyllus
Holly Olive
Holly Osmanthus

'Armatus'   'Purpureus'
'Gulftide'   'Variegatus'

7–10 i.1856 Japan

background
barrier
formal garden
hedge
house plant
screen
seacoast
sheared

P C Si Sa L
4 5 6 7 8
M P A W E
W WM M MD D
vT T M I vI
slow moderate
dense

Penstemon cordifolius
Vine Penstemon
Heartleaf Penstemon

7–10 i.1848 s. California

climbing vine
container
cut flowers
naturalizing
seacoast

P C Si Sa L
4 5 6 7 8
M P A W E
W WM M MD D
vT T M I vI
fast short
open

Picea pungens 'Compacta'
Dwarf Colorado Spruce

3–8 c.1863 cultivar

formal garden
oriental garden
rock gardens
specimen / accent

P C Si Sa L
4 5 6 7 8
M P A W E
W WM M MD D
vT T M I vI
very slow long
dense

Pieris forresti
Chinese Pieris

8–10 Himalayas

background
border mass
specimen / accent
woodland garden

P C Si Sa L
4 5 6 7 8
M P A W E
W WM M MD D
vT T M I vI
moderate moderate
dense

…evergreen S4–24

LARGE SHRUB	FORM	BARK	LEAF	FLOWER	FRUIT	CULTURE	USES	REGION

Pieris 'Forest Flame'
Forest Flame Pieris
Flame-of-the-Forest
'Bisbee Dwarf'

FORM: dense, 6-12
CULTURE: P C Si Sa L · 4 5 6 7 8 · M P A W E · W WM M MD D · vT T M I vl · moderate / moderate
USES: background / border mass / specimen / accent / woodland garden
REGION: cultivar · 7–9 · i.1957

Pieris japonica
Japanese Pieris
Lily-of-the-Valley

FORM: dense, 6-12
CULTURE: P C Si Sa L · 4 5 6 7 8 · M P A W E · W WM M MD D · vT T M I vl · moderate / moderate
USES: background / border mass / specimen / accent / woodland garden
REGION: Japan · 6–9 · i.1870

Pinus mugo mughus
Mugo Swissmountain Pine

FORM: dense, 12-20
CULTURE: P C Si Sa L · 4 5 6 7 8 · M P A W E · W WM M MD D · vT T M I vl · very slow / long
USES: background / bonsai / container / hedge / rock garden / screen / sculptural / specimen / accent
REGION: Switzerland · 2–7 · i.1779

Pinus pumila
Dwarf Stone Pine
Dwarf Siberian Pine

FORM: dense, 6-12
CULTURE: P C Si Sa L · 4 5 6 7 8 · M P A W E · W WM M MD D · vT T M I vl · slow / short
USES: bonsai / oriental garden / sculptural / specimen / accent
REGION: Japan · 4–7 · i.1791

Pinus sylvestris 'Watereri'
Waterer Scotch Pine
Columnar Scotch Pine

FORM: dense, 0 6-12
CULTURE: P C Si Sa L · 4 5 6 7 8 · M P A W E · W WM M MD D · vT T M I vl · fast / short
USES: bonsai / formal gardens / screen
REGION: cultivar · 4–8 · 0.1865

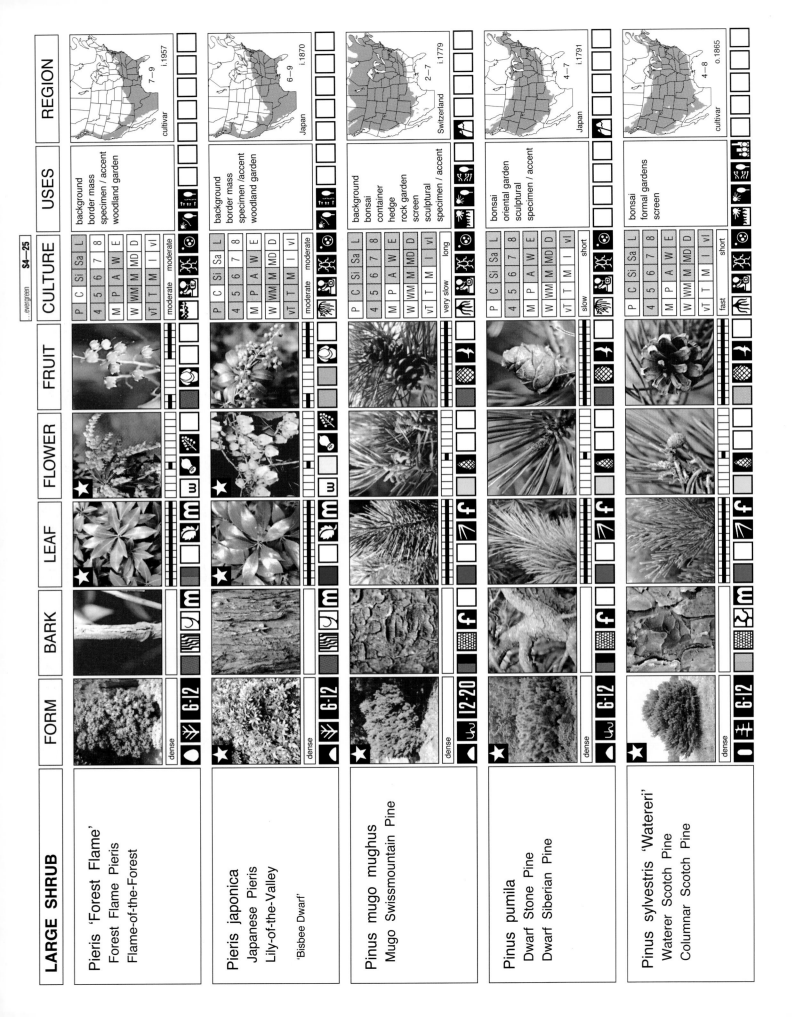

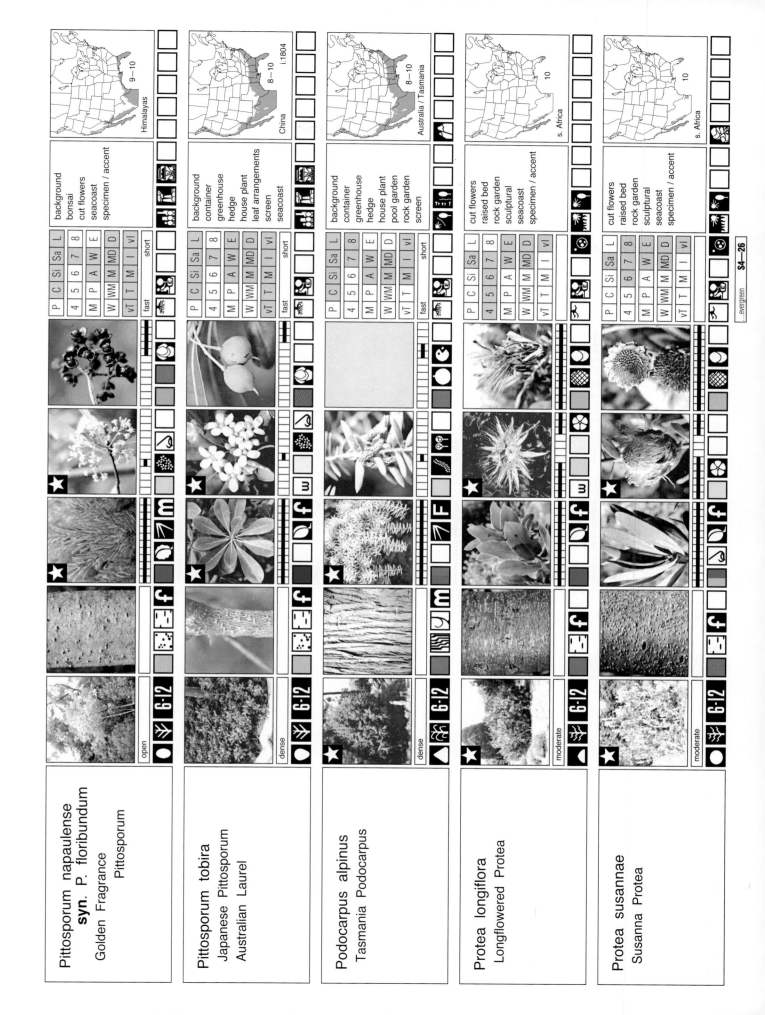

Pittosporum napaulense **syn.** P. floribundum
Golden Fragrance
Pittosporum

background
bonsai
cut flowers
seacoast
specimen / accent

Himalayas
9–10

Pittosporum tobira
Japanese Pittosporum
Australian Laurel

background
container
greenhouse
hedge
house plant
leaf arrangements
screen
seacoast

China
i.1804
8–10

Podocarpus alpinus
Tasmania Podocarpus

background
container
greenhouse
hedge
house plant
pool garden
rock garden
screen

Australia / Tasmania
8–10

Protea longiflora
Longflowered Protea

cut flowers
raised bed
rock garden
sculptural
seacoast
specimen / accent

s. Africa
10

Protea susannae
Susanna Protea

cut flowers
raised bed
rock garden
sculptural
seacoast
specimen / accent

s. Africa
10

...evergreen

S4—26

LARGE SHRUB	FORM	BARK	LEAF	FLOWER	FRUIT	CULTURE	USES	REGION

Purshia glandulosa
Desert Bitterbrush
Waxy Bitterbrush

dense · 6-12

CULTURE:
P C Si Sa L
4 5 6 7 8
M P A W E
W WM M MD D
vT T M I vl
fast · long

USES:
bank erosion
naturalizing
reclamation

REGION: 8–10 · w. N.America

Purshia tridentata
Antelope Bitterbrush
Antelopebrush

dense · 6-12

CULTURE:
P C Si Sa L
4 5 6 7 8
M P A W E
W WM M MD D
vT T M I vl
fast · long

USES:
bank erosion
naturalizing
reclamation

REGION: 6—10 · w. N.America

Pyracantha coccinea
Scarlet Firethorn
Scarlet Pyracantha

'Kasan'   'Lowboy'
'Lalendei'   'Rutgers'

dense · 6-12

CULTURE:
P C Si Sa L
4 5 6 7 8
M P A W E
W WM M MD D
vT T M I vl
moderate · short

USES:
background
barrier
espalier
hedge
screen
specimen / accent

REGION: 6—9 · i.1629 · Asia

Pyracantha fortuneana
Chinese Firethorn

'Graberi'

dense · 6-12

CULTURE:
P C Si Sa L
4 5 6 7 8
M P A W E
W WM M MD D
vT T M I vl
slow · short

USES:
background
barrier
espalier
hedge
screen
specimen / accent

REGION: 7—9 · i.1906 · China

Quercus dumosa
California Scrub Oak

moderate · 6-12

CULTURE:
P C Si Sa L
4 5 6 7 8
M P A W E
W WM M MD D
vT T M I vl
slow · long

USES:
bank erosion
specimen / accent
wild garden

REGION: 8–10 · California

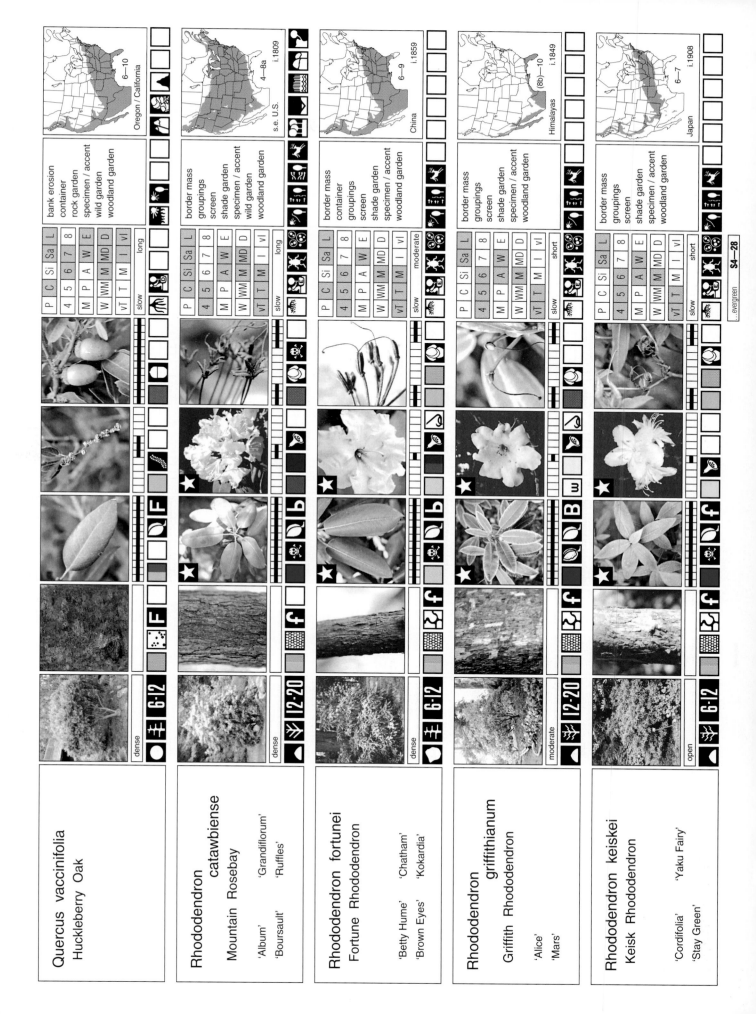

Quercus vaccinifolia
Huckleberry Oak

Oregon / California
6—10

bank erosion
container
rock garden
specimen / accent
wild garden
woodland garden

P	C	Si	Sa	L
4	5	6	7	8
M		P	A	E
W		WM	M	D
vT	T	M	I	vI

slow   long

dense   6-12

Rhododendron
catawbiense
Mountain Rosebay

'Album'   'Grandiflorum'
'Boursault'   'Ruffles'

s.e. U.S.
i.1809
4—8a

border mass
groupings
screen
shade garden
specimen / accent
wild garden
woodland garden

P	C	Si	Sa	L
4	5	6	7	8
M		P	A	E
W	WM	M	MD	D
vT	T	M	I	vI

slow   long

dense   12-20

Rhododendron fortunei
Fortune Rhododendron

'Betty Hume'   'Chatham'
'Brown Eyes'   'Kokardia'

China
i.1859
6—9

border mass
container
groupings
screen
shade garden
specimen / accent
woodland garden

P	C	Si	Sa	L
4	5	6	7	8
M		P	A	E
W	WM	M	MD	D
vT	T	M	I	vI

slow   moderate

dense   6-12

Rhododendron
griffithianum
Griffith Rhododendron

'Alice'
'Mars'

Himalayas
i.1849
(8b)—10

border mass
groupings
screen
shade garden
specimen / accent
woodland garden

P	C	Si	Sa	L
4	5	6	7	8
M		P	A	E
W	WM	M	MD	D
vT	T	M	I	vI

slow   short

moderate   12-20

Rhododendron keiskei
Keisk Rhododendron

'Cordifolia'   'Yaku Fairy'
'Stay Green'

Japan
i.1908
6—7

border mass
groupings
screen
shade garden
specimen / accent
woodland garden

P	C	Si	Sa	L
4	5	6	7	8
M		P	A	E
W	WM	M	MD	D
vT	T	M	I	vI

slow   short

open   6-12

...evergreen   S4—28

LARGE SHRUB	FORM	BARK	LEAF	FLOWER	FRUIT	CULTURE	USES	REGION

Rhododendron smirnowi
Smirnow Rhododendron

FORM: open — 6-12

CULTURE:
P	C	Si	Sa	L
4	5	6	7	8
M	P	A	W	E
W	WM	M	MD	D
vT	T	M	I	vI
slow / short

USES:
border mass
groupings
screen
shade garden
specimen / accent
woodland garden

REGION: 4b—8a i:1886 Caucasus

Rhus ovata
Sugarbush
Sugar Sumac

FORM: open-dense — 20-35

CULTURE:
P	C	Si	Sa	L
4	5	6	7	8
M	P	A	W	E
W	WM	M	MD	D
vT	T	M	I	vI
fast / short

USES:
background
bank erosion
berverage
espalier
hedge
screen

REGION: 7—10 Arizona / California

Sabal minor
Dwarf Palmetto

FORM: open — 6-12

CULTURE:
P	C	Si	Sa	L
4	5	6	7	8
M	P	A	W	E
W	WM	M	MD	D
vT	T	M	I	vI
slow / moderate

USES:
sculptural
specimen / accent

REGION: (7b)—10 s.e. U.S.

Sasa palmata
Palmata Bamboo

'Nebulosa'

FORM: dense — 12-20

CULTURE:
P	C	Si	Sa	L
4	5	6	7	8
M	P	A	W	E
W	WM	M	MD	D
vT	T	M	I	vI
very fast / long

USES:
bank erosion
container
greenhouse
oriental garden
rarley flowers
screen
specimen / accent
woodland garden

REGION: 6—10 i:1889 Japan

Senecio petasitis
Velvet Groundsell
California Geranium

FORM: dense — 6-12

CULTURE:
P	C	Si	Sa	L
4	5	6	7	8
M	P	A	W	E
W	WM	M	MD	D
vT	T	M	I	vI
fast / short

USES:
container
greenhouse
screen
specimen / accent

REGION: 9—10 Mexico

Sophora tomentosa
Silverbush

P	C	Si	Sa	L
4	5	6	7	8
M	P	A	W	E
W	WM	M	MD	D
vT	T	M	I	vl

fast | short

seacoast
specimen / accent

10b
Old World Tropics

open | 6-12

Taxus baccata 'Elegantissima'
Elegant English Yew

P	C	Si	Sa	L
4	5	6	7	8
M	P	A	W	E
W	WM	M	MD	D
vT	T	M	I	vl

slow | moderate

background
formal garden
hedge
poisonous leaves
screen
seacoast
specimen / accent
topiary

6b—8a   c.1852
cultivar

dense | 6-12

Taxus baccata 'Fowle'
Fowle English Yew

P	C	Si	Sa	L
4	5	6	7	8
M	P	A	W	E
W	WM	M	MD	D
vT	T	M	I	vl

slow | moderate

background
bonsai
formal garden
hedge
screen
seacoast
specimen / accent
topiary

6b—9a
cultivar

dense | 12-20

Taxus x media 'Browni'
Brown's Anglojapanese Yew

P	C	Si	Sa	L
4	5	6	7	8
M	P	A	W	E
W	WM	M	MD	D
vT	T	M	I	vl

slow | long

background
formal garden
hedge
screen
seacoast
topiary

5—8a   c.1940
cultivar

dense

Taxus x media 'Hatfieldi'
Hatfield Anglojapanese Yew

P	C	Si	Sa	L
4	5	6	7	8
M	P	A	W	E
W	WM	M	MD	D
vT	T	M	I	vl

slow | long

background
formal garden
hedge
screen
seacoast
topiary

5—8a   c.1923
cultivar

dense | 6-12

LARGE SHRUB	FORM	BARK	LEAF	FLOWER	FRUIT	CULTURE	USES	REGION

Taxus x media 'Viridis'
Viridus Anglojapanese Yew

FORM: dense · 6-12
CULTURE:
P	C	Si	Sa	L
4	5	6	7	8
M	P	A	W	E
W	WM	M	MD	D
vT	T	M	I	vI
slow — long
USES: background, formal garden, hedge, screen, seacoast, topiary
REGION: 5—8a · cultivar · c.1948

Thevetia peruviana
Lucky Nut
Yellow Oleander

FORM: open · 6-12
CULTURE:
P	C	Si	Sa	L
4	5	6	7	8
M	P	A	W	E
W	WM	M	MD	D
vT	T	M	I	vI
fast
USES: background, container, greenhouse, hedge, lucky charm, patio garden, screen, specimen / accent
REGION: 9b—10 · Tropical America

Tsuga canadensis 'Nana'
Dwarf Eastern Hemlock

FORM: dense · 6-12
CULTURE:
P	C	Si	Sa	L
4	5	6	7	8
M	P	A	W	E
W	WM	M	MD	D
vT	T	M	I	vI
slow — long
USES: bonsai, formal garden, hedge, screen, shearing, specimen / accent, topiary
REGION: 3—8a · cultivar · c.1855

Viburnum x burkwoodi
Burkwood Viburnum

'Chenaultii'
'Mohawk'

FORM: dense · 6-12
CULTURE:
P	C	Si	Sa	L
4	5	6	7	8
M	P	A	W	E
W	WM	M	MD	D
vT	T	M	I	vI
moderate — short
USES: background, border mass, espalier, hedge, patio garden, screen, specimen / accent
REGION: (5b) — 8 · hybrid · o.1924

Viburnum rhytidophyllum
Leatherleaf Viburnum

FORM: dense · 6-12
CULTURE:
P	C	Si	Sa	L
4	5	6	7	8
M	P	A	W	E
W	WM	M	MD	D
vT	T	M	I	vI
fast — short
USES: background, border mass, formal garden, hedge, screen, specimen / accent
REGION: (5b) — 9 · China · c.1927

Viburnum suspensum
Sandankwa Viburnum

Japan i:1850 8–10

P	C	Si	Sa	L
4	5	6	7	8
M	P	A	W	E
W	WM	M	MD	D
vT	T	M	I	vI

moderate / short

border mass
formal garden
hedge
screen
sculptural
specimen / accent

dense 6-12

Viburnum tinus
Laurustinus Viburnum

'Compactum' 'Robustum'
'Spring Bouquet'

Mediterranean c.1500 7–9

P	C	Si	Sa	L
4	5	6	7	8
M	P	A	W	E
W	WM	M	MD	D
vT	T	M	I	vI

fast / short

background
container
hedge
screen
seacoast
specimen / accent
topiary

open 12-20

Xylosma heterophylla
Holly Xylosma

Colombia 10

P	C	Si	Sa	L
4	5	6	7	8
M	P	A	W	E
W	WM	M	MD	D
vT	T	M	I	vI

fast / short

background
container
barrier
espalier
hedge
screen
shearing

open 20-35

Yucca gloriosa
Spanish Dagger
Roman Candle

s.e. U.S. i:1550 6–10

P	C	Si	Sa	L
4	5	6	7	8
M	P	A	W	E
W	WM	M	MD	D
vT	T	M	I	vI

slow / long

border mass
preservation
sculptural
specimen / accent

moderate 3-6

...evergreen

P	C	Si	Sa	L
4	5	6	7	8
M	P	A	W	E
W	WM	M	MD	D
vT	T	M	I	vI

MEDIUM SHRUB	FORM	BARK	LEAF	FLOWER	FRUIT	CULTURE	USES	REGION

Abelia floribunda
Mexican Abelia

CULTURE: P C Si Sa L / 4 5 6 7 8 / M P A W E / W WM M MD D / vT T M I vl — fast / short

USES: background, hedge, screen, seacoast, specimen / accent

REGION: 7–10 · Mexico · i.1841

dense · 3·6

Abelia × grandiflora
Glossy Abelia
'Compacta'
'Sherwoodii'

CULTURE: P C Si Sa L / 4 5 6 7 8 / M P A W E / W WM M MD D / vT T M I vl — fast / short

USES: background, border mass, fragrant leaves, hedge, screen, sheared, specimen / accent

REGION: 5–10 · hybrid · o.b.1880

dense · 3·6

Abies concolor
'Compacta'
Compact White Fir

CULTURE: P C Si Sa L / 4 5 6 7 8 / M P A W E / W WM M MD D / vT T M I vl — slow / moderate

USES: formal garden, oriental garden, rock garden, specimen / accent

REGION: 4–8 · cultivar · c.1891

dense · 3·6

Abies koreana
'Compact Dwarf'
Dwarf Korean Fir

CULTURE: P C Si Sa L / 4 5 6 7 8 / M P A W E / W WM M MD D / vT T M I vl — slow / moderate

USES: formal garden, oriental garden, rock garden, specimen / accent

REGION: 6–8 · cultivar · unknown

dense · 6·12

Agave americana
Centuryplant
American Aloe
marginata   mexico-picata
variegata

CULTURE: P C Si Sa L / 4 5 6 7 8 / M P A W E / W WM M MD D / vT T M I vl — slow / moderate

USES: barrier, container, fire retardant, greenhouse, rock garden, sculptural, seacoast, specimen / accent

REGION: 9b–10 · Mexico · i.1561

open · 3·6

Agave attenuata

open

3-6

container
dies after flower
fire retardant
rock garden
sculptural
specimen / accent
pool garden

P	C	Si	Sa	L
4	5	6	7	8
M	P	A	W	E
W	WM	M	MD	D
vT	T	M	I	vl

slow   long

Mexico   9b–10

Agave ferox

open

6-12

barrier
conservatory
dies after flower
fire retardant
rock garden
sculptural
specimen / accent

P	C	Si	Sa	L
4	5	6	7	8
M	P	A	W	E
W	WM	M	MD	D
vT	T	M	I	vl

slow   long

Mexico   9b–10

Alyogyne huegelii
Blue Hibiscus
Desert Rose

'Monterey Bay'
'Santa Cruz'

open

6-12

specimen / accent

P	C	Si	Sa	L
4	5	6	7	8
M	P	A	W	E
W	WM	M	MD	D
vT	T	M	I	vl

moderate   short

s. Australia   10

Arctostaphylos densiflora
Sonoma Manzanita
Vine Hill Manzanita

'Howard McMinn'
'Sentinel'

dense

6-12

background
bank erosion
naturalizing
preservation
seacoast
specimen / accent

P	C	Si	Sa	L
4	5	6	7	8
M	P	A	W	E
W	WM	M	MD	D
vT	T	M	I	vl

moderate   short

California   7–10

Arctostaphylos stanfordiana
Stanford Manzanita

'Louis Edmunds'

dense

6-12

background
bank erosion
low maintenance
naturalizing
specimen / accent

P	C	Si	Sa	L
4	5	6	7	8
M	P	A	W	E
W	WM	M	MD	D
vT	T	M	I	vl

moderate   short

California   8–10

...evergreen

MEDIUM SHRUB	FORM	BARK	LEAF	FLOWER	FRUIT	CULTURE	USES	REGION

Ardisia crenata syn. A. crenulata

Coral Ardisia
Coralberry

'Alba'

FORM: open, 3·6

CULTURE: P C Si Sa L / 4 5 6 7 8 / M P A W E / W WM M MD D / vT T M I vl / slow

USES: container, greenhouse, hedge, house plant, patio garden, rock garden, specimen / accent, sunroom

REGION: India, 7–10

Artemisia abrotanum

Southernwood
Oldman Wormwood

'Camphor'
'Tangerine'

FORM: dense, 3·6

CULTURE: P C Si Sa L / 4 5 6 7 8 / M P A W E / W WM M MD D / vT T M I vl / fast

USES: bank erosion, border edging, border mass, dried flowers, dried leaves, herb garden, historic garden, naturalizing

REGION: s. Europe, 3b–10, c.1500

Artemisia arborescens

Shrubby Wormwood

FORM: dense, 3·6

CULTURE: P C Si Sa L / 4 5 6 7 8 / M P A W E / W WM M MD D / vT T M I vl / fast

USES: border edging, border mass, container, dried leaves, herb garden, patio garden, rock garden, seacoast

REGION: Mediterranean, 8b–10, i.1640

Atriplex canescens

Fourwing Saltbush
Chamiso

FORM: open-dense, 6·12

CULTURE: P C Si Sa L / 4 5 6 7 8 / M P A W E / W WM M MD D / vT T M I vl / fast

USES: bank erosion, border mass, hedge, naturalizing, restoration, screen, sheared

REGION: w. U.S., 5–10, c.1870

Berberis x chenaulti

Chenault Barberry

FORM: dense, 3·6

CULTURE: P C Si Sa L / 4 5 6 7 8 / M P A W E / W WM M MD D / vT T M I vl / fast

USES: background, barrier, hedge, screen, sheared, specimen / accent

REGION: hybrid, 6–9, o.1928

Berberis gagnepaini
Black Barberry

w. China
6b – 9
i.1904

background
bank erosion
barrier
hedge
specimen / accent

P	C	Si	Sa	L
4	5	6	7	8
M	P	A	W	E
W	WM	M	MD	D
vT	T	M	I	vI

fast short
dense 3·6

Berberis hookeri
Hooker's Barberry

Himalayas
6 – 9
i.1844

background
bank erosion
barrier
border mass
hedge
specimen / accent

P	C	Si	Sa	L
4	5	6	7	8
M	P	A	W	E
W	WM	M	MD	D
vT	T	M	I	vI

fast short
dense 3·6

Berberis julianae
Wintergreen Barberry
'Nana'

China
6b – 9a
i.1900

background
barrier
border mass
hedge
low maintenance
screen
seacoast
specimen / accent

P	C	Si	Sa	L
4	5	6	7	8
M	P	A	W	E
W	WM	M	MD	D
vT	T	M	I	vI

moderate short
dense 3·6

Berberis x mentorensis
Mentor Barberry

hybrid
5 – 9
o.1924

background
bank erosion
barrier
border mass
hedge
low maintenance
specimen / accent

P	C	Si	Sa	L
4	5	6	7	8
M	P	A	W	E
W	WM	M	MD	D
vT	T	M	I	vI

moderate short
dense 3·6

Berberis triacanthophora
Threespine Barberry

China
5 – 9
i.1907

background
bank erosion
barrier
border mass
hedge
screen
seacoast

P	C	Si	Sa	L
4	5	6	7	8
M	P	A	W	E
W	WM	M	MD	D
vT	T	M	I	vI

fast short
dense 3·6

...evergreen S3—4

MEDIUM SHRUB

	FORM	BARK	LEAF	FLOWER	FRUIT	CULTURE	USES	REGION

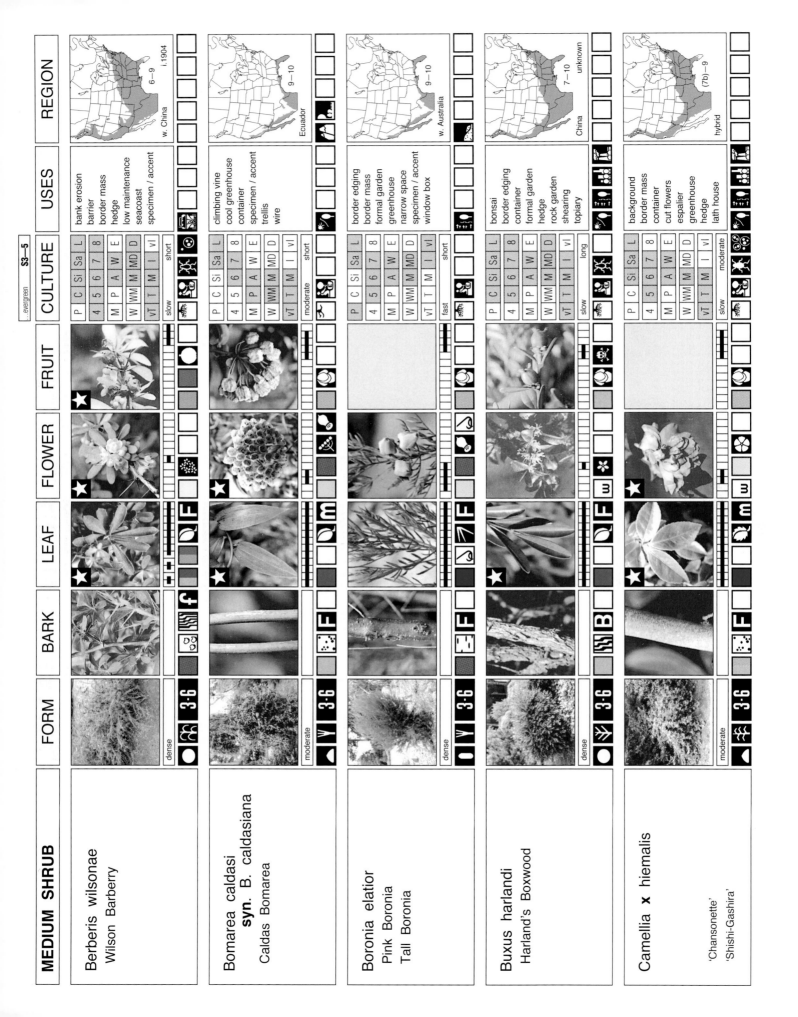

Berberis wilsonae
Wilson Barberry

- FORM: dense — 3-6
- CULTURE: P C Si Sa L / 4 5 6 7 8 / M P A W E / W WM M MD D / vT T M I vl — slow, short
- USES: bank erosion, barrier, border mass, hedge, low maintenance, seacoast, specimen / accent
- REGION: w. China — 6—9, i.1904

Bomarea caldasi **syn.** B. caldasiana
Caldas Bomarea

- FORM: moderate — 3-6
- CULTURE: P C Si Sa L / 4 5 6 7 8 / M P A W E / W WM M MD D / vT T M I vl — moderate, short
- USES: climbing vine, cool greenhouse, container, specimen / accent, trellis, wire
- REGION: Ecuador — 9—10

Boronia elatior
Pink Boronia
Tall Boronia

- FORM: dense — 3-6
- CULTURE: P C Si Sa L / 4 5 6 7 8 / M P A W E / W WM M MD D / vT T M I vl — fast, short
- USES: border edging, border mass, formal garden, greenhouse, narrow space, specimen / accent, window box
- REGION: w. Australia — 9—10

Buxus harlandi
Harland's Boxwood

- FORM: dense — 3-6
- CULTURE: P C Si Sa L / 4 5 6 7 8 / M P A W E / W WM M MD D / vT T M I vl — slow, long
- USES: bonsai, border edging, container, formal garden, hedge, rock garden, shearing, topiary
- REGION: China — 7—10, unknown

Camellia **x** **hiemalis**
'Chansonette'
'Shishi-Gashira'

- FORM: moderate — 3-6
- CULTURE: P C Si Sa L / 4 5 6 7 8 / M P A W E / W WM M MD D / vT T M I vl — slow, moderate
- USES: background, border mass, container, cut flowers, espalier, greenhouse, hedge, lath house
- REGION: hybrid — (7b)—9

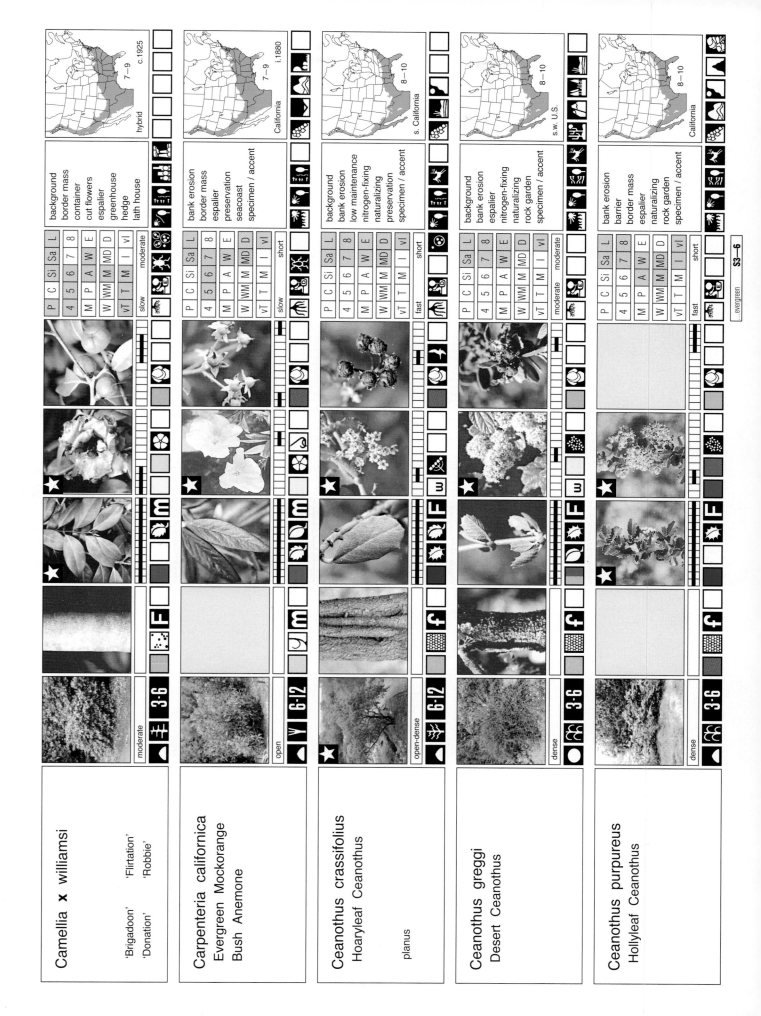

MEDIUM SHRUB	FORM	BARK	LEAF	FLOWER	FRUIT	CULTURE	USES	REGION

Ceanothus ramulosus
Coast Ceanothus

fasciculatus

USES: espalier, naturalizing, seacoast

CULTURE: P C Si Sa L · 4 5 6 7 8 · M P A W E · W WM M MD D · vT T M I vl · moderate / short

REGION: California · 8–10

**Chamaecyparis obtusa
'Compacta'**
Compact Hinoki Falsecypress
Compact Hinoki Cypress

dense

USES: bonsai, container, formal garden, oriental garden, rock garden, specimen / accent

CULTURE: P C Si Sa L · 4 5 6 7 8 · M P A W E · W WM M MD D · vT T M I vl · slow / long

REGION: cultivar · 4–9 · c.1875

**Chamaecyparis obtusa
'Nana Gracilis'**
Dwarf Slender Hinoki
         Falsecypress

dense

USES: bonsai, container, formal garden, oriental garden, rock garden, specimen / accent

CULTURE: P C Si Sa L · 4 5 6 7 8 · M P A W E · W WM M MD D · vT T M I vl · slow / long

REGION: cultivar · 4b–8 · c.1863

**Chamaecyparis obtusa
'Nana Torulosa'**

dense

USES: bonsai, container, formal garden, oriental garden, rock garden, specimen / accent

CULTURE: P C Si Sa L · 4 5 6 7 8 · M P A W E · W WM M MD D · vT T M I vl · slow / long

REGION: cultivar · 4–8

**Chamaedorea brachypoda
syn. C. stolonifera**

USES: container, greenhouse, house plant, pool garden, screen, seacoast, specimen / accent

CULTURE: P C Si Sa L · 4 5 6 7 8 · M P A W E · W WM M MD D · vT T M I vl · fast / moderate

REGION: Guatemala · 9–10

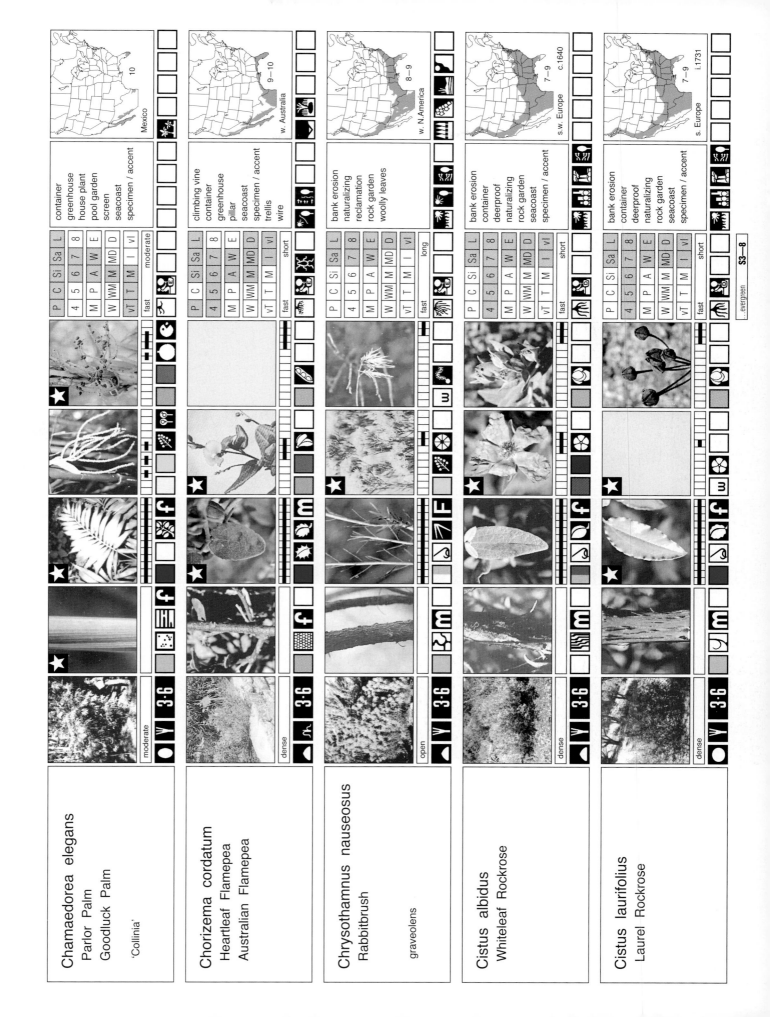

Chamaedorea elegans
Parlor Palm
Goodluck Palm

'Collinia'

container
greenhouse
house plant
pool garden
screen
seacoast
specimen / accent

P	C	Si	Sa	L
4	5	6	7	8
M	P	A	W	E
W	WM	M	MD	D
vT	T	M	I	vl

fast ___ moderate

Mexico 10

moderate · 3·6

Chorizema cordatum
Heartleaf Flamepea
Australian Flamepea

climbing vine
container
greenhouse
pillar
seacoast
specimen / accent
trellis
wire

P	C	Si	Sa	L
4	5	6	7	8
M	P	A	W	E
W	WM	M	MD	D
vT	T	M	I	vl

fast ___ short

w. Australia 9–10

dense · 3·6

Chrysothamnus nauseosus
Rabbitbrush

graveolens

bank erosion
naturalizing
reclamation
rock garden
woolly leaves

P	C	Si	Sa	L
4	5	6	7	8
M	P	A	W	E
W	WM	M	MD	D
vT	T	M	I	vl

fast ___ long

w. N.America 8–9

open · 3·6

Cistus albidus
Whiteleaf Rockrose

bank erosion
container
deerproof
naturalizing
rock garden
seacoast
specimen / accent

P	C	Si	Sa	L
4	5	6	7	8
M	P	A	W	E
W	WM	M	MD	D
vT	T	M	I	vl

fast ___ short

s.w. Europe c.1640 7–9

dense · 3·6

Cistus laurifolius
Laurel Rockrose

bank erosion
container
deerproof
naturalizing
rock garden
seacoast
specimen / accent

P	C	Si	Sa	L
4	5	6	7	8
M	P	A	W	E
W	WM	M	MD	D
vT	T	M	I	vl

fast ___ short

s. Europe i.1731 7–9

dense · 3·6

...evergreen   **S3—8**

MEDIUM SHRUB	FORM	BARK	LEAF	FLOWER	FRUIT	CULTURE	USES	REGION

Cistus populifolius
Poplarleaf Rockrose

- FORM: dense — 3·6
- CULTURE: P C Si Sa L / 4 5 6 7 8 / M P A W E / W WM M MD D / vT T M I vl — fast / short
- USES: bank erosion, border mass, container, deerproof, rock garden, screen, seacoast, specimen / accent
- REGION: France — c.1634 — 8–10

Cistus x purpureus
Purple Rockrose
Orchid Rockrose

- FORM: dense — 3·6
- CULTURE: P C Si Sa L / 4 5 6 7 8 / M P A W E / W WM M MD D / vT T M I vl — fast / short
- USES: bank erosion, border mass, container, deerproof, rock garden, screen, seacoast, specimen / accent
- REGION: hybrid — i.1790 — 8b–9

Clerodendrum bungei
syn. C. foetidum
Cashmere Bouquet
Rose Glorybower

- FORM: moderate — 3·6
- CULTURE: P C Si Sa L / 4 5 6 7 8 / M P A W E / W WM M MD D / vT T M I vl — fast / short
- USES: border mass, greenhouse, screen, specimen / accent
- REGION: China — i.1844 — 8–10

Codiaeum variegatum
Croton
Variegated Croton
'Kentucky'   'Pitcairn'
'Monarch'   'Polychrome'

- FORM: open — 3·6
- CULTURE: P C Si Sa L / 4 5 6 7 8 / M P A W E / W WM M MD D / vT T M I vl — slow / moderate
- USES: border mass, container, leaf arrangements, greenhouse, house plant, patio garden, pool garden, seacoast
- REGION: Pacific Islands — 10

Colletia armata

- FORM: open — 3·6
- CULTURE: P C Si Sa L / 4 5 6 7 8 / M P A W E / W WM M MD D / vT T M I vl — fast / short
- USES: barrier, container, cool greenhouse, specimen / accent
- REGION: Chile — 7–10

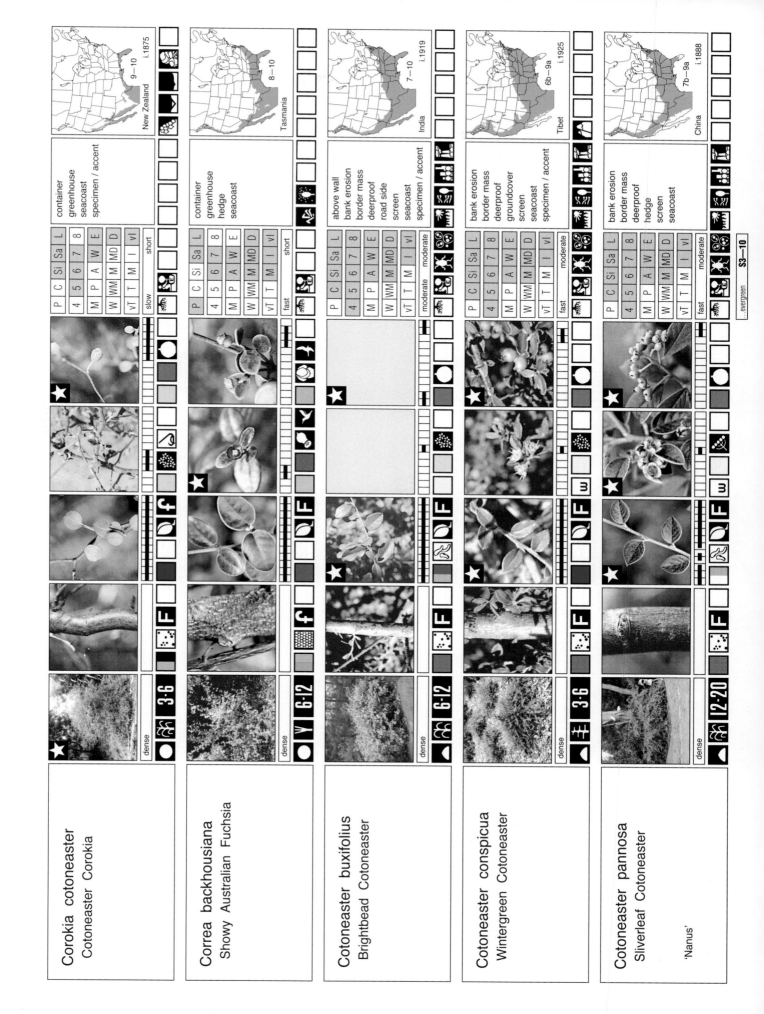

Corokia cotoneaster — Cotoneaster Corokia

container / greenhouse / seacoast / specimen / accent

P	C	Si	Sa	L
4	5	6	7	8
M		P	A	E
W	WM	M	MD	D
vT	T	M	I	vI

slow · short · dense · 3-6

New Zealand · 9–10 · i.1875

Correa backhousiana — Showy Australian Fuchsia

container / greenhouse / hedge / seacoast

P	C	Si	Sa	L
4	5	6	7	8
M		P	A	E
W	WM	M	MD	D
vT	T	M	I	vI

fast · short · dense · 6-12

Tasmania · 8–10

Cotoneaster buxifolius — Brightbead Cotoneaster

above wall / bank erosion / border mass / deerproof / road side / screen / seacoast / specimen / accent

P	C	Si	Sa	L
4	5	6	7	8
M		P	A	E
W	WM	M	MD	D
vT	T	M	I	vI

moderate · moderate · dense · 6-12

India · 7–10 · i.1919

Cotoneaster conspicua — Wintergreen Cotoneaster

bank erosion / border mass / deerproof / groundcover / screen / seacoast / specimen / accent

P	C	Si	Sa	L
4	5	6	7	8
M		P	A	E
W	WM	M	MD	D
vT	T	M	I	vI

fast · moderate · dense · 3-6

Tibet · 6b–9a · i.1925

Cotoneaster pannosa — Silverleaf Cotoneaster

'Nanus'

bank erosion / border mass / deerproof / hedge / screen / seacoast

P	C	Si	Sa	L
4	5	6	7	8
M		P	A	E
W	WM	M	MD	D
vT	T	M	I	vI

fast · moderate · dense · 12-20

China · 7b–9a · i.1888

MEDIUM SHRUB	FORM	BARK	LEAF	FLOWER	FRUIT	CULTURE	USES	REGION

Daphne x burkwoodi
Burkwood Daphne

'Carol Mackie'
'Somerset'

FORM: open · 3-6
CULTURE:
P	C	Si	Sa	L
4	5	6	7	8
M	P	A	W	E
W	WM	M	MD	D
vT	T	M	l	vl
moderate · short

USES: border mass / container / patio garden / rock garden / shade garden / specimen / accent

REGION: hybrid · 4b–9 · o.1935

Daphne odora
Winter Daphne

'Alba'
'Aureo-Marginata'

FORM: open · 3-6
CULTURE:
P	C	Si	Sa	L
4	5	6	7	8
M	P	A	W	E
W	WM	M	MD	D
vT	T	M	l	vl
slow · short

USES: border mass / container / greenhouse / rock garden / seacoast / shade garden / specimen / accent

REGION: China · 7–9 · i.1771

Dasylirion wheeleri
Desert Spoon
Spoonflower

FORM: open · 3-6
CULTURE:
P	C	Si	Sa	L
4	5	6	7	8
M	P	A	W	E
W	WM	M	MD	D
vT	T	M	l	vl
slow · moderate

USES: container / dried flowers / leaf arrangements / patio garden / pool garden / rock garden / specimen / accent / warm greenhouse

REGION: s.w. U.S. · 8–10

Dioon edule
Chestnut Dioon

FORM: dense · 3-6
CULTURE:
P	C	Si	Sa	L
4	5	6	7	8
M	P	A	W	E
W	WM	M	MD	D
vT	T	M	l	vl
very slow · long

USES: barrier / container / greenhouse / house plant / must cook fruit / specimen / accent

REGION: Central America · 9b–10

Dracaena umbragulifera

FORM: open · 3-6
CULTURE:
P	C	Si	Sa	L
4	5	6	7	8
M	P	A	W	E
W	WM	M	MD	D
vT	T	M	l	vl
slow · long

USES: container / greenhouse / house plant / narrow space / sculptural / specimen / accent

REGION: Java · 9–10

Echium fastuosum
Pride-of-Madeira

Canary Islands · 9—10

bank erosion
border mass
container
groupings
naturalizing
sculptural
seacoast
specimen / accent

P	C	Si	Sa	L
4	5	6	7	8
M	P	A	W	E
W	WM	M	MD	D
vT	T	M	I	vI

fast · short
dense · 6-12

Encelia farinosa
Brittlebush
Desert Encelia

s.w. U.S. · 9—10

groupings
naturalizing
seacoast
specimen / accent

P	C	Si	Sa	L
4	5	6	7	8
M	P	A	W	E
W	WM	M	MD	D
vT	T	M	I	vI

fast · short
moderate · 3-6

Encephalartos ferox
Kaffirbread

s. Africa · 10

container
greenhouse
house plant
specimen / accent

P	C	Si	Sa	L
4	5	6	7	8
M	P	A	W	E
W	WM	M	MD	D
vT	T	M	I	vI

slow · long
dense · 3-6

Erica terminalis
Corsican Heather

Italy · i.1765 · 7—8

border edge
container
heath garden
seacoast
specimen / accent

P	C	Si	Sa	L
4	5	6	7	8
M	P	A	W	E
W	WM	M	MD	D
vT	T	M	I	vI

slow · short
dense · 3-6

Euonymus fortunei 'Sarcoxie'
Sarcoxie Wintercreeper

China · 5b—9

background
climbing vine
groupings
hedge
screen

P	C	Si	Sa	L
4	5	6	7	8
M	P	A	W	E
W	WM	M	MD	D
vT	T	M	I	vI

slow · short
moderate · 6-12

...evergreen

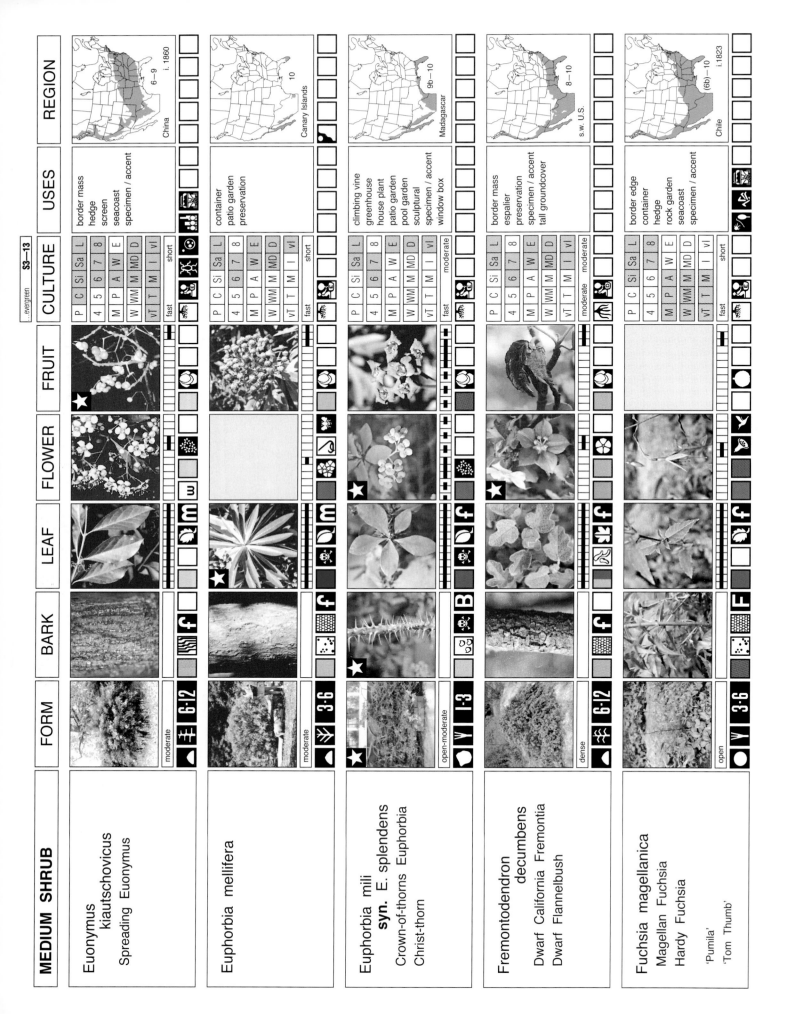

...evergreen **S3—13**

MEDIUM SHRUB	FORM	BARK	LEAF	FLOWER	FRUIT	CULTURE	USES	REGION

Euonymus kiautschovicus
Spreading Euonymus

- moderate — 6-12
- CULTURE: P C Si Sa L / 4 5 6 7 8 / M P A W E / W WM M MD D / vT T M I vl / fast — short
- USES: border mass / hedge / screen / seacoast / specimen / accent
- REGION: China 6—9 i. 1860

Euphorbia mellifera

- moderate — 3-6
- FLOWER: m
- CULTURE: P C Si Sa L / 4 5 6 7 8 / M P A W E / W WM M MD D / vT T M I vl / fast — short
- USES: container / patio garden / preservation
- REGION: Canary Islands 10

Euphorbia mili
syn. E. splendens
Crown-of-thorns Euphorbia
Christ-thorn

- open-moderate — 1-3
- CULTURE: P C Si Sa L / 4 5 6 7 8 / M P A W E / W WM M MD D / vT T M I vl / fast — moderate
- USES: climbing vine / greenhouse / house plant / patio garden / pool garden / sculptural / specimen / accent / window box
- REGION: Madagascar 9b—10

Fremontodendron decumbens
Dwarf California Fremontia
Dwarf Flannelbush

- dense — 6-12
- CULTURE: P C Si Sa L / 4 5 6 7 8 / M P A W E / W WM M MD D / vT T M I vl / moderate — moderate
- USES: border mass / espalier / preservation / specimen / accent / tall groundcover
- REGION: s.w. U.S. 8—10

Fuchsia magellanica
Magellan Fuchsia
Hardy Fuchsia

- 'Pumila'
- 'Tom Thumb'
- open — 3-6
- CULTURE: P C Si Sa L / 4 5 6 7 8 / M P A W E / W WM M MD D / vT T M I vl / fast — short
- USES: border edge / container / hedge / rock garden / seacoast / specimen / accent
- REGION: Chile (6b)—10 i.1823

Galphimia glauca
Rain-of-Gold

Mexico — 10

Uses: border edge, container, greenhouse, specimen / accent

P	C	Si	Sa	L
4	5	6	7	8
M	P	A	W	E
W	WM	M	MD	D
vT	T	M	I	vl

short — fast — moderate — 3·6

Gardenia jasminoides
Cape Jasmine
Common Gardenia
'Mystery'
'Radicans'

China — 8–10 — i.1761

Uses: container, dried flowers, espalier, hedge, raised beds, screen, seacoast, specimen / accent

P	C	Si	Sa	L
4	5	6	7	8
M	P	A	W	E
W	WM	M	MD	D
vT	T	M	I	vl

moderate — moderate — moderate — 3·6

Gaultheria shallon
Salal Wintergreen
Shallon

w.N.America — 7–8 — i.1826

Uses: bank erosion, border mass, leaf arrangements, seacoast, specimen / accent, tall groundcover

P	C	Si	Sa	L
4	5	6	7	8
M	P	A	W	E
W	WM	M	MD	D
vT	T	M	I	vl

moderate — short — fast — open — 3·6

Gordonia axillaris

Vietnam — 8b–10

Uses: screen, specimen / accent

P	C	Si	Sa	L
4	5	6	7	8
M	P	A	W	E
W	WM	M	MD	D
vT	T	M	I	vl

moderate — moderate — moderate — 3·6

Grevillea aquifolium
Hollyleaved Grevillea

Australia — 9–10

Uses: bank erosion, barrier, container, greenhouse, hedge, house plant, patio garden

P	C	Si	Sa	L
4	5	6	7	8
M	P	A	W	E
W	WM	M	MD	D
vT	T	M	I	vl

slow — moderate — dense — 6·12

...evergreen

MEDIUM SHRUB

	FORM	BARK	LEAF	FLOWER	FRUIT	CULTURE	USES	REGION

Grevillea lanigera
Woolly Grevillea

- FORM: dense, 6-12
- CULTURE: P C Si Sa L / 4 5 6 7 8 / M P A W E / W WM M MD D / vT T M I vl / slow — moderate
- USES: bank erosion, barrier, container, fruit arrangement, greenhouse, hedge, patio garden, screen
- REGION: 9–10, Australia

Grevillea rosmarinifolia
Rosemary Grevillea

- FORM: dense, 12-20
- CULTURE: P C Si Sa L / 4 5 6 7 8 / M P A W E / W WM M MD D / vT T M I vl / slow — moderate
- USES: bank erosion, barrier, border mass, container, greenhouse, hedge, patio garden, screen
- REGION: 9–10, Australia

Grevillea thelemanniana
Hummingbird-bush
Spidernet Grevillea

- FORM: dense, 6-12
- CULTURE: P C Si Sa L / 4 5 6 7 8 / M P A W E / W WM M MD D / vT T M I vl / slow — moderate
- USES: attract butterflies, border mass, container, fruit arrangements, greenhouse, house plant, patio garden, seacoast
- REGION: 9–10, w. Australia

Grevillea victoriae
syn. G. miqueliana

- FORM: dense, 6-12
- CULTURE: P C Si Sa L / 4 5 6 7 8 / M P A W E / W WM M MD D / vT T M I vl / slow — moderate
- USES: bank erosion, border mass, container, greenhouse, hedge, screen, specimen / accent
- REGION: 9–10, Australia

Hakea purpurea
Purple Pincushion
Purple Hakea

- FORM: dense, 3-6
- CULTURE: P C Si Sa L / 4 5 6 7 8 / M P A W E / W WM M MD D / vT T M I vl / fast — short
- USES: barrier, background, fruit arrangements, screen
- REGION: 10, e. Australia

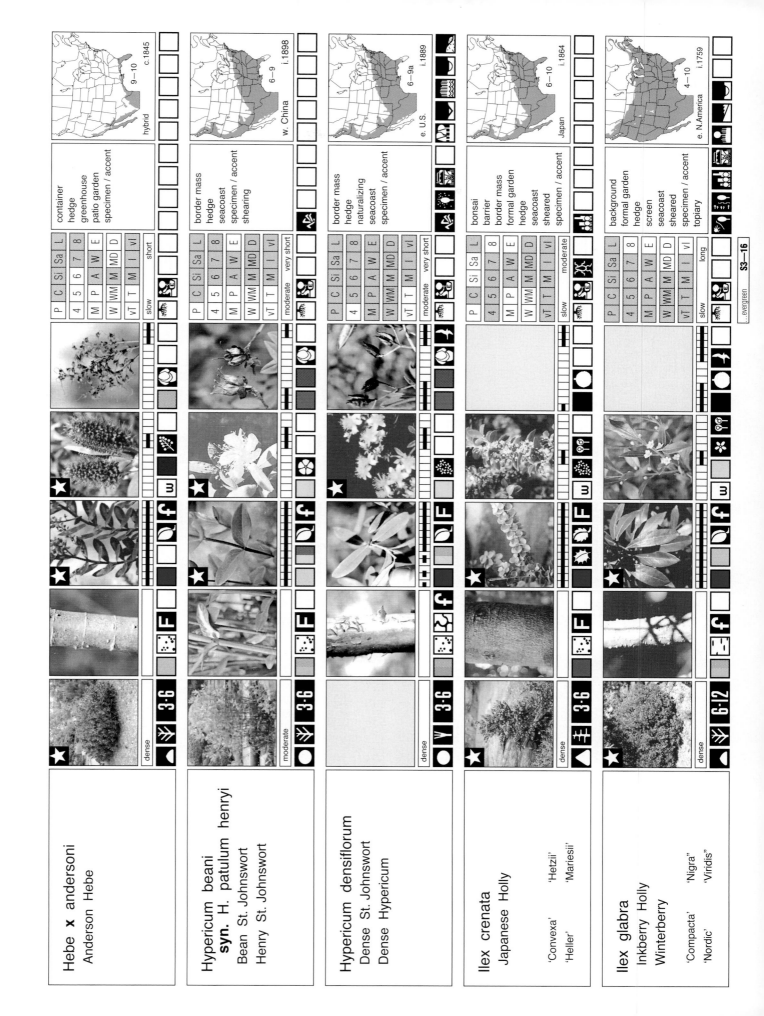

Hebe x andersoni
Anderson Hebe

container
hedge
greenhouse
patio garden
specimen / accent

hybrid   c.1845
9–10

Hypericum beani
syn. H. patulum henryi
Bean St. Johnswort
Henry St. Johnswort

border mass
hedge
seacoast
specimen / accent
shearing

w. China   i.1898
6–9

Hypericum densiflorum
Dense St. Johnswort
Dense Hypericum

border mass
hedge
naturalizing
seacoast
specimen / accent

e. U.S.   i.1889
6–9a

Ilex crenata
Japanese Holly

'Convexa'   'Hetzii'
'Heller'   'Mariesii'

bonsai
barrier
border mass
formal garden
hedge
seacoast
sheared
specimen / accent

Japan   i.1864
6–10

Ilex glabra
Inkberry Holly
Winterberry

'Compacta'   'Nigra'
'Nordic'   'Viridis'

background
formal garden
hedge
screen
seacoast
sheared
specimen / accent
topiary

e. N. America i.1759
4–10

...evergreen   S3—16

MEDIUM SHRUB	FORM	BARK	LEAF	FLOWER	FRUIT	CULTURE	USES	REGION

Ilex x meserveae
Blue Holly

'Blue Boy' 'Blue Maid'
'Blue Girl'

FORM: dense — 6-12

CULTURE:
P	C	Si	Sa	L
4	5	6	7	8
M	P	A	W	E
W	WM	M	MD	D
vT	T	M	I	vl

slow — moderate

USES:
background
border mass
formal garden
hedge
seacoast
sheared
specimen / accent
topiary

REGION: hybrid — 4b–8

Illicium parviflorum
Yellow Anisetree

FORM: moderate — 3-6

CULTURE:
P	C	Si	Sa	L
4	5	6	7	8
M	P	A	W	E
W	WM	M	MD	D
vT	T	M	I	vl

moderate — short

USES:
novelty
preservation
screen
specimen / accent

REGION: s.e. U.S. — 8b–10

Jasminum floridum
Showy Jasmine

FORM: open-moderate — 6-12

CULTURE:
P	C	Si	Sa	L
4	5	6	7	8
M	P	A	W	E
W	WM	M	MD	D
vT	T	M	I	vl

moderate

USES:
arbor
bank erosion
border mass
climbing vine
greenhouse
pillar
tall groundcover
trellis

REGION: China / Japan — 7–10   i.1850

Juniperus chinensis
'Ames'
Ames Juniper

FORM: dense — 3-6

CULTURE:
P	C	Si	Sa	L
4	5	6	7	8
M	P	A	W	E
W	WM	M	MD	D
vT	T	M	I	vl

slow — short

USES:
background
barrier
bonsai
formal garden
screen
seacoast

REGION: cultivar — 3b–8   c.1935

Juniperus chinensis
'Sea Green'
Sea Green Juniper

FORM: dense — 3-6

CULTURE:
P	C	Si	Sa	L
4	5	6	7	8
M	P	A	W	E
W	WM	M	MD	D
vT	T	M	I	vl

slow — moderate

USES:
bank erosion
barrier
bonsai
tall groundcover

REGION: cultivar — 3–9

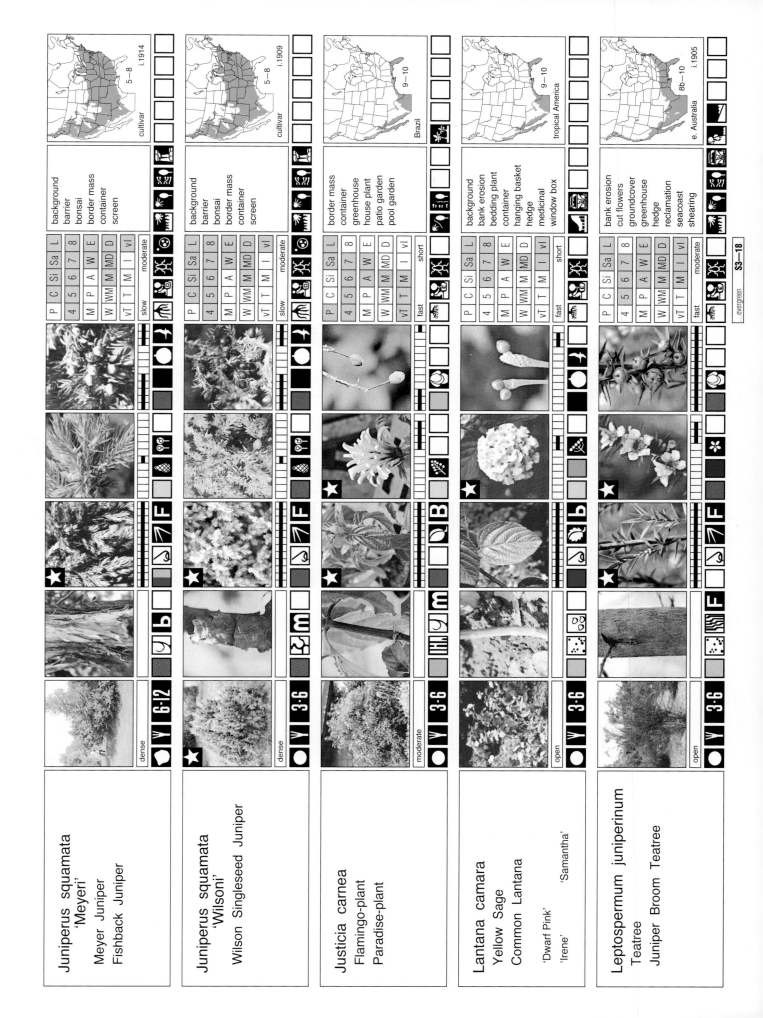

Juniperus squamata
'Meyeri'
Meyer Juniper
Fishback Juniper

background
barrier
bonsai
border mass
container
screen

P	C	Si	Sa	L
4	5	6	7	8
M	P	A	W	E
W	WM	M	MD	D
vT	T	M	I	vI

slow   moderate

cultivar   i.1914   5—8

dense   6-12

Juniperus squamata
'Wilsoni'
Wilson Singleseed Juniper

background
barrier
bonsai
border mass
container
screen

P	C	Si	Sa	L
4	5	6	7	8
M	P	A	W	E
W	WM	M	MD	D
vT	T	M	I	vI

slow   moderate

cultivar   i.1909   5—8

dense   3-6

Justicia carnea
Flamingo-plant
Paradise-plant

border mass
container
greenhouse
house plant
patio garden
pool garden

P	C	Si	Sa	L
4	5	6	7	8
M	P	A	W	E
W	WM	M	MD	D
vT	T	M	I	vI

fast   short

Brazil   9—10

moderate   3-6

Lantana camara
Yellow Sage
Common Lantana

'Dwarf Pink'
'Irene'   'Samantha'

background
bank erosion
bedding plant
container
hanging basket
hedge
medicinal
window box

P	C	Si	Sa	L
4	5	6	7	8
M	P	A	W	E
W	WM	M	MD	D
vT	T	M	I	vI

fast   short

tropical America   9—10

open   3-6

Leptospermum juniperinum
Teatree
Juniper Broom Teatree

bank erosion
cut flowers
groundcover
greenhouse
hedge
reclamation
seacoast
shearing

P	C	Si	Sa	L
4	5	6	7	8
M	P	A	W	E
W	WM	M	MD	D
vT	T	M	I	vI

fast   moderate

e. Australia   8b—10

open   3-6

...evergreen   **S3—18**

...evergreen **S3—19**

MEDIUM SHRUB	FORM	BARK	LEAF	FLOWER	FRUIT	CULTURE	USES	REGION

Leucospermum cordifolium
syn. L. nutans
Nodding Pincushion
Broadleaved Pincushion

open — 3·6

USES: cut flowers, sculptural, specimen / accent

REGION: 10

Leucothoe axillaris
syn. L. catesbaei
Coastal Leucothoe
'Compacta'

moderate — 6·12

CULTURE: slow

USES: bog garden, naturalizing, poisonous leaves, seacoast, sculptural, shade garden, specimen / accent, woodland garden

REGION: 7 — 9   i.1765   s.e. U.S.

Leucothoe fontanesiana
Fountain Leucothoe
Drooping Leucothoe
'Rainbow'
'Scarletta'

moderate — 6·12

CULTURE: slow

USES: bank erosion, border mass, cut flowers, hedge, sculptural, specimen / accent, tall groundcover, woodland garden

REGION: 5 — 8   i.1793   s.e. U.S.

Leucothoe keiskei
Keisk Leucothoe

moderate — 6·12

CULTURE: slow

USES: bank erosion, border mass, rock garden, specimen / accent, shade garden, tall groundcover, woodland garden

REGION: 6 — 9   i.1915   Japan

Ligustrum delavayanum
Delavay Privet

open-dense — 3·6

CULTURE: fast

USES: background, barrier, bonsai, border mass, hedge, screen, sheared, windbreak

REGION: 8 — 10   i.1890   w. China

CULTURE columns: P C Si Sa L | 4 5 6 7 8 | M P A W E | W WM M MD D | vT T M I vl | short / moderate / fast

Loropetalum chinense

China / Japan — i.1880 — 7b–10

Uses:
- container
- greenhouse
- hanging basket
- seacoast
- shade garden
- specimen / accent
- tall groundcover
- woodland garden

P	C	Si	Sa	L
4	5	6	7	8
M	P	A	W	E
W	WM	M	MD	D
vT	T	M	I	vl

moderate · short

dense · 3–6

Luculia pinceana

Nepal — i.1843 — 9–10

Uses:
- container
- cool greenhouse

P	C	Si	Sa	L
4	5	6	7	8
M	P	A	W	E
W	WM	M	MD	D
vT	T	M	I	vl

moderate · short

moderate · 3–6

Lupinus arboreus
Tree Lupine

California — c.1793 — 8–10

Uses:
- bank erosion
- border mass
- container
- hedge
- nitrogen-fixing
- naturalizing
- reclamation
- rock garden

P	C	Si	Sa	L
4	5	6	7	8
M	P	A	W	E
W	WM	M	MD	D
vT	T	M	I	vl

fast · short

dense · 6–12

X Mahoberberis aquacandidula

hybrid — i.1943 — 6–9a

Uses:
- armed leaves
- background
- barrier
- border edge
- leaf arrangement
- hedge
- specimen / accent

P	C	Si	Sa	L
4	5	6	7	8
M	P	A	W	E
W	WM	M	MD	D
vT	T	M	I	vl

slow · short

open-moderate · 3–6

X Mahoberberis aquisargentii

hybrid — 6b–9a

Uses:
- armed leaves
- background
- barrier
- border edge
- leaf arrangement
- hedge
- specimen / accent

P	C	Si	Sa	L
4	5	6	7	8
M	P	A	W	E
W	WM	M	MD	D
vT	T	M	I	vl

slow · short

moderate · 3–6

...evergreen

MEDIUM SHRUB	FORM	BARK	LEAF	FLOWER	FRUIT	CULTURE	USES	REGION

Mahonia aquifolium
Oregongrape Mahonia
Hollyleaf Mahonia

'Compacta'
'Mayhan'

moderate · 3·6

CULTURE: P C Si Sa L / 4 5 6 7 8 / M P A W E / W WM M MD D / vT T M I vl / slow short

USES: armed leaves / background / barrier / border mass / specimen / accent / seacoast / woodland garden / tall groundcover

REGION: n.w. N America / 5–9 / i.1823

Mahonia fremonti
Fremont Mahonia
Desert Mahonia

moderate · 3·6

CULTURE: P C Si Sa L / 4 5 6 7 8 / M P A W E / W WM M MD D / vT T M I vl / slow short

USES: bank erosion / background / barrier / border mass / hedge / naturalizing / specimen / accent

REGION: w. U.S. / 8–10 / c.1895

Mahonia higginsiae
Higgin's Mahonia

moderate · 3·6

CULTURE: P C Si Sa L / 4 5 6 7 8 / M P A W E / W WM M MD D / vT T M I vl / slow short

USES: background / bank erosion / barrier / border mass / hedge / naturalizing / preservation / specimen / accent

REGION: s. California / 8b–10

Mahonia lomariifolia
Burmese Mahonia

open-moderate · 3·6

CULTURE: P C Si Sa L / 4 5 6 7 8 / M P A W E / W WM M MD D / vT T M I vl / very slow

USES: background / barrier / border mass / hedge / sculptural / specimen / accent / seacoast

REGION: China / 8–10 / i.1931

Mahonia nevini
Nevin Mahonia

open · 3·6

CULTURE: P C Si Sa L / 4 5 6 7 8 / M P A W E / W WM M MD D / vT T M I vl / slow short

USES: background / bank erosion / barrier / border mass / hedge / naturalizing / preservation / specimen / accent

REGION: s. California / (7b)–10 / i.1928

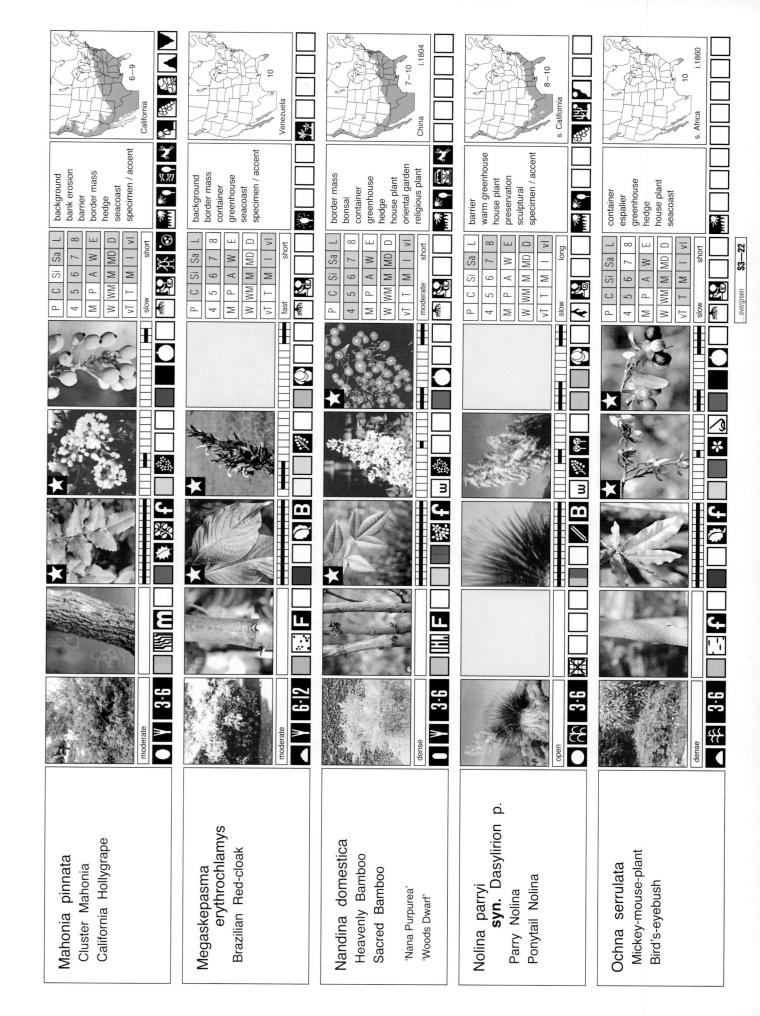

Mahonia pinnata
Cluster Mahonia
California Hollygrape

California — 6–9
moderate — 3·6

background
bank erosion
barrier
border mass
hedge
seacoast
specimen / accent

P	C	Si	Sa	L
4	5	6	7	8
M	P	A	W	E
W	WM	M	MD	D
vT	T	M	I	vI

slow — short

Megaskepasma erythrochlamys
Brazilian Red-cloak

Venezuela — 10
moderate — 6·12

background
border mass
container
greenhouse
seacoast
specimen / accent

P	C	Si	Sa	L
4	5	6	7	8
M	P	A	W	E
W	WM	M	MD	D
vT	T	M	I	vI

fast — short

Nandina domestica
Heavenly Bamboo
Sacred Bamboo

'Nana Purpurea'
'Woods Dwarf'

China — 7–10 i.1804
dense — 3·6

border mass
bonsai
container
greenhouse
hedge
house plant
oriental garden
religious plant

P	C	Si	Sa	L
4	5	6	7	8
M	P	A	W	E
W	WM	M	MD	D
vT	T	M	I	vI

moderate — short

Nolina parryi **syn.** Dasylirion p.
Parry Nolina
Ponytail Nolina

s. California — 8–10
open — 3·6

barrier
warm greenhouse
house plant
preservation
sculptural
specimen / accent

P	C	Si	Sa	L
4	5	6	7	8
M	P	A	W	E
W	WM	M	MD	D
vT	T	M	I	vI

slow — long

Ochna serrulata
Mickey-mouse-plant
Bird's-eyebush

s. Africa — 10 i.1860
dense — 3·6

container
espalier
greenhouse
hedge
house plant
seacoast

P	C	Si	Sa	L
4	5	6	7	8
M	P	A	W	E
W	WM	M	MD	D
vT	T	M	I	vI

slow — short

...evergreen

MEDIUM SHRUB	FORM	BARK	LEAF	FLOWER	FRUIT	CULTURE	USES	REGION

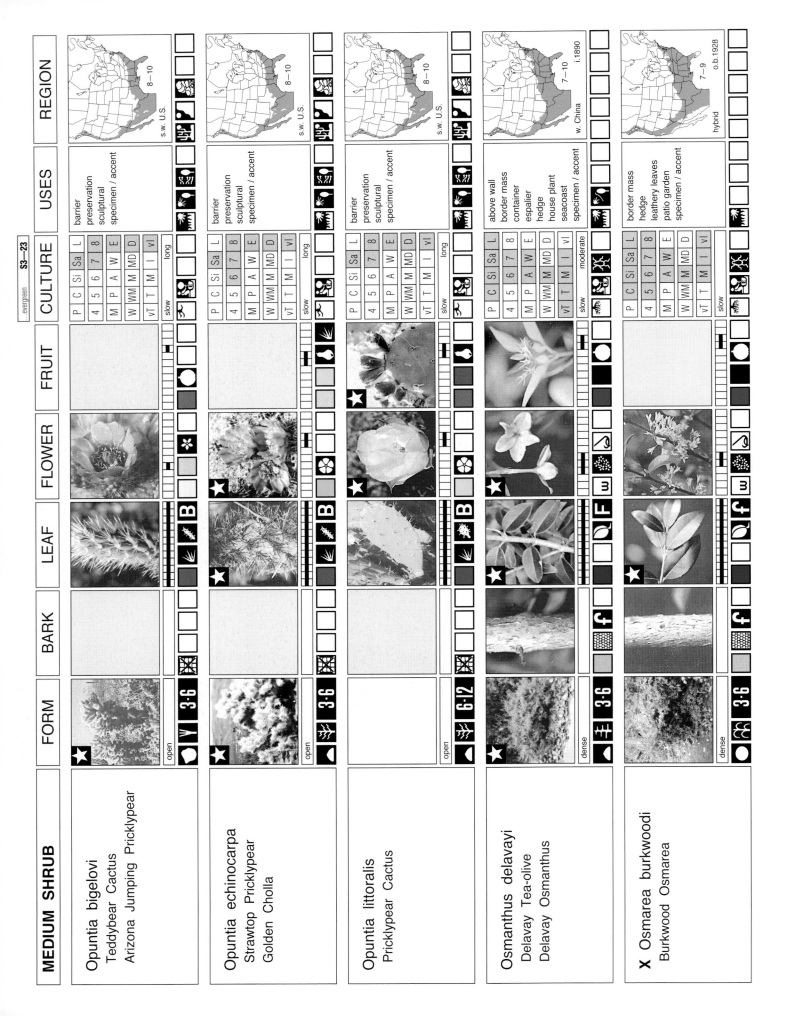

Opuntia bigelovi
Teddybear Cactus
Arizona Jumping Pricklypear

CULTURE: P C Si Sa L · 4 5 6 7 8 · M P A W E · W WM M MD D · vT T M I vl · slow · long
USES: barrier · preservation · sculptural · specimen / accent
REGION: 8–10 · s.w. U.S.
FORM: open · 3-6

Opuntia echinocarpa
Strawtop Pricklypear
Golden Cholla

CULTURE: P C Si Sa L · 4 5 6 7 8 · M P A W E · W WM M MD D · vT T M I vl · slow · long
USES: barrier · preservation · sculptural · specimen / accent
REGION: 8–10 · s.w. U.S.
FORM: open · 3-6

Opuntia littoralis
Pricklypear Cactus

CULTURE: P C Si Sa L · 4 5 6 7 8 · M P A W E · W WM M MD D · vT T M I vl · slow · long
USES: barrier · preservation · sculptural · specimen / accent
REGION: 8–10 · s.w. U.S.
FORM: open · 6-12

Osmanthus delavayi
Delavay Tea-olive
Delavay Osmanthus

CULTURE: P C Si Sa L · 4 5 6 7 8 · M P A W E · W WM M MD D · vT T M I vl · slow · moderate
USES: above wall · border mass · container · espalier · hedge · house plant · seacoast · specimen / accent
REGION: 7–10 · i.1890 · w. China
FORM: dense · 3-6

x Osmarea burkwoodi
Burkwood Osmarea

CULTURE: P C Si Sa L · 4 5 6 7 8 · M P A W E · W WM M MD D · vT T M I vl · slow
USES: border mass · hedge · leathery leaves · patio garden · specimen / accent
REGION: 7–9 · o.b.1928 · hybrid
FORM: dense · 3-6

Pelargonium quercifolium
Oakleaf Geranium
Almond Geranium

'Chocolate Mint'
'Fair Ellen'

aromatic bark
aromatic leaves
container
greenhouse
house plant
seacoast

s. Africa   9–10

Philodendron selloum **syn** P. evansi
Selloum Philodendron

'German Selloum'
'Miniature Selloum'   'Seaside'

container
climbing vine
exotic leaves
greenhouse
house plant
pool garden

s. Brazil   10

Phlomis fruiticosa
Jerusalem Sage

historic garden
hedge
seacoast

Mediterranean   8–10   c.1596

Phormium tenax
New Zealand Flax
New Zealand Hemp

'Purpureum'
'Variegatum'

border mass
container
greenhouse
house plant
pool garden
seacoast
specimen / accent

New Zealand   9–10   i.1789

Phygelius capensis
Cape Fuchsia

above wall
border edge
container
cool greenhouse
perennial garden
trellis

s. Africa   7–9   i.1855

...evergreen   S3–24

MEDIUM SHRUB	FORM	BARK	LEAF	FLOWER	FRUIT	CULTURE	USES	REGION

Picea abies 'Clanbrasiliana'

Barry Spruce

FORM: dense · 6-12

CULTURE: P C Si Sa L / 4 5 6 7 8 / M P A W E / W WM M MD D / vT T M I vl · very slow · long

USES: bonsai, background, formal garden, hedge, oriental garden, rock garden, screen, specimen / accent

REGION: cultivar · 4—7 · c.1798

Pieris floribunda

Mountain Pieris

Fetterbush

'Karenoma'

'Spring Snow'

FORM: dense · 6-12

CULTURE: P C Si Sa L / 4 5 6 7 8 / M P A W E / W WM M MD D / vT T M I vl · slow · short

USES: border mass, cut flowers, specimen / accent

REGION: s.e. U.S. · 5—7 · i.1800

Pinus strobus 'Nana'
syn. P. s. umbraculifera

Dwarf Eastern White Pine

FORM: dense · 6-12

CULTURE: P C Si Sa L / 4 5 6 7 8 / M P A W E / W WM M MD D / vT T M I vl · slow · moderate

USES: background, bonsai, container, formal garden, hedge, oriental garden, specimen / accent, rock garden

REGION: cultivar · 3b—9 · o.1855

Podocarpus nivalis

Snow Podocarpus

Alpine Totara Pine

FORM: dense · 3-6

CULTURE: P C Si Sa L / 4 5 6 7 8 / M P A W E / W WM M MD D / vT T M I vl · fast · moderate

USES: alpine garden, background, greenhouse, hedge, house plant, rock garden, screen, sheared

REGION: New Zealand · 7b—10

Polygala x dalmaisiana

Dalmais Polygala

Sweet Peashrub

FORM: dense · 3-6

CULTURE: P C Si Sa L / 4 5 6 7 8 / M P A W E / W WM M MD D / vT T M I vl · fast · short

USES: border edging, container, cool greenhouse, hedge, sheared

REGION: hybrid · 9—10

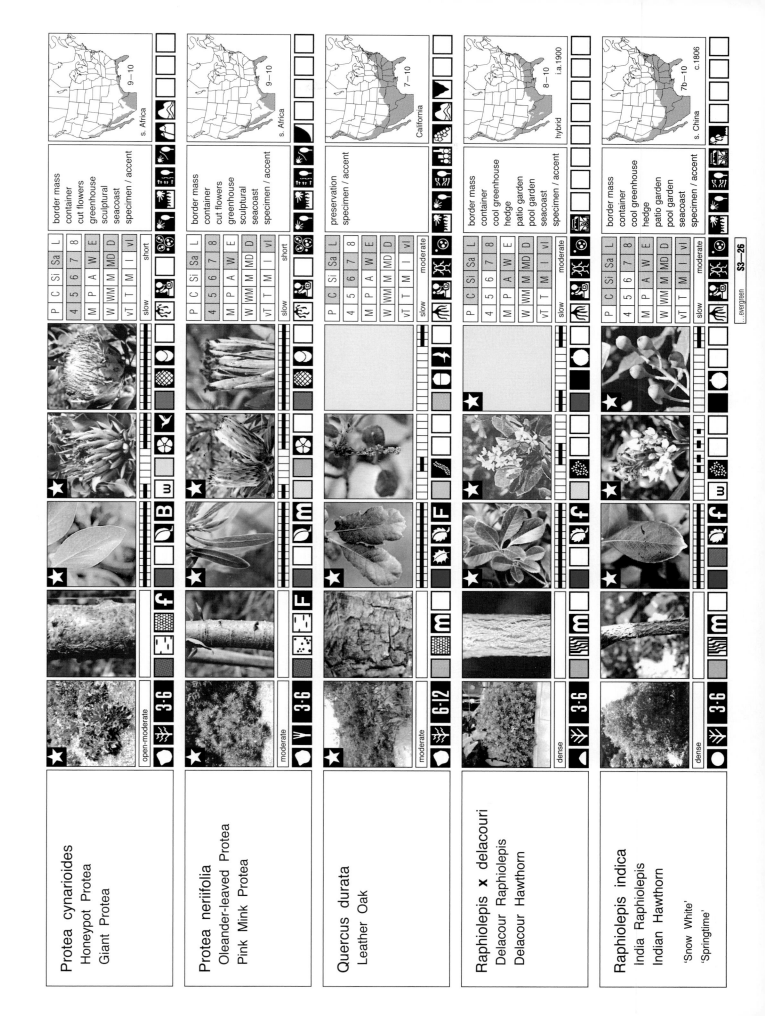

Protea cynarioides
Honeypot Protea
Giant Protea

border mass
container
cut flowers
greenhouse
sculptural
seacoast
specimen / accent

s. Africa   9—10

Protea neriifolia
Oleander-leaved Protea
Pink Mink Protea

border mass
container
cut flowers
greenhouse
sculptural
seacoast
specimen / accent

s. Africa   9—10

Quercus durata
Leather Oak

preservation
specimen / accent

California   7—10

Raphiolepis x delacouri
Delacour Raphiolepis
Delacour Hawthorn

border mass
container
cool greenhouse
hedge
patio garden
pool garden
seacoast
specimen / accent

hybrid   i.a.1900   8—10

Raphiolepis indica
India Raphiolepis
Indian Hawthorn

'Snow White'
'Springtime'

border mass
container
cool greenhouse
hedge
patio garden
pool garden
seacoast
specimen / accent

s. China   c.1806   7b—10

...evergreen   S3—26

MEDIUM SHRUB	FORM	BARK	LEAF	FLOWER	FRUIT	CULTURE	USES	REGION

Raphiolepis umbellata
Yeddo Raphiolepis
Yeddo Hawthorn
ovata

CULTURE: P C Si Sa L | 4 5 6 7 8 | M P A W E | W WM M MD D | vT T M I vl — slow · moderate
USES: border mass, container, cool greenhouse, hedge, patio garden, pool garden, seacoast, specimen / accent
REGION: Japan 8–9 i.1862
FORM: dense

Rhapis excelsa
syn. Chamaerops excelsa
Lady Palm

CULTURE: P C Si Sa L | 4 5 6 7 8 | M P A W E | W WM M MD D | vT T M I vl — slow
USES: border mass, container, greenhouse, house plant, patio garden, pool garden, shade garden, specimen / accent
REGION: Japan 10
FORM: moderate-dense

Rhododendron calophytum
Bigleaf Rhododendron

CULTURE: P C Si Sa L | 4 5 6 7 8 | M P A W E | W WM M MD D | vT T M I vl — slow
USES: border mass, poisonous leaves, shade garden, specimen / accent, woodland garden
REGION: w. China 7–8 i.1904
FORM: moderate-dense

Rhododendron
carolinianum
Carolina Rhododendron
'Album'
'M.L. Webb'

CULTURE: P C Si Sa L | 4 5 6 7 8 | M P A W E | W WM M MD D | vT T M I vl — moderate · short
USES: border mass, container, poisonous leaves, specimen / accent
REGION: N. Carolina 5b–8 c.1815
FORM: dense

Rhododendron ferrugineum
Rock Rhododendron
Alpine Rose

CULTURE: P C Si Sa L | 4 5 6 7 8 | M P A W E | W WM M MD D | vT T M I vl — slow · short
USES: alpine garden, border mass, poisonous leaves, rock garden, specimen / accent
REGION: Switzerland (4b)–7a c.1752
FORM: dense

Rhododendron indicum
Indian Rhododendron
Macranthum Azalea

'Balsaminiflorum'
'Rosaflora'

border mass
container
poisonous leaves
rock garden
shade garden
specimen / accent
woodland garden

P	C	Si	Sa	L
4	5	6	7	8
M	P	A	W	E
W	WM	M	MD	D
vT	T	M	I	vl

moderate   short

dense   6-12

6b—9   s. Japan   i.1883

Rhododendron japonicum
Japanese Azalea

border mass
container
poisonous leaves
shade garden
specimen / accent
woodland garden

P	C	Si	Sa	L
4	5	6	7	8
M	P	A	W	E
W	WM	M	MD	D
vT	T	M	I	vl

moderate   short

dense   3-6

5—8   Japan   i.1861

Rhododendron
    Kurume Hybrids
Kurume Hybrid Azaleas

'Hexe'   'Coral Bells'
'Snow'

border mass
container
poisonous leaves
shade garden
specimen / accent
woodland garden

P	C	Si	Sa	L
4	5	6	7	8
M	P	A	W	E
W	WM	M	MD	D
vT	T	M	I	vl

moderate   short

dense   3-6

6—9   hybrids   i.1920

Rhododendron x
    laetevirens
Wilson Rhododendron

'Laetevirens'

border mass
container
poisonous leaves
rock garden
shade garden
specimen / accent
woodland garden

P	C	Si	Sa	L
4	5	6	7	8
M	P	A	W	E
W	WM	M	MD	D
vT	T	M	I	vl

slow   short

dense   3-6

5—(8a)   hybrid

Rhododendron
    mucronatum
Snow Azalea

border mass
container
poisonous leaves
rock garden
shade garden
specimen / accent
woodland garden

P	C	Si	Sa	L
4	5	6	7	8
M	P	A	W	E
W	WM	M	MD	D
vT	T	M	I	vl

moderate   short

moderate   3-6

(6b)—9   Japan   i.1819

...evergreen   S3—28

MEDIUM SHRUB	FORM	BARK	LEAF	FLOWER	FRUIT	CULTURE	USES	REGION

Rhododendron 'P.J.M.'
P.J.M. Rhododendron
'Donna Totten'
'Split Rock'

- FORM: moderate, 3·6
- USES: border mass, container, poisonous leaves, rock garden, shade garden, specimen / accent, woodland garden
- CULTURE: P C Si Sa L / 4 5 6 7 8 / M P A W E / W WM M MD D / vT T M I vl / slow / short
- REGION: (4a)—7, cultivar

Rhododendron racemosum
Mayflower Rhododendron

- FORM: moderate, 3·6
- USES: border mass, container, poisonous leaves, rock garden, shade garden, specimen / accent, woodland garden
- CULTURE: P C Si Sa L / 4 5 6 7 8 / M P A W E / W WM M MD D / vT T M I vl / moderate / short
- REGION: 5—8, i.1889, Yunnan / China

Rosmarinus officinalis
Rosemary
'Albus'   'Arp'
'Prostratus'

- FORM: open, 1·3
- USES: background, bonsai, container, culinary, herb garden, medicinal, kitchen garden, patio garden
- CULTURE: P C Si Sa L / 4 5 6 7 8 / M P A W E / W WM M MD D / vT T M I vl / slow / moderate
- REGION: 7—9, Mediterranean, long c.

Salvia apiana
White Sage

- FORM: dense, 3·6
- USES: bank erosion, rock garden, seacoast, specimen / accent
- CULTURE: P C Si Sa L / 4 5 6 7 8 / M P A W E / W WM M MD D / vT T M I vl / fast / short
- REGION: 8—10, s. California

Salvia clevelandi
Cleveland Sage

- FORM: dense, 3·6
- USES: bank erosion, rock garden, seacoast, specimen / accent
- CULTURE: P C Si Sa L / 4 5 6 7 8 / M P A W E / W WM M MD D / vT T M I vl / fast / short
- REGION: 8—10, s. California

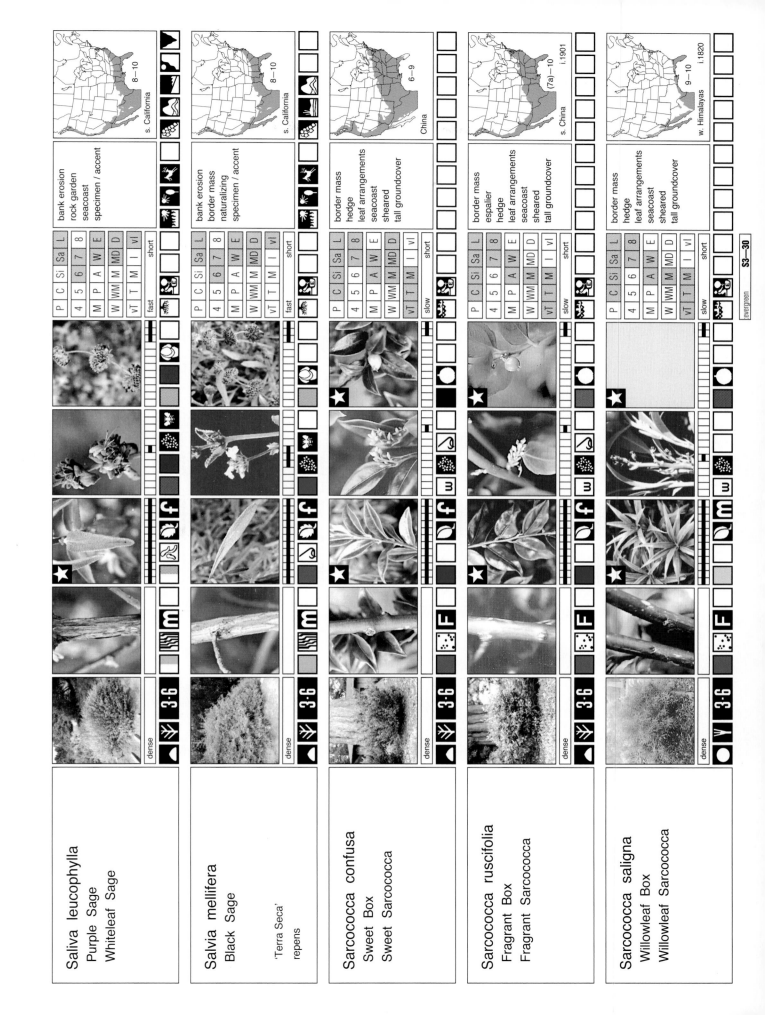

Salvia leucophylla
Purple Sage
Whiteleaf Sage

s. California
8–10

P	C	Si	Sa	L
4	5	6	7	8
M	P	A	W	E
W	WM	M	MD	D
vT	T	M	I	vI

fast   short   dense

3·6

bank erosion
rock garden
seacoast
specimen / accent

Salvia mellifera
Black Sage

'Terra Seca'
repens

s. California
8–10

P	C	Si	Sa	L
4	5	6	7	8
M	P	A	W	E
W	WM	M	MD	D
vT	T	M	I	vI

fast   short   dense

3·6

bank erosion
border mass
naturalizing
specimen / accent

Sarcococca confusa
Sweet Box
Sweet Sarcococca

China
6–9

P	C	Si	Sa	L
4	5	6	7	8
M	P	A	W	E
W	WM	M	MD	D
vT	T	M	I	vI

slow   short   dense

3·6

border mass
hedge
leaf arrangements
seacoast
sheared
tall groundcover

Sarcococca ruscifolia
Fragrant Box
Fragrant Sarcococca

s. China
(7a)–10   i.1901

P	C	Si	Sa	L
4	5	6	7	8
M	P	A	W	E
W	WM	M	MD	D
vT	T	M	I	vI

slow   short   dense

3·6

border mass
espalier
hedge
leaf arrangements
seacoast
sheared
tall groundcover

Sarcococca saligna
Willowleaf Box
Willowleaf Sarcococca

w. Himalayas
9–10   i.1820

P	C	Si	Sa	L
4	5	6	7	8
M	P	A	W	E
W	WM	M	MD	D
vT	T	M	I	vI

slow   short   dense

evergreen

border mass
hedge
leaf arrangements
seacoast
sheared
tall groundcover

MEDIUM SHRUB	FORM	BARK	LEAF	FLOWER	FRUIT	CULTURE	USES	REGION

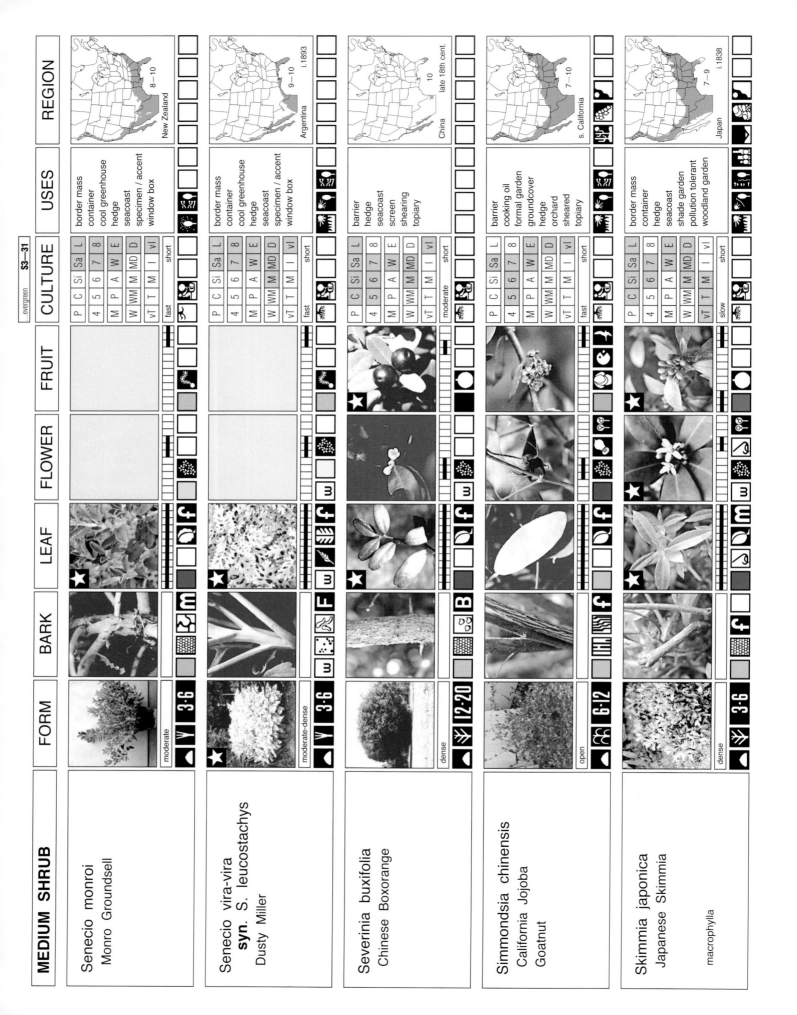

Senecio monroi
Monro Groundsell

moderate · 3-6

CULTURE: P C Si Sa L / 4 5 6 7 8 / M P A W E / W WM M MD D / vT T M I vI / fast / short

USES: border mass, container, cool greenhouse, hedge, seacoast, specimen / accent, window box

REGION: New Zealand 8–10

Senecio vira-vira
syn. S. leucostachys
Dusty Miller

moderate-dense · 3-6

CULTURE: P C Si Sa L / 4 5 6 7 8 / M P A W E / W WM M MD D / vT T M I vI / fast / short

USES: border mass, container, cool greenhouse, hedge, seacoast, specimen / accent, window box

REGION: Argentina i.1893 9–10

Severinia buxifolia
Chinese Boxorange

dense · 12-20

CULTURE: P C Si Sa L / 4 5 6 7 8 / M P A W E / W WM M MD D / vT T M I vI / moderate / short

USES: barrier, hedge, seacoast, screen, shearing, topiary

REGION: China late 18th cent. 10

Simmondsia chinensis
California Jojoba
Goatnut

open · 6-12

CULTURE: P C Si Sa L / 4 5 6 7 8 / M P A W E / W WM M MD D / vT T M I vI / fast / short

USES: barrier, cooking oil, formal garden, groundcover, hedge, orchard, sheared, topiary

REGION: s. California 7–10

Skimmia japonica
Japanese Skimmia

macrophylla

dense · 3-6

CULTURE: P C Si Sa L / 4 5 6 7 8 / M P A W E / W WM M MD D / vT T M I vI / slow / short

USES: border mass, container, hedge, seacoast, shade garden, pollution tolerant, woodland garden

REGION: Japan i.1838 7–9

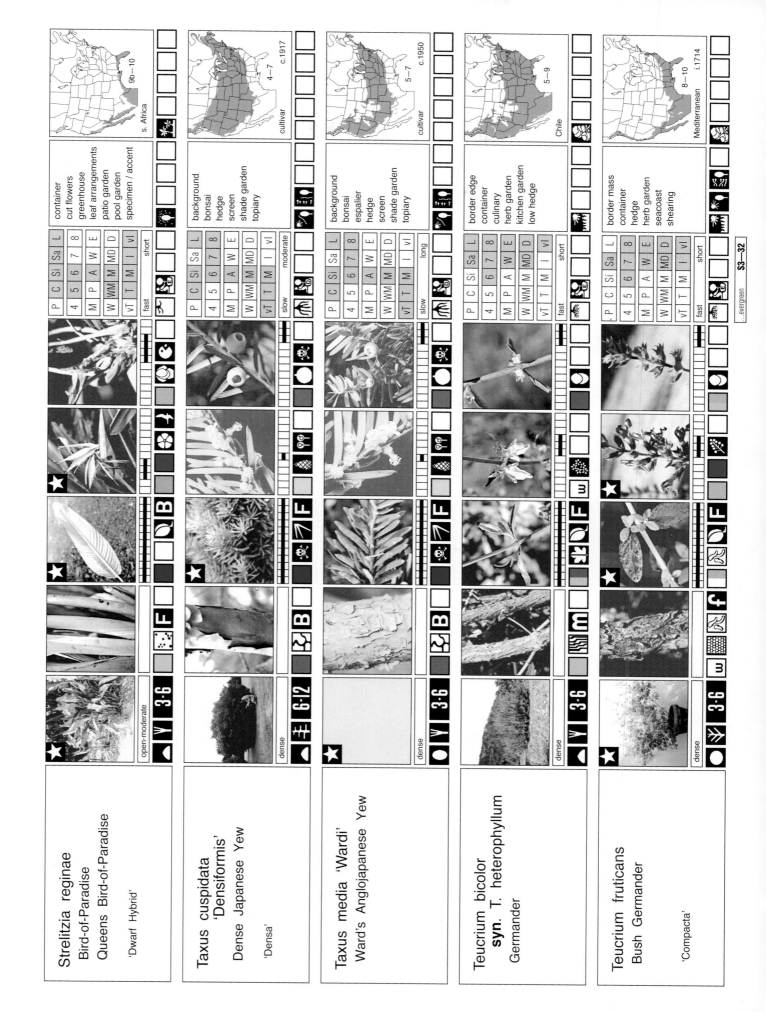

Strelitzia reginae
Bird-of-Paradise
Queens Bird-of-Paradise
'Dwarf Hybrid'

s. Africa — 9b–10

container / cut flowers / greenhouse / leaf arrangements / patio garden / pool garden / specimen / accent

P	C	Si	Sa	L
4	5	6	7	8
M	P	A	W	E
W	WM	M	MD	D
vT	T	M	I	vI

fast — short
open-moderate — 3-6

Taxus cuspidata 'Densiformis'
Dense Japanese Yew
'Densa'

cultivar — 4–7 — c.1917

background / bonsai / hedge / screen / shade garden / topiary

P	C	Si	Sa	L
4	5	6	7	8
M	P	A	W	E
W	WM	M	MD	D
vT	T	M	I	vI

slow — moderate
dense — 6-12

Taxus media 'Wardi'
Ward's Anglojapanese Yew

cultivar — 5–7 — c.1950

background / bonsai / espalier / hedge / screen / shade garden / topiary

P	C	Si	Sa	L
4	5	6	7	8
M	P	A	W	E
W	WM	M	MD	D
vT	T	M	I	vI

slow — long
dense — 3-6

Teucrium bicolor **syn.** T. heterophyllum
Germander

Chile — 5–9

border edge / container / culinary / herb garden / kitchen garden / low hedge

P	C	Si	Sa	L
4	5	6	7	8
M	P	A	W	E
W	WM	M	MD	D
vT	T	M	I	vI

fast — short
dense — 3-6

Teucrium fruticans
Bush Germander
'Compacta'

Mediterranean — 8–10 — i.1714

border mass / container / hedge / herb garden / seacoast / shearing

P	C	Si	Sa	L
4	5	6	7	8
M	P	A	W	E
W	WM	M	MD	D
vT	T	M	I	vI

fast — short
dense — 3-6

...evergreen — S3—32

MEDIUM SHRUB	FORM	BARK	LEAF	FLOWER	FRUIT	CULTURE	USES	REGION

Thuja occidentalis 'Globosa'
Globe Eastern Arborvitae

dense · 3-6

P	C	Si	Sa	L
4	5	6	7	8
M	P	A	W	E
W	WM	M	MD	D
vT	T	M	I	vI

moderate · long

Uses: background, bonsai, formal garden, hedge, screen, sheared

cultivar · 4–7 · c.1875

Thuja occidentalis 'Hoveyi'
Hovey Eastern Arborvitae

dense · 6-12

P	C	Si	Sa	L
4	5	6	7	8
M	P	A	W	E
W	WM	M	MD	D
vT	T	M	I	vI

moderate · moderate

Uses: bonsai, background, formal garden, hedge, screen, sheared

cultivar · 4–7 · c.1868

Thuja occidentalis 'Umbraculifera'
Umbrella Eastern Arborvitae

dense · 3-6

P	C	Si	Sa	L
4	5	6	7	8
M	P	A	W	E
W	WM	M	MD	D
vT	T	M	I	vI

moderate · moderate

Uses: background, bonsai, formal garden, hedge, screen, sheared, specimen / accent

cultivar · 4–7 · c.1892

Thuja occidentalis 'Woodwardi'
Woodward Arborvitae

dense · 6-12

P	C	Si	Sa	L
4	5	6	7	8
M	P	A	W	E
W	WM	M	MD	D
vT	T	M	I	vI

moderate · moderate

Uses: background, bonsai, formal garden, hedge, screen, sheared

cultivar · 4–7 · c.1871

Trichostema lanatum
Woolly Bluecurls
Romero

open · 3-6

P	C	Si	Sa	L
4	5	6	7	8
M	P	A	W	E
W	WM	M	MD	D
vT	T	M	I	vI

fast · short

Uses: border edging, perennial border, naturalizing, wild garden

California · 9–10

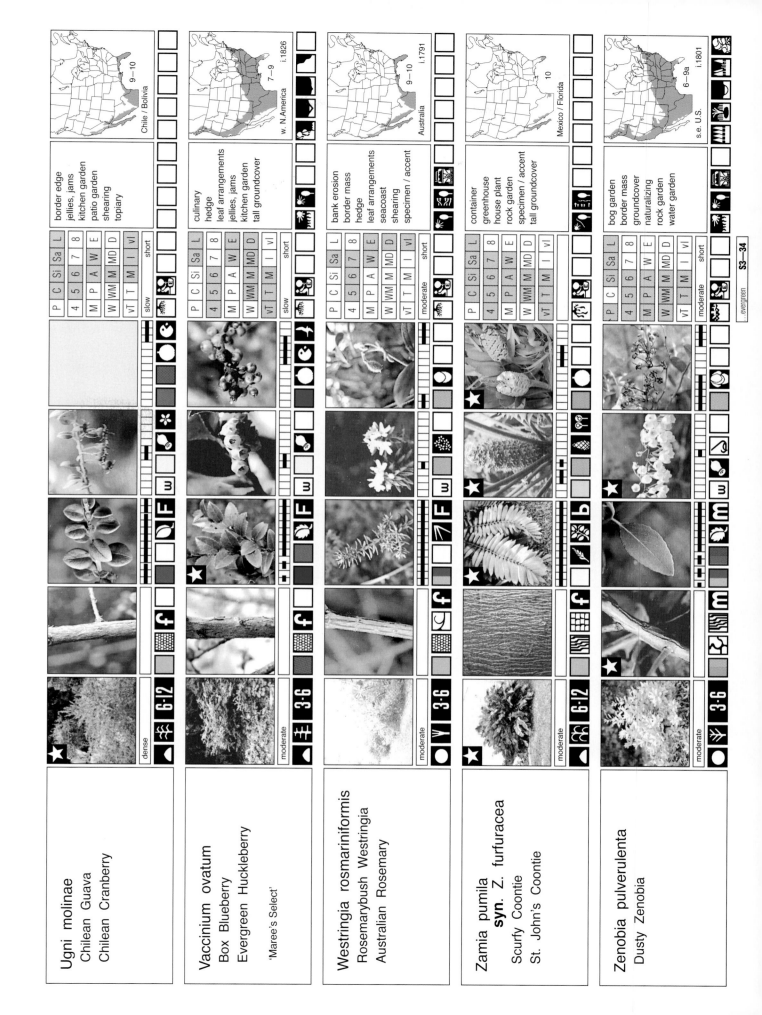

Ugni molinae
Chilean Guava
Chilean Cranberry

Chile / Bolivia 9-10

border edge
jellies, jams
kitchen garden
patio garden
shearing
topiary

P	C	Si	Sa	L
4	5	6	7	8
M	P	A	W	E
W	WM	M	MD	D
vT	T	M	I	vI

slow

dense 6-12

Vaccinium ovatum
Box Blueberry
Evergreen Huckleberry
'Maree's Select'

w. N.America i.1826 7-9

culinary
hedge
leaf arrangements
jellies, jams
kitchen garden
tall groundcover

P	C	Si	Sa	L
4	5	6	7	8
M	P	A	W	E
W	WM	M	MD	D
vT	T	M	I	vI

slow

moderate 3-6

Westringia rosmariniformis
Rosemarybush Westringia
Australian Rosemary

Australia i.1791 9-10

bank erosion
border mass
hedge
leaf arrangements
seacoast
shearing
specimen / accent

P	C	Si	Sa	L
4	5	6	7	8
M	P	A	W	E
W	WM	M	MD	D
vT	T	M	I	vI

moderate

moderate 3-6

Zamia pumila syn. Z. furfuracea
Scurfy Coontie
St. John's Coontie

Mexico / Florida 10

container
greenhouse
house plant
rock garden
specimen / accent
tall groundcover

P	C	Si	Sa	L
4	5	6	7	8
M	P	A	W	E
W	WM	M	MD	D
vT	T	M	I	vI

short

moderate 6-12

Zenobia pulverulenta
Dusty Zenobia

s.e. U.S. i.1801 6-9a

bog garden
border mass
groundcover
naturalizing
rock garden
water garden

P	C	Si	Sa	L
4	5	6	7	8
M	P	A	W	E
W	WM	M	MD	D
vT	T	M	I	vI

moderate

moderate 3-6

.. evergreen

SMALL SHRUB	FORM	BARK	LEAF	FLOWER	FRUIT	CULTURE	USES	REGION

Agapetes serpens
syn. Pentapterygium s.

- FORM: dense, 3-6
- CULTURE: P C Si Sa L / 4 5 6 7 8 / M P A W E / W WM M MD D / vT T M I vl — fast, short
- USES: above wall / bank erosion / container / greenhouse / hanging basket / heath garden
- REGION: Himalayas, 9–10

Agave deserti
Desert Agave

- FORM: dense, 1-3
- CULTURE: P C Si Sa L / 4 5 6 7 8 / M P A W E / W WM M MD D / vT T M I vl — slow, long
- USES: barrier / container / formal garden / greenhouse / rock garden / sculptural / specimen / accent
- REGION: w. U.S., 8b–10

Agave parryi
Mescal
Parry Agave

- FORM: dense, 1-3
- CULTURE: P C Si Sa L / 4 5 6 7 8 / M P A W E / W WM M MD D / vT T M I vl — slow, long
- USES: barrier / container / formal garden / greenhouse / rock garden / sculptural / specimen / accent
- REGION: s.w. U.S. / Mexico i.1868, 10–

Agave shawi
Shaw Agave

- FORM: dense, 1-3
- CULTURE: P C Si Sa L / 4 5 6 7 8 / M P A W E / W WM M MD D / vT T M I vl — slow, long
- USES: container / formal garden / greenhouse / preservation / rock garden / seacoast
- REGION: s.w. U.S., 8b–10

Agave utahensis
Utah Agave

- FORM: moderate, 1-3
- CULTURE: P C Si Sa L / 4 5 6 7 8 / M P A W E / W WM M MD D / vT T M I vl — slow, long
- USES: barrier / container / formal garden / greenhouse / rock garden / sculptural / specimen / accent
- REGION: s.w. U.S., 7a–10

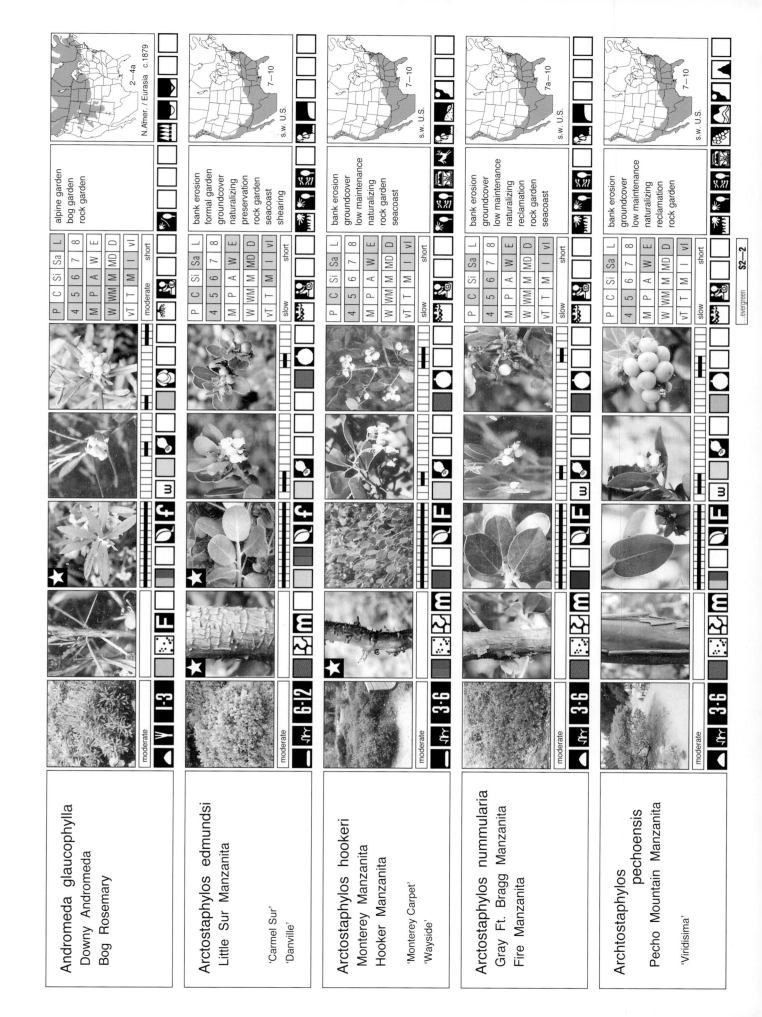

Andromeda glaucophylla
Downy Andromeda
Bog Rosemary

P	C	Si	Sa	L
4	5	6	7	8
M	P	A	W	E
W	WM	M	MD	D
vT	T	M	I	vI

moderate · short

alpine garden
bog garden
rock garden

2—4a
N. Amer. / Eurasia   c.1879

Arctostaphylos edmundsi
Little Sur Manzanita

'Carmel Sur'
'Danville'

P	C	Si	Sa	L
4	5	6	7	8
M	P	A	W	E
W	WM	M	MD	D
vT	T	M	I	vI

moderate · slow · short

bank erosion
formal garden
groundcover
naturalizing
preservation
rock garden
seacoast
shearing

7—10
s.w. U.S.

Arctostaphylos hookeri
Monterey Manzanita
Hooker Manzanita

'Monterey Carpet'
'Wayside'

P	C	Si	Sa	L
4	5	6	7	8
M	P	A	W	E
W	WM	M	MD	D
vT	T	M	I	vI

moderate · slow · short

bank erosion
groundcover
low maintenance
naturalizing
rock garden
seacoast

7—10
s.w. U.S.

Arctostaphylos nummularia
Gray Ft. Bragg Manzanita
Fire Manzanita

P	C	Si	Sa	L
4	5	6	7	8
M	P	A	W	E
W	WM	M	MD	D
vT	T	M	I	vI

moderate · slow · short

bank erosion
groundcover
low maintenance
naturalizing
reclamation
rock garden
seacoast

7a—10
s.w. U.S.

Archtostaphylos pechoensis
Pecho Mountain Manzanita

'Viridisima'

P	C	Si	Sa	L
4	5	6	7	8
M	P	A	W	E
W	WM	M	MD	D
vT	T	M	I	vI

moderate · slow · short

bank erosion
groundcover
low maintenance
naturalizing
reclamation
rock garden

7—10
s.w. U.S.

...evergreen   **S2—2**

SMALL SHRUB	FORM	BARK	LEAF	FLOWER	FRUIT	CULTURE	USES	REGION

Arctostaphylos pumila
Dune Manzanita
Sandmat Manzanita

dense-moderate · 3-6

bank erosion
border mass
groundcover
naturalizing
preservation
rock garden
seacoast
specimen / accent

P	C	Si	Sa	L
4	5	6	7	8
M	P	A	W	E
W	WM	M	MD	D
vT	T	M	I	vl

slow

s.w. U.S.   7–10   c.1933

Ardisia crispa
Coral Ardisia
Spiceberry

moderate · 3-6

bonsai
border mass
container
greenhouse
house plant
patio garden
specimen / accent
sunroom

P	C	Si	Sa	L
4	5	6	7	8
M	P	A	W	E
W	WM	M	MD	D
vT	T	M	I	vl

slow

Japan / Asia   9–10

Arundinaria variegata
syn. Pleioblastus fortunei
Dwarf Whitestripe Bamboo

dense · 6-12

bank erosion
bog garden
container
groundcover
pool garden
rock garden
seacoast
water garden

P	C	Si	Sa	L
4	5	6	7	8
M	P	A	W	E
W	WM	M	MD	D
vT	T	M	I	vl

fast

Japan   6b–10   c.1863

Arundinaria viridistriata
Dwarf Yellowstripe Bamboo

dense · 6-12

bank erosion
bog garden
container
groundcover
pool garden
rock garden
seacoast
water garden

P	C	Si	Sa	L
4	5	6	7	8
M	P	A	W	E
W	WM	M	MD	D
vT	T	M	I	vl

fast

Japan   7b–10   i.1870

Bauera rubioides
Dog Rose Bauera
River Rose Bauera

open · 6-12

bog garden
container
greenhouse
groundcover
hedge
rock garden
seacoast

P	C	Si	Sa	L
4	5	6	7	8
M	P	A	W	E
W	WM	M	MD	D
vT	T	M	I	vl

fast

Australia / s.Wales   9a–10

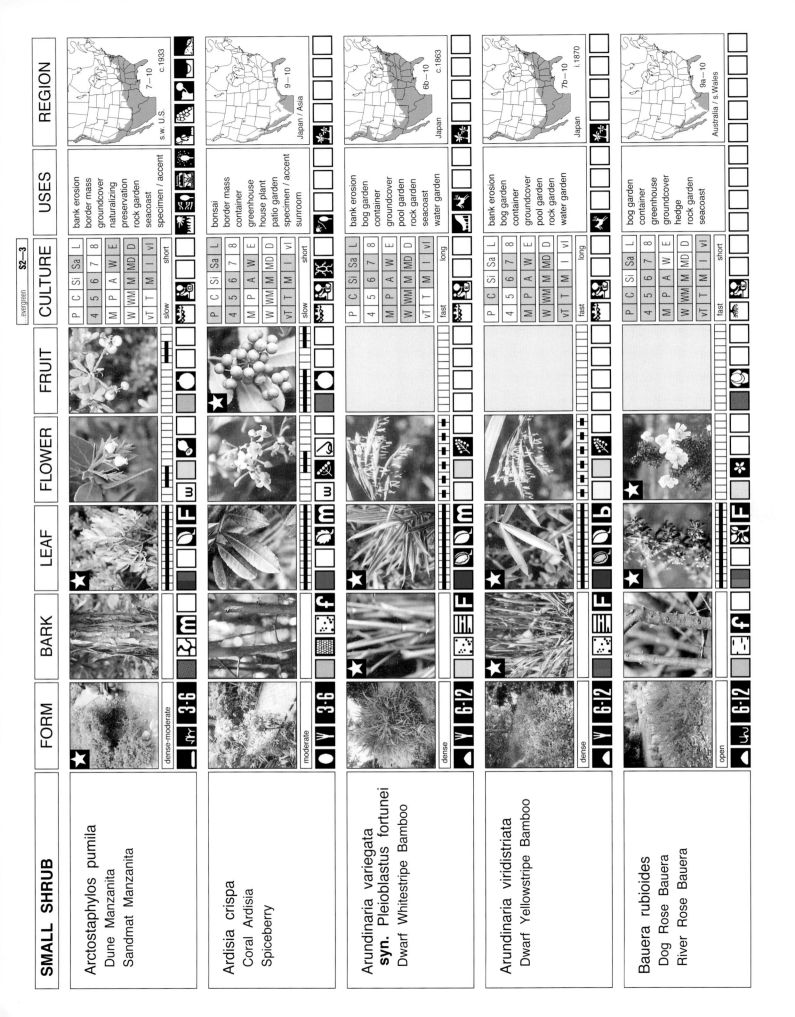

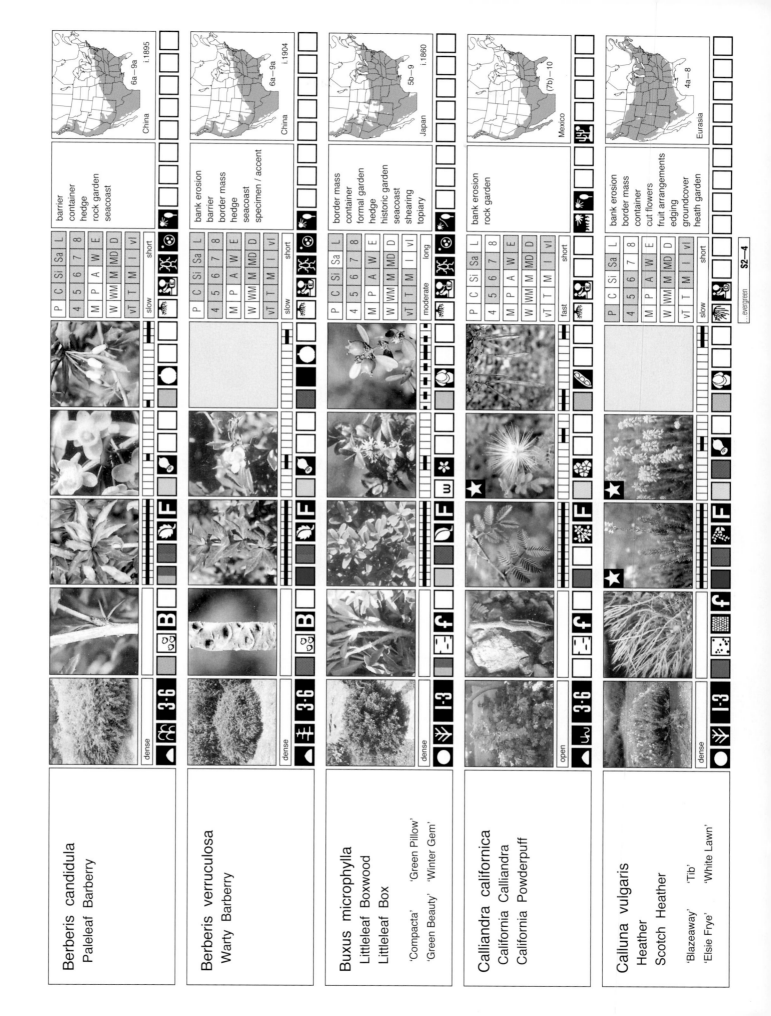

Berberis candidula — Paleleaf Barberry
barrier · container · hedge · rock garden · seacoast
6a–9a · i.1895 · China

P C Si Sa L / 4 5 6 7 8 / M P A W E / W WM M MD D / vT T M I vl · slow · short
dense · 3–6 · B · F

Berberis verruculosa — Warty Barberry
bank erosion · barrier · border mass · hedge · seacoast · specimen / accent
6a–9a · i.1904 · China

P C Si Sa L / 4 5 6 7 8 / M P A W E / W WM M MD D / vT T M I vl · slow · short
dense · 3–6 · B · F

Buxus microphylla — Littleleaf Boxwood · Littleleaf Box
'Compacta' · 'Green Pillow' · 'Green Beauty' · 'Winter Gem'
border mass · container · formal garden · hedge · historic garden · seacoast · shearing · topiary
5b–9 · i.1860 · Japan

P C Si Sa L / 4 5 6 7 8 / M P A W E / W WM M MD D / vT T M I vl · moderate · long
dense · I–3 · F

Calliandra californica — California Calliandra · California Powderpuff
bank erosion · rock garden
(7b)–10 · Mexico

P C Si Sa L / 4 5 6 7 8 / M P A W E / W WM M MD D / vT T M I vl · fast · short
open · 3–6 · F

Calluna vulgaris — Heather · Scotch Heather
'Blazeaway' · 'Tib' · 'Elsie Frye' · 'White Lawn'
bank erosion · border mass · container · cut flowers · fruit arrangements · edging · groundcover · heath garden
4a–8 · Eurasia

P C Si Sa L / 4 5 6 7 8 / M P A W E / W WM M MD D / vT T M I vl · slow · short
dense · I–3 · F

…evergreen

SMALL SHRUB	FORM	BARK	LEAF	FLOWER	FRUIT	CULTURE	USES	REGION

Calocephalus browni
Cushionbush
Silver Cushionbush
Browns Garlandflower

CULTURE: P C Si Sa L / 4 5 6 7 8 / M P A W E / W WM M MD D / vT T M I vI / fast / short
USES: border mass / edging / rock garden / seacoast / specimen / accent
REGION: Australia / 10

Catharanthus roseus
Rose Periwinkle
Old-Maid
'Dixieland' 'Little Hybrids'
'Linda' 'Morning Mist'

CULTURE: P C Si Sa L / 4 5 6 7 8 / M P A W E / W WM M MD D / vT T M I vI / fast / very short
USES: annual garden / border mass / container / greenhouse / groundcover / medicinal / seacoast / window box
REGION: India / 9a—10

Ceanothus leucodermis
Chaparral Ceanothus
Whitethorn Ceanothus

CULTURE: P C Si Sa L / 4 5 6 7 8 / M P A W E / W WM M MD D / vT T M I vI / fast / short
USES: bank erosion / barrier / groundcover / reclamation / rock garden
REGION: s.w. U.S. / 8—10

Ceratostigma griffithi
Burmese Plumbago
Griffith Ceratostigma

CULTURE: P C Si Sa L / 4 5 6 7 8 / M P A W E / W WM M MD D / vT T M I vI / fast / short
USES: border mass / container / edging / rock garden
REGION: Himalayas / 9a—10

Chamaecyparis lawsoniana 'Forsteckensis'
Forsteck Falsecypress
Forsteck Cypress

CULTURE: P C Si Sa L / 4 5 6 7 8 / M P A W E / W WM M MD D / vT T M I vI / slow / long
USES: aromatic leaves / formal garden / rock garden / shearing / specimen / accent
REGION: cultivar / 5—9 / c.1904

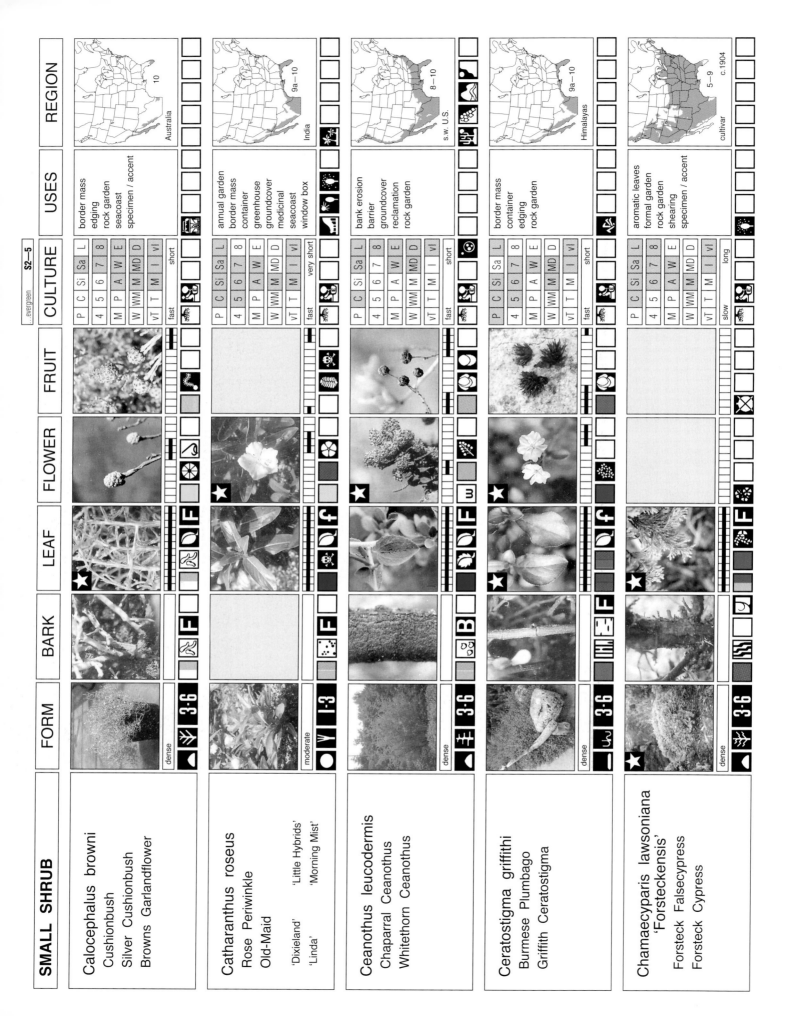

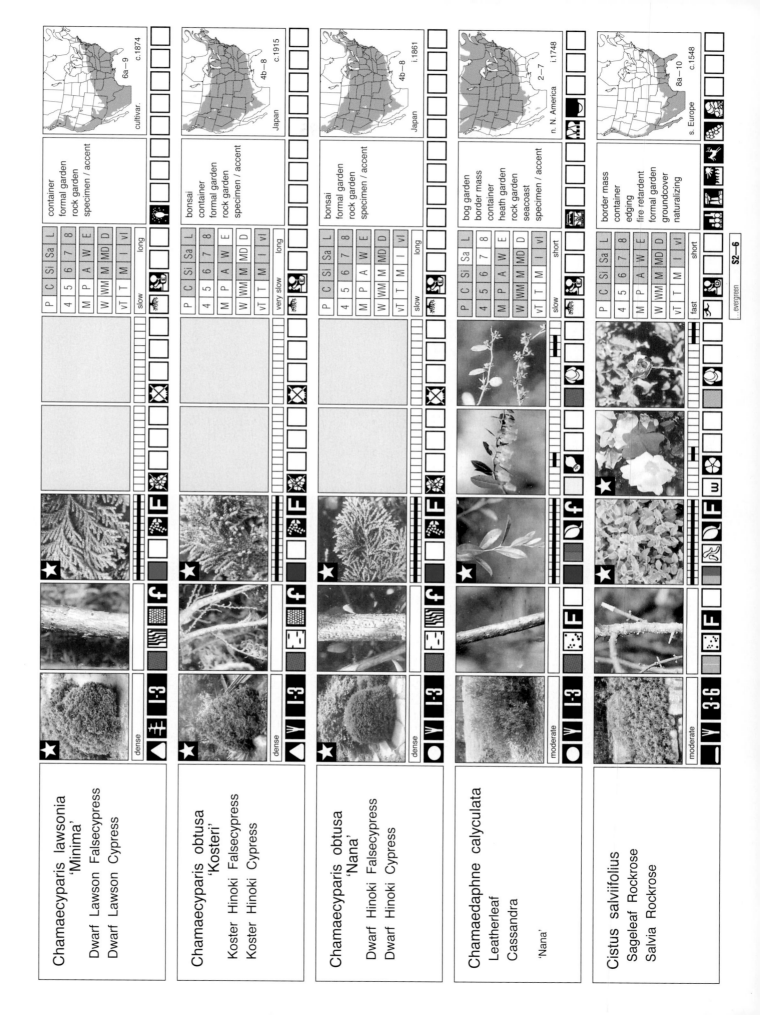

Chamaecyparis lawsonia 'Minima'

Dwarf Lawson Falsecypress
Dwarf Lawson Cypress

cultivar. c.1874 6a—9

container
formal garden
rock garden
specimen / accent

P	C	Si	Sa	L
4	5	6	7	8
M	P	A	W	E
W	WM	M	MD	D
vT	T	M	I	vI

slow • long
dense • 1-3

Chamaecyparis obtusa 'Kosteri'

Koster Hinoki Falsecypress
Koster Hinoki Cypress

Japan c.1915 4b—8

bonsai
container
formal garden
rock garden
specimen / accent

P	C	Si	Sa	L
4	5	6	7	8
M	P	A	W	E
W	WM	M	MD	D
vT	T	M	I	vI

very slow • long
dense • 1-3

Chamaecyparis obtusa 'Nana'

Dwarf Hinoki Falsecypress
Dwarf Hinoki Cypress

Japan i.1861 4b—8

bonsai
formal garden
rock garden
specimen / accent

P	C	Si	Sa	L
4	5	6	7	8
M	P	A	W	E
W	WM	M	MD	D
vT	T	M	I	vI

slow • long
dense • 1-3

Chamaedaphne calyculata

Leatherleaf
Cassandra

'Nana'

n. N. America i.1748 2—7

bog garden
border mass
container
heath garden
rock garden
seacoast
specimen / accent

P	C	Si	Sa	L
4	5	6	7	8
M	P	A	W	E
W	WM	M	MD	D
vT	T	M	I	vI

slow • short
moderate • 1-3

Cistus salviifolius

Sageleaf Rockrose
Salvia Rockrose

s. Europe c.1548 8a—10

border mass
container
edging
fire retardent
formal garden
groundcover
naturalizing

P	C	Si	Sa	L
4	5	6	7	8
M	P	A	W	E
W	WM	M	MD	D
vT	T	M	I	vI

fast • short
moderate • 3-6

evergreen .... **S2—6**

SMALL SHRUB	FORM	BARK	LEAF	FLOWER	FRUIT	CULTURE	USES	REGION

Coprosma x kirki
Kirks Coprosma
Creeping Coprosma
'Variegata'
'Verde Vista'

FORM: dense · 3·6
CULTURE: P C Si Sa L / 4 5 6 7 8 / M P A W E / W WM M MD D / vT T M I vI / fast short
USES: bank erosion, container, greenhouse, groundcover, hedge, house plant, rock garden, seacoast
REGION: Australia / N.Zealand · 9a–10

Correa alba
White Correa

FORM: open · 3·6
CULTURE: 4 5 6 7 8 / M P A W E / W WM M MD D / vT T M I vI / fast short
USES: container, edging, greenhouse, rock garden, seacoast
REGION: Australia · 8a–10 · i.1793

Correa x harrisi
Harris Correa

FORM: open · 3·6
CULTURE: P C Si Sa L / 4 5 6 7 8 / M P A W E / W WM M MD D / vT T M I vI / fast short
USES: container, edging, greenhouse, rock garden
REGION: hybrid · 9a–10

Cuphea hyssopifolia
False Heather
Hyssop Cuphea
'Purpurea'

FORM: dense · 3·6
CULTURE: P C Si Sa L / 4 5 6 7 8 / M P A W E / W WM M MD D / vT T M I vI / fast short
USES: bedding plant, border mass, container, cut flowers, edging, greenhouse, rock garden, window box
REGION: Mexico · 9b–10

Cuphea llavea **syn.** C. miniata
Cinnabar Cuphea

FORM: dense · 3·6
CULTURE: P C Si Sa L / 4 5 6 7 8 / M P A W E / W WM M MD D / vT T M I vI / fast short
USES: bedding plant, container, cut flowers, edging, rock garden, window box
REGION: Mexico · 10

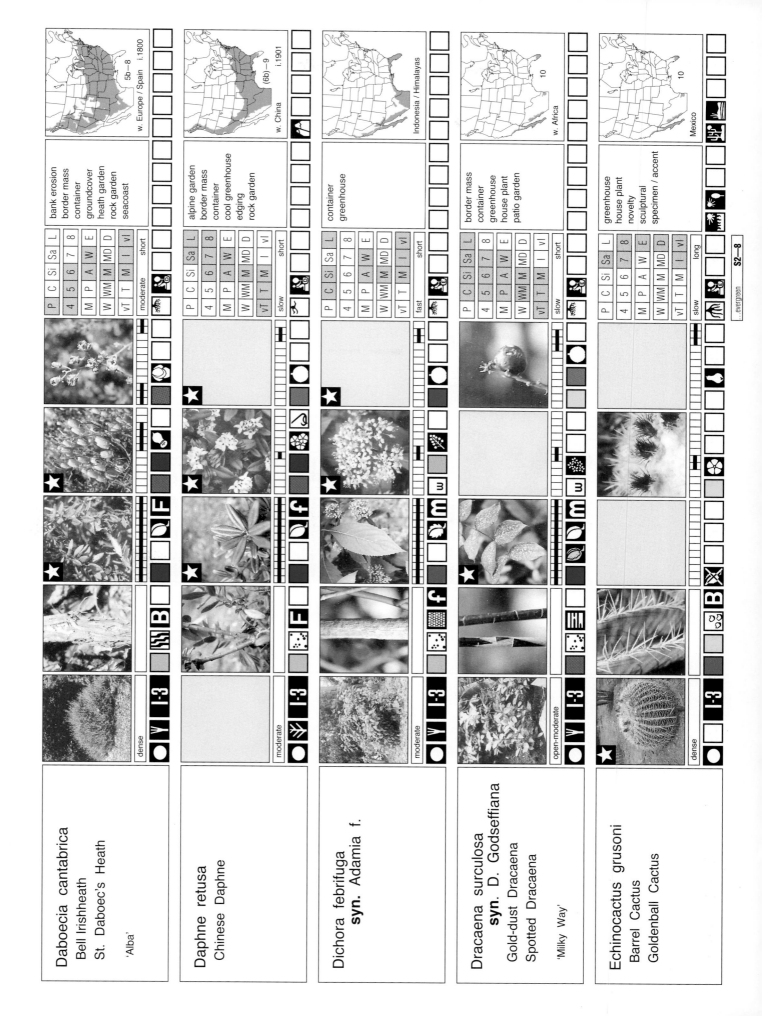

Daboecia cantabrica
Bell Irishheath
St. Daboec's Heath
'Alba'

w. Europe / Spain i:1800 5b–8

bank erosion
border mass
container
groundcover
heath garden
rock garden
seacoast

P C Si Sa L
4 5 6 7 8
M P A E
W WM M D
vT T M I VI

short · moderate · dense

Daphne retusa
Chinese Daphne

w. China i:1901 (6b)–9

alpine garden
border mass
container
cool greenhouse
edging
rock garden

P C Si Sa L
4 5 6 7 8
M P A E
W WM M MD D
vT T M I VI

short · slow · moderate

Dichora febrifuga
syn. D. Adamia f.

Indonesia / Himalayas

container
greenhouse

P C Si Sa L
4 5 6 7 8
M P A E
W WM M MD D
vT T M I VI

short · fast · moderate

Dracaena surculosa
syn. D. Godseffiana
Gold-dust Dracaena
Spotted Dracaena
'Milky Way'

w. Africa 10

border mass
container
greenhouse
house plant
patio garden

P C Si Sa L
4 5 6 7 8
M P A E
W WM M MD D
vT T M I VI

short · slow · open-moderate

Echinocactus grusoni
Barrel Cactus
Goldenball Cactus

Mexico 10

greenhouse
house plant
novelty
sculptural
specimen / accent

P C Si Sa L
4 5 6 7 8
M P A E
W WM M MD D
vT T M I VI

long · slow · dense

...evergreen S2—8

SMALL SHRUB	FORM	BARK	LEAF	FLOWER	FRUIT	CULTURE	USES	REGION

Ephedra distachya
Jointfir Ephedra

CULTURE: P C Si Sa L / 4 5 6 7 8 / M P A W E / W WM M MD D / vT T M I vl — slow

USES: bank erosion, groundcover, medicinal, novelty

REGION: s.Europe / w. Asia — 8–10

Ephedra viridus
Green Ephedra
Mexican Tea

CULTURE: P C Si Sa L / 4 5 6 7 8 / M P A W E / W WM M MD D / vT T M I vl — slow

USES: bank erosion, beverage, groundcover, medicinal, novelty

REGION: s.w. U.S. — 9–10

Eranthemum pulchellum
Blue Sage
Blue Eranthemum

CULTURE: P C Si Sa L / 4 5 6 7 8 / M P A W E / W WM M MD D / vT T M I vl — fast

USES: container, edging, greenhouse, patio garden, seacoast

REGION: India — 9b–10

Erica hyemalis
White Winter Heather
French Heather

CULTURE: P C Si Sa L / 4 5 6 7 8 / M P A W E / W WM M MD D / vT T M I vl — slow

USES: border mass, container, groundcover, heath garden, rock garden, seacoast

REGION: s. Africa — 9a–10

Erica tetralix
Crossleaf Heath
Bog Heather
'Alba'   'Pink Star'
'Mollis' 'Rosea'

CULTURE: P C Si Sa L / 4 5 6 7 8 / M P A W E / W WM M MD D / vT T M I vl — slow

USES: bog garden, border edge, border mass, container, garden, heath, rock garden, seacoast

REGION: n. Europe — 4a–7a — i.1789

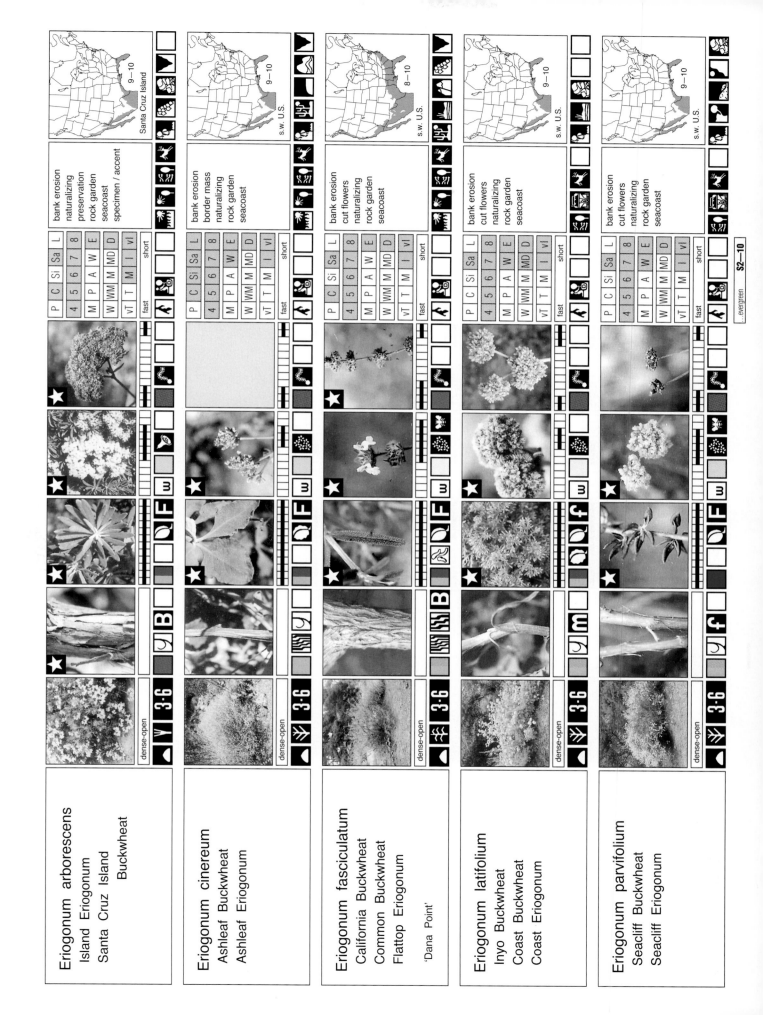

Eriogonum arborescens
Island Eriogonum
Santa Cruz Island Buckwheat

P	C	Si	Sa	L
4	5	6	7	8
M	P	A	W	E
W	WM	M	MD	D
vT	T	M	I	vI

bank erosion
naturalizing
preservation
rock garden
seacoast
specimen / accent

Santa Cruz Island
9—10

fast · short · dense-open · 3-6

Eriogonum cinereum
Ashleaf Buckwheat
Ashleaf Eriogonum

P	C	Si	Sa	L
4	5	6	7	8
M	P	A	W	E
W	WM	M	MD	D
vT	T	M	I	vI

bank erosion
border mass
naturalizing
rock garden
seacoast

s.w. U.S.
9—10

fast · short · dense-open · 3-6

Eriogonum fasciculatum
California Buckwheat
Common Buckwheat
Flattop Eriogonum
'Dana Point'

P	C	Si	Sa	L
4	5	6	7	8
M	P	A	W	E
W	WM	M	MD	D
vT	T	M	I	vI

bank erosion
cut flowers
naturalizing
rock garden
seacoast

s.w. U.S.
8—10

fast · short · dense-open · 3-6

Eriogonum latifolium
Inyo Buckwheat
Coast Buckwheat
Coast Eriogonum

P	C	Si	Sa	L
4	5	6	7	8
M	P	A	W	E
W	WM	M	MD	D
vT	T	M	I	vI

bank erosion
cut flowers
naturalizing
rock garden
seacoast

s.w. U.S.
9—10

fast · short · dense-open · 3-6

Eriogonum parvifolium
Seacliff Buckwheat
Seacliff Eriogonum

P	C	Si	Sa	L
4	5	6	7	8
M	P	A	W	E
W	WM	M	MD	D
vT	T	M	I	vI

bank erosion
cut flowers
naturalizing
rock garden
seacoast

s.w. U.S.
9—10

fast · short · dense-open · 3-6

...evergreen **S2—10**

SMALL SHRUB	FORM	BARK	LEAF	FLOWER	FRUIT	CULTURE	USES	REGION

Eriophyllum confertiflorum
Golden Yarrow
Goldenyarrow Eriophyllum

dense | 3·6

P	C	Si	Sa	L
4	5	6	7	8
M	P	A	W	E
W	WM	M	MD	D
vT	T	M	I	vl

fast / short

Uses: bank erosion, naturalizing, rock garden, seacoast, specimen / accent

Region: w. U.S. 9–10

Eriophyllum staechadifolium
Lizard-tail
Lizardtail Eriophyllum

dense | 3·6

P	C	Si	Sa	L
4	5	6	7	8
M	P	A	W	E
W	WM	M	MD	D
vT	T	M	I	vl

fast / short

Uses: bank erosion, naturalizing, rock garden, seacoast

Region: w. U.S. 9–10

Escallonia virgata
Twiggy Escalonia

dense | 3·6

P	C	Si	Sa	L
4	5	6	7	8
M	P	A	W	E
W	WM	M	MD	D
vT	T	M	I	vl

fast / short

Uses: border edge, espalier, hedge, seacoast, shearing, specimen / accent

Region: Chile 7a–10 i.1866

Euphorbia characias
Euphorbia

dense | 3·6

P	C	Si	Sa	L
4	5	6	7	8
M	P	A	W	E
W	WM	M	MD	D
vT	T	M	I	vl

fast / short

Uses: greenhouse, rock garden, specimen / accent, window box

Region: Mediterranean 7a–10

Euryops pectinatus
Gray-leaved Euryops

'Viridis'

open | 3·6

P	C	Si	Sa	L
4	5	6	7	8
M	P	A	W	E
W	WM	M	MD	D
vT	T	M	I	vl

fast / short

Uses: background, container, greenhouse, screen, seacoast

Region: s. Africa 8a–10

Gaultheria veitchiana
Veitch Wintergreen

w. China — 6–9

border mass
rock garden
woodland garden

P	C	Si	Sa	L
4	5	6	7	8
M	P	A	W	E
W	WM	M	MD	D
vT	T	M	I	vI

fast — short

moderate — 1-3

Globularia cordifolia
Heartleaf Globularia

s. Europe — 5a–7

alpine garden
rock garden

P	C	Si	Sa	L
4	5	6	7	8
M	P	A	W	E
W	WM	M	MD	D
vT	T	M	I	vI

slow — short

dense — 1-3

Hakea incrassata
Pincushion
Swan River Hakea

w. Australia

specimen / accent

P	C	Si	Sa	L
4	5	6	7	8
M	P	A	W	E
W	WM	M	MD	D
vT	T	M	I	vI

fast — short

moderate — 1-3

Homalocladium platycladum
Centipede Plant
Ribbonbush

Solomon Islands — 9b–10

container
greenhouse
house plant
novelty
raised bed

P	C	Si	Sa	L
4	5	6	7	8
M	P	A	W	E
W	WM	M	MD	D
vT	T	M	I	vI

fast — short

open — 1-3

Hypericum 'Hidcote'
Hidcote St. Johnswort

cultivar — c.1920 — 6b–10

border mass
container
groupings
hedge
seacoast

P	C	Si	Sa	L
4	5	6	7	8
M	P	A	W	E
W	WM	M	MD	D
vT	T	M	I	vI

fast — short

dense — 3-6

SMALL SHRUB	FORM	BARK	LEAF	FLOWER	FRUIT	CULTURE	USES	REGION
Hypericum kouytchense 'Sungold'	dense 1-3					P C Si Sa L 4 5 6 7 8 M P A W E W WM M MD D vT T M I vl fast short	border mass groupings rock garden seacoast specimen / accent	6a—9a w.China
Hypericum x moserianum Gold Flower 'Tri-color'	dense 3-6					P C Si Sa L 4 5 6 7 8 M P A W E W WM M MD D vT T M I vl fast short	border mass container groundcover groupings rock garden seacoast	7a—10 hybrid o.1877
Hypericum patulum Goldencup St. Johnswort 'Sunshine'	dense 1-3					P C Si Sa L 4 5 6 7 8 M P A W E W WM M MD D vT T M I vl fast short	border mass groundcover groupings rock garden specimen / accent	7a—9a w. China i.1898
Juniperus chinensis 'Armstrongi' Armstrong Juniper	dense 1-3					P C Si Sa L 4 5 6 7 8 M P A W E W WM M MD D vT T M I vl fast moderate	bonsai	5b—8 cultivar i.1932
Juniperus chinensis 'Pfitzeriana Compacta' Nicks Compact Juniper	dense 3-6					P C Si Sa L 4 5 6 7 8 M P A W E W WM M MD D vT T M I vl fast moderate	bonsai	4a—9 cultivar c.1930

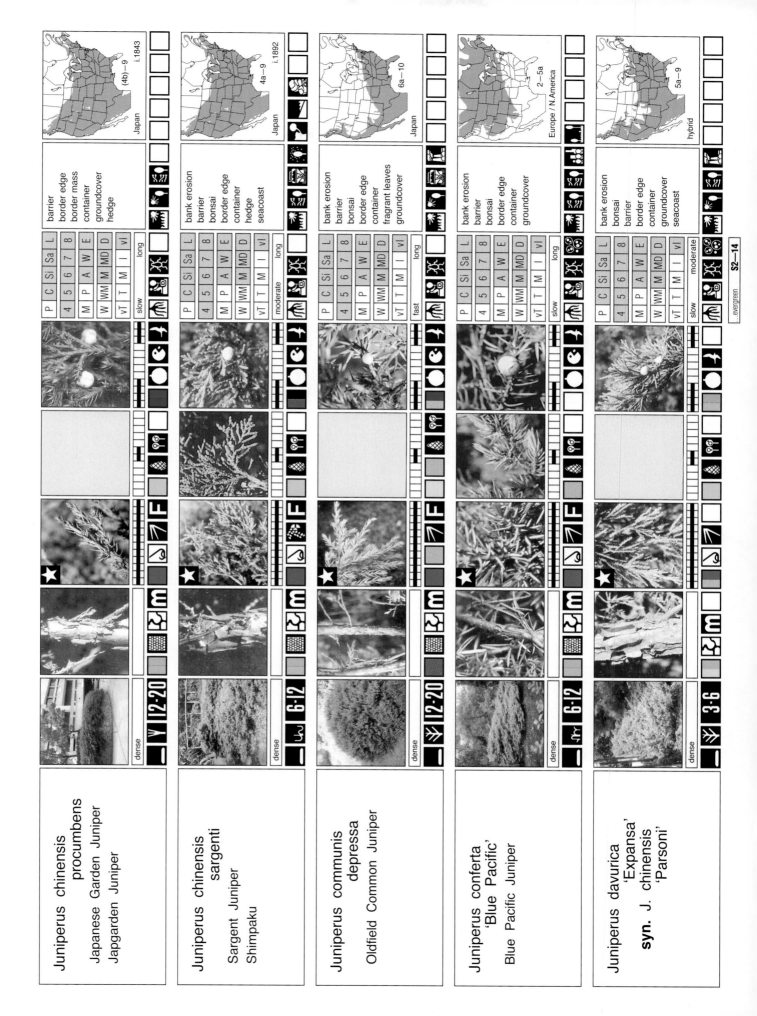

Juniperus chinensis procumbens
Japanese Garden Juniper
Japgarden Juniper

barrier
border edge
border mass
container
groundcover
hedge

P	C	Si	Sa	L
4	5	6	7	8
M	P	A	W	E
W	WM	M	MD	D
vT	T	M	I	vl

slow — long

Japan
(4b)–9
i. 1843

dense 12-20

Juniperus chinensis sargenti
Sargent Juniper
Shimpaku

bank erosion
barrier
bonsai
border edge
container
hedge
seacoast

P	C	Si	Sa	L
4	5	6	7	8
M	P	A	W	E
W	WM	M	MD	D
vT	T	M	I	vl

moderate — long

Japan
4a–9
i. 1892

dense 6-12

Juniperus communis depressa
Oldfield Common Juniper

bank erosion
barrier
bonsai
border edge
container
fragrant leaves
groundcover

P	C	Si	Sa	L
4	5	6	7	8
M	P	A	W	E
W	WM	M	MD	D
vT	T	M	I	vl

fast — long

Japan
6a–10

dense 12-20

Juniperus conferta 'Blue Pacific'
Blue Pacific Juniper

bank erosion
barrier
bonsai
border edge
container
groundcover

P	C	Si	Sa	L
4	5	6	7	8
M	P	A	W	E
W	WM	M	MD	D
vT	T	M	I	vl

slow — long

Europe / N.America
2–5a

dense 6-12

Juniperus davurica 'Expansa'
syn. J. chinensis 'Parsoni'

bank erosion
bonsai
barrier
border edge
container
groundcover
seacoast

P	C	Si	Sa	L
4	5	6	7	8
M	P	A	W	E
W	WM	M	MD	D
vT	T	M	I	vl

slow — moderate

hybrid
5a–9

dense 3-6

...evergreen **S2–14**

SMALL SHRUB

	FORM	BARK	LEAF	FLOWER	FRUIT	CULTURE	USES	REGION

Juniperus horizontalis
Creeping Juniper
Trailing Juniper
'Bar Harbor' 'Hughes'
'Blue Chip' 'Wiltonii'

dense 6-12

Culture: P C Si Sa L / 4 5 6 7 8 / M P A W E / W WM M MD D / vT T M I vl — slow / long

Uses: above wall, alpine garden, bank erosion, barrier, groundcover, rock garden, seacoast

Region: 2—9, c. 1830, n.N America

Juniperus horizontalis 'Douglasi'
Waukegan Creeping Juniper

dense 6-12

Culture: P C Si Sa L / 4 5 6 7 8 / M P A W E / W WM M MD D / vT T M I vl — moderate

Uses: above wall, bank erosion, barrier, fragrant leave, groundcover, rock garden, seacoast

Region: 3a—8b, c.1916, cultivar

Juniperus horizontalis 'Plumosa'
Andorra Creeping Juniper

dense 6-12

Culture: P C Si Sa L / 4 5 6 7 8 / M P A W E / W WM M MD D / vT T M I vl — moderate

Uses: above wall, bank erosion, barrier, bonsai, groundcover, rock garden, seacoast, specimen / accent

Region: 4a—8b, c.1907, cultivar

Juniperus sabina 'Tamariscifolia'
Savin Juniper
Tamarix Juniper

dense 12-20

Culture: P C Si Sa L / 4 5 6 7 8 / M P A W E / W WM M MD D / vT T M I vl — slow / moderate

Uses: bank erosion, barrier, bonsai, border mass, groundcover, specimen / accent

Region: 4a—9b, cultivar

Juniperus scopulorum 'Silver King'
Silver King Juniper

dense 6-12

Culture: P C Si Sa L / 4 5 6 7 8 / M P A W E / W WM M MD D / vT T M I vl — moderate / moderate

Uses: bank erosion, barrier, bonsai, border mass, groundcover, specimen / accent

Region: 4a—7b, cultivar

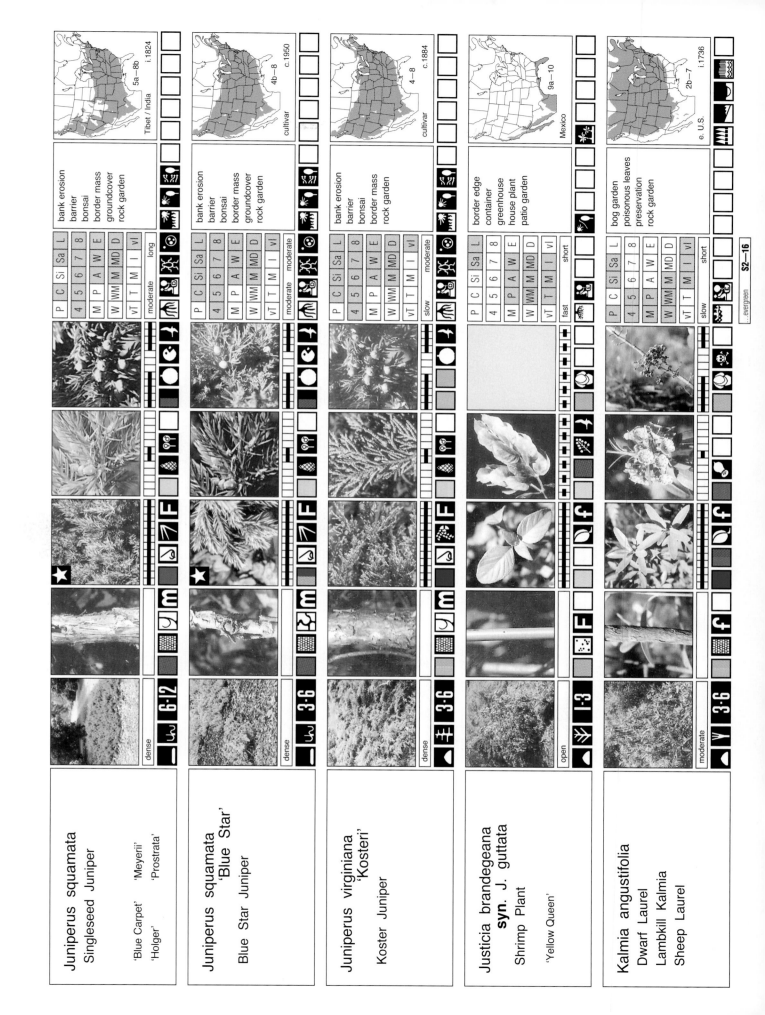

Juniperus squamata — Singleseed Juniper

'Blue Carpet' 'Meyerii'
'Holger' 'Prostrata'

Tibet / India i:1824 5a–8b

bank erosion / barrier / bonsai / border mass / groundcover / rock garden — moderate / long — dense — 6·12

Juniperus squamata 'Blue Star' — Blue Star Juniper

cultivar c.1950 4b–8

bank erosion / barrier / bonsai / border mass / groundcover / rock garden — moderate / moderate — dense — 3·6

Juniperus virginiana 'Kosteri' — Koster Juniper

cultivar c.1884 4–8

bank erosion / barrier / bonsai / border mass / rock garden — slow / moderate — dense — 3·6

Justicia brandegeana syn. J. guttata — Shrimp Plant

'Yellow Queen'

Mexico 9a–10

border edge / container / greenhouse / house plant / patio garden — fast / short — open — 1·3

Kalmia angustifolia — Dwarf Laurel / Lambkill Kalmia / Sheep Laurel

e. U.S. i:1736 2b–7

bog garden / poisonous leaves / preservation / rock garden — slow / short — moderate — 3·6

SMALL SHRUB	FORM	BARK	LEAF	FLOWER	FRUIT	CULTURE	USES	REGION

Kalmia polifolia
Bog Kalmia
Bog Laurel

FORM: moderate · 3-6

CULTURE: P C Si Sa L / 4 5 6 7 8 / M P A W E / W WM M MD D / vT T M I vl · slow

USES: alpine garden / aquatic garden / bog garden / container / rock garden

REGION: 2 – (6b) · Canada

Lavandula angustifolia
English Lavender
Common Lavender

'Hidcote'   'Nana'
'Munstead'   'Spica'

FORM: dense · 1-3

CULTURE: P C Si Sa L / 4 5 6 7 8 / M P A W E / W WM M MD D / vT T M I vl · moderate

USES: accent / border edge / border mass / container / groundcover / herb garden / rock garden / seacoast

REGION: 6 – 8 · w. Mediterranean

Lavandula dentata
French Lavender
Toothed Lavender

'Silver Form'

FORM: open · 1-3

CULTURE: P C Si Sa L / 4 5 6 7 8 / M P A W E / W WM M MD D / vT T M I vl · fast

USES: accent / border edge / border mass / groundcover / herb garden / rock garden / seacoast

REGION: 8 – 9 · Balearick

Lavandula latifolia
Spike Lavender

FORM: moderate · 1-3

CULTURE: P C Si Sa L / 4 5 6 7 8 / M P A W E / W WM M MD D / vT T M I vl · fast

USES: accent / border edge / border mass / groundcover / herb garden / rock garden / seacoast

REGION: 8 – 10 · Portugal

Lavandula multifida
Jagged Lavender

'French Lace'

FORM: moderate · 1-3

CULTURE: P C Si Sa L / 4 5 6 7 8 / M P A W E / W WM M MD D / vT T M I vl · fast

USES: border mass / edging / groundcover / herb garden / rock garden / seacoast / specimen / accent

REGION: 7 – 10 · Portugal

Lavandula stoechas
Spanish Lavender
'Quast'

Portugal 7–9

accent
border edge
border mass
container
groundcover
herb garden
rock garden
seacoast

P	C	Si	Sa	L
4	5	6	7	8
M	P	A	W	E
W	WM	M	MD	D
vT	T	M	I	vI

short
fast
dense
1-3

Ledum groenlandicum
Labrador Tea
'Compactum'

Greenland 2–6 i.1763

alpine garden
beverage
bog garden
border mass
container
kitchen garden
rock garden
seacoast

P	C	Si	Sa	L
4	5	6	7	8
M	P	A	W	E
W	WM	M	MD	D
vT	T	M	I	vI

short
slow
open
3-6

Leiophyllum buxifolium
Sandmyrtle
Box Sandmyrtle
'Pine Cake'

e. U.S. 6–8 i.1736

border mass
container
groundcover
heath garden
preservation
reclamation
rock garden
specimen / accent

P	C	Si	Sa	L
4	5	6	7	8
M	P	A	W	E
W	WM	M	MD	D
vT	T	M	I	vI

short
slow
open
1-3

Leucothoe davisiae
Sierra Laurel
Blacklaurel Leucothoe

w. U.S. 6–8 i.1853

bog garden
preservation
woodland garden

P	C	Si	Sa	L
4	5	6	7	8
M	P	A	W	E
W	WM	M	MD	D
vT	T	M	I	vI

short
slow
dense
3-6

Mahonia nervosa
Longleaf Mahonia
Cascades Mahonia

n.w. N.America 6b–9a i.1822

barrier
groundcover
rock garden
seacoast
woodland garden

P	C	Si	Sa	L
4	5	6	7	8
M	P	A	W	E
W	WM	M	MD	D
vT	T	M	I	vI

short
slow
moderate
3-6

...evergreen   **S2—18**

SMALL SHRUB	FORM	BARK	LEAF	FLOWER	FRUIT	CULTURE	USES	REGION

Opuntia microdasys
Bunny-Ears
Goldplush Pricklypear

'Minor'
'Lemon'

CULTURE: P C Si Sa L / 4 5 6 7 8 / M P A W E / W WM M MD D / vT T M I vl — slow ... long

USES: bank erosion, container, greenhouse, house plant, rock garden, sculptural

REGION: Mexico 10

Pelargonium crispum
Lemon Geranium
Fingerbowl Pelargonium

'Minor'
'Lemon'

CULTURE: P C Si Sa L / 4 5 6 7 8 / M P A W E / W WM M MD D / vT T M I vl — fast ... short

USES: container, greenhouse, herb garden, house plant, seacoast

REGION: 9–10

Penstemon barbatus
Beardlip Penstemon
Beard-tongue

'Albia'   'Torre'
'Elfin Pink'

CULTURE: P C Si Sa L / 4 5 6 7 8 / M P A W E / W WM M MD D / vT T M I vl — fast ... very short

USES: container, cut flowers, edging, naturalizing, rock garden, seacoast, specimen / accent, wild garden

REGION: s.w. U.S. / Mexico 4–8

Penstemon heterophyllus
Chaparral Penstemon
Blue Penstemon

'Blue Spring'
'Tree Blue'

CULTURE: P C Si Sa L / 4 5 6 7 8 / M P A W E / W WM M MD D / vT T M I vl — fast ... very short

USES: accent, bank erosion, border edge, container, naturalizing, rock garden, seacoast, wild garden

REGION: California 7–8

Penstemon procerus
Littleflower Penstemon

CULTURE: P C Si Sa L / 4 5 6 7 8 / M P A W E / W WM M MD D / vT T M I vl — fast ... very short

USES: alpine garden, container, cut flowers, edging, naturalizing, rock garden, seacoast, specimen / accent

REGION: n.w. America

FORM: open   3-6 (Opuntia, Penstemon barbatus); open   1-3 (Pelargonium, Penstemon heterophyllus, Penstemon procerus)

Pernettya ciliaris
syn. P. cillata

7–9
s. Chile

P	C	Si	Sa	L
4	5	6	7	8
M	P	A	W	E
W	WM	M	MD	D
vT	T	M	I	vl

fast short moderate

border mass
container
groundcover
heath garden
persisting fruit
rock garden
window box

3-6

Pernettya mucronata
Chilean Pernettya

'Rubra'

7b–9a
i.1828
Chile

P	C	Si	Sa	L
4	5	6	7	8
M	P	A	W	E
W	WM	M	MD	D
vT	T	M	I	vl

fast short moderate

border mass
container
groundcover
heath garden
persisting fruit
rock garden
seacoast
window box

3-6

Pernettya poeppigi

7–9
Chile

P	C	Si	Sa	L
4	5	6	7	8
M	P	A	W	E
W	WM	M	MD	D
vT	T	M	I	vl

fast short moderate

aggressive
border mass
container
groundcover
heath garden
rock garden
seacoast

3-6

Philesia magellanica
Magellan Boxlily

7–8
s. Chile

P	C	Si	Sa	L
4	5	6	7	8
M	P	A	W	E
W	WM	M	MD	D
vT	T	M	I	vl

slow short moderate

bog garden
climbing vine
groundcover
seacoast

1-3

Picea abies 'Maxwelli'
Maxwell Norway Spruce

4–7
c.1860
cultivar

P	C	Si	Sa	L
4	5	6	7	8
M	P	A	W	E
W	WM	M	MD	D
vT	T	M	I	vl

slow long dense

bonsai
formal garden
oriental garden
rock garden

...evergreen

3-6

SMALL SHRUB	FORM	BARK	LEAF	FLOWER	FRUIT	CULTURE	USES	REGION

Picea abies 'Procumbens'
Prostrate Norway Spruce

- FORM: dense, 6·12
- CULTURE:
P	C	Si	Sa	L
4	5	6	7	8
M	P	A	W	E
W	WM	M	MD	D
vT	T	M	I	vl

  slow
- USES: bank erosion, bonsai, groundcover, oriental garden, rock garden
- REGION: cultivar, 4–7, c.1850

Picea pungens 'Globosa'
Globe Colorado Spruce
Globe Colorado Blue Spruce

- FORM: dense, 1·3
- CULTURE:
P	C	Si	Sa	L
4	5	6	7	8
M	P	A	W	E
W	WM	M	MD	D
vT	T	M	I	vl

  very slow
- USES: bonsai, formal garden, oriental garden, rock garden
- REGION: cultivar, 3–8, c.1937

Picea pungens montgomery
Montgomery Colorado Spruce

- FORM: dense, 3·6
- CULTURE:
P	C	Si	Sa	L
4	5	6	7	8
M	P	A	W	E
W	WM	M	MD	D
vT	T	M	I	vl

  very slow
- USES: bonsai, formal garden, oriental garden, rock garden
- REGION: 3–8, c.1934

Pimelea ferruginea
Rosy Riceflower

- FORM: dense, 3·6
- CULTURE:
P	C	Si	Sa	L
4	5	6	7	8
M	P	A	W	E
W	WM	M	MD	D
vT	T	M	I	vl

  moderate, moderate, long
- USES: container, cool greenhouse, ground bed, rock garden, seacoast
- REGION: w. Australia, 7–9, i.1824

Pinus sylvestris 'Beauvronensis'
Very Dwarf Scotch Pine

- FORM: dense, 3·6
- CULTURE:
P	C	Si	Sa	L
4	5	6	7	8
M	P	A	W	E
W	WM	M	MD	D
vT	T	M	I	vl

  slow, long
- USES: bonsai, formal garden, oriental garden, rock garden, specimen / accent
- REGION: 3–8, c.1891

Rhamnus crocea — Redberry Buckthorn

s.w. U.S. 6b–10

P	C	Si	Sa	L
4	5	6	7	8
M	P	A	W	E
W	WM	M	MD	D
vT	T	M	I	vI

fast · short

bank erosion · barrier · border mass · groundcover · rock garden · seacoast

dense · 3-6

Rhododendron × altaclerense — Altaclerense Rhododendron

hybrid 6–8

P	C	Si	Sa	L
4	5	6	7	8
M	P	A	W	E
W	WM	M	MD	D
vT	T	M	I	vI

slow · short

border mass · groupings · sculptural · specimen / accent · woodland garden

moderate · 3-6

Rhododendron yakusimanum

'Ken Janeck'
'Mist Maiden'

Japan (5b)–8a   i.1934

P	C	Si	Sa	L
4	5	6	7	8
M	P	A	W	E
W	WM	M	MD	D
vT	T	M	I	vI

slow · short

border mass · groupings · sculptural · specimen / accent · woodland garden

moderate · 3-6

Ribes viburnifolium — Catalina Currant, Viburnumleaf Currant

w. U.S. 8b–10   i.1897

P	C	Si	Sa	L
4	5	6	7	8
M	P	A	W	E
W	WM	M	MD	D
vT	T	M	I	vI

fast · short

bank erosion · groundcover · preservation

dense · 6-12

Ruscus aculeatus — Butcher's Broom, Jew's Myrtle

Azores (7b)–9   i.1750

P	C	Si	Sa	L
4	5	6	7	8
M	P	A	W	E
W	WM	M	MD	D
vT	T	M	I	vI

moderate · short

barrier · edging · florist ornament · groundcover · hedge · house plant · sculptural · seacoast

dense · 1-3

...evergreen

SMALL SHRUB	FORM	BARK	LEAF	FLOWER	FRUIT	CULTURE	USES	REGION

Ruscus hypoglossum

- moderate
- 3-6

CULTURE:
P	C	Si	Sa	L
4	5	6	7	8
M	P	A	W	E
W	WM	M	MD	D
vT	T	M	I	vl

fast ... short

USES: border mass, edging, groundcover, hedge, seacoast

REGION: s. Eur / Turkey   7–9   c.b.1508

Salvia elegans
Pineapple-scented Sage
Pineapple Sage

- moderate
- 3-6

CULTURE:
P	C	Si	Sa	L
4	5	6	7	8
M	P	A	W	E
W	WM	M	MD	D
vT	T	M	I	vl

fast ... short

USES: border mass, container, culinary, fragrant leaves, herb garden, kitchen garden, seacoast

REGION: Mexico   9–10

Salvia greggi
Autumn Sage
Cherry Sage

'Rosea'

- moderate
- 1-3

CULTURE:
P	C	Si	Sa	L
4	5	6	7	8
M	P	A	W	E
W	WM	M	MD	D
vT	T	M	I	vl

fast ... short

USES: border mass, container, groundcover, hedge, herb garden, kitchen garden, leathery leaves, sheared

REGION: Mexico   9–10   c.1885

Salvia leucantha
Mexican Bush Sage

'Emerald'
'Point Sal'

- moderate
- 3-6

CULTURE:
P	C	Si	Sa	L
4	5	6	7	8
M	P	A	W	E
W	WM	M	MD	D
vT	T	M	I	vl

fast ... short

USES: border mass, container, edging, greenhouse, groundcover, hedge

REGION: Mexico   9–10

Salvia microphylla
Baby Sage

- moderate
- 1-3

CULTURE:
P	C	Si	Sa	L
4	5	6	7	8
M	P	A	W	E
W	WM	M	MD	D
vT	T	M	I	vl

fast ... short

USES: border mass, container, edging, groundcover, hedge

REGION: Mexico   10   i.1829

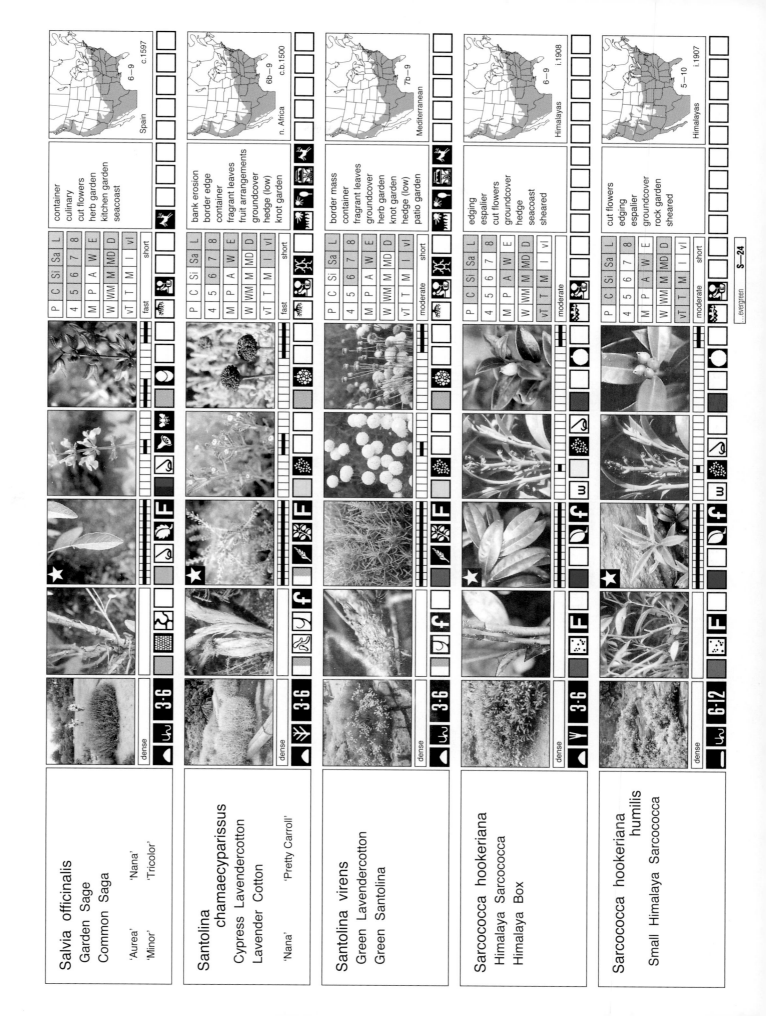

Salvia officinalis — Garden Sage, Common Saga
'Aurea', 'Nana', 'Minor', 'Tricolor'
Spain — 6–9 — c.1597

container / culinary / cut flowers / herb garden / kitchen garden / seacoast
P C Si Sa L / 4 5 6 7 8 / M P A W E / W WM M MD D / vT T M I vI
fast — short
dense — 3·6

Santolina chamaecyparissus — Cypress Lavendercotton, Lavender Cotton
'Nana', 'Pretty Carroll'
n. Africa — 6b–9 — c.b.1500

bank erosion / border edge / container / fragrant leaves / fruit arrangements / groundcover / hedge (low) / knot garden
P C Si Sa L / 4 5 6 7 8 / M P A W E / W WM M MD D / vT T M I vI
fast — short
dense — 3·6

Santolina virens — Green Lavendercotton, Green Santolina
Mediterranean — 7b–9

border mass / container / fragrant leaves / groundcover / herb garden / knot garden / hedge (low) / patio garden
P C Si Sa L / 4 5 6 7 8 / M P A W E / W WM M MD D / vT T M I vI
moderate — short
dense — 3·6

Sarcococca hookeriana — Himalaya Sarcococca, Himalaya Box
Himalayas — 6–9 — i.1908

edging / espalier / cut flowers / groundcover / hedge / seacoast / sheared
P C Si Sa L / 4 5 6 7 8 / M P A W E / W WM M MD D / vT T M I vI
moderate
dense — 3·6

Sarcococca hookeriana humilis — Small Himalaya Sarcococca
Himalayas — 5–10 — i.1907

cut flowers / edging / espalier / groundcover / rock garden / sheared
P C Si Sa L / 4 5 6 7 8 / M P A W E / W WM M MD D / vT T M I vI
moderate — short
dense — 6·12

SMALL SHRUB	FORM	BARK	LEAF	FLOWER	FRUIT	CULTURE	USES	REGION

Sasa veitchi
Kuma Bamboo Grass
Veitch Bamboo
Veitch Saga

FORM: dense · 12-20

CULTURE: P C Si Sa L / 4 5 6 7 8 / M P A W E / W WM M MD D / vT T M I vl / short · fast

USES: bank erosion, groundcover, winter garden

REGION: Japan · 6–10 · i.1880

Serissa foetida
Yellowrim

'Cherry Blossom'   'Mt. Fuji'
'Kyoto'

FORM: moderate · 1-3

CULTURE: P C Si Sa L / 4 5 6 7 8 / M P A W E / W WM M MD D / vT T M I vl / short · fast

USES: bonsai, border edge, container, greenhouse, hedge, house plant, rock garden

REGION: India · 9–10

Skimmia reevesiana
Reeves Skimmia

FORM: dense · 1-3

CULTURE: P C Si Sa L / 4 5 6 7 8 / M P A W E / W WM M MD D / vT T M I vl / short · slow

USES: border edge, border mass, container, fruit arrangement, greenhouse, patio garden, seacoast

REGION: China · (7a)–9 · i.1849

Taxus canadensis
Canada Yew
Ground Hemlock

'Verkades Recurved'

FORM: open · 6-12

CULTURE: P C Si Sa L / 4 5 6 7 8 / M P A W E / W WM M MD D / vT T M I vl / long · slow

USES: above wall, bank erosion, espalier, groundcover, seacoast, shade garden

REGION: e. N. America · 3–6 · i.1800

Taxus cuspidata 'Nana'
Dwarf Japanese Yew

FORM: dense · 3-6

CULTURE: P C Si Sa L / 4 5 6 7 8 / M P A W E / W WM M MD D / vT T M I vl / long · slow

USES: barrier, bonsai, espalier, hedge, seacoast, shearing

REGION: Japan · 4–7 · c.1861

Teucrium flavum
Yellow Germander

4–9
Mediterranean

- greenhouse
- herb garden
- kitchen garden
- medicinal
- rock garden
- window box

P	C	Si	Sa	L
4	5	6	7	8
M	P	A	W	E
W	WM	M	MD	D
vT	T	M	I	vI

fast · very short
moderate · 1·3

Tsuga canadensis 'Coles Prostrate'
Cole's Prostrate Hemlock

2–7
c.1927
cultivar

- bonsai
- rock garden
- specimen / accent

P	C	Si	Sa	L
4	5	6	7	8
M	P	A	W	E
W	WM	M	MD	D
vT	T	M	I	vI

very slow · long
dense · 3·6

Tsuga canadensis 'Pendula'
Sargent Weeping Hemlock

2–8
i:1876
cultivar

- bonsai
- formal garden
- oriental garden
- rock garden
- sculptural
- specimen / accent

P	C	Si	Sa	L
4	5	6	7	8
M	P	A	W	E
W	WM	M	MD	D
vT	T	M	I	vI

very slow · long
dense · 3·6

Vaccinium delavayi
Delavay Blueberry

7–10
i:1923
w. China

- kitchen garden

P	C	Si	Sa	L
4	5	6	7	8
M	P	A	W	E
W	WM	M	MD	D
vT	T	M	I	vI

moderate · short
moderate · 1·3

Veronica incana
Woolly Speedwell

3–7
Russia

- border edge
- border mass
- bouquets
- cut flowers
- flower border
- groundcover
- rock garden
- wall garden

P	C	Si	Sa	L
4	5	6	7	8
M	P	A	W	E
W	WM	M	MD	D
vT	T	M	I	vI

fast · short
open · 1·3

'Nana'
'Rosea'

...evergreen **S2—26**

SMALL SHRUB	FORM	BARK	LEAF	FLOWER	FRUIT	CULTURE	USES	REGION

Veronica spicata
Spike Speedwell

'Blue Fox'   'Nana'
'Erica'   'Red Fox'

FORM: open / I-3
CULTURE: P C Si Sa L / 4 5 6 7 8 / M P A W E / W WM M MD D / vT T M I vl / short · fast

USES: border edge / border mass / bouquets / cut flowers / rock garden / wall garden

REGION: n. Eur / Asia · 4—10

Viburnum davidi
David Viburnum

FORM: dense / 3-6
CULTURE: P C Si Sa L / 4 5 6 7 8 / M P A W E / W WM M MD D / vT T M I vl / short · moderate

USES: border edge / border mass / groundcover / specimen / accent

REGION: China · 7—9 · i.1904

Yucca filamentosa
syn. Y. smalliana
Adamsneedle Yucca
Needle Palm

'Bright Edge'   'Golden Sword'

FORM: dense / I-3
CULTURE: P C Si Sa L / 4 5 6 7 8 / M P A W E / W WM M MD D / vT T M I vl / long · slow

USES: barrier / container / greenhouse / patio garden / reclamation / sculptural / seacoast / specimen / accent

REGION: s.e. U.S. · (5a)—10 · c.1675

Yucca flaccida
Weakleaf Yucca

'Ivory Tower''

FORM: dense / 3-6
CULTURE: P C Si Sa L / 4 5 6 7 8 / M P A W E / W WM M MD D / vT T M I vl / long · slow

USES: barrier / container / greenhouse / patio garden / sculptural / seacoast / specimen / accent

REGION: s. U.S. · 5b—10 · i.1816

Yucca glauca
Small Soapweed
Soapwell

'Pendula'

FORM: open / I-3
CULTURE: P C Si Sa L / 4 5 6 7 8 / M P A W E / W WM M MD D / vT T M I vl / long · slow

USES: barrier / container / greenhouse / patio garden / sculptural / specimen / accent

REGION: w. U.S. · 4b—7 · c.1811

Zamia integrifolia

Coontie

Sago Cycad

Seminole-Bread

w. Indies / Florida

9—10

border mass
container
greenhouse
groundcover
patio garden
rock garden
sculptural
specimen / accent

slow

long

dense

3·6

P	C	Si	Sa	L
4	5	6	7	8
M	P	A	W	E
W	WM	M	MD	D
vT	T	M	I	vI

P	C	Si	Sa	L
4	5	6	7	8
M	P	A	W	E
W	WM	M	MD	D
vT	T	M	I	vI

P	C	Si	Sa	L
4	5	6	7	8
M	P	A	W	E
W	WM	M	MD	D
vT	T	M	I	vI

P	C	Si	Sa	L
4	5	6	7	8
M	P	A	W	E
W	WM	M	MD	D
vT	T	M	I	vI

VERY SMALL SHRUB	FORM	BARK	LEAF	FLOWER	FRUIT	CULTURE	USES	REGION

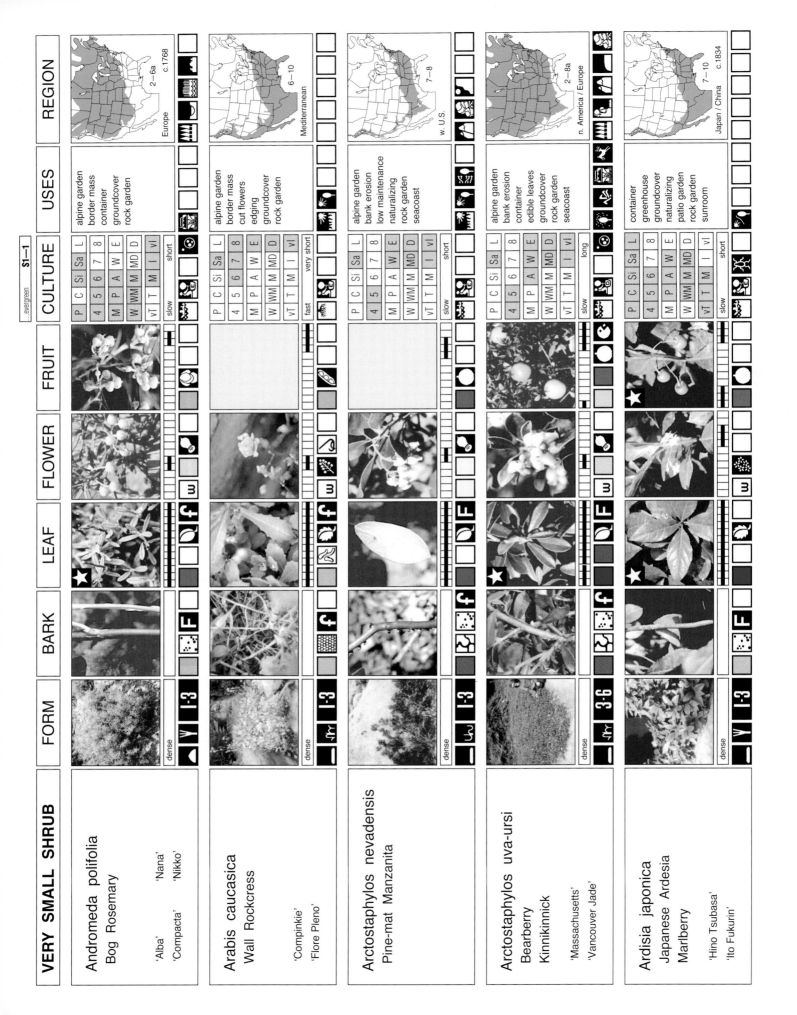

Andromeda polifolia
Bog Rosemary

'Alba'   'Nana'
'Compacta' 'Nikko'

CULTURE: P C Si Sa L / 4 5 6 7 8 / M P A W E / W WM M MD D / vT T M I vl / slow / dense / 1-3

USES: alpine garden, border mass, container, groundcover, rock garden

REGION: Europe 2–6a c.1768

Arabis caucasica
Wall Rockcress

'Compinkie'
'Flore Pleno'

CULTURE: P C Si Sa L / 4 5 6 7 8 / M P A W E / W WM M MD D / vT T M I vl / fast / very short / dense / 1-3

USES: alpine garden, border mass, cut flowers, edging, groundcover, rock garden

REGION: Mediterranean 6–10

Arctostaphylos nevadensis
Pine-mat Manzanita

CULTURE: P C Si Sa L / 4 5 6 7 8 / M P A W E / W WM M MD D / vT T M I vl / slow / dense / 1-3

USES: alpine garden, bank erosion, low maintenance, naturalizing, rock garden, seacoast

REGION: w. U.S. 7–8

Arctostaphylos uva-ursi
Bearberry
Kinnikinnick

'Massachusetts'
'Vancouver Jade'

CULTURE: P C Si Sa L / 4 5 6 7 8 / M P A W E / W WM M MD D / vT T M I vl / slow / long / dense / 3-6

USES: alpine garden, bank erosion, container, edible leaves, groundcover, rock garden, seacoast

REGION: n. America / Europe 2–8a

Ardisia japonica
Japanese Ardesia
Marlberry

"Hino Tsubasa'
'Ito Fukurin'

CULTURE: P C Si Sa L / 4 5 6 7 8 / M P A W E / W WM M MD D / vT T M I vl / slow / short / dense / 1-3

USES: container, greenhouse, groundcover, naturalizing, patio garden, rock garden, sunroom

REGION: Japan / China 7–10 c.1834

Artemisia frigida
Fringed Sagebrush
Fringed Wormwood

P	C	Si	Sa	L
4	5	6	7	8
M	P	A	W	E
W	WM	M	MD	D
vT	T	M	I	vl

dense · I-3 · fast · short

bank erosion
border mass
nitrogen-fixing
rock garden

n. America   5–8   i.1597

Baccharis pilularis
Coyotebush
Kidneywort
'Pigeon Point'
'Twin Peaks'

P	C	Si	Sa	L
4	5	6	7	8
M	P	A	W	E
W	WM	M	MD	D
vT	T	M	I	vl

dense · 3-6 · fast · long

bank erosion
groundcover
low maintenance
naturalizing
nitrogen-fixing
restoration

California   7–10   c.1910

Ballota pseudodictammus

P	C	Si	Sa	L
4	5	6	7	8
M	P	A	W	E
W	WM	M	MD	D
vT	T	M	I	vl

dense · I-3 · fast · short

bank erosion
border edging
rock garden

Mediterranean   7–9

Bruckenthalia spiculifolia
Spikeheath

P	C	Si	Sa	L
4	5	6	7	8
M	P	A	W	E
W	WM	M	MD	D
vT	T	M	I	vl

dense · I-3 · slow · short

container
groundcover
heath garden
rock garden
seacoast

Eurasia   6–8   i.1888

Cassiope lycopodioides
Alaska Cassiope

P	C	Si	Sa	L
4	5	6	7	8
M	P	A	W	E
W	WM	M	MD	D
vT	T	M	I	vl

dense · I-3 · slow · short

alpine garden
container
heath garden
rock garden

n.e. Asia / Japan   3b–7   c.1933

...evergreen   **S1—2**

VERY SMALL SHRUB	FORM	BARK	LEAF	FLOWER	FRUIT	CULTURE	USES	REGION

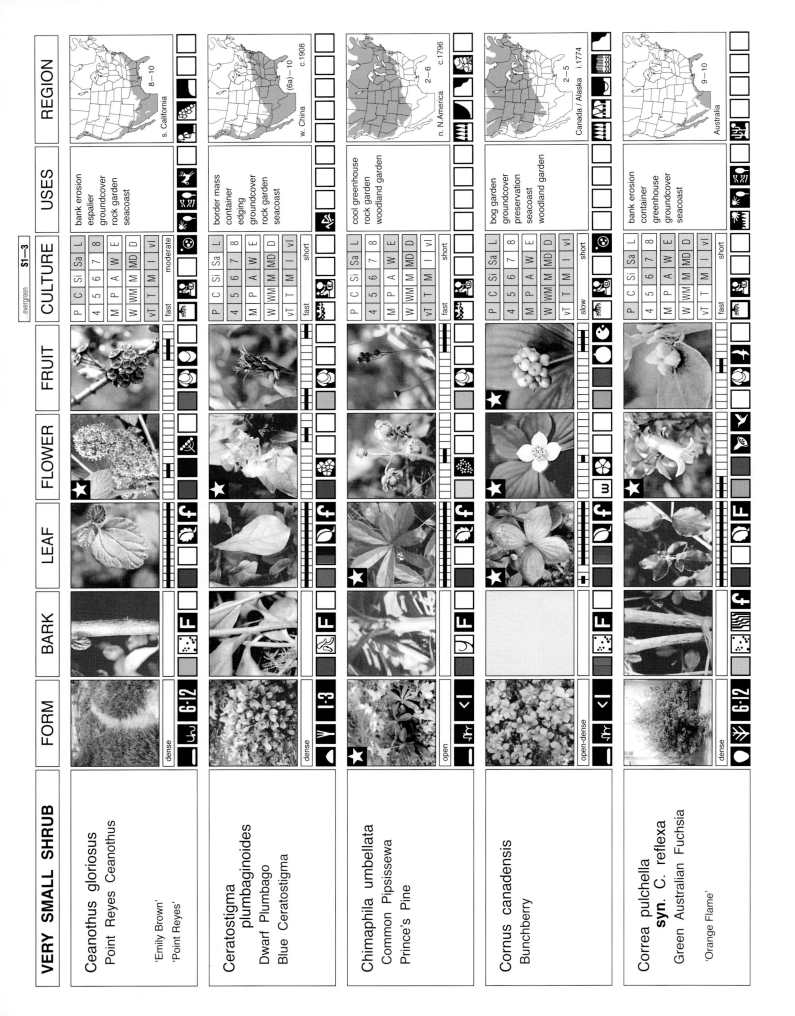

Ceanothus gloriosus
Point Reyes Ceanothus

'Emily Brown'
'Point Reyes'

dense

6–12

s. California
8–10

bank erosion
espalier
groundcover
rock garden
seacoast

P C Si Sa L
4 5 6 7 8
M P A W E
W WM M MD D
vT T M I vl
fast   moderate

Ceratostigma plumbaginoides
Dwarf Plumbago
Blue Ceratostigma

dense

1–3

w. China
(6a)–10   c.1908

border mass
container
edging
groundcover
rock garden
seacoast

P C Si Sa L
4 5 6 7 8
M P A W E
W WM M MD D
vT T M I vl
fast   short

Chimaphila umbellata
Common Pipsissewa
Prince's Pine

open

<1

n. N.America
2–6   c.1796

cool greenhouse
rock garden
woodland garden

P C Si Sa L
4 5 6 7 8
M P A W E
W WM M MD D
vT T M I vl
fast   short

Cornus canadensis
Bunchberry

open–dense

<1

Canada / Alaska
2–5   i.1774

bog garden
groundcover
preservation
seacoast
woodland garden

P C Si Sa L
4 5 6 7 8
M P A W E
W WM M MD D
vT T M I vl
slow   short

Correa pulchella
syn. C. reflexa
Green Australian Fuchsia

'Orange Flame'

dense

6–12

Australia
9–10

bank erosion
container
greenhouse
groundcover
seacoast

P C Si Sa L
4 5 6 7 8
M P A W E
W WM M MD D
vT T M I vl
fast   short

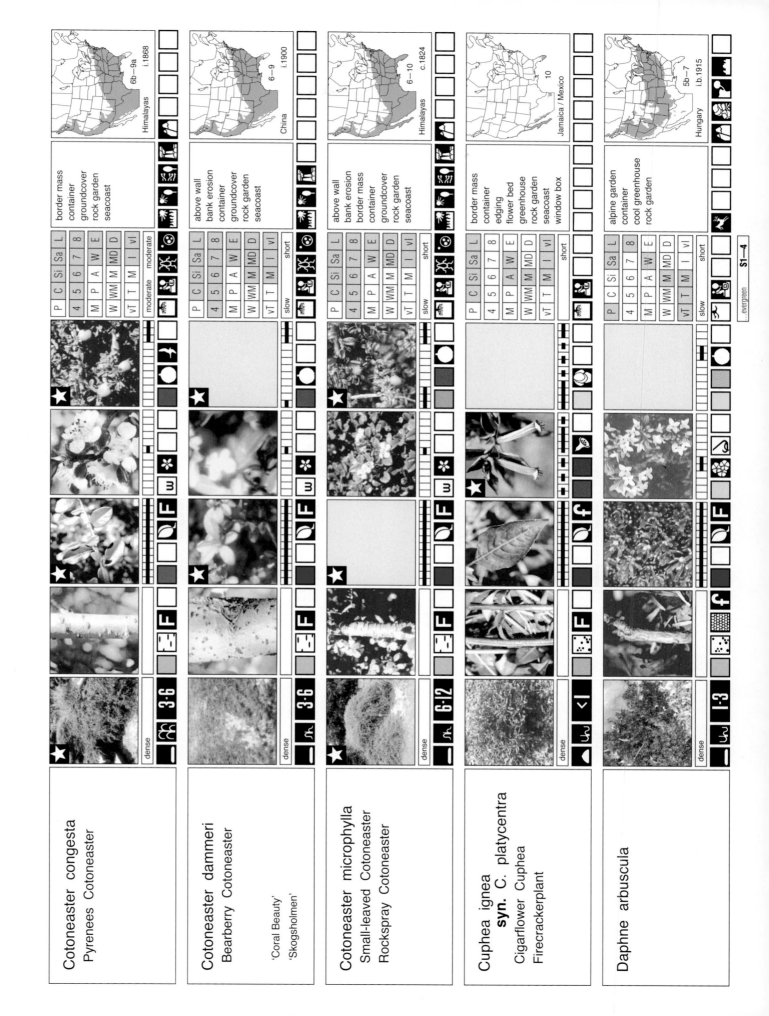

Cotoneaster congesta
Pyrenees Cotoneaster

P	C	Si	Sa	L
4	5	6	7	8
M	P	A	W	E
W	WM	M	MD	D
vT	T	M	I	vl

border mass
container
groundcover
rock garden
seacoast

6b–9a
i.1868
Himalayas

moderate moderate
slow short
dense
3·6

Cotoneaster dammeri
Bearberry Cotoneaster

'Coral Beauty'
'Skogsholmen'

P	C	Si	Sa	L
4	5	6	7	8
M	P	A	W	E
W	WM	M	MD	D
vT	T	M	I	vl

above wall
bank erosion
container
groundcover
rock garden
seacoast

6–9
i.1900
China

slow short
dense
3·6

Cotoneaster microphylla
Small-leaved Cotoneaster
Rockspray Cotoneaster

P	C	Si	Sa	L
4	5	6	7	8
M	P	A	W	E
W	WM	M	MD	D
vT	T	M	I	vl

above wall
bank erosion
border mass
container
groundcover
rock garden
seacoast

6–10
c.1824
Himalayas

slow short
dense
6·12

Cuphea ignea syn. C. platycentra
Cigarflower Cuphea
Firecrackerplant

P	C	Si	Sa	L
4	5	6	7	8
M	P	A	W	E
W	WM	M	MD	D
vT	T	M	I	vl

border mass
container
edging
flower bed
greenhouse
rock garden
seacoast
window box

10
Jamaica / Mexico

short
dense
<I

Daphne arbuscula

P	C	Si	Sa	L
4	5	6	7	8
M	P	A	W	E
W	WM	M	MD	D
vT	T	M	I	vl

alpine garden
container
cool greenhouse
rock garden

5b–7
i.b.1915
Hungary

slow short
dense
1·3

...evergreen

S1—4

VERY SMALL SHRUB

	FORM	BARK	LEAF	FLOWER	FRUIT	CULTURE	USES	REGION

Daphne blagayana
Balkan Daphne

CULTURE: P C Si Sa L / 4 5 6 7 8 / M P A W E / W WM M MD D / vT T M I vl — slow

USES: alpine garden, container, groundcover, rock garden

REGION: Greece 2—6 i.1875

Daphne cneorum
Rose Daphne
Garlandflower

'Alba' 'Eximia'
'Ruby Glow'

CULTURE: P C Si Sa L / 4 5 6 7 8 / M P A W E / W WM M MD D / vT T M I vl — slow

USES: alpine garden, container, groundcover, rock garden

REGION: Europe (4b)—8a i.1752

Echinocereus engelmanni
Hedgehog Cactus
Engelmann Cactus

CULTURE: P C Si Sa L / 4 5 6 7 8 / M P A W E / W WM M MD D / vT T M I vl — slow

USES: house plant, greenhouse, window box

REGION: s.w. U.S. 9—10

Empetrum nigrum
Black Crowberry

CULTURE: P C Si Sa L / 4 5 6 7 8 / M P A W E / W WM M MD D / vT T M I vl — moderate

USES: groundcover, heath garden, rock garden, seacoast

REGION: n. N.America 2—6 i.b.1700

Epigaea repens
Trailing Arbutus
Mayflower

CULTURE: P C Si Sa L / 4 5 6 7 8 / M P A W E / W WM M MD D / vT T M I vl — slow

USES: alpine garden, edible flower, fragrant flowers, naturalizing, preservation, rock garden, seacoast

REGION: e. U.S. 2b—8 i.1736

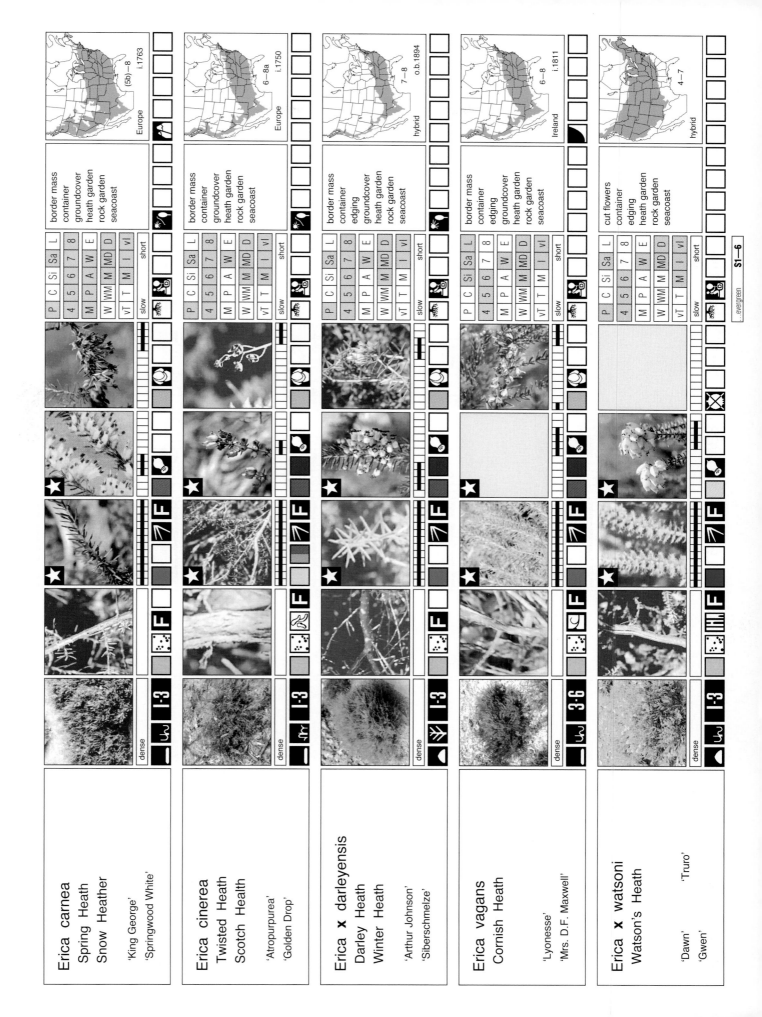

Erica carnea
Spring Heath
Snow Heather

'King George'
'Springwood White'

P	C	Si	Sa	L
4	5	6	7	8
M	P	A	W	E
W	WM	M	MD	D
vT	T	M	I	vl

slow — short

border mass
container
groundcover
heath garden
rock garden
seacoast

Europe   (5b)—8   i.1763

dense   1-3

Erica cinerea
Twisted Heath
Scotch Health

'Atropurpurea'
'Golden Drop'

P	C	Si	Sa	L
4	5	6	7	8
M	P	A	W	E
W	WM	M	MD	D
vT	T	M	I	vl

slow — short

border mass
container
groundcover
heath garden
rock garden
seacoast

Europe   6—8a   i.1750

dense   1-3

Erica x darleyensis
Darley Heath
Winter Heath

'Arthur Johnson'
'Siberschmelze'

P	C	Si	Sa	L
4	5	6	7	8
M	P	A	W	E
W	WM	M	MD	D
vT	T	M	I	vl

slow — short

border mass
container
edging
groundcover
heath garden
rock garden
seacoast

hybrid   7—8   o.b.1894

dense

Erica vagans
Cornish Heath

'Lyonesse'
'Mrs. D.F. Maxwell'

P	C	Si	Sa	L
4	5	6	7	8
M	P	A	W	E
W	WM	M	MD	D
vT	T	M	I	vl

slow — short

border mass
container
edging
groundcover
heath garden
rock garden
seacoast

Ireland   6—8   i.1811

dense   3-6

Erica x watsoni
Watson's Heath

'Dawn'   'Truro'
'Gwen'

P	C	Si	Sa	L
4	5	6	7	8
M	P	A	W	E
W	WM	M	MD	D
vT	T	M	I	vl

slow — short

cut flowers
container
edging
heath garden
rock garden
seacoast

hybrid   4—7

dense   1-3

VERY SMALL SHRUB	FORM	BARK	LEAF	FLOWER	FRUIT	CULTURE	USES	REGION

Eriogonum umbellatum
Sulfurflower
Sulfur Eriogonum
'Ute'

FORM: dense · 1-3
CULTURE: P C Si Sa L · 4 5 6 7 8 · M P A W E · W WM M MD D · vT T M I vl · fast · short
USES: bank erosion / groundcover / rock garden
REGION: Rocky Mts. · 7—9

Euphorbia myrsinites
Myrtle Euphorbia

FORM: moderate · 1-3
CULTURE: P C Si Sa L · 4 5 6 7 8 · M P A W E · W WM M MD D · vT T M I vl · fast · short
USES: container / rock garden / specimen / accent / window box
REGION: s.Europe · 4—9

Gaultheria hispidula syn. Chiogenes h.
Creeping Pearlberry
Creeping Snowberry

FORM: open-dense · 1-3
CULTURE: P C Si Sa L · 4 5 6 7 8 · M P A W E · W WM M MD D · vT T M I vl · slow · short
USES: alpine garden / groundcover / leather leaves / rock garden / terrarium / woodland garden
REGION: n. N. America · 2—6 · c.1927

Gaultheria miqueliana
Miquel Wintergreen

FORM: dense · 3-6
CULTURE: P C Si Sa L · 4 5 6 7 8 · M P A W E · W WM M MD D · vT T M I vl · slow · short
USES: alpine garden / groundcover / rock garden / seacoast / terrarium / woodland garden
REGION: Japan · (5b)—8 · i.1892

Gaultheria ovatifolia
Oregon Wintergreen

FORM: dense · 1-3
CULTURE: P C Si Sa L · 4 5 6 7 8 · M P A W E · W WM M MD D · vT T M I vl · slow
USES: alpine garden / groundcover / rock garden
REGION: w. U.S. · 5—8 · c.1890

...evergreen

Gaultheria procumbens
Checkerberry Wintergreen

alpine garden
aromatic leaves
edible leaves
groundcover
naturalizing
rock garden
seacoast

e. N. America   i.b.1762   2–8a

P C Si Sa L | 4 5 6 7 8 | M P A W E | W WM M MD D | vT T M I vl
slow   short   open   <1

Gaylussacia brachycera
Box-huckleberry

groundcover
preservation
rock garden

e. U.S.   i.1796   3–7

P C Si Sa L | 4 5 6 7 8 | M P A W E | W WM M MD D | vT T M I vl
slow   short   dense   6-12

Grevillea gaudicnaudi

bank erosion
greenhouse
groundcover
house plant
patio garden

9–10

P C Si Sa L | 4 5 6 7 8 | M P A W E | W WM M MD D | vT T M I vl
slow   moderate   dense   1-3

Halimium umbellatum
syn. Helianthemun u.
Lineleaf Falsesunrose

bank erosion
rock garden
seacoast

Spain   i.1731   8–10

P C Si Sa L | 4 5 6 7 8 | M P A W E | W WM M MD D | vT T M I vl
fast   short   moderate   1-3

Helianthemum apenninum
Apennine Sunrose

'Roseum'

bank erosion
border edging
container
flower bed
rock garden
seacoast

s. Eurasia   i.1731   6–8

P C Si Sa L | 4 5 6 7 8 | M P A W E | W WM M MD D | vT T M I vl
fast   short   moderate   1-3

VERY SMALL SHRUB	FORM	BARK	LEAF	FLOWER	FRUIT	CULTURE	USES	REGION

Helianthemum nummularium
Common Sunrose
'Apricot'
'Gold Rush'

- FORM: dense, 1-3
- CULTURE: P C Si Sa L / 4 5 6 7 8 / M P A W E / W WM M MD D / vT T M I vl / fast / short
- USES: bank erosion, container, edging, flower bed, groundcover, rock garden, seacoast
- REGION: Europe, 5—10

Hypericum calycinum
Aaronsbeard
Creeping St. Johnswort

- FORM: dense, 1-3
- CULTURE: P C Si Sa L / 4 5 6 7 8 / M P A W E / W WM M MD D / vT T M I vl / fast / short
- USES: aromatic leaves, bank erosion, border mass, groundcover, naturalizing, rock garden, seacoast, specimen / accent
- REGION: Bulgaria, i.1676, 6—10

Ilex rugosa
Tsuru Holly
Rugose Holly

- FORM: dense, 3-6
- CULTURE: P C Si Sa L / 4 5 6 7 8 / M P A W E / W WM M MD D / vT T M I vl / slow / moderate
- USES: bank erosion, bonsai, fruit arrangements, groundcover, rock garden, seacoast
- REGION: Japan, i.1895, 4—7

Jasminum mesnyi
Primrose Jasmine
Yellow Jasmine
'Variegata'

- FORM: open, 6-12
- CULTURE: P C Si Sa L / 4 5 6 7 8 / M P A W E / W WM M MD D / vT T M I vl / fast / short
- USES: above wall, bank erosion, border mass, container, espalier, greenhouse, groundcover, hanging basket
- REGION: China, i.1900, (8b)—10

Juniperus chinensis procumbens nana
Dwarf Japangarden Juniper

- FORM: dense, 3-6
- CULTURE: P C Si Sa L / 4 5 6 7 8 / M P A W E / W WM M MD D / vT T M I vl / slow / long
- USES: above wall, alpine garden, aromatic leaves, bank erosion, bonsai, groundcover, reclamation, rock garden
- REGION: Japan, i.1922, (2b)—9

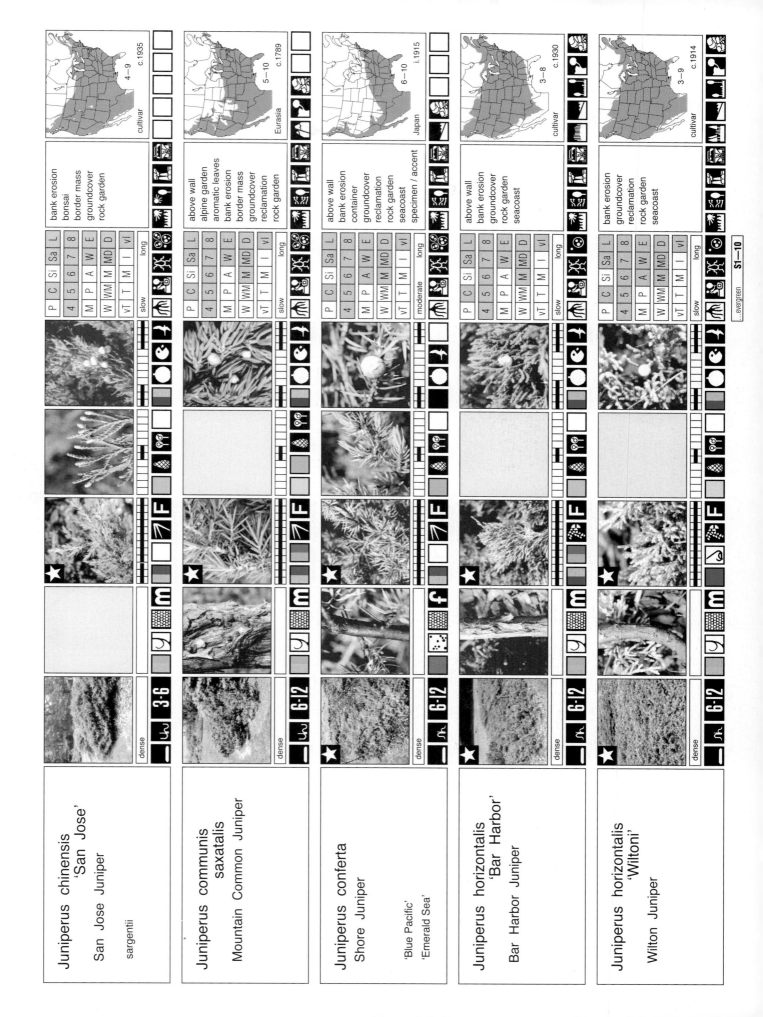

Juniperus chinensis 'San Jose'
San Jose Juniper
sargentii

cultivar
4—9
c.1935

bank erosion
bonsai
border mass
groundcover
rock garden

P C Si Sa L
4 5 6 7 8
M P A W E
W WM M MD D
vT T M I vl
slow · long
dense · 3-6

Juniperus communis saxatalis
Mountain Common Juniper

Eurasia
5—10
c.1789

above wall
alpine garden
aromatic leaves
bank erosion
border mass
groundcover
reclamation
rock garden

P C Si Sa L
4 5 6 7 8
M P A W E
W WM M MD D
vT T M I vl
slow · long
dense · 6-12

Juniperus conferta
Shore Juniper

'Blue Pacific'
'Emerald Sea'

Japan
6—10
i.1915

above wall
bank erosion
container
groundcover
reclamation
rock garden
seacoast
specimen / accent

P C Si Sa L
4 5 6 7 8
M P A W E
W WM M MD D
vT T M I vl
moderate · long
dense · 6-12

Juniperus horizontalis 'Bar Harbor'
Bar Harbor Juniper

cultivar
3—8
c.1930

above wall
bank erosion
groundcover
rock garden
seacoast

P C Si Sa L
4 5 6 7 8
M P A W E
W WM M MD D
vT T M I vl
slow · long
dense · 6-12

Juniperus horizontalis 'Wiltoni'
Wilton Juniper

cultivar
3—9
c.1914

bank erosion
groundcover
reclamation
rock garden
seacoast

P C Si Sa L
4 5 6 7 8
M P A W E
W WM M MD D
vT T M I vl
slow · long
dense · 6-12

...evergreen   S1—10

VERY SMALL SHRUB	FORM	BARK	LEAF	FLOWER	FRUIT	CULTURE	USES	REGION

Juniperus sabina 'Arcadia'
Arcadia Juniper

- FORM: dense, 6-12
- CULTURE: P C Si Sa L / 4 5 6 7 8 / M P A W E / W WM M MD D / vT T M I Vl / long / slow
- USES: aromatic leaves / bank erosion / groundcover / reclamation / rock garden / seacoast
- REGION: 4–(8a) / cultivar / i.1949

Juniperus sabina 'Broadmoor'
Broadmoor Juniper

- FORM: dense, 12-20
- CULTURE: P C Si Sa L / 4 5 6 7 8 / M P A W E / W WM M MD D / vT T M I Vl / long / slow
- USES: aromatic leaves / bank erosion / groundcover / reclamation / rock garden / seacoast
- REGION: 4–(9a) / cultivar / i.1963

Linnaea borealis
Twinflower

- FORM: open, 1-3
- CULTURE: P C Si Sa L / 4 5 6 7 8 / M P A W E / W WM M MD D / vT T M I Vl / short / fast
- USES: alpine garden / bog garden / groundcover / moss garden / rock garden / woodland garden
- REGION: 2–6 / Circumboreal / c.1762

Loiseleuria procumbens
Alpineazalea

- FORM: moderate, 1-3
- CULTURE: P C Si Sa L / 4 5 6 7 8 / M P A W E / W WM M MD D / vT T M I Vl / short / slow
- USES: alpine garden / rock garden / specimen / accent
- REGION: 2–5 / Circumpolar / c.1800

Mahonia repens
Creeping Mahonia

- FORM: dense, 3-6
- CULTURE: P C Si Sa L / 4 5 6 7 8 / M P A W E / W WM M MD D / vT T M I Vl / short / slow
- USES: bank erosion / cut foliage / leaf arrangement / groundcover / jellies, jams / low maintenance
- REGION: 5b–10 / Pacific Mts. / i.a.1890

Margyricarpus setosus syn. **M. pinnatus**

Pearlberry
Pearlfruit

Ecuador 7–9 i.1829

container
fruit arrangement
greenhouse
groundcover
rock garden
seacoast

| P | C | Si | Sa | 4 | 5 | 6 | 7 | 8 | L | M | P | A | W | E | W | WM | M | MD | D | vT | T | M | I | vI |

slow · short · open · 1-3

Microbiota decussata
Siberian Carpet Cypress

'Siberian Carpet'

Siberia 2–8

bank erosion
container
groundcover
rock garden
seacoast

| P | C | Si | Sa | 4 | 5 | 6 | 7 | 8 | L | M | P | A | W | E | W | WM | M | MD | D | vT | T | M | I | vI |

slow · long · dense · 6-12

Myoporum debile

Australia 9–10

bank erosion
groundcover
rock garden
seacoast

| P | C | Si | Sa | 4 | 5 | 6 | 7 | 8 | L | M | P | A | W | E | W | WM | M | MD | D | vT | T | M | I | vI |

fast · short · dense · 3-6

Myoporum parvifolium

'Carsonii'
'Putah Creek'

Australia 9–10

bank erosion
groundcover
patio garden
seacoast

| P | C | Si | Sa | 4 | 5 | 6 | 7 | 8 | L | M | P | A | W | E | W | WM | M | MD | D | vT | T | M | I | vI |

fast · short · dense · 6-12

Opuntia fragilis
Brittle Pricklypear

c. U.S. 5–10 i.1814

bank erosion
greenhouse
house plant
rock garden
seacoast

| P | C | Si | Sa | 4 | 5 | 6 | 7 | 8 | L | M | P | A | W | E | W | WM | M | MD | D | vT | T | M | I | vI |

slow · long · dense · 1-3

VERY SMALL SHRUB	FORM	BARK	LEAF	FLOWER	FRUIT	CULTURE	USES	REGION

Opuntia polyacantha
Plains Pricklypear

- FORM: dense
- CULTURE: P C Si Sa L / 4 5 6 7 8 / M P A W E / W WM M MD D / vT T M I vl — long, slow
- USES: bank erosion, greenhouse, house plant, rock garden, seacoast
- REGION: w. U.S. — 4–9 — c.1814

Pachysandra terminalis
Japanese Spurge
Japanese Pachysandra
'Green Carpet'
'Silver Edge'

- FORM: open-dense, slow
- CULTURE: P C Si Sa L / 4 5 6 7 8 / M P A W E / W WM M MD D / vT T M I vl
- USES: bank erosion, groundcover, rock garden
- REGION: Japan — 4–10 — i.1822

Parahebe lyalli
syn. Hebe l.

- FORM: dense, slow, short
- CULTURE: P C Si Sa L / 4 5 6 7 8 / M P A W E / W WM M MD D / vT T M I vl
- USES: container, groundcover, leathery leaves, rock garden, seacoast
- REGION: New Zealand — 8–9 — i.1870

Paxistima canbyi
syn. Pachistima c.
Canby Pachistima
'Compacta'

- FORM: moderate, slow, short
- CULTURE: P C Si Sa L / 4 5 6 7 8 / M P A W E / W WM M MD D / vT T M I vl
- USES: bank erosion, border mass, groundcover, preservation, rock garden, woodland garden
- REGION: e.U.S. Mts. — 4b–7 — c.1800

Paxistima myrsinites
syn. Pachistima m.
Myrtle Pachistima
Oregon Boxwood

- FORM: open, slow, short
- CULTURE: P C Si Sa L / 4 5 6 7 8 / M P A W E / W WM M MD D / vT T M I vl
- USES: bank erosion, border mass, groundcover, preservation, rock garden, seacoast, woodland garden
- REGION: Rocky Mts. — 6b–8 — c.1879

Penstemon fruticosus
Bush Penstemon

s.w. U.S. — 6–8 — c.1838

container
cut flowers
edging
flower beds
naturalizing
rock garden
seacoast
specimen / accent

P	C	Si	Sa	L
4	5	6	7	8
M	P	A	W	E
W	WM	M	MD	D
vT	T	M	I	vI

short — fast — moderate — 1-3

Penstemon newberryi
Newberry Penstemon
Mountain Pride

California — 6–9 — c.1872

container
cut flowers
edging
flower bed
leathery leaves
naturalizing
rock garden
seacoast

P	C	Si	Sa	L
4	5	6	7	8
M	P	A	W	E
W	WM	M	MD	D
vT	T	M	I	vI

very short — fast — open — 1-3

Petrophytum caespitosum **Syn.** Spiraea s.
Tufted Rockmat
Rock Spirea

w. U.S. — 6–9 — c.1900

dry wall (stone)
rock garden

P	C	Si	Sa	L
4	5	6	7	8
M	P	A	W	E
W	WM	M	MD	D
vT	T	M	I	vI

short — slow — open — 1-3

Phyllodoce empetriformis
Red Mountainheath

Pacific. Mts. — 2b–5 — c.1830

container
groundcover
heath garden
rock garden
seacoast
wild garden

P	C	Si	Sa	L
4	5	6	7	8
M	P	A	W	E
W	WM	M	MD	D
vT	T	M	I	vI

short — slow — open — 1-3

Picea abies 'Repens'
Creeping Norway Spruce

cultivar — 2b–7

above wall
formal garden
groundcover
oriental garden
rock garden
specimen / accent

P	C	Si	Sa	L
4	5	6	7	8
M	P	A	W	E
W	WM	M	MD	D
vT	T	M	I	vI

long — slow — dense — 3-6

...evergreen **S1—14**

VERY SMALL SHRUB	FORM	BARK	LEAF	FLOWER	FRUIT	CULTURE	USES	REGION

Pinus sylvestris 'Repens'
Dwarf Scotch Pine

dense 3·6

CULTURE:
P C Si Sa L
4 5 6 7 8
M P A W E
W WM M MD D
vT T M I vl
slow moderate

USES:
formal garden
groundcover
oriental garden
rock garden
specimen / accent

REGION:
3—8b
cultivar

Polygala paucifolia
Fringed Milkwort
Flowering Wintergreen
Fringed Polygala

dense 3·6

CULTURE:
P C Si Sa L
4 5 6 7 8
M P A W E
W WM M MD D
vT T M I vl
fast short

USES:
container
cool greenhouse
groundcover
preservation
rock garden

REGION:
5—9
e. N. America

Potentilla tabernaemontani

dense 1·3

CULTURE:
P C Si Sa L
4 5 6 7 8
M P A W E
W WM M MD D
vT T M I vl

USES:
edging
groundcover
oriental garden
rock garden
specimen / accent

REGION:
6—9
Europe

Potentilla tridentata
Wineleaf Cinquefoil
Three-toothed Cinquefoil

'Minima'
'White Cloud'

dense 1·3

CULTURE:
P C Si Sa L
4 5 6 7 8
M P A W E
W WM M MD D
vT T M I vl
moderate long

USES:
alpine garden
groundcover
leathery leaves
rock garden
seacoast

REGION:
3—8a
c.1789
c. N. America

Rhododendron impeditum
Cloudland Rhododendron

'Little Imp'
'Moerheim'

moderate 1·3

CULTURE:
P C Si Sa L
4 5 6 7 8
M P A W E
W WM M MD D
vT T M I vl
slow moderate

USES:
border mass
container
groundcover
rock garden
specimen / accent

REGION:
5b—7
i.1911
w. China

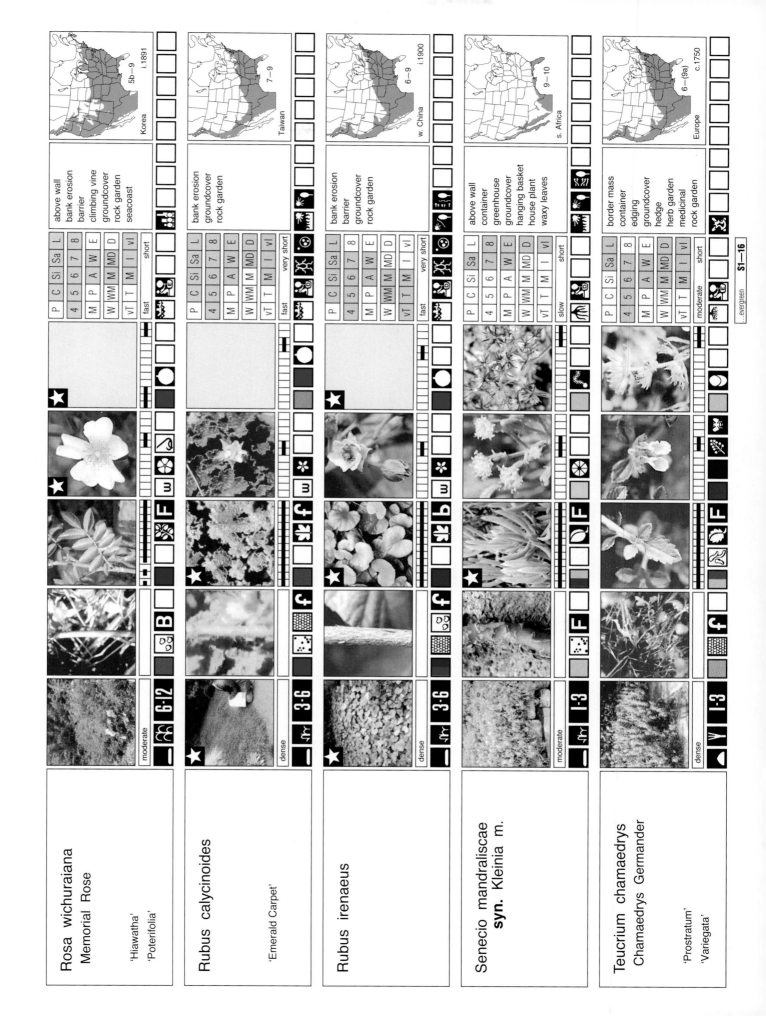

Rosa wichuraiana
Memorial Rose

'Hiawatha'
'Poterifolia'

Korea 5b—9 i.1891

above wall
bank erosion
barrier
climbing vine
groundcover
rock garden
seacoast

moderate

6-12

Rubus calycinoides

'Emerald Carpet'

Taiwan 7—9

bank erosion
groundcover
rock garden

dense

3-6

Rubus irenaeus

w. China 6—9 i.1900

bank erosion
barrier
groundcover
rock garden

dense

3-6

Senecio mandraliscae
syn. Kleinia m.

s. Africa 9—10

above wall
container
greenhouse
groundcover
hanging basket
house plant
waxy leaves

moderate

1-3

Teucrium chamaedrys
Chamaedrys Germander

'Prostratum'
'Variegata'

Europe 6—(9a) c.1750

border mass
container
edging
groundcover
hedge
herb garden
medicinal
rock garden

dense

1-3

...evergreen   S1—16

VERY SMALL SHRUB	FORM	BARK	LEAF	FLOWER	FRUIT	CULTURE	USES	REGION

Teucrium massiliense
Rose Germander

dense · I-3

P	C	Si	Sa	L
4	5	6	7	8
M	P	A	W	E
W	WM	M	MD	D
vT	T	M	I	vI

short · slow

USES: container, dry wall (stone), edging, greenhouse, herb garden

REGION: 2–6 · Crete

Thymus x citriodorus
Lemon Thyme

'Aureus'
'Silver Queen'

dense · I-3

P	C	Si	Sa	L
4	5	6	7	8
M	P	A	W	E
W	WM	M	MD	D
vT	T	M	I	vI

very short · fast

USES: cool greenhouse, dry wall (stone), groundcover, herb garden, kitchen garden, rock garden

REGION: 5–10 · hybrid

Thymus herba-barona
Caraway Thyme

dense · I-3

P	C	Si	Sa	L
4	5	6	7	8
M	P	A	W	E
W	WM	M	MD	D
vT	T	M	I	vI

very short · fast

USES: cool greenhouse, dry wall (stone), flavoring, groundcover, herb garden, kitchen garden, rock garden

REGION: 5–10 · Sardinia

Thymus lanuginosus
Creeping Thyme
Woolly Mother-of-Thyme

dense · I-3

P	C	Si	Sa	L
4	5	6	7	8
M	P	A	W	E
W	WM	M	MD	D
vT	T	M	I	vI

very short · fast

USES: cool greenhouse, culinary, groundcover, herb garden, kitchen garden, rock garden, rock wall

REGION: 5–10 · Europe / France

Thymus serphyllum
Lemon Thyme
Mother-of-Thyme

dense · I-3

P	C	Si	Sa	L
4	5	6	7	8
M	P	A	W	E
W	WM	M	MD	D
vT	T	M	I	vI

very short · fast

USES: bank erosion, cool greenhouse, dry wall, groundcover, kitchen garden, rock garden, seacoast

REGION: 4–10 · n. w. Europe

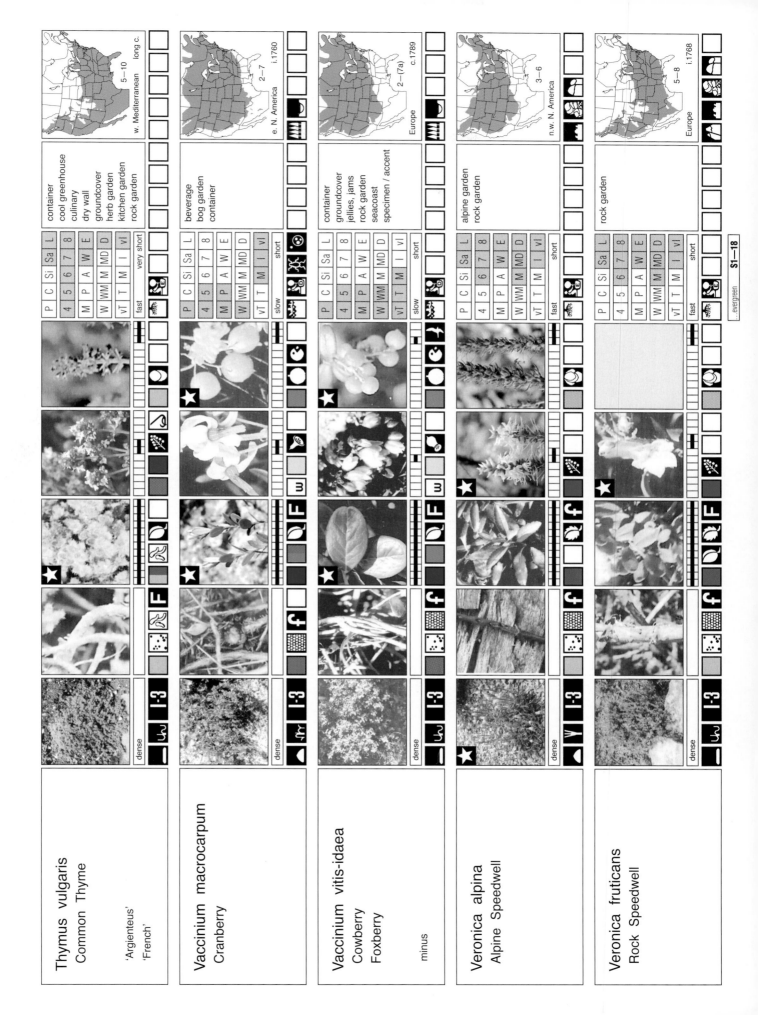

Thymus vulgaris
Common Thyme

'Argenteus'
'French'

container
cool greenhouse
culinary
dry wall
groundcover
herb garden
kitchen garden
rock garden

w. Mediterranean   long c.   5–10

P	C	Si	Sa	L
4	5	6	7	8
M	P	A	W	E
W	WM	M	MD	D
vT	T	M	I	vI

very short   fast   dense

Vaccinium macrocarpum
Cranberry

beverage
bog garden
container

e. N. America   i.1760   2–7

P	C	Si	Sa	L
4	5	6	7	8
M	P	A	W	E
W	WM	M	MD	D
vT	T	M	I	vI

short   slow   dense

Vaccinium vitis-idaea
Cowberry
Foxberry

minus

container
groundcover
jellies, jams
rock garden
seacoast
specimen / accent

Europe   c.1789   2–(7a)

P	C	Si	Sa	L
4	5	6	7	8
M	P	A	W	E
W	WM	M	MD	D
vT	T	M	I	vI

short   slow   dense

Veronica alpina
Alpine Speedwell

alpine garden
rock garden

n.w. N. America   3–6

P	C	Si	Sa	L
4	5	6	7	8
M	P	A	W	E
W	WM	M	MD	D
vT	T	M	I	vI

short   fast   dense

Veronica fruticans
Rock Speedwell

rock garden

Europe   i.1768   5–8

P	C	Si	Sa	L
4	5	6	7	8
M	P	A	W	E
W	WM	M	MD	D
vT	T	M	I	vI

short   fast   dense

...evergreen   **S1—18**

VERY SMALL SHRUB	FORM	BARK	LEAF	FLOWER	FRUIT	CULTURE	USES	REGION

Veronica repens
Creeping Speedwell

FORM: dense

CULTURE:

P	C	Si	Sa	L
4	5	6	7	8
M	P	A	W	E
W	WM	M	MD	D
vT	T	M	I	vI

fast

USES:
alpine garden
groundcover
rock garden

REGION:
Spain
3—6

TALL VINE	FORM	BARK	LEAF	FLOWER	FRUIT	CULTURE	USES	REGION

Bignonia capreolata
Crossvine
Quartervine
'Atrosanguinea'
'Crimson Trumpet'

open — 20-35

CULTURE: P C Si Sa L · 4 5 6 7 8 · M P A W E · W WM M MD D · vT T M I vI · very fast · moderate

USES: arbor, container, fence, pergola, screen, seacoast

REGION: s.e. U.S. · 6—10 · c.1653

Clytostoma callistegioides
Argentine Trumpetvine
Love Charm

moderate — 20-35

CULTURE: P C Si Sa L · 4 5 6 7 8 · M P A W E · W WM M MD D · vT T M I vI · fast · short

USES: bank erosion, fence, greenhouse, groundcover, pergola, trellis, wires

REGION: Argentina · 9—10

Distictis buccinatoria
Blood-Trumpetvine
Mexican Blood Trumpet

moderate — 35-50

CULTURE: P C Si Sa L · 4 5 6 7 8 · M P A W E · W WM M MD D · vT T M I vI · fast · short

USES: arbor, container, fence, greenhouse, pillar, seacoast, screen, wall

REGION: Mexico · 10

Distictis 'Rivers'
Royal Trumpetvine

moderate — 35-50

CULTURE: P C Si Sa L · 4 5 6 7 8 · M P A W E · W WM M MD D · vT T M I vI · fast · short

USES: arbor, container, fence, greenhouse, pillar, screen, seacoast, wall

REGION: cultivar · 7—10

Hedera colchica
Colchis Ivy
Fragrant Ivy
'Dentata'
'Paddy's Pride'

dense — 20-35

CULTURE: P C Si Sa L · 4 5 6 7 8 · M P A W E · W WM M MD D · vT T M I vI · moderate · long

USES: bank erosion, building wall, container, groundcover, fragrant leaves, sculptural, seacoast, wall

REGION: Iran · (7b)—9 · c.1860

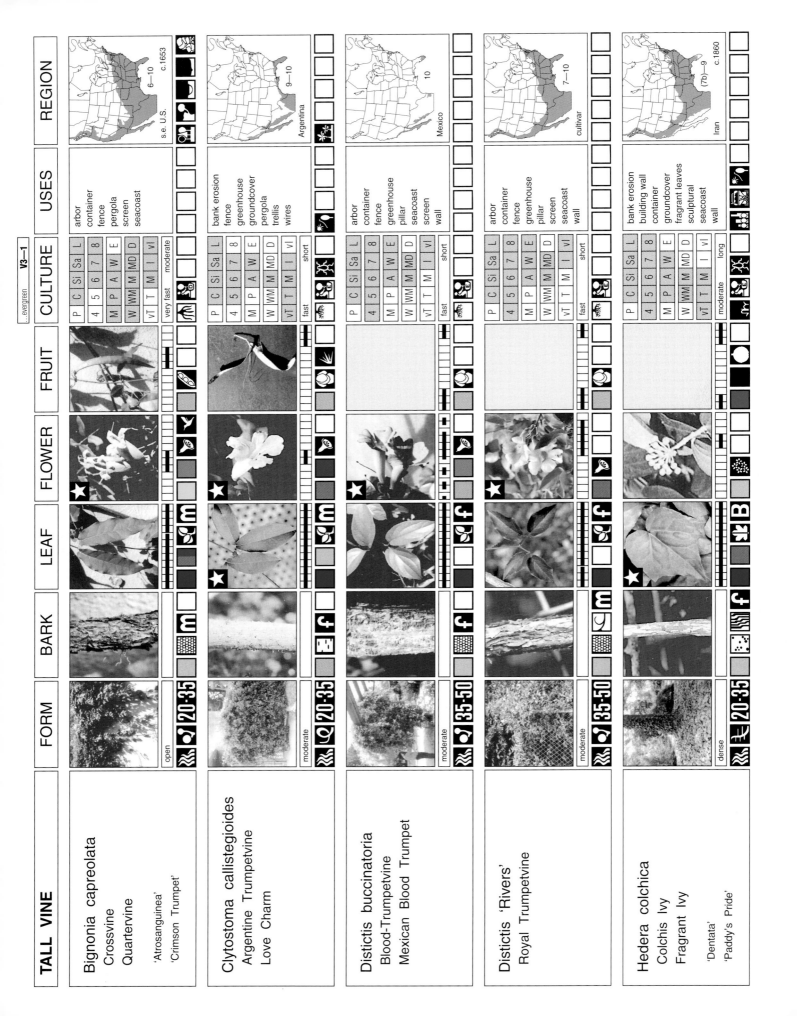

Hedera helix
English Ivy

bank erosion
building wall
container
groundcover
pillar
seacoast
wall

P	C	Si	Sa	L
4	5	6	7	8
M	P	A	W	E
W	WM	M	MD	D
vT	T	M	I	vl

long
fast
dense
20-35
Europe
6-10
long c.

Hedera helix 'Baltica'
Baltic English Ivy
Baltic Ivy

bank erosion
building wall
container
groundcover
pillar
seacoast
wall

P	C	Si	Sa	L
4	5	6	7	8
M	P	A	W	E
W	WM	M	MD	D
vT	T	M	I	vl

moderate long
dense
12-20
cultivar
(5a)—10

Lonicera hildebrandiana
Giant Honeysuckle
Giant Burmese Honeysuckle

'Bulgaria'   'Stardust'
'Pixie'   'Thorndale'

arbor
fence
trellis
wall

P	C	Si	Sa	L
4	5	6	7	8
M	P	A	W	E
W	WM	M	MD	D
vT	T	M	I	vl

fast
open
20-35
Burma
i.1888
9—10

Lonicera japonica
Japanese Honeysuckle
Gold-and-Silverflower

'Halliana'

arbor
bank erosion
barrier
container
fence
groundcover
seacoast

P	C	Si	Sa	L
4	5	6	7	8
M	P	A	W	E
W	WM	M	MD	D
vT	T	M	I	vl

moderate
dense
20-35
Japan
i.1806
4—10

Lonicera sempervirens
Trumpet Honeysuckle
Coral Honeysuckle

'Coral'   'Sulphurea'
'Magnifica'   'Superba'

arbor
fence
pergola
seacoast
trellis

P	C	Si	Sa	L
4	5	6	7	8
M	P	A	W	E
W	WM	M	MD	D
vT	T	M	I	vl

moderate long
moderate
6-12
e. U.S.
i.1656
4—10

...evergreen   **V3—2**

TALL VINE	FORM	BARK	LEAF	FLOWER	FRUIT	CULTURE						USES	REGION

Monstera deliciosa
Ceriman
Monstera

FORM: open, 20-35
CULTURE:
P	C	Si	Sa	L
4	5	6	7	8
M	P	A	W	E
W	WM	M	MD	D
vT	T	M	I	vl
moderate

USES:
container
greenhouse
groundcover
house plant
pool garden
shrub-like

REGION: central America, 10

Passiflora manicata
Red Passionflower

FORM: dense, 6-12
CULTURE:
P	C	Si	Sa	L
4	5	6	7	8
M	P	A	W	E
W	WM	M	MD	D
vT	T	M	I	vl
fast, short

USES:
arbor
bank erosion
container
fence
religious plant
screen
seacoast
trellis

REGION: Peru / Venezuela, 9–10

Passiflora mollisima
Softleaf Passionflower
Banana Passionfruit

FORM: dense, 6-12
CULTURE:
P	C	Si	Sa	L
4	5	6	7	8
M	P	A	W	E
W	WM	M	MD	D
vT	T	M	I	vl
fast

USES:
arbor
bank erosion
container
fence
groundcover
screen
seacoast
trellis

REGION: Venezuela / Bolivia, 9–10

**Philodendron
melanochrysum
syn. P. andreanum**
Black-Gold Philodendron

FORM: open, 6-12
CULTURE:
P	C	Si	Sa	L
4	5	6	7	8
M	P	A	W	E
W	WM	M	MD	D
vT	T	M	I	vl
fast, moderate

USES:
container
greenhouse
house plant
pillar
pool garden
sunroom

REGION: Columbia, 9–10

Philodendron selloum
Splitleaf Philodendron

FORM: dense, 6-12
CULTURE:
P	C	Si	Sa	L
4	5	6	7	8
M	P	A	W	E
W	WM	M	MD	D
vT	T	M	I	vl
fast, moderate

USES:
container
greenhouse
house plant
pillar
pool garden
shrub-like
sunroom

REGION: Brazil, 10

Pileostegia viburnoides
Tangleweed

Himalayas
i.1908
7b–10

seacoast
tree trunk
wall

P	C	Si	Sa	L
4	5	6	7	8
M	P	A	W	E
W	WM	M	MD	D
vT	T	M	I	vl

moderate
short

moderate

20·35

Tetrastigma voinierianum
Chestnut Vine

Laos
10

arbor
bank erosion
container
greenhouse
groundcover
pillar
pool garden
seacoast

P	C	Si	Sa	L
4	5	6	7	8
M	P	A	W	E
W	WM	M	MD	D
vT	T	M	I	vl

very fast
short

dense

20·35

P	C	Si	Sa	L
4	5	6	7	8
M	P	A	W	E
W	WM	M	MD	D
vT	T	M	I	vl

P	C	Si	Sa	L
4	5	6	7	8
M	P	A	W	E
W	WM	M	MD	D
vT	T	M	I	vl

P	C	Si	Sa	L
4	5	6	7	8
M	P	A	W	E
W	WM	M	MD	D
vT	T	M	I	vl

...evergreen **V3–4**

MEDIUM VINE	FORM	BARK	LEAF	FLOWER	FRUIT	CULTURE	USES	REGION

Akebia quinata
Fiveleaf Akebia
Chocolatevine

'Williamsii'
hendersonii

FORM: open 6-12
CULTURE: P C Si Sa L / 4 5 6 7 8 / M P A W E / W WM M MD D / vT T M I vI — moderate / moderate
USES: balustrades, bank erosion, groundcover, pergola, pillar, rock garden, screen, trellis
REGION: 4b–9 / i:1845 / Japan / China

Allamanda cathartica
Common Allamanda
Golden Trumpet

'Williamsii'
hendersonii

FORM: dense 12-20
CULTURE: P C Si Sa L / 4 5 6 7 8 / M P A W E / W WM M MD D / vT T M I vI — fast
USES: arches, clipped hedge, container, greenhouse, groundcover, hedge, pergola, pillar
REGION: 9b–10 / s.America / Brazil

Beaumontia grandiflora
Herald's Trumpet
Easter-Lilyvine

FORM: dense 12-20
CULTURE: P C Si Sa L / 4 5 6 7 8 / M P A W E / W WM M MD D / vT T M I vI — fast / moderate
USES: cut flowers, espalier, greenhouse, pool garden, pergola
REGION: 9b–10 / Himalayas

Berberidopsis corallina
Coralplant
Coral Chilevine

FORM: open 12-20
CULTURE: P C Si Sa L / 4 5 6 7 8 / M P A W E / W WM M MD D / vT T M I vI — slow / short
USES: cool greenhouse, pillars, post, preservation, wire
REGION: 8–9b / i:1862 / Chile

Bougainvillea x buttiana
Hybrid Bougainvillea

'Orange King'

FORM: dense 12-20
CULTURE: P C Si Sa L / 4 5 6 7 8 / M P A W E / W WM M MD D / vT T M I vI — fast / moderate
USES: above wall, border mass, container, espalier, fence, greenhouse, pergola, trellis
REGION: 10 / hybrid

Bougainvillea spectabilis
Brazil Bougainvillea

Brazil — 9–10

above wall
border mass
espalier
fence
greenhouse
patio garden
pergola
trellis

P	C	Si	Sa	L
4	5	6	7	8
M	P	A	W	E
W	WM	M	MD	D
vT	T	M	I	vl

fast · moderate · dense · 12-20

Cissus rhombifolia
Grape Ivy

Brazil — (9b)–10

container
greenhouse
groundcover
hanging basket
house plant
pergola
trellis
window box

P	C	Si	Sa	L
4	5	6	7	8
M	P	A	W	E
W	WM	M	MD	D
vT	T	M	I	vl

fast · short · dense · 12-20

Cobaea scandens
Monastrybells
Cup-and-Saucer

'Alba'

Mexico — 9–10

arbor
climbing vine
greenhouse
pergola
trellis

P	C	Si	Sa	L
4	5	6	7	8
M	P	A	W	E
W	WM	M	MD	D
vT	T	M	I	vl

fast · short · moderate · 6-12

Euonymus fortunei
Wintercreeper Euonymus

'Colorata'   'Minima'
'Greenlane'   'Sarcoxie'

w.China — i.1907 — 4b–9

bank erosion
border mass
climbing vine
container
lawn substitute
low wall
screen
shrub-like

P	C	Si	Sa	L
4	5	6	7	8
M	P	A	W	E
W	WM	M	MD	D
vT	T	M	I	vl

moderate · slow · dense · 12-20

Euonymus fortunei
radicans
Common Wintercreeper
Euonymus

'Argenteo-Marginata'

Japan — i.1865 — 4b–9

border mass
building
climbing vine
container
erosion control
lawn substitute
rock garden
screen

P	C	Si	Sa	L
4	5	6	7	8
M	P	A	W	E
W	WM	M	MD	D
vT	T	M	I	vl

moderate · short · dense · 12-20

MEDIUM VINE	FORM	BARK	LEAF	FLOWER	FRUIT	CULTURE	USES	REGION

Euonymus fortunei vegetus
Bigleaf Wintercreeper
Euonymus
'Minima' 'Variegata'
'Quercifolia'

- FORM: 20-35, dense
- CULTURE: P C Si Sa L / 4 5 6 7 8 / M P A W E / W WM M MD D / vT T M I vl — slow, moderate
- USES: building wall, climbing vine, low wall, seacoast
- REGION: Japan, 4b–9, i.1876

Ficus pumila
Creeping Fig
Climbing Fig

- FORM: 12-20, dense
- CULTURE: P C Si Sa L / 4 5 6 7 8 / M P A W E / W WM M MD D / vT T M I vl — moderate, fast
- USES: container, cool greenhouse, groundcover, seacoast, wall
- REGION: Asia / Indochina, 8b–10, i.1721

Gelsemium sempervirens
Yellow Jessamine
Evening Trumpetflower
'Floraplena'
'Pride-of-Augusta'

- FORM: 12-20, moderate
- CULTURE: P C Si Sa L / 4 5 6 7 8 / M P A W E / W WM M MD D / vT T M I vl — moderate, fast
- USES: bank erosion, fence, greenhouse, groundcover, pergola, screen, toxic leaves, trellis
- REGION: s. U.S., 7–10, i.1640

Jasminum humile
Italian Jasmine
'Revolutum'

- FORM: 12-20, open
- CULTURE: P C Si Sa L / 4 5 6 7 8 / M P A W E / W WM M MD D / vT T M I vl — short, fast
- USES: bank erosion, groundcover, hedge, patio garden, shrub-like, trellis
- REGION: Himalayas, 7b–9, c.1650

Jasminum officinale
Common White Jasmine
Poet's Jessamine
'Grandiflorum'

- FORM: 12-20, open
- CULTURE: P C Si Sa L / 4 5 6 7 8 / M P A W E / W WM M MD D / vT T M I vl — short, fast
- USES: arbor, container, greenhouse, hedge, post, shrub-like, trellis
- REGION: Himalayas, 7b–10, i.1548

Jasminum polyanthum
Pink Jasmine

container
greenhouse
groundcover
pillar
trellis

w. China — i.1891 — 9–10

P C Si Sa L | 4 5 6 7 8 | M P A W E | W WM M MD D | vT T M I Vl

open — fast — short — 12-20

Jasminum x stephanense
Stephan Jasmine

arbor
climbing vine
container
espalier
greenhouse
post
trellis

hybrid — o.1920 — 8b–10

P C Si Sa L | 4 5 6 7 8 | M P A W E | W WM M MD D | vT T M I Vl

moderate — fast — short — 12-20

Lapageria rosea
Chilean Bellflower
Copihue

cool greenhouse
cut flowers
fence
trellis
wire

Chile — i.1847 — 10

P C Si Sa L | 4 5 6 7 8 | M P A W E | W WM M MD D | vT T M I Vl

dense — moderate — short — 12-20

Lonicera henryi
Henry Honeysuckle

arbor
fence
trellis
woodland garden

China — i.1908 — 5–9

P C Si Sa L | 4 5 6 7 8 | M P A W E | W WM M MD D | vT T M I Vl

dense — fast — short — 20-35

Mandevilla x amabilis

arbor
container
greenhouse
house plant
pergola
pillars
seacoast
trellis

hybrid — 9b–10

P C Si Sa L | 4 5 6 7 8 | M P A W E | W WM M MD D | vT T M I Vl

open — moderate — moderate — 6-12

...evergreen   V2—4

MEDIUM VINE	FORM	BARK	LEAF	FLOWER	FRUIT	CULTURE	USES	REGION

Mutisia decurrens

open · 6-12

CULTURE: P C Si Sa L · 4 5 6 7 8 · M P A W E · W WM M MD D · vT T M I vI · fast · very short

USES: cool greenhouse · specimen / accent · trellis

REGION: Chile · 8–10

Pandorea jasminoides
Jasmine Pandorea
Bowervine
'Lady Di'

open · 20-35

CULTURE: P C Si Sa L · 4 5 6 7 8 · M P A W E · W WM M MD D · vT T M I vI · fast · short

USES: archways · container · greenhouse · pergola · pillars · seacoast · walls

REGION: Australia · 10

Passiflora antioquiensis
Banana Passionfruit

dense · 20-35

CULTURE: P C Si Sa L · 4 5 6 7 8 · M P A W E · W WM M MD D · vT T M I vI · fast · short

USES: arbor · bank erosion · fence · greenhouse · orchard · religious plant · screen · trellis

REGION: Columbia · 10

Passiflora caerulea
Blue Passionflower
Bluecrown Passionflower

dense · 20-35

CULTURE: P C Si Sa L · 4 5 6 7 8 · M P A W E · W WM M MD D · vT T M I vI · fast · short

USES: arbor · container · fence · greenhouse · religious plant · screen · seacoast · trellis

REGION: Brazil · i.1699 · (7b)–10

Passiflora coccinea
Red Passionflower
Scarlet Passionflower

dense · 20-35

CULTURE: P C Si Sa L · 4 5 6 7 8 · M P A W E · W WM M MD D · vT T M I vI · fast · short

USES: arbor · fence · greenhouse · religious plant · screen · trellis

REGION: Venezuela · 10

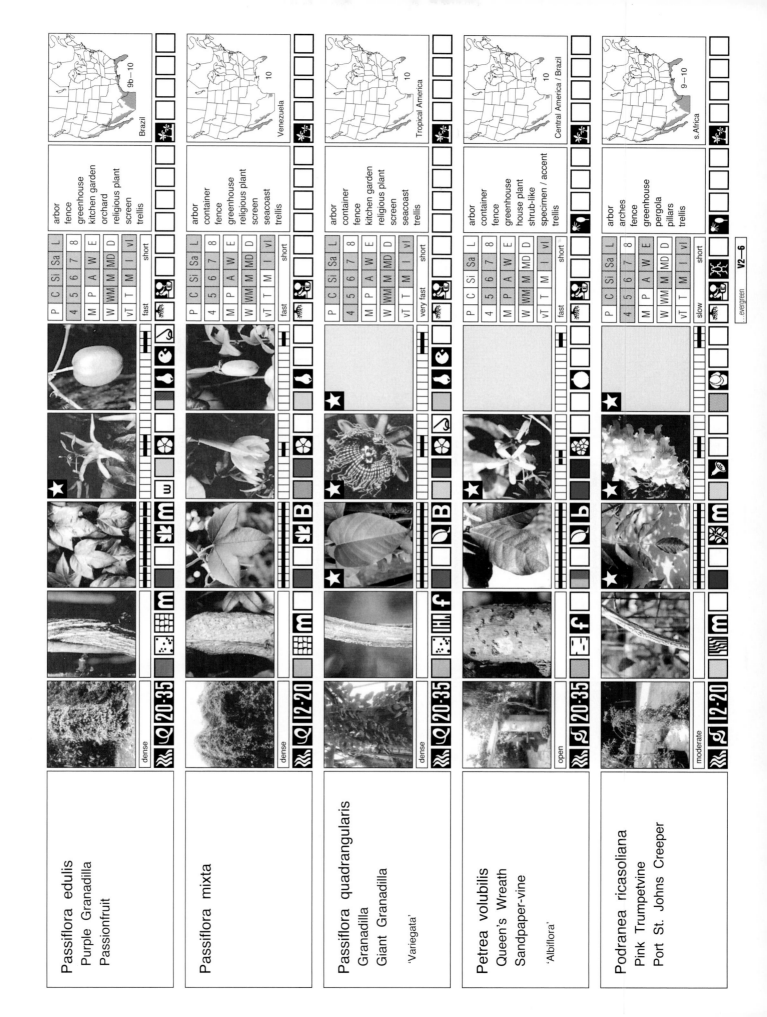

Passiflora edulis — Purple Granadilla, Passionfruit
Brazil · 9b–10
arbor, fence, greenhouse, kitchen garden, orchard, religious plant, screen, trellis
P C Si Sa L · 4 5 6 7 8 · M P A W E · W WM M MD D · vT T M I vI
short · fast · dense · 20-35

Passiflora mixta
Venezuela · 10
arbor, container, fence, greenhouse, religious plant, screen, seacoast, trellis
P C Si Sa L · 4 5 6 7 8 · M P A W E · W WM M MD D · vT T M I vI
short · fast · dense · 12-20

Passiflora quadrangularis — Granadilla, Giant Granadilla · 'Variegata'
Tropical America · 10
arbor, container, fence, kitchen garden, religious plant, screen, seacoast, trellis
P C Si Sa L · 4 5 6 7 8 · M P A W E · W WM M MD D · vT T M I vI
short · very fast · dense · 20-35

Petrea volubilis — Queen's Wreath, Sandpaper-vine · 'Albiflora'
Central America / Brazil · 10
arbor, container, fence, greenhouse, house plant, shrub-like, specimen / accent, trellis
P C Si Sa L · 4 5 6 7 8 · M P A W E · W WM M MD D · vT T M I vI
short · fast · open · 20-35

Podranea ricasoliana — Pink Trumpetvine, Port St. Johns Creeper
s.Africa · 9–10
arbor, arches, fence, greenhouse, pergola, pillars, trellis
P C Si Sa L · 4 5 6 7 8 · M P A W E · W WM M MD D · vT T M I vI
short · slow · moderate · 12-20

...evergreen

MEDIUM VINE	FORM	BARK	LEAF	FLOWER	FRUIT	CULTURE	USES	REGION

Pyrostegia venusta syn. Bignonia v.
Flameflower
Golden-Shower

FORM: open · 35-50

CULTURE: P C Si Sa L · 4 5 6 7 8 · M P A W E · W WM M MD D · vT T M I vl · fast · short

USES: arbor, balastrades, bank erosion, container, groundcover, pergola, rock garden, screen

REGION: 9b–10 · Brazil

Rosa banksiae
Banksia Rose
Lady Banks' Rose
'Alba Plena'

FORM: dense · 12-20

CULTURE: P C Si Sa L · 4 5 6 7 8 · M P A W E · W WM M MD D · vT T M I vl · moderate · short

USES: arbor, bank erosion, barrier, groundcover, metal arches, naturalizing, trellis

REGION: 7b–9 · i.1807 · China

Rosa laevigata
Cherokee Rose
'Anemone'

FORM: open · 20-35

CULTURE: P C Si Sa L · 4 5 6 7 8 · M P A W E · W WM M MD D · vT T M I vl · moderate · short

USES: arbor, barrier, fence, metal arches, naturalizing, trellis

REGION: 7b–10 · i.b.1780 · China

Solandra grandiflora
Showy Chalicevine

FORM: moderate · 20-35

CULTURE: P C Si Sa L · 4 5 6 7 8 · M P A W E · W WM M MD D · vT T M I vl · very fast · moderate

USES: climbing vine, container, fence, greenhouse, pergola, pillar, seacoast

REGION: 9b–10 · Puerto Rico

Solandra maxima
Milkcup Chalicevine
Cup-of-gold

FORM: open · 20-35

CULTURE: P C Si Sa L · 4 5 6 7 8 · M P A W E · W WM M MD D · vT T M I vl · very fast · moderate

USES: bank erosion, container, fence, greenhouse, pergola, pillar, pool garden, shrub-like

REGION: 9b–10 · Mexico

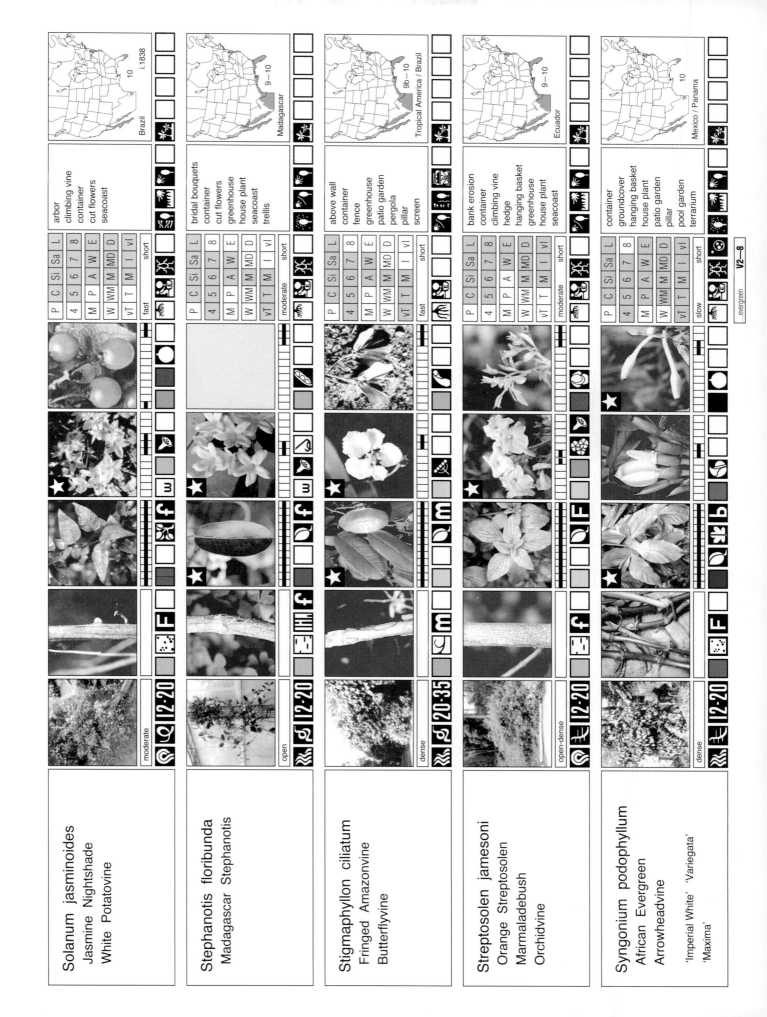

Solanum jasminoides
Jasmine Nightshade
White Potatovine

arbor
climbing vine
container
cut flowers
seacoast

Brazil
10
i.1838

P	C	Si	Sa	L
4	5	6	7	8
M	P	A	W	E
W	WM	M	MD	D
vT	T	M	I	vI

fast   short

moderate   12-20

Stephanotis floribunda
Madagascar Stephanotis

bridal bouquets
container
cut flowers
greenhouse
house plant
seacoast
trellis

Madagascar
9—10

P	C	Si	Sa	L
4	5	6	7	8
M	P	A	W	E
W	WM	M	MD	D
vT	T	M	I	vI

moderate   short

open   12-20

Stigmaphyllon ciliatum
Fringed Amazonvine
Butterflyvine

above wall
container
fence
greenhouse
patio garden
pergola
pillar
screen

Tropical America / Brazil
9b—10

P	C	Si	Sa	L
4	5	6	7	8
M	P	A	W	E
W	WM	M	MD	D
vT	T	M	I	vI

fast   short

dense   20-35

Streptosolen jamesoni
Orange Streptosolen
Marmaladebush
Orchidvine

bank erosion
container
climbing vine
hedge
hanging basket
greenhouse
house plant
seacoast

Ecuador
9—10

P	C	Si	Sa	L
4	5	6	7	8
M	P	A	W	E
W	WM	M	MD	D
vT	T	M	I	vI

moderate   short

open-dense   12-20

Syngonium podophyllum
African Evergreen
Arrowheadvine

container
groundcover
hanging basket
house plant
patio garden
pillar
pool garden
terrarium

Mexico / Panama
10

P	C	Si	Sa	L
4	5	6	7	8
M	P	A	W	E
W	WM	M	MD	D
vT	T	M	I	vI

slow   short

'Imperial White' 'Variegata'
'Maxima'

dense   12-20

...evergreen   **V2—8**

MEDIUM VINE	FORM	BARK	LEAF	FLOWER	FRUIT	CULTURE	USES	REGION

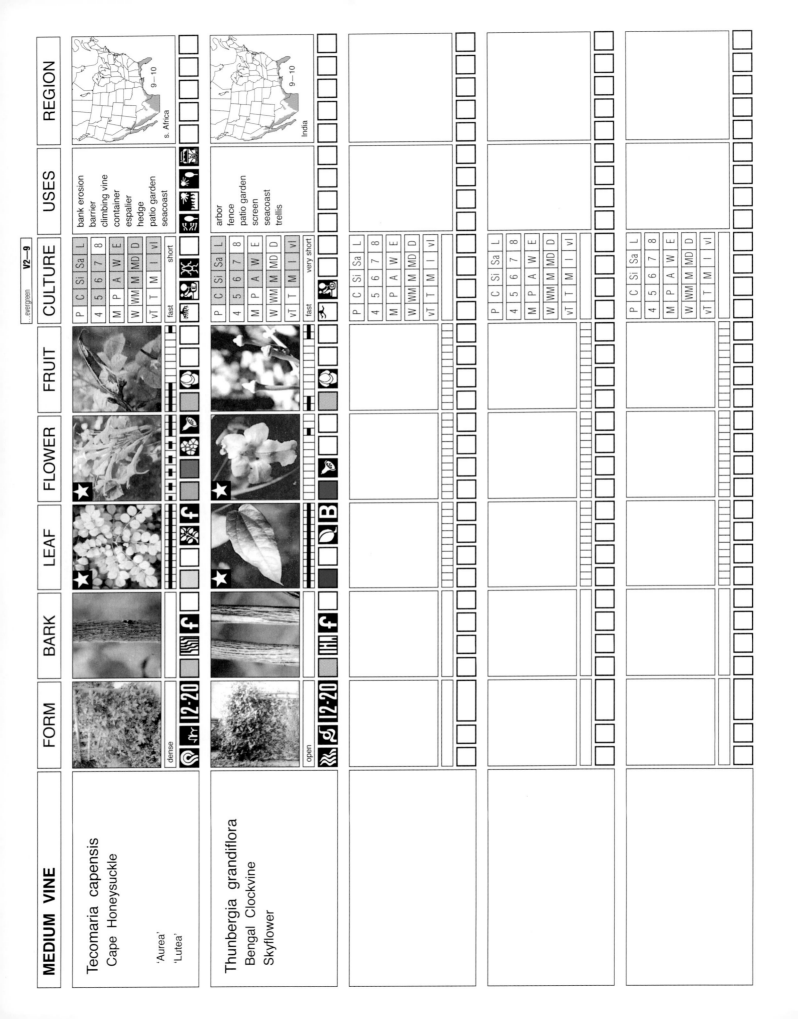

Tecomaria capensis
Cape Honeysuckle

'Aurea'
'Lutea'

CULTURE: P C Si Sa L / 4 5 6 7 8 / M P A W E / W WM M MD D / vT T M I vl / fast / dense

USES: bank erosion, barrier, climbing vine, container, espalier, hedge, patio garden, seacoast

REGION: 9—10 / s. Africa

FORM: 12-20

Thunbergia grandiflora
Bengal Clockvine
Skyflower

CULTURE: P C Si Sa L / 4 5 6 7 8 / M P A W E / W WM M MD D / vT T M I vl / fast / very short / open

USES: arbor, fence, patio garden, screen, seacoast, trellis

REGION: 9—10 / India

FORM: 12-20

CULTURE: P C Si Sa L / 4 5 6 7 8 / M P A W E / W WM M MD D / vT T M I vl

CULTURE: P C Si Sa L / 4 5 6 7 8 / M P A W E / W WM M MD D / vT T M I vl

CULTURE: P C Si Sa L / 4 5 6 7 8 / M P A W E / W WM M MD D / vT T M I vl

...evergreen **VI—1**

LOW VINE

LOW VINE	FORM	BARK	LEAF	FLOWER	FRUIT	CULTURE	USES	REGION
Aristolochia elegans Calico Flower Calico Dutchmanspipe	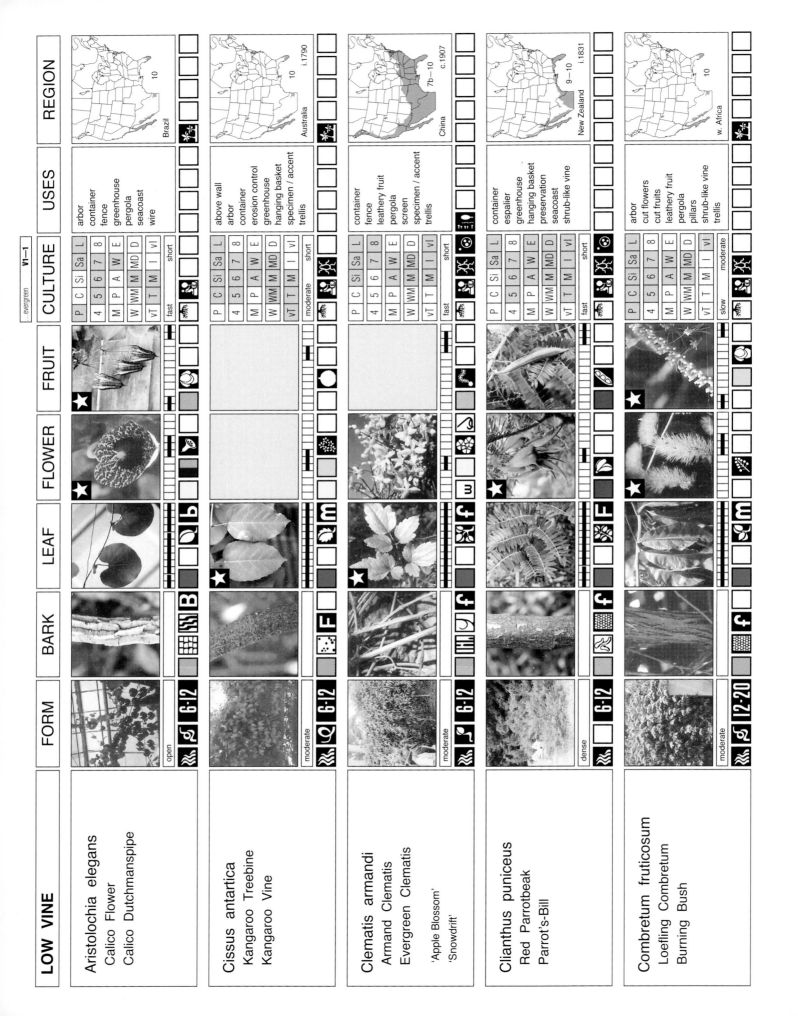open 6-12					P C Si Sa L 4 5 6 7 8 M P A W E W WM M MD D vT T M I vl short · fast	arbor container fence greenhouse pergola seacoast wire	Brazil 10
Cissus antartica Kangaroo Treebine Kangaroo Vine	moderate 6-12					P C Si Sa L 4 5 6 7 8 M P A W E W WM M MD D vT T M I vl short · moderate	above wall arbor container erosion control greenhouse hanging basket specimen / accent trellis	Australia 10 i.1790
Clematis armandi Armand Clematis Evergreen Clematis 'Apple Blossom' 'Snowdrift'	moderate 6-12					P C Si Sa L 4 5 6 7 8 M P A W E W WM M MD D vT T M I vl short · fast	container fence leathery fruit pergola screen specimen / accent trellis	China 7b–10 c.1907
Clianthus puniceus Red Parrotbeak Parrot's-Bill	dense 6-12					P C Si Sa L 4 5 6 7 8 M P A W E W WM M MD D vT T M I vl short · fast	container espalier greenhouse hanging basket preservation seacoast shrub-like vine	New Zealand 9–10 i.1831
Combretum fruticosum Loefling Combretum Burning Bush	moderate 12-20					P C Si Sa L 4 5 6 7 8 M P A W E W WM M MD D vT T M I vl moderate · slow	arbor cut flowers cut fruits leathery fruit pergola pillars shrub-like vine trellis	w. Africa 10

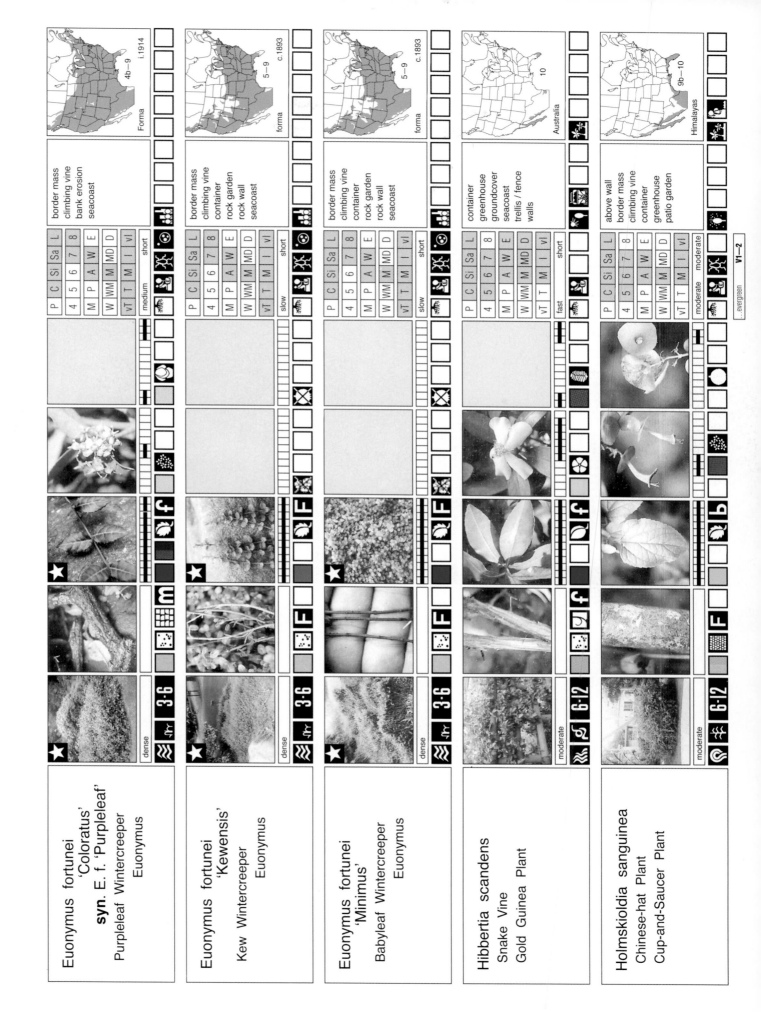

Euonymus fortunei
syn. E. f. 'Purpleleaf'
'Coloratus'
Purpleleaf Wintercreeper
Euonymus

border mass
climbing vine
bank erosion
seacoast

P	C	Si	Sa	L
4	5	6	7	8
M	P	A	W	E
W	WM	M	MD	D
vT	T	M	I	vI

medium · short

4b–9 · i.1914 · Forma

dense · 3·6

Euonymus fortunei
'Kewensis'
Kew Wintercreeper
Euonymus

border mass
climbing vine
container
rock garden
rock wall
seacoast

P	C	Si	Sa	L
4	5	6	7	8
M	P	A	W	E
W	WM	M	MD	D
vT	T	M	I	vI

slow · short

5–9 · c.1893 · forma

dense · 3·6

Euonymus fortunei
'Minimus'
Babyleaf Wintercreeper
Euonymus

border mass
climbing vine
container
rock garden
rock wall
seacoast

P	C	Si	Sa	L
4	5	6	7	8
M	P	A	W	E
W	WM	M	MD	D
vT	T	M	I	vI

slow · short

5–9 · c.1893 · forma

dense · 3·6

Hibbertia scandens
Snake Vine
Gold Guinea Plant

container
greenhouse
groundcover
seacoast
trellis / fence
walls

P	C	Si	Sa	L
4	5	6	7	8
M	P	A	W	E
W	WM	M	MD	D
vT	T	M	I	vI

fast · short

10 · Australia

moderate · 6·12

Holmskioldia sanguinea
Chinese-hat Plant
Cup-and-Saucer Plant

above wall
border mass
climbing vine
container
greenhouse
patio garden

P	C	Si	Sa	L
4	5	6	7	8
M	P	A	W	E
W	WM	M	MD	D
vT	T	M	I	vI

moderate · moderate

9b–10 · Himalayas

moderate · 6·12

...evergreen · V1–2

LOW VINE

	FORM	BARK	LEAF	FLOWER	FRUIT	CULTURE	USES	REGION

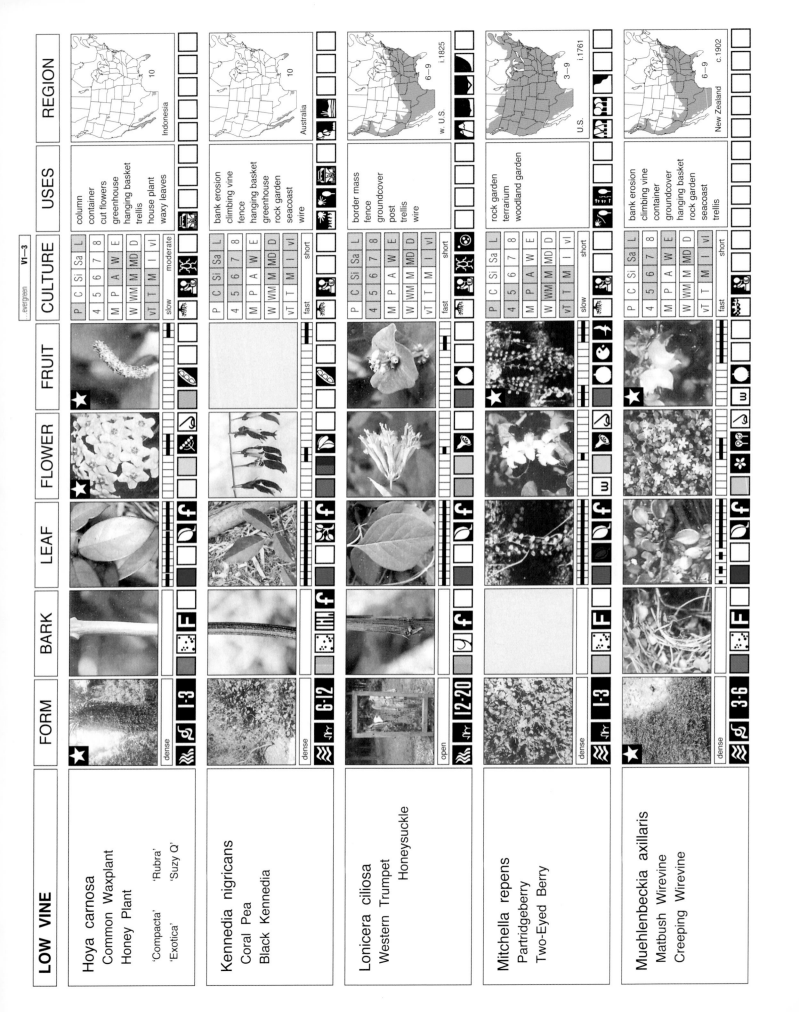

Hoya carnosa
Common Waxplant
Honey Plant
'Compacta' 'Rubra'
'Exotica' 'Suzy Q'

FORM: dense · 1-3
CULTURE: P C Si Sa L / 4 5 6 7 8 / M P A W E / W WM M MD D / vT T M I vl / slow moderate
USES: column, container, cut flowers, greenhouse, hanging basket, trellis, house plant, waxy leaves
REGION: Indonesia · 10

Kennedia nigricans
Coral Pea
Black Kennedia

FORM: dense · 6-12
CULTURE: P C Si Sa L / 4 5 6 7 8 / M P A W E / W WM M MD D / vT T M I vl / fast short
USES: bank erosion, climbing vine, fence, hanging basket, greenhouse, rock garden, seacoast, wire
REGION: Australia · 10

Lonicera ciliosa
Western Trumpet
Honeysuckle

FORM: open · 12-20
CULTURE: P C Si Sa L / 4 5 6 7 8 / M P A W E / W WM M MD D / vT T M I vl / fast short
USES: border mass, fence, groundcover, post, trellis, wire
REGION: w. U.S. · 6-9 · i.1825

Mitchella repens
Partridgeberry
Two-Eyed Berry

FORM: dense · 1-3
CULTURE: P C Si Sa L / 4 5 6 7 8 / M P A W E / W WM M MD D / vT T M I vl / slow short
USES: rock garden, terrarium, woodland garden
REGION: U.S. · 3-9 · i.1761

Muehlenbeckia axillaris
Matbush Wirevine
Creeping Wirevine

FORM: dense · 3-6
CULTURE: P C Si Sa L / 4 5 6 7 8 / M P A W E / W WM M MD D / vT T M I vl / fast short
USES: bank erosion, climbing vine, container, groundcover, hanging basket, rock garden, seacoast, trellis
REGION: New Zealand · 6-9 · c.1902

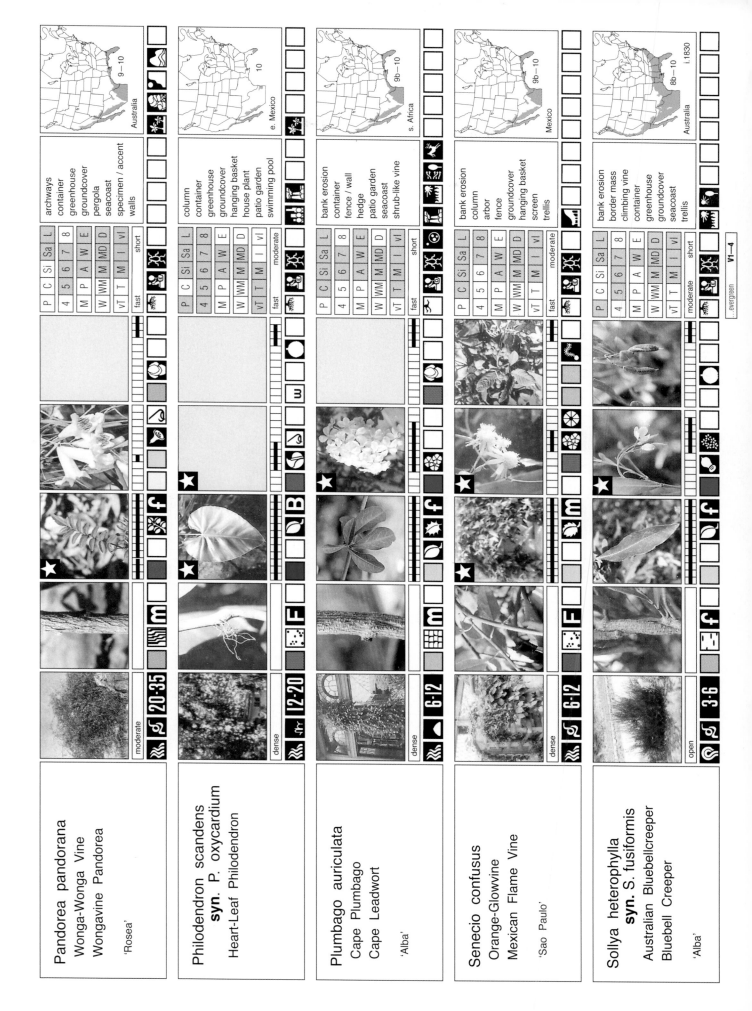

Pandorea pandorana
Wonga-Wonga Vine
Wongavine Pandorea
'Rosea'

archways
container
greenhouse
groundcover
pergola
seacoast
specimen / accent
walls

P	C	Si	Sa	L
4	5	6	7	8
M	P	A	W	E
W	WM	M	MD	D
vT	T	M	I	vl

fast   short

moderate   20-35

Australia   9–10

Philodendron scandens
syn. P. oxycardium
Heart-Leaf Philodendron

column
container
greenhouse
groundcover
hanging basket
house plant
patio garden
swimming pool

P	C	Si	Sa	L
4	5	6	7	8
M	P	A	W	E
W	WM	M	MD	D
vT	T	M	I	vl

fast   moderate

dense   12-20

e. Mexico   10

Plumbago auriculata
Cape Plumbago
Cape Leadwort
'Alba'

bank erosion
container
fence / wall
hedge
patio garden
seacoast
shrub-like vine

P	C	Si	Sa	L
4	5	6	7	8
M	P	A	W	E
W	WM	M	MD	D
vT	T	M	I	vl

fast   short

dense   6-12

s. Africa   9b–10

Senecio confusus
Orange-Glowvine
Mexican Flame Vine
'Sao Paulo'

bank erosion
column
arbor
fence
groundcover
hanging basket
screen
trellis

P	C	Si	Sa	L
4	5	6	7	8
M	P	A	W	E
W	WM	M	MD	D
vT	T	M	I	vl

fast   moderate

dense   6-12

Mexico   9b–10

Sollya heterophylla
syn. S. fusiformis
Australian Bluebellcreeper
Bluebell Creeper
'Alba'

bank erosion
border mass
climbing vine
container
greenhouse
groundcover
seacoast
trellis

P	C	Si	Sa	L
4	5	6	7	8
M	P	A	W	E
W	WM	M	MD	D
vT	T	M	I	vl

moderate   short
...evergreen   V1—4

open   3-6

Australia   8b–10   i.1830

LOW VINE	FORM	BARK	LEAF	FLOWER	FRUIT	CULTURE	USES	REGION

Thunbergia gregori
Orange Clockvine

dense · 6-12

CULTURE: P C Si Sa L / 4 5 6 7 8 / M P A W E / W WM M MD D / vT T M I vl — fast short

USES: above wall · container · fence · greenhouse · groundcover · hanging basket · lath house · seacoast

REGION: Africa 9b—10

Trachelospermum asiaticum
Japanese Starjasmine

'Variegata'

open-moderate · 12-20

CULTURE: P C Si Sa L / 4 5 6 7 8 / M P A W E / W WM M MD D / vT T M I vl — moderate short

USES: container · groundcover · house plant · seacoast · shrub-like vine · walls / fence

REGION: Korea / Japan (7b)—10   i.1880

Trachelospermum jasminoides
Chinese Starjasmine
Confederate Jasmine

'Madison'   'Variegatum'

open-moderate · 12-20

CULTURE: P C Si Sa L / 4 5 6 7 8 / M P A W E / W WM M MD D / vT T M I vl — moderate short

USES: arbor · border edging · gazebo · groundcover · raised beds · screen · shrub-like vine · trellis

REGION: China (8b)—10

Vinca major
Bigleaf Periwinkle

'Morning Glory'
'Variegata'

dense · 3-6

CULTURE: P C Si Sa L / 4 5 6 7 8 / M P A W E / W WM M MD D / vT T M I vl — moderate short

USES: bank erosion · container · naturalizing · seacoast · window box

REGION: Mediterranean 8—10   i.1789

Vinca minor
Common Periwinkle
Dwarf Periwinkle

'Alba'   'Rubra'
'Purpurea'   'Shademaster'

dense · 3-6

CULTURE: P C Si Sa L / 4 5 6 7 8 / M P A W E / W WM M MD D / vT T M I vl — fast short

USES: bank erosion · naturalizing · window box

REGION: Europe 4b—(8a)   c. ancient x

Appendix — A

FORM

orm: Each plant species has a characteristic adult form when grown in the open field under favorable environmental conditions. Qualities of plant form include shape, branching pattern, spread, and mass. The pictorial symbols (38 — icons) that represent the form data in the plantfile are described below.

Star = showy ornamental quality

Photograph of characteristic Form

Mass

Shape, Branching Pattern, Spread.

Shape: The shape of a particular tree, shrub, or vine refers to the typical outline of the crown as perceived in silhouette. Volumetric description (trees, shrubs) and life-form (vines) best express the adult crown shape for each species. Thirteen basic crown forms for natural, open-grown plants are possible.

 broad conical: approaching triangular in outline; broad at the base, vertical axis about equal to or somewhat exceeding the horizontal.

 climbing: tall growing vines that use other plants or objects for vertical support.

 columnar: narrow cylindrical outline; vertical axis greatly exceeding the horizontal.

 elliptic: upright elliptic outline; broadest through the middle, vertical axis exceeding the horizontal by a 2 to 1 ratio.

 globular: rounded, circular outline with vertical and horizontal axis about equal.

 ground cover: very low-growing vines that trail on the ground, resembling herbaceous ground cover.

 irregular: uneven outline; assymetrical.

 mat: prostrate, low, wide-spreading outline; horizontal axis greatly exceeding the vertical, from a 3 to 1 up to or beyond a 10 to 1 ratio.

 mound: broad triangular or elliptic outline; horizontal axis exceeding the vertical by a 2 to 1 ratio.

 narrow conical: approaching triangular in outline; very narrow at the base, vertical axis greatly exceeding the horizontal; spire-like or steeple-like.

 obovoid: upright elliptic to egg-shaped outline; broadest at the crown apex, vertical axis exceeding the horizontal by a 2 to 1 ratio.

 ovoid: upright elliptic to egg-shaped outline; broadest at the crown base, vertical axis exceeding the horizontal by a 2 to 1 ratio.

 shrub-like: multibranched vines that resemble a shrub in appearance and outline.

Branching Pattern: The visual form of a plant is greatly affected by the structure and orientation of the main trunk and of the lower branches (trees) or stems (shrubs). Similarly the form of a climbing vine is influenced by the way it climbs. Branching pattern and the method by which vines climb can be an important design consideration. Trees with descending branches, for example, function poorly as street trees. Only vines with suction discs or aerial rootlets can successfully cover the walls of a stone or brick building. Sixteen branching patterns are most common.

 aerial roots: small, root-like organs along the stems of some climbing vines, used for support.

 arching: branches or stems changing from erect near the plant base, curving horizontal near the middle, and becoming descending at the tips; umbrella-like.

 ascending: main branches or stems diverging from the trunk at a 45 degree angle above the horizontal.

 descending: main branches or stems diverging from the trunk at an angle below the horizontal.

 erect: main branches or stems stiffly upright and diverging at a slight angle (up to 25 degrees) from the vertical.

 horizontal: main branches or stems predominantly oriented parallel with the ground.

 picturesque: naturally irregular or contorted branching occurring occasionally in most species but common to some species.

 recurving: main branches or stems arching, then recurving, becoming ascending at the tips.

 suction disks: a suction, cup-like organ by which some climbing vines fasten to an object for support.

 tendrils: a coiling, thread-like organ by which certain vines grasp an object for support.

 trailing: horizontal orientation, but with most branches/stems hugging the ground.

trailing ascending: most branches/stems trailing horizontally across the ground, then diverging to a 45 degree angle or becoming erect at the tips.

 trailing rooting: most branches trailing horizontally across the ground, commonly rooting and forming extensive patches.

 twining: clasping method by which certain climbing vines wind stems around an object for support.

 twisting leafstalk: clasping method by which certain climbing vines wind leafstalks around an object for support.

 weeping: secondary branchlets or tertiary branch tips and twigs pendant.

Spread: Knowledge of a species' typical adult spread is essential. Installing a young plant in a place that it is likely to outgrow can be a costly and embarrassing error in judgment. This often necessitates severe and unsightly pruning to keep the plant in bounds, which alters the natural form of the plant and the intent of the design. Knowing the spread of the adult plant is prerequisite if proper scale and proportion are to be achieved in landscape design.

Nine categories of adult crown spread are presented for designer review. The unit of measure is in feet.

Mass: The intricacy of foliage and branching, which is controlled by the genetic code of each species, produces a predictable density, which can be measured and quantified. Density is measured as a ratio of positive to negative space within the plant crown. Positive space includes branching, foliage, and other plant parts perceived as line or area. Negative space is the illusory space between the branching and foliage perceived as sky or light. Three categories of mass are classified.

dense: extremely well developed branching, or heavily clothed with foliage, negative space minimal.

moderate: branching and foliage of intermediate density, positive to negative space ranging between a 2 to 1 and a 1 to 1 ratio.

open: sparce branching, or clothed with a small quantity of foliage, high percentage of negative space visible.

Appendix – B

BARK

Bark: The bark of some plants is their most ornamental feature. The eucalypts, stewartias, planetrees, and birches are valued primarily for their showy bark. These and many others are excellent specimens for entry courts and other conspicuous places where their stems, trunks, or branches can be displayed to advantage. While a few plants have outstanding bark ornament, the bark of any plant can be interesting when viewed close at hand. Plant identification is enhanced through bark recognition because each plant species has its own characteristic bark pattern, coloration, and texture.

Photograph of characteristic Bark

Color or color range, Pattern, Texture.

Pattern: The pattern of the bark of woody plants is remarkably varied. Some plants are easily identified by their bark. Sixteen characteristic bark types are observed.

 armed: bark with sharp defenses including ornamental prickles, barbs, spines, thorns, or sharp modified twigs.

 blocky: knobby, warty, or convex squarish blocks or ridges.

 corky: elongated warty or wing-like strips of soft spongy wood.

 deep furrowed: grooved by deep, longitudinal cracks with narrow to wide rounded or flattened ridges or becoming checked across into elongated rectangular segments.

 horizontal exfoliating: exfoliating into broad shaggy, papery, or pencil thin string-like or fiber-like strips that peel horizontally.

 lenticels: numerous and conspicuous round or elongated pock-like markings that admit air to the interior tissues of a plant.

 patchy: exfoliating into irregular mottled patches with puzzle-like configuration and often exposing a colorful inner bark.

 persisting leaf stems: characteristic of some palm trees whose dead leaf stalks do not detach when replaced with new leaf growth; typically these are cut off near the trunk.

 platy: thick squarish or rectangular plates of large size and separated by coarse, deep fissures.

 ringed: usually smooth bark marked with pronounced horizontal lines that ring or encircle the trunk /stem.

 scaly: regular, thin, loose papery flakes or scales separated by a mesh pattern of fine, shallow cracks.

 shallow furrowed: grooved by shallow longitudinal cracks with narrow to wide rounded or flattened ridges, or becoming checked across into elongated linear to rectangular segments.

 smooth: having a continuous, even surface with a minimum of protuberances or cracks.

striped: usually smooth bark marked with fine, vertical lines of contrasting color.

vertical exfoliating: exfoliating into broad shaggy, papery, or pencil thin string-like or fiber-like strips that peel vertically.

woolly: with dense hair-like or downy covering.

Coloration: The vast color palette in plants is a basic aesthetic consideration in their use. The use of plants with colorful bark can achieve emphasis, decoration, and accent in the landscape. Bark and stem coloration is one of the most striking visual features of the winter landscape when contrasted with the white background of snow or the green background of evergreens. The primary bark color(s) for each species of plant is/are presented in the plantfile. Seventeen colors are presented for designer consideration. Light, medium, and dark hues of some of those are also featured in the bark section of the plantfile. A combination or range of bark colors is characteristic of many plants and is shown when appropriate.

black	gray (medium)	purple
blue (light)	gray (dark)	red
blue	green (light)	red-brown
blue-green	green (medium)	silver
brown (light)	green (dark)	violet
brown (medium)	orange	yellow
brown (dark)	pink (light)	yellow-green
cream	pink	white
gray (light)	purple (light)	

Texture: The variation in the smoothness or roughness of the bark throughout the files of trees, shrubs, and vines accounts for their textural appearance. Incorporating plants with extra fine or extra coarse bark texture as specimen or accent is greatly enhanced if contrasted against the fine, medium, or bold textures of other plants. Similarly, the manipulation of bark textures can create rhythm, surprise, or emphasis in the detailed landscape close at hand.

B   **extra bold:** grooved by deep, wide cracks and fissures or having thick squarish or rectangular plates of large size; includes corky, platy, deep furrowed, persisting leaf stems, armed, and some exfoliating bark types.

b   **bold:** having knobby, warty, or blocky appearance; includes blocky bark type.

m   **medium:** grooved by shallow, narrow cracks and fissures or becoming checked across into elongated linear or rectangular segments; includes shallow furrowed bark type.

f   **fine:** having numerous and conspicuous pock-like markings, thin loose papery flakes or scales, thin irregular patches or pencil thin string-like strips; includes lenticels, patchy, scaly, and many exfoliating bark types.

F   **extra fine:** having a continuous, even surface with a minimum of cracks or markings or covered with fine downy hairs; includes smooth, woolly, striped, and ringed bark types.

Appendix — C

LEAF

L **leaf**: Leaves, with their variety of shape, structure, texture, and coloration are the most important visual interest in the summer landscape. Where temperate climate prevails, summer is a season when relatively few plants exhibit colorful flowers or fruit. Plant selection based on flower merit has long been popular, but there is little to justify it. The flowering season for most plants is only a two week period in the year. However, plant selection based on leaf characteristics has much to recommend it. The constancy of evergreen foilage and the changing seasonal dynamics of deciduous foliage as leaves emerge, mature, and color brilliantly in autumn must be considered two of the most enriching landscape perceptions in the human experience.

Star —showy ornamental quality

Photograph of characteristic Leaf

Season (leaf emergence through drop)

Summer —Autumn color (expressed as single or range of color), Type, Texture.

Structure and Shape: The most conspicuous feature of foliage is leaf structure and shape. The structure and shape of a leaf or leaflet is usually characteristic of a species. Botanists, foresters and landscape architects commonly analyze these characteristics to correctly identify and inventory plant species in forest, park or field. The following structure and shape terminology has the authority and precedence of wide acceptance in usage in those professions.

 bifoliate: compound leaf with two leaflets.

 bipinnate: several individual leaflets arranged along each side of a branched axis of a twice compound leaf.

 club: thick, fleshy, club-like, jointed stems; such as those common to certain species of cacti. These plants do not have leaves or they have leaves on juvenile plants that soon fall.

 dagger: thick, fleshy, knife-like leaf; such as those common to yucca.

 fan: similar to palmate-lobed but with many sharp-pointed, radially displayed partitions; such as those common to many species of palm.

 fern-like: long leaves with fine and deeply-lobed margins; such as those common to many species of fern.

 needle: long, slender to thick, and sharp-pointed needle, like a sewing or crochet needle.

 pad: thick, fleshy, modified, jointed stems that resemble a pad or beaver's tail; such as those common to many species of cacti. These plants do not have leaves or they have leaves on juvenile plants that soon fall.

 palmate-compound: several individual leaflets radiating from a single point.

 palmate-lobed: major lobes of a simple leaf radiating from a central point at the leaf base, like fingers on the human hand.

 pinnate-compound: several individual leaflets arranged along each side of a common, unbranched axis (rachis), resembling the pattern of a feather.

pinnate-lobed: major lobes of a simple leaf at more or less right angles along parallel leaf margins.

 scaly: small, short leaves resembling scales and overlapping one another like shingles on a roof.

 simple-entire: leaf having only one blade united continuously along the margin.

 simple-prickly: leaf having only one blade and armed with sharp prickles along the margin.

 simple-toothed: leaf having only one blade with bold to fine jagged-toothed margin, resembling teeth on a saw blade.

 simple-wavy: leaf having only one blade with shallow, rounded, undulating or wavy margin.

trifoliate: compound leaf with three leaflets.

Coloration: The tremendous spectrum of leaf colors, along with a wide assortment of hues, intensities, and values, equips the designer with a color palette that changes with the season. Designers create plant compositions that feature muted or vivid color combinations in much the same way that an artist uses paints on canvas. The spectacular leaf colors of deciduous plants in the fall season are, for many people, the most memorable and celebrated image of the natural landscape.

The first box shows the coloration of the mature leaf as it would appear in mid-summer. The second box shows the typical autumn coloration for deciduous plants or winter coloration for broadleaf and coniferous evergreens when different from summer. Sixteen colors are presented below for designer consideration. Light, medium, and dark hues of some colors are also featured in the leaf section of the plantfile. A combination or range of leaf color is characteristic of many plant species and varieties and is shown when appropriate.

■	black	■	blue-green	■	brown (dark)
■	blue (light)	■	brown (light)	■	cream
■	blue	■	brown (medium)	■	gray (light)

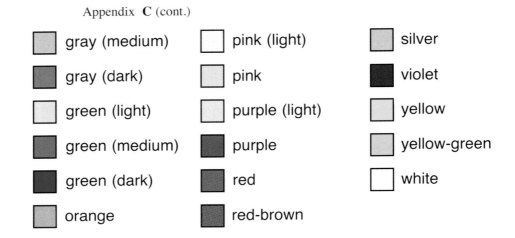

gray (medium) pink (light) silver

gray (dark) pink violet

green (light) purple (light) yellow

green (medium) purple yellow-green

green (dark) red white

orange red-brown

Season: Different deciduous plants have different timing in their leaf emergence, development, maturity, and drop. These stages correlate with seasonal climatic changes in temperate regions. The calendar month during which a certain plant typically comes into leaf or drops its leaves are shown. Correlating those events with a particular season can be an important design consideration, such as identifying all those plants that come into leaf in mid-spring (April) or hold their leaves into late fall (November). The bargraph calendar displays the twelve months of the year, starting with the winter season and the month of **December.** In the illustration below, leaf emergence occurs in May (late spring), develops and matures over a five month period, and drops in September (early autumn).

Texture: Texture in the landscape is primarily attributed to the size and shape of plant leaves. Trees, shrubs, and vines appear bold, medium, or fine textured because of leaf size, which is a function of leaf surface area in deciduous and broadleaved evergreen plants or length of leaves in coniferous evergreen plants. Bold textures are usually featured in moderation as a foliage accent. Conversely, finer textured plants predominate most natural and cultural landscape settings. They function as background for the bolder accent plants. Five categories of leaf texture are classified.

B   **extra bold:** deciduous —leaf blades expansive, greater than 100 square centimeters (15 square inches) in total leaf surface area.

conifers —leaf blades greater than 16 centimeters (6 inches) long.

b **bold:** deciduous —leaf blades between 60 and 100 square centimeters (9 and 15 square inches) in total leaf surface area.

conifers —leaf blades between 10 and 15 centimeters (4 and 6 inches) long.

m **medium:** deciduous —leaf blades between 20 and 60 square centimeters (3 and 9 square inches) in total leaf surface area.

conifers —leaf blades between 5 and 10 centimeters (2 and 4 inches) long.

f **fine:** deciduous —leaf blades between 10 and 15 centimeters (1 and 3 square inches) in total leaf surface area.

conifers —leaf blades between 2.5 and 5 centimeters (1 and 2 inches) long.

F **extra fine:** deciduous —leaf blades compact or divided, less than 6 square centimeters (1 square inch) in total leaf surface area.

conifers —leaf blades less than 2.5 centimeters (1 inch) long.

Aromatic: The leaves of certain plants exude pleasant scents which are enhanced when they are crumpled or torn or shed. Pine, spruce, (most coniferous evergreens, for that matter) pricklyash, spicebush, and lemon are representative species with aromatic leaves.

  aromatic: having a spicy aroma.

Appendix — D FLOWER

F **lower:** A child's first awareness of plants can often be attributed to his/her discovery of the bright colors, perfumed fragrances, and exotic appearances of their flowers. For many people the appearance of a pageant of flowers in meadow and woodland are the most heralded event of the spring season. Flower qualities—structure, color, fragrance, season, and the nectar-feeding birds and insects they attract—have traditionally been some of the most popular design criteria influencing plant selection.

Star —showy ornamental quality

Photograph of characteristic Flower

Season

Color or color range, Structure, Fragrance, Attracts insects/birds, Dioecious plant.

Structure: The diversity of flower shape and arrangement of parts is captivating. The fourteen flower structures listed below are of the most commonly observed.

 bell: cup-like or bell-shaped.

 catkin: tiny blossoms crowded together in slender elongated catkins.

 cone: small male or female "flowers" of coniferous plants crowded into cylindrical cones.

 daisy: composite with disk flowers in a central head-like cluster and surrounded by strap-like ray flowers.

 flat-topped: small flowers in rounded or flattened clusters mostly at the branch tips.

 hidden: tiny flowers hidden from view inside a fruit-like closure, like the flowers of the fig.

 hood: a large bract enveloping the flower spike (spadix), like the 'hood' of Jack-in-the-Pulpit.

 large cluster: large flowers in clusters along or at the ends of branches.

 large solitary: large flower more than 15 centimeters (1 inch) across, borne singularly along or at the ends of branches.

 pea-like: lipped flower typical of legume family and resembling the blossom. of the garden pea.

 small cluster: small flowers in clusters along or at the ends of branches.

 small solitary: small flower less than 15 centimeters (1 inch) across, borne singularly along or at the ends of branches.

 spike: flowers crowded in elongated, pyramidal clusters mostly at branch ends.

 sterile: not or rarely producing flowers.

trumpet: elongated tubular blossom with broad, flared mouth, resembling a trumpet.

Coloration: The great spectrum of brilliant to muted flower colors and the dramatic visual impact achieved in mass plantings of same or mixed colors have an arresting power that has long had popular appeal. Sixteen colors are presented for designer consideration. Light and dark hues of some of those are also featured in the flower section of the plantfile. A combination or range of leaf color is characteristic of many plant species and varieties and is shown when appropriate. Letter symbols distinguish between pistillate (p) and staminate (s) flower colors for some plants, whichever is featured in the accompanying photograph.

■ black	gray (medium)	purple
blue (light)	gray (dark)	red
blue	green (light)	red-brown
blue-green	green (medium)	silver
brown (light)	green (dark)	violet
brown (medium)	orange	yellow
brown (dark)	pink (light)	yellow-green
cream	pink	white
gray (light)	purple (light)	

Season: Flower season refers to the period of time the blossoms remain ornamentally effective. The calendar month(s) in which a certain plant is in bloom are shown as a bargraph. The calendar displays the twelve months of the year and starts with the winter season and month of **December**. In the illustration below, the flower season occurs in May.

Fragrance: The flowers of many trees, shrubs, and vines exude pleasant scents. The spicy sweet blossoms of lilac, plum, linden, and crabapple are well known. Cut flower arrangements from those kinds decorate many kitchen counters and dining tables during the season when they are available. Some kinds are dried for wall decoration and potpourri.

 having a spicy sweet to pungent fragrance.

Attract nectar feeding insects/birds: An abundance of nectar is produced by many flowering plants. This nectar attracts nectar feeding insects including honeybees and butterflies. Some flowering plants have evolved special trumpet shapes with bright coloration that attract nectar feeding birds, hummingbirds, and honeycreepers in particular.

 attract honeybees.

 attract butterflies and sphinx moths.

 attract hummingbirds and honeycreepers.

Dioecious Plant: Most plants have both staminate (male) and pistillate (female) flowers on the same plant allowing self-fertilization. Some groups of plants are dioecious and bear staminate flowers on one plant and pistillate on another. The selection of a staminate plant might be desirable where fruits become a messy nuisance or a health concern, as is the case with plants that produce fruits that are poisonous if eaten by humans. Conversely, if heavy fruit crops serve a useful purpose or are an ornamental feature, then a staminate plant must be planted near the pistillate to enhance the probability of a heavy fruit crop. Mulberry, bayberry, ginkgo, and yew are dioecious plants.

 dioecious: indicates plants with pistillate or staminate flowers only.

Appendix — E $\qquad$ FRUIT

ruit: Ornamental fruits are often as showy as the flowers they follow. Many display bright colors and exotic appearance. Some produce edible fruits and are grown commercially for human consumption around the world. Others are eagerly consumed by many species of wildlife. While most flower displays last, at best, a few weeks, many species exhibit ornamental fruits over several months and yet others for a year or longer. Plant selection based on fruit merit with long duration should be favored over flower merit of short duration.

Star —showy ornamental quality

Photograph of characteristic Fruit

Season

Color or range of color, Structure, Human value, Wildlife value.

Structure: Twelve categories of fruit structure are classified.

 achene: a small, dry, hard, nonsplitting fruit with one seed, often with a long, plume-like tail, such as in clematis.

 acorn: a one-seeded, hard and bony fruit partially enclosed by a cap-like cover at the base, such as in oak.

 berry: fruits with soft, fleshy covering over the seed and less than 15 centimeters (1 inch) in diameter, such as in cherry.

 capsule: fruit of more than one chamber, usually splitting lengthwise along multiple seams from one end, such as in bittersweet.

 cone: woody fruit, primarily of conifers and cycads, having stiff overlapping scales which support naked seeds, such as in pine.

 follical: aggregate of small, fleshy pods on stout, short, erect stem; resembles a cucumber when immature, such as in magnolia.

 large fleshy: fruits with soft to firm, fleshy covering over the seed(s) and more than 15 centimeters (1 inch) in diameter, such as in apple and persimmon.

 multiple: small unwinged, one-celled, one-seeded fruit compounded to form a globose or ball-like head, such as in sweetgum.

 nut: a one-seeded, hard, bony fruit partially or wholly enclosed in a husk which may be papery, woody, leafy, or spiny in character, such as in hickory and buckeye.

 nutlet: a small, hard, bony fruit that does not split, such as in hornbeam and ceanothus.

 pod: elongated, bean-like pod splitting along two seams at maturity, such as in redbud and locust.

 samara: naked seeds with thin membranous wing, such as in maple and linden.

 strobile: slender, pendant, or erect catkin-like or cone-like fruit with papery, overlapping seeds, such as in birch and alder.

 sterile: not producing fruit; flowers are not fertile.

Coloration: Sixteen colors are presented for designer consideration. Light and dark hues of some of those are also featured in the fruit section of the plantfile. A combination or range of fruit coloration is characteristic of many plant species and varieties and is shown when appropriate.

■	black	▨	gray (medium)	■	purple
□	blue (light)	▦	gray (dark)	▦	red
■	blue	□	green (light)	▨	red-brown
■	blue-green	▨	green (medium)	□	silver
□	brown (light)	■	green (dark)	■	violet
▨	brown (medium)	▨	orange	□	yellow
■	brown (dark)	□	pink (light)	▨	yellow-green
□	cream	▨	pink	□	white
□	gray (light)	□	purple (light)		

Season: Fruit season refers to the period of time during which the ripe fruits remain ornamentally effective. The calendar month(s) during which a plant displays ornamental fruit are shown. The calendar shows the twelve months of the year, beginning with the winter season and the month of **December.** In the illustration below, the season of ornamental fruit display occurs from mid-July through September.

Human Value: Growing plants in the home landscape that yield edible fruits and seeds (and other edible parts for that matter) is increasing in popularity. Planting, caring for, and harvesting the bounty of kitchen gardens, herb gardens, berry gardens, and nut trees are satisfying and economical. Such gardens can be more energy efficient and healthful than commercial operations. Reduction or avoidance of chemical fertilizers, herbicides, insecticides, irrigation, and preservatives are environmental and human health benefits.

A few plants have fruits that are poisonous to humans if consumed. The use of such plants in areas where children play or walk is an unnecessary health risk. On the other hand, many of those are relished by wildlife with no apparent side-affects. The use of those plants will depend on each landscape situation. If the designer has any doubt regarding their appropriateness, then they should **not** be used.

 fruits **edible** by humans and nutritious.

 fruits **poisonous** to humans if consumed.

Wildlife Value: It has been estimated that 60 percent of Americans have an active interest in attracting wildlife around the home for the purposes of observing, identifying, photographing, and feeding them. Planting trees, shrubs, and vines that provide cover and food is the most successful way to attract wildlife close-up. Those plants that produce fruits that are favored by a variety of wildlife species and that are an important part of their diet are featured in the plantfile.

 high value: plants that are known to comprise an important measure of the diet of 15 or more species of birds or mammals.

Appendix — F   CULTURE

Culture: Culture is a term used by landscape architects and horticulturists to describe the factors of environment in which a plant grows and flourishes. Important factors of the soil include structure, chemical reaction, drainage, and plant available soil moisture. The amount of shade overhead and susceptibility to damage from insects and disease are other factors that impact the normal rate of growth and longevity of a plant. The characteristic root pattern of a species and ease of transplanting it to a new location are additional information that can affect plant vigor and survival.

The cultural information is organized in the plantfile as shown. The gray or shaded boxes represent that plant's most suitable cultural environment.

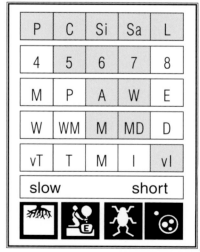

P	C	Si	Sa	L

Soil structure

4	5	6	7	8

Soil chemical reaction (pH)

M	P	A	W	E

Soil drainage

W	WM	M	MD	D

Soil moisture capacity

vT	T	M	I	vl

Shade tolerance

slow .... short

Growth rate and longevity

Root type, Transplant ease,
insect susceptibility and Disease susceptibility.

Soil Structure: Structure refers to the composition and size of soil particles. These particles are classified in five general categories: gravel and sands, medium loams, silts, clays, and peat. Soil composition with high percentages of any given particle size determine its overall structure.

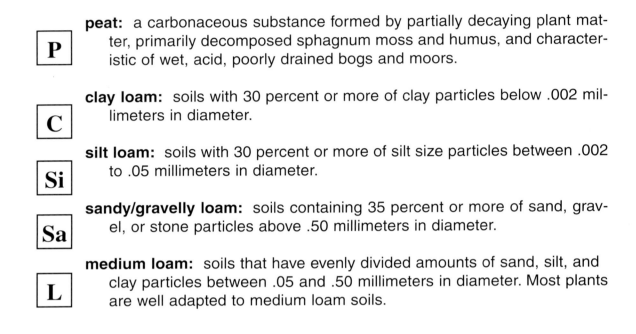

peat: a carbonaceous substance formed by partially decaying plant matter, primarily decomposed sphagnum moss and humus, and characteristic of wet, acid, poorly drained bogs and moors.

clay loam: soils with 30 percent or more of clay particles below .002 millimeters in diameter.

silt loam: soils with 30 percent or more of silt size particles between .002 to .05 millimeters in diameter.

sandy/gravelly loam: soils containing 35 percent or more of sand, gravel, or stone particles above .50 millimeters in diameter.

medium loam: soils that have evenly divided amounts of sand, silt, and clay particles between .05 and .50 millimeters in diameter. Most plants are well adapted to medium loam soils.

Soil Reaction: Soils can be divided into five classes based on measurable differences in chemical reaction. The degree of acidity or alkalinity of a soil is expressed in pH values. A soil that tests pH 7.0 is described as precisely neutral in reaction, because it is neither acid nor alkaline. Most plants are adapted to slightly acid and neutral soils. Some demand strong acid soils. A few tolerate alkaline.

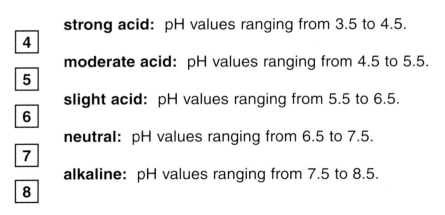

strong acid: pH values ranging from 3.5 to 4.5.

moderate acid: pH values ranging from 4.5 to 5.5.

slight acid: pH values ranging from 5.5 to 6.5.

neutral: pH values ranging from 6.5 to 7.5.

alkaline: pH values ranging from 7.5 to 8.5.

Soil Drainage: Drainage refers to the frequency and duration of saturation or partial saturation of the soil. Five classes of natural soil drainage are recognized.

| M |

minimally drained: Water is removed from the soil so slowly that free water remains at or on the surface during most of the growing season. Very poorly drained soils are commonly level or depressed and are frequently ponded. Yet, where rainfall is high and nearly continuous, they can have moderate or high slope gradients, as for example in "hill-peats" and "climatic moors". Minimally drained soils are cold, which results in a much shorter growing season.

| P |

poorly drained: Water is removed slowly enough that the soil is wet for significant periods during the growing season. Poorly drained soils commonly have a slowly pervious layer, a high water table, additional water from seepage, nearly continuous rainfall, or a combination of these.

| A |

average drainage: Water is removed from the soil somewhat slowly during some periods. Average drained soils are wet for only a short time during the growing season. They commonly have a slowly pervious layer within or directly below the solum, or periodically receive high rainfall, or both. Most plants attain their best development in average to well drained soils.

| W |

well drained: Water is removed from the soil readily, but not rapidly. It is available to plants throughout most of the growing season, and wetness does not inhibit growth of plant roots for significant periods during most growing seasons. Well drained soils are commonly medium textured.

| E |

excessively drained: Water is removed from the soil very rapidly. Soils are commonly very coarse textured, rocky or sandy, and shallow. Some are on slopes so steep that much of the water they receive is lost as runoff.

Soil Moisture Capacity: Soil moisture capacity refers to the capacity of soils to hold water available for use by most plants. It is commonly defined as the difference between the amount of soil water at field moisture capacity and the amount at wilting point. Field moisture capacity is the moisture content of a soil held between the soil particles by surface tension after the gravitational or free water has drained away two or three days after a soaking rain. It is commonly expressed as inches of water per given depth of soil. The capacity, in inches, in a 150 centimeter (60-inch) profile is expressed as:

wet: More than 30 cm (12 inches).

| W | **moderately wet:** 22.5 to 30 cm (9 to 12 inches). |

| WM | **moist:** 15 to 22.5 cm (6 to 9 inches). |

| M | **moderately dry:** 7.5 to 15 cm (3 to 6 inches). |

| MD | **dry:** 0 to 7.5 cm (0 to 3 inches). |

| D |

Shade Tolerance: Most plants do well in full sun exposure. Where plants are being considered for shaded or partially shaded sites, however, it becomes important to know those that will perform best and how much shade each will endure. Yet, other plants demand some shade in order to grow well. Five classes of shade tolerance have been delineated.

very tolerant: plants that grow well beneath continuous dense, canopy shade including those that dehydrate, scorch, or burn in sun and therefore demand shade protection.

| vT |

tolerant: plants that grow well beneath mostly shaded canopy with flecks of sun.

| T |

moderately tolerant: plants that grow well in part-day shade caused by a building or beneath canopy trees with continuous and somewhat equivalent proportions of sun and shade.

| mT |

intolerant: plants that grow well in mostly sunny areas with flecks of shade.

| I |

very intolerant: plants that grow well in continuous full sun, including those that become suppressed in shade and therefore demand full sun exposure.

| vI |

Growth Rate: The predictable vertical increase in the height of a plant during one growing season determines its rate of growth. Different species have correspondingly varying rates of growth. Rate is also influenced by numerous variables such as age and factors of the plant's physical environment. Generally, young trees grow rapidly, adding a great deal of height before slowing with maturity.

fast: having the potential to produce 60 centimeters (24 inches) or more of stem growth annually.

moderate: having between 30 and 60 centimeters (12 to 24 inches) of stem growth in one year.

slow: having less than 30 centimeters (12 inches) of stem growth in one year.

Longevity: Refers to the length of time a selected plant can be expected to live where environmental conditions are most favorable.

very long: living 500 years or more, having the potential to endure for one or more millennia.

long: living for centuries, from 100 to 500 years.

moderate: living for decades, from 20 to 100 years.

short: living for years, from 5 to 20.

very short: living 5 years or less, having an extremely short life expectancy due to genetic constitution.

Root Structure: The roots of a plant perform two primary functions. The work of large lateral roots anchor and brace the plant. Fine roots and roothairs filter and draw in a steady supply of oxygen, water, and minerals, which nourishes the growth of the plant. Generally, plants have a tendency to develop root system arrangements of six types.

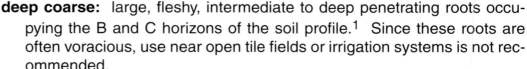

deep coarse: large, fleshy, intermediate to deep penetrating roots occupying the B and C horizons of the soil profile.[1] Since these roots are often voracious, use near open tile fields or irrigation systems is not recommended.

deep fibrous: fibrous mass of fine lateral roots that penetrate to considerable depth into the B and C horizons of the soil profile.

shallow coarse: large, fleshy roots and rhizomes with shallow depth, commonly less than 12 inches.

shallow fibrous: dividing and redividing, the roots form a fibrous mat commonly less than 12 inches in depth and from 1 1/2 to 3 times the spread of the canopy. In the Midwest, shallow-rooted plants suffer early injury during periods of low precipitation. Prolonged drought can result in the eventual death of many individual plants. Similarly, reduced vigor and mortality result when soil is compacted beneath heavy vehicular, animal, or human traffic. An impermeable crust forms which greatly reduces oxygen and moisture in the upper soil layers.

stoloniferous: a horizontal stem, just above or beneath the soil, from the tip of which a plant will sprout. Plants with stoloniferous roots often form large patches in extent.

taproot: plants with deep, carrot-like taproot that may grow to a depth of 15 feet or more. Few plants develop taproots. The notable exception are desert plants including yucca and agave. Plants having deep tap or lateral root systems are considerably more tolerant of drought because root penetration is to a depth where moisture is available from ground water sources.

[1] Differences in color, acidity, nutrient content, and organic matter are in horizontal layers within the soil called horizons. The horizons or layers occur in a vertical sequence from the surface down several feet and make up the soil profile. Three major horizons are in most soils, designated A (surface), B (subsoil), and C (parent material).

Ease of Transplanting: Most ornamental garden plants are transplanted at some time in their life. Established plants generally transplant with ease or difficulty. Species with large taproots, deep lateral spreading roots, fleshy roots, rhizomes, or ultra fine and delicate roots, generally transplant with difficulty. Those plants frequently go into shock, followed by rapid decline and death. Plants that do recover from the shock may lack vigor and health for many years. Generally, valued specimens of those kinds should not be transplanted, or only when very small.

difficult: high risk species with taproot, deep lateral, fleshy, or ultrafine roots and generally poor rate of recovery after transplanting.

easy: low risk, resilient species with shallow fibrous roots and generally quick rate of recovery after transplanting.

Insect Susceptibility: Plant health is affected by the frequency and severity of insect infestation. Sucking, boring, and feeding insects may severely injure leaves, twigs, branches, bark, or roots causing stunting, decadence, and eventual death in severe cases. Two categories of insect susceptibility are presented.

frequent: species whose visual appearance, health, and survival are seriously threatened by insects.

occasional: species with only occasional or minor insect problems that do not significantly alter visual appearance, or threaten health or survival.

Disease Susceptibility: Severe injury to leaves, twigs, branches, or roots may cause stunting, decline, and death of the infected plant in the worst cases. Three of the most virulent diseases are Chestnut blight, Dutch elm disease, and Oak wilt. These usually cause rapid decline and result in death. Two categories of disease susceptibility are presented.

frequent: species whose visual appearance, health, and survival are frequently threatened by disease.

occasional: species hosting only occasional or minor diseases which do not significantly alter visual appearance, or threaten health or survival.

USES

Uses: The 3,600 plants described in the American Plant*f*ile include an almost infinite combination of color, texture, size, and shape. Finding just the right plant for each design situation can lead to bewilderment. To help guide the designer in choosing appropriate plants for specific landscape functions, special effects, or for solutions to garden problems —over 60 landscape situations for which a plant is well suited are featured in the uses section of the plantfile.

beverage
bog garden
border mass
container
kitchen garden
rock garden
seacoast

Key word listing of popular Uses

Tolerance / Sensitivity index.

above wall	espalier	reclamation
allee	forestry	religious significance
alpine garden	formal	rock garden
arbor	fragrance garden	screen
autumn color	greenhouse	sculptural affect
background	groundcover	seashore garden
bank erosion	hanging basket	shade garden
barrier	heath garden	shade tree
beverage plant	hedge	shearing
bog garden	herb garden	shrub-like vine
bonsai	houseplant	specimen/accent
border edging	jams, jellies	standard
border mass	kitchen garden	street tree
bosque	medicinal	terrarium plant
climbing vine	narrow space	trellis
column/post	naturalizing	wall garden
container	orchard	windbreak
culinary	oriental garden	window box
cut flowers	patio garden	window glass
cut foliage	pergola	wire/fence
cut fruits	pool garden	woodland garden
dried arrangements	prairie garden	
dye plant	preservation	

Tolerance/sensitivity index for selected environmental factors:

Plants are remarkably resilient and tolerant of the adverse conditions within their natural environment. Cultural environments are often more hostile. The tolerance of plants introduced to those sites varies considerably between genera and species. The levels of sensitivity to or tolerance of the 13 different factors of natural or cultural environments are described below.

 air pollution tolerant: plants tolerant of excessive smoke, toxic gases, smog, dust, and soot that encrust leaves and injure plant tissues.

 city tolerant: plants tolerant of a hostile urban environment characterized by poor soil, insufficient light, improper drainage, air pollution, extended photo periods from night lighting, and excessive heat and wind, to name the major problems.

 deerproof: plants that deer generally find less palatable or with pungent repelling odor, particularly valued in areas with an overpopulation of deer.

drought tolerant/water conserving: plants that thrive with little or no water in a normal dry year (less than 12 inches of rainfall) or periodic occurring drought.

 dieback: plants that commonly suffer death of the branch tips caused by abnormal heat, cold, or drought.

 fire resistant: plants that will not burn suddenly and easily when ignited by fire. When planted in strips or borders, such plants can function as a fire break. Fire insurance rates have been reduced in instances where such plants have been used in fire prone areas, such as southern California.

 heat tolerant: plants that thrive under conditions of intense solar heat, including reflected heat exposure from buildings, streets, and parking lots.

 humidity demanding: plants of tropical and semitropical origin that demand a humid atmosphere to grow well.

 invasive: plants with primarily stoloniferous root systems that quickly spread and colonize adjacent areas where they compete with other plants for available resources.

 salt tolerant: plants tolerant of natural or cultural saline environments, including salts leached into soils or deposited as aerial drift from urban and rural road deicing programs in northern states.

 sun sensitive: plants that are subject to bark scald, leaf scorch, and browning or dehydration in full sun and therefore benefit from shade protection.

 wind sensitive: shallow rooted or weak/brittle wooded plants that frequently suffer wind throw or broken limbs in ice or wind storms and therefore benefit from wind protection.

 wind tolerant: plants that are decidedly wind firm in the wind-swept landscapes of the great plains, the timberline barrens in the high mountains, and on the headlands and cliffs facing the ocean tempest.

Appendix — H   REGION

Floristic Region: Through evolution, all plant species have adapted with the physical environment of a particular region. Broad regional factors influencing plant distribution include those of climate, such as precipitation, humidity, solar radiation, measures of daylight, and patterns of wind. Bedrock and glacial geology, topography and soils also have a major influence on the plants at regional scale. Within a region, the assemblage of plant (and animal) species are distributed more or less uniformly throughout the area. Collectively the plant species of a region are called flora. The more or less uniform pattern they form is called a floristic region. Fourteen floristic regions are most common in the United States, Canada, and northern Mexico.

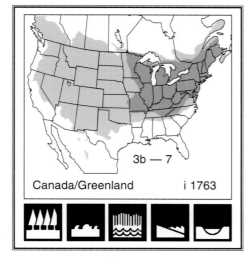

Region of plant nativity (red) and/or adaptability (green)

Numeric zone(s) of hardiness

Country of origin, Date of introduction

Floristic region, —Local habitat. (North American Plants only)

boreal forest: largely coniferous forest of fir, pine, and spruce; landscape characterized by short growing season, cold winters with heavy snowfall, permafrost in the subsoil, even in mid-summer.

 coastal forest: largely coniferous forest of hemlock, fir, and redwood; landscape characterized by high humidity, mild ocean climate, rare frosts, heavy fog, or heavy rainfall of 150 inches or more a year.

 cool desert: great basin, high desert of sagebrush and mesquite; landscape characterized by low and erratic rainfall of less than 10 inches a year, high winds, low humidity, scattered spacing between plants, and cool/cold temperature at night.

 deciduous forest: temperate deciduous forest of maple, beech and oak; landscape characterized by high humidity, 40 plus inches of rainfall a year at regular intervals, mild summers/winters.

 glade: grassland with invading groves of coniferous trees including cedar, pine, and arborvitae; landscape characterized by rock outcroppings or shallow soils over bedrock, alkaline soils; rare fire occurrance.

 grassland: largely short to tall grasses with a few fire-tolerant woody plants such as ceanothus, rose, and leadplant; landscape characterized by hot summers, periodic drought, low yearly rainfall (between 10 to 30 inches), strong winds, and frequent fire.

 mixed forest: transition forest of mixed coniferous and deciduous species of pine, birch, and maple; landscape characterized by many glacial lakes, cool summers, and cold winters with heavy snow fall.

 mountain forest: largely coniferous forest of spruce, pine, and Douglafir; landscape characterized by rocky barrens, cool summers, heavy snow and extreme cold in winter, short growing season, and strong winds.

 savanna: grassland with scattered groves of deciduous trees including oak, poplar, and willow; landscape characterized by hot, dry summers, periodic drought, occasional fire, and 30 to 40 inches of rainfall yearly.

 shrub lands: grasslands with mostly broadleaf evergreen shrubs including ceanothus, manzanita, and oak; low, hilly landscape characterized by long, hot summers with frequent fire, 10 to 30 inches of rainfall yearly.

 southern forest: mixed coniferous, deciduous, and broadleaf evergreen forest of pine, live oak, cypress, and magnolia; coastal plain and Florida peninsula landscape characterized by swamps and sand barrens, high humidity, hot summers, warm winters.

 tropical forest: broadleaf evergreen forest of mangrove, palm, and holly; landscape characterized by high humidity, high water table, floating vegetation, swamps, lakes, bays, tidal marsh, and everglades, 60 to 100 inches of yearly rainfall.

 tundra: alpine and arctic barrens with low, dwarfed, mat-like sedges and shrubs including willow, heaths, and blueberries; landscape characterized by extreme wind and cold exposure, very short growing season and depth to permafrost of only a few inches.

 warm desert: southwest, low desert of California, Arizona, New Mexico, and Mexico with cacti, yucca, and agave; low, erratic rainfall of less than 10 inches yearly, extreme high daily temperature from 100 to 130 degrees in summer, low humidity and strong winds.

Local Habitat: Within a floristic region there are local assemblages of plants called plant communities that respond to very different local environments or habitats. These habitats are characterized by local differences of microclimate and soil conditions that are dramatically influenced by landscape position and slope aspect. Most habitats vary from less than one to several hundred acres in size. The habitats and adapted plant species and communities consistently recur in a mosaic pattern and make up the floristic region. The nature of 20 of the most common habitats are described below.

 alluvial plain: floodplains and terraces of major streams, intermittent yearly flooding of short duration.

 balds: open, treeless, low mountain meadows and dwarf shrub lands above timberline.

 bluff/head slope: often rugged, wind-swept head lands and bluffs.

 bog/swamp: shallow depressions with permanent standing brackish water.

 beach/dune: unstable, hot, droughty and windy sand or gravel beaches and dunes along large, freshwater lakes or seashore.

canyon/arroyo: deep, steep-walled rocky canyons, arroyos, and gorges with free-flowing or intermittent stream at bottom.

 cliff: shear, near vertical rock face to shallow sloping ledges of dolomite, sandstone, quartzite, or granitic rock.

 cool slope: sheltered coves, generally north- and east-facing slope aspects, protection from direct sun exposure with cool, moist soils.

 fencerow: linear corridor with limited width along fences in agricultural landscapes.

 footslope: base of hill or valley side-slope where sediments and moisture from up-slope habitats result in increased soil depth, fertility, and available moisture.

 foothills: transitional hills between the plains and mountains with habitat intermediate between the two.

 old field: abandoned agricultural fields with colonizing plants tolerant of soil disturbance and open exposed sites.

 ridge: narrow, rocky, or sandy ridge crests with severe wind and sun exposure, excessive drainage, and minimal soil.

 river, stream, lake margin: water's edge habitat subject to high water table, poor drainage, and rare (lake) to frequent and violent (river, stream) inundation due to flooding.

 rocky barrens: steep to flat, shallow soils over bedrock with many rock outcroppings at the surface and with hot, droughty and wind-swept microclimate.

 sand barrens: disturbed, wind influenced areas including blowouts, sand deserts and inland dunes with unstable, excessively hot, and droughty microclimate.

 spring: wet, cool springs with outflows from underground streams and caverns.

 warm slope: generally south- and west-facing slope aspects with direct sun exposure and warm, dry soils.

 wet meadow: open, treeless habitat with wet soils, high water table, and organic over-wash from surrounding uplands.

woods edge: narrow, mostly linear, transitional habitat between forest and open field or meadow.

Plant Hardiness Map: Although the combined effects of many environmental factors determine whether a plant will grow, winter hardiness is the most important single governing factor according to many contemporary authorities. The United States Department of Agriculture (USDA) publishes a hardiness map that shows the average annual minimum temperatures for most of North America. Each zone delineated on the USDA map includes 10 degree increments. The plantfile hardiness maps (displayed in green) help the designer determine at a glance whether a particular species or variety is generally adaptable to the project site and region. Since many factors in addition to temperature influence plant adaptability, it is necessary to consult a nurseryman, horticulturist, or landscape architect in the project locale to confirm the appropriateness of your choice(s). Each general hardiness zone can be further divided into an "a" and "b" subzone with 5 degree increments and with the lower temperature occurring in the "a" subzone. The subzone description more accurately depicts the hardiness of a plant at the limits of its adaptable range. These limits can be stretched somewhat if additional protection is afforded the plant. When a plant demands protection, those subzones are bracketed, (6b) for example.

Zone **2**:	-50 to -40 F		Zone **7**:	0 to +10 F
Zone **3**:	-40 to -30 F		Zone **8**:	+10 to +20 F
Zone **4**:	-30 to -20 F		Zone **9**:	+20 to +30 F
Zone **5**:	-20 to -10 F		Zone **10**:	+30 to +40 F
Zone **6**:	-10 to 0 F			

Native Range Map: The natural range of each native tree (displayed in red) is mapped and shows its geographic distribution in the lower 48 states and adjacent portions of Canada and Mexico. The distribution maps are to be used as general guides to the conservation, preservation, and restoration of our native landscape heritage, and is encouraged.

Plant Habitat and Cultivation: As previously discussed, the locale and region where a plant grows naturally or is indigenous is its habitat. However, a plant can often be cultivated far from its habitat where climate and soils are similar. Plants native to eastern Australia, China, Chile, Turkey and South Africa have been introduced and cultivated successfully in the United States. Nurserymen, florists, and arboreta propagate and disseminate the new introductions. These may be wild species, natural variations, or newly originated horticultural varieties. Natural variations or subspecies are geographical variants of a species. They are identified in the plantfile as a three-part botanic name, *Juniperus chinensis sargenti* , for example.

Most horticultural varieties, cultivars, or hybrids are originated by gardeners, nurserymen or plant breeders. Varieties retain most of the characteristics of their species parentage while differing in some particular way, such as narrower form, weeping habit, or flower color. Varietal names are expressed as *Juniperus chinensis 'San Jose'*. Cultivars are horticultural varieties propagated by vegetative means. They are listed in the plantfile by genus name followed by the cultivar name, as in *Malus 'Blanche Ames'*. Hybrid plants are a cross between two species, subspecies, varieties, or cultivars, or any combination of those. They appear in the plantfile as *Malus x zumi* or *x Fatshedera lizei*. The last is a hybrid between two different genera.

The native habitat and dates of introduction (i.), cultivation (c.), or origination (o.) are additional information presented in the region section of the plantfile for those plants that are not native to the United States. This information can be helpful in the restoration or re-creation of historic gardens of a particular period. Use of the dates of introduction for this purpose must be considered with caution, however. Many of the dates are English. A comparison of English and American dates of introduction for selected species with records in both countries revealed a majority with the same date or differences of only a few years. However, differences of several decades are also apparent for some species.

ibliography

Adams, James. *Landscaping with Herbs.* Portland, OR: Timber Press, 1987.

American Horticultural Society. *Houseplants.* Mount Vernon, VA: American Horticultural Society, 1980.

_____. *Shrubs and Hedges.* Mount Vernon, VA: American Horticultural Society, 1982.

Bailey, Liberty Hyde. *Hortus Third: A Concise Dictionary of Plants Cultivated in the United States and Canada.* New York, NY: MacMillan, 1976.

Batson, Wade T. *Landscape Plants for The Southeast.* 1st Ed. Columbia, SC: University of South Carolina Press, 1984.

Bean, William Jackson. *Trees and Shrubs Hardy in the British Isles.* 8th Ed. London: J. Murray, 1980.

Benson, Lyman and **Robert Darrow**. *Trees and Shrubs of the Southwestern Deserts.* 3 rd Ed. Tucson, AZ: University of Arizona Press, 1981.

Briggs, George B. *Indoor Plants.* New York, NY: Wiley, 1987.

Brookes, John. *The Gardener's Index of Plants and Flowers.* New York, NY: MacMillan Books, 1987.

Brown, Dennis Albert. *The Encyclopedia Botanica: The Definitive Guide to Indoor Blossoming and Foliage Plants.* New York, NY: Dial Press, 1978.

Brown, George Ernest. *Shade Plants for Garden and Woodland.* London; Boston: Faber and Faber, 1980.

Chamberlin, Susan. *Hedges, Screens and Espaliers: How To Select, Grow and Enjoy.* Tucson, AZ: HP Books, 1983.

Courtright, Gordon. *Trees and Shrubs for Temperate Climates.* 3rd Rev. Ed. Portland, OR: Timber Press, 1988.

_____. *Trees and Shrubs for Western Gardens.* Forest Grove, OR: Timber Press, 1979.

Craighead, Frank Cooper. *The Trees of South Florida.* Coral Gables, FL: University of Miami Press, 1971.

DeGraaf, Richard M. *Trees, Shrubs, and Vines for Attracting Birds: A Manual for the Northeast.* Amherst, MA: University of Massachusetts Press, 1979.

Dirr, Michael. *Manual of Woody Landscape Plants: Their Identification, Ornamental Characteristics, Culture, Propagation and Uses.* 2nd Ed. Champaign, IL: Stipes Publishing Co., 1977.

_____. *Photographic Manual of Woody Landscape Plants: Form and Function in the Landscape.* Champaign, IL: Stipes Publishing Co., 1978.

Duffield, Mary Rose. *Plants for Dry Climates: How to Select, Grow, and Enjoy.* Tucson, AZ: H.P. Books, 1981.

Elias, Thomas S. *The Complete Trees of North America: Field Guide and Natural History.* New York: Outdoor Life Nature Books; Van Nostrand Reinhold, 1980.

Eliovson, Sima. *Shrubs, Trees, and Climbers.* 9th Ed., Rev. Johannesburg MacMillan South Africa; Beaverton, OR: Exclusive Distributor, ISBS, 1981.

Enari, Leonid. *Ornamental Shrubs of California: 277 Native and Introduced Ornamental Shrubs Grown in California.* Los Angeles, CA: W. Ritchie, 1962.

Everett, Thomas H. *The New York Botanical Garden Illustrated Encyclopedia of Horticulture.* New York, NY: Garland Publishing, 1980.

Fish, Margery. *Gardening in the Shade.* London; Boston: Faber and Faber, 1983.

Flint, Harrison Leigh. *Landscape Plants for Eastern North America: Exclusive of Florida and the Immediate Gulf Coast.* New York: Wiley, 1983.

Fogg, Harry and **George Witham**. *Cut Flowers and Foliage Plants.* New York, NY: Drake Publishers, 1973.

Foote, Leonard E. *Native Shrubs and Woody Vines of the Southeast: Landscaping Uses and Identification.* Portland, OR: Timber Press, 1989.

Garnock, Jamie. *Trellis: The Creative Way to Transform Your Garden.* New York, NY: Rizzoli, 1991.

Gentry, Harvard Scott. *Agaves of Continental North America.* Tucson, AZ: University of Arizona Press, 1982.

Gilbertie, Sal. *Kitchen Herbs: The Art and Enjoyment of Growing Herbs and Cooking with Them.* Toronto, NY: Bantam Books, 1988.

Graf, Alfred Byrd. *Tropica: Color Cyclopedia of Exotic Plants and Trees for Warm-Region Horticulture—In Cool Climate The Summer Garden or Shelter Indoors*. 3rd Ed., Rev. and Enl. East Rutherford, NJ: Roehrs Co., 1981.

Grey-Wilson, C. *A Manual of Alpine and Rock Garden Plants*. London: C. Helm; Portland, OR: Timber Press, 1989.

Gruffydd, Bodfan. *Tree Form, Size and Colour: A Guide to Selection, Planting, and Design*. London; New York: E. & F. N. Spon, 1987.

Harrod, Julie. *The Garden Wall: Fences, Hedges, and Walls —Their Planning and Planting*. New York, NY: Atlantic Monthly Press, 1991.

Herwig, Rob. *The Good Housekeeping Encyclopedia of House Plants*. 1st U.S. Ed. New York, NY: Hearst Books, 1984.

_____. *2850 House and Garden Plants*. New York, NY: Crescent Books; Distributed by Crown Publishers, 1985.

Hightshoe, Gary L. *Native Trees, Shrubs, and Vines for Urban and Rural America: A Planting Design Manual for Environmental Designers*. New York, NY: Van Nostrand Reinhold, 1988.

Hillier Nurseries. *The Hillier Manual of Trees and Shrubs*. 6th Ed. Newton Abbot, Devon: David & Charles, 1991.

Holliday, Ivan. *A Field Guide to Australian Native Shrubs*. Adelaide, Australia: Rigby, 1978.

Holt, Geraldene. *Geraldene Holt's Complete Book of Herbs*. 1st American Ed. New York, NY: Henry Holt, 1991.

Huxley, Anthony J., Editor-In-Chief. *The New Royal Horticultural Society Dictionary of Gardening*. London: New York: Stockton Press, 1992.

Ingwersen, Will. *Alpine and Rock Plants*. London: J. M. Dent, 1983.

Jekyll, Gertrude. *Wall, Water, and Woodland Gardens, Including the Rock Garden and the Heath Garden*. 8th Ed. Rev. Woodbridge, Suffolk: Antique Collectors' Club, 1982.

Joyce, David. *Rock Gardens and Alpine Plants*. New York, NY: Arco, 1985.

Kawasumi, Masakuni. *Bonsai with American Trees*. 1st Ed. Tokyo; New York: Kodansha, 1975.

Lenz, Lee W. *California Native Trees and Shrubs: For Garden and Environmental Use in Southern California and Adjacent Areas.* Claremont, CA: Rancho Santa Ana Botanic Garden, 1981.

Loewenfeld, Claire. *The Complete Book of Herbs and Spices.* 2nd Rev. Ed. Newton Abbot, Devon: David & Charles, 1978.

Lunardi, Costanza. *Simon & Schuster's Guide to Shrubs and Vines and Other Small Ornamentals.* New York, NY: Simon and Schuster, 1988.

Martin, Alexander Campbell. *American Wildlife and Plants: A Guide to Wildlife Food Habits: The Use of Trees, Shrubs, Weeds, and Herbs by Birds and Mammals of the United States.* New York, NY: Dover Publications, 1961.

McClintock, Elizabeth and **Andrew Leiser**. *Woody Ornamental Plants of California, Oregon and Washington.* Berkeley, CA: University of California Press, 1979.

Mitchell, Alan F. *A Field Guide to the Trees of Britain and Northern Europe.* 2nd Ed. London: Collina, 1978.

Molyneux, Bill. *The Austraflora Book of Australian Plants: A Guide to Selecting and Growing Australian Native Flora.* Ringwood, Victoria, Australia; New York: Viking O'Neil, 1988.

Morton, Julia Frances. *Major Medicinal Plants: Botany, Culture, and Uses.* Springfield, IL: Thomas, 1977.

National Wildlife Federation. *Butterfly Gardening: Creating Summer Magic in Your Garden.* San Francisco: Sierra Club Books, 1990.

Nokes, Jill. *How to Grow Native Plants of Texas and the Southwest.* Austin, TX: Texas Monthly Press, 1986.

Odenwald, Neil and **James Turner**. *Identification, Selection and Use of Southern Plants for Landscape Design.* Baton Rouge, LA: Claitor's Publishing Division, 1993.

Palmer, Eve. *A Field Guide to the Trees of Southern Africa.* London,: William Collins Sons & Co. Ltd., 1977.

Perkins, Harold Oliver. *Espaliers and Vines for the Home Gardener.* Princeton, NJ: D. Van Nostrand Company, Inc.,1964.

Perry, Bob. *Trees and Shrubs for Dry California Landscapes: Plants for Water Conservation: An Introduction to More Than 360 California Native and Introduced Plants which Survive.* San Dimas, CA: Land Design Pub., 1981.

Petrides, George A. *A Field Guide to Western Trees: Western United States and Canada.* Boston: Houghton Mifflin Co., 1992.

Phillips, Judith. *Southwestern Landscaping with Native Plants.* Santa Fe, NM: Museum of New Mexico Press, 1987.

Preston, Richard Joseph. *North American Trees: Exclusive of Mexico and Tropical Florida.* 4th Ed. Ames, IA: Iowa State University Press, 1989.

Prockter, Noel J. *The Collingridge Handbook of Climbing and Screening Plants.* Rev. Ed. Feltham, Middlesex: Collingridge, 1983.

Reader's Digest Association. edited by. *Reader's Digest Encyclopedia of Garden Plants and Flowers.* 2nd Ed. New York, NY: Reader's Digest Association Limited, 1978.

Reisch, Kenneth W. *Woody Ornamentals for the Midwest (Deciduous).* Dubuque, IA: Kendall/Hunt Publishing Co., 1975.

Resnick, Susan M. Bachenheimer. *Bonsai: In Cooperation with the Brooklyn Botanic Garden.* 1st American Ed. Boston: Little, Brown, 1992.

Saratoga Horticultural Foundation. *Success List of Water Conserving Plants.* San Martin, CA: Saratoga Horticultural Foundation, 1982.

Schauenberg, Paul. *Guide to Medicinal Plants.* New Canaan, CT: Keats Pub., 1990.

Schmidt, Marjorie G. *Growing California Native Plants.* Berkeley, CA: University of California Press, 1980.

Sinnes, A. Cort. *Container Gardening.* Sunset Books, Menlo Park, CA: Lane Publishing Co., 1984.

Smith, Alice Upham. *Patios, Terraces, Decks and Roof Gardens.* New York: Beekman House Books, 1969.

Snyder, Leon Carleton. *Trees and Shrubs for Northern Gardens.* Minneapolis: University of Minnesota Press, 1980.

Soil Conservation Society of America, Arizona Chapter. *Natural Vegetation Committee. Landscaping with Native Arizona Plants.* Tucson, AZ: University of Arizona Press, 1973.

Spangler, Ronald L. *Landscape Plants for Central and Northeastern United Sates Including Lower and Eastern Canada.* Minneapolis, MN: Burgress Publishing Co., 1977.

Squire, David. *Window-Boxes, Pots and Tubs: A Growing Guide.* Newton Abbot; North Pomfret, VT: David & Charles, 1983.

Stein, Deni W. *Ortho's Complete Guide to Successful Gardening.* San Francisco, CA: Ortho Books, 1983.

Sunset Magazine Editors. *Sunset Western Garden Book.* Menlo Park, CA: Lane Magazine and Book Co., 1989.

Taylor, Norman. *Taylor's Guide to Ground Covers, Vines and Grasses.* 1st Ed. Boston: Houghton Mifflin, 1987.

_____.*Taylor's Guide to Houseplants.* 1st Ed. Boston: Houghton Mifflin, 1987.

_____.*Taylor's Guide to Shrubs.* 1st Ed. Boston: Houghton Mifflin, 1987.

_____.*Taylor's Guide to Trees.* 1st Ed. Boston: Houghton Mifflin, 1988.

Tucker, David M. *Kitchen Gardening in America: A History.* 1st Ed. Ames, IA: Iowa State University Press, 1993.

Van der Spuy, Una. *South African Shrubs and Trees for the Garden.* 1st Ed. Johannesburg; San Francisco, CA: H. Keartland Publishers, 1971.

Vines, Robert A. *Trees, Shrubs and Woody Vines of the Southeast.* 6th Ed. Austin, TX: University of Texas Press, 1986.

Walters, James E. and **Balbir Backhous.** *Shade and Color with Water Conserving Plants.* Portland, OR: Timber Press, 1992.

Wasowski, Sally and **Andy Wasowski.** *Native Texas Plants: Landscaping Region by Region.* Austin, TX: Texas Monthly Press, 1988.

Watkins, John Vertrees. *Florida Landscape Plants: Native and Exotic.* Rev. Ed. Gainesville, FL: University Presses of Florida, 1975.

Wernert, Susan J. editor. *Reader's Digest Eastern American Wildlife.* Pleasantville, New York; Reader's Digest Association, 1982.

Wrigley, John W. *Australian Native Plants: A Manual for Their Propagation, Cultivation and Use in Landscaping.* Sydney: Collins, 1979.

Wyman, Donald. *Hedges, Screens and Windbreaks: Their Uses, Selection and Care.* New York; London: Whittlesey House, McGraw Hill Book Company, Inc., 1938.

_____. *Shrubs and Vines for American Gardens.* Rev. and Enl. Ed. New York: MacMillan, 1969.

_____. *Trees for American Gardens.* 3rd Ed. Toronto: Collier MacMillan; New York: Maxwell MacMillan International, 1990.

_____. *Wyman's Gardening Encyclopedia.* New Expanded 2nd Ed. New York: MacMillan; London: Collier MacMillan Publishers, 1986.

Common Name INDEX

Black Crowberry	e...S1—5	Bougainvillea		California	e...S2—10
Black Jetbead	d...S3—21	Brazil	e...V2—2	Coast	e...S2—10
Black Kennedia	e...V1—3	Hybrid	e...V2—1	Common	e...S2—10
Black Sally	e...T6—10	Bowervine	e...V2—5	Inyo	e...S2—10
Black Sapote	e...T8—8	Bowwood	d...T7—17	Santa Cruz Island	e...S2—10
Black Titi	d...S5—7	Box		Seacliff	e...S2—10
Black Treefern	e...T7—7	Fragrant	e...S3—30	Bufflaloberry	
Black Tupelo	d...T8—15	Himalaya	e...S2—24	Russet	d...S3—26
Blackberry		Littleleaf	e...S2—4	Silver	d...S4—25
Allegany	d...S4—23	Sweet	e...S3—30	Bull Bay	e...T8—10
Cutleaf	d...S2—12	Willowleaf	e...S3—30	Bullocksheart Custardapple	e...T6—2
Blackthorn	d...S5—18	Boxwood		Bumelia	
Bladderbush	e...S4—18	Common	e...S5—4	Buckthorn	e...T6—4
Bladdernut		English	e...S5—4	Gum	d...T7—8
American	d...S4—27	Harland's	e...S3—5	Bunchberry	e...S1—3
Chinese	d...S5—21	Littleleaf	e...S2—4	Bunny-ears	e...S2—19
Colchis	d...S4—27	Tree	e...S5—4	Bunya Bunya	e...T8—4
Sierra	d...S4—27	Bracelet Honeymyrtle	e...T6—14	Burning Bush	e...V1—1
Bleeding-heartvine	d...V1—4	Brazilian Red-cloak	e...S3—22	Burro-fat	e...S4—18
Blood-trumpetvine	e...V3—1	Brazilian Skyflower	e...S4—13	Bursting-heart	d...S4—9
Blue		Brittlebush	e...S3—12	Bush Anemone	e...S3—6
Ceratostigma	e...S1—3	Broom		Bush Chinquapin	e...S4—10
Eranthemum	e...S2—9	Bigflower	d...S2—5	Bush Frostwort	d...S2—7
Mist	d...S2—2	Easter	d...S2—5	Bushclover	
Potatobush	d...S3—26	Kew	d...S1—1	Japanese	d...S4—13
Bluebeard	d...S2—2	Mount Aetna	d...S5—9	Maximowiczi	d...S4—13
Common	d...S3—5	Pink	e...S5—16	Shrub	d...S4—13
Bluebell Creeper	e...V1—4	Portuguese	d...S1—1	Thunberg	d...S4—13
Blueberry		Provence	d...S2—4	Bush-honeysuckle	
Blueridge	d...S2—14	Purple	d...S2—4	Dwarf	d...S2—5
Box	e...S3—34	Scotch	d...S4—8	Southern	d...S2—5
Delavay	e...S2—26	Southern	e...S5—16	Bushcherry Eugenia	e...T6—23
Dryland	d...S2—14	Spike	d...S2—4	Bushpoppy	
Highbush	d...S5—22	Warminster	d...S3—8	Island	e...S5—8
Bluebush	e...S5—9	Broombrush	d...S3—12	Stiff	e...S4—12
Bocconia		Browns Garlandflower	e...S2—5	Bushy Sea-oxeye	d...S3—4
South-American	e...T6—3	Buckeye		Bushy Yate	d...T6—12
Bog Rosemary	e...S1—1	Bottlebrush	d...S4—1	Butchersbroom	e...S2—22
Bog Rosemary	e...S2—1	California	d...T6—4	Butterflybush	
Bokaravine	d...V2—6	Early	d...S3—32	Colville	d...S5—3
Bomarea		Georgia	d...S5—2	Fallow's	d...S4—3
Caldas	e...S3—5	Mexican	d...T6—31	Fountain	d...S4—2
Boronia		Ohio	d...T7—4	Orange-eye	d...S3—4
Pink	e...S3—5	Painted	d...S5—2	Butterflytree	e...T6—3
Tall	e...S3—5	Red	d...T6—4	Butterflyvine	e...V2—8
Bottlebrush		Sweet	d...T8—2	Butternut	d...T8—11
Crimson	e...S5—4	Texas	d...S5—1	Buttonbush	
Lemon	e...S5—4	Yellow	d...T8—2	Common	d...S4—4
Narrowleaved	e...S4—6	Buckthorn		Buttonwood	d...T8—15
Natal	d...S5—10	Alder	d...T6—27		
Showy	e...S4—7	California	e...S5—19		
Stiff	e...S5—5	Cascara	d...T6—27		
Transvaal Natal	d...S5—10	Coffeeberry	e...S5—19		
Weeping	e...T6—4	Common	d...T6—27		
Bottletree	e...T7—3	Dahurian	d...T6—27		
Flame	e...T7—3	European	d...T6—27		
Kurrajong	e...T7—3	Glossy	d...T6—27		
Lacebark	d...T7—7	Longleaf	d...S5—18	Cactus	
Bottonwood	e...T8—7	Redberry	e...S2—22	Barrel	e...S2—8
		Rock	d...S2—10		
		Buckwheat			
		Ashleaf	e...S2—10		

Cactus (cont.)		Hoaryleaf	e…S3—6	Mountain	d…S5—17
Engelmann	e…S1—5	Hollyleaf	e…S3—6	Nanking	d…S4—18
Goldenball	e…S2—8	Inland	d…S2—2	Oriental	d…T8—18
Hedgehog	e…S1—5	Pallidus	d…S2—2	Pin	d…T7—24
Pricklypear	e…S3—23	Point Reyes	e…S1—3	Portugese Laurel	e…T6—21
Spineless	e…S5—17	Ray Hartman	e…S5—5	Potomac	d…T7—24
Teddybear	e…S3—23	San Diego	e…S4—8	Purpleleaf Sand	d…S4—18
Whisker	e…S5—14	Santa Barbara	e…S4—8	Rosebud	d…T6—25
Cajeputtree	e…T8—11	Whitethorn	e…S2—5	Sand	d…S3—18
Calico Flower	e…V1—1	Whitethorn	e…S4—8	Sand	d…S4—18
Calicobush	e…S5—13	Cedar		Sargent	d…T7—24
California Holly Toyon	e…T6—12	Atlas	e…T8—6	St. Lucie	d…T7—23
California Hollygrape	e…S3—22	California Insense	e…T8—5	Surinam	e…T6—23
California Powderpuff	e…S2—4	Deerhorn	e…T8—23	Sweet	d…T7—23
Calliandra		Deodar	e…T8—6	Tibetan	d…T7—24
California	e…S2—4	Globe Eastern Red	e…S4—20	Western Sand	d…S3—18
Camelthorn	d…T6—1	Eastern Red	e…T7—12	Yoshino	d…T7—24
Camellia		Hiba	e…T8—23	Chestnut	
Common	e…T6—4	Japanese Red	e…T8—8	American	d…T8—6
Magnolia	e…T6—4	Northern White	e…T7—22	Chinese	d…T7—9
Sasanqua	e…S5—5	Summit	e…T7—3	European	d…T8—6
Taperleaf	e…S5—5	Western Red	e…T8—23	Japanese	d…T6—6
Camelthorn	d…T6—1	Cedar-of-Lebanon	e…T8—6	Spanish	d…T8—6
Camphortree	e…T7—6	Centuryplant	e…S3—1	Chestnutvine	e…V3—4
Nepal	e…T6—7	Ceriman	e…V3—3	Chile Mayten	e…T6—14
Canary Date	e…T7—16	Cestrum		Chilean Bellflower	e…V2—4
Canaryclover	d…S2—5	Chilean	e…S4—9	Chinaberry	d…T8—14
Candleberry	d…S4—15	Nightblooming	e…S4—9	Chinese Cinnamon	e…T7—6
Candlebush	d…S3—5	Orange	e…S4—8	Chinese Fanpalm	e…T7—13
Candlenut-tree	e…T8—4	Red	e…S4—9	Chinese Fountainpalm	e…T7—13
Capechestnut	e…T7—4	Chalicevine		Chinese Leptodermis	d…S3—14
Cape Leadwort	e…V1—4	Cup-of-gold	e…V2—7	Chinese Neillia	d…S3—16
Carambola	e…T6—2	Milkcup	e…V2—7	Chinese Parasoltree	d…T6—13
Caricatureplant	e…S4—16	Showy	e…V2—7	Chinese Scholartree	d…T8—24
Carob	e…T7—5	Chamise	e…S4—1	Chinese Silkvine	d…V1—5
Carolina Moonseed	d…V2—4	Chamiso	e…S3—3	Chinese Snowball	e…S5—24
Cashmere Bouquet	e…S3—9	Chastetree		Chinese Toon	d…T7—9
Cassandra	e…S2—6	Cutleaved	d…S5—24	Chinese-hat Plant	e…V1—2
Cassiabarktree	e…T7—6	Lilac	d…S5—24	Chittamwood	d…T7—8
Cassie	d…S5—1	Checkerberry	e…S1—8	Chocolate Puddingtree	e…T8—8
Cassiope		Chenilleplant	e…S4—1	Chocolatevine	e…V2—1
Alaska	e…S1—2	Cherimoya	d…T6—5	Chokeberry	
Catalina Ironwood	e…T7—13	Cherry		Black	d…S3—2
Catalina Lyontree	e…T7—13	Almond	d…S3—18	Purple	d…S4—2
Catalpa		Australian Brush	e…T6—23	Red	d…S4—2
Chinese	d…T6—7	Birch-bark	d…T7—24	Chokecherry	
Northern	d…T8—6	Black	d…T8—18	Amur	d…T7—23
Southern	d…T8—6	Brush	e…T6—23	Common	d…T6—25
Ceanothus		Carolina Laurel	e…T6—20	Cholla	
Blueblossom	e…S5—6	Catalina	e…T7—20	Golden	e…S3—23
Carmel	e…S4—8	Conradina	d…T6—23	Jumping	e…S5—17
Catalina	e…T6—6	Dwarf	d…S4—18	Christ-thorn	e…S3—13
Chaparral	e…S2—5	Evergreen	e…S5—19	Christmasberry	e…T6—22
Coast	e…S3—7	Fire	d…T7—24	Christmas-candle	d…S3—5
Coast	e…S4—8	Fuji	d…T6—24	Christmas-cosmos	e…S5—15
Desert	e…S3—6	Higan	d…T6—25	Christmas-daisy	e…S5—15
Feltleaf	e…T6—6	Hollyleaf	e…S5—19	Christmas-flower	e…S4—15
Greenbark	e…S5—5	Japanese Flowering	d…T8—18	Cinnabar Cuphea	e…S2—7
		Laurel	e…S5—19		
		Mahaleb	d…T7—23		
		Manchu	d…S4—18		
		Mazzard	d…T7—23		

Cinquefoil			California	d...S2—1	
Northern	d...S2—10		Painted	e...S4—1	
Old Field	d...S2—10		Coprosma		
Shrubby	d...S3—18		Creeping	e...S2—7	
Three-toothed	e...S1—15		Kirk's	e...S2—7	
Wineleaf	e...S1—15		Coral Ardisia	e...S2—3	
Clammy Hopseedbush	e...S4—12		Coral Chilevine	e...V2—1	
Clematis			Coralbeads	d...V2—4	
Alpine	d...V1—1		Coralberry	e...S3—3	
Anemone	d...V2—3		Chenault	d...S2—13	
Armand	e...V1—1		Indiancurrant	d...S2—14	
Bigpetal	d...V1—3		Coral Pea	e...V1—3	
Cream	d...V1—2		Coralplant	e...V2—1	
Downy	d...V1—3		Coraltree		
Evergreen	e...V1—1		Cockspur	d...T6—11	
Fragrant Tube	d...S2—3		Kaffirboom	d...T6—11	
Golden	d...V1—3		Coralvine	d...V3—1	
Goldwool	d...V1—2		Corkscrewflower	d...V2—7	
Italian	d...V1—4		Corkwood	d...S5—12	
Jackman	d...V1—2		Corokia		
Japanese	d...V2—3		Bigfruit	e...S5—7	
Jouin	d...V1—2		Cotoneaster	e...S3—10	
Lilac	d...V1—3		Correa		
Manycolor	d...V1—3		Harris	e...S2—7	
Ningpo	d...V1—2		White	e...S2—7	
October	d...V2—3		Cotoneaster		
Scarlet	d...V1—3		Bearberry	e...S1—4	
Solitary	d...S2—3		Brightbead	e...S3—10	
Sweetautumn	d...V2—3		Cherryberry	d...S3—7	
Texas	d...V1—3		Chinese	d...S4—8	
Clethra			Cranberry	d...S2—4	
Cinnamon	d...S5—5		Creeping	d...S1—1	
Japanese	d...T6—7		Diel'	d...S3—7	
Cliff Fendlerbush	d...S3—10		European	d...S3—7	
Cliffrose	e...S4—12		Franchet	e...S4—11	
Clockvine			Glossy	d...S4—7	
Bengal	e...V2—9		Hedge	d...S4—7	
Orange	e...V1—5		Parney	e...S4—11	
Coach Whip	d...S5—9		Peking	d...S4—7	
Cochinealplant	e...S5—16		Pyrenees	e...S1—4	
Coconut	e...T8—7		Redbox	e...S4—11	
Coffea			Rock	d...S2—4	
Arabian	e...S5—7		Rockspray	d...S2—4	
Coffeetree			Rockspray	e...S1—4	
Kentucky	d...T8—11		Sliverleaf	e...S3—10	
Common Allamanda	e...V2—1		Small-leaved	e...S1—4	
Common Boxelder	d...T7—2		Soongori Redbead	d...S4—8	
Common Jasminorgane	e...S5—15		Spreading	d...S3—7	
Common Moonseed	d...V1—5		Willowleaf	e...S4—11	
Common Papermulberry	d...T7—7		Wintergreen	e...S3—10	
Common Pipsissewa	e...S1—3		Cottonwood		
Common Sausagetree	e...T7—12		Black	d...T8—18	
Common Seabuckthorn	d...T6—14		Eastern	d...T8—16	
Common Waxplant	e...V1—3		Fremont	d...T8—17	
Confederate Jasmine	e...V1—5		Plains	d...T8—17	
Coontie			Western	d...T8—17	
Scurfy	e...S3—34		Coyotebush	e...S1—2	
St. John'	e...S3—34		Crabapple		
Copihue	e...V2—4		Adams	d...S5—14	
Copperleaf			Arnold	d...S5—14	
			Bechtel	d...T6—19	

Bigfruit	d...S5—15
Biltmore	d...T6—18
Blanche Ames	d...T6—17
Bob White	d...S5—14
Carmine	d...T6—16
Cherry	d...T6—20
Chinese Flowering	d...T6—21
Cutleaf	d...T6—21
Dolgo	d...T7—19
Dorothea	d...T6—17
Double-flowered Iowa	d...T6—19
Dupont	d...T6—18
Evelyn	d...S5—14
Flame	d...T6—17
Georgia	d...S5—15
Gorgeous	d...T6—18
Hupeh	d...T6—18
Iowa	d...T6—18
Japanese Flowering	d...T6—17
John Downie	d...S5—15
Katherine	d...T6—19
Lemoine	d...T6—20
Makamik	d...T6—19
Marshall Oyama	d...T6—19
Nippon	d...S5—14
Oregon	d...T7—19
Ormiston Roy	d...T6—19
Parkman	d...S5—15
Pearleaf	d...T6—20
Plumleaf	d...T6—20
Prairie	d...T6—18
Prince Georges	d...T6—20
Radiant	d...T6—20
Red Jade	d...S5—15
Red Silver	d...S5—15
Redbud	d...T6—22
Rosseau	d...T7—20
Sargent	d...S4—15
Scheidecker	d...S5—16
Siberian	d...T7—19
Sissipuk	d...T7—20
Snowdrift	d...T6—21
Tanner	d...S5—16
Tea	d...T6—18
Toringo	d...S4—15
Tschonoski	d...T7—20
Van Eseltine	d...S5—16
Weeping	d...T7—20
Wild Sweet	d...T6—17
Winter Gold	d...S5—16
Zumi	d...T6—21
Crapemyrtle	d...T6—16
Creambush	d...S4—11
Creeper	
Japanese	d...V3—2
Port St. Johns	e...V2—6
Silvervein	d...V2—5
Thicket	d...V1—5
Virginia	d...V3—1
Creeping Pearlberry	e...S1—7
Creosotebush	e...S4—20
Crossvine	e...V3—1
Croton	e...S3—9

H

Rose (cont.)			**Sage**			Pacific	d...S5—2
Carolina	d...S2—11		Autumn	e...S2—23		Roundleaved	d...S3—1
Cherokee	e...V2—7		Baby	e...S2—23		Running	d...S3—2
Chestnut	d...S4—23		Black	e...S3—30		Saskatoon	d...S4—1
Climbing	d...S4—23		Blue	e...S2—9		Shadblow	d...T7—5
Cottage	d...S3—23		Cherry	e...S2—23		Utah	d...S5—2
Dog	d...S4—21		Cleveland	e...S3—29		**Sevenbark**	d...S3—11
Drophip	d...S3—24		Common	e...S2—24		**Shallon**	e...S3—14
Erectprickle	d...S3—23		Garden	e...S2—23		**Shellflower**	e...S4—1
Father Hugo	d...S4—22		Jerusalem	e...S3—24		Red	e...S5—1
French	d...S3—24		Mexican Bush	e...S2—23		**SheOak**	
Froebel	d...S4—22		Pineapple	e...S2—23		Bluebrush	e...S5—6
Harison's Yellow	d...S3—24		Pineapple-scented	e...S2—23		River	e...T8—5
Helen	d...S5—19		Purple	e...S3—30		Rose	e...T6—5
Holland	d...S3—23		Texas	e...S4—20		**Shimpaku**	e...S2—14
Japanese	d...S3—13		White	e...S3—29		**Shower Orchid**	d...V3—1
Japanese	d...S4—22		Whiteleaf	e...S3—30		**Shrub Althaea**	d...S5—11
Kamtchatka	d...S3—23		Yellow	e...S3—18		**Siberian Salttree**	d...S3—11
Lady Banks'	e...V2—7		Veitch	e...S2—25		**Sierra Chinquapin**	e...S4—10
Leatherleaf	d...S4—22		**Sagebrush**			**Silkoak**	e...T8—10
Malva	e...S5—14		Basin	e...S4—2		**Silktree**	d...T6—4
Meadow	d...S3—23		California	d...S3—2		**Silver Leucodendron**	e...T6—14
Memorial	e...S1—16		Coast	d...S2—1		**Silver Wattle**	e...T7—1
Moyes	d...S4—22		Common	e...S4—2		**Silvertree**	e...T6—14
Multiflora	d...S4—22		Fringed	e...S1—2		**Silvervine**	d...V2—1
Omei	d...S4—23		Sandhill	d...S2—1		**Skimmia**	
Pasture	d...S2—11		**Sago Fern**	e...T7—7		Japanese	e...S3—31
Prairie	d...S4—23		**Saguaro**	e...T7—4		Reeves	e...S2—25
Primrose	d...S4—23		**Sakaki**	e...S4—10		**Skunkbush**	d...S4—20
Red	d...S3—24		**Saltbush**			**Skyflower**	e...S5—9
Redleaf	d...S3—25		Big	e...S4—3		**Skyflower**	e...V2—9
Roxburgh	d...S4—23		Brewer	e...S4—2		**Sloe**	d...S5—18
Rugosa	d...S3—25		Fourwing	e...S3—3		**Small-leaf Coriaria**	d...S3—6
Scotch	d...S2—12		**Sandmyrtle**	e...S2—18		**Smokebush**	
Shining	d...S2—12		Box	e...S2—18		American	d...T6—8
Smooth	d...S3—23		**Sandpaper-vine**	e...V2—6		Common	d...S5—6
Swamp	d...S3—24		**Sapota**	e...T8—19		**Snailflower**	d...V2—7
Turkestan	d...S3—25		**Sarcococca**			**Snailseed**	d...V2—4
Virginia	d...S3—25		Fragrant	e...S3—30		**Snake Vine**	e...V1—2
Wood	d...S4—22		Himalaya	e...S2—24		**Snowbell**	
Rose Periwinkle	e...S2—5		Small Himalaya	e...S2—24		American	d...S5—21
Rose-of-Sharon	d...S5—11		Sweet	e...S3—30		Chinese	d...S4—27
Rosy Riceflower	e...S2—21		Willowleaf	e...S3—30		Fragrant	d...T6—31
Royal Paulownia	d...T7—22		**Sassafras**			Japanese	d...T6—30
Royal Poinciana	d...T7—12		Common	d...T7—28		**Snowberry**	
Rubberplant	e...T7—9		**Scarlet Angel's Trumet**	e...S4—5		Common	d...S3—29
Small-leaved	e...T7—9		**Scarlet Bouvardia**	d...S3—4		Creeping	d...S1—4
Rubbertree			**Schefflera**	e...T6—4		Mountain	d...S3—29
Hardy	d...T7—13		**Screwpine**	e...T6—16		Pink	d...S4—27
Russianolive	d...T7—13		**Seagrape**	e...S5—6		Spreading	d...S1—4
			Seminole-Bread	e...S2—28		Western	d...S3—29
			Senna			**Snow-in-Summer**	e...T6—15
			Appleblossom	d...T6—6		**Snowdrop**	d...T7—15
			Bladder	d...S5—5		**Snowwreath**	d...S3—17
			Scorpion	d...S4—6		**Snowy Mintbush**	d...S2—10
			Wormwood	d...S3—5		**Soapbarktree**	e...T7—21
			Sequoia			**Sophora**	
			Giant	e...T8—22		Fourwing	d...T7—29
Saga Fern	e...T7—7		**Serviceberry**				
			Allegany	d...T7—6			
			Apple	d...T6—5			

Botanic Name INDEX

A

Acer (cont.)			deserti	e...S2—1	**Amorpha**		
saccharinum	d...T8—1		ferox	e...S3—2	californica	d...S5—2	
'Blair'			parryi	e...S2—1	canescens	d...S2—1	
'Pyramidale'			shawi	e...S2—1	fruticosa	d...S5—3	
'Silver Queen'			utahensis	e...S2—1	nana	d...S1—1	
'Wieri'			**Agonis flexuosa**	e...T7—2	occidentalis	d...S5—3	
saccharum	d...T8—1		**Ailanthus altissima**	d...T7—4	**Ampelopsis**		
'Bonfire'			**Akebia**		brevipedunculata	d...V2—1	
'Globosum'			quinata	e...V2—1	'Elegans'		
'Green Mountain'			trifoliata	d...V2—1	'Variegata'		
'Temple's Upright'			**Albizzia**		cordata	d...V2—2	
spicatum	d...S5—1		julibrissin	d...T6—4	humulifolia	d...V2—2	
tataricum	d...T6—3		'E.H. Wilson'		megalophylla	d...V1—1	
triflorum	d...T6—3		'Rosea'		**Andromeda**		
truncatum	d...T7—3		lebbeck	d...T7—4	glaucophylla	e...S2—2	
'Akikaza-Nishiki'			**Aleurites moluccana**	e...T8—4	polifolia	e...S1—1	
'Mayrii'			**Allamanda cathartica**	e...V2—1	'Alba'		
Acmena smithi	e...T6—2		hendersonii		'Compacta'		
Acoelorraphe wrighti	e...T6—17		'Williamsii'		'Nana'		
Actinidia			**Alnus**		'Nikko'		
arguta	d...V3—1		cordata	d...T7—5	**Annona**		
'Akin #3'			glutinosa	d...T7—5	cherimola	d...T6—5	
'Ananasnaja'			'Imperialis'		glabra	d...T6—5	
'Anna'			incana	d...T7—5	reticulata	e...T6—2	
callosa	d...V2—1		'Pendula'		squamosa	d...T6—5	
chinensis	d...V2—1		maritima	d...T6—4	**Antigonon leptopus**	d...V3—1	
'Tomuri'			oregona	d...T8—2	**Arabis caucasica**	e...S1—1	
'Vincent'			rubra	d...T8—2	'Compinkie'		
kolomikta	d...V1—1		rugosa	d...S5—2	'Flore Pleno'		
'Arctic Beauty'			rhombifolia	d...T7—5	**Aralia**		
'Krupnopladnaya'			serrulata	d...S5—2	elata	d...T7—6	
polygama	d...V2—1		sinuata	d...T6—4	spinosa	d...T7—6	
Adenostoma			sitchensis	d...T6—4	**Araucaria**		
fasciculatum	e...S4—1		tenuifolia	d...T6—5	angustifolia	e...T7—2	
sparsifolium	e...S5—1		**Aloysia triphylla**	d...S4—1	araucana	e...T8—4	
Adina rubella	d...S3—1		**Alpinia**		bidwilli	e...T8—4	
Adolphia californica	d...S2—1		purpurata	e...S5—1	cunninghami	e...T8—4	
Aesculus			speciosa	e...S4—1	excelsa	e...T8—5	
arguta	d...S5—1		zerumbet	e...S4—1	'Magestic Beauty'		
californica	d...T6—4		**Alyogyne huegeli**	e...S3—2	heterophylla	e...T8—5	
x carnea	d...T7—3		'Monterey Bay'		**Arbutus**		
'Briotii'			'Santa Cruz'		menziesi	e...T7—2	
'O'neill Red'			**Amelanchier**		unedo	e...T6—2	
glabra	d...T7—4		alnifolia	d...S4—1	'Compacta'		
hippocastanum	d...T7—4		'Honeywood'		**Archontophoenix acuminata**	e...T7—4	
'Baumanii'			'Northline'		**Arctostaphylos**		
'Rubra'			'Regent'		andersoni	e...S4—2	
indica	d...T8—2		'Smokey'		densiflora	e...S3—2	
'Sidney Pierce'			canadensis	d...T7—5	'Howard McMinn'		
octandra	d...T8—2		'Prince William'		'Sentinel'		
parviflora	d...S4—1		'Tradition'		edmundsi	e...S2—2	
serotina			florida	d...S5—2	'Carmel Sur'		
pavia	d...T6—4		x grandiflora	d...T6—5	'Danville'		
'Rubra'			'Ballarina'		glandulosa	e...S4—2	
sylvatica	d...S5—2		'Cole Select'		glauca	e...S5—1	
turbinata	d...T7—4		'Rubescens'		hookeri	e...S2—2	
Agapetes serpens	e...S2—1		'Strata'		'Monterey Carpet'		
Agave			laevis	d...T7—6	'Wayside'		
americana	e...S3—1		'Prince Charles'		manzanita	e...S5—2	
marginata			sanguinea	d...S3—1	'Dr. Hurd'		
mexico-picata			stolonifera	d...S3—2	nevadensis	e...S1—1	
variegata			utahensis	d...S5—2	nummularia	e...S2—2	
attenuata	e...S3—2						

Bougainvillea
  x buttiana   e...V2—1
    'Orange King'
  spectabilis   e...V2—2
Bouvardia ternifolia   d...S3—4
    'Christmas Red'
    'Fire Chief'
Brachychiton
  acerifolia   e...T7—3
  discolor   d...T7—7
  populneum   e...T7—3
Brachyglottis
  repanda   e...S5—3
Brahea armata   e...T7—7
Brassaia actinophylla   e...T6—4
    'Compacta'
Broussonetia papyrifera   d...T7—7
Bruckenthalia spiculifolia   e...S1—2
Brugmansia
  x candida   e...S5—3
    'Double White'
  sanguinea   e...S4—5
    flava
  suaveolens   e...S5—3
Brunfelsia
  australis   e...S4—5
  grandiflora   e...S4—5
  pauciflora 'Floribunda'   e...S4—5
Buddleia
  alternifolia   d...S4—2
    'Argentea'
  colvillei   d...S5—3
  davidi   d...S3—4
    'Burgundy'
    'Charming'
    'Royal Red'
    'Showbank'
  fallowiana   d...S4—3
    'Lochinch'
Bumelia
  lanuginosa   d...T7—8
  lycoides   e...T6—4
Bursera simaruba   d...T8—4
Butia capitata   e...S5—4
Buxus
  harlandi   e...S3—5
  microphylla   e...S2—4
    'Compacta'
    'Green Beauty'
    'Green Pillow'
    'Winter Gem'
  sempervirens   e...S5—4
    'Arborescens'   e...S5—4
    'Newport Blue'
    'Salicifolia'
    'Suffruticosa'
    'Vardar Valley'

Caesalpinia
  gilliesi   e...S5—4
  mexicana   e...S4—6
  pulcherrima   e...S4—6
Calliandra
  californica   e...S2—4
  haematocephala   e...S4—6
    alba
  tweedi   e...S4—6
Callicarpa
  bodinieri   d...S4—3
    'Profusion'
  dichotoma   d...S3—4
  japonica   d...S3—5
    'Leucocarpa'
Callistemon
  citrinus   e...S5—4
    'Jeffersii'
  linearis   e...S4—6
  pallidus   e...S4—7
  rigidus   e...S5—5
  speciosus   e...S4—7
  viminalis   e...T6—4
    'Red Cascade'
Callitris
  rhomboidea   e...T7—3
  tasmanica   e...T7—3
Calluna vulgaris   e...S2—4
    'Blazeaway'
    'Elsie Frye'
    'Tib'
    'White Lawn'
Calocedrus decurrens   e...T8—5
Calocephalus browni   e...S2—5
Calodendron capense   e...T7—4
Calycanthus
  fertilis   d...S4—3
  floridus   d...S4—3
    'Athens'
  occidentalis   d...S4—3
Camellia
  cuspidata   e...S5—5
  hiemalis   e...S3—5
    'Chansonette'
  japonica   e...T6—4
    'Magnoliaeflora'   e...T6—4
    'Alba Plena'
    'Debutante'
    'Magnoliaeflora'
    'Tom Knudsen'
  saluenensis   e...S4—7
    'Appleblossom'
  sasanqua   e...S5—5
    'Jean May'

    'Rosea'
    'Yuletide'
    'White Doves'
  sinensis   e...T6—5
  x williamsi   e...S3—6
    'Brigadoon'
    'Donation'
    'Flirtation'
    'Robbie'
Campsis
  chinensis   d...V1—1
  grandiflora   d...V1—1
  radicans   d...V3—1
    'Crimson Trumpet'
    'Flava'
  x tagliabuana   d...V2—2
    'Madame Galen'
Caragana
  arborescens   d...S5—4
    'Green Globe'
    'Walker'
  aurantiaca   d...S4—4
  frutex   d...S4—4
    'Globosa'
  maximowicziana   d...S3—5
Carica papaya   e...T6—5
    'Kapoho'
    'Solo'
    'Sunset'
    'Waimanalo'
Carissa
  grandiflora   e...S4—7
  macrocarpa   e...S4—7
Carnegiea gigantea   e...T7—4
Carpentaria
  acuminata   e...T7—4
  californica   e...S3—6
Carpinus
  betulus   d...T7—8
    'Columnaris'
    'Fastigiata'
    'Pendula'
  caroliniana   d...T7—8
  japonica   d...T7—8
  orientalis   d...S5—4
Carya
  cordiformis   d...T8—4
  glabra   d...T8—5
  illinoensis   d...T8—5
    'Cheyene'
    'Chickasaw'
    'Elliot'
    'Stuart'
  laciniosa   d...T8—5
    'Bradley'
    'Chetopa'
    'Fayette'
    'Nieman'
  ovata   d...T8—5
    'Abundance'
    'Fox'
    'Porter'
    'Wilcox'

texana	d...T8—5	'Ceres'		occidentalis	d...T7—10
tomentosa	d...T8—6	'Indigo'		siliquastrum	d...T6—7
Caryopteris		'Perle Rose'		Cercocarpus	
x clandonensis	d...S2—2	'Topaz'		betuloides	e...T6—6
'Azure'		purpureus	e...S3—6	ledifolius	e...T7—5
'Dark Knight'		ramulosus	e...S3—7	montanus	e...T6—6
incana	d...S3—5	fasciculatus		traskiae	e...T6—7
Caryota urens	e...T8—5	'Ray Hartman'	e...S5—5	Cereus	
Casimiroa edulis	e...T7—4	spinosus	e...S5—5	gigantea	e...T7—4
Cassia		thyrsiflorus	e...S5—6	peruvianus	e...T7—5
alata	d...S3—5	repens		Cestrum	
artemisioides	d...S3—5	'Skylark'		aurantiacum	e...S4—8
brewsteri	d...T7—8	Cedrela sinensis	d...T7—9	elegans	e...S4—9
excelsa	e...T6—5	Cedrus		nocturnum	e...S4—9
javanica	d...T6—6	atlantica	e...T8—6	parqui	e...S4—9
leptophylla	e...T6—5	'Aurea'		Chaenomeles	
roxburghi	d...T6—6	'Fastigiata'		japonica	d...S2—3
marginata	d...T6—6	'Glauca'		'Coles Red'	
Cassinia vauvilliersi	e...S4—7	deodara	e...T8—6	'Maulei'	
Cassiope lycopodioides	e...S1—2	'Cream Puff'		'Minerva'	
Castanea		'Kashmir'		'Super Red'	
crenata	d...T6—6	'Pendula'		japonica alpina	d...S1—1
dentata	d...T8—6	'Pygmaea'		lagenaria	d...S4—4
mollissima	d...T7—9	libani stenocoma	e...T8—6	'Cameo'	
'Crane'		'Nana'		'Nivalis'	
'Eaton'		'Green Prince'		'Rubra'	
'Fords Sweet'		'Pendula'		'Spit Fire'	
'Norm Higgens'		'Sargentii'		speciosa	d...S4—4
pumila	d...T7—9	Celastrus		x superba	d...S3—6
sativa	d...T8—6	orbiculatus	d...V2—3	'Hollandia'	
Castanopsis sempervirons	e...S4—10	scandens	d...V2—3	'Jet Trail'	
Casuarina		'Indian Brave'		'Pink Lady'	
cunninghamiana	e...T8—5	'Indian Maiden'		'Texas Scarlet'	
torulosa	e...T6—5	Celtis		Chamaebatiaria millefolium	d...S3—6
Catalpa		australis	d...T8—7	Chamaecyparis	
bignonioides	d...T8—6	bungeana	d...T7—9	lawsoniana	e...T8—6
ovata	d...T6—7	jessoensis	d...T8—7	'Allumnii'	
speciosa	d...T8—6	laevigata	d...T8—7	'Ellwoodi'	
Catharanthus roseus	e...S2—5	'All Seasons'		'Fletcheri'	
'Dixieland'		occidentalis	d...T8—7	'Forsteckensis'	e...S2—5
'Linda'		'Prairie Pride'		'Minima'	e...S2—6
'Little Hybrids'		reticulata	d...T7—9	nootkatensis	e...T8—6
'Morning Mist'		sinensis	d...T8—7	'Aurea'	
Ceanothus		Cephalanthus occidentalis	d...S4—4	'Compacta'	
americanus	d...S2—2	californica		'Glauca'	
arboreus	e...T6—6	Cephalotaxus		'Pendula'	
crassifolius	e...S3—6	fortunei	e...T6—6	obtusa	e...T8—7
planus		harringtonia	e...T6—6	'Compacta'	e...S3—7
cyaneus	e...S4—8	Ceratonia siliqua	e...T7—5	'Crippsii'	
gloriosus	e...S1—3	Ceratostigma		'Kosteri'	e...S2—6
'Emily Brown'		griffithi	e...S2—4	'Lycopodiodes'	e...S4—9
'Point Reyes'		plumbaginoides	e...S1—3	'Nana'	e...S2—6
greggi	e...S3—6	willmottianum	d...S2—2	'Nana Gracilis'	e...S3—7
griseus	e...S4—8	Cercidophyllum japonicum	d...T7—10	'Nana Torulosa'	e...S3—7
'Louis Edmonds'		'Pendulum'		'Spiralis'	
'Santa Ana'		Cercis		pisifera	e...T8—7
impressus	e...S4—8	canadensis	d...T7—10	'Boulevard'	e...S4—9
'Victoria'		'Alba'		'Filifera'	e...S5—6
incanus	e...S4—8	Forest Pansy'		'Aurea'	
leucodermis	e...S2—5	chinensis	d...T6—7	'Mops'	
ovatus	d...S2—2	'Avondale'		'Nana'	
x pallidus	d...S2—2	'Nana'		'Plumosa'	e...T6—7
				'Snow'	

Chamaecyparis (cont.)			'Eureka'			versicolor	d...V1—3
thyoides	e...T8—7		'Meyer'			virginiana	d...V2—4
'Andelyensis'			'Ponderosa'			vitalba	d...V2—4
'Conica'			'Sun Gold'			viticella	d...V1—4
'Ericoides'			reticulata	e...T6—8		'Abundance'	
'Little Jamie'			'Calamondin'			'Purpurea'	
Chamaedaphne calyculata	e...S2—6		'Changsha'			'Rubra'	
'Nana'			'Dancy'			Cleome arborea	e...S4—18
Chamaedorea			'Kara'			Clerodendrum	
brachypoda	e...S3—7		sinensis	e...T7—6		bungei	e...S3—9
elegans	e...S3—8		'G.C. Wilson'			foetidum	e...S3—9
'Collinia'			'Moro'			x speciosum	e...S4—10
stolonifera	e...S3—8		'Valencia'			thomsoniae	d...V1—4
Chamaerops			'Washington'			'Delectum'	
excelsa	e...S3—27		Cladrastis lutea	d...T7—11		'Variegata'	
humilis	e...S5—6		'Rosea'			trichotomum	d...S5—4
Chamelaucium uncinatum	e...S4—10		Clematis			Clethra	
'Vista'			alpina	d...V1—1		acuminata	d...S5—5
Chilopsis linearis	d...S5—4		'Columbine'			alnifolia	d...S4—5
'Barranca'			'Pamela Jack'			'Paniculata'	
Chimaphila umbellata	e...S1—3		'Ruby'			'Pink Spire'	
Chimonanthus			'White Moth'			'Rosea'	
praecox	d...S4—4		armandi	e...V1—1		barbinervis	d...T6—7
praecox	e...S4—10		'Apple Blossom'			Cleyera japonica	e...S4—10
Chiogenes hispidula	e...S1—7		'Snowdrift'			'Hosoba Fukurin'	
Chionanthus			apiifolia	d...V2—3		'Tricolor'	
retusus	d...S5—4		chrysocoma	d...V1—2		Clianthus puniceus	e...V1—1
virginicus	d...T6—7		'Sericea'			Clytostoma callistegioides	e...V3—1
Chiranthodendron			dioscoreifolia	d...V2—3		Cobaea scandens	e...V2—2
pentadactylon	e...T7—5		florida	d...V1—2		'Alba'	
Chorisia			'Plena'			Coccoloba uvifera	e...S5—6
insignis	d...T7—10		heracleifolia	d...S2—3		Cocculus	
speciosa	d...T7—10		'Davidiana'			carolinus	d...V2—4
'Majestic Beauty'			integrifolia	d...S2—3		laurifolius	e...S5—7
Chorizema cordatum	e...S3—8		x jackmani	d...V1—2		Cocos nucifera	e...T8—7
Chrysobalanus icaco	e...T6—7		'Alba'			Codiaeum variegatum	e...S3—9
Chrysolepis sempervirens	e...S4—10		'Henryi'			'Kentucky'	
Chrysophyllum cainito	e...T7—5		'Rubra'			'Monarch'	
Chrysothamnus nauseosus	e...S3—8		'Superba'			'Pitcairn'	
graveolens			x jouiniana	d...V1—2		'Polychrome'	
Cinnamomum			'Praecox'			Coffea arabica	e...S5—7
camphora	e...T7—6		lanuginosa	d...V1—2		'Brazilian Bush'	
cassia	e...T7—6		'Candida'			'Kona'	
glanduliferum	e...T6—7		'Fairy Queen'			Colletia	
Cissus			'Henryi'			armata	e...S3—9
antarctica	e...V1—1		macropetala	d...V1—3		cruciata	e...S4—11
rhombifolia	e...V2—2		'Markham's Pink'			Colutea arborescens	d...S5—5
Cistus			'Pink'			Comarostaphylis diversifolia	e...S5—7
albidus	e...S3—8		'Snowbird'			planifolia	
laurifolius	e...S3—8		montana	d...V2—3		Combretum fruticosum	e...V1—1
populifolius	e...S3—9		'Alba'			Comptonia peregrina	d...S2—3
x purpureus	e...S3—9		'Elizabeth'			Congea tomentosa	d...V3—1
salviifolius	e...S2—6		'Marjorie'			Conocarpus erecta	e...T8—7
Citrus			'Tetrarose'			Copernicia baileyana	e...T7—6
aurantifolia	e...T6—8		paniculata	d...V2—3		Coprosma x kirki	e...S2—7
'Bears'			patens	d...V1—3		'Variegata'	
'Key Lime'			'Fortunei'			'Verde Vista'	
'Persian Lime'			'Grandiflora'			Cordia boissieri	e...T6—8
aurantium	e...T6—8		'Standishii'			Cordyline australis	e...T6—8
limon	e...S5—6		tangutica	d...V1—3		'Purpureus'	
			'Aurolin'				
			texensis	d...V1—3			
			'Duchess of Albany'				
			'Gravetye Beauty'				

Coriaria microphylla	d...S3—6
Cornus	
alternifolia	d...T6—8
amomum	d...S4—5
canadensis	e...S1—3
capitata	e...T7—6
controversa	d...T7—11
florida	d...T7—11
'Alba'	
'First Lady'	
'Pendula'	
'Rubra'	
kousa	d...T6—8
'Cascade'	
'Doubloom'	
'Gold Spot'	
'Milky Way'	
macrophylla	d...T7—11
mas	d...T6—8
'Golden Glory'	
nuttali	d...T8—8
'Colrigo Giant'	
'Goldspot'	
officinalis	d...S5—5
paucinervis	d...S4—5
racemosa	d...S4—5
'Heaven Sent'	
rugosa	d...S4—5
sericea	d...S4—6
baileyi	
'Cardinal'	
'Flaviramea'	d...S4—6
'Isanti'	
'Kelseyi'	d...S2—3
stolonifera	d...S4—6
Corokia	
cotoneaster	e...S3—10
macrocarpa	e...S5—7
Coronilla emerus	d...S4—6
Correa	
alba	e...S2—7
backhousiana	e...S3—10
x harrisi	e...S2—7
pulchella	e...S1—3
reflexa	e...S1—3
'Orange Flame'	
Corylopsis	
glabrescens	d...S5—5
pauciflora	d...S3—6
platypetala	d...S4—6
sinensis	d...S5—5
spicata	d...S3—6
veitchiana	d...S3—7
willmottiae	d...S4—6
'Spring Purple'	
Corylus	
americana	d...S4—7
avellana	d...S5—6
'Atropurpurea'	
'Contorta'	
'Pendula'	
colurna	d...T8—8
'Jacquemonti'	

cornuta	d...S4—7
Corynocarpus laevigata	e...T6—9
Cotinus	
americanus	d...T6—8
coggygria	d...S5—6
purpureus	
obovatus	d...T6—8
Cotoneaster	
acutifolia	d...S4—7
'Nana'	
adpressa	d...S1—1
apiculata	d...S2—4
'Blackburn'	
'Tom Thumb'	
buxifolius	e...S3—10
congesta	e...S1—4
conspicua	e...S3—10
dammeri	e...S1—4
'Coral Beauty'	
'Skogsholmen'	
dielsiana	d...S3—7
'Major'	
divaricata	d...S3—7
foveolata	d...S4—7
francheti	e...S4—11
cinerascens	
horizontalis	d...S2—4
'Beni Shitan'	
'Little Gem'	
'Prostratus'	
'Robusta'	
integerrimus	d...S3—7
lacteus	e...S4—11
parneyi	
lucida	d...S4—7
microphylla	e...S1—4
multiflora	d...S4—8
pannosa	e...S3—10
'Nanus'	
racemiflora soongorica	d...S4—8
rotundifolia	e...S4—11
'Prostratus'	
salicifolia	e...S4—11
'Emerald Carpet'	
'Repandens'	
'Repens'	
'Scarlet Leader'	
zabeli	d...S3—7
Couroupita guianensis	d...T7—11
Cowania mexicana	e...S4—12
Crataegus	
arnoldiana	d...S5—6
cerronis	d...S5—7
chrysocarpa	d...S5—6
coccinea	d...T6—10
coccinoides	d...S5—6
crus-galli	d...T7—12
'Cockspur Crusader'	
'Inermis'	
'Splendens'	
douglasi	d...T6—8
erythropoda	d...S5—7
laevigata	d...T6—9

x lavallei	d...T6—9
'Carrieri'	
mollis	d...T7—12
monogyna	d...T6—9
'Flexuosa'	
'Inermis'	
'Pendula Rosa'	
'Stricta'	
oxyacantha	d...T6—9
'Autumn Glory'	
'Contorta'	
'Crimson Cloud'	
'Pauls Scarlet'	d...T6—9
pedicellata	d...T6—10
phaenopyrum	d...T6—10
'Fastigiata'	
pinnatifida	d...S5—7
pruinosa	d...T6—10
x prunifolia	d...T6—10
punctata	d...T6—10
'Ohio Pioneer'	
nitida	d...T6—9
succulenta	d...S5—7
viridis	d...T7—12
'Winter King'	
Crinodendron hookerianum	e...S5—7
Cryptomeria japonica	e...T8—8
'Bandai Sugi'	
'Compressa'	
'Lobii Nana'	
'Tansii'	
Cunninghamia lanceolata	e...T8—8
'Glauca'	
'Nana'	
Cuphea	
hyssopifolia	e...S2—7
'Purpurea'	
ignea	e...S1—4
platycentra	e...S1—4
llavea	e...S2—7
Cuphea miniata	e...S2—7
X Cupressocyparis leylandi	e...T8—8
'Castlewellen'	
'Naylor Blue'	
'Silver Dust'	
Cupressus	
bakeri	e...T6—9
goveniana	e...T7—7
guadalupensis	e...T7—7
macnabiana	e...T7—7
macrocarpa	e...T8—8
'Contorta'	
sargenti	e...S5—8
Cyathea	
cooperi	e...S5—22
medullaris	e...T7—7
Cycas revoluta	e...S5—8
Cydonia	
oblonga	d...T6—11
sinensis	d...S5—7
Cyrilla racemiflora	d...S5—7

Cytisus	
albus	d...S1—1
x kewensis	d...S1—1
nigricans	d...S2—4
praecox	d...S3—8
'Allgold'	
'Bronze Eyes'	
'Hollandii'	
purgans	d...S2—4
purpureus	d...S2—4
racemosa	d...S2—5
scoparius	d...S4—8
'Burkwoodii'	
'Carla'	
'Lena'	
'Pomona'	
supinus	d...S2—5

Daboecia cantabrica	e...S2—8
'Alba'	
Daphne	
alpina	d...S1—2
arbuscula	e...S1—4
blagayana	e...S1—5
x burkwoodi	e...S3—11
'Carol Mackie'	
'Somerset'	
cneorum	e...S1—5
'Alba'	
'Eximia'	
'Ruby Glow'	
mezereum	d...S3—8
'Alba'	
odora	e...S3—11
'Alba'	
'Aureo-Marginata'	
retusa	e...S2—8
Dasylirion	
parryi	e...S3—22
wheeleri	e...S3—11
Datura	
x candida	e...S5—3
suaveolens	e...S5—3
Davidia involucrata	d...T7—12
'Vilmoriana'	
Decaisnea fargesi	d...S5—8
Decumaria barbara	d...V2—4
Delonix regia	d...T7—12
Dendromecon	
'Harfordi'	e...S5—8

rigida	e...S4—12
Deutzia	
gracilis	d...S3—8
'Nana'	
'Rosea'	
grandiflora	d...S3—8
x lemoinei	d...S3—8
'Compacta'	
parviflora	d...S3—9
x rosea	d...S3—9
'Carminea'	
'Eximia'	
scabra	d...S4—8
'Godsall Pink'	
'Pride of Rochester'	
Dichroa febrifuga	e...S2—8
Diervilla	
lonicera	d...S2—5
sessilifolia	d...S2—5
Dioon edule	e...S3—11
Diospyros	
digyna	e...T8—8
kaki	d...T7—13
'Great Wall'	
'Hachiya'	
'Sheng'	
virginiana	d...T8—8
'Early Golden'	
'Meader'	
'John Rick'	
'Sweet Lent'	
Dipelta floribunda	d...S5—8
Diplacus glutinosus	d...S3—16
Dirca palustris	d...S3—9
Distictis	
buccinatoria	e...V3—1
'Rivers'	e...V3—1
Dizygotheca elegantissima	e...S4—12
Dodonaea viscosa	e...S4—12
'Purpurea'	
Dombeya cacuminum	e...T6—9
Dorycnium suffruticosum	d...S2—5
Dovyalis caffra	e...S5—8
Dracaena	
draco	e...S5—8
godseffiana	e...S2—8
'Milky Way'	
marginata	e...S4—12
'Colorama'	
'Tricolor'	
surculosa	e...S2—8
umbragulifera	e...S3—11
Drimys winteri	e...T6—9
Duranta	
repens	e...S5—9
plumieri	e...S5—9
stenostachya	e...S4—13

Echinocactus grusoni	e...S2—8
Echinocereus engelmanni	e...S1—5
Echium fastuosum	e...S3—12
Ehretia	
acuminata	d...T6—11
thyrsiflora	d...T6—11
Elaeagnus	
angustifolia	d...T7—13
'King Red'	
x ebbingei	e...S4—13
'Gilt Edge'	
multiflora	d...S3—9
pungens	e...S4—13
'Fruitlandii'	
'Reflexa'	
'Rotundifolia'	
'Variegata'	
umbellata	d...S5—8
'Cardinal'	
'Jazbo'	
'Titan'	
Elliottia racemosa	d...S4—8
Elsholtzia stauntoni	d...S3—9
Empetrum nigrum	e...S1—5
Encelia farinosa	e...S3—12
Encephalartos ferox	e...S3—12
Enkianthus	
campanulatus	d...T6—11
'Hollandia Red'	
'Red Bells'	
perulatus	d...S3—10
Enterolobium cyclocarpum	d...T8—8
Ephedra	
distachya	e...S2—9
viridus	e...S2—9
Epigaea repens	e...S1—5
Eranthemum pulchellum	e...S2—9
Erica	
arborea	e...S5—9
australis	e...S4—13
carnea	e...S1—6
'King George'	
'Springwood White'	
cinerea	e...S1—6
'Atropurpurea'	
'Golden Drop'	
x darleyensis	e...S1—6
'Arthur Johnson'	
'Siberschmelze'	
hyemalis	e...S2—9
terminalis	e...S3—12
tetralix	e...S2—9
'Alba'	
'Mollis'	
'Pink Star'	

'Rosea'		Eucommia ulmoides	d...T7—13
vagans	e...S1—6	Eucryphia	
'Lyonesse'		cordifolia	e...S5—10
'Mrs. D.F. Maxwell'		lucida	e...T6—10
x watsoni	e...S1—6	Eugenia	
'Dawn'		australis	e...T6—23
'Gwen'		uniflora	e...T6—23
'Truro'		Euonymus	
Eriobotrya		alatus	d...S4—9
deflexa	e...S5—9	'Compacta'	
'Bronze Improved'		'Nordine'	
japonica	e...T6—9	'Tures'	
'Gold Nugget'		americana	d...S4—9
Eriogonum		atropurpureus	d...T6—12
arborescens	e...S2—10	bungeana	d...T6—12
cinereum	e...S2—10	'Pendula'	
fasciculatum	e...S2—10	europaea	d...T6—12
'Dana Point'		'Aldenhamensis'	
giganteum	e...S4—13	'Red Cap'	
formosum		'Red Cascade'	
latifolium	e...S2—10	fortunei	e...V2—2
parvifolium	e...S2—10	'Coloratus'	e...V1—2
umbellatum	e...S1—7	'Greenlane'	
'Ute'		'Kewensis'	e...V1—2
Eriophyllum		'Minimus'	e...V1—2
confertiflorum	e...S2—11	radicans	e...V2—2
staechadifolium	e...S2—11	'Argenteo-Marginata'	
Erythea armata	e...T7—7	'Purpleleaf'	e...V1—2
Erythrina		'Sarcoxie'	e...S3—12
caffra	d...T6—11	vegetus	e...V2—3
constantiana	d...T6—11	kiautschovicus	e...S3—13
crista-galli	d...T6—11	latifolia	d...S5—8
falcata	d...T6—12	nikoensis	d...T7—13
Escallonia		obovatus	d...V1—4
bifida	e...S4—14	sachalinensis	d...S4—9
herrerae	e...T6—10	sanguinea	d...S5—8
leucantha	e...S5—9	yedoensis	d...S4—9
myrtilloides	e...S4—14	Eupatorium ligustrinum	e...S5—10
rubra	e...S4—14	Euphorbia	
virgata	e...S2—11	characias	e...S2—11
Eucalyptus		leucocephala	e...S4—15
calopylla	e...T7—8	mellifera	e...S3—13
camaldulensis	e...T8—9	mili splendens	e...S3—13
erythrocorys	e...T6—10	myrsinites	e...S1—7
ficifolia	e...T7—8	pulcherrima	e...S4—15
globulus	e...T8—9	'Brilliant'	
'Compacta'		'Gutbier Hybrid'	
gunni	e...T8—9	'Jingle Bell'	
intertexta	d—T7—13	'Marble'	
lehmanni	d...T6—12	splendens	e...S3—13
leucoxylon	e...T7—8	tirucalli	e...S5—10
'Rosea'		trigona	e...S5—10
macrocarpa	e...S5—9	Euryops pectinatus	e...S2—11
maculata	d...T8—8	'Viridis'	
niphophila	e...S5—10	Evodia	
pauciflora	e...T7—8	danielli	d...T6—13
perriniana	e...T6—10	hupehensis	d...T7—14
pulverulenta	e...T7—8	Exochorda	
x rhodantha	e...S4—14	giraldi	d...S4—9
sideroxylon	e...T7—9	'Wilsonii	
'Rosea'		x macrantha	d...S4—10
stellulata	e...T6—10	'The Bride'	
tetraptera	e...S4—14		

racemosa	d...S4—10

Fabiana imbricata	e...S4—15
Fagus	
grandifolia	d...T8—9
orientalis	d...T8—9
sylvatica	d...T8—9
'Asplenifolia'	
'Atropunicia'	
'Fastigiata'	
'Pendula'	
Fallugia paradoxa	d...S3—10
Fatsia japonica	e...S4—15
Feijoa sellowiana	e...S5—11
'Coolidge'	
'Nazemetz'	
'Triumph'	
Fendlera rupicola	d...S3—10
Ficus	
aurea	d...T8—9
benghalensis	e...T8—9
benjamina	e...T7—9
'Major'	
'Variegata'	
carica	d...T6—13
'Abidjan'	
'Alma'	
'Asahi'	
'Beall'	
lyrata	e...T7—9
macrophylla	e...T7—9
pumila	e...V2—3
'Minima'	
'Quercifolia'	
'Variegata'	
religiosa	d...T8—9
Firmiana simplex	d...T6—13
Fontanesia	
fortunei	d...S4—10
phillyreoides	d...S4—10
Forestiera	
acuminata	d...T6—13
angustifolia	d...T6—13
neomexicana	d...S5—9
Forsythia	
'Arnold Dwarf'	d...S2—6
'Beatrix Farrand'	d...S4—10
ovata	d...S3—10
'Ottawa'	
'Tetragold'	
'Spring Glory'	d...S4—11
suspensa	d...S4—11
'Sieboldii'	

salicifolia	e…S4—17
Hedera	
colchica	e…V3—1
'Dentata'	
'Paddy's Pride'	
helix	e…V3—2
'Baltica'	e…V3—2
Helianthemum	
apenninum	e…S1—8
'Roseum'	
nummularium	e…S1—9
'Apricot'	
'Gold Rush'	
umbellatum	e…S1—8
scoparium	d…S2—7
Helichrysum bracteatum	d…S2—7
'Dragon Hill'	
'Monstrosum'	
Heliconia rostrata	e…S4—17
Hemiptelea davidi	d…S5—11
Heptapleurum arboricola	e…S5—20
Heteromeles arbutifolia	e…T6—12
Hibbertia scandens	e…V1—2
Hibiscus	
elatus	e…T7—10
rosa-sinensis	e…S4—17
'Empire'	
'Full Moon'	
'Red Dragon'	
'White Wings'	
syriacus	d…S5—11
'Ardens'	
'Diana	
'Red Heart'	
'Rubis'	
Hippophae rhamnoides	d…T6—14
Holmskioldia sanguinea	e…V1—2
Holodiscus	
discolor	d…S4—11
dumosus	d…S3—11
Homalocladium platycladum	e…S2—12
Hovenia dulcis	d…T6—14
Howea belmoreana	e…T6—12
Hoya carnosa	e…V1—3
'Compacta'	
'Exotica'	
'Rubra'	
'Suzy Q'	
Hydrangea	
anomala petiolaris	d…V2—4
arborescens	d…S3—11
'Annabelle'	
'Grandiflora'	d…S3—11
radiata	
aspera	d…S3—11
'Robusta'	
sargentiana	
heteromalla	d…S3—12
involucrata	d…S3—12
macrophylla	d…S3—12
'Nikko Blue'	

'Otaksa'	
'Tosca'	
'Tricolor'	
paniculata	d…S5—11
'Floribunda'	
'Grandiflora'	
'Tardiva'	
quercifolia	d…S3—12
'Harmony'	
'Snowflake'	
'Snow Queen'	
Hymenosporum flavum	e…T6—12
Hypericum	
androsaemum	d…S2—8
beani	e…S3—16
buckleyi	d…S1—2
calycinum	e…S1—9
canariense	d…S4—12
densiflorum	e…S3—16
frondosum	d…S2—8
'Sunburst'	
'Hidcote'	e…S2—12
kalmianum	d…S2—8
kouytchense	e…S2—13
'Sungold'	
x moserianum	e…S2—13
'Tricolor'	
olympicum	d…S1—3
uniflorum	
patulum	e…S2—13
henryi	e…S3—16
'Sunshine'	
prolificum	d…S3—12
uralum	d…S2—8
Hyptis emoryi	d…S3—13

I

Idesia polycarpa	d…T7—15
Ilex	
x altaclarensis	e…T7—10
aquifolium	e…T7—10
'Ciliata Major'	
'Gold Coast'	
'Pinto'	
'San Gabriel'	
x aquipernyi	e…S5—11
'Brilliant'	
'Lydia Morris'	
cassine	e…T7—10
'Lowei'	
ciliospinosa	e…S5—11
cornuta	e…S4—17
'Burfordi'	e…S5—12
'B. Nana'	
'B. Willowleaf'	

'Carrissa'	
'Fineline'	
'Rotunda'	
crenata	e…S3—16
'Convexa'	
'Heller'	
'Hetzii'	
'Mariesii'	
decidua	d…T6—15
'Council Fire'	
'Pocahontas'	
'Warren's Red'	
fargesi	e…T6—12
glabra	e…S3—16
'Compacta'	
'Nigra'	
'Nordic'	
'Viridis'	
integra	e…T6—12
laevigata	d…S4—12
latifolia	e…T7—10
x meserveae	e…S3—17
'Blue Boy'	
'Blue Girl'	
'Blue Maid'	
opaca	e…T7—11
'Fosteri'	
'Greenleaf'	
'Miss Helen'	
'Satyr Hill'	
pedunculosa	e…S5—12
perado	e…T6—13
pernyi	e…T6—13
'Compacta'	
rugosa	e…S1—9
serrata	d…S5—11
'Bonfire'	
'Subtilis Ohwi'	
verticillata	d…S4—12
'Aurantiaca'	
'Compacta'	
'Sunset'	
'Winter Red'	
yunnanensis	e…S4—17
Illicium	
floridanum	e…S4—18
'Alba'	
'Hally's Comet'	
parviflorum	e…S3—17
Indigofera	
amblyantha	d…S3—13
decora	d…S1—3
'Alba'	
incarnata	d…S1—3
kirilowii	d…S2—8
'Coreana'	
Iochroma cyaneum	e…S4—18
Isomeris arborea	e…S4—18
Itea virginica	d…S3—13
'Henry's Garnet'	
Ixora duffi	e…S4—18

Lupinus (cont.)	
albifrons	d...S3—15
Lycium	
chinense	d...V1—4
halimifolium	d...V1—5
Lyonia	
ligustrina	d...S4—14
mariana	d...S3—15
Lyonothamnus floribundus	e...T7—13
Lysiloma latisiliqua	d...T7—17

M

Maackia amurensis	d...S5—13
'Buergeri'	
Macadamia ternifolia	e...T7—14
Maclura pomifera	d...T7—17
'Park'	
Magnolia	
acuminata	d...T8—13
'Golden Glow'	
'Miss Honeybee'	
campbelli	d...T8—14
'Alba'	
'Charles Raefill'	
'Late Pink'	
'Strybing White'	
cordata	d...T6—16
dawsoniana	d...T7—17
'Chyverton'	
'Clarke'	
delavayi	e...T7—14
denudata	d...T7—17
fraseri	d...T7—17
grandiflora	e...T8—10
'Edith Bogue'	
'Samual Sommer'	
'Victoria'	
heptapeta	d...T7—17
'Purple Eye'	
'Swada'	
'Wada'	
kobus	d...T7—18
liliflora	d...S4—15
quinquepeta	d...S4—15
'Lyons'	
'Nigra'	
'O'neill'	
x loebneri	d...T7—18
'Ballerina'	
'Merrill'	
'Messel'	
'Spring Snow'	
macrophylla	d...T7—18
salicifolia	d...T7—18
'Elsie Frye'	

'Kochanakee'	
'Miss Jack'	
'W.B. Clarke'	
x soulangiana	d...T6—16
'6-B'	
'Brozzonii'	
'Lennei'	
'Speciosa'	
sprengeri	d...T7—18
'Diva'	
stellata	d...S5—13
'Centennial'	
'King Rose'	
'Rosea'	
'Royal Star'	
x thompsoniana	d...S3—16
'Urbana'	
tripetala	d...T7—19
x veitchi	d...T7—19
virginiana	e...T7—14
X Mahoberberis	
aquacandidula	e...S3—20
aquisargentii	e...S3—20
Mahonia	
aquifolium	e...S3—21
'Compacta'	
'Mayhan'	
bealei	e...S4—21
fremonti	e...S3—21
higginsiae	e...S3—21
japonica	e...S4—22
lomariifolia	e...S3—21
nervosa	e...S2—18
nevini	e...S3—21
pinnata	e...S3—22
repens	e...S1—11
Malosma laurina	e...T6—22
Malus	
'Adams'	d...S5—14
x arnoldiana	d...S5—14
x atrosanguinea	d...T6—16
baccata	d...T7—19
'Columnaris'	
'Jackii'	
'Midwest'	
'Walters'	
'Blanche Ames'	d...T6—17
'Bob White'	d...S5—14
brevipes	d...S5—14
coronaria	d...T6—17
'Charlotta'	
'Nieuwlandiana'	
'Dolgo'	d...T7—19
'Dorothea'	d...T6—17
'Evelyn'	d...S5—14
'Flame'	d...T6—17
floribunda	d...T6—17
'Calloway'	
fusca	d...T7—19
glabrata	d...T6—18
'Gorgeous'	d...T6—18
halliana 'Parkmani'	d...S5—15
'Henry F. Dupont'	d...T6—18
hupehensis	d...T6—18

ioensis	d...T6—18
'Klehm's'	
'Plena'	d...T6—19
'Prairiefire'	
'Prairie Crab'	
'Prairie Rose'	
'John Downie'	d...S5—15
'Katherine'	d...T6—19
'Makamik'	d...T6—19
'Marshall Oyama'	d...T6—19
'Ormiston Roy'	d...T6—19
'Oekonomierat Echtermeyer'	d...T7—20
platycarpa	d...S5—15
'Prince Georges'	d...T6—20
prunifolia	d...T6—20
pumila	d...T7—20
x purpurea 'Lemoinei'	d...T6—20
'Radiant'	d...T6—20
'Red Jade'	d...S5—15
'Red Silver'	d...S5—15
x robusta	d...T6—20
'Persicifolia'	
'Rosseau'	d...T7—20
sargenti	d...S4—15
'Rosea'	
'Sargentina'	
'Tina'	
x scheideckeri	d...S5—16
sieboldi	d...S4—15
arborescens	
'Sissipuk'	d...T7—20
'Snowdrift'	d...T6—21
spectabilis	d...T6—21
'Alba'	
'Riversii'	
sylvestris	d...T6—21
'Tanner'	d...S5—16
toringoides	d...T6—21
'Macrocarpa'	
tschonoski	d...T7—20
'Van Eseltine'	d...S5—16
'Winter Gold'	d...S5—16
x zumi	d...T6—21
'Calocarpa'	d...T6—22
'Glen Mills'	
'Indian Magic'	
Malvaviscus arboreus	e...S4—22
drummondii	
mexicanus	
Mandevilla x amabilis	e...V2—4
Mangifera indica	e...T7—14
Margyricarpus	
setosus	e...S1—12
pinnatus	e...S1—12
Maurandya scandens	d...V1—1
Maytenus boaria	e...T6—14
Megaskepasma erythrochlamys	e...S3—22
Melaleuca	
armillaris	e...T6—14
decora	e...S5—14
decussata	e...S4—22

Parrotia persica	d...T7—21		'Sharwil'		pubescens	e...T8—11
Parthenocissus			borbonia	e...T7—15	nigra	e...T6—18
henryana	d...V2—5		Petrea volubilis	e...V2—6	'Bory'	
'Silvervein Creeper'			'Albiflora'		'Henon'	
inserta	d...V1—5		Petrophytum caespitosum	e...S1—14	viridus	e...T7—16
quinquefolia	d...V3—1		Phellodendron amurense	d...T7—22	'Robert Young'	
'Engelmannii'			'Macho'		Physocarpus	
tricuspidata	d...V3—2		Philadelphus		capitatus	d...S4—17
'Green Spring'			coronarius	d...S4—16	opulifolius	d...S4—17
'Lowii'			'Aureus'		'Aureus'	
'Robusta'			incanus	d...S4—16	'Darts Gold'	
'Veitchii'			inodorus	d...S4—16	'Luteus'	
Passiflora			x lemoinei	d...S3—17	'Nanus'	
antioquiensis	e...V2—5		'Belle Etoile'		Picea	
caerulea	e...V2—5		'Enchantment'		abies	e...T8—11
coccinea	e...V2—5		'Erectus'		'Clanbrasiliana'	e...S3—25
edulis	e...V2—6		'Sylvaine'		'Little Gem'	
manicata	e...V3—3		lewisi	d...S4—16	'Maxwelli'	e...S2—20
mixta	e...V2—6		'Waterton'		'Nidiformis'	
mollisima	e...V3—3		mexicanus	d...V2—5	'Procumbens'	e...S2—21
quadrangularis	e...V2—6		microphyllus	d...S3—18	'Repens'	e...S1—14
'Variegata'			purpurascens	d...S4—16	asperata	e...T8—12
Paulownia tomentosa	d...T7—22		schrenki	d...S4—17	'Pendula'	
Paurotis wrighti	e...T6—17		x virginalis	d...S4—17	breweriana	e...T8—12
Paxistima			'Natchez'		engelmanni	e...T8—12
canbyi	e...S1—13		'Virginal'		'Blue Pyramid'	
'Compacta'			Philesia magellanica	e...S2—20	'Vanderwolfs'	
myrsinites	e...S1—13		Phillyrea latifolia	e...T6—17	glauca	e...T8—12
Pelargonium			Philodendron		'Conica'	e...S5—18
crispum	e...S2—19		andreanum	e...V3—3	'C. Albertiana'	
'Minor'			evansi	e...S3—24	'C. Globosa'	
'Lemon'			meanochrysum	e...V3—3	densata	e...T6—18
'Orange'			oxycardium	e...V1—4	'Echiniformis'	
quercifolium	e...S3—24		scandens	e...V1—4	'Sanders Blue'	
'Chocolate Mint'			selloum	e...S3—24	jezoensis hondoensis	e...T8—12
'Fair Ellen'			'German Selloum'		koyamai	e...T8—13
Peltophorum africanum	e...T6—17		'Miniature Selloum'		mariana	e...T7—16
Penstemon			'Seaside'		'Doumeti'	e...T7—17
barbatus	e...S2—19		Phlomis fruiticosa	e...S3—24	'Corbet'	
'Albia'			Phoenix		'Golden'	
'Elfin Pink'			canariensis	e...T7—16	'Nana'	
'Torre'			dactylifera	e...T7—16	omorika	e...T8—13
cordifolius	e...S4—24		reclinata	e...T6—17	'Nana'	
fruticosus	e...S1—14		Phormium tenax	e...S3—24	'Pendula'	
heterophyllus	e...S2—19		'Purpureum'		orientalis	e...T8—13
'Blue Spring'			'Variegatum'		'Aurea Compacta'	
'Tree Blue'			Photinia		'Gowdy'	
newberryi	e...S1—14		x fraseri	e...S5—17	'Nana'	
procereus	e...S2—19		'Indian Princess'		pungens	e...T8—13
Pentapterygium serpens	e...S2—1		'Red Robin'		'Bakeri'	
Periploca sepium	d...V1—5		serrulata	e...T7—16	'Compacta'	e...S4—24
Pernettya			villosa	d...S5—17	'Fat Albert'	
ciliaris	e...S2—20		Phygelius capensis	e...S3—24	glauca	e...T8—13
cillata	e...S2—20		Phyllodoce empetriformis	e...S1—14	'Globosa'	e...S2—21
mucronata	e...S2—20		Phyllostachys		'Hoopsii'	
'Rubra'			aurea	e...S5—18	'Koster'	
poeppigi	e...S2—20		'Flavacens Inversa'		montgomery	e...S2—21
Persea			'Koi'		rubens	e...T8—14
americana	e...T7—15		aureosulcata	e...T6—18	'Pocono'	
'Fuerta'			bambusoides	e...T8—11	sitchensis	e...T8—14
'Gwen'			'White Crookstem'		'Nana'	
'Hass'			flexuosa	e...S5—18	'Papoose'	
					'Tenas'	
					'Upright Dwarf'	

smithiana	e...T8—14	'Pygmaea'		occidentalis	d...T8—15
wilsoni	e...T8—14	'Pyramidalis'		orientalis	d...T8—15
Pieris		palustris	e...T8—17	racemosa	d...T8—15
floribunda	e...S3—25	parviflora	e...T7—18	wrighti	d...T8—16
'Karenoma'		'Glauca'		Plumbago auriculata	e...V1—4
'Spring Snow'		'Glauca Nana'		'Alba'	
forresti	e...S4—24	'Koko-no-e'		Plumeria	
'Bisbee Dwarf'		'Templehof'		obtusa	e...S5—19
'Forest Flame'	e...S4—25	patula	e...T7—18	rubra	e...S5—19
japonica	e...S4—25	peuce	e...T8—17	Podocarpus	
Pileostegia viburnoides	e...V3—4	'Nana'		alpinus	e...S4—26
Pimelea ferruginea	e...S2—21	pinaster	e...T8—17	andinus	e...T7—20
Pinus		pinea	e...T8—17	henkeli	e...T7—20
aristata	e...T7—17	ponderosa	e...T8—18	macrophyllus	e...T7—20
banksiana	e...T7—17	pumila	e...S4—25	'Buddhist Pink'	
'Fastigiata'		pungens	e...T7—18	nivalis	e...S3—25
'Nana'		radiata	e...T8—18	totara	e...T8—19
'Schoodic'		resinosa	e...T8—18	Podranea ricasoliana	e...V2—6
'Uncle Foggy'		rigida	e...T8—18	Poinciana	
bungeana	e...T8—14	'Sherman Eddy'		gilliesi	e...S5—4
cembra	e...T7—17	sabiniana	e...T7—19	pulcherrima	e...S4—6
'Broom'		serotina	e...T6—19	Polygala	
'Compacta'		strobus	e...T8—18	x dalmaisiana	e...S3—25
'Nana'		'Fastigiata'		paucifolia	e...S1—15
'Siberica'		'Nana'	e...S3—25	Polygonum	
cembroides	e...T6—18	'Pendula'	e...S5—18	auberti	d...V2—6
contorta	e...T6—18	'Umbraculifera'		baldschuanicum	d...V2—6
'Murrayana'		sylvestris	e...T8—19	cuspidatum	d...S4—17
'Spaan's Dwarf'		'Beauvronensis'	e...S2—21	'Compactum'	
contorta latifolia	e...T8—15	'Fastigiata'		'Spectabile'	
coulteri	e...T8—15	'Repens'	e...S1—15	Poncirus trifoliata	d...S5—17
densiflora	e...T8—15	'Watereri'	e...S4—25	'Flying Dragon'	
'Globosa'		taeda	e...T8—19	Populus	
'Oculus Draconis'		thunbergiana	e...T8—19	alba	d...T8—16
'Pendula'		'Pygmaea'		'Bolleana'	
'Umbraculifera'		'Thunderhead'		'Nivea'	
echinata	e...T8—15	'Yatsubusa'		'Raket'	
edulis	e...T6—19	torreyana	e...T7—19	balsamifera	d...T8—16
elliotti	e...T8—15	umbraculifera	e...S3—25	'Idahoensis'	
flexilis	e...T7—17	virginiana	e...T6—19	'Mojave Hybrid'	
'Glauca'		'Nashawena'		x candicans	d...T8—16
'Pendula'		'Wates Golden'		'Aurora'	
'Reflexa'		Pistacia		'Eugenei'	
griffithi	e...T8—16	atlantica	d...T7—22	'Robusta'	
halepensis	e...T7—18	chinensis	d...T7—22	deltoides	d...T8—16
jeffreyi	e...T8—16	Pithecellobium flexicaule	e...T7—19	'Carolina'	
koraiensis	e...T8—16	Pittosporum		'Mighty Moe'	
'Dragon Eye'		bicolor	e...T6—19	'Platte'	
'Glauca'		crassifolium	e...T6—20	'Souixland'	
'Jack Corbet'		'Compactum'		fremonti	d...T8—17
lambertiana	e...T8—16	eugenioides	e...T7—19	'Nevada'	
monophylla	e...T6—19	'Platinum'		'Texana'	
monticola	e...T8—16	floribundum	e...S4—26	grandidentata	d...T8—17
'Pygmaea'		napaulense	e...S4—26	maximowiczi	d...T8—17
'Rigby's Weeping'		rhombifolium	e...T7—19	nigra 'Italica'	d...T8—17
mugo	e...S5—18	tobira	e...S4—26	sargenti	d...T8—17
'Mops'		truncatum	e...T7—20	'Souixland'	
mughus	e...S4—25	undulatum	e...T6—20	simoni	d...T7—22
'Prostrata'		viridiflorum	e...T6—20	'Fastigiata'	
pumillo		Platanus		tremuloides	d...T7—23
muricata	e...T7—18	x acerifolia	d...T8—15	'Kiabab'	
nigra	e...T8—17	'Bloodgood'		'Swede'	
'Globosa'		'Pyramidalis'			
'Hornibrookiana'		'Yarwood'			

Populus (cont.)		lusitanica	e...T6—21	taxifolia	e...T8—20
trichocarpa	d...T8—18	lyoni	e...T7—20	Psidium	
Potentilla		maacki	d...T7—23	cattleianum	e...T6—21
fruticosa	d...S3—18	mahaleb	d...T7—23	'Lucidum'	
'Abbotswood'		maritima	d...S3—19	littorale	e...T6—21
'Buttercup'		mume	d...T6—24	Ptelea trifoliata	d...T6—25
'Goldfinger'		'Bonita'		Pterocarya	
'Tangerine'		'Dawn'		fraxinifolia	d...T8—18
gracilis	d...S2—10	'Kobai'		x rehderana	d...T8—19
simplex	d...S2—10	'Peggy Clarke'		Pterostyrax hispida	d...T7—25
'Snowflake Coronation'	d...S2—10	padus	d...T7—24	Punica granatum	d...T6—25
tabernaemontani	e...S1—15	'Dropmore'		'Alba'	
tridentata	e...S1—15	'Rancho'		'Chico'	
'Minima'		'Summer Glow'		'Nana'	
'White Cloud'		pensylvanica	d...T7—24	'Wonderful'	
Puoteria sapota	e...T8—19	persica	d...T6—24	Purshia	
Prinsepia uniflora	d...S3—18	'Alba'		glandulosa	e...S4—27
Prosopis		'Lovell'		tridentata	e...S4—27
alba	e...T6—20	'Rubria'		Pyracantha	
glandulosa	d...T6—23	'Versicolor'		coccinea	e...S4—27
velutina	d...T7—23	pumila	d...S4—18	'Kasan'	
Prostanthera nivea	d...S2—10	sargenti	d...T7—24	'Lalendei'	
Protea		'Columnaris'		'Lowboy'	
cynaroides	e...S3—26	'Rancho'		'Rutgers'	
longiflora	e...S4—26	serotina	d...T8—18	fortuneana	e...S4—27
neriifolia	e...S3—26	'Spring Sparkle Rum'		'Graberi'	
susannae	e...S4—26	serrula	d...T7—24	Pyrostegia	
Prunus		serrulata	d...T8—18	ignea	e...V2—7
americana	d...T6—23	'Amanogawa'		venusta	e...V2—7
angustifolia	d...S5—17	'Kwanzan'		Pyrus	
armeniaca	d...T6—23	'Shirofugen'		calleryana	d...T6—25
'Mandshurica'		'Shirotae'		'Bradford'	
'Morden 604'		spinosa	d...S5—18	'Capital'	
avium	d...T7—23	subhirtella	d...T6—25	'Chanticlear'	
'Plena'		'Accolade'		'Redspire'	
besseyi	d...S3—18	'Autumnalis'		communis	d...T6—26
'Rocky Mountain'		'Pendula'		ussuriensis	d...T7—25
caroliniana	e...T6—20	'Rosy Cloud'			
'Bright 'n Tight'		tenella	d...S3—19		
'Compacta'		alba			
cerasifera	d...T6—23	'Firehill'			
'Newport'		tomentosa	d...S4—18		
'Nigra'		'Hansens'			
'Thundercloud'		'Pink Cloud'			
'Vesuvius'		triloba	d...S4—18		
x cistena	d...S4—18	'Flore Pleno'			
'Big Cis'		'Multiplex'			
conradinae	d...T6—23	virginiana	d...T6—25		
davidiana	d...T6—24	'Canada Red'		Quercus	
glandulosa	d...S3—18	'Colorata'		acutissima	d...T7—25
'Alboplena'		'Johnson'		agrifolia	e...T8—20
'Prairie Pink'		'Red Select'		alba	d...T8—19
'Rosea'		yedoensis	d...T7—24	arizonica	e...T7—21
'Sinensis'		'After Glow'		bicolor	d...T8—19
hortulana	d...T6—24	'Akebono'		borealis	d...T8—19
ilicifolia	e...S5—19	'Yoshino'		cerris	d...T8—19
incisa	d...T6—24	Pseudolarix kaemferi	d...T8—18	chrysolepis	e...T8—20
'Midori'		Pseudotsuga		'Vaccinifolia'	
laurocerasus	e...S5—19	menziesi	e...T8—20	coccinea	d...T8—20
'Ottoluyken'		'Caesia'		'Splendens'	
'Portugal'		'Fastigiata'		douglasi	d...T7—25
'Schipkaesis'		glauca	e...T8—20	dumosa	e...S4—27
'Zabeliana'		'Pendula'			
		'Pumila'			

durata   e...S3—26
ellipsoidalis   d...T8—20
engelmanni   e...T8—20
falcata   d...T8—20
frainetto   d...T8—20
gambeli   d...T6—26
garryana   d...T8—20
glandulifera   d...T7—25
ilicifolia   d...S4—18
imbricaria   d...T7—26
kelloggi   d...T8—21
laurifolia   e...T8—21
liaotungensis   d...T6—26
libani   d...T6—26
lobata   d...T8—21
lyrata   d...T8—21
macrocarpa   d...T8—21
   'Sweet Idaho'
marilandica   d...T7—26
muehlenbergi   d...T7—26
nuttalli   d...T8—21
palustris   d...T8—22
   'Crownright'
   'Sovereign'
phellos   d...T8—22
prinoides   d...S3—19
robur   d...T8—22
   'Concordia'
   'Fastigiata'
   'Filicifolia'
   'Pendula'
shumardi   d...T8—22
stellata   d...T7—26
suber   e...T8—21
texana   d...T6—26
vaccinifolia   e...S4—28
variabilis   d...T8—22
velutina   d...T8—23
virginiana   e...T8—21
wislizeni   e...T8—21

Quillaja saponaria   e...T7—21

Radermachia sinica   e...T6—21
Raphiolepis
  x delacouri   e...S3—26
  indica   e...S3—26
   'Snow White'
   'Springtime'
  umbellata   e...S3—27
   ovata
Ravenala madagascariensis   e...T6—21
Rhapis excelsa   e...S3—27

Rhamnus
  californica   e...S5—19
   'Eve Case'
   'Little Sur'
   'Seaview Improved'
  carolinianum   e...S3—27
   'Album'
   'M.L. Webb'
  cathartica   d...T6—27
  crocea   e...S2—22
  davurica   d...T6—27
  frangula   d...T6—27
   'Asplenifolia'
   'Columnaris'
  pallasi   d...S5—18
  purshiana   d...T6—27
  saxatilis   d...S2—10

Rhododendron
  x altaclerense   e...S2—22
  arborescens   d...S5—18
   'Camdon'
   'White Lightening'
  arboreum   e...T7—21
   'Barto White'
   'Sir Charles Lemon'
  atlanticum   d...S2—11
   'Choptank'
   'Marydel'
  bakeri   d...S4—19
  calendulaceum   d...S4—19
  calophytum   e...S3—27
  canadense   d...S2—11
  carolinianum   e...S3—27
  catawbiense   e...S4—28
   'Album'
   'Boursault'
   'Grandiflorum'
   'Ruffles'
  decorum   e...S5—20
   'Caroline'
  discolor   e...S5—20
   doshongense
  Exbury hybrids   d...S4—19
   'Balzac'
   'Gibraltar'
   'Pink Ruffles'
   'Rocket'
  ferrugineum   e...S3—27
  flavum   d...S4—19
   'Batumi Gold'
  fortunei   e...S4—28
   'Betty Hume'
   'Brown Eyes'
   'Chatham'
   'Kokardia'
  x gandavense   d...S4—19
  Ghent hybrids   d...S3—19
   'Daviesi'
   'Flamboyant'
   'Nancy Waterer'
   'Pucella'
  Glenn Dale hybrids   d...S3—19
   'Anchorite'
   'Everest'

   'Geisha'
   'Glacier'
  griffithianum   e...S4—28
   'Alice'
   'Mars'
  impeditum   e...S1—15
   'Little Imp'
   'Moerheim'
  indicum   e...S3—28
   'Balsaminiflorum'
   'Rosaflora'
  japonicum   e...S3—28
  kaempferi   d...S2—11
  keiskei   e...S4—28
   'Cordifolia'
   'Stay Green'
   'Yaku Fairy'
  Kurume hybrids   e...S3—28
   'Apple Blossom'
   'Coral Bells'
   'Hexe'
   'Snow'
  x laeteivirens   e...S3—28
   'Laeteivirens'
  luteum   d...S4—19
  maximum   e...T6—21
   'Lady Clementine Mitford'
   'Prides Pink'
   'Roseum'
  micranthum   d...S3—20
  minus   e...S5—20
   chapmanii
   minus
  molle   d...S3—20
  mucronatum   e...S3—28
  mucronulatum   d...S3—20
   'Alba'
   'Cornell Pink'
   'Crater's Edge'
   'Pink Panther'
  nudiflorum   d...S3—20
  occidentale   d...S5—18
  periclymenoides   d...S3—20
  'P.J.M.'   e...S3—29
  ponticum   e...S5—20
   'Blue Jay'
   'Chionoides'
   'Daphanoides'
   'Lemon Ice'
  prinophyllum   d...S4—20
  prunifolium   d...S4—20
   'S.D. Coleman'
  racemosum   e...S3—29
   'Donna Totten'
   'Split Rock'
  roseum   d...S4—20
  schlippenbachi   d...S5—18
   'Sids Royal Pink'
  smirnowi   e...S4—29
  vaseyi   d...S5—19
   'Alba'
  viscosum   d...S4—20
   'Deleware Blue'
   'Lemon Drop'

microphylla	e…S2—23	
officinalis	e…S2—23	
'Aurea'		
'Minor'		
'Nana'		
'Tricolor'		
Sambucus		
caerulea	d…T7—28	
callicarpa	d…S5—20	
canadensis	d…S4—24	
'Adams'		
'Aurea'		
'Nova'		
'York'		
mexicana	d…T6—29	
nigra	d…T6—29	
pubens	d…S5—20	
racemosa	d…S4—25	
'Arborescens'		
'Plumosa Aurea'		
Santolina		
chamaecyparissus	e…S2—24	
'Nana'		
'Pretty Carroll'		
virens	e…S2—24	
Sapindus drummondi	d…T7—28	
Sapium sebiferum	d…T7—28	
Sarcococca		
confusa	e…S3—30	
hookeriana	e…S2—24	
humilis	e…S2—24	
ruscifolia	e…S3—30	
saligina	e…S3—30	
Sasa		
palmata	e…S4—29	
'Nebulosa'		
veitchi	e…S2—25	
Sassafras albidum	d…T7—28	
Schefflera arboricola	e…S5—20	
'Manita Ripple'		
Schinus		
latifolia	e…T6—22	
lentiscifolia	e…S5—21	
molle	e…T7—21	
terebinthifolia	e…T6—22	
Schisandra chinensis	d…V2—6	
Sciadopitys verticillata	e…T8—22	
Semiarundinaria fastuosa	e…S5—21	
Senecio		
confusus	e…V1—4	
'Sao Paulo'		
leucostachys	e…S3—31	
mandraliscae	e…S1—16	
monroi	e…S3—31	
petasitis	e…S4—29	
vira-vira	e…S3—31	
Sequoia sempervirens	e…T8—22	
Sequoiadendron giganteum	e…T8—22	
'Pendula'		
Serissa foetida	e…S2—25	
'Cherry Blossom'		

'Kyoto'		
'Mt. Fuji'		
Severinia buxifolia	e…S3—31	
Shepherdia		
argentea	d…S4—25	
'Commutata'		
canadensis	d…S3—26	
Simmondsia chinensis	e…S3—31	
Sinarundinaria nitida	e…S5—21	
Skimmia		
japonica	e…S3—31	
macrophylla		
reevesiana	e…S2—25	
Smilax		
hispida	d…V2—6	
rotundifolia	d…V2—6	
tamnoides hispida	d…V2—6	
Solandra		
grandiflora	e…V2—7	
maxima	e…V2—7	
Solanum		
crispum	e…S5—21	
jasminoides	e…V2—8	
rantonneti	d…S3—26	
lycianthes	d…S3—26	
'Royal Robe'		
wendlandi	d…V2—7	
Sollya		
fusiformis	e…V1—4	
'Alba'		
heterophylla	e…V1—4	
Sophora		
davidi	d…S4—25	
japonica	d…T8—24	
'Fastigiata'		
'Pendula'		
'Princeton Upright'		
'Regent'		
tetraptera	d…T7—29	
tomentosa	e…S4—30	
viciifolia	d…S4—25	
Sorbaria		
aitchisoni	d…S4—25	
assurgens	d…S4—25	
sorbifolia	d…S3—26	
Sorbus		
alnifolia	d…T7—29	
americana	d…T6—29	
aria	d…T7—29	
'Lutescens'		
'Magnifica'		
aucuparia	d…T7—29	
'Blackhawk'		
'Cardinal Royal'		
commixta	d…T6—30	
decora	d…T6—30	
discolor	d…T6—30	
domestica	d…T7—29	
hupehensis	d…T7—30	
x hybrida	d…T6—30	
scopulina	d…S5—20	
tianshanica	d…S5—20	

'Red Cascade'		
Sparmannia africana	e…S5—21	
'Variegata'		
Spathodea campanulata	e…T8—22	
Sphaeropteris		
cooperi	e…S5—22	
medullaris	e…T7—7	
Spiraea		
alba	d…S2—12	
albiflora	d…S2—13	
x arguta	d…S3—26	
'Compacta'		
'Graciosa'		
bullata	d…S2—13	
x bumalda	d…S2—13	
'Coccinea'		
'Froebelii'		
'Goldenflame'		
'Norman'		
caespitosum	e…S1—14	
canescens	d…S4—26	
cantoniensis	d…S2—13	
chamaedrifolia	d…S3—27	
decumbens	d…S1—4	
douglasi	d…S3—27	
japonica	d…S3—27	
'Alpina'		
'Coccinea'		
'Gold Mound'		
'Shirobana'		
latifolia	d…S3—27	
menziesi	d…S3—27	
nipponica	d…S3—28	
'Halward's Silver'		
'Snowmound'		
prunifolia	d…S3—28	
'Plena'		
reevesiana	d…S2—13	
'Flora Plena'		
'Lanceata'		
thunbergi	d…S3—28	
tomentosa	d…S3—28	
trilobata	d…S3—28	
'Fairy Queen'		
'Swan Lake'		
x vanhouttei	d…S4—26	
veitchi	d…S4—26	
wilsoni	d…S4—26	
Stachyurus praecox	d…S4—26	
Staphylea		
bolanderi	d…S4—27	
colchica	d…S4—27	
holocarpa	d…S5—21	
trifolia	d…S4—27	
Stenocarpus sinuatus	e…T6—24	
Stephanandra		
incisa	d…S3—29	
'Crispa'		
'Crispifolia Nana'		
tanakae	d…S3—29	
Stephanotis floribunda	e…V2—8	

Stewartia	
koreana	d...T7—30
'Rutger's Gold'	
ovata	d...S5—21
grandifolia	
pseudocamellia	d...T7—30
'Cascade'	
sinensis	d...T6—30
Stigmaphyllon ciliatum	e...V2—8
Stranvaesia davidiana	e...S5—22
Strelitzia	
nicolai	e...S5—22
reginae	e...S3—32
'Dwarf Hybrid'	
Streptosolen jamesoni	e...V2—8
Styrax	
americanus	d...S5—21
pulverulentus	
japonica	d...T6—30
'Carillon'	
'Kusan'	
'Pendula'	
'Pink Charm'	
obassia	d...T6—31
rothomagensis	d...S5—21
wilsoni	d...S4—27
Syagrus orinocensis	e...T8—23
Symphoricarpos	
albus	d...S3—29
'Jewell'	
laevigatus	d...S4—28
x chenaulti	d...S2—13
'Hancock'	
microphyllus	d...S4—27
mollis	d...S1—4
occidentalis	d...S3—29
orbiculatus	d...S2—14
'Variegatus'	
oreophilus	d...S3—29
rotundifolius	d...S3—29
rivularis	d...S4—28
Symplocos paniculata	d...T6—31
Syngonium podophyllum	e...V2—8
'Imperial White'	
'Maxima'	
'Variegata'	
Syringa	
amurensis japonica	d...T7—30
x chinensis	d...S5—21
alba	
'Suageana'	
x josiflexa	d...S4—28
josikaea	d...S4—28
'Pallida'	
laciniata	d...S3—30
meyeri	d...S3—30
'Palibin'	
microphylla	d...S3—30
'Superba'	
oblata dilatata	d...S4—28
patula	d...S4—28
'Miss Kim'	

x persica	d...S3—30
'Laciniata'	
'Purple Dark'	
potanini	d...S4—29
x prestoniae	d...S5—21
'Donald Wyman'	
'Hiawatha'	
'Nocturne'	
'Royalty'	
reflexa	d...S4—29
reticulata	d...T7—30
'Ivory Silk'	
'Summer Snow'	
x swegiflexa	d...S4—29
'James McFarland'	
villosa	d...S4—29
vulgaris	d...S5—22
'Alba'	
'Charles Jolly'	
'Edith Cavell'	
'Sensation'	
Syzygium	
cumini	e...T7—21
paniculata	e...T6—23
'Globulus'	
'Teenie Genie'	
uniflora	e...T6—23

Tamarix parviflora	d...S5—22
Taxodium	
ascendens	d...T8—24
distichum	d...T8—24
'Pendens'	
'Prairie Sentinel'	
'Shawnie Brave'	
Taxus	
baccata	e...T6—23
'Elegantissima'	e...S4—30
'Fowle'	e...S4—30
'Repandens'	
'Standishii'	
brevifolia	e...T7—22
canadensis	e...S2—25
'Verkades Recurved'	
cuspidata	e...T7—22
'Capitata'	e...S5—22
'Densiformis'	e...S3—32
'Densa'	
'Greenwave'	
'Nana'	e...S2—25
'Wardii'	
x media	e...S5—22
'Browni'	e...S4—30
'Hatfieldi'	e...S4—30
'Hicksi'	e...S5—23

'Mooni'	
'Nigra'	
'Viridis'	e...S4—31
'Wardi'	e...S3—32
Tecoma stans	e...S5—23
Tecomaria capensis	e...V2—9
Tetrapanax papyriferus	e...S5—23
Tetrastigma voinierianum	e...V3—4
Teucrium	
bicolor	e...S3—32
heterophyllum	e...S3—32
flavum	e...S2—26
fruticans	e...S3—32
'Compacta'	
chamaedrys	e...S1—16
'Prostratum'	
'Variegata'	
massiliense	e...S1—17
Thespesia grandiflora	e...T7—15
Thevetia peruviana	e...S4—31
Thuja	
occidentalis	e...T7—22
'Globosa'	e...S3—33
'Hoveyi'	e...S3—33
'Nigra'	
'Pyramidalis'	
'Umbraculifera'	e...S3—33
'Woodwardi'	e...S3—33
orientalis	e...T7—22
'Aurea Nanus'	
'Blue Cone'	
'Excelsus'	
'Ramsayi'	
plicata	e...T8—23
'Atrovirens'	
'Elegantissima'	
'Hillerii'	
'Stoneham Gold'	
standishi	e...T8—23
Thujopsis dolabrata	e...T8—23
'Nana'	
Thunbergia	
grandiflora	e...V2—9
gregori	e...V1—5
Thymus	
x citriodorus	e...S1—17
'Aureus'	
'Silver Queen'	
herba-barona	e...S1—17
lanuginosus	e...S1—17
serpyllum	e...S1—17
vulgaris	e...S1—18
'Argienteus'	
'French'	
Tibouchina urvilleana	e...S5—23
Tilia	
americana	d...T8—24
'Capitol'	
'Fastigiata'	
'Redmond'	
cordata	d...T8—24
'Chancellor'	

'Greenspire'		
'Morden'		
'Rancho'		
x euchlora	d...T8—25	
'Redmond'		
mongolica	d...T7—30	
oliveri	d...T7—31	
petiolaris	d...T8—25	
platyphyllos	d...T8—25	
'Pyramidal'		
'Rubra'		
tomentosa	d...T8—25	
'Green Mountain'		
'Princeton'		
'Sterling Silver'		
Torreya		
californica	e...T7—22	
nucifera	e...T6—23	
taxifolia	e...T7—23	
Toxicodendron		
diversilobum	d...V1—6	
radicans	d...V3—2	
Trachelospermum		
asiaticum	e...V1—5	
'Variegata'		
jasminoides	e...V1—5	
'Madison'		
'Minuma'		
'Variegatum'		
Trachycarpus fortunei	e...T6—23	
Trichostema lanatum	e...S3—33	
Tripterygium regeli	d...V2—7	
Tristania laurina	e...T6—24	
Tsuga		
canadensis	e...T8—24	
'Coles Prostrate'	e...S2—26	
'Hussii'		
'Nana'	e...S4—31	
'Jeddeloh'		
'Pendula'	e...S2—26	
'Sargentii'		
caroliniana	e...T7—23	
'Arnold Pyramid'		
'Labar's Weeping'		
diversifolia	e...T7—23	
heterophylla	e...T8—24	
mertensiana	e...T8—24	
'Elizabeth'		
'Vans Prostrate'		
Tupidanthus calyptratus	e...S5—23	

Ugni molinae e...S3—34

Ulmus
alata	d...T7—31	
americana	d...T8—25	
'Augustine'		
'Column'		
carpinifolia	d...T8—26	
'Christine Buiseman'		
'Koopmanii'		
'Umbraculifera'		
crassifolia	d...T7—31	
fulva	d...T8—27	
glabra	d...T8—26	
'Dumont'		
'Klemmer'		
x hollandica	d...T8—26	
'Bea Schwartz'		
'Groenveldt'		
'Urban'		
parvifolia	d...T8—26	
'Brea'		
'Drake'		
'Dynasty'		
'Prairie Shade'		
procera	d...T8—26	
'Louis van Houtte'		
pumila	d...T8—27	
'Autumn Gold'		
'Coolshade'		
'Dropmore'		
'Sapparo'		
rubra	d...T8—27	
thomasi	d...T7—31	
x vegeta 'Camperdowni'	d...T6—31	

Umbellularia californica e...T8—24

Ungnadia speciosa d...T6—31

Vaccinium
corymbosum	d...S5—22	
'Tomahawk'		
delavayi	e...S2—26	
macrocarpum	e...S1—18	
ovatum	e...S3—34	
'Maree's Select'		
pallidum	d...S2—14	
parvifolium	d...S4—29	
stamineum	d...S5—22	
vitis-idaea	e...S1—18	
minus		

Vauquelinia californica e...S5—24

Veitchia joannis e...T8—24

Veronica
alpina	e...S1—18	
fruticans	e...S1—18	
incana	e...S2—26	
repens	e...S1—19	
spicata	e...S2—27	
'Blue Fox'		
'Erica'		
'Nana'		
'Red Fox'		

Viburnum
acerifolium	d...S3—30	
alnifolium	d...S4—30	
bitchiuense	d...S4—30	
x bodnantense	d...S4—30	
'Dawn'		
x burkwoodi	e...S4—31	
'Chenaulti'		
'Mohawk'		
x carlcephalum	d...S4—30	
carlesi	d...S3—31	
'Aurora'		
'Compactum'		
cassinoides	d...S3—31	
davidi	e...S2—27	
dentatum	d...S4—30	
dilatatum	d...S4—31	
'Erie'		
'Oneida'		
ellipticum	d...S4—31	
farreri	d...S4—31	
fragrans	d...S4—31	
'Bowles'		
'Nanum'		
x juddi	d...S4—31	
lantana	d...S5—22	
'Mohican'		
lentago	d...T6—31	
lobophyllum	d...S5—23	
macrocephalum	e...S5—24	
'Sterile'		
nudum	d...S5—23	
odoratissimum	e...S5—24	
opulus	d...S5—23	
'Compactum'	d...S3—14	
'Nanum'	d...S2—14	
'Roseum'		
'Xanthocarpum'		
plicatum	d...S5—23	
tomentosum	d...S4—31	
'Casade'		
'Mariesii'		
'Shasta'		
'Watanabe'		
'Shoshoni'		
prunifolium	d...T6—32	
'Summer Magic'		
rafinesquianum	d...S3—31	
x rhytidophylloides	e...S5—24	
'Alleghany'		
'Willowwood'		
rhytidophyllum	e...S4—31	
rufidulum	d...T6—32	
sargenti	d...S4—32	
'Onandago'		
'Susquehanna'		
setigerum	d...S4—32	
'Aurantiacum'		

Viburnum (cont.)
  sieboldi   d...S5—23
    'Seneca'
  suspensum   e...S4—32
  trilobum   d...S5—24
    'Alfredo'
    'Compactum'   d...S4—32
    'Hahs'
    'Wentworth'
  tinus   e...S4—32
    'Compactum'
    'Robustum'
    'Spring Bouquet'
  veitchi   d...S3—31
  wrighti   d...S4—32
Vigna caracalla   d...V2—7
Vinca
  major   e...V1—5
    'Morning Glory'
    'Variegata'
  minor   e...V1—5
    'Alba'
    'Purpurea'
    'Rubra'
    'Shademaster'
Vitex
  agnus-castus   d...S5—24
    latifolia
  negundo   d...S5—24
    heterophylla
Vitis
  aestivalis   d...V3—2
  amurensis   d...V3—2
  californica   d...V3—2
  labrusca   d...V2—7
    'Catawba'
    'Concord'
  riparia   d...V3—3
  vinifera   d...V3—3
    'Chardonnay'
    'Gewurztraminer'
    'Merlot'
  vulpina   d...V3—3

Washingtonia
  filifera   e...T7—23
  robusta   e...T8—25
Weigela
  florida   d...S4—32
    'Pink Delight'
    'Rosea'
    'Vanidek'
    'Variegata'

praecox   d...S3—32
Westringia rosmariniformis e...S3—34
Wigandia caracasana   d...S4—33
Wisteria
  floribunda   d...V2—8
    'Alba'
    'Macrobotrys'
    'Plena'
    'Rosea'
  frutescens   d...V3—3
  macrostachya   d...V2—8
  sinensis   d...V3—3
    'Alba'
    'Caroline'
    'Plena'
    'Rosea'
  venusta   d...V2—8

Xanthoceras sorbifolium d...S5—23
Xanthorhiza simplicissima d...S2—14
Xylosma
  congesta   e...T6—24
  heterophylla   e...S4—32
  japonica   e...T6—24
    'Compactum'

Yucca
  brevifolia   e...T6—24
  elephantipes   e...T6—24
  elata   e...S5—25
  filamentosa   e...S2—27
  flaccida   e...S2—27
    'Ivory Tower'
  glauca   e...S2—27
    'Pendula'
  gloriosa   e...S4—32
  schidigera   e...S5—25
  smalliana   e...S2—27
    'Bright Edge'
    'Golden Sword'

Zamia
  integrifolia   e...S2—28
  furfuracea   e...S3—34
  pumila   e...S3—34
Zanthoxylum
  americanum   d...T6—32
  piperitum   d...S5—24
  simulans   d...S5—25
Zelkova serrata   d...T8—27
    'Green Vase'
    'Village Green'
Zenobia pulverulenta   e...S3—34
Ziziphus jujuba   d...T6—32
    'Sherwood'